Rapid Innovation and Development in the Global Cannabis Market

Pfano Mashau
University of KwaZulu-Natal, South Africa

Jabulani Nyawo
University of KwaZulu-Natal, South Africa

IGI Global
PUBLISHER of TIMELY KNOWLEDGE

A volume in the Advances in Business Strategy and Competitive Advantage (ABSCA) Book Series

Published in the United States of America by
IGI Global
Business Science Reference (an imprint of IGI Global)
701 E. Chocolate Avenue
Hershey PA, USA 17033
Tel: 717-533-8845
Fax: 717-533-8661
E-mail: cust@igi-global.com
Web site: http://www.igi-global.com

Library of Congress Cataloging-in-Publication Data

Names: Mashau, Pfano, 1991- editor. | Nyawo, Jabulani, 1987- editor.
Title: Rapid innovation and development in the global cannabis market / Pfano Mashau, and Jabulani Nyawo, editors.
Description: Hershey, PA : Business Science Reference, [2023] | Includes bibliographical references and index. | Summary: "The book aims to package studies around the innovations and opportunities of the cannabis industry in South Africa to identify current trends and benefits"-- Provided by publisher.
Identifiers: LCCN 2022039904 (print) | LCCN 2022039905 (ebook) | ISBN 9781668463468 (hardcover) | ISBN 9781668463475 (paperback) | ISBN 9781668463482 (ebook)
Subjects: LCSH: Marijuana industry--South Africa. | Cannabis--South Africa.
Classification: LCC HD9019.M382 S57 2023 (print) | LCC HD9019.M382 (ebook) | DDC 362.29/50968--dc23/eng/20221020
LC record available at https://lccn.loc.gov/2022039904
LC ebook record available at https://lccn.loc.gov/2022039905

This book is published in the IGI Global book series Advances in Business Strategy and Competitive Advantage (ABSCA) (ISSN: 2327-3429; eISSN: 2327-3437)

British Cataloguing in Publication Data
A Cataloguing in Publication record for this book is available from the British Library.

For electronic access to this publication, please contact: eresources@igi-global.com.

Advances in Business Strategy and Competitive Advantage (ABSCA) Book Series

Patricia Ordóñez de Pablos
Universidad de Oviedo, Spain

ISSN:2327-3429
EISSN:2327-3437

Mission

Business entities are constantly seeking new ways through which to gain advantage over their competitors and strengthen their position within the business environment. With competition at an all-time high due to technological advancements allowing for competition on a global scale, firms continue to seek new ways through which to improve and strengthen their business processes, procedures, and profitability.

The **Advances in Business Strategy and Competitive Advantage (ABSCA) Book Series** is a timely series responding to the high demand for state-of-the-art research on how business strategies are created, implemented and re-designed to meet the demands of globalized competitive markets. With a focus on local and global challenges, business opportunities and the needs of society, the **ABSCA** encourages scientific discourse on doing business and managing information technologies for the creation of sustainable competitive advantage.

Coverage

- Innovation Strategy
- Co-operative Strategies
- Outsourcing
- Business Models
- Entrepreneurship & Innovation
- Economies of Scale
- Strategy Performance Management
- Resource-Based Competition
- Small and Medium Enterprises
- Customer-Orientation Strategy

IGI Global is currently accepting manuscripts for publication within this series. To submit a proposal for a volume in this series, please contact our Acquisition Editors at Acquisitions@igi-global.com or visit: http://www.igi-global.com/publish/.

The Advances in Business Strategy and Competitive Advantage (ABSCA) Book Series (ISSN 2327-3429) is published by IGI Global, 701 E. Chocolate Avenue, Hershey, PA 17033-1240, USA, www.igi-global.com. This series is composed of titles available for purchase individually; each title is edited to be contextually exclusive from any other title within the series. For pricing and ordering information please visit http://www.igi-global.com/book-series/advances-business-strategy-competitive-advantage/73672. Postmaster: Send all address changes to above address.

Titles in this Series

For a list of additional titles in this series, please visit: http://www.igi-global.com/book-series/advances-business-strategy-competitive-advantage/73672

Handbook of Research on Business Model Innovation Through Disruption and Digitalization
Erik Stavnsager Rasmussen (University of Southern Denmark, Denmark) and Nicolaj Hannesbo Petersen (UCL Professional College and Business Academy, Denmark)
Business Science Reference • © 2023 • 400pp • H/C (ISBN: 9781668448953) • US $325.00

Intellectual Capital as a Precursor to Sustainable Corporate Social Responsibility
Bartolomé Marco-Lajara (University of Alicante, Spain) Patrocinio Zaragoza-Sáez (University of Alicante, Spain) and Javier Martínez-Falcó (University of Alicante, Spain)
Business Science Reference • © 2023 • 291pp • H/C (ISBN: 9781668468159) • US $250.00

The Transformation of Global Trade in a New World
Bartolomé Marco-Lajara (University of Alicante, Spain) Ahu Coşkun Özer (Marmara University, Turkey) and Javier Martínez Falcó (University of Alicante, Spain)
Business Science Reference • © 2023 • 308pp • H/C (ISBN: 9781668459508) • US $250.00

Exploring the Economic Opportunities and Impacts of Migrant Entrepreneurship Success Stories and Case Studies
Meena Chavan (Macquarie University, Australia) and Sheba Nandkeolyar (Multiconnexions, Australia)
Business Science Reference • © 2022 • 231pp • H/C (ISBN: 9781668449868) • US $215.00

Analyzing the Relationship Between Corporate Governance, CSR, and Sustainability
Ayberk Soyer (Istanbul Technical University, Turkey) and Umut Asan (Istanbul Technical University, Turkey)
Business Science Reference • © 2022 • 315pp • H/C (ISBN: 9781799842347) • US $215.00

Handbook of Research on Digital Innovation and Networking in Post-COVID-19 Organizations
Ana Pego (Nova University of Lisbon, Portugal)
Business Science Reference • © 2022 • 539pp • H/C (ISBN: 9781668467626) • US $315.00

Antecedents and Outcomes of Employee-Based Brand Equity
Muhammad Waseem Bari (Government College University, Faisalabad, Pakistan) Muhammad Abrar (Government College University, Faisalabad, Pakistan) and Emilia Alaverdov (Tbilisi State University, Georgia)
Business Science Reference • © 2022 • 297pp • H/C (ISBN: 9781668436219) • US $250.00

IGI Global
PUBLISHER of TIMELY KNOWLEDGE

701 East Chocolate Avenue, Hershey, PA 17033, USA
Tel: 717-533-8845 x100 • Fax: 717-533-8661
E-Mail: cust@igi-global.com • www.igi-global.com

Table of Contents

Detailed Table of Contents

The demand for cannabis is at present increasing and the business globally is really evolving and expanding. With newcomers such as big corporate businesses, investors, and entrepreneurs, there has been a new standard of sophistication and level in the cannabis market worldwide. Several business providers of cannabis are confronted with a consortium of challenges and intend to have any form of insurance coverage to reduce those hiccups. However, there has been noted challenges in insuring the cannabis-allied business providers as they are considered a high-geared risk and embrace the so-called risk of specialty. Insuring the cannabis related businesses market is nowadays more complex as the market trend takes a difficult turn due to regulatory and supervisory challenges. Since cannabis indeed is used for multi-purposes and plays a huge role in enhancing businesses nowadays, it will be wise that the government officials, policymakers, and others work closely with the insurance market players or providers so that these challenges can be reduced.

Cannabis policy controls and regulatory changes have attracted a lot of attention across the world as the drive for full cannabis commercialization gathers momentum. The diversity of views on cannabis regulation reflects a melting pot of regulatory regimes (Aguilar et al., 2018; Seddon and Floodgate, 2020). This chapter is therefore an attempt to converge fragmented pieces of knowledge on cannabis policies and regulations. Using a qualitative research approach, the study found that cannabis policies and regulations in Zimbabwe and most countries of the world are at experimental stages and have to negotiate a family of challenges to succeed. For the cannabis industry sector to flourish, making sense of the policy tools that have worked in other countries and adopting supportive policy best practices to strengthen the cannabis policy and regulatory framework in Zimbabwe is crucial. The chapter ends by proposing ways of strengthening the cannabis policy framework in Zimbabwe.

The legal cannabis industry has been the fastest-growing industry in the United States of America and across the world. The marketing structure for cannabis production, supply, and sale in the USA was underground and illegal for the majority of the twentieth century. This study aims to identify the online and offline marketing techniques providing opportunities for cannabis entrepreneurs. This study was conducted using the desktop research method to identify the online and offline marketing techniques for cannabis entrepreneurs and the analysis of challenges faced by entrepreneurs in the marketing of cannabis.

The topic of cannabis has been widely researched over the years, but still remains a controversial yet interesting field of study. As an industry, the cannabis industry has evolved and developed over the years. The plant was previously utilized mainly by individuals for personal consumption, but following much research and development into the topic it has now become a lucrative market. Some countries have legalized cannabis or have gone through the decriminalization process. In recent times, the recreational usage of the cannabis plant has become a major source of interest as more investment and research has been made into the industry as a means to innovate more recreational cannabis products. There are now cannabis products like oil, beauty and skin care products, beverages, chocolate, capsules, gummies, and dog treats. The chapter is based on a qualitative approach as the aim is to gather a greater understanding of the phenomenon and provide insight for future research.

The chapter proposes a vigilant approach towards the demand of legalising cannabis. It explains the opportunities of Fintech to develop legal, safe, and flexible transactions in the industry which is considered illegal in many countries. The chapter presents the cases of the Jammu and Kashmir, India to grow and manufacture licensed cannabis compounds, making upon indigenous knowledge, culture, and nourishing environment. It also accounts to mitigate the risk around related illegal activities. There are a few pharmaceutical manufacturing companies producing cannabis-based drugs, but they do not own farms, and source it from a few tilizing farmlands. Some big companies have started tilizing blockchain technologies, raising opportunity to test further possibilities through blockchain, cryptography, digital identity cards, etc. The chapter presents findings from a survey in the Jammu and Kashmir, India, capturing perceptions about cannabis farming, cannabis-based medicine, financial transaction challenges, and the use of Fintech in legal use of cannabis.

In recent years, cannabis has been one of the substances that many countries around the world have taken or are taking steps to legalise for certain kinds of consumption. In some countries, it is only legal in certain parts and still illegal in others. There is literature to suggest that idea of legalising cannabis tends to divide opinion with some people being for its legalisation and others being against it. The reason for the division of opinion regarding the legalisation of cannabis can be traced back to the many challenges and benefits that stem from cannabis being legal in any given society. There is sparse literature addressing the contextual dynamics of these resulting challenges and benefits. In this chapter, the authors present a commentary of some of the challenges and benefits that may result from the legalisation of cannabis in South Africa.

The possibilities of legalizing cannabis for commercial use in South Africa is investigated in this study using desktop research from documents, newsletters, and existing literature. Indigenous communities would gain immensely from the legalization of producing cannabis-infused products, as it would help to enhance the rural economy by producing jobs and create wealth. Cannabis is a significant component of African religion, culture, and beliefs, having been used by indigenous communities for generations and believed to have curative properties. Moreover, legalizing cannabis for industrial use makes sense not only for economic development but also for further medical research. According to the 2022 February speech of the Republic of South Africa's president, Mr. Cyril Ramaphosa, cannabis has the potential to be industrialized and commercialized in South Africa in the near future. The speech came after the Constitutional Court (ConCourt) in 2018 had already decriminalized and permitted cannabis use for both personal and medical purposes, which was previously illegal.

The aim of the chapter is to provide knowledge on the opportunities that the cannabis market has for South Africa. It further provides new models developed from the current literature on the related subjects. The industry also plans to improve the current products, which requires a lot of training and development from the existing people in the market. Therefore, this chapter will cover a range of topics such as the employment relation act, entrepreneurship competencies, human resource planning, training and development, recommendable diversity and motivational models, national qualifications framework (NQF), as well as to look at the future jobs within the cannabis industry.

This chapter aims to understand the opportunities that are available for the industrialisation of cannabis in South Africa from the developmental state perspective. The exclusion of Black people in the economy is still the main theme of the South African economy 28 years into democracy. Therefore, the intersection between the state and its importance in terms of guiding the private sector to achieve industrialisation and redistribution is a theme worthy of exploring. Interestingly, cannabis being a nascent sector in the economy, can either create opportunities for inclusion of those previously excluded, or it could sustain the dominance of those who presently control the status quo. Hence to facilitate such inclusion the state needs to play a pivotal facilitative role. Therefore, three themes are the focus of this chapter: i) developmental state; ii) opportunity for the cannabis industry in South Africa; and iii) redistribution - what form of distribution is required to occur in the industry to benefit the entire South African population.

The most critical and mainly inherent objective of this chapter is to afford a fresh insight into the economic realm that denotes cannabis potentially through its ploughing, refinery, nurture, multifaceted functions, in relation to job opportunities, employment creation, and subsequently generating revenues. Otherwise, it provides a variety of information depicted from various expert sources regarding the subject matter. Essentially, it presents researched work in the form of surveys which identify not only key debates, challenges, and trends, but also constructs and argue for a future agenda. The selected topic deliberately provides a constellation of perspectives aimed at exploring, yet also debating crucial issues as raised.

Preface

Cannabis research has primarily concentrated on the medicinal benefits and legality of using it for recreational purposes. In recent years, the general public has been acquainted with different benefits of cannabis following the legalization of the use of cannabis-based products such as medicinal products, skincare, body products, CBD and other developments. This has resulted in an economically viable industry that requires high-level investigation in order for countries fully benefit from it. For instance, in South Africa alone, the war on cannabis cost taxpayers over USD$223.7 million in 2014 and 2015; the industry is vital for medical cannabis in reducing the country's reliance on imported pharmaceuticals (Kitchen, Kabba, & Fang, 2022). The decriminalization or legalization of medical or recreational use of cannabis offers South Africa an opportunity to recover some of the money lost during the war on cannabis. As alluded to in the study titled 'Decriminalizing Marijuana: The Science and Social Sustainability Behind the use of Marijuana (Cannabis) in India" there is a need to comprehensively study and understand the benefits of this industry in terms of; 1. Policy to govern the sector, 2. Rapid innovation on related products and 3. processes and other development in the cannabis sector (Kuppuram, 2021). As governments industrialize cannabis, the public should beware that where there are investments, innovation follows Gosch (2019). Investment in the Cannabis industry has been increasing as countries legalize and decriminalize this industry. In North America alone, 43 billion US dollars are invested in the industry (Abara, 2021). South Africa has started legalizing the cannabis trade, and the market for cannabis-based products has emerged, notwithstanding the inherent challenges faced by prospective growers and traders. During the 2022 State of the Nation Address, the president of South Africa announced the industrialization of the cannabis industry (Presidency, 2022). As this sector mushrooms in different economies coupled with good governance, research shows that there are economic benefits that follow and the industry's entire value chain is realized. As investments in this industry are increasing, jobs are created, new products are developed, current products are improved, the market for products increases and the need for complementing government intervention arises. For instance, in the newly decriminalized South African cannabis industry, the Department of Agriculture, Land Reform and Rural Development (2020) reported that South Africa has a cannabis industry worth R28 billion and the potential to create about 20 000 to 30000 jobs.

The main objective of this book is to provide chapters that capture the recent innovation and development in the Global Cannabis Market. The general public is still debating the significance of the cannabis industry and its developments. Therefore, the book will contribute to the dialogue by providing chapters that introduce readers to the world cannabis industry, provide knowledge of the industry, capture the effects of different policies governing the industry, and document products and processes innovations. The main target audience include general members of the public, policy makers, academics and researchers.

The central thesis of this book is cannabis, and this publication is a product of different scholars in different fields. Majority of the scholars have published extensively both nationally and internationally. The book consists of sixteen chapters:

Chapter 1 is titled "Does the Industry for Cannabis Provide More Challenges in Its Insurance Provision? A Case of Global Perspective."

The demand for cannabis is currently increasing and the business globally is evolving and expanding. With new comers such as big corporate businesses, investors and entrepreneurs, there has been a new standard of sophistication and level in the cannabis market worldwide. Several business providers of cannabis are confronted with a consortium of challenges and intend to have any form of insurance cover to reduce those hiccups. However, there have been noted challenges in insuring the cannabis-allied business providers as they are considered high-geared risk and embrace the so-called risk of specialty. Insuring the cannabis related businesses market is nowadays more complex as the market trend takes a difficult turn due to regulatory and supervisory challenges. The chapter shows that cannabis has multipurposes and plays a huge role in enhancing businesses nowadays, it will be wise that government officials, policymakers and others work closely with the insurance market players or providers so that these challenges can be reduced.

Chapter 2 is titled "Cannabis Industry Policy Controls and Regulations in Zimbabwe."

Cannabis policy controls and regulatory changes have attracted a lot of attention across the world as the drive for full cannabis commercialization gathers momentum. The diversity of views on cannabis regulation reflects a melting pot of regulatory regimes. This chapter is therefore an attempt to converge fragmented pieces of knowledge on cannabis policies and regulations. Using a qualitative research approach the study found that cannabis policies and regulations in Zimbabwe and most countries of the world are at the experiment stage and have to negotiate a family of challenges to succeed. For the cannabis industry sector to flourish, making sense of the policy tools that have worked in other countries and adopting supportive policy best practices to strengthen the cannabis policy and regulatory framework in Zimbabwe is crucial. The chapter ends by proposing ways of strengthening the cannabis policy framework in Zimbabwe.

Chapter 3 is titled "Contemporary Marketing Techniques for Cannabis Entrepreneurs."

The legal cannabis industry has been the fastest-growing in the United States of America (USA) and worldwide. The marketing structure for cannabis production, supply and sale in the USA was underground and illegal for the majority of the twentieth century. This study aims to identify the online and offline marketing techniques providing opportunities for cannabis entrepreneurs. This study was conducted using the desktop research method to identify the online and offline marketing techniques for cannabis entrepreneurs and the analysis of challenges faced by entrepreneurs in marketing cannabis.

Chapter 4 is titled "Twenty-First Century Innovation of Cannabis Products."

The topic of cannabis has been widely researched over the years, but still remains a controversial yet interesting field of study. As an industry, the cannabis industry has evolved and developed over the years. The plant was previously utilized mainly by individuals for personal consumption, but following much research and development into the topic, it has become a lucrative market. Some countries have legalized cannabis or have gone through the decriminalization process. In recent times, the recreational usage of the cannabis plant has become a major source of interest as more investment and research has been made into the industry as a means to innovate more recreational cannabis products. There are now cannabis products like oil, beauty and skin care products, beverages, chocolate, capsules, gummies and dog treats. The chapter is based on a qualitative approach as the aim is to gather a greater understanding of the phenomenon and provide insight for future research.

Chapter 5 is titled "Indian Cannabis Farming Policies and Use of FinTech to Improve Related Legalities."

The chapter proposes a vigilant approach towards the demand for legalising cannabis. It explains the opportunities of Fintech to develop legal, safe, and flexible transactions in the industry which is considered illegal in many countries. The chapter presents the case of Jammu and Kashmir, India to grow and manufacture licensed cannabis compounds, making upon indigenous knowledge, culture, and a nourishing environment. It also accounts for mitigating the risk around related illegal activities. Few pharmaceutical manufacturing companies produce cannabis-based drugs but do not own farms, and they source it from few authorised farmlands. Some big companies have started utilising blockchain technologies, raising opportunity to test further possibilities through blockchain, cryptography, digital identity cards, etc. The chapter presents finding from a survey in the Jammu and Kashmir, India, capturing perceptions about cannabis farming, cannabis-based medicine, financial transaction challenges, and the use of Fintech in legal use of cannabis.

Chapter 6 is titled "The Legalisation of Cannabis in South Africa."

The recent legalisation of cannabis in South Africa has created a sizable market for the importation of cannabis products into the country. The Cannabis-Masterplan explains how the value creation features must be reflected in legislation. Cannabis products may already be imported with approval. This causes yet another delay and issue because it disadvantages the local market would be primary, secondary and tertiary producers. Small-scale cannabis producers are a secondary segment of the value chain that can best solve this. Consequences that can be anticipated from making cannabis farming the main source feeding into the value chain. The chapter suggests a value conceptual framework that creates new players, creating markets and jobs for the local women and the youth, thus addressing one of the sustainable developmental goals of creating employment.

Chapter 7 is titled "The Role of the South African Government in Advancing the Cannabis Industry to Assist the Ailing Economy and Improve Unemployment."

The cannabis industry, although shrouded with controversy due to stigmatization, has the potential to enhance countries' economies substantially and assist with alleviating unemployment. The industry is projected to be worth some two hundred and seventy-two billion dollars by 2028. Besides the commonly understood medicinal properties, the plant has broad applications for use in construction, food products, toiletries, paper, and furniture. Following the devastation of the coronavirus pandemic and the looting in July 2021, the South African government needs to pursue alternative revenue streams. Public debt is mounting, unemployment figures continue to rise and the economy is strained. This chapter thus seeks to offer insight into the contribution that the cannabis industry could provide in assisting the ailing economy and in alleviating unemployment.

Chapter 8 is titled "Empowering South African Rural Stakeholders to Participate in the Cannabis Legal Market: A Sustainable Livelihoods Approach."

The chapter aimed to contribute to understanding the roles of the cannabis industry's stakeholders/transforming structures/institutions to empower and sustain local rural Small, Medium & Micro Enterprises (SMMEs) in South Africa (SA). The lessons learned from the literature reviewed in this chapter is that local stakeholders/institutions/transforming structures can either play a positive role or be a negative force. A force in the empowerment and sustainability (using available resources/assets) of the cannabis-related SMMEs. It is therefore concluded that for South African cannabis stakeholders to effectively empower and sustain (using their resources) local rural SMMEs, they ought to embrace cannabis-related SMMEs' local values and assumptions alongside their regulations and laws. This chapter contributes to how key local rural-based institutions/stakeholders/structures can effectively use their resources/assets, rules, regulations, local values and assumptions to transform each other positively in pursuit of cannabis-related SMME's empowerment and sustainability in SA.

Chapter 9 is titled "Analysis of Lessons That Can Be Learnt by South African Government Leaders in Their Role in Advancements Within the Cannabis Industry of South Africa."

Government leaders have a key role in leading a diverse economy towards alleviating poverty. Throughout the years cannabis has contributed to improved livelihoods even with strong legislative policies preventing its cultivation. In efforts to grow its economy South Africa has joined many countries in changing its legislative policies to allow for legalization of hemp and cannabis under certain conditions. This chapter provides an analysis of the lessons that can be learnt by South African government leaders from the cannabis industry and their role in advancements within the Cannabis industry of South Africa.

Chapter 10 is titled "Addressing the Cannabis Stigma: South African Perspective."

There is confusion leading to the stigmatization of Cannabis topics. Cannabis is referred to as 'marijuana', weed, and dagga among other names depending on the adjoining audience. Consumption of cannabis leads to social devaluation of the user within communities. The cannabis industry is known for being illegal, scheduled as an illicit drug, and associated with brain damage leading to criminal activities. There is zero to less information available for the public regarding the topic. Cannabis use is associated with negativity arising from the consequences of substance abuse. The researcher followed the commonly practiced stigmas toward cannabis. The stigmas accumulate from the familiarity of the topic following the media, word of mouth, and local experience. The uneasiness and discrimination of users. RSA policies were used as a guide in addressing the cannabis stigmas. The names: cannabis, marijuana, dagga, etc. were clarified. The chapter aims to address the stigma by giving insights into the legislation, medical cannabis, and clarifying the commonly identified stigmas.

Chapter 11 is titled "The Role of Supply Chain Technology in the Growth of the Cannabis Industry."

Technological innovations seem to contribute to improving lifestyle, better resource allocation, and ensuring intensive economic growth. The purpose is to cogitate on technological transformation's essence and encapsulate innovation activities' value propositions to improve the producer value and socio-economic growth. The first objective is to establish the role of technology and innovations in the development of the cannabis and help industry to analyse how supply chain technology influences the socio-economic growth of the cannabis industry. The systematic literature review method synthesises the industry's existing conceptual approaches. The study embodied the review protocol, identified the inclusion exclusion criteria for relevant publications, performed an in-depth search for studies, followed by a critical appraisal, data extraction, and a synthesis of past findings. The study reveals that the role of technology and innovation invigorates the propensity to innovativeness in the cannabis industry to generate new ideas and operations methods.

Chapter 12 is titled "The Legalisation of Cannabis: Prevailing Challenges and Benefits for the South African Society."

In recent years, cannabis has been one of the substances that many countries around the world have taken or are taking steps to legalise for certain kinds of consumption. In some countries, it is only legal in certain parts and still illegal in others. There is literature to suggest that idea of legalising cannabis tends to divide opinion with some people being for its legalisation and others being against it. The reason for the division of opinion regarding the legalisation of cannabis can be traced back to the many challenges and benefits that stem from cannabis being legal in any given society. There is sparse literature addressing the contextual dynamics of these resulting challenges and benefits. In this chapter, the authors present a commentary of some of the challenges and benefits that may result from the legalisation of Cannabis in South Africa.

Chapter 13 is titled "The Process Towards Cannabis Commercialization by Indigenous Communities for Medicinal Purposes in South Africa."

The possibilities for legalizing cannabis for commercial use in South Africa is investigated in this study using desktop research from documents, newsletters and existing literature. Indigenous communities would gain immensely from the legalization of producing cannabis-infused products, as it would help to enhance the rural economy by producing jobs and create wealth. Cannabis is a significant component of African religion, culture, and beliefs, having been used by indigenous communities for generations and believed to have curative properties. Moreover, legalizing cannabis for industrial use makes sense for economic development and further medical research. According to the republic of South Africa's president, Mr Cyril Ramaphosa's 2022 February speech, cannabis has the potential to be industrialized and commercialized in South Africa in the near future. The speech came after the Constitutional Court (ConCourt) in 2018 has already decriminalized and permitted cannabis use for both personal and medical purposes, which was previously illegal.

Chapter 14 is titled "Possible Employment and Career Development in the South African Cannabis Market."

The aim of the chapter is to provide knowledge on the opportunities that the cannabis market has for South Africa. It further provides new models developed from the current literature on the related subjects. The industry also plans to improve the current products which requires a lot of training and development from the existing people in the market. Therefore, this chapter will cover a range of topics such as Employment Relation Act, entrepreneurship competencies, human resource planning, training and development, recommendable diversity and motivational models, National Qualifications Framework (NQF) as well as to look at the future jobs within the cannabis industry.

Chapter 15 is titled "The Industrialization of Cannabis in South Africa: A State-Led Case for High-Powered Redistribution."

This chapter aims to understand the opportunities that are available for the industrialisation of cannabis in South Africa from the developmental state perspective. The exclusion of Black people in the economy is still the main theme of the South African economy 28 years into democracy. Therefore, the intersection between the state and its importance in terms of guiding the private sector to achieve industrialisation and redistribution is a theme worthy of exploring. Interestingly, cannabis being a nascent sector in the economy, can either create opportunities for inclusion of those previously excluded or it could sustain the dominance of those who presently control the status quo. Hence to facilitate such inclusion the state needs to play a pivotal facilitative role. Therefore, three themes are the focus of this chapter: i) developmental state; ii) opportunity for the cannabis industry in South Africa; and iii) redistribution - what form of distribution is required to occur in the industry to benefit the entire South African population.

Chapter 16 is titled "Envisaged Cannabis Economic Value-Chain for South Africa."

The most critical and mainly inherent objective of this chapter is to afford a fresh insight into the Economic realm that denotes cannabis potentially through its ploughing, refinery, nurture, multi-fated functions, in relation to job opportunities, employment creation, and subsequently generating revenues. Otherwise, it provides various information from various expert sources regarding the subject matter. Essentially, it presents researched work in the form of surveys that identify key debates, challenges, and trends and construct and argue for a future agenda. The selected topic deliberately provides a constellation of perspectives aimed at exploring and debating crucial issues as raised.

This book advances the narrative on the cannabis industry around the globe from the perspective of different researchers. The book forms part of the background information required to study the viability of the cannabis sector to the economy and businesses. The cannabis sector offers a lot of opportunities for the economy and the businesses in it. The book broadly contributes to subjects relating to regulation, stigma, products and economic benefits of the Cannabis sector.

Pfano Mashau
University of KwaZulu-Natal, South Africa

Jabulani Nyawo
University of KwaZulu-Natal, South Africa

REFERENCES

Abara, E. (2021, February 7). *Africa's cannabis industry could potentially grow beyond $7 billion valuation by 2023 as opportunities abound.* https://africa.businessinsider.com/local/markets/africas-cannabis-industry-could-potentially-grow-beyond-dollar7-billion-valuation-by/evlxmqz

Gosch, I. (2019, March 1). *5 Key Innovations Driving the Future of Cannabis.* Visual Capitalist. Available at: https://protect-za.mimecast.com/s/cI_0CNx1WPS9Dv97tmIORy?domain=visualcapitalist.com/

Kitchen, C., Kabba, J. A., & Fang, Y. (2022). Status and Impacts of Recreational and Medicinal Cannabis Policies in Africa: A Systematic Review and Thematic Analysis of Published and "Gray" Literature. *Cannabis and Cannabinoid Research.*

Kuppuram, G. (2021). Decriminalizing Marijuana: The Science and Social Sustainability Behind the use of Marijuana (Cannabis) in India. *Journal of the Association of Researchers*, *26*(2), 10–27.

The Business Fortune. (2022 February 16). *Cannabis Market Size, Research | Marijuana Industry Growth 2028.* https://www.fortunebusinessinsights.com/industry-reports/cannabis-marijuana-market-100219

The Department of Agriculture, Land Reform, and Rural Development. (2022, February 8). *Trends in the Agricultural Sector.* https://www.dalrrd.gov.za/Portals/0/Statistics%20and%20Economic%20Analysis/Statistical%20Information/Trends%20in%20the%20Agricultural%20Sector%202020.pdf

The Presidency. (2022, February 8). *State of the Nation Address 2022.* South African Government. https://www.gov.za/SONA2022

Chapter 1
Does the Industry for Cannabis Provide More Challenges in Its Insurance Provision?
A Case of Global Perspective

Bibi Zaheenah Chummun
University of KwaZulu-Natal, South Africa

ABSTRACT

The demand for cannabis is at present increasing and the business globally is really evolving and expanding. With newcomers such as big corporate businesses, investors, and entrepreneurs, there has been a new standard of sophistication and level in the cannabis market worldwide. Several business providers of cannabis are confronted with a consortium of challenges and intend to have any form of insurance coverage to reduce those hiccups. However, there has been noted challenges in insuring the cannabis-allied business providers as they are considered a high-geared risk and embrace the so-called risk of specialty. Insuring the cannabis related businesses market is nowadays more complex as the market trend takes a difficult turn due to regulatory and supervisory challenges. Since cannabis indeed is used for multi-purposes and plays a huge role in enhancing businesses nowadays, it will be wise that the government officials, policymakers, and others work closely with the insurance market players or providers so that these challenges can be reduced.

INTRODUCTION

Insurance or so-called cover relates to a tool of risk management which is utilized by organizations namely insurers and banks or individuals whether it is traditional or conventional . The term insurance is so common these days that it is classified to be a decent legal service that is proposed to the various stakeholders including the public as a whole. Life or long-term assurance, for instance, was considered to be rude to many religions as buying an insurance policy was seen to go against the divine forces in the 1700s (Clark & Clark, 1999). However, Britain allowed life insurance to develop, mainly because the

DOI: 10.4018/978-1-6684-6346-8.ch001

protestants needed to find some measures of generating some type of life cover to protect their families in case of an unexpected hardships. It was motivated that long-term life insurance is equipped with many benefits, thus a culture was then generated of having a long-term cover to bet on third persons' life. The enactment of a piece of legislation namely, Life Assurance Act of 1774 by parliament required a subscriber to convey an "insured interest" on the life of an insured, then started the conventional regulatory and supervisory balance of allowing insurance to receive socially and mentally beneficial-related results and simultaneously regulating the insurance industry to reduce challenges. The roots of insurance embodied important principles and measures that keep on informing conventional regulation of insurance through supervisory, judicial and legislative efforts to counteract the unwanted consequences that cover has on behavior of people. For instance, a subscriber of an insurance life policy having another insured on his policy can have a motive of bad faith to end that person life and received all the benefits of the policy. Tackling the concept of moral hazard has been an important aspect of regulation in the insurance sector. In South Africa the long-term insurance Ombudsman deals with these scenarios and in other countries there is a pool of funds that is put by the government to assist the victims for his public good in case the insurer refused to pay the claim.

Over the years, several important life insurance principles have been brought into the relief and arena of the law of insurance and have even been applied especially now that the cannabis market of several legalized states has emerged recently with so much determination in some countries. The so-called famous cannabis also known as marijuana, is a term used interchangeably in different contexts. Marijuana contains a psychoactive component known as Tetrahydrocannabinol (THC) derived from the cannabis plant. Over 100 different cannabinoids have been identified in the cannabis Sativa plant (Bogdanovic, Borisev, & Ivana, 2017). Cannabidiol (CBD) contains chemical substance and is meant for therapeutic use by an authorised prescriber. Native to South Asia and central Asia, cannabis has over the years been utilized for entheogenic, recreational and traditional medicines purposes.

On a worldwide font, the need and importance to understand the requirements of a respective cannabis market and also consider the steps to address insurance needs in their respective state markets in their integral terms has never been felt like nowadays in view of their challenges. In an attempt to stimulate future growth, it is needless to mention that many regulators of cannabis related insurance have emphasized the needs to encourage successfully the participation of insurers to offer the legal cannabis business providers some sort of cover. Although the participation rate and level of cannabis business providers has increased, there is still a huge insurance gap related to cannabis in many parts of a country or states where it has been legalised. Cannabis has been classified as a product that is unique. Any product, including a cannabis product that is marketed with a claim of therapeutic benefit, or with any other disease claim, is considered to be a drug . Generally, a new drug must be approved by the Food and Drug Administration (FDA) for its intended use before it may be introduced into the activities of inter- states. The United States Food and Drug Administration (FDA or USFDA) is a federal agency of the Department of Health and Human Services. The FDA is responsible for protecting and promoting public health. It Protects the public from harmful products Many parts of the country consider cannabis as not legal in the United States. The Development of drugs has focused on using particles in cannabis: Cannabidiol(CBD) and Tetrahydrocannabinol (THC)

Four products have been approved in 2021 by the FDA:

1. Marinol (dronabinol) (1985): nausea from cancer chemotherapy.
2. Cesamet (nabilone) (1985 (2006)): nausea & neuropathic pain.

3. Syndros (dronabinol) (2016): nausea from cancer chemotherapy.
4. Epidiolex (CBD) (2018): for childhood seizures. Schedule V

The emphasis remains that the study on the cannabis paradigm should not be generalized (Adebisi & Olaoye, 2022) as there are so many fluctuations in the legalization of the local and federal, state, and local level and it is a continually evolving market with many types of products.

In South Africa, SAHPRA (South African Health Product Regulatory Authority) is the regulatory body appointed by the department of health of the Republic of South Africa. The government of South Africa has developed policies, collaborated with United Nations (INBC), and employed a regulating body (SAHPRA) to regulate the cannabis industry however many people are not informed about such policies including law government officials.

In South Africa the possession, legalization of private cultivation, and the utilization of cannabis were discussed in September 2018 at the Constitutional Court in South Africa. That discussion had potential of amending the insurance law which will transform the insurance market as a whole (Businesstech, 2021). The utilization of cannabis for religious and medical purposes, the privacy right of someone to use it for these purposes was considered by the South African Constitutional court. Canada has also considered these approaches.

As the maturity and growth of the cannabis related activities in different countries and market continue, so are the challenges which keep on becoming pressing to the extent that it is obvious that these issues have put pressures on the government to persistently tackle them and find solutions within the regimes. The legal people have been much involved and concerned in this process of conflict resolution in an attempt to assist their respective customers to subscribe imperatively to insurance cover wherever applicable related to these risks of cannabis-related activities. As the cannabis market become more intensive nowadays in their business dealings, the need to secure a relevant insurance cover becomes even more pressing. However, due the uniqueness of the cannabis product and market which is considered as a high level risk component in its specificity, acquiring insurance cover is heading towards more difficulties as ever due to the complex structures of the regulatory and supervisory challenges cropping its way.

Therefore, the main aim of the study is to examine the different criteria that insurers mainly intermediaries, should really become abreast with in the process of looking for appropriate cover for the cannabis specialty line industry and also the different obstacles they are likely to be confronted with and subsequently address them when dealing in cannabis insurance operations.

This chapter is divided into five main sections: The first section provides a snapshot of different types of cannabis insurance policies that cover in terms of cannabis-related risks and customized to generate cover to providers of cannabis related activities. Section two provides some key challenges related to cannabis consumption including the different usage risk factor of cannabis. Section three discusses recommendations based on the findings. Section four provides the future research directions of the study and a conclusion will be found in section five.

BACKGROUND

The demand for cannabis is at present increasing and the business globally is really evolving and expanding. The global cannabis market revenue is expected to increase to $24 Billion in 2024 and $33.6 billion by 2025 compared to $17.5 Billion 2019 and $20 Billion in 2020(National Association of Insurance

Commissioners, 2022). According to the United Nations(2021), 158.8 million people around the world have used marijuana more than 3.8% of the planet's population and from the pool, more than 94 million people in the United States have admitted using it at least once. Data from the 2007 National Survey on Drug Use and Health indicated that 2.4 million people in the United States have used marijuana for the first time that year, among whom the youngsters were 6.7% between the age of 12 to 17(Azofeifa et al., 2016).

There has been a surge in the production of domestic marijuana which has increased drastically over the last twenty-five years from the survey of the National Survey on Drug Use and Health in 2007. Next to alcohol, cannabis is the second most frequently found substance in the bodies of drivers involved in fatal automobile accidents (Damsere, 2017). 242,200 emergency vehicles accidents cases visited in the United States involved marijuana consumption . Further, according to the US Drug Enforcement Administration, a large percentage of those arrested for crimes tested positive for marijuana. Nationwide, 40% of adult males tested positive at the time of their arrest.

In South Africa, The South African Health Products Regulatory Authority (SAHPRA) controls the sale, possession and manufacture of any medicine or Scheduled substance in South Africa. This is regulated by the Medicines and Related Substances Act, 1965 (the Medicines Act). SAHPRA is the new name for the old Medicines Control Council (MCC). There was a recent study on the growing cannabis industry(CNN, 2019). On the verge of becoming a multi-billion-dollar industry, countries around the world have started to legalise cannabis. In South Africa, farmers are trading in traditional crops in favour of growing cannabis but navigating this expanding industry is challenging. Like many countries, cannabis regulation in South Africa is not without challenges. According to a Cannabis Expo in Pretoria, South Africa in 2019 the legal issues around cannabis with farmers and sellers who are benefitting from the growing industry were discussed. There are so many pessimisms around the cannabis activities, Many pregnancies for teenagers and dropouts of schools have been part of these negativities. The consumption of marijuana keeps on hiking as mentioned by many authors such as Destrebecq (2007) and Mujuru & Sekhejane, (2014). The South African Department of Transport and the Council for Scientific and Industrial Research in South Africa made a survey on 400 drivers. The surveys were conducted on various roads and 60 drivers out the 400 tested positive for cannabis. In many countries, drivers involved are injured due to accidents commonly are found positive for cannabis Tetrahydrocannabinol and alcohol (Perkel, 2005).

In 2018, South Africa decriminalised smoking and cultivating cannabis in private spaces, with the caveat that all cannabidiol (CBD) products must be registered. According to the South African Health Products Regulatory Authority (2018), which explained the process to register, four medical cannabis cultivation licences with the aim to eventually produce locally made CBD oil were granted to the farmers. The cannabis industry in South Africa is a big opportunity that generates into a global marketplace. For many farmers in South Africa, cannabis is more than just a business, it is a philosophy for many farmers with similar thoughts that their desire to work in collaboration in unity to create value for each other and some called it, a canna-abundance, canna-fever and there is no shortage in the world (Jonckie, 2019).

Cannabis is decriminalized and allowed for medical use in several regions of North America, Africa, Australia, Europe and South America(Hacienda, 2021). However, it remains prohibited in Middle Eastern countries and Asia (Hacienda, 2021). It is essential for every individual that uses cannabis to have an understanding of these cannabis laws, especially if they are traveling or relocating to another country. One can avoid the possibility of randomly getting caught in a cannabis search by vaping discreetly.

However the smell of cannabis is still very divisive, and if caught in areas with strict anti-cannabis rules, one may face some legal issues.

Generally, to be on the safe part, individuals who consume cannabis normally buy insurance cover protection against to protect them from unexpected hardships. For instance, the availability of an insurance called third-party cover gives cover for liability occurring related to injury of a person by the insured.

The next section takes into account some of the insurance policies the hurdles cropping up around the risks of cannabis. The regulators in conjunction with insurers have addressed the aspects and the extent to which those insurance cover which are allowed to insure losses with regard to cannabis related risks but some areas are still lying in the grey side. Therefore, the next section looks at different types of insurance policies related to cannabis risks

A SNAPSHOT OF SOME CURRENT INSURANCE POLICIES AND CANNABIS RELATED RISKS.

Liability Insurance

In general term, liability cover policies give protection to the subscriber against the claims put forward by someone whom the insured has negligently injured (Business Insurance, 2022). The availability of an auto-liability cover gives cover to the injured people due to inadmissible behaviour or to the trade of illegal drugs in general. Liability cover normally does not cover claims that is generated by the transfer, possession, use, sale or manufacture of a substance except that the person complies that it is a health care practitioner that has prescribed the medical prescription. The auto liability cover generally remove losses that arise by the subscriber's intoxication of illegal drugs (Bartlome, 2018).

Property Insurance

The presence of homeowners policies allows the insured to claim if his/her personal building is brought to damages. The availability of a property cover is a more complicated situation when it is associated to the cultivation of cannabis. The challenges that arises is when the courts consider a ban on the sale, production and use of cannabis as an enforced public policy. In 2012, a court of the federal in Hawaii maintained that a subscriber of insurance who cultivated cannabis for his/her private use could not claim under his/her homeowners insurance policy (Kobayashi, 2012). After a dozen plants that were robbed,on the premises, it was argued that the state cannabis laws did not legalise the cannabis ownership(Sparkling, 2019).

Employment-Related Insurance Coverages

The implications of insurance cover in the use of legal cannabis have been dealt by the courts in some states for instance in the case of employment relationship. Workplaces or sites of employment have been territories for the use of cannabis by employees for many years although employers have made it clear that workers do not consume alcohol together with their food (Reckner & Brighton, 1999). By the same token, after the medical sector and their employees such as doctors and pharmaceuticals have been using cannabis for several years for many diseases, it became obvious of the ban of cannabis use in the products (Mootz, 2018). Further, recently, the legislatures have ensured that the workplaces are free of the use of illegal drugs consumed for the enhancement of productivity and safety at work. However, it is not certain that these protocols and rules at work will be maintained consistently as workers continue to use cannabis in their places of work.

CHALLENGES IN THE CANNABIS MARKET

The whole market whether national or international of legal cannabis is growing. As more businesses in the cannabis sector are implanted, the need to increase these potential risks is more felt. However, because of the unique and specialty risk nature of the business of cannabis there are more challenges in insuring the businesses resulting from the regulatory and supervisory challenges.

Although the cannabis industry has made important improvement especially in the area of legalisation, it continues to be confronted with challenges. Further, for intermediaries to meet successfully the objectives of extending the right cover to their customers dealing in cannabis businesses is quite a hard task. This section takes into consideration what intermediaries need to be aware of when they accept to offer the insurance to the cannabis businesses. Although the legal and regulatory aspects continue to be the driving forces of the cannabis market, different states and countries address the sale and use of cannabis on a different basis in the United States. On an overall basis the cannabis industry is a complicated one for many investors, suppliers and stakeholders (Johnston 2021).

As the sector for cannabis business activities to grow, it has to adjust to the speedy complex market trends including its legal implications. Different states as well as different countries have different laws and rules that apply to the sale, use, distribution of cannabis. It is a fact that the "addiction" sector namely the liquor, tobacco, pharmaceuticals, have been encouragingly advised to invest in the cannabis market. The players of the cannabis sector have been encoraged to purchase shares in the cannabis market or merging/partnering with them in an attempt to sell cannabis on large scale production as they do with their own services. It is expected that this market trend could drastically change the cannabis industry in its integral form (Johnston 2021). Below we look at the different key challenges facing the cannabis industry.

Cannabis Usage as a Risk Factor

There are different factors that affect the way the premium charged for a cannabis insurance policy. For instance, the use of cannabis by someone may impinge the way that the premiums of insurance is calculated and determined. The insurer may at his discretion want to increase the premiums for insurance of cannabis users because of the severe risks that can be associated with performing certain activities such as driving or any actions being under cannabis influence.

The constitutional court in South Africa has been stringent when it comes to the consumption of cannabis by the users (SAPHRA, 2020). The utilisation of cannabis made in an excessive manner can generate harm to the consumer. However, there is a certain amount that when consumed by a customer is likely to lead to minimal or no harm at all according to some medical evidence, although the amount is still not clear. Users of cannabis are required to fully reveal all necessary information in good faith and fairness to their insurer when subscribing to a new contract of insurance or upon renewal of the contract. Further, it is the responsibility of the insured to fully reveal all aspects which are important to the risk for which the insurance policy is being applied or taken. The purpose of full disclosure is an advantage to the consumer although it does increase the premium if high risk is being exposed to. For instance, the life style the consumer is exposed to is a key determinant when calculating the insurance premium for the subscriber although there could be an increase in the premium. Failure to disclose all the important information could lead to the claims being rejected by the insurer at a later date.

Complex Structures of Business and Different Requirements

Every cannabis provider/operator is very unique business scenarios depending on which state and country they belong to. By the same token are their different tax treatment and federal legalities they are confronted with (FDA, 2021).

Complexity of Knowledgeable Markets

Cannabis is a difficult market to understand and intermediaries such as brokers and agents at times see it as a challenge to engage to the risks. Training and development have been seen as very important for the personnel. Further, it is wiser to work with the experts in the industry who can grasp the specific underwriting process of cannabis operation activities.

Preliminary stages of the Cannabis Industry

The cannabis market is still at its preliminary stages for some countries or states and there are not many criteria, actuarial tables or guidelines to calculate insurance premiums. Resultantly at times there is no transparency in the practices, processes, and systems in place from an insurance organisation or from the view of the industry as a whole. This is a big challenge for both the carriers and underwriters to set up their own guidelines.

Exhausting Process of Sales

The market of cannabis is always targeted by the sales or turnover and as time elapsed the pressure is more felt. This follows the same process of sales target like in other fields of insurance like the low-income insurance cover (Chummun, 2012). It is a trend that the intermediaries are charging more than the traditional insurance seller of cannabis. The sales process of cannabis is becoming more competitive within a short space of time as they want to keep a specific niche market for their customers and also build on the potential ones. So is the insurance process of cannabis, the insurers want to demarcate their insurance policies from other players on the market to be more competitive whether in terms of their services or on their insurance premiums.

The Inconsistencies in Policies

A cannabis policy of insurance is not very consistent when it comes to adequate cover for the cannabis businesses. Further the language can differ in some policies which does not make it easy. Finding enough cover in a cannabis policy can be very challenging. According to National Association of Insurance Commissioners (2022), too many cannabis businesses that receive an insurance cover policy has inadequate cover or limits. According to National Association of Insurance Commissioners (2022), the hardest challenges is that the cannabis businesses face robbery product or general liability. In the field of insurance segments, intermediaries are struggling to extend the cover needed by the cannabis businesses due to the risks of theft, product and general liability that occur often.

Banking Challenges

The banking aspect related to the cannabis businesses can be a hurdle as many companies cannot access traditional banking services in the United States (Johnston, 2021). The federal regulations have restricted the amount of capital that cannabis businesses are allowed to(Johnston, 2021). In the financing cannabis development industry, the most innovative ideas and implementation thereof will come from the biggest funders or investors and the developed nations. The banking industry in the emerging countries has not put forward a financing offer to aspiring cannabis businesses in the developing countries such as South Africa. The African continent has a great opportunity to benefit from the industry. It is revealed that around seventy percent of Cannabis businesses transact only on a cash basis and are less likely to have a formal connection with banks in their business dealings (the Secure and Fair Enforcement Banking Act). It is anticipated that this will change or relaxed in the near future, and it will be made clear the amount of capital the cannabis businesses are allowed to.

Interest Rates

The cannabis sector is still in its early phase of development and like any starting business, the cannabis businesses require to increase capital to invest in the future growth. Since the cannabis businesses have limited capital and do not have financing options by the banks, the process of getting capital is harder and it increases their costs also.

Lack of Complete Insurance Cover for Cannabis Operators

The market of cannabis is a specific market on its own and the entry of cannabis businesses can be challenging to obtain surplus lines insurance covering all risks is important to the effective management of risk process. In specificity, the outdoor cultivators of cannabis and logistics businesses that carry cannabis from one destination to another location have seen that it is very difficult to find appropriate insurance cover. For instance, the businesses dealing in outdoor cultivation have had difficulties finding theft, product and general liability cover covering any hiccups due to theft (Moorcraft, 2018). The insurance companies are not very willing to insure the risks should there be a theft along the way of cultivation as the cannabis cultivation is perceived to be often held in a hazard manner outside. This is due to the operators sometimes lacking protective equipment related to greenhouse cultivation and solid equipment available on the cultivation site such as strong barriers surrounding the cultivation and a proper roof. Further, the use of pesticides which is not allowed in most cases in the growing of outdoor cannabis may be used sometimes (Perkowski, 2018) .The effect of bad weather due to climate change can also affect the harvests badly.

Lack of Products Liability Cover and Occurrence Claims

From an operations standpoint of the risk management process, products liability cover represents mainly the most pertinent need of insurance for cannabis businesses through the whole supply chain. The product liability cover protects businesses in case of the product being defective and claimed by the insureds in the marketplace.

According to Levenson (2016), for products like cannabis that are consumable, the product liability provides an important risk that businesses should cope around carefully with much tools and expertise including the product liability cover. The risks embedded in the consumption of cannabis normally takes some time to manifest or show that it can be harmful, and this has been demonstrated by the consumers or insureds. The cannabis products such as edibles can be placed somewhere for some time before it is used by the consumers or insureds and resultantly the product in generate injury to the body or damage to the property that cannot be identified for a period of time before a claim is associated with the products can be made to the insurer. There have been many claims received so far for the sold faulty cannabis products which have been placed for some time before being used for the consumption of third party or insureds. For instance, a consumer can report the faulty product to the retailer or supplier soon after buying a pen in the form of a vape that consequently burnt the insured or third-party throat. Therefore it is important for the operators of cannabis to buy enough insurance cover for their products to protect them against the potential "occurrences" that may arise during the period of policy in place.

The Inadequacy of Available Coverage

In general terms, traditional cover for cannabis businesses is restricted to fully cover the whole business activities as there are underwriting challenges on the part of insurers. First and foremost, some policies do not make it clear and is difficult to understand in their formatted standard language to some consumers. Secondly, at times when the insurance policies are formatted in standard language, it becomes complexed to interpret the inclusions and exclusions due to how cannabis activities are regulated in some states. Last but not least, the insurance policies that are available to the cannabis market nowadays normally contain terms and conditions that are customised to remove some the risks that are pertinent to the cannabis businesses. The increased under insurance gap of $500 to $750 million among cannabis operators is more likely affecting the stability of the industry on a financial front, certainty of several cannabis and the customers safety (NACB, 2021). However, the entry of many carriers of cannabis to the industry have not reduced these challenges although that more competition in the sector among the players would provide more adequate and appropriate cover at reasonable costs.

General Challenges

Cannabis businesses are confronted with many risks and challenges, in brief robbery, and product liability due to manufacturing, crop failure due to climate change and fire, damage to the property or injury to the insureds or third party. Further, legalisation or regulation are the most common obstacles in the sector of cannabis and insurance to these are challenging too due to the reasons mentioned above.

RECOMMENDATIONS

Some Innovative Measures and Practices on how can Cannabis Insurance be Placed

As mentioned below, since many hurdles are happening in the cannabis market and becoming more complex as time is elapsing, the insurers should accordingly adopt a reasonable way they deal with those difficulties in an innovative and effective way. The need to apply innovation is much needed in this market nowadays to deal with the wicked problem of Covid-19. Therefore, one needs the insights and input without forgetting the assistance of different stakehoders in due time as time goes by slowly but certainly rather than spot on the solution upfront. The next section looks at different recommendations based on the challenges identified and related to the findings of the study.

Develop Good Working Relationships with experts in the field such as Knowledgeable Retailers and Wholesalers

A retailer or supplier who is knowledgeable or has got the competencies and expertise in the field of cannabis does not only understand the content of a standard policy of insurance but also is equipped to convey the information to other stakeholders including intermediaries/insureds/agents on how to maximise the limited cover that are being placed. For retailers or brokers who transact mainly in the standard market of cannabis, extending their activities in the space of cannabis requires partnering with a wholesaler as the latter is deemed to be knowledgeable and can assist in the understanding process of the insurance policy and also how to protect their business activities in the cannabis market. This is very demanding as it requires a big learning curve process to be set in place in view that underwriting and covering risks as well as finding the right mix of products and services can be vital.

As was mentioned earlier, it is pertinent for intermediaries to determine some cover gaps in the insurance policies of cannabis. Nowadays, the top three liability-related policy gaps in most cannabis-related insurance policies are:

1. Lack of cover for vaping products. Nowadays some standard insurance policies specifically have the exclusions of vaping products. Many insurance policies do not transparently stipulate about the inclusions and exclusions of the vaping products related policy.
2. Minimal -risk hazard endorsements. These appendices exclude insurance cover for the health-related claims and this compromises the level standard of quality of a product liability cover.
3. Limits in the injury cover. For organisations that employ security guards for instance, the misconduct of employees or customers can result in costly liability claims. It is a fact that the limits which are on the lower side can put the cannabis businesses at jeopardized financial risk.

The South African government has so far developed some policies and even liaised with the United Nations (INBC), and employed a regulating body (SAHPRA) to regulate the cannabis industry however many people are not informed about such policies including law government officials. Below are some recommendations where the cannabis legalization and insurance should be considered.

Home Insurance

In South Africa the homeowners' insurance does not cover for claims which occur from non-legal business activities although when an act of crime happens without the intention to make the damage. The submission of a claim related to a damage or loss of with regard to cannabis is not generally insured in a homeowner policy of insurance. Insurers can at times be challenged with claims submitted related to damage, theft or loss of a cannabis supply. Thus, it is crucial for insurance companies to properly revise the language used or wording of the homeowners policy of insurance by considering the legalization of the possession, use and cultivation of marijuana/cannabis for private purposes by adults. Insurance companies must also review their policies in terms of their wordings related to all perils basis or only a name peril basis and to what extent can the sum be insured. Further the categories of cultivators and users can be exempt from cover . It is therefore important that the legislation place a certain limits and parameters when ironing out the grey points in the present legislation.

Motor Insurance

It is not clear and certain so far the way that driving a motor vehicle while being under the cannabis influence will be approached by insurers. As intoxication rules its ways; it is said that driving under the influence of alcohol has the same effects when driving under the cannabis/marijuana influence. While being under the cannabis influence, a person senses are reduced and being placed as a hazard to his own self and other users of the road. The National Road Traffic Act (1996) in South Africa put it forward and clear that nobody can drive a vehicle while under the influence of alcohol intoxication or intoxicating drug which has a narcotic effect. Insurers bank a lot on the level of alcohol in the blood test when it comes to paying or not in the event of a claim. Many motor insurance policies generally set as exclusions liabilities if the driver is under the influence of intoxicating drugs or liquor.

A person who is found to have traces of cannabis in their system while driving can be arrested and prosecuted according to SAPHRA(2020). It is not certain what means of testing the authorities can employ to determine whether a person is under the influence of cannabis other than performing an oral fluid or blood test.

The insurance industry must carefully consider the underwriting implications of more widespread marijuana use. The key underwriting considerations will include the frequency, purpose, and admission of use, as well as the type of marijuana used, the applicant's age, history of accidents, risky behaviour, and other substance abuse. Given the many different forms of marijuana (vapes, edibles and oils), an underwriter needs to be able to quantify not only the dosage but the strength of the substance involved. Although some companies are considering offering non-smoker rates to the occasional marijuana user who does not smoke or combine tobacco or nicotine products, this remains a challenge.

The competitive marketplace has driven a number of these changes, however, their effects on insurance cover is still not known. Although some research studies have been undertaken and support of these underwriting changes have been made, there can be trade-offs such as potential price hikes, unexpected morbidity and death results and also there could be a paradigm change in insurance applications from the niche targets.

Know the Niche Market

While this insurance market may be new for many independent agents, understanding everything from the terminology that is used to the carriers that offer coverage is essential. If one wants to get involved into the insurance marketplace one must know the space. That means learning the terminology, the classes of business and how they operate.

Cannabis operations require a range of insurance policies, including property and liability cover. It is wise for one to take his/her time and ask lots of questions as the diversity in the way cannabis businesses operate. While most cannabis businesses have common security protections, alarms, safes, cameras, they will also have uniquely different operations and approaches to their business.

Additionally, when it comes to the product itself different forms of solvent-based extraction and types of lighting and drying processes will all vary from one license holder to the next and will play a dynamic role in evaluating the risk profile of an insured. Helping the insured accurately represents their operations on a supplemental application is critical to placing effective and relevant coverage for the insured.

Development of Partnerships

Creating relationships with carriers will give an agent aiming to specialize in the cannabis market space to grow. The more accounts and savings they work together on and the more committed each party is to the business activities, the more successful they will be (Chummun & Ojah, 2016). Almost everyone is serving the same markets, so it truly comes down to expertise and relationships. It will be wiser that carriers and the programs in the market get familiar with their applications and their submission requirements and appointment process.

However, agents should still sharpen their risk management knowledge because the insurance offerings do not cover everything like in the standard market and clients will need to fill those gaps.

FUTURE RESEARCH DIRECTIONS

Despite that the global pandemic of COVID-19 has stabilized a bit of its negative effects on the welfare of people, it has left the post math effects on the life of many. As such it has affected a growing number of increased persons using cannabis for medical uses. This is because the 2019-nCoV pandemic has taken its toll on peoples' mental health on a global basis. There were 53.2 million additional major cases of depressive disorder and 76.2 million additional cases of anxiety disorders globally due to the pandemic in 2020, according to a study by The Lancet in October 2021(The Lancet, 2021). This obviously shows the rising use of medicinal cannabis. Specifically, the study found that people with mental health conditions increased their use of medicinal cannabis by 91% since COVID-19 was declared a pandemic on March 11, 2020. The emergence in November 2021 of Omicron, a new variant of the coronavirus has kept marijuana use at high levels among mental health patients to counteract their health disorders such as depression being one of the unexpected hits on their overall health. Obviously, this has led to the rising use of cannabis market activities on a global basis. Therefore, the insurance sector needs redress for the cannabis industry to be the game changer for the emerging markets in this sector. It is imperative that the government and other stakeholders find new ways of identifying appropriate new insurance policies, processes and systems to be set in place. This is a very challenging task for the providers of cannabis insurance due to the restrictions or rapid changes in the legal frameworks . Furthermore, the insurers have an immense task to ensure that the messages through training and development are being conveyed properly to the cannabis insurance intermediaries offering cannabis cover on the global market wherever applicable and relevant. Thus, the government and other insurance providers can factor those mentioned aspects mentioned above to create, innovate participation and uptake in the cannabis insurance market with the objective of driving sustainability in some countries and states and that still leave room for potential future research directions on this subject-matter.

CONCLUSION

This paper gives a snapshot and an overview of how the industry for cannabis provide more challenges its insurance provision including the obstacles of a fully-fledged related insurance cover on a global perspective. The insurance market for cannabis has grown much during the last decade and has still potential to expand in the near future. Although its recorded growth, the insurance market for cannabis is at present struggling as per the findings of this study due to fluctuation in the legal frameworks of cannabis in some states and countries, inadequacy of cover and inconsistencies in the insurance policies, banking challenges and other complexities as mentioned in the paper among others. The regulators of cannabis wherever applicable approve the application of cannabis dealings and insurance cover types and as a matter of context the market need immediate redress. To bring innovation to the font, it is high time that the government of the respective countries and policy makers work closely with the insurance companies to bring relevant and adequate insurance cover into the cannabis market place as these risks inherent in the product is unique in nature and can have serious consequences. It is pertinent the proper cover gives confidence to the insureds and various stakeholders in case if a claim is submitted at a later stage, it can be honoured and paid. Hence the study takes into consideration that the first section provides a snapshot of different types of cannabis insurance policies that cover in terms of cannabis-related risks and insurance policies customized to generate appropriate cover to providers of cannabis related activities. Section two provides some key challenges related to cannabis consumption including the different usage risk factor of cannabis. Section three discusses recommendations based on the findings of the study. Section four provides the future research directions of the study. Since there is still a lot of work that needs to be done in the sector of cannabis on a global basis, the policymakers need to be proactive to bring innovation to the forth as has been discussed in the content of the paper.

REFERENCES

Adebisi, Y. A., & Olaoye, D. Q. (2022). Medical Use of Cannabis in Africa: The Pharmacists' Perspective. *Innovations in Pharmacy*, *13*(1), 8. doi:10.24926/iip.v13i1.4430 PMID:36304681

Azofeifa, A., Mattson, M. E., Schauer, G., McAfee, T., Grant, A., & Lyerla, R. (2016). National estimates of marijuana use and related indicators—National Survey on Drug Use and Health, United States, 2002–2014. *MMWR. Surveillance Summaries*, *65*(11), 1–25. doi:10.15585/mmwr.ss6511a1 PMID:27584586

Bartlome, L. R. (2018). *Insurance for the Marijuana Industry*. Dilworth Paxson. https://www.dilworthlaw.com/blog/insurance-for-the-marijuana-industry-pg-38/

Bogdanovic, V., Mrdjanović, J., & Borišev, I. (2017). A review of the Therapeutic antitumor potential of cannabinoids. *Journal of Alternative and Complementary Medicine (New York, N.Y.)*, *23*(11), 831–836. doi:10.1089/acm.2017.0016 PMID:28799775

Business insurance. (2022). Liability Insurance. *Business Insurance*. https://businessinsurance.co.za/employer-insurance/liability-insurance/

BusinessTech. (2021). New cannabis rules proposed for South Africa – to be introduced within next 2 years. *Business Tech*. https://businesstech.co.za/news/lifestyle/482625/new-cannabis-rules-proposed-for-south-africa-to-be-introduced-within-next-2-years/

Chummun, B., & Ojah, K. (2016). Aggregate savings and financial inclusion: Lessons for developing African economies. *AfricaGrowth Agenda Journal*, *13*(3), 4–9.

Chummun, B. Z. (2012). *Evaluating business success in the Microinsurance industry of South Africa* [Doctoral dissertation, North-West University, Africa].

Clark, G., & Clark, G. W. (1999). *Betting on lives: the culture of life insurance in England, 1695-1775*. Manchester University Press.

Damsere Derry, J. (2017). *The prevalence of alcohol use among road users and its impact on traffic crash severity in Ghana* (Doctoral dissertation, Queensland University of Technology).

Destrebecq, D. (2007). *CANNABIS IN AFRICA; An Overview*. UNODC.

Federal Drug Administration. (2021). *FDA Role in Regulation of Cannabis Products*. FDA. https://www.fda.gov/media/128156/download

Hacienda, T. (2021). *The 2021 guide to cannabis laws around the world*. Tribute Content Agency.

Jonckie (2019). CNN's Marketplace Africa explores South Africa's cannabis industry. *Insurance Chat*. https://www.insurancechat.co.za/2019-07/cnns-marketplace-africa-explores-south-africas-cannabis-industry/

Kobayashi, L. (2012). *Tracy v. USAA Cas. Ins. Co.* Casetext. https://casetext.com/case/tracy-v-usaa-cas-ins-co

Levenson, D. (2016). *Asbestos Cases Illustrate Claims-Made vs. Occurrence Insurance Policies*. Insure Your Company. https://www.insureyourcompany.com/blog/asbestos- cases-illustrate-claims-made-vs-occurrence-insurance-policies/

Moorcraft, B. (2018). Outdoor Cannabis Growers Lack Insurance Options-What Can Be Done? Insurance Business Magazine. https://www.insurancebusinessmag.com/ca/market-analysis/outdoor-cannabis growers-lack-insurance-options—what-can-be-done-113996.aspx.

Mootz, F. J. (2018). Ethical Cannabis Lawyering in California. *Mary's J. on Legal Malpractice & Ethics*, *9*, 2.

Mujuru, M., & Sekhejane, P. (2014). Legalising Cannabis for Cancer: Benefits of Indigenous Cannabis Therapeutics (Briefing NO 110 ed.). Africa Institute Of South Africa.

NACB. (2021). The Cannabis Industry's massive under Insurance Gap and Need for more coverage. *NACB*. https://nacb.com/blog/the-cannabis-industrys-massive-under-insurance-gap-and-need-for-core-coverages/

National Association of Insurance Commissioners. (2022). *Cannabis and Insurance*. NAIC. https://content.naic.org/cipr-topics/cannabis-and-insurance

Perkel, C. (2005). Cannabis- the debate continues: A South African perspective. *South African Psychiatry Review*, *8*, 25–30.

Perkowski, M. (2018). Marijuana Pesticide Contamination Worries Oregon Farmers. *Capitol Press*. https://www.capitalpress.com/state/oregon/marijuana-pesticide- contamination-worries-oregon-farmers/article_303327ce-fa5d-11e8-b01f-d3b7bdf5bfde.html

Reckner, P. E., & Brighton, S. A. (1999). "Free from all vicious habits": Archaeological perspectives on class conflict and the rhetoric of temperance. *Historical Archaeology*, *33*(1), 63–86. doi:10.1007/BF03374280

SAHPRA. (2020, January 01). *Cannabis_and_related_substances_A5_final*. SAHPRA. https://www.sahpra.org.za/wp content/uploads/2020/01/Cannabis_and_related_substances_A5_final-1.pdf

Sprankling, J. G. (2019). Owning Marijuana. *Duke Journal of Constitutional Law and Public Policy*. https://scholarship.law.duke.edu/cgi/viewcontent.cgi?article=1153&context=djclpp

The Lancet. (2021). Global prevalence and burden of depressive and anxiety disorders in 204 countries and territories in 2020 due to COVID-19 pandemic. *The Lancet*. https://www.thelancet.com/journals/lancet/article/PIIS0140-6736(21)02143-7/fulltext

KEY TERMS AND DEFINITIONS

Cannabis: a genus type of flowering plant and the product is made from the cannabis plant or synthetic cannabis composites.

FDA(Federal drug administration): is an agency within the U.S. Department of Health and Human Services

Insurance: an agreement by which a person pays a company and the company promises to pay money if the person becomes injured or dies or to pay for the value of property lost or damaged

Risk Management: Risk management is the process of identifying, assessing and controlling threats to a company's resources

Risks: the chance of loss or the perils to the subject matter of an insurance contract

SAHPRA (South African Health Product Regulatory Authority): regulatory body appointed by the department of health of the Republic of South Africa

Specialty Risks: jargon used by commercial insurers to describe unusual coverage features or types of risks not underwritten by most insurers for instance cannabis insurance.

Surplus Insurance Lines: insurance protects against a financial risk that is too high for a regular insurance company to cover. Surplus line insurance can be used by companies or purchased individually. Unlike traditional insurance, this insurance can be bought from an insurer not licensed in the insured's state.

TetraHydroCannabinol (THC): a type of cannabinoid that contains high stimulation constituents known as "high effects", hail from the Cannabis Sativa plant.

Chapter 2
Cannabis Industry Policy Controls and Regulations in Zimbabwe

Taurai Muparadzi
University of KwaZulu-Natal, South Africa

Pfano Mashau
https://orcid.org/0000-0003-0490-1925
University of KwaZulu-Natal, South Africa

ABSTRACT

Cannabis policy controls and regulatory changes have attracted a lot of attention across the world as the drive for full cannabis commercialization gathers momentum. The diversity of views on cannabis regulation reflects a melting pot of regulatory regimes (Aguilar et al., 2018; Seddon and Floodgate, 2020). This chapter is therefore an attempt to converge fragmented pieces of knowledge on cannabis policies and regulations. Using a qualitative research approach, the study found that cannabis policies and regulations in Zimbabwe and most countries of the world are at experimental stages and have to negotiate a family of challenges to succeed. For the cannabis industry sector to flourish, making sense of the policy tools that have worked in other countries and adopting supportive policy best practices to strengthen the cannabis policy and regulatory framework in Zimbabwe is crucial. The chapter ends by proposing ways of strengthening the cannabis policy framework in Zimbabwe.

INTRODUCTION

In the 1970s it was generally unacceptable to legalize cannabis use (Plant, 1977), but the review of prohibitive policies and laws is long overdue in this regard. In fact, Kay et al. (2020, p. 27) suggest that the construction of prohibitive cannabis regimes was a historic mistake and transition towards liberal frameworks should be carefully calculated to include all players in the cannabis industry. Cannabis industry policies and regulations are still at experiment stage in most countries and most of what existed as

DOI: 10.4018/978-1-6684-6346-8.ch002

drug policies have been condemned as wrong and subjected to reviews considered necessary to make the policy and regulatory environment rational (Coombes, 2014). Several current and past scholarly works for example Plant (1977), Van het Loo et al (2003), Hurley (2018) and Kay et al. (2020) among others confirm that cannabis industry policies in most countries are still emerging from policy laboratories. Resultantly, policy implementation results have triggered policy and regulatory reviews across the globe based on the premises that cannabis is beneficial and that legal access and value addition through improved regulatory protocol is crucial. World-wide calls, including in Zimbabwe, for fundamental reforms in the cannabis industry have been noted by Hurley (2018). Van het Loo et al. (2003) also confirm that cannabis policies have endured debate for several decades now but a unified policy remains out of reach. As a result, different nations have made different policy decisions regarding possession and use of cannabis.

While some countries such as the USA, Spain, Uruguay and Netherlands (Aguilar et al., 2018; Lindblom, 2019 and Crick et al., 2013), ended up with stable policies, policies in other countries continue to change. Generally, cannabis policy and regulatory reforms have taken a political, medical, recreational, industry and economic dimension in countries such as the Netherlands, Spain, Uruguay and the United States of America (USA) (Mansson et al., 2021; Hall, 2020; Crick et al. (2013). To accommodate these diverse perspectives, fundamental reforms to existing cannabis policies are needed and these may even include abandonment of international treaties that prohibit the use of cannabis for industrial purposes. Such changes should be driven by the fact that the cannabis industry has huge economic potential of up to one trillion dollars in the USA, over 56 billion Euros in Europe (Coombes, 2014). In fact, Kay et al (2020:28) agree that even a rough estimate of global cannabis users is notoriously difficult to obtain despite that around 2017, a conservative estimate was placed at 188 million users of cannabis around the world but a figure which largely excludes the Global South. Buttressed by this economic reality and by the argument that the war against the use of cannabis has been lost and that dedication to building the cannabis industry is growing at both national and global levels (Herley, 2018), this Chapter examines cannabis policy in Zimbabwe and policies from selected countries in order to build a case for fit for purpose policies that support the emerging potential of the cannabis industry sector. The problem is that the cannabis policy framework in Zimbabwe has gaps which may prematurely block rapid growth of the cannabis industry. By proposing recommendations based on evidence from Zimbabwe and other countries at the end of the chapter, it is intended that new cannabis policy ideas will be added to the current stock of knowledge on cannabis regulation.

Research Methodology and Analytical Framework

This section provides a clear description of the study procedures followed during data collection and analysis. A qualitative research approach in which case studies were analysed was adopted in order to fully capture the state of cannabis regulation in Zimbabwe. The study sought to answer questions that include the following: What are the key policy instruments used to regulate cannabis use in Zimbabwe? What are some of the major cannabis policy changes recorded in other countries? What are the challenges affecting cannabis policy improvement to accommodate cannabis use for recreational purposes and how can cannabis policies be improved? In order to provide answers to these questions, the research methodology followed included a thorough review of relevant literature on the topic between the period 1 May 2022 and 31 July 2022. Online databases, institutional websites and other online libraries were used for this purpose. The search was done to obtain views and commentaries on cannabis policies and laws as well as cannabis use and these included book publications, peer reviewed journals, and reports on specific case studies. Every book section, book chapter, journal article, and report was read and what it emphasized was noted in line with predefined themes that included cannabis laws and controls, cannabis regulatory framework in Zimbabwe, cannabis laws and policies in selected case studies, cannabis industry growth opportunities and challenges affecting the design and implementation of cannabis policies among others. The key issues emerging from literature were then analysed and compared in order to identify areas of convergence and divergence. The study also relied on views from informal discussions with cannabis industry experts designed to gain a clear understanding of the cannabis policy framework in Zimbabwe. The intensity of the analysis done assisted the researchers to set a firm and realistic basis of the findings and recommendations on cannabis policy presented in the last segment of this Chapter.

LITERATURE REVIEW

Cannabis Industry Laws and Controls: An Overview

This section provides an overview of the history of cannabis controls at a global level and at the African and Zimbabwean levels. This discussion on laws and regulations is rooted in the reality that countries have obligations to control the cannabis industry. The current pressure to reform is largely fueled by the need to allow cannabis value addition and use for recreational purposes (Omare et al. 2021). Modern cannabis control laws have roots in early 20th Century laws (Aguilar et al., 2018). International drug laws can be traced to The Hague Convention of 1912 and the Second Opium Convention of 1925 (League of Nations, 1925), (European Monitoring Centre for Drugs and Drug Addiction (EMCDDA), 2018; Aguilar et al., 2018). These conventions, in particular the Second Opium Convention of 1925 among other things introduced a ban on the export of cannabis resin to countries where its use was prohibited, introduced domestic controls and required that countries impose adequate penalties and punishment for unauthorised possession of cannabis extracts (Articles 1; 4 7; 11a and 28).

These Conventions were succeeded by United Nations Conventions/Treaties regulating the production, trade, acquisition or possession of psychoactive drugs with known and proven medical use. In the European Union for example, all member states have signed these treaties. These UN Conventions include the UN Convention of 1961, 1971 and 1988 which recommend that the use of all controlled drugs should be limited to medical and scientific uses. The Conventions also classify controlled drugs into four schedules based on their levels of risk of abuse and ban the illicit cultivation of cannabis. Cannabis is listed as a schedule I and IV drug and this reflects that it is considered a dangerous drug and a serious threat to public health. Kay et al (2020) also flag the fact that international conventions schedule and label cannabis as a dangerous drug with no use value. Likewise, Aguilar et al (2018) also note that the 1971 Convention further extended the prohibitionist regime on the reasoning that the therapeutic value of cannabis is limited to non-existent. In addition, the 1988 convention further introduced criminal penalties on production, manufacture, supply, distribution, sale, transportation, import, export, cultivation and acquisition of any narcotic drug. As a result, these Conventions caused more harm to the cannabis industry and society as a whole through criminalization and social profiling of different races and attendant enforcement costs borne by governments around the world. This also further restrained the use of the drug for medical purposes.

Based on these Conventions, most national laws criminalize the unauthorised production, possession, trade and acquisition of cannabis among other issues. In addition, most national laws punish offenders by deprivation of liberty. While these conventions act as universal guidelines on dealing with controlled drugs, it should be noted that they do not dictate the specific content of national laws hence individual countries have room to draft laws that do not hinder the legal trade of such drugs for scientific and industrial purposes. Evidence from recent past and current policy reforms reflects a deviation from the restrictions imposed by the UN Conventions as is the case in Canada. Kay et al (2020:27) note that recent policy changes have reshaped the global cannabis market by opening up legal markets for medical and recreational cannabis use and this has created a rush by established firms from the Global North to capture the licit market but in a manner that threatens to squeeze out small firms in the Global South.

Cannabis Policies and Laws in Selected Case Studies

This section first examines policies and regulations in selected case studies and lastly in Zimbabwe. Selected case studies which include selected countries from Europe, selected states from the USA, Uruguay and Canada among others provide evidence supporting successful cannabis regulation in these countries as well as cannabis policy and regulation challenges and failures. Cross case analysis in this section provides a benchmark for judging the efficacy of policies adopted by the Zimbabwean government. According to Mansson et al (2021), views from literature on cannabis laws and regulation point in different directions and this diversity of approaches shows differences on cannabis use and regulation. In fact, Aguilar et al (2018) agree that regulations are not the same and do not have the same impact across the world. It is also important to note the observation of Coombes (2014) that though widely available, cannabis use and production is illegal in most countries. However, most countries are moving from absolute cannabis prohibition to legalized and regulated production, distribution and retailing despite cannabis being one of the world's most illicit drugs (Aguilar et al., 2018). The emergence of these permissive models in countries such as Uruguay, Spain, Chile, Colombia, Jamaica, Belgium, Netherlands, and USA confirm a calculated shift in the cannabis value addition and prohibition debate (Hall, 2020; Aguilar et al., 2018 and Cyrenne & Shanahan, 2018). This is confirmed by Hall (2020) who suggests that the dominance of prohibitive policies on cannabis use in most developed countries ended around the year 2012. Aguilar et al (2018) however notes that the current tide of policy changes to more cannabis tolerant policies is caused by court rulings from individual cases seeking permission to use cannabis-based medicines, democratic processes such as referendums on the use of cannabis, pressure from companies seeking licit use of cannabis-based medicines following successful research and development of medicinal products and public policy making processes in some countries.

In addition, the regulatory architecture in different countries also depends on the type of society, the quality of educational and academic institutions and dedicated research on cannabis issues, the level of technological advancement, the history of cannabis use and demand for cannabis products in the country. In line with the views above, this section therefore examines cannabis regulatory experiences in selected case studies in order to explain the trade-off between full legalization informed by the benefits of commercialization and strict prohibition of cannabis use for recreational purposes. This section further provides ideas about cannabis regulation and sets the foundation for further cannabis policy improvement in Zimbabwe.

The United Nations Drug Control Conventions

The international ban on cannabis use started in 1912 at the international opium convention (Aguilar et al., 2018). The UN drug control laws as already noted above include the the 1961 UN Single Convention on Narcotic Drugs, the 1971 UN Convention on Psychotropic Substances, and the 1988 UN Convention against Illicit Traffic in Narcotic Drugs and Psychotropic Substances. These treaties shape international laws on drug control because they are binding agreements that require countries to impose bans on the supply of controlled drugs for non-medical or scientific use. These conventions serve two critical functions: firstly, to prevent the production, supply and use of specific drugs for non-medical and scientific use and to ensure limited supplies of those drugs for legal use.

According to the Transform drug policy foundation (TDPF), the 1961 Single Convention on Narcotic Drugs identified and listed drugs in the narcotic drugs group and classified these drugs based on their risks and potential benefits. At this convention, cannabis was classified as a schedule I and schedule IV drug (Aguilar et al., 2018). Accordingly, the convention outlawed or required countries to outlaw the production and supply or transportation of those drugs for non-medical or scientific purposes (www.transform.org). Key outcomes of this convention were the establishment of the Commission on Narcotic Drugs (CND) and the International Narcotics Control Board (INCB) responsible for guiding global policy, amendments to the treaties and monitoring the implementation of the treaty respectively. Similarly, the 1971 Convention on Psychotropic Substances established further scheduling for specified drugs while the 1988 Convention Against Illicit Traffic in Narcotic Drugs and Psychotropic Substances imposed restrictions on cross-border transportation of scheduled drugs. Commenting on the UN drug control treaties, Hall (2020) notes that since 1961, countries that signed these laws adopted a prohibitive policy approach based on the reasoning that cannabis use is harmful and that the drug had no medical use.

Cannabis Controls and Regulations in the European Union

The EU has specific regulations on the production, trade and possession or acquisition of Cannabis. Under the Common Agricultural Policy (CAP), it is legal to cultivate and supply Cannabis seeds in the European Union for hemp fibre as long as they have low levels of tetrahydrocannabinol (THC) which under EU Regulation 1307/2013 should not exceed 0.2%. This condition and the specific procedures for testing the THC levels on imported hemp are also provided for under EU regulation 1308/2013. However, the European Union (EU) does not have a universal law on cannabis use but individual member states have the responsibility to enact laws that provide an adequate response, both criminal and administrative, to drug use offenses. Article 168 of the Treaty on the Functioning of the EU however provides that the EU shall complement member states in reducing drugs related health damage. In that context, there is renewed debate about the legalization of the supply and use of cannabis in Europe but concerns still remain about the public health impact of cannabis use (EMCDDA, 2018). As a result, some opposition to decriminalization and legalization of cannabis still remains. Notwithstanding anti-decriminalization and anti-legalization voices in Europe, cannabis policies and laws across the world are entering a period of change and proposals for full legalization are under consideration as is the case in Latin America where successive changes have occurred in a sort of domino effect (Aguilar et al., 2018). Evidence shows that there is very little harmonization of these laws and this clearly shows that member states treat cannabis use differently. For example, even in countries that have decriminalized possession of cannabis such as Portugal and Croatia, cultivation of cannabis remains a criminal offence. Generally, laws in the European

Union punish possession and use of cannabis for recreational purposes. Punishments however vary from counselling to imprisonment depending on country specific legislation.

In performing its complementary role in the control of drugs considered harmful to public health, the EU developed the 2004 EU Framework Decision (2004/757/JHA) based on Article 83 of the TFEU which provides minimum provisions on what constitutes a criminal offense and the related penalties for drug trafficking. More specifically the framework obliges member states to ensure that punishment for drug trafficking is 'effective, proportionate and dissuasive' and that minimum and maximum levels of penalties are defined. Effectively, this left member states with space to craft laws compliant with country specific conditions. The overall effect was however that this ensured a common approach to fighting drug trafficking.

Evidence from the EU also shows that legal approaches to handling cannabis issues vary from country to country. In some EU countries, the severity of penalties for unauthorised dealing in cannabis is high while in other EU countries they are low. Hall (2020) notes that cannabis policy in the Netherlands is liberal and since the 1970s, penalties for cannabis use and small scale sales of cannabis have not been enforced. This confirms the view of Lindblom (2019) that some countries adopted policy tolerance and enforcement discretion in the regulation of cannabis use. EMCDDA (2018) reveals that in the Netherlands, the government licenses all producers while the Office of Medicinal Cannabis (OMC) holds the monopoly to supply and distribute medical Cannabis products. Apart from the Opium Act, Netherlands introduced the Controlled Cannabis Supply Chain Experiment Act of 2019 which sought to create a uniform environment for experimentation with cannabis use for recreational purposes through coffee shops. In the context of decriminalization, the principles of the Act provide for quality controlled cultivation and supply chain of cannabis for recreational use; the introduction of coffee shops for purposes of retailing cannabis; disables prohibitions provided for by the Opium Act; sets four years as the time frame for the duration of the experiment from date of designation; provides for licensing of cannabis producers by the state; provides for the maximum number of municipalities to participate in the experiment subject to approval after screening; provides for rules governing cannabis production, delivery and sale in coffee shops and other ancillary issues such as record keeping for evaluation purposes; allows for setting of additional rules to fine tune the experiment; gives mayors powers to determine the number of coffee shops to operate in their jurisdiction; provides for sanctions in the event of infringement of the rules and provisions of the law; provides for amendment of sections in other laws that may contradict the legislative intent set out in the supply chain experiment and finally provides for evaluation for purposes of informing government's position on the cannabis supply chain experiment. Key features from this framework include the requirement for registration after screening, disabling prohibitions set out in other laws, decriminalizing cannabis cultivation, delivery and sales of cannabis, decentralizes authority to local governments and provides for evaluation of the policy after a specific period. In the Czech Republic, the State Agency for Medical Cannabis, in line with the Ministerial Notice of 2013, sets rules for e-prescription and for pharmacies. In Italy, the Ministry of Health is the primary regulator and coordinator for medical cannabis with the sole responsibility to issue permits for cultivating, producing, using and possessing medical cannabis. In Croatia, new regulations now allow the use of cannabis for medical purposes but the ordinance sets specific requirements related to the procedure for prescription for compliance purposes.

In Sweden, the national drug policy relies on criminal control and prohibition and is very strict (Mansson et al., 2021). Cannabis debate among politicians and in the Swedish media remains controversial and divided between two clashing perspectives. Despite a hard stance on cannabis use in Sweden, cannabis use shows an increasing trend which has attracted attention (Public Health Agency, 2019). Mansson et al further note that the Swedish drug policy has ideological roots in that its strict policy stance is constructed on the beliefs that cannabis causes psychosocial problems and acts as a gateway to hard drugs. The belief that cannabis leads to escalation or progression to other more harmful drugs has long been noted by Plant (1977) who confirms that this culminated in the introduction of the Misuse of Drugs Act (1971) in the United Kingdom (UK), a law which severely penalized cultivation, possession and trafficking of cannabis. In addition, drug use is also perceived to be contagious and a major potential cause of social disaster if not controlled. This mindset led to the adoption of police-oriented strategies and restrictive cannabis policies in the UK and Sweden. Moreover, the political leadership still maintains that Sweden is not a cannabis society and shall not be. As a result, the country favours a restrictive policy approach than a liberalized approach to cannabis regulation. Because of this policy stance, Mansson et al (2021 reasons that such policies may divide society among users and non-users, a scenario which may ferment discrimination, exclusion and marginalization of cannabis users. Moderate but positive policy changes have also been noted in Germany, Denmark, Ireland, Poland, Slovenia, Czech Republic and Greece (Aguilar et al., 2018). Such evidence from Europe clearly shows that cannabis policies are no longer stuck in absolute prohibition but are undergoing transformation.

Cannabis Controls and Regulation in the United States of America

This section traces cannabis legalization models in selected states in the USA. While Ramírez (2018) and Senovaityte et al (2021) note that the USA still maintains staunch prohibition on cannabis using both international and federal laws, Aguilar et al (2018) confirm that the USA is a pioneer in the development of an advanced cannabis industry with twenty-nine (29) states having laws permitting the use of cannabis for medical and scientific purposes at the time. Policy changes in the USA are basically responses to different needs and interests initiated through a mix of referenda (voter initiatives) and legislative processes (Cyrenne and Shanahan, 2018). Lindblom (2019) directs attention to the Federal Food, Drug and Cosmetics Act as one of the primary laws that regulate cannabis use in the USA and the Food and Drug Administration as the authority empowered to regulate drugs including cannabis-based preparations. Hall (2020) notes that the USA has adopted the model used for alcohol regulation as a common approach to legalization and regulation of cannabis use. In this model, producers, processors and retailers are licensed to operate for profit. Legalization of cannabis use in the USA has created a vibrant cannabis industry that now seeks to displace the illicit cannabis market. However, though pressure for liberalizing cannabis use is increasing at state level, cannabis prohibition laws at federal level have continued. This has created a regulatory double standard which restrains full commercialization of the cannabis industry sector. Evidence also shows that some states in the USA have widely legalized cannabis use through citizen initiatives while some still restrict the number and location of cannabis outlets and this has prevented effective federal regulation of cannabis use. The impact according to Lindblom (2019) is that interstate trade is adversely affected as long as there is contradiction between state and federal laws despite that the federal policy of regulatory forbearance has been in place since 1996 and that the USA has visible regulatory discretion that prevents the enforcement of federal anti-drug laws in some states. In essence US state cannabis markets operate free from federal enforcement. This has indirectly promoted the growth of cannabis markets in the USA.

Agitation for a cannabis policy shift in the USA began with proposals for the ending of the hard stance (zero-tolerance) in favour of a soft stance on cannabis in line with the Sharter Commission recommendations that harsh laws on cannabis should be removed. Since then, cannabis policies have shifted towards removal of cannabis prohibitions as supported by evidence from Colorado. Hall (2020) acknowledges that the push for cannabis legalization triggered referenda across many states in the USA and obtained massive support at state levels. According to Coombes (2014, p. 3), Colorado had the most overtly commercial model for cannabis production by 2014. According to Crick et al (2013), cannabis policy changes in the USA have been incremental and multi-layered and experiments with cannabis policy in Colorado and Washington signalled a shift from the zero-tolerance approach. While the new policies in these states contradicted federal laws and international drug control agreements, federal regulatory forbearance signalled US interest in experimenting with new cannabis policy ideas apart from the need to avoid the political implications attached to challenging the initiatives at the time. Cannabis policies in Colorado and Washington therefore provided scope for generating evidence needed to influence policy shifts elsewhere. Apart from seeking to establish legally regulated markets for cannabis production, experiments in Colorado and Washington tested the taxation of the cannabis industry as well. Unlike the tolerated cannabis coffee shop model in the Netherlands, the Colorado and Washington models were enshrined in law. The votes for legalized cannabis markets in Colorado and Washington also proved politically sensitive for the federal government. Political calculations became necessary as many states also sought to legalize cannabis use thereby placing cannabis legislation on the policy agenda. Crick et al (2013), further note that the success of cannabis policies in Washington and Colorado is linked to high level support from politicians, academics and legal professionals in a largely top-down approach, the availability of clarity on where cannabis tax money would go, and tracking cannabis from seed to store to avoid leakages on to the black market through high-tech surveillance systems. However, major pitfalls along the cannabis policy reform journey and the drive towards legally established cannabis markets included creating systems motivated by market privileges for a few major participants in the cannabis industry that ignored opinions on cannabis production from the ordinary citizens and poorly crafted proposed laws as was the case in Oregon's Measure 80 (M80) and lack of funding for proposed initiatives. The above clearly suggests the need for cannabis policies clear on taxation principles, socio-political preferences, funding, political will, and use of information communication technologies in supporting activities in the cannabis value chain.

The Cannabis Production Model in Uruguay

Uruguay is the first country to completely legalize the use of cannabis for medical and scientific as well as industrial and recreational purposes (Aguilar et al., 2018). The approach to cannabis regulation is largely statist and that means the government maintains a monopoly on the wholesale of cannabis. This model according to Hall (2020) limits the legal supply of cannabis by limiting the number of cannabis producers, maintaining licensing at state level, allowing cannabis growers' clubs and allowing the purchase of cannabis products from licensed pharmacies. Coombes (2014) notes that the Uruguay model is more restrictive compared to the Colorado and Washington models. In Uruguay, production is licensed by the state. Licensed firms produce cannabis and sell to authorised pharmacies. Non-medical use of cannabis is allowed but regulated and limited to 40 grams a month. Personal cultivation of cannabis is allowed. Advertising of cannabis product is banned and smoking is prohibited in smoke free areas. The model also allows limited home production of up to six plants and cannabis clubs that can plant up to ninety-nine plants are allowed. All buyers of Cannabis in Uruguay are registered and regulated by the Institute of Regulation and Control of Cannabis (IRCC). The major weakness of the model noted is that it leads to increased availability and consumption of cannabis. The influence of this model has also been noted in Chile and Colombia where adopted cannabis models closely mimic the Uruguay model. Notable features of these models include state control, authorization of cultivation for personal use, support for traditional growers of cannabis, authorization of collective cannabis growing clubs, and government mediated pricing of cannabis products. Several other Latin American countries such as Argentina, Brazil, Mexico and Bolivia have also amended their drug control laws to allow cannabis use for medicinal and scientific uses. It is evident therefore that cannabis policy changes in Latin America favour both medical and scientific and recreational use of cannabis.

Cannabis Control and Regulation in Canada

According to Cyrenne and Shanahan (2018), some of the main goals of the cannabis policy framework in Canada include creating a responsible and vibrant supply chain and maintaining medical access. In addition, the cannabis legalization framework was founded on strong political commitment. As a result, Canada's cannabis policy approach quickly gained momentum and has received notable attention from cannabis policy analysts and is widely seen as well advanced and progressing ahead of many cannabis policies around the world (Cyrenne and Shanahan, 2018). Research in Canada has shown that though cannabis is regarded as one of the most illicit drugs, a very small proportion of Canadians use cannabis to the extent that is problematic (Leos-Toro et al., 2017). Based on findings from similar researches, recommendations for sensitive cannabis policies became prominent and by 2018 Canada had forty-four licenced producers and thousands licensed to possess and consume cannabis for medical purposes (Aguilar et al., 2018, p. 8). As pointed out by Kay et al (2020, p. 29), modern cannabis policy should be anchored in a development, public health and human rights-based approach. Hall (2020) notes that cannabis use and sale is allowed in Canada but the regulations do not permit advertising of cannabis. The laws make plain packaging mandatory and impose taxes depending on THC content levels. The Canadian policy framework also allows provinces to choose between a for profit cannabis industry or to allow the sale of cannabis through state monopolies where alcohol monopolies exist but evidence shows that states prefer the first option.

The Cannabis Regulatory Framework in Zimbabwe

This section is a condensed analysis of relevant policies and laws related to the cannabis industry in Zimbabwe. The aim of this section is to provide a summative analysis of the relevance and effectiveness of existing laws and policies. As recent as 2017, cannabis use in Zimbabwe was banned. The new cannabis policy which specifically allows cannabis production for medical and scientific purposes is a step towards decriminalization or legalization of cannabis use for medical and industrial purposes. The cannabis regulatory ecosystem in Zimbabwe is made up of laws, regulations and institutions. Institutions include the Ministry of Health and Child Care, the Ministry of Home Affairs, the Zimbabwe Republic Police, the Zimbabwe Revenue Authority, the Medicines Control Authority of Zimbabwe, the National Prosecuting Authority of Zimbabwe, individuals and companies licenced to produce cannabis. The ban on cannabis use remains mainly imposed by laws that include international law provisions on control of cannabis plants and products, the Criminal Law (Codification and Reform) Act Chapter 9:23, the Dangerous Drugs Act Chapter 15:02, the Dangerous Drugs regulations of 1975 and Statutory Instrument 62 Dangerous Drugs (Production of Cannabis for Medicinal and Scientific Use) Regulations, 2018.

The Criminal Law (Codification and Reform) Act Chapter 9:23 prohibits cultivating, producing or manufacturing and possession of cannabis or anything related to the production or manufacturing of cannabis for purposes of dealing in cannabis. The Act also criminalises the incitement of one to consume, procure or offer to procure cannabis on behalf of another person. Generally, the performance of any activity related to the cultivation and processing of cannabis is banned in terms of this law. The Dangerous Drugs Act Chapter 15:02 and the Dangerous Drugs Regulations 1975, when read together prohibit anyone who is not licensed or authorized from acquiring, possessing, supplying or procuring cannabis for another person.

Important features of the cannabis legal and institutional framework in Zimbabwe are discussed below. Cannabis cultivation, production, value addition, distribution and selling in Zimbabwe is licensed by the state as provided by Statutory Instrument 62 of 2018 Dangerous Drugs (Production of Cannabis for Medicinal and Scientific Use) Regulations, 2018. According to these regulations, cannabis production in Zimbabwe is authorised for medicinal and scientific purposes only. The policy also imposes the need to comply with international drug control treaties and any other conditions set by the responsible authority in the country. This clearly shows that cannabis production in Zimbabwe is tied to international drug control laws. These regulations control the dispensing of prescriptions of drug preparations from controlled drugs. The cannabis production policy also provides for stringent licensing requirements for both individuals and companies intending to participate in the cannabis industry sector. For example, the application fee is set at fifty thousand United States Dollars (USD50, 000.00), (Statutory Instrument 62 of 2018 Dangerous Drugs (Production of Cannabis for Medicinal and Scientific Use) Regulations, 2018) a figure which may be restrictive and discriminative for the ordinary citizen wanting to participate in the budding cannabis industry.

Cannabis regulations in Zimbabwe also set minimum cannabis production site security requirements that the individual or entity requiring licensing must comply with before a licence can be granted. These include visual monitoring systems and intrusion detection systems for the perimeter of the cannabis production site, restricted access, visual monitoring and intrusion detection in specific areas where cannabis handling is done, physical barriers to the cannabis production site, and uninterrupted surveillance of all areas where cannabis is present by company personnel (Statutory Instrument 62 of 2018 Dangerous Drugs (Production of Cannabis for Medicinal and Scientific Use) Regulations, 2018).

The cannabis regulations further impose compliance requirements on issues related to cannabis cultivation, soil quality, fertilizers used, irrigation methods and water quality, pest control, and harvesting and drying. The regulations also set minimum expectations on processing, processing equipment, sanitation requirements, product recall procedures and basic standard operating procedures and quality assurance standards in the cannabis production value chain. In addition, the regulations also impose a ban on advertising of cannabis products and stipulate penalties applicable in cases of breaches of the law (Statutory Instrument 62 of 2018 Dangerous Drugs (Production of Cannabis for Medicinal and Scientific Use) Regulations, 2018).

The cannabis regulations also further regulate the packaging, labelling, and shipping of cannabis products (Statutory Instrument 62 of 2018 Dangerous Drugs (Production of Cannabis for Medicinal and Scientific Use) Regulations, 2018). More specifically the regulations in Section 53 deal with packaging of fresh or dried cannabis or cannabis oil, cannabis seeds, and cannabis plants. The policy also further provides for other packaging related issues such as accuracy of weight, security seals, accuracy of number of plants, product labels and expiry dates. In addition, the regulations provide for matters related to the import and export of cannabis and cannabis products in Section 63. Moreover, the regulations also set basic record keeping and records retention requirements for individuals and companies operating in the cannabis industry sector. The regulations in part IV finally deal with other ancillary issues such as fees, penalties and appeals. While the regulations are comprehensive, they are restrictive, discriminative and likely to be overtaken by current developments in the global cannabis industry which is already gliding towards full legalization of cannabis for recreational purposes.

Cannabis Industry Growth Opportunities: Informing Cannabis Policies from an Economic Value Stand-point

Though the cannabis industry is at its infancy (Browne, 2018), available evidence already indicates that numerous benefits can be realized from the sector. Cannabis industry policies and regulations encounter the prominent question on why cannabis was initially prohibited but is now the subject of world-wide legalization initiatives. According to Miller (2013) this clearly shows that cannabis has both beneficial and negative effects. Creating supportive policies and regulations is often moderated by the need to undo prohibition laws. This section brings to the fore, cannabis industry growth potential and economic benefits that Zimbabwe and other countries can realize through strategic policy positioning of the cannabis industry sector. These benefits are located in the medical, agriculture, recreational, crime management and law enforcement, public health and taxation discourses.

Kay et al. (2020:29) agree that with the right policies, cannabis can deliver jobs, income, food security, reduce the health bill and free up resources for other developmental needs. Though tremendous business interest in the cannabis industry is rapidly growing, there is no doubt that the cannabis industry emerges from a system laden with prohibitive regulations and restrictions. Navigating these restrictions often requires undoing or aligning existing laws with current or emerging trends and thinking about the potential attached to the cannabis industry. Coombes (2014) confirms that expanding and liberalizing cannabis production and value addition has potential to create tax windfalls from a potentially multi-billion-dollar cannabis market as shown by unfolding market dynamics (Kay et al., 2020). Similarly, Hall (2020) notes that pro-liberal cannabis policy arguments are anchored on the reasoning that legalizing cannabis use has less health effects than other drugs and that legalization opens up opportunities to better regulate and tax the cannabis industry sector. For this to be possible, the large-scale commercial cannabis production should be opened to reforms. Pro-cannabis legalization campaigners in the Netherlands for example argue that legalizing cannabis cultivation, production and value addition could be a lasting solution to the criminal market problem characterized by illegal plantations, organized crime and backdoor supplies. However, counter arguments are that increased liberalization results in increased cannabis use that has potential to increase access to other drugs and worsen the health burden in most countries.

Hall (2020) writes that cannabis policy variations include those policies which deal with cannabis for commercial use, cannabis for medical purposes and cannabis for adult use. Jin et al. (2019) also suggests that cannabis growing opportunities can be linked to stages of the entire cannabis growing process. While these stages are ideally used to explain optimal growing environments for cannabis, an attempt to identify cannabis industry opportunities at each stage is reasonable for purposes of fulfilling the objectives of this chapter. These stages include material, growth and harvest stages. The material sage provides opportunities related to training cannabis growers, seed processing or cloning, certification and distribution. The growth stage provides opportunities related to construction of green houses, irrigation (plant management), research and development on plant nutrients that is both organic and chemical fertilizers. The harvesting stage provides opportunities for processing, marketing and distribution of cannabis products. Cannabis farming clearly opens up multiple opportunities and according to Aguilar et al (2018), since the year 2000, cannabis production has leaped upwards to several hundreds of tones. In that regard, policies that support cannabis farming opportunities and comply with the current direction of cannabis policy trending across the globe are vital.

The medicinal value of cannabis is now widely acknowledged including its use in traditional or alternative medicine (Aguilar et al., 2018; Senovaityte et al., 2021). The push for legalization of cannabis for medical purposes has generally precipitated the abandonment of prohibition policies in many countries of the world. According to Kay et al (2020:28), policy changes in the cannabis industry triggered an unprecedented boom in the medical markets. Omare et al. (2021) acknowledge that many scholars have reported the efficacy of cannabis use for medical purposes. Aguilars et al. (2018) confirm that intensified efforts to introduce laws that permit the medicinal use of cannabis have been noted in the Americas. Likewise, Hall (2020, p. 283) writes that governments may legislate to permit cannabis use for medical purposes by allowing patients to buy cannabis medical products from pharmacies. Kinyungu et al. (2022) also write that medical marijuana is now widely accepted and has risen in popularity over the last few decades. Their study concluded that medical marijuana is efficacious in chronic pain patients. Similarly, Jin et al. (2019, p. 927) note that since the turn of the 21st century, medicinal cannabis has trended globally and is well established in North America. In the USA for example, cannabis for medical use is widely accepted as a remedy for chronic pain while elsewhere evidence has shown that cannabis reduces muscle spasms in multiple sclerosis and nausea and vomiting in patients receiving chemotherapy (Hall, 2020, p. 282). Omare et al (2021) also predicted cannabis pharmaceutical potential in areas such Coronavirus-2019 (Covid-19), HIV and cancer treatment. While access to approved cannabis medicines is a major challenge in most countries because of strict regulations, it is easier under more liberal cannabis regulations but with the effect of increasing adult cannabis use. Given arguments above, it is imperative that cannabis policy design should be based on broad based research on the value of cannabis for medical purposes.

Finally, cannabis use for recreational purposes provides opportunities in the wholesale and retail of cannabis products. According to Omare et al. (2021), cannabis use for recreation purposes is one of the prominent reasons for legalization being advanced by pro-legalization policy makers. Evidence from some states in the USA, Uruguay, the Netherlands, Spain, Italy, and even in South Africa support this view. Overall, Aguilar et al. (2018) acknowledge that the cannabis sector has potential to create jobs and boost income for local producers as well as improving national export earnings through export of cannabis end products to international markets as is the case in Netherlands which supplies medicinal cannabis products to Germany. Deloitte (2022, p. 3) notes that in Cannada, between 2018 and 2021, the cannabis industry generated eleven billion in sales, created one hundred and fifty-one thousand jobs, added fifteen point one billion dollars tax to the national purse and added a total forty-three-point five billion dollars to Canada's GDP. The economic potential of the cannabis industry is therefore immense.

Challenges Affecting the Design and Implementation of Cannabis Industry Policies

This segment of the chapter describes the challenges that complicate cannabis industry policy development and implementation. It is important to interrogate some of the major causes of cannabis industry policy failure that include political, socio-economic, technological, environmental and legal factors (Browne, 2018). Learning from Miller (2013), this section proceeds from the understanding that the use and regulation of cannabis is not completely free from problems and its status should emerge from informed discussion of all critical issues.

The primary challenge affecting policy experiments in most countries is that while new policies intent to legalize cannabis value addition, such moves create tension with UN treaties (Kay et al., 2020). This creates multifaceted challenges such as complications with access to international markets, international funds transfers and opening of bank accounts, access to credit lines and loan guarantees, promotion of inter-state trade and grants. In addition, the current prohibitive policy regimes that are well established in most countries continue to encounter the reality that support for cannabis legalization has been increasing across the globe but more specifically in the USA since the year 2011. According to Hall (2020, p. 284) the surge in support for legalization was rooted in three main arguments which are that cannabis use is not as harmful as previously thought, that cannabis prohibition laws and penalties have more harm on youth than cannabis use and that legalization is a better policy than prohibition because it has low enforcement costs. This has created tension between prohibition laws and pro-legalization proponents that makes it difficult to enforce prohibition laws. The tension has potential to slow progressive policy development with the consequence that in the absence of bold policy steps, the global south will remain at the tail end of benefiting from a liberalized cannabis market.

The cannabis industry also faces challenges related to lack of coherent policy implementation at both state and national levels. Van het Loo et al. (2003) note that there is a sizeable gap between formal policy and actual policy implemented. Limitations in financial and human resources also impede implementation of the formal policy. As a result, uniform implementation is seldom achieved. Lack of sufficient data to measure the impact of cannabis policies is another major limitation. In that regard, van het Loo et al. (2003) suggest that cannabis policy should be based as much as possible on evidence regarding their effectiveness. Mansson et al. (2021) also suggest that most of the challenges affecting cannabis policy development and the achievement of a unified global cannabis policy are rooted in the expressed descriptions of cannabis in different parts of the global society and the widely shared perception that cannabis is a health hazard (Hassunah & McIntosh, 2016). Miller (2013) points out that mixed perceptions about cannabis affect the legal status of the drug resulting in a confusing mix of regulations in different countries. Back in the 1930s, the origin of restrictive US policies is traced to the political influence of Anslinger who popularized the idea that smoking cannabis turns people into murdering rapists. Browne (2018) also notes that in Canada, inconsistent legal status created problems for cannabis farming. The overall result was a hard policy response to cannabis regulation. In Sweden, a clash of interest between policy makers and users of cannabis ferments sharp differences that interrupt successful policy implementation. While policy makers in Sweden argue that Sweden is not a cannabis state, adult users think that restrictive policies against cannabis users are undemocratic, unfair and irrational. This has potential to create a hunter-hunted relationship between regulators and users of cannabis. Empirical evidence from Sweden actually shows that cannabis users are warming up to cannabis use for recreational purposes even in a restrictive and strict drug policy environment. Ultimately, governments may be seen as oppressive if the regulatory intent is to crack down on illegal cannabis users.

Enforcement of cannabis specific regulations and laws also remains a major challenge for the cannabis industry sector. In the UK, Plant (1977) pointed out three major problems settled at the cannabis policy foundation but still evident in contemporary cannabis policy enforcement and these include that cannabis users are hard to detect and only a few are detected, that a distinction between penalties for users and suppliers is erroneous because in most cases cannabis users are also suppliers and finally that the application of cannabis laws and regulations can never be uniform. Hassuna and McIntosh (2016) also note that the intention to make marijuana legal is complicated by the uncertainty of policy and enforcement outcomes. Implied is that most cannabis prohibition laws may be bad laws but not to the extent of discrediting the intention of policy makers in wanting to control drug use but have evidently failed to stop cannabis use.

Other challenges affecting cannabis policy across the globe include lack of funding, evidential double standards and lack of policy craft competence among policy lakers. Hall (2020) suggests that cannabis policy problems may be a result of the reality that there is very little funding for research needed to evaluate the impact of policies that legalize cannabis use even in developed countries. Hall further suggests that evidential double standards account for some cannabis policy problems. This is because there are contradictions on the evaluation of evidence on benefits of cannabis use and adverse effects caused by cannabis use. Lack of enlightened policy makers in developing countries is another challenge that may complicate cannabis industry growth. In this context, Kay et al. (2020, p. 30) notes that aspirations to grow the cannabis industry and to implement strategies to achieve that require political will and vision. Politicians should understand how the cannabis market works and that it requires active creation, regulation and guidance. However, the risk that the hype the cannabis market has received so far may be hijacked by speculative investors is high. In that regard Kay cautions that developing countries must avoid the "danger of attracting investors and asking questions later". This clearly directs attention to the need for smart policy makers.

Cannabis policies have also been challenged for failing to address energy efficiency and climate change issues especially in countries that legislate cannabis growing conditions (Browne, 2018; Harper, 2019). Indoor cannabis growing under controlled conditions is more energy intensive than partially or wholly open space farming (Cyrenne & Shanahan, 2018). Harper (2019) also notes that recent scholarship agrees that "cannabis prohibition is terrible for the environment" because it perpetuates illegal farming which happens with no oversight. Learning from the US experience, cannabis policy conversations that do not address the environmental impact of indoor cannabis farming and energy consumption sustainability concerns complicate the growth of the cannabis industry in countries already affected by power supply deficits such as Zimbabwe which face the risk of remaining under the burden of unnecessary costs of failed policies.

STRATEGIES FOR IMPROVING CANNABIS POLICY FORMULATION AND IMPLEMENTATION

This section draws on cannabis industry best practices found in literature and obtained from formal and informal discussions with industry experts. Based on findings of the study, the segment triangulates findings from literature and research data to generate sound proposals for the effective implementation of Cannabis policies in Zimbabwe.

A careful analysis of research evidence indicates the need for strengthening cannabis policies to make them more supportive of the growth of cannabis markets and to improve the implementation of these policies. In his analysis of cannabis policy, Hall (2020) concludes that designing cannabis policy requires a careful compromise trade-off between the goal of minimizing the negative public health impact and maximizing the economic benefits of cannabis use. Implied is that policy makes cannot escape the need to strike a compromise between competing socially desirable goals when formulating cannabis policies because both governments and citizens are still uncertain about the benefits and risks of cannabis legalization. Accordingly, research and development funding for the cannabis industry is needed to inform policy fine tuning before wholesale legalization is entrenched making it difficult to reverse the policies should research data turn out to be adverse.

Learning from van het Loo et al. (2003), cannabis policy has two dimensions that deal with supply and demand side issues. The analytic framework by MacCoun and Reuter adopted in their study shows that cannabis supply side policies mainly focus on supply reduction while demand side policies focus on prevention, sanctions, and treatment policies. The implementation of these policies should therefore focus on enforcement of criminal laws and design and implementation of prevention and treatment programs. The model further lists cannabis policy outcomes and their direct and indirect consequences. While the model remains practical from a prohibitionist point of view, its relevance in a more liberalized cannabis industry is limited without further upgrading. For example, the framework is silent on outcomes related to the positive economic benefits offered by a vibrant cannabis industry sector.

To help shape the emerging cannabis market, Kay et al. (2020, p. 31) recommends a broad-based approach in which all stakeholders are involved in particular small and traditional growers in an approach they term leveraging a broader community of practice. Miller (2013) pointed out that lawyers and politicians contributed to US cannabis policy more than the scientists who study the drug resulting in mismatches between scientific data and political positions, a scenario which resulted in faulty policies. Harper (2019) also condemns US cannabis prohibition for its lack of a scientific basis. Based on these arguments, Aguilar et al. (2018) show that the involvement of local and traditional growers of cannabis in Uruguay and Colombia aided the success of the cannabis policies and regulations. Implied is that governments must allow small cannabis growers to have a stake in the licit cannabis space and to self-regulate and form alliances that enable them to lobby for policies that support their participation in the licit cannabis market (Kay et al., 2020). The reasoning used by Kay to support this argument is that many small cannabis growers are the traditional suppliers of illicit markets and should be first in line to benefit from legalized cannabis market spaces. This has the benefit of growing the local industry first before foreign entities dominate and takeover local production and markets. Given this line of reasoning, it is not far-fetched to suggest that policies that recognize and prioritize such social justice receive wide acceptance. From a family of suggestions made by Kay and others, one can infer that good cannabis policies may need to: provide for quotas for small and traditional cannabis growers; be based on affirmative licensing that gives local players a head start ahead of corporate players and foreign players; provide for setting up of a cannabis development fund to be reinvested in cannabis growing communities; lessen barriers to entry in particular for local cannabis players; allow registration of cooperative cannabis producers; legalize the production of alternative cannabis health products; provide for land allocation to cannabis growers; allow traditional small cannabis growers to transition out of illegality without penalties in order to comply with new laws; prevent predatory behaviour by foreign companies and provide for research and development including the use of technology to support the cannabis value chain. Cannabis policies and laws in Zimbabwe should therefore be tested for compliance with some of these noble suggestions.

The success of cannabis policies is highly dependent on the level of success of its implementation (Van het Loo et al., 2003). It must be known upfront that cannabis policies are influenced by many exogenous and endogenous factors which require policy experts to question deviations during implementation, to interrogate the consequences of cannabis policy on individuals and society as a whole, and the impact of policies on cannabis use. The above reasoning aligns well with the suggestion of Hall (2020, p. 283) that when designing cannabis policies, policy makers have options that include "removing criminal penalties for personal use while retaining the prohibition on commercial cannabis supply; the legalization of cannabis for medical use only; and the legalization of adult cannabis use." In fact, Aguilar et al (2018) stress that the design and implementation of cannabis policies matters. Based on these observations, effective cannabis policy design requires a clear understanding of the factors likely to affect the cannabis industry and the solutions to identified challenges and taking a clear position on the policy intent desired by policy makers.

Partitioning the licensing system to ensure that licenses are given for a specific activity related to cannabis production is a crucial consideration with potential to stimulate the cannabis industry sector. Aguilar et al. (2018) suggest that regulation of cannabis supply can be enhanced by issuing licenses to individuals or private entities according to the type of activity they engage in that is whether it is production, manufacture, export, transport, research, processing or sale. Economic benefits generated by cannabis accrue at different stages and in relation to different activities. It is therefore vital to issue specific licences designed to support meaningful activity at each value addition stage.

Based on the observation that indoor cannabis growing is energy intensive and potentially harmful to the environment through carbon emissions and cannabis farming outside oversight (Harper, 2019), cannabis policies must set energy efficiency standards, encourage businesses to invest in energy saving equipment, encourage cannabis producers to rely on renewable energy, and introduce penalties for energy consumption above specific thresholds. In the case of Zimbabwe, such a forward-looking policy stance is crucial given decades long power supply challenges already affecting other sectors of the economy. Incentivising energy efficiency among cannabis producers and environmental protection is therefore a vital component of any ideal cannabis policy.

The current cannabis policy regimes also make cannabis production a high-cost market due to stringent licensing requirements, stratospheric establishment costs, high production costs related to electricity, irrigation, plant management, storage and transportation costs (Cyrenne and Shanahan, 2018). Evidence from most cannabis growing jurisdictions shows that lowest cost markets have not been achieved as the global cannabis market becomes a reality. An additional issue is that the current expensive cannabis markets limit supply and help provide a ready market for illegal suppliers. While this creates a predicament on how to manage demand apart from increasing taxes, it also threatens to halt the rapid growth of the licit cannabis sector in emerging markets such as Zimbabwe. A policy philosophy that addresses this quandary is needed.

DISCUSSION OF FINDINGS

This segment provides a condensed analysis of arguments emerging from literature review and data collected using thematic, historical, cross case analysis and informal discussions. This section also provides a basis for study conclusions and recommendations. Notable findings from literature are that the cannabis industry is a trillion-dollar market that is currently characterised by policy discord and lack of a unified global cannabis policy that negotiates tension with UN prohibition conventions now viewed as notorious road blocks to cannabis value addition. One major barrier to decriminalizing and legally regulating the production, distribution and sale of cannabis noted in literature is the existence of drug treaties less supportive of rapid growth of the cannabis industry mostly in countries that are not ready to breach the treaties in search of viable models supportive of rapid growth in local cannabis markets. Implied is that countries making progress in reforming their cannabis policies by allowing decriminalization and legalization of cultivation, production, possession and sell of cannabis for recreational use are willing to flout international treaties for the benefit of their economies and socio-political ecosystems. Evidence from Uruguay, Colorado, Washington, the Netherlands, and Spain suggests that more countries will weigh the costs of breaching international treaties against the potential economic benefits generated by local policies that support a lucrative cannabis industry sector. Moreover, Hall (2020, p. 283) notes that in countries such as Australia, the Netherlands, France, Portugal and some states in the USA, depenalization has not markedly led to increased cannabis use as argued by anti-legalization policy analysts. This clearly shows that the international drug landscape is changing towards greater latitude for more policy experiments.

Findings also show that there is general consensus on legalizing cannabis for medical use but there is disagreement on recreational use. As suggested by Mansson et al. (2021), cannabis users generally agree with the principles of legalizing cannabis for medical and scientific use but they think differently about the strict stance adopted by many cannabis policies on cannabis use for recreational purposes. As cannabis users increase across the globe, the likelihood of clashes between cannabis users and pro-restrictive cannabis policy makers and systems is high. Learning from arguments by Coombes (2014), policies that fall short of fully legalizing cultivation and distribution of cannabis leave the supply side open to manipulation by criminal gangs whose activities may tarnish good policies. Arguments presented in literature also suggest that governments need to recognize the reality that millions of cannabis users around the world are supplied by unregulated illicit markets (Plant, 1977), a factor which complicates cannabis use problems. In that regard, Hassunah and McIntosh (2016) suggest that legalization of cannabis use should be accompanied by educational programmes, counselling services and a delivery system which minimizes cannabis usage by juveniles and young adults. Making cannabis policies acceptable to both anti and pro cannabis legalization camps is therefore crucial.

Evidence from literature also shows that cannabis regulation has become a political issue and the likelihood that it will further slip into high level political agendas is supported by evidence from Spain, Sweden and the Netherlands where demands for cannabis social clubs and coffee shops respectively have generated serious politically motivated campaigns. An extension of this argument is that cannabis regulation is plagued by many questions that could be solved by learning from existing regulations for the tobacco, liquor and other controlled markets for related drugs (Cyrenne & Shanahan, 2018). Arguments from literature also suggest that repressive cannabis policies are counter-productive and drain scarce resources from the fiscus. In fact, Coombes (2014) concludes that coffee shops in the Netherlands and cannabis social clubs are grassroots initiatives to get around bad policies and laws. Evidence from Sweden also shows that a strict policy on drug use does not achieve 100% control on illicit drug use and trade due to increased clashes between policy preferences and cannabis user motives in which policy intentions are perceived as violating social settings.

Empirical findings from Mansson et al. (2021, p. 284) and Ramírez (2018) show that cannabis has both recreational and medical uses. Using these lenses, cannabis policy should therefore provide for both recreational and medical or scientific uses. Implied is that the cannabis policy environment should change towards a more liberalized policy stance because there is nothing fundamentally scientifically rational about prohibitionist policies which do not take into consideration alternative ways of controlling cannabis use. Ideal policies should remove regulatory vulnerabilities and open doors for rapid growth in the cannabis sector by giving direction to all cannabis uses including for medical, industrial and recreational purposes. The government of Zimbabwe should seriously consider a similar policy and regulatory approach.

Evidence from literature (Kay et al., 2020; Plant, 1977, Mansson et al., 2021; Coombes, 2014; Aguilar et al., 2018) has shown that with the right policies the cannabis industry promises to provide substantial benefits for most countries. However, from the analysis of the cannabis policy and regulations in Zimbabwe the study found that the laws and regulations do not provide for cannabis use for recreational purposes and remains stuck in the prohibitionist regulatory frame. In addition, the law enforcement strategy remains largely harsh and while the regulatory framework in Zimbabwe mimics policies in other countries, it is not far-fetched to conclude that the regulatory framework is restrictive and in the long term may not support the growth of the local cannabis industry. A radical shift in the cannabis regulatory and law enforcement doctrine is therefore urgently needed if the cannabis industry is to flourish while realizing political, social, environmental, legal and economic benefits.

Based on the observation made by Kay et al. (2020) that the rush for profits may benefit well established firms in the global north which may use their capital muscle to squeeze out traditional small growers in the global south and the reality that the law in Zimbabwe, by virtue of stringent licensing requirements and restrictive establishment requirements beyond the reach of small growers, there is need for the government to develop a friendly legislative and regulatory environment that accommodates small growers to avoid worsening the already damaged legacy of prohibitive cannabis laws.

CONCLUSION AND RECOMMENDATIONS

In line with the observation that most countries are now experimenting with their cannabis policies with the goal of legalizing cannabis for both medical and recreational use, it is reasonable to conclude that cannabis cultivation, processing, distribution and retailing are no longer untouchable areas. As pointed out by Aguilar et al (2018, p. 8), the cannabis regulatory environment reflects a melting pot of regulatory regimes oscillating between prioritizing public health issues and pursuing legitimate commercial ends and revenue generating goals. Hassunah and McIntosh (2016) note that the highly visible hesitation to radically change cannabis policies emanates from the fear that wholesome legalization may lead to increased use of cannabis that leads to more public health problems. By extension, cannabis regulation reflects a winding and complex political trail and a cautious approach to cannabis regulation (Ramírez, 2018). In that regard, the Zimbabwean government needs to shift to a more liberal and supportive cannabis policy in order to support meaningful growth in the sector. Regulatory forbearance as well as enforcement discretion in the USA have already proved important indicators for pursuing that option. In addition, evidence from the Netherlands and Uruguay confirm that taking a radical policy shift potentially pays off. Given such evidence, the Zimbabwean government should work on the provisions for the full commercialization of cannabis end products to support a vibrant cannabis industry. However, regulation remains necessary to maintain the integrity of cannabis products and the cannabis sector. Finally, future research should examine the feasibility of a fair and unified cannabis industry policy acceptable to all cannabis producers and developed based on analysis of complete data on licit and illicit cannabis use across the world.

Recommendations for Further Research

This chapter examined the cannabis regulatory framework in Zimbabwe and compared the provisions that form the rule of law with those in other countries but the analysis was not conclusive. There is need for further analysis that relies on thorough legal interpretation of the laws used to regulate cannabis use in Zimbabwe. In addition, the case studies used are few and therefore not adequate to give a whole of the world view on global cannabis regulation. There is need for research that tracks cannabis regulation across the globe to fully capture the state of cannabis regulation. Further research that adopts other research approaches such as mixed methods approaches or purely quantitative approaches is also crucial to establish the impact of the cannabis industry on global economies.

REFERENCES

Aguilar, S., Gutiérrez, V., Sánchez, L. and Nougier, M. (2018*) Medicinal cannabis policies and practices around the world* (Briefing Paper). International Drug Policy Consortium.

Browne, A. (2018). Power Hungry: The Energy Demands of the Growing Cannabis Industry. *Renewable Energy Law and Policy Review*, *8*(4), 7–11. doi:10.4337/relp.2018.03.01

Coombes, R. (2014). Cannabis Regulation: High Time for Change? *British Medical Journal*, *348*, 1–4. PMID:24850823

Crick, E., Haase, H. J., & Bewley-Taylor, D. (2013). Legally Regulated Cannabis Markets in the US: Implications and Possibilities. Global drug Policy Observatory.

Cyrenne, P., & Shanahan, M. (2018). Toward a Regulatory Framework for the Legalization of Cannabis. *Canadian Public Policy*, *44*(1), 54–76. doi:10.3138/cpp.2017-026

Deloitte (2022). *An Industry Makes its Mark: The Economic and Social Impact of Cannabis of Canada's Cannabis Sector*. DeLoitte..

European Monitoring Centre for Drugs and Drug Addiction. (2018). *Cannabis Legislation in Europe: An Overview*. Publications Office of the European Union.

Hall, W. (2020). The Costs and Benefits of the Cannabis Control Policies. *Dialogues in Clinical Neuroscience*, *22*(3), 281–287. doi:10.31887/DCNS.2020.22.3/whall PMID:33162771

Harper, C. (2019). All Is for the Best in the Best of all Possible Worlds, *Vermont. Journal of Environmental Law*, *21*(1), 55–89.

Hurley, R. (2018). Cannabis, Cannabis Everywhere: UK to Review Medical Cannabis Policy as Cannada plans Imminent Legalisation for all uses. *British Medical Journal*, *361*, 1–4.

Jin, D., Jin, S. X., & Chen, J. (2019). Cannabis Indoor Growing Conditions, Management Practices, and Post-Harvest Treatment: A Review. *American Journal of Plant Sciences*, *10*(06), 925–946. doi:10.4236/ajps.2019.106067

Kay, S., Jelsma, M., & Bewley-Taylor, D. (2020). Fair Trade cannabis: A road map for meeting the socio-economic needs and interests of small and traditional growers. *Journal of Fair Trade*, *2*(1), 27–34. doi:10.13169/jfairtrade.2.1.0027

Kinyungu, N. M., Gikungi, J., & Davson, A. (2022). Medical Marijuana Efficacy: A Survey. *Open Journal of Anesthesiology, 12*(03), 91–98. doi:10.4236/ojanes.2022.123008

Leos-Toro, C., Rynard, V., & Hammond, D. (2017). Prevalence of problematic cannabis use in Canada [Revue Canadienne de Santé Publique]. *Canadian Journal of Public Health, 108*(5-6), e516–e522. doi:10.17269/CJPH.108.5955 PMID:29356658

Lindblom, E. N. (2019). How FDA Could Use Its Existing Authorities to Make State Legalization of Cannabis. *Food and Drug Law Journal, 74*(2), 191–211.

Månsson, J., Ekendahl, M., & Karlsson, P. (2021). Clashing Perspectives: Cannabis Users and Swedish Drug Policy. In H. Tham (Ed.), *Retreat or Entrenchment? Drug Policies in the Nordic Countries at a Crossroads* (pp. 267–290). Stockholm University Press. doi:10.16993/bbo.k

Miller, R. J. (2013). The cannabis conundrum. *Proceedings of the National Academy of Sciences of the United States of America, 110*(43), 17165. doi:10.1073/pnas.1317663110 PMID:24151330

Number, R. N. (1975). *1111 of 1975*. Dangerous Drugs Regulations.

Omare, M. O., Kibet, J. K., Cherutoi, J. K., & Kengara, F. O. (2021). Current Trends in the Use of Cannabis Sativa: Beyond Recreational and Medicinal Applications. *Open Access Library Journal, 8*(06), 1–17. doi:10.4236/oalib.1107132

Plant, M. A. (1977). Decriminalising Cannabis. *British Journal of Law and Society, 4*(2), 252–256. doi:10.2307/1409678

Ramírez, M. (2018). New Mexico tribal cannabis: Policy, politics, & guidance for government-to-Government cooperation in state-tribal cannabis compacting. *Natural Resources Journal, 58*(1), 75–124.

Senovaityte, S., Nguyen, A., Han, S., La, B., Anane-Asane, F., Mohran, R., Lee, S., Monzon, A., Samara, O., Murcia, D., & Purohit, S. (2021). The Safety of Cannabis Use in Pregnancy. *Open Journal of Obstetrics and Gynecology, 11*(11), 1437–1445. doi:10.4236/ojog.2021.1111133

Statutory, Z. (2018). *62, Dangerous Drugs (Production of Cannabis for Medicinal and Scientific Use)*. Regulations.

Van het Loo, M., Hoorens, S., van 't Hof, C., & Kahan, J. P. (2003). *Cannabis Policy, Implementation and Outcomes*. RAND Corporation.

Chapter 3
Contemporary Marketing Techniques for Cannabis Entrepreneurs

Andrisha Beharry Ramraj
University of KwaZulu-Natal, South Africa

Thobeka Nomcebo Mnyandu
University of KwaZulu-Natal, South Africa

ABSTRACT

The legal cannabis industry has been the fastest-growing industry in the United States of America and across the world. The marketing structure for cannabis production, supply, and sale in the USA was underground and illegal for the majority of the twentieth century. This study aims to identify the online and offline marketing techniques providing opportunities for cannabis entrepreneurs. This study was conducted using the desktop research method to identify the online and offline marketing techniques for cannabis entrepreneurs and the analysis of challenges faced by entrepreneurs in the marketing of cannabis.

INTRODUCTION

In many countries, there has been a great demand for commercial cannabis legalisation. When countries like Australia and some states in the United States of America (USA) legalised cannabis growing and use for medical reasons, the movement gained a lot of traction (Manu, 2021). Legal recreational cannabis sales have been increasing all over the world and its use has become more normalised in the USA in the years since California became the first state to legalise medical cannabis (Manu, 2021). The Constitutional Court of South Africa legalised recreational cannabis in September 2018 after centuries of cannabis prohibition. However, some departments and other citizens were against this ruling because they believe that cannabis legalisation has a lot of unintended consequences that may cause harm to citizens' health and well-being (Volkow, Swanson, Evins, 2016). Adolescent health faces new challenges as policy, social norms and the marketing environment change. It is important to keep an eye on the

DOI: 10.4018/978-1-6684-6346-8.ch003

intersection of emerging policy and large-scale cannabis marketing as it represents the new frontier of marketing challenges and research opportunities.

In the year 2020, the legal cannabis industry was the fastest-growing industry in the USA and across the world, creating approximately 77 300 jobs (Bhattarai, 2021). In 2016, legal cannabis sales brought in about $200 million in tax revenue for the state of Colorado (McCarthy, 2017). The cannabis industry has changed the way in which people think about health and wellness to a point where it is becoming a rich industry. As the cannabidiol (CBD) segment of cannabis keeps on increasing the market research has estimated that by 2024 it will exceed US$20 billion (Disa, 2020). Despite the fact that more states are legalising cannabis, it is still illegal at the federal level. As a result, each state has a different set of restrictions. Cannabis businesses such as medical marijuana dispensaries, CBD shops and many more, have a chance to experiment with new marketing strategies to expand and improve business.

As cannabis has been penetrating the market in recent years all over the world, despite the public attention on its legalisation, there is a lack of research on the marketing perspective. Cannabis marketing techniques are almost non-existent due to the federal government's prohibition of cannabis (Manu, 2021). However, there are published studies that could help identify online and offline marketing techniques for cannabis entrepreneurs. This study will contribute to the understanding of which marketing techniques cannabis entrepreneurs can use to promote their products and how these techniques can influence consumer purchasing behaviour. Cannabis entrepreneurs have begun to use some marketing techniques to promote their products, and this study will focus on identifying online and offline marketing techniques for cannabis entrepreneurs. It will also discuss the challenges that entrepreneurs face in cannabis marketing.

BACKGROUND

The marketing structure for cannabis production, supply and sale in the USA was underground and illegal for the majority of the twentieth century. Access to the product was highly erratic for consumers; transactions occurred outside of the official economy and there were uncertainties about locations and times consumers could get the products (Klein, 2017). The situation began to change after the passing of a state ballot initiative in California in 1996 which allowed people to consume cannabis for medical purposes. According to Layton (2015), a small number of fixed-location brick-and-mortar dispensaries began to sprout in California after a few years. However, the progress was slow. Instead, in 2005 there were only four medicinal cannabis dispensaries in Los Angeles (Layton, 2015). However, over the years there have been extreme changes in the medical cannabis market.

There were dramatic changes in the California cannabis marketing system, from operating underground and illegally to a major semi-legal business that operates publicly and visibly. Surprisingly, this shift took place while the legality of cannabis storefront sales in California was still up in the air. Even in places where medical cannabis was authorised, the legislation failed to provide clear protection for individuals selling cannabis to patients. During this period, dispensary owners and operators faced rigorous policing and criminal prosecution on both the municipal and federal levels for their market activities. Many businesses were raided, their funds were taken away and their property was taken away or destroyed. A lot of businesses decided to open dispensaries despite knowing all the risks of entering this business; there was a lot of growth and transformation in cannabis marketing strategies (Emmanuel, Mbuyiselo, Mohlomi, & Tarkang, 2021).

It was argued that the legalisation of cannabis would not only assist the developing countries economies but also reduce the use of other dangerous drugs like opioids. Colorado's state government received over $135 million in tax income from recreational and medical marijuana sales in 2015. Tax income might be utilised to fund drug addiction and marijuana control in order to ensure that positive effects coexist with the large economic boost that recreational marijuana legalisation could bring (Zvonarev, Fatuki, Tregubenko, 2019). A major decision by South Africa's Constitutional Court in September 2018 legalised some cannabis-related actions. The court decided that an adult's private production, possession and use of cannabis for personal purposes should no longer be considered a crime. This decision acknowledged the constitutional right to privacy. Importantly, any commercial usage of cannabis must be legal cannabis, defined as cannabis grown under the supervision of the South African Health Products Regulatory Authority (SAHPRA) (Smit & Van Wyk, 2021). However, Lesotho was the first country in Africa to obtain a permit for the cultivation of medical cannabis in May 2017.

The first business to establish legitimate plantations in the nation was Medigrow Lesotho, and the license allows for the production, supply, export, and transportation of medicinal cannabis and cannabis products from the nation (Boak, 2017). Since then, other businesses have done the same. Investors wishing to expand their enterprises from Canada, Israel, and Europe are drawn to Lesotho by its favorable environment and affordable labor costs (Rupert & Michel, 2021). The government has made initiatives to create regulatory infrastructure, such as creating the Lesotho Narcotics Bureau (LNB), which is in charge of awarding and renewing licenses, in order to entice international investment. Zimbabwe legalized the production of medical cannabis in April 2018, becoming the second nation in Africa to do so. The industrial hemp laws were published in the gazette in September 2020. These laws create an atmosphere that supports industrial hemp cultivation, acquisition, distribution, possession, sale, and transportation. Some countries have only legalized cannabis for medical reasons, while others have gone as far as to legalize it for recreational use (Oniwe, 2021). Businesses are under a lot of pressure from the soaring demand for products containing cannabis to successfully negotiate the confusing patchwork of laws related to the emerging sector.

The Coronavirus (Covid-19) outbreak presented an opportunity to help the sector while also relaxing rules for cannabis companies, as there were more than 50 countries in 2020 that regulated the product's cultivation, manufacture or sales for therapeutic reasons. A legal market for the product will enable access to knowledge and greater consumption among customers, which will bring about market opportunities in the coming years (Hall, 2020). As the market is growing, there are marketing techniques that entrepreneurs use in cannabis businesses. The rise of CBD marketing is evident wherever you turn on the internet, whether it be in the shape of an eye-catching Facebook ad focusing on CBD, a Google ad campaign promoting CBD products, or an engaging Instagram story with a "Swipe-up" link directing viewers to a website.

Studies on the cannabis has either focused on its medical legalization, restrictions or either the impact it has on minors or youngsters, there is little to nothing that has been studied on cannabis marketing techniques. As the cannabis market has been growing rapidly, this study aims to show that it is possible for marketers to promote cannabis products online and offline without breaching the advertising regulations at the place.

PURPOSE OF THE STUDY

The purpose of this study is to obtain a better understanding of the cannabis industry and to identify and discuss possible opportunities provided by online/offline marketing techniques for cannabis entrepreneurs. The study aims to understand challenges that the entrepreneurs are facing in marketing cannabis and determine possible solutions to deal with those shortcomings. This research will help cannabis entrepreneurs who already exist and those who are new in the business to decide on which marketing techniques are the most suitable or effective for the marketing of cannabis products and how to implement them without violating federal restriction rules.

LITERATURE REVIEW

Cannabis is sometimes referred to as marijuana and is a psychoactive drug produced from the *Cannabis sativa* plant which is indigenous to Central and South Asia (Roussell, 2012). It has long been used as a recreational and entheogen drug, as well as in a variety of traditional treatments. According to Roussell (2012), hemp and marijuana are frequently confused socially and legally. They are both *Cannabis sativa* and are technically similar, except for differences in physical structure and chemical composition. Apart from the chemical makeup of the plants, the greatest source of misunderstanding is the social and legal element of the distinction between hemp and marijuana (Roussell, 2012). This makes the law, which is often driven by mutually exclusive, organised classes, extremely problematic.

The term 'medicinal cannabis' refers to goods that are lawful, high-quality and consistent and that are derived from crude or raw cannabis. Doctors cannot prescribe crude cannabis since the amount and strength of the drug are not examined or known in each patient (Smit & Van Wyk, 2021). According to Jenkins (2021), pharmaceutical cannabis preparations use modified active components of cannabis in medical formulations to optimise therapeutic efficacy while reducing side effects. Pharmaceutical preparations such as tablets, capsules and sprays enable concentration and dose control uniformity. In medicinal cannabis products, tetrahydrocannabinol (THC) and cannabidiol (CBD) are frequently found combined. Some CBD-only products are available, while others primarily include THC. Medical cannabis is grown under rigorous pharmacological guidelines (Jenkins, Kelly, Binger & Moreno, 2021).

The psychopharmacological qualities and consumption effects of the cannabis market are all different and complicated. For example, the main psychoactive qualities of cannabis are attributed to the cannabinoid THC, which is the most prevalent component of cannabis and is responsible for the commonly recognised intoxication effects. It can be found in two medications that are used to treat Acquired Immunodeficiency Syndrome (AIDS) patients' nausea and appetite suppression caused by chemotherapy; these medications are approved by the Food and Drug Administration known as the FDA (National Institute on Drug Abuse 2019). Previous studies have found that CBD is the most common active element in cannabis (Chagas, Marcos, Eckeli, Zuardi, Waldo & Pena-Pereira, 2014). It has been demonstrated that it has psychoactive and non-psychoactive effects that have been reported to help consumers with pain relief, sadness and insomnia. In 2018, the FDA approved and made available a CBD oral solution for the treatment of epileptic seizures (FDA, 2018).

Doctors and pharmacists are well-versed in the contents of the drug. The components, strength and quality of illegal recreational cannabis have not been well investigated. Microbes, insecticides and heavy metals can all cause contamination. Oils, sprays, tinctures and capsules are the most common forms of medicinal cannabis. Illicit cannabis, on the other hand, is generally smoked. Because of these distinctions, cannabis obtained through illegal means cannot be classified as therapeutic cannabis (Piet & Sanja, 2021). In the USA, marijuana is the most often used illicit drug. In 2014, 22.2 million people (8.4%) said they had used marijuana, up 35% from 2002. Recreational marijuana was legalised in California in 2016 following the legislation changes. Regardless of the debate over marijuana legalisation and decriminalization and its repercussions, the evolving regulatory framework, especially recreational cannabis legalisation, is conducive to the rapid establishment of a new cannabis retail industry (Berg, 2018).

In the USA cannabis has become the most rapidly expanding industry. Cannabis products have become more diverse as a result of this growing industry. Although marijuana is commonly assumed to be smoked like cigarettes, it can be ingested in a variety of ways including smoking or inhaling it in joints, bowls, pipes, bongs, water pipes and blunts, vaporizing it and using it as topicals such as lotions and lip balms (Jenkins, Kelly, Binger & Moreno, 2021). Some users think that various products like herbs, edibles and oil provide distinct highs based on the amount of CBD and THC present as well as whether the strain is physically sedating, mentally invigorating or a combination of the two (Volkow, 2014). Furthermore, cannabis legalisation and the diversity of state and local cannabis policies may influence cannabis usage and modes of use (Berg, 2018). As the recreational marijuana industry grows more established, surveillance research is needed to better understand how sellers position themselves in the market.

The sector has seen an astounding transformation from a global shadow business to an agro-industrial powerhouse, with South Africa being most recent nation to take a firm stance in its favor. The African Cannabis Report from market analysts Prohibition Partners estimates that if nine African countries legalize both the recreational and medical use of cannabis by 2023, the market for the drug will be worth at least 7.1 USD billion. Cannabis sales broke records across the globe during the Covid-19 lockdown period in several different geographic areas. According to the report, sales of medical cannabis, adult-use (recreation), and CBD, an important component in cannabis that is commonly used as a natural treatment, exceeded 37.4 USD billion in 2021 and may reach 102 USD billion by 2026 (Thomas, 2022). Given the bureaucracy and the regulations that the digital platforms have implemented around the cannabis sector, cannabis marketing and advertising are a little subtler but they are still the most important aspect of the lead generation and prospecting efforts.

Research surrounding the online and offline strategies that entrepreneurs can use in their businesses is very scarce. According to D'Amico (2018), cannabis marketing puts youth at risk and preliminary studies are limited because they use inexact measures such as general awareness of marketing and receptivity to marketing that rely on retrospective calls which are subject to participant recall and bias (D'Amico, 2018). Additionally, current research only discusses marketing exposures as a whole, obscuring details about how and when each exposure occurs as well as other psychosocial variables that may have an impact on its outcomes (Noël et al., 2021). In particular, previous research does not go into details about the techniques or channels whereby cannabis marketing exposures take place or the means by which federal marketing regulations are broken (Rupert & Michel, 2021). The effectiveness of various cannabis marketing and distribution methods on teenagers should also be investigated by policymakers.

The current literature on licit drug retail may be used to guide research, which emphasizes the influence of geographical access to tobacco and alcohol shops, as well as exposure to cigarette and alcohol marketing, on smoking and drinking (Gilphin, 2007). Indeed, research reveals that there are similar characteristics of districts where these merchants are concentrated and that retail marketing methods differ depending on these contextual elements. To evaluate the retail marketplace for tobacco and alcohol, researchers looked at product availability, promotion, placement and pricing as well as analysed major differences in marketing by local demographics. According to the tobacco literature, marketing is important for attracting new customers, sustaining the old ones, establishing brand loyalty and molding consumer views of goods, especially for new or unique products (Berg, 2018). Therefore, entrepreneurs could use some of the marketing techniques that are used by the tobacco and alcohol industry to promote their cannabis products as they relate to some of the legal market restrictions.

ONLINE AND OFFLINE MARKETING TECHNIQUES FOR CANNABIS ENTREPRENEURS

The legal cannabis business has grown significantly in recent years all over the world, with a market value of $52.8 billion anticipated in 2019 (Maharaj, 2021). The global legal cannabis market is expected to grow at a compound annual growth rate of 14.5% from 2020 to 2024, reaching $103.9 billion. North America was the largest market in terms of revenue share in 2019, accounting for 88.4% of total sales. However, medical cannabis is expected to propel the European industry to become the largest regional market in the next five years (Insight Survey, 2021). The rise of this market has been primarily driven by the liberalisation of legislation and growing awareness of the potential health benefits of cannabis, similar to that of the global market.

For the past few years, the cannabis industry has been flourishing, more businesses are turning to social media to market their products, spread educational information about cannabis use and promote decriminalisation, social justice and stigma reduction. On sites like Google, Instagram and Facebook there are limits on promoting cannabis-derived CBD products online (Kavya, 2020). With all the online marketing restrictions, businesses can still create business profiles to interact with customers and promote their cannabis goods without violating the restrictions. Entrepreneurs must understand what they can and cannot put online, they must always comply with the rules of cannabis marketing. Cannabis entrepreneurs who do not adapt quickly and think outside the box, or understand the rules of engagement on these platforms, will be surpassed by those who do. When it comes to marketing and promotion, hemp-derived goods such as tinctures, capsules, candies and sublingual strips, face more scrutiny (Sebastian, 2020).

According to Anderson (2018), social media exposure to cannabis marketing information is particularly concerning because virtually all teenagers use social media (e.g. Instagram, Facebook, Twitter) and 45% report being online extremely frequently. By the end of 2021, cannabis revenues reached about $25 billion. Colorado's cannabis marketing laws are modeled on the voluntary code of the alcohol industry, which prohibits corporations from advertising via channels (such as television, radio, print and the Internet) where more than 30% of the audience can be reasonably believed to be under the age of 21. Seven other jurisdictions with legal retail cannabis marketplaces have adopted a similar rule, with varying degrees of specificity (Anderson, 2018). According to a review of Instagram posts that are related to cannabis hashtags, 43% of them were explicitly about cannabis. This included cannabis images in classic and novel forms, cannabis advertising and some images of it being swallowed (Cavazos-Rehg et al., 2016). These findings are alarming due to the risk of teenage exposure since there are children as young as 13 on Instagram. Cannabis looks to have a well-established and sophisticated online presence, raising consumer protection issues for vulnerable groups like teenagers (Bierut, Krauss, Sowles & Cavazos-Rehg, 2017). Regardless of legality or media company restrictions, there are creative commercials, online influencer promotions and tailored mail-order boxes.

With the steady influx of new entrants, the cannabis industry is getting increasingly crowded, making a brand's attractiveness to its target demographic all the more important. There are always new cannabis products introduced to the already existing products and that is overwhelming the market. Everything from face cleansers to hand lotions to CBD drinks and chocolate is CBD-infused. Building brand identity requires creating a product that meets your clients' wants and promoting it properly (Klein, 2017). Brands must establish their reputation in the market through consistent messages and images, making design engagement a crucial aspect of branding. In this sense, distinctiveness is also important for keeping cannabis brands in forefront of customers' minds, especially considering the crowded industry. The health advantages of CBD are so numerous that many companies are driven to manufacture one-size-fits-all solutions (Sebastian, 2020). The market should reflect this diversity and brands should seek to stand out among competitors.

There are a variety of methods to communicate with customer regardless of who they are. Packaging may define your brand in three ways from a marketing standpoint: user experience, content and logo design (Sebastian, 2020). A logo is a distinctive design feature that usually consists of letter forms (logotype), and signs sometimes consist of both. This is the most effective visual representation of the message and positioning of the brand. While there are numerous other aspects that influence how buyers view your CBD brand, the logo and packaging are frequently the first messengers of this opinion. When a logo is designed properly with a brand strategy, it may help cannabis entrepreneurs reach out to their target audience, express the message, value and advantages and aesthetically draw more attention. With the CBD industry rapidly getting saturated, it is critical to have a logo that is both creative and unique (Klein, 2017).

Creating content is undoubtedly the most important strategy for establishing a brand. It does not matter if it is a blog, posts on social media or physical brochures, the material that is published by the business should consistently portray and reflect the brand. Anything that is published provides relevant information to the targeted audience; it draws the audience to the website and helps the business retain current consumers by engaging with them. The pages, websites and blogs are all supposed to be keyword-optimized in order to drive traffic to the created content, particularly on e-commerce sites that sell cannabis products. As a result, content should distinguish a firm from its competition. Creating branded material on the particular benefits and attractions of CBD products will help distinguish your company from the competition as well as improve conversation and search engine results (Disa, 2020).

Many aspects go into building and positioning a brand, especially in the cannabis market where there is a lot of possibility for development and opportunity. Given the lack of understanding about the distinctions between THC and CBD, for example, a business that educates its customer base about its products might improve the user experience. Customers may make educated and responsible purchasing decisions by knowing where a tincture is coming from and what the contents are (Berg, 2018). Quality may also add to a brand's implicit information. When considering product pricing, consumers believe that when the price is greater, so is the quality of the product. Though the identity of a brand is important for any company, getting a CBD company off the ground presents significant obstacles. Many individuals are unaware of the distinctions between cannabis and CBD because it is a new market. As a result of the link between hemp and cannabis, CBD products have a stigma attached to them, making many hesitant to incorporate them into their daily lives (Nicholls, 2015). This information gap also presents distinct hurdles when it comes to the marketing success of cannabis businesses that have strong brand awareness and identity. There are other online and offline marketing techniques for cannabis entrepreneurs.

Print and Media

Cannabis products are a sensory experience by nature, especially as marijuana becomes more closely associated with health and wellbeing. Visual material is crucial for enhancing your brand and attracting clients to your items. For businesses to separate their brand from others they should use distinctive, eye-catching print and media assets that would allow them to display their products and services and also engage with the customers. A few examples an entrepreneur should think about when employing print and media are product packaging, video, promotional messages, photographs and display marketing (Kavya, 2020).

Product Packaging, Promotional Materials and Collateral

The success of the marketing mix depends on the use of high-quality graphic assets in digital marketing. Print advertising is not extinct. Original print advertising strategies, from packaging design to promotional materials and marketing collateral, can dramatically improve the way the brand is presented, especially with cannabis products and all of the surrounding legalities (Jenkins, Kelly, Binger & Moreno, 2021). For advertising the brand at special events, business cards, brochures, direct mailings, flyers, posters and stationery, among other promotional goods and collateral, are essential. The cannabis and medical marijuana businesses, for example, gain a lot of exposure at tradeshows and conferences where entrepreneurs can present their brands. Distributing pamphlets and business cards at such events could increase brand awareness of the cannabis business.

The overall message that entrepreneurs want to convey should be incorporated into the design of the product packaging for cannabis brands. Regulation around cannabis and cannabis-related product packaging is something CBD businesses should pay special attention to. Packaging and advertising limitations apply in countries where selling cannabis and CBD products is authorised (Smit & Van Wyk, 2021). Most countries, for example, require that some warning labels and writing on product packaging be legible, with some regulations specifying font style and size. Other countries have likewise made it illegal to use colorful packaging or neon or any artwork that promotes the cannabis product to children. To learn the best procedures for packaging your CBD products in general, examine your country's regulations or reference the National Cannabis Industry Association's literature.

E-Commerce

It is important for a cannabis business to adopt e-commerce strategies. A website serves as a wide platform for people to purchase your items in addition to promoting your company values. To genuinely inspire a purchase choice, your website's e-commerce layouts should be simple to use and attractive, offering your clients a unique and personalised shopping experience (Jenkins et al., 2021). Customers should also have confidence in the security of their personal information and data. The website should be user-friendly, professional and tidy. In that way, there would be more recurring customers and a larger return on investment can be achieved by providing an excellent and consistent user experience (Kavya, 2020).

Search Engine Optimisation (SEO)

To effectively reach the target demographic, cannabis entrepreneurs should update the content more often on websites. Businesses should always be on the search engine top page in a way that customers can easily locate your products while searching for cannabis or anything else connected to the company. This is where keywords come into play in conjunction with the designing of the website and its development as these relate to the user experience (Jenkins et al., 2021). Overall, a complete SEO plan considers mobile and local SEO, as well as social media optimisation. Paid advertising for cannabis-related or CBD goods is prohibited on the internet because cannabis is not legalised at a federal level. Google, for example, has regulations in place for pay-per-click advertisements, shopping campaigns, in-app adverts, video ads and many more. Because of these prohibitions, paid promotion for CBD businesses is both difficult and risky (Jenkins et al., 2021). However, some companies have become inventive and have been able to get around the restriction by swapping phrases like 'herb' and 'greens' for prohibited ones like THC and cannabis.

CHALLENGES THAT ARE FACED BY ENTREPRENEURS IN MARKETING CANNABIS

The cannabis sector has the potential to enhance state and national economies, but it still confronts several legal and political obstacles when it comes to online cannabis product marketing. Many regulations and tight requirements limit how companies may sell their cannabis brand. To begin with, advertising cannabis near schools is prohibited. That means cannabis companies are not able to promote cannabis goods on traditional media like radio, automobiles or television. Despite the fact that marijuana has been around for a long time, the cannabis business is still relatively new. Cannabis businesses must adapt to these changes when marketing CBD products since the cannabis landscape is always evolving. For instance, in the USA cannabis rules on cultivation, legality, distribution and usage are different from state to state. Marketing cannabis goods or CBD-related enterprises is difficult for cannabis companies since regulations are always changing (Jenkins et al., 2021).

Society is gradually accepting cannabis usage as a 'normal' drug as more countries allow it for recreational and medicinal purposes. However, because cannabis has been outlawed for so long, no policy can ever completely remove the stigma associated with it. Cannabis businesses must remove this stigma while advertising their products online. Under YouTube's standards on harmful or hazardous content, content targeted at selling regulated or illegal items or services (whether via direct sales or to sites offering these things) is prohibited. Prescription medications, narcotics, alcohol, internet gambling casinos, nicotine products and other commodities are controlled or outlawed. Although YouTube previously appeared to welcome cannabis advertising, that changed when YouTube began flagging cannabis-related channels without warning or explanation. In 2018, Leafly and Lift & Co, both well-known names in the cannabis sector, were briefly stopped (Baxter, 2020). YouTube claimed that the impacted channels had broken its rules. Those channels, ironically, had no problems on the platform for many years and prospered under their supervision. Most of these channels were eventually reinstalled on YouTube, however, they now notify users that their video may not be appropriate for all audiences before they watch it and, in that way, users may then choose whether to watch an ad or not (Nicholls, 2015).

When it comes to ad material for drugs or drug-related items, Instagram follows Facebook's lead. The use or selling of prescription, illicit or recreational drugs is prohibited under Instagram's ad policy. If you do not follow these rules, social media networks may delete your account. You may still share cannabis material without being suspended, much like Google AdWords and Facebook, depending on the type of content you post. Instagram has no problems with instructional and informative material and will always accept it (Bourque, 2019). On the other hand, you should avoid including a call to action in your cannabis marketing material on Instagram. When advertising cannabis advertisements on Instagram, another effective suggestion is to employ influencers as part of your marketing plan.

Few research studies have used qualitative methodologies to investigate cannabis marketing efforts on social media. By assessing adherence to cannabis advertising rules on social media in Washington State, one researcher applied content analysis to better understand cannabis marketing material on social media. Although this study focused on distinct, preset categories appropriate for policy application, thematic components of postings that may be influential to teenagers were not captured using this technique. This content analysis research, for example, caught categories such as the presence of mandatory warnings based on regulation text but was unable to catch emergent categories or themes such as tone. As a result, a new technique for analyzing more complex or emerging themes linked with online cannabis marketing material is required (Moreno et al., 2018).

METHODOLOGY

This study used a desktop research technique to identify the marketing techniques for cannabis entrepreneurs' marketing and the analysis of challenges faced by entrepreneurs in the marketing of cannabis. This approach is typically used to investigate, describe or explain a social phenomenon, which is exactly what this research is attempting to achieve. To properly comprehend the marketing strategies for cannabis, the analysis period is from 2014 to date. As a result, any relevant internet articles on cannabis relations at this time were included in the population. The key phrases for cannabis marketing, branding, digital trends, legalisation and marijuana were found in 89 articles collected from the University of KwaZulu-Natal (UKZN) library from March-August 2022. Bloggers, reports and newspaper articles provided some of the information. This scoping study contained 44 articles after the full-text review. The systematic review was employed in this study as its purpose was to find and analyse relevant papers, both published and unpublished, to answer the research questions. The focus of this research was on secondary data sources and textual sources such as textbooks, journals and magazines as well as blogs and website postings were used to create secondary data.

Several search engines were utilised to discover articles, and keywords were employed to identify relevant information. To search, Google Scholar, PubMed and, most importantly, academic search via Ebscohost via the University of KwaZulu-Natal and Cochrane library were used. It was necessary to develop a way for removing unnecessary articles while searching for useful material. To put it another way, criteria for inclusion and exclusion must be developed to aid in the inclusion and exclusion of certain things. As a result, the technique outlined below was used. Search engines like Ebscohost and Google Scholar were used to discover relevant publications using keywords. Following that, certain articles were chosen based on their titles. Articles with titles that were relevant were chosen. The abstracts were chosen based on the titles of the articles. After reviewing all of the papers, only those that were pertinent to the research were used.

FINDINGS AND DISCUSSION

In this research, the entrepreneurs were identified as members of a medicinal cannabis community. Although they were conscious of the stigma attached to them as members of what society perceived as a deviant group, the entrepreneurs eventually came to reject that label as well as the factual foundation upon which it was based. They considered medical cannabis stigma and cannabis prohibition in general as the result of ignorance, often deliberate, and this perception served as a basis for rejecting the validity of the entire prohibition apparatus. They refuted three grounds used to justify cannabis prohibition: cannabis is a harmful substance, cannabis is ineffective as a medication and standard medicines are safer than cannabis. According to social identity theory, rejection of these reasons, as well as the perception that prohibition was founded on fundamental ignorance, provided a foundation for redefining the social status of medicinal cannabis users as a group in relation to prohibition advocates. They depict proponents of prohibition as uneducated persons able or unable to accept reality, believing themselves to have a better comprehension of the facts. Their decisions to open cannabis stores were portrayed as attempts to live up to their identities.

According to Webb, Tihanyi, Ireland and Sirmon (2009), collective identity is important in black market entrepreneurship. They claim that belonging to a social group that denies the legitimacy of limits on certain types of market exchanges allows entrepreneurs to recognise and profit from such transactions. However, these theories are mainly unsupported by actual evidence. Furthermore, their model ignores efforts to overturn such legal restrictions. This study tries to fill up a gap in the restriction of cannabis marketing techniques. It contributes to macro-marketing by shedding light on the individual and group-level identification processes at work in motivating entrepreneurs to transform both marketing systems and society in general. While individual and group identification procedures are micro in nature, macro-level changes in marketing systems are typically predicated on micro-level activity (Layton, 2015).

A study by Kavya (2021) indicates that one of the most successful methods to convince consumers to sign up for newsletters or give their contact information is through education. When signing up for newsletters, entrepreneurs might give out gifts like e-books that explain the difference between CBD and cannabis. For entrepreneurs to grow their market while they gather the information that is important such as what interests their potential customers they should allow them to subscribe to the newsletters of their choice whether it is weekly or monthly. This information would allow entrepreneurs to personalise emails for each customer effectively.

The explanation of a unique methodological technique for analysing information online is another significant addition to this research. In future studies, this technique might be especially beneficial for describing the effect and tactics of content linked to drug use that the youth may be exposed to. While prior research employed content analysis to examine non-medical cannabis firms' conformity to advertising restrictions in Washington, this is the first attempt to subjectively analyse internet cannabis marketing material. Many concerns with this content can be resolved to utilise the cyber-ethnographic method, which does not require pre-defined categories with narrow definitions and can make it difficult to capture more nuanced or emerging topics.

RECOMMENDATIONS

As adolescents are active and engaged consumers of digital media, it is critical to evaluate the consequences of exposure to influencing marketing, such as cannabis promotion, at a young age. More innovative techniques, such as the ones given here, are needed to evaluate cannabis firms' tactics for promoting and normalising cannabis usage in ways that may affect the youth. For individuals exposed to these messages, cannabis firms' focus on normalisation may have a substantial influence on the attitudes of the youth toward cannabis usage. Healthcare providers, educators and prevention experts who work with children and adolescents should be aware of the possible impact of internet marketing strategies that promote marijuana use. Understanding this material may assist individuals in these positions to teach youngsters to be more suspicious of marketing in order to prevent unwanted impacts. Furthermore, much of the particular targeting displayed by cannabis firms on social media, such as in group marketing and pop culture allusions, may appeal to teenagers and their interests. This discovery might be utilised to tighten cannabis advertising standards and regulations as well as to monitor internet content that could be harmful to children (Jenkins et al., 2021).

There should also be ongoing education and awareness of the detrimental consequences of marijuana abuse, particularly among minors. Furthermore, raising the retail price of marijuana might reduce its use, particularly among youngsters. For example, a 10% decrease in price is expected to result in a 3% rise in cannabis use (Kilmer, 2014). As a result, guaranteeing that marijuana costs do not fall might potentially reduce its use.

FUTURE RESEARCH

As businesses hoped that the commercial legalisation of marijuana growing and trade would enhance their economic fortunes, they were equally concerned about the policy's potential ramifications for their livelihood and community. As a result, it is urged that future discussions in South Africa on commercial marijuana cultivation and trading be conducted in consultation with illegal marijuana farmers and merchants to guarantee that their interests are protected. There is not much information on cannabis marketing research due to many restrictions on marketing techniques. Researchers must focus on the effectiveness of cannabis marketing strategies used by entrepreneurs and also on the impact of cannabis on marketing and branding. The references are up-to-date even though there is a lack of research on the offline and online marketing of cannabis. This study is properly directed to the targeted audience (cannabis marketers), it can help a lot of marketers who want to enter the market or who are already in the market, with the right marketing techniques the cannabis industry will boom even further.

CONCLUSION

Marijuana legalisation trends are extremely important for all countries in the world. Many of the commercial issues connected with recreational marijuana legalisation relate to the drug's unlawful status at the federal level, despite the fact that individual states have legalised it and implemented rules and countermeasures. State-level rules follow an industry-led voluntary self-regulation paradigm with no federal control. However, learning from tobacco control policies and best practices may be a superior way. When all of these marketing umbrellas are combined, CBD entrepreneurs, without resorting to illegal marketing tactics, have a fantastic opportunity to educate customers and raise brand awareness. A holistic marketing approach includes branding and the use of print, media, site design and development, SEO, social media and email. When all these channels are consistent, they not only increase the reputation and identity of a CBD business but also improve customers' experiences with the brand in a variety of ways. Customer should feel as if they are going along with a business, from discovering its latest product through an Instagram post to scanning their inbox for a discount code to visit the business's site to purchase that product.

REFERENCES

Anderson, M., & Jiang, J. (2018). ATeens, social media, and technology. *Pew Research Center.* https://www.forbes.com/sites/andrebourque/2019/05/06/under-the-influence-of-instagram-cannabis-in-the-age-of-social-medi
a/?sh=3871ad684746

Baxter, B. (2020). Cannabis Companies Tap Top Lawyers as CEOs Amid Legal Challenges. *Bloomberg Law.* https://news.bloomberglaw.com/business-and-practice/cannabis-companies-tap-top-lawyers-as-ceos-amid-legal-challenges

Berg, C. J. (2018). The Emerging Marijuana Retail Environment: Key Lessons Learned from Tobacco and Alcohol Retail Research. *Addictive Behaviors, 81,* 26-31.

Bierut, T., Krauss, M., Sowles, S. J., & Cavazos-Rehg, P. A. (2017). Advertising on Weedmaps, a Popular Online Directory. *Prevention Science, 18*(2), 183–192. doi:10.100711121-016-0702-z PMID:27534665

Boak, A. (2017). Drug Use among Ontario students: Ontario drug use and health survey 1977–2017: Detailed findings from the Ontario Student Drug Use and Health Survey (OSDUHS) *CAMH Research Document Series No.46.*

Bourque, A. (2019). Under The Influence Of Instagram: Cannabis In The Age Of Social Media. *Forbes.* https://www.forbes.com/sites/andrebourque/2019/05/06/under-the-influence-of-instagram-cannabis-in-the-age-of-social-medi
a/

Cavazos-Rehg, P. A., Krauss, M. J., Sowles, S. J., & Bierut, L. J. (2016). Marijuana-related posts on Instagram. *Prevention Science, 17*(6), 710–720. doi:10.100711121-016-0669-9 PMID:27262456

Chagas, M. H. N., Eckeli, A. L., Zuardi, A. W., Pena-Pereira, M. A., Sobreira-Neto, M. A., Sobreira, E. T., Camilo, M. R., Bergamaschi, M. M., Schenck, C. H., Hallak, J. E. C., Tumas, V., & Crippa, J. A. S. (2014). Cannabidiol Can Improve Complex Sleep-Related Behaviours Associated with Rapid Eye Movement Sleep Behaviour Disorder in Parkinson's Disease Patients: A Case Series. *Journal of Clinical Pharmacy and Therapeutics, 39*(5), 564–566. doi:10.1111/jcpt.12179 PMID:24845114

Cova. (2019). *Colorado Medical and Recreational Marijuana Laws and Licensing Procedures.* Cova. https://www. covasoftware.com/us-dispensary-laws/colorado.

Disa. (2020). *Map of Marijuana Legality by State.* https://bit.ly/3aM3CPu

Emmanuel, M., Mbuyiselo, D., Mohlomi, J. N., & Enowbeyang Tarkang, E. (2021). *The perspective of illicit marijuana growers and traders on commercial legislation in South Africa: considerations for policy formulation*. Substance Abuse Treatment, Prevention, and Policy. BMC.

Federal Trade Commission. (2018). *Federal Trade Commission Smokeless Tobacco Report for 2016.* Federal Trade Commission. https://www.ftc.gov/system/files/documents/reports/federal-trade-commission-cigarette-report-2016-federal-trade-commission-smokeless-tobacco-report/ftc_smokeless_tobacco_report_for_2016_0.pdf

Gilpin, E., White, M., Messer, K., & Pierce, J. (2007). Receptivity to Tobacco Advertising and Promotions Among Young Adolescents as a Predictor of Established Smoking in Young Adulthood. *American Journal of Public Health, 97*(8), 1489–1495. doi:10.2105/AJPH.2005.070359 PMID:17600271

Hall, W. (2020). The costs and benefits of cannabis control policies. *National Center for Biotechnology Information.* https://www.ncbi.nlm.nih.gov/pmc/articles/PMC7605025/

Katherine, W. (2021). *4 Top Marketing Trends Affecting The Cannabis Industry in 2021.* Cannabis Marketing Association. https://thecannabismarketingassociation.com/4-top-marketing-trends-affecting-the-cannabis-industry-in-2021/

Kilmer, B. (2014). Policy designs for cannabis legalization: Starting with the eight Ps. *The American Journal of Drug and Alcohol Abuse, 40*(4), 259–261. doi:10.3109/00952990.2014.894047 PMID:24853283

Klein, K. (2017). Entrepreneurship, Identity, and the Transformation of Marketing Systems: Medical Cannabis in California. *Journal of Macromarketing, 37*(1), 85–86. doi:10.1177/0276146716655848

Layton, R. A. (2015). Formation, Growth, and Adaptive Change in Marketing. *Journal of Macromarketing,* 316. Jenkins, M.C., Kelly, L., Binger, K. & Moreno, M.A. (2021). Cyber-ethnography of cannabis marketing on social media. *Substance Abuse Treatment, Prevention, and Policy.*

Maharaj, Y. . (2021). Is SA's cannabis industry predicted to become 'green gold' or 'fool's gold'? *Biz Community.*https://www.bizcommunity.com/Article/196/744/212607.html

McCarthy, J. (2017). Record-High Support for Legalizing Marijuana Use in U.S. *GALLUP.* https://news.gallup.com/poll/221018/record-high-support-legalizing-marijuana.aspx

Moreno, M. A., Gower, A. D., Jenkins, M. C., Scheck, J., Sohal, J., Kerr, B., Young, H. N., & Cox, E. (2018). Social media posts by recreational marijuana companies and administrative code regulations in Washington state. *JAMA Network Open, 1*(7), e182242. doi:10.1001/jamanetworkopen.2018.2242 PMID:30646364

National Institute on Drug Abuse. (2019). What Is Medical Marijuana? *National Institute on Drug Abuse.* https://www.drugabuse.gov/publications/drugfacts/marijuana-medicine

Nicholls, A. (2012). Everyday, Everywhere: Alcohol Marketing and Social Media—Current Trends. *Alcohol and Alcoholism (Oxford, Oxfordshire)*, *47*(4), 486–493. doi:10.1093/alcalc/ags043 PMID:22532575

Noël, C., Armiento, C., Péfoyo, A. K., Klein, R., Bédard, M., & Scharf, D. (2021). Adolescent exposure to cannabis marketing following recreational cannabis legalization in Canada: A pilot study using ecological momentary assessment. *Addictive Behaviors Reports*, *14*, 100383. doi:10.1016/j.abrep.2021.100383 PMID:34938841

Oniwe, L. (2021). *Cannabis*. Revolutionising the Global Consumer Sector.

Piet, Bester. & Sonja, Els. (2021). The legalization of cannabis: A security-vetting dilemma. *South African Journal of Military Studies*.

Roussell, A. (2012). Forensic Identification of Marijuana: Suspicion, Mortal Danger, and the Creation of Non-Psychoactive THC. *Albany Law Journal of Science & Technology*.

Rupert Klein & Michel Bédard. (2021). *Adolescent exposure to cannabis marketing following recreational cannabis legalization in Canada: A pilot study using ecological momentary assessment. Kavya, S, (2020). The ultimate guide to CBD marketing*. Cannabis Creative Groups.

Smit & Van Wyk. (2021). *South Africa: Legalisation Of Private Use Of Cannabis In South Africa*. MONDAQ. https://www.mondaq.com/southafrica/cannabis-hemp/1107436/legalisation-of-private-use-of-cannabis-in-south-africa

Volkow, N. D., Swanson, J. M., Evins, A. E., DeLisi, L. E., Meier, M. H., Gonzalez, R., Bloomfield, M. A., Curran, H. V., & Baler, R. (2016). Effects of Cannabis Use on Human Behavior, Including Cognition, Motivation, and Psychosis: A Review. *JAMA Psychiatry*, *73*(3), 292–297. doi:10.1001/jamapsychiatry.2015.3278 PMID:26842658

Webb, J. W., Tihanyi, L. R., Ireland, D., & Sirmon, D. G. (2009). *You Say Illegal, I Say Legitimate: Entrepreneurship in the Informal Economy*. Academy of Management. https://www.jstor.org/stable/27760016

Zvonarev, V., Fatuki, T.A., Tregubenko, P. (2019). The public health concerns of marijuana legalization: an overview of current trends. *DISA*.

Chapter 4
Twenty-First Century Innovation of Cannabis Products

Andrisha Beharry Ramraj
University of KwaZulu-Natal, South Africa

Mxolisi Ngcobo
University of KwaZulu-Natal, South Africa

ABSTRACT

The topic of cannabis has been widely researched over the years, but still remains a controversial yet interesting field of study. As an industry, the cannabis industry has evolved and developed over the years. The plant was previously utilized mainly by individuals for personal consumption, but following much research and development into the topic it has now become a lucrative market. Some countries have legalized cannabis or have gone through the decriminalization process. In recent times, the recreational usage of the cannabis plant has become a major source of interest as more investment and research has been made into the industry as a means to innovate more recreational cannabis products. There are now cannabis products like oil, beauty and skin care products, beverages, chocolate, capsules, gummies, and dog treats. The chapter is based on a qualitative approach as the aim is to gather a greater understanding of the phenomenon and provide insight for future research.

INTRODUCTION

The cannabis industry is becoming an attractive industry for investors around the world as the regulators are minimizing the restrictions and this is paving the way for new innovations in the industry to emerge. The cannabis industry remains controversial around the world as the use of cannabis is prohibited in certain countries like Algeria and Angola, while it is regulated to be used only for medical purposes in other countries like Chile and Croatia (Freeman & Lorenzetti, 2020). Cannabis remains forbidden amongst some conservative societies and cultures around the world but is accepted in liberal and mod-

DOI: 10.4018/978-1-6684-6346-8.ch004

ern societies. This contrast is very much evident in the United States of America (USA), where certain liberal states (Florida and New Jersey) have decriminalized the use of the plant, yet it is still criminalized in conservative states like Alabama and South Carolina (Freeman & Hindocha, 2019). The use of cannabis has evolved over the years, from mainly being used for personal consumption in the form of smoking, to being used for medical purposes (Albright & Johnson, 2018). There have been numerous innovations in the cannabis industry and more new products, or services are expected to be invented due to the continued investment in research and development (R&D) on cannabis. Most of the literature on cannabis focuses on the medical use of cannabis and there is not a lot of data on the recreational use of cannabis. This is the identified gap in the literature that this chapter will seek to address.

The recreational usage of cannabis has been prevalent for a very long time and regulators have been trying to prevent the proliferation of the use of the plant without any significant success. This has paved the way for businesses and innovators to come up with sustainable approaches to commercialize the cannabis industry. There have been numerous attempts by regulators to legalize or decriminalize the cannabis industry as it is proving to be a very lucrative market. It can enable governments to increase their sources of revenue which can in turn be channeled toward public service delivery, for example. South Africa has become one of the few countries to decriminalize cannabis for both medical and recreational purposes (Riley et al., 2020).

The chapter will be framed within the constructivist paradigm as the aim is to understand the multiple realities across the world associated with the topic of cannabis and to understand the 21st century innovations of cannabis products. The paper will first provide a background on cannabis, literature on the topic will then be reviewed, the research methodology for the paper will be stated, the research findings and discussion will be detailed and lastly, recommendations and future research on the topic will then be discussed.

BACKGROUND

Cannabis is made from the desiccated flowering heads and leaves of a plant called Cannabis sativa (Chouvy & Macfarlane, 2018). The plant is utilized as both a medical and a recreational drug. The usage of cannabis is regulated and banned by the government in some countries or states. Most countries around the world have legalized the use of cannabis for medical purposes but only a few have legalized the use of cannabis for recreational purposes. Countries like Canada, Netherlands, Spain, Uruguay and South Africa are some of the prominent countries to legalize the use of cannabis for recreational purposes (Uwakonye, 2020). There are instances where there are contradicting viewpoints within countries like the USA, where states have different legislations with regard to the usage of the cannabis plant (Chouvy & Macfarlane, 2018). Regulators are pressured by lobby groups and businesses to change the regulations with regards to cannabis as the plant is already prevalent in the unregulated black market and yet the industry demonstrates huge economic potential. The decriminalization of cannabis for medical and recreational purposes has resulted in a surge of investment in the industry as businesses are seeking to innovate with products that yield an exceptional return on investment.

South Africa has taken huge strides toward changing the legislation guiding the usage of cannabis in the country. The plant has been decriminalized for medical and recreational usage subject to adhering to all the regulations stipulated in the legislation (Lewis, 2020). There are still regulations around the usage of cannabis in South Africa for recreational purposes including that the user must be over the age of 18, the quantity that an individual can keep in their private space is less than 600 grams, individuals can have up to 100 grams in person in a public space but must not consume it in the public space (Gerwel, 2018). The government is currently assessing the prospect of fully legalizing the use of cannabis for medical purposes subject to adhering to all the legislations. This will have a huge impact on the country's economy as this will attract investment, create employment and generate tax revenue (Gerwel, 2018). The move to legalize cannabis for both medical and recreational purposes has a positive effect on introducing new innovations in the cannabis industry. The cannabis industry is already huge as there are shops or retailers devoted to selling cannabis products. The prospect of acquiring more investment results in the emergence of new innovations and this proves very essential for boosting the economy of South Africa.

PURPOSE OF THE STUDY

This chapter will seek to provide insight into the evolving nature of cannabis by investigating the contemporary innovations of cannabis products in South Africa compared to the rest of the world in the 21st century. This assists with understanding the rationale behind the growing interest, research and development in the cannabis industry. By virtue of providing knowledge of contemporary cannabis products, more individuals, groups, policymakers and investors become more informed on the subject and this can result in the further development of modern cannabis products. The cannabis industry can be utilized as a catalyst for rural and township economic growth by providing entrepreneurs with information and by supporting them with adequate funding. The study provides insight to investors and businesses about the economic prospects of the cannabis industry in South Africa. Furthermore, through this study, consumers become more aware of the emerging cannabis products in the market that they can utilize. The study can also be utilized by lobby groups and business forums to challenge the notion of criminalizing the use of cannabis as this is hindering economic growth and the creation of employment opportunities in South Africa.

LITERATURE REVIEW

Cannabis is a plant that is used by individuals and businesses for medical or recreational purposes (Hannah & Mallinson, 2018). The cultivation, use and distribution of cannabis remain forbidden in most states, however, the legal framework on cannabis is shifting and governments are displaying more acceptance. The most notable recent development is the move by state governors in the USA in the states of Alaska, Colorado, Oregon and Washington to legalize cannabis for personal use, which was followed by California decriminalizing the recreational use of cannabis (Chouvy & Macfarlane, 2018). Canada has also taken considerate strides towards legalizing the use of cannabis for both recreational and medical purposes. Uruguay introduced a licensed retail and production system for cannabis in 2014 to legalize the use of cannabis.

The abovementioned regions demonstrate the economic benefits of institutional innovations in cannabis legislation. The most notable benefits are evident in increased tax revenues from cannabis sales and also research provides evidence of reduced cannabis use among minors as the sale of cannabis can be monitored by the retailers. The principal goal of legalization must be the eradication of the illicit trade in cannabis and maximizing market participation through open markets and personal cultivation

(Chouvy & Macfarlane, 2018). Ongoing public backing for the legalization of recreational marijuana continues to rise across the USA and globally. The study demonstrates public opinion support for marijuana legalization has continued to significantly increase. The dispute around the legalization of cannabis is firmly situated within the context of harm reduction and potential social impact. The arguments made by those opposing the legalization of cannabis are that it is a drug and contributes to social issues like crime and violence in South Africa.

Transformation is on the horizon, as governments around the world continue to liberalize their laws and regulations in relation to cannabis as a means to encourage research and development (R&D) in the sector. In the United Kingdom (UK), research and development of cannabis-based products are anticipated to surge significantly resulting from the UK government's recent announcement to "build a greater research base on the therapeutic benefit of these products to maximize their potential as medicines" (Manthey, 2019). Companies looking to develop or sell cannabis products must source funding for their businesses. Depending on the developmental stage of the product, this can either be through preliminary funding by university research grants, venture capital investment or intellectual property commercialization, joint ventures, further rounds of private investment, or public capital markets. Small to medium-sized businesses in particular may not have adequate funds to enter into the market which is capital intensive, in regards to covering the costs of the regulatory and licensing requirements for the sector or developing their business (Chouvy & Macfarlane, 2018). They may wish to pursue investment from private, corporate or institutional investors or look to raise capital by way of an Initial Public Offering (IPO) of equity shares on public markets.

Medical cannabis was legalized in 2016 in South Africa. The South African Health Products Regulation Authority (SAHPRA) approved cultivation licenses and these formal sector licensees were permitted to export their crops (Gerwel, 2018). SAHPRA is geared up to regulate the usage and trade of medicines but also regulates the cultivation of medicinal cannabis because of the outdated Medicines Act (1965). The system remains subject to elite capture but must be mitigated to make cannabis cultivation an inclusive, pro-poor industry in South Africa. Lesotho has taken the role of precursor in using the changing international institutional framework in cannabis markets, permitting licenses to numerous commercial cultivators to export medical cannabis to the USA (Uwakonye, 2020). This is a fertile opportunity for the South African government to overhaul its present prohibitionist stance against cannabis cultivation to further the goals of poverty reduction and inclusive growth of the rural economy as articulated in the National Development Plan 2030 (NDP). The South African government has since decriminalized the personal use of cannabis but it is still regulated. There are a lot of barriers to entry to the market including funding, legislation and lack of information inter alia.

Capitalizing on a high-growth opportunity, cannabis manufacturing is a powerful example of how exterior circumstances can drive industry expansion. During the pandemic, nine million people consumed cannabidiol (CBD) for the first time, while 46% of usual consumers purchased at least one new type of CBD product. These noteworthy sales upsurges are sparking new sector interest. The increased consumer demand presents business growth opportunities, but it can also yield difficulties. Nearly two-thirds (63%) of present CBD manufacturers admit to having been incapable of efficiently meeting customer demand during the period 2020 to 2021 (Aptean, 2021). The CBD sales are forecast to increase by 21% until 2028, thus keeping pace with market appetite could become an even greater issue (Aptean, 2021). CBD manufacturers must understand how market forces are impacting their distribution competencies and why digital conversion is essential to comprehending the legal cannabis manufacturing opportunity. Building on the CBD industry's current momentum, optimism is high in the legal cannabis product sector. After strong growth in 2020/21, 89% of CBD manufacturers predict their sales and revenue will increase further in 2022 (Aptean, 2021).

Cannabis is mostly decriminalized in various countries or states for medical purposes. Research over the years has provided valuable insights and information on the positive impact of cannabis on medical practice. The prominent use of cannabis for medical purposes will be discussed below.

DIFFERENCES BETWEEN MEDICINAL AND RECREATIONAL CANNABIS

Medicinal cannabis is lawfully manufactured under strict pharmaceutical conditions (Balthazar, Joly & Filion, 2022). Doctors and pharmacists know accurately what medicine encompasses. The ingredients, effectiveness and quality of unlawful recreational cannabis are untested. Contamination with microbes, pesticides and heavy metals can occur. Medicinal cannabis products are generally available as oils, sprays, tinctures and capsules (Manthey, 2019). By contrast, illicit cannabis is usually smoked. These differences mean cannabis sourced through illicit channels cannot be described as medicinal cannabis. The use of cannabis for medical purposes has evolved and advanced over the years through research and development which has led to new innovations. The processing of cannabis for the treatment of cancer and other chronic diseases is well documented and this innovation has played an essential role in decriminalizing cannabis, which has resulted in the emergence of further innovations (Balthazar et al., 2022).

MEDICINAL CANNABIS

Medicinal cannabis is a term that refers to the legal, extraordinary quality and standardized products made from crude or raw cannabis (Freeman & Hindocha, 2019). Crude cannabis is a difficult drug for doctors to recommend because the dosage and effectiveness of the drug in each case are not tested or known. Pharmaceutical preparations of cannabis use reformed active mechanisms of cannabis in medical formulations, which maximize the healing benefit and decrease side effects (Whiting et al., 2015). Pharmaceutical preparations, such as a tablet, capsule or spray, mean the concentration can be standardized and the dose controlled. Many medicinal cannabis products comprise a blend of Tetrahydrocannabinol (THC) and CBD. Some products have CBD only, whilst others contain predominantly THC.

MEDICAL CANNABIS MARKET

The cannabis market is attractive to investors in both the medical and recreational sectors (Erickson, 2021). In the first place, international cannabis demand is met by contemporary supply, even if it has been illegal. There is therefore a huge and established recreational supply market and the growers in this subdivision will most likely be able to meet legal recreational demand over the medium term. The second motivation is that in the future, medical cannabis will have to be cultivated in laboratory-like environments and hence, will require extensive greenhouse environments and pesticide-free soil (Freeman & Lorenzetti, 2020). The extended hours of sunshine are a substantial boost to natural growth circumstances with artificial lighting only used periodically during winter months. Based on various expectations, the legal cannabis market is expected to grow at approximately 20% per annum for the next

10 years (Angulo-Cuentas et al., 2019). For this reason, there has been a global explosion in cannabis-related investment. In the short term, there will more than likely be an oversupply of both recreational and medical materials, but as high-cost suppliers are eliminated, low-cost suppliers will flourish, thereby creating thousands of new jobs and propelling economic growth significantly (Erickson, 2021). Some of the medical conditions that cannabis is useful for will be outlined below.

INNOVATIVE MEDICAL USE OF CANNABIS

Cannabis is widely utilized across the world for medical purposes as studies have found that the plant possesses medical benefits. There has been widespread research and innovation in the industry of cannabis for medicinal usage and the regulators are constantly decreasing the regulations around the use of the cannabis plant for medical reasons. The most prominent innovative medical usage of cannabis will be outlined in this section.

Nausea and Vomiting due to Chemotherapy

Cannabis has proved to be effective for cancer patients experiencing nausea and vomiting (Angulo-Cuentas, Ramírez-Vergara, & Charris-Polo, 2019). Patients that have been treated with cannabinoids (CBD) showed a great response towards treating nausea and vomiting compared to other conventional drugs. Additional patients consuming cannabinoids had reduced pain compared to those patients being treated with the normal drugs utilized to treat nausea and vomiting.

Chronic Pain

Cannabis has been proven to have a substantial impact on managing chronic pain (Bala, Rademan, Kevin, Maharaj, & Matsabisa, 2019). Patients using cannabinoids have been reported to have reduced chronic pain levels as compared to those being treated with other forms of drugs.

Appetite Stimulation in HIV/AIDS Patients

Cannabis is perceived to have a positive influence on stimulating appetite in HIV/AIDS positive patients (Angulo-Cuentas et al., 2019). There was a report of a change in weight associated with cannabinoid treatment. The researchers report that there was some evidence that is associated with weight gain for patients being treated with (CBD) infused medication compared to a placebo. Evidence for increased appetite, increase in body fat percentage, and reduction in nausea was more limited and was mostly assessed in single studies (Bala et al., 2019).

INNOVATIVE PRODUCTS MADE FROM CANNABIS

The medical innovations of cannabis are well-documented and accepted in numerous states. Over the past decades, there has been immense interest and investment in the innovation of cannabis products. The plant has become an attractive industry for investment and R & D. In this chapter, the most prominent contemporary cannabis product innovations will be outlined and discussed.

Cannabis Oil

This is the most diverse and arguably the most comprehensive cannabis product classification. The cannabis products introduced below contain cannabidiol (CBD) oil to achieve the anticipated effect of comfort and healthy alternative products (Ciolino, Ranieri & Taylor, 2018). However, hemp oil can be taken in many forms. This versatility has made it the most desirable cannabis product for those looking for legal use. CBD oil has very few traces of THC and does not affect a person's abilities like raw cannabis used for smoking (Benelli et al., 2018). It states that in theory, the expected effects of pain relief, anxiety relief, nausea relief and so on can be achieved without being treated with a drug that affects behavior, mood, thoughts, or perception (Benelli et al., 2018). According to Benelli et al. (2018), CBD oil is also beneficial for pain relief, cancer treatment, anxiety, depression, and sleep problems, among other things. E-liquid in a vape pen is the most common form of cannabis oil, and tinctures are also used. CBD tincture is a drop of balanced CBD extract that is positioned under the tongue and absorbed into the mouth. Some capsules can be taken with water, like a normal pill.

Cannabis Beauty and Skin Care Products

Corporations and businesspersons have innovations and concepts for selling CBD products to customers who are often not part of the target market (Koltai et al., 2019). The CBD beauty product industry is growing exponentially every year and women in the suburbs are not the only ones using CBD (Ciolino et al., 2018). According to Ciolino et al. (2018), CBD has anti-inflammatory effects due to cannabinoid receptors on the skin. It also helps with acne treatment, pain relief, hydration and even exhilarated relaxation (Ciolino et al., 2018). The combination of these effects which these products promise to offer is very attractive to potential customers. Cannabis oil lotion promises to relieve muscle pain and lotions and ointments provide the appeal of clearer skin (Ciolino et al., 2018). Bath bombs and bath salts bring comfort and relaxation to the bathtub. The cannabis market is constantly growing and expanding. There are products such as cannabis body wash, lip gloss and mascara (Ciolino et al., 2018). The types of cannabinoids in cosmetic products help determine the effect. Many of these products focus on CBD and the health benefits it offers.

Cannabis Beverages

Cannabis beverages have not yet reached the height of mainstream cosmetic products, but are becoming more popular. Cannabis-injected cocktails are still in their infancy and can be found in some bars that allow recreational cannabis, but there is a huge market for cannabis-based beverages in South Africa (Ciolino et al., 2018). Beverages infused with cannabis are only permitted in countries where cannabis is completely ecrimina or ecriminalized for recreational consumption.

Cannabis Chocolates

Eating cannabis is a common method mainly for getting a feeling of euphoria because it is more effective than other methods (Freeman & Lorenzetti, 2020). It allows consumers to eat light meals while taking their supplements, which is perceived as favourable by the consumers. The most well-known edible foods are standard weed brownies, pot cookies, and marijuana gummies (Qian et al., 2019). Cannabis chocolate has become a trend since it is legal and companies are eager to sell cannabis treats (Qian et al., 2019). Chocolate can be sold to those who are interested in trying out legitimate cannabis products but who are not eager to do so via smoking. These chocolates are sold in limited quantities as they contain THC.

Cannabis Gummies

Cannabis gummies are the most popular CBD-specific product since the use of marijuana is criminalised in most states. This is an unregulated area and thus it is difficult to determine with accuracy how much CBD is actually contained in them across the various suppliers (Qian et al., 2019). As a result, anyone living in a state where medical marijuana is permitted and who has a medical marijuana card can consume cannabis 'gummies', cannabis 'worms' and various other types of confectionary infused with CBD only or also THC and can buy these from the retailers (Benelli et al., 2018).

Cannabis Capsules

Cannabis capsules are not sweet like gummies or chocolate and are not as refreshing as cannabis-infused beer but are another option for those who want to uplift their mood or relieve pain (Hammond, 2021). The capsules are most common with people who are not looking for a treat but want to experience the same sensation without smoking, and instead choose to take it like a medicine (Hammond, 2021). This method is surprisingly popular all over the world, and in areas where the use of cannabis has been legalised.

Cannabis Dog Treats

There are general concerns about giving dogs a cannabis treat, but it's completely safe if the treat is purchased or sourced from an authorised supplier (Freeman & Lorenzetti, 2020). While the focus should be on circumventing the high of THC, there are several companies working on the development of pet-specific hemp and CBD products (Davis, Tzanidis & Saltzman, 2018). There are many examples of pets being actively treated with marijuana, but it turns out that getting such a permit is difficult in most countries. Still, many scientists continue to study the effects of medical marijuana on pets. Additional detailed research will provide scientists with more data to prove or test this hypothesis. According to Davis et al. (2018), preliminary results show that CBD helps treat cancer, epilepsy, osteoporosis, joint pain and anxiety in pets. Hemp and CBD are acceptable for dogs, as long as owners are cautious and keep in mind that not all companies claiming that CBD products contain minimal THC are telling the truth (Qian et al., 2019).

CANNABIS REGULATIONS IN SOUTH AFRICA

South Africa is amongst the countries around the world with less stringent regulations when it comes to the usage of cannabis. There are numerous alternatives to the prohibition of cannabis ranging from regulation to decriminalization and legalization. Decriminalization refers to the elimination of the illegal status for personal possession or use, regulation denotes the limit on access and limitations on advertising (Freeman & Hindocha, 2019). Legalization refers to cannabis use and cannabis supply, making lawful what was previously forbidden. Cannabis usage in most countries is only limited to medical usage under strict regulations. On the contrary, cannabis usage is permitted for both medical and recreational purposes in South Africa subject to adhering to the legalized quantities and purposes for the use of the plant. The cannabis regulations for medical use in South Africa are divided into eight categories, with schedule 8 being the strongest substance. The usage of schedule 8 and 7 substances requires a permit from the Director-General of the health department, schedule 6 up to 4 substances are only available subject to a prescription from a medical practitioner and the others are available over the counter (Riley et al., 2020). Cannabis usage for recreational purposes is permitted for adults to consume within a private environment, for personal consumption and to cultivate on private property for personal consumption only (Riley et al., 2020).

Cannabis CBD Oil

CBD-containing products (with zero or negligible THC) are permitted to be legally imported or manufactured and sold, subject to having a SAHPRA license (Gerwel, 2018). In May 2020, the Government Gazette published amendments to the schedules of the 1965 Medicines Act. CBD remains schedule 4 (requiring a prescription) but CBD products containing less than 0.001% THC and less than 0.0075% CBD are moved to schedule 0 (uncontrolled). Fourteen retail chains such as Clicks and Dischem are presently legally selling CBD-containing products. The oil mined from hemp seeds is extremely healthy because it is rich in polyunsaturated fatty acids of which some are essential fatty acids that individuals must obtain from their diet (Riley et al., 2020). Edible oil can be acquired by cold-pressing the hemp seeds and is added to human food, cosmetics and industrial fluids, while the residual seed cake can be transformed into protein-rich flour or livestock feed supplements.

Industrial Hemp Cultivation

According to Lewis (2020), the cultivation, processing and sale of industrial hemp "cannabis containing zero or negligible THC" were illegal in terms of the Medicines Act (1965) and the Drugs and Drug Trafficking Act (1992). In terms of the Gazette May 2020 regulation amendments, industrial hemp containing less than 0.1% THC is no longer regulated (Riley et al., 2020). Nevertheless, the cannabis plant with seeds inclusive and related products remains schedule 7 as a regulated substance. From the above brief policy review, it is evident that the national government seeks to lawfully enable the growth of an inclusive cannabis economy. Existing legislation is still to be amended to allow this industry to flourish. The most notable legislations that require amendments are the Medicines and Related Substances Act of 1965, The Drugs and Drug Trafficking Act of 1992, and the Traditional Health Practitioners Act of 2007 (Riley et al., 2020). There is a need for better policy coordination between drug policy and policies relating to cannabis business development and formalization processes (Parry et al., 2019).

The decriminalization of cannabis for personal consumption has opened the door for more research and development to be conducted and innovations to emerge from South Africa, beyond the exportation of raw cannabis plants alone (Riley et al., 2020).

METHODOLOGY

Research methodology refers to the practical manner in which the research was conducted (Lewis, Thornhill & Saunders, 2019). More precisely, it is about how a researcher systematically designs a study to ensure valid and reliable results that address the research aims and objectives. Desktop research was used for this chapter due to the fact that there have been numerous studies already conducted on this topic. Desktop research is also referred to as secondary research since it involves reviewing the available research findings of existing papers. Desktop research involves collecting data from existing resources hence it is often considered a low-cost technique as compared to field research (Schindler, 2018). The systematic review procedure is utilized to assemble the available empirical research on the topic. According to Bengtsson (2016), a systematic review seeks to collect all accessible empirical research by utilizing evidently defined, systematic approaches to acquire solutions to a particular problem. The data was collected by reviewing research papers from a global perspective and a South African perspective with regards to the topic of cannabis in recent years dating from 2018 to 2022. Content analysis was used to analyse and code the collected data. Content analysis is a research tool used to determine the presence of certain words, themes, or concepts within some given qualitative data (Bengtsson, 2016). By virtue of utilizing content analysis, the researcher is able to quantify and analyze the occurrence, meanings and connections of certain arguments, themes or theories. The data was collected online as this is a desktop research platform. Google Scholar, Ebscohost and Jstor were used to collect data. There were 64 articles that were found and only 27 were used as they were more closely related to this study. The articles used were published between 2018 and 2022 as a method of gathering more updated data and the key search phrases were "cannabis innovation, medical cannabis, recreational cannabis, developments in cannabis products and new cannabis products".

FINDINGS AND DISCUSSION

The use and stigma around cannabis have evolved over the years, as cannabis was conventionally used for recreational purposes as an illegal and unregulated drug. Regulators across the world are constantly limiting the restrictions on the use of cannabis as more research and development is occurring around the world. Cannabis is widely decriminalized in most countries for medical purposes as extensive research has been conducted on this product or good and research proves that cannabis has positive medical benefits if utilized in a proper manner. South Africa is amongst the countries that have decreased the extent of regulations around the use of cannabis for both medical and recreational purposes. The medical use of cannabis is well documented and it is a highly regulated sector that requires extensive research and funding (Freeman & Lorenzetti, 2020). Medicine produced from cannabis is showing positive results based on the effective rate of patients treated for cancer, chronic pain, appetite stimulation for HIV/AIDS individuals and for treating pain in pets (Davis et al., 2018).

There has been growing interest, investment, research and development in the cannabis industry. Some of the most prominent contemporary product innovations include cannabis oil, cannabis beauty and skin care products, beverages, chocolates, gummies, capsules and cannabis dog treats (Hammond, 2021). These cannabis products are regulated in most states around the world and are only permitted in a few countries. Based on observation around the world, there has been no widely reported negative impact of the products on individuals or societies. This asserts that essential research and development were conducted prior to producing these products and there has been substantial growth in the market as people prefer to consume cannabis in a processed state rather than conventional smoking of the plant as previously done in the past.

South Africa is amongst the few countries that have legalized or decriminalized cannabis usage for both medical and recreational purposes (Riley et al., 2020). There are still regulations around the quantity of cannabis an individual should be in possession of and the type of plant that can be utilized for research and development. There is an issue of unequal distribution of information and lack of access to funding to promote cannabis innovation in South Africa (Gerwel, 2018). This is hindering the process of research and development in the country which results in the compliant cannabis growers exporting it without adding value to the plant. There should be more effort made by regulators to promote this industry through providing workshops, training and information to the rural and township areas as this industry could be used to alleviate poverty.

There is a huge gap between South Africa and developed countries in terms of cannabis innovation. Based on the available literacy, there is minimal information or lack of innovation in South Africa in regard to cannabis innovations beyond medical purposes. Most of the cannabis innovations are within the medical field. This is a huge concern as the market is available and has substantial potential for growth. Cannabis plants are grown all over the country, especially in rural settlements. This ends up not yielding to rural economic development as there is no lucrative market to purchase all that output. Business-to-business (B2B) is more lucrative and results in long-term business sustainability. The absence or minimal innovations of cannabis products in South Africa is depriving the rural communities of the opportunity to alleviate poverty and become essential contributors to the country's economy.

The economic prospect of cannabis is very huge in South Africa and the available cannabis products are showing good economic viability. The number of cannabis retailers is constantly increasing due to the interest and consumer demand for cannabis goods and services. Hair and beauty cannabis products are proving viable in the market as consumers are becoming more aware of the positive effect of organic products. More research and development are still required to further improve the product quality to attract more consumers. Cannabis gummies are very popular amongst the youth in South Africa in urban areas, mostly among university students based on observation. The demand is huge for this type of innovation and there are only a few suppliers of the product. With more marketing and further product development, cannabis capsules have the potential to become a very lucrative product. Other innovations include vaping supplements used by the consumers of e-cigarettes and numerous types of vaping products. These products are usually utilized in clubs, parties and for private consumption.

RECOMMENDATIONS

The cannabis industry is lucrative, and more research should be done to allow the industry to reach its full potential. Government should reduce restrictions on the industry and provide funding opportunities to researchers for the industry to be legalised. This can be achieved through providing information to the public more often and inviting public participation in the bill amendments as this results in a more inclusive decision-making process. The lack of information for the citizens regarding the economic potential of cannabis is the source of uncertainty which is hindering the innovation process in South Africa and around the world. The prospect of more information and data becoming available results in more innovations and the growth of the industry. This can be achieved through proving training and workshops on cannabis products innovation and development. South Africa must observe the successful innovations from other counties and innovate products that have economic viability in the country's market.

Government departments like economic development, small business enterprise development and agriculture must prioritise the cannabis industry as a means of promoting innovation in SMMEs and rural and township economic development. Access to funding is a major issue for SMMEs in South Africa and making it available ensures that more companies become active in the industry and this yields an increase in the output of cannabis products. Reducing the barriers to entry in the industry asserts that more people gain entry to the market and more innovations emerge. The process of applying for permits and licensing is time-consuming and costly. By virtue of the regulators making it more accessible, the underprivileged and former marginalized communities can participate as this industry possesses the prospect of becoming a catalyst for rural and township development. Providing access to markets for the farmers of cannabis is one step toward making the industry become economically viable. The critical stage is providing funding opportunities to businesses for innovations to emerge. The prospect of the industry flouring results in employment opportunities both directly and indirectly from the industry.

FUTURE RESEARCH

The vast majority of literature on the topic of cannabis focuses on the medical use of cannabis and there is not a lot of information on the recreational purposes of cannabis. More research is required on the recreational use of cannabis as this paves way for the emergence of more innovations. The negative and positive effects of the drug must be studied further so that the public can make more informed decisions regarding the use of cannabis. There is insufficient literature on breeding cannabis, the different types of cannabis that exist, licensing requirements and the economy of cannabis in South Africa. It is essential to study the role that can be played by the cannabis industry in poverty alleviation and enabling an inclusive economy that can also benefit disadvantaged communities, providing that they meet the requirement set by regulators.

CONCLUSION

There have been numerous innovations in cannabis products in the 21st century and the industry is bound to continue evolving in the coming years. Government regulations have a major impact on the innovation and use of cannabis in their jurisdictions. Countries around the world, including South Africa, are starting to legalise the use of cannabis products for either medical reasons, recreational purposes or both. Further reduction of regulations in the industry is required for additional innovations to emerging through research and development. Some of the most prominent contemporary innovations are cannabis oil, beauty and skin care products, beverages, chocolate, gummies, capsules and dog treats. Technology is constantly improving and this enables more innovations to emerge which further increases the quantity and quality of cannabis product offerings. These innovations prove the market viability of the industry and the role it can play in the quest for economic growth of both developed and developing countries. More research and development are still required for the industry to reach its full potential, but regulations are still required to mitigate the prospect of drug abuse and criminal activities. Small and emerging businesses are excluded from the industry through a lack of funding and information in South Africa. By virtue of making the industry more inclusive, the marginalised groups can utilise this opportunity to alleviate poverty. More research and investment are still needed to add further innovations in the cannabis industry as it has already proven its worth in both recreational and medical usage.

REFERENCES

Albright, V. A., & Johnson, E. O. (2018). Emerging Topics and Innovative Methodologies in Cannabis Research. *Substance Abuse: Research and Treatment, 12*, 117822181877426. doi:10.1177/1178221818774264 PMID:29795983

Angulo-Cuentas, G., Ramírez-Vergara, J., & Charris-Polo, M. (2019). Cannabis: Innovation Opportunities for its Medical Use. *Recent Patents on Engineering, 13*(3), 212–223. doi:10.2174/1872212112666181022155150

Bala, A., Rademan, S., Kevin, K. N., Maharaj, V., & Matsabisa, M. G. (2019). UPLC-MS Analysis of Cannabis sativa Using Tetrahydrocannabinol (THC), Cannabidiol (CBD), and Tetrahydrocannabinolic Acid (THCA) as Marker Compounds: Inhibition of Breast Cancer Cell Survival and Progression. *Natural Product Communications, 14*(8), 1934578X1987290. doi:10.1177/1934578X19872907

Balthazar, C., Joly, D. L., & Filion, M. (2022). Exploiting Beneficial Pseudomonas spp. for Cannabis Production. *Frontiers in Microbiology, 12*, 833172. doi:10.3389/fmicb.2021.833172 PMID:35095829

Benelli, G., Pavela, R., Petrelli, R., Cappellacci, L., Santini, G., Fiorini, D., Sut, S., Dall'Acqua, S., Canale, A., & Maggi, F. (2018). The essential oil from industrial hemp (Cannabis sativa L.) by-products as an effective tool for insect pest management in organic crops. *Industrial Crops and Products, 122*, 308–315. doi:10.1016/j.indcrop.2018.05.032

Bengtsson, M. (2016). How to plan and perform a qualitative study using content analysis. *Nursing Plus Open, 2*, 8–14. doi:10.1016/j.npls.2016.01.001

Bernstein, M. (2002). 10 tips on writing the living Web. *A List Apart: For People Who Make Websites, 149*. http://www.alistapart.com/articles/writeliving

Chouvy, P.-A., & Macfarlane, J. (2018). Agricultural innovations in Morocco's cannabis industry. *The International Journal on Drug Policy, 58*, 85–91. doi:10.1016/j.drugpo.2018.04.013 PMID:29885594

Ciolino, L. A., Ranieri, T. L., & Taylor, A. M. (2018a). Commercial cannabis consumer products part 1: GC–MS qualitative analysis of cannabis cannabinoids. *Forensic Science International, 289*, 429–437. doi:10.1016/j.forsciint.2018.05.032 PMID:29954632

Davis, S. J., Tzanidis, A., & Saltzman, D. (2018). Medicinal marijuana: Commercialisation and innovation in a complex regulatory environment. *Australasian Biotechnology*, *28*(1), 60–62. https://search.informit.org/doi/10.3316/informit.553969626513007

Deloitte. (2020). Nurturing new growth, Canada gets ready for Cannabis 2.0. *Deloitte.* http://www.deloitte.com

Erickson, D. (2021). How Will CBD Manufacturers Drive Sector Growth in 2022? *Aptean*. https://www.aptean.com/en-EU/insights/blog/cannabis-manufacturers-drive-growth-2022

Freeman, T. P., Hindocha, C., Green, S. F., & Bloomfield, M. A. P. (2019). Medicinal use of cannabis based products and cannabinoids. *BMJ (Clinical Research Ed.)*, *1141*, l1141. doi:10.1136/bmj.l1141 PMID:30948383

Freeman, T. P., & Lorenzetti, V. (2019). 'Standard THC units': A proposal to standardize dose across all cannabis products and methods of administration. *Addiction (Abingdon, England)*, *115*(7), 1207–1216. doi:10.1111/add.14842 PMID:31606008

Gerwel, H. (2018). Institutional innovation and pro-poor agricultural growth: cannabis cultivation in the Eastern Cape province of South Africa as fertile opportunity. In *Crop Production/Industries.* https://ageconsearch.umn.edu/record/284784?ln=en

Hammond, D. (2019). Communicating THC levels and 'dose' to consumers: Implications for product labelling and packaging of cannabis products in regulated markets. *The International Journal on Drug Policy*, *102509*. doi:10.1016/j.drugpo.2019.07.004 PMID:31351756

Hannah, A. L., & Mallinson, D. J. (2017). Defiant Innovation: The Adoption of Medical Marijuana Laws in the American States. *Policy Studies Journal: the Journal of the Policy Studies Organization*, *46*(2), 402–423. doi:10.1111/psj.12211

Koltai, H., Poulin, P., & Namdar, D. (2019). Promoting cannabis products to pharmaceutical drugs. *European Journal of Pharmaceutical Sciences*, *132*, 118–120. doi:10.1016/j.ejps.2019.02.027 PMID:30851400

Lewis, M. (2020, June). *Cannabis in the East Cape.* ECSECC - Eastern Cape Socio Economic Consultative Council. https://www.ecsecc.org/documentrepository/informationcentre/cannabis-in-the-eastern-cape-paper-web_76550.pdf

Lewis, P., Thornhill, A., & Saunders, M. N. K. (2019). *Research Methods for Business Students*. Pearson Education, Limited.

Lloyd, D. H., & Horn, P. G. (2001). Local economic development in rural Eastern cape towns. *Africa Insight*, *31*(1). doi:10.4314/ai.v31i1.22354

Manthey, J. (2019). Cannabis use in Europe: Current trends and public health concerns. *The International Journal on Drug Policy*, *68*, 93–96. doi:10.1016/j.drugpo.2019.03.006 PMID:31030057

Parry, C., Myers, B., & Caulkins, J. (2019). Decriminalisation of recreational cannabis in South Africa. *Lancet*, *393*(10183), 1804–1805. doi:10.1016/S0140-6736(19)30011-X PMID:31057166

Qian, Y., Gurley, B. J., & Markowitz, J. S. (2019). The Potential for Pharmacokinetic Interactions Between Cannabis Products and Conventional Medications. *Journal of Clinical Psychopharmacology, 39*(5), 462–471. doi:10.1097/JCP.0000000000001089 PMID:31433338

Riley, S., Vellios, N., & van Walbeek, C. (2019). An economic analysis of the demand for cannabis: Some results from South Africa. *Drugs Education Prevention & Policy*, *27*(2), 123–130. doi:10.1080/09687637.2019.1581139

Schindler, P. S. (2018). *Business Research Methods*. McGraw-Hill Education.

Uwakonye, D. (2020). *Strengthening Capacity Of Youth In Support Of Emerging Agricultural Industries In Africa: Lesotho's Cannabis Industry And The Role Of Higher Education In Its Human Resource Development* [Masters Thesis, Cornell University, USA]. https://ecommons.cornell.edu/bitstream/handle/1813/72648/DeAndre_Uwakonye_MPS_Capstone.pdf?sequence=1

Whiting, P. F., Wolff, R. F., Deshpande, S., Di, N. M., Duffy, S., Hernández, A. V., Keurentjes, J. C., Lang, S., Misso, K., Ryder, S., Schmidlkofer, S., Westwood, M., & Kleijnen, J. (2015). *Cannabinoids for Medical Use A Systematic Review and Meta-analysis*. American Medical Association. http://hdl.handle.net/10757/558499

Chapter 5
Indian Cannabis Farming Policies and Use of FinTech to Improve Related Legalities

Ali Hussain Mir
University of Huddersfield, UK

Sammar Javed
https://orcid.org/0000-0002-3000-936X
University of Derby, UK

ABSTRACT

The chapter proposes a vigilant approach towards the demand of legalising cannabis. It explains the opportunities of Fintech to develop legal, safe, and flexible transactions in the industry which is considered illegal in many countries. The chapter presents the cases of the Jammu and Kashmir, India to grow and manufacture licensed cannabis compounds, making upon indigenous knowledge, culture, and nourishing environment. It also accounts to mitigate the risk around related illegal activities. There are a few pharmaceutical manufacturing companies producing cannabis-based drugs, but they do not own farms, and source it from a few tilizing farmlands. Some big companies have started tilizing blockchain technologies, raising opportunity to test further possibilities through blockchain, cryptography, digital identity cards, etc. The chapter presents findings from a survey in the Jammu and Kashmir, India, capturing perceptions about cannabis farming, cannabis-based medicine, financial transaction challenges, and the use of Fintech in legal use of cannabis.

INTRODUCTION

Modern era advancement is not mere technological advancement but with advent of new illnesses. Manmade systems have caused in various ailments and so pushed the pharmaceutical business progress. Demand of medicines has raised whether allopathic, homeopathic or ayurvedic, Chinese medicine, naturopathic, traditional medicine etc. Pharmaceutical manufacturing is heavily dependent on ingredients

DOI: 10.4018/978-1-6684-6346-8.ch005

from plants. Moreover, sustainable development goals have raised the awareness and trend towards vegan/vegetarian products, natural rather than synthetic elements, carbon footprints of manufacturing and so on. This chapter focuses on cannabis industry, its challenges and opportunities, its use for medical purposes, status of its legalisation, and adoption of technological advancement. The cannabis plant is abundant in chemical substances (about 540) and have various types. A key species Cannabis Sativa, also known as marijuana, contains substantial amount tetrahydrocannabinol (THC) and is known for its effects on persona mental state (National Institute of Health, 2022). Many times, marijuana and cannabis are used as interchangeable terminology.

BACKGROUND

In most countries of the world, the business of growing cannabis is illegal. The prohibition speeded in current century, despite cannabis been known as one of the oldest agricultural crops, with history of over 10,000 years. The reasons behind illegal status of cannabis are complicated, prejudiced, and disturbing (Wilcox, 2020). The first ban imposed on cannabis was in 1913 in California, passed by board of pharmacy whilst they were heavily influenced by the biggest anti-narcotics campaign, in US past. Henry Finger introduced cannabis in the bill reflecting clearly on his prejudice against Hindus. The law and then Mexican revolution gave rise to the cannabis popularity in US. The racism of legislators and media extended to other minorities including African Americans and Filipinos. With the establishment of Federal bureau of Narcotics 1930 harsh history of legislation to restrict production and consumption of cannabis begin in 1937 without scientific evidence and consideration towards the gained and potential benefits. Meanwhile, in some countries, the cultivation and use of cannabis are legal for its medical properties. United States, Italy, Canada, Spain, Israel, Uruguay, and the United Kingdom are among those countries where medical use of cannabis has been approved. Further few countries have encouraged its therapeutic use and thus stands out. Though little is known yet about the impact of this legalisation including the purchase process, accessibility to the regulated producers, and open availability of medicinal products (Pacek, Towe, Hobkirk, Nash, and Goodwin, 2018). Various studies have identified that the cannabis business is high in Indian region, and it is illegal in this region (For example Arya et al., 2022; Balhara et al., 2016; Balhara et al., 2020). Central Asia had been historic hub for cannabis, bound with faith related mysticism and terminologies like *bhanga* have origin with historic *Arya* people (Russo, 2005).

Indian Context

The Ministry of Social Justice, India's report 2019 presented that 31 million Indians claimed to use cannabis within a year. The India's National Survey 2004 confirmed the alignment to global statistics, that cannabis is the most used illicit psychoactive substance and is second most used by treatment seekers at rehabilitation centres (Balhara et al., 2016). Hundreds of sub species of Sativa, Indica and Ruderalis types of cannabis grows wild in India around highways and parks, despite the fact there is no legally grown cannabis. Bombay Hemp Company (BOHECO) claims to have 3000 products of cannabis (APSA, 2019) and estimates 240 tons only collected in state of Madhya Pradesh (Merelli, 2020) and every year tons of cannabis are sold through governmental channels. They further estimate the economic potential of industrial and medicinal cannabis of \$500-\$750 million over next 5 years, where they will be extending production over thousands of acres (Merelli, 2020). BOHECO is one of the pioneer's cannabis businesses in India started in 2013, exploring the vast potential of the industry. According to Section 8 of the Law on Narcotic Drugs and Psychotropic Substances, manufacturing, and trade of cannabis in India is classified as an offence. This legislation also does not permit the import and export of cannabis to and from India. The state of Uttarakhand legalised the cultivation of cannabis for industrial purposes despite a federal cannabis ban in India. This was first reported in the Cannabis Times India, which is the first news portal on Hemp and Cannabis production in India (Cannabis Times India, 2020). The Indian Industrial Hemp association IIHA was licensed to plant 1,000 hectares of cannabis to support seed bank resultantly cultivating 10,000 hectares within 5 years for textile fibre, in July 2018 (APSA, 2019). Medical and research usage of cannabis is an exception under the NDPS Act (Oultram et al., 2021). Moreover, cross border exchange of products falling in the category of drugs and and psychopharmaceutical are governed by the PML Act 2002 (Prevention of Money Laundering Law) (Pedrazzi et al., 2021).

Despite the challenges, the demand for cannabis for its medical use is soaring in India. Arya, Ghosh and Kazhungil (2022) measured views of early career psychiatrists about cannabis legislation and found that 55% respondents agree for medical cannabis and 23% agreed for the recreational cannabis. Early career Psychiatrists with past use of cannabis have more positivity towards legalising recreational use of cannabis. The potential market for cannabis products is considerable for India, with a population of around 1.4 billion and a growing middle class. According to Farinon, Molinari, Costantini, and Merendino (2020) it is high time that we had a consensus about its immense medical potential by using cannabis completely embedded in the Indian Ayurveda and Atharvaveda system for medical consumption. In February 2020, a funding of $ 1 million was raised by the India-based health care starter HempStreet, to support research on the use of cannabis in ayurvedic medicine (Oultram et al., 2021). Hempstreet plan to make use of technological development to expand research on new series of cannabis-based products. They claim to re-define industry standards through their network of 60,000 ayurvedic practitioners serving 10,000+ ayurvedic clinics and have successful 300+ ayurvedic formulations (Hempstreet, 2022). The co-founder of HempStreet, Abhishek Mohan, said that the company plans to set new milestones in the country's medical cannabis sector and is already working on blockchain technology to track cannabis from seed to sale to eliminate the risk of substance abuse (Rupasinghe et al., 2020).

The supply chain and use of cannabis has revealed various issues like cannabis use disorder (Schlag et al., 2021) and demand for further research and awareness regarding the safe medical cannabis prescription. Another issue is illegal trafficking for example, on average 16 kg of cannabis was transported each month during April – July 2020, even though Covid lockdown was implemented in the end of March 2020, as the cargo activity of essential materials remained in action (Salami, Martinelli, Giovino, Bachari, Arad, and Mantri, 2020). According to Leinow and Birnbaum (2017), the legalisation of cannabis and the development of a new industry have taken great steps over recent years. It appears that every day the dynamics of the industry change, with rapid mergers and acquisitions, the start-up of new companies and the urge for better products. The industry has massive progress margin with the improvement of related laws (Parker et al., 2019).

The study aims to discuss challenges and opportunities of cannabis industry, cannabis medical benefits, its state of legalisation and possibilities of using Fintech within Jammu and Kashmir, a golden Cannabis Indian region. The chapter explores the need for ratification of the related legislation to avoid the abuse related to cannabis use and business. Moreover, the exploration suggests that the advancements in Fintech and blockchain could revolutionise the cannabis industry by tackling drug trafficking and pave way for amazing medical benefits hidden in the Cannabis plant. The economic impact of the cannabis industry and its advancement on the local economy is also discussed. Moreover, the study attempts to contribute to the huge data gap (Arya, Ghosh and Kazhungil, 2022) of cannabis industry in India more specifically the region of Jammu and Kashmir.

CHALLENGES OF GROWING CANNABIS AND TECHNOLOGICAL POSSIBILITIES IN THE CANNABIS SECTOR

This section starts with a discussion about challenges of growing Cannabis in India. Discussion around some of the challenges faced by the Cannabis industry provides the basis for discussion of future cannabis industry sector possibilities. This segment proceeds to examine the use of Fintech in the cannabis supply chain as well as other technological possibilities that include blockchain, cryptography, digital payment systems and digital identity cards etc.

Challenges and Opportunities of Cannabis Industry

The cannabis industry faces numerous safety issues, including limiting youthful consumption of cannabis, illegal trade, and the adulteration of commodities (Farinon et al., 2020). The possible advances in the cannabis industry could be hampered by such safety issues. Appropriate legal provisions along the technological advancements could be promising for socio-economic betterment. Kavousi et al., (2022) studied cannabis governance and presented opportunities and challenges associated with the industry. They include raise in tax returns and land price, business growth, employment boost, improved health and wellbeing, and potential for inclusion and diversity, as opportunities. Whereas the challenges include less than expected economic benefit, complex regulations, increased demand, increased health and safety risks, slow rate improvements for inclusion and diversity. A traditional reason for the criminalisation for cannabis use is that it results in the habit of using other damaging drugs. Tulsyan's (2022) analysis proved NDPC Act as unconstitutional, which implements criminalisation for the cannabis use in India. International obligations and being signatory of 1961 convention, India introduced NDPC Act which was maiden for cannabis criminalisation.

Cannabis usefulness is proven since thousands of years and covers range of leisure, spiritual, societal, and healing objectives (Badiola, Doshi, and Narouze, 2021). In comparison the formal research and legalisation has history of last 2-3 decades. Recent legalisation of cannabis use for pain management in US states, has brought some change in the scenario. Illegal stature of cannabis proves a hurdle in the way research advancement towards pain management any many other medical and social benefits. Cannabis is considered as multi-use crop with several potential applications and its history since 18th century in Bangladesh has been analysed by Rahman et al., (2022). In 1987 it ceased because of Bangladesh's commitment to international narcotics agreement. Wealth of knowledge about related cultivation, regulation, sale, use was put on risk due to a week response to a foreign agenda.

India also has a long history of cultivating cannabis and its medical usage (Kuddus et al., 2013), as presented in folk tales and testimony since 1,000 BC (Kuppuram, 2021) but has suffered about for a century due to its illegal status. The growing demand to legalise cannabis, raising awareness towards the potential socio-economic benefits and the advancement in Fintech to ease the supply chain challenges, has brought back the industry in attention. According to Ritter, Zadik-Weiss, Almogi-Hazan and Or (2020), India is wedged between the Golden Crescent and Golden Triangles, the two largest illicit opium areas in the world. This proximity has traditionally been seen as a source of vulnerability because both India and the opiate producer in these regions have been made a destination and a transit route. The fact remains important in defining trends in drug trafficking in the subcontinent. But the extent of the diversion of lawful opium grown in the country from heroin seized in the country is still under debate. Another level of challenge is the definitional consideration by the NDPS Act as it treats ganja, charas, and bhang differently and need to be looked in comparison to tobacco and alcohol which are more lethal (Kuppuram, 2021). Moreover, there are some state-based Act putting restrictions on distinct categories of cannabis for example, The Assam Ganja and Bhang Prohibition Act, 1958, and the Bombay Prohibition Act, 1949.

Status Quo of Cannabis Industry in India

Hemp Foundation claims that Indian hemp start-ups have global access and list top 10 start-ups as: Health horizons in Delhi, Bombay Hemp Company (BOHECO) in Mumbai, Hemp Foundation in Uttarakhand, Hempsters in Hyderabad, Satliva in Bangalore, Vedi in Bhubaneswar, GreenJams in Vizag, Namrata Hemp Company in Bangalore, B.E Hemp in Bangalore, Hemp Cann in Bhubaneswar (Vivek, 2021). Hemp foundation and other start-ups are manufacturing range of cannabis products including plastic, paper, yarn, fabric, fibres, accessories, clothing, food, home furnishings, ropes, herds, webbings, twine etc. Sheel (2021) shared a database of companies working in India under the categories of manufacturers, research and development organisations, media companies, community centric collectives, cannabis aggregators (marketplaces, resellers), ayurvedic cannabis, CBD, and Hemp companies. During 2020, cannabis start-ups remained in limelight in national media, but this did not help the confusion prevailing throughout the country regarding use of distinct parts of the plants from Cannabaceae family (Sharma, 2020). She clarified that hemp cultivation is legal in India but its flowering part of the plant which is leisurely smoked is illicit as per NDPS Act. Wildly grown plant through out the country is extensively used in rituals and home remedies along associated rich indigenous knowledge. Indian government license businesses to produce and sell cannabis (bhang), whereas cannabis resin (charas) and the bud (Ganja) are illegal, and anyone found guilty will face imprisonment of up to 20 years (Sinha and Fogla, 2020). Describing the legal status, they specified that the only state of Uttar Pradesh and Uttarakhand holds the license of hemp cultivation, followed by Madhya Pradesh legalising the cultivation. Since early 2020, NGOs and the activists had filed petitions for cannabis legalisation and Bangalore become the home of legalisation movement. A license has been issued to The Indian Institute of Integrative Medicine (IIIM) to cultivate cannabis for research and medical purpose especially developing medication of epilepsy and cancer.

Cannabis Medicinal Benefits

In India, over 1000 descriptions of cannabis and its compounds have been used to describe its use as a hypnotic and tranquillizer in the treatment of anxiety, hysteria, and mania (Farinon et al., 2020). Likewise, patients with multiple sclerosis or intractable neurogenic pain reported the benefits of cannabinoids, including reduced anxiety, depression, as well as muscle spasm and pain (Groce, 2018). Russo, (2017) listed effects and actions of Cannabis and Cannabinoids, including anxiolytic and euphoric effects, for anxiety and depression; anticonvulsant action; analgesia, including dysesthesia; decreased pain perception, increased pain tolerance; appetite stimulation in the cachexia state; antiemetic action; saliva reduction in patients (ALS); muscle relaxation for spasticity relief; decreased intraocular pressure, useful in glaucoma cases; epilepsy and neurological disorders; anti-tumour and anti-inflammatory activity in cancer. Crescioli, Lombardi, Bettiol, Menniti-Ippolito, Da Cas, Parrilli, and Vannacci (2020) found the treatment possibilities for AIDS, cancer, ADHD (attention deficit hyperactivity disorder), multiple sclerosis, nausea from chemotherapy, Crohn's disease, glaucoma, epilepsy, insomnia, migraine, arthritis and poor appetite, anorexia, Tourette syndrome, Alzheimer's disease, muscular dystrophy, fibromyalgia, cachexia, and amyotrophic lateral sclerosis, using cannabis.

Cannabis is used in treatment of 'chronic pain, chemotherapy- induced nausea and vomiting, and multiple sclerosis spasticity'. Recent study of Przybycień, Gąsior-Perczak and Placha, (2022) claimed that cannabinoid components play considerable role in disorders related to glucose-lipid metabolism, obesity, and fertility. In England alone from 2000 to 2019, women obesity has increased from 21% to 29%, and US is the 12th most obese country in the world (Djordjevic, 2021). Lyoo, Renshaw and Yurgelun-Todd (2022) analysed therapeutic use of cannabis and emphasised the need to understand neurobiological dynamics. They further suggested that two major cannabinoids (delta-9-tetrahydrocannabinol and cannabidiol) have distinctive impact on the brain metabolite levels. Deaths due to neoplasms have causes where lung cancer is top on the list, worldwide. Drozd, et al., (2022) were convinced that certain components of Cannabis Sativa establish anticancer pursuit towards breast, prostate, colorectal, etc., it has huge potential to treat lung cancer. They suggested cannabis as supplementary agent in future cancer treatments.

In discussing clinical use of cannabis in UK, Couch (2020) emphasised therapeutic potential especially for physiological issues and urged authorities to fund related products. He highlighted a policy change to prevent illegal medical use of street cannabis. Current policies globally restrict Cannabis farming and so the production of drugs using Cannabis compounds. Among very few, Hempstreet is a health tech start up in India aiming to become India's first research and retail venture in ayurvedic medicine utilising Cannabis in production (HempStreet, 2022). One of the biggest operators in the Indian cannabis market, HempStreet tends to leverage blockchain technology for tracking the production chain ranging from sourcing to manufacturing and extended distribution to the clinics (HempStreet, 2022).

State of Legalisation of Cannabis

Legal position of cannabis farming is ambiguous in many countries including India, even its production and use is banned in most forms. Most policies globally consider cannabis-related activities illegal (Decorte et al., 2020) and so the cross-border investment in Cannabis is a legitimate challenge. It was in 1986, when sale, production and transportation of cannabis and related products were brought under the Narcotics law under the influence of international drug cartel, damaging a legal income stream (Kuppuram, 2021). According to a new report in the Financial Express (2020) titled 'India's cannabis problem is not just about its use' concerning the arrest of an actress under NDPS Act, recounted misuse of the Cannabis as the biggest challenge for the industry. A report by UN office on Drugs and Crime has unveiled the illegal cultivation of cannabis in Jammu and Kashmir, Tamil Nadu, Manipur, Kerala, Uttar Pradesh, Himachal Pradesh and other states (UNODC, 2021). The illegal flow of various chemicals and drugs violate rules at Indian borders and causes a significant threat to national security (Sharma and Ravikumar, 2017). Moreover, wild growth of cannabis and its trafficking across India has also been identified as a major threat.

According to Salami et al., (2020), Cannabis law varies concerning possession, delivery, cultivation, consumption from country to country. Israel has prohibition for the use of cannabis, but since 1992 certain treatments have been allowed the use of drugs containing cannabis compound. Recreational use of cannabis has been legalised in 36 US states (Kavousi, 2022). Malta was first among the European countries to legalise cultivation and possession of cannabis for personal usage (The Week, 2021). Canada legalised cannabis use in 2018 for non-medical purposes along introduction of cannabis Act specifying goals for public health and National Cannabis survey collecting data about cannabis consumption (Rotermann, 2020).

After legalisation of the recreational use of cannabis in the 36 US States the project sale was at $92 billion during 2021 (Kavousi, 2022). In February 2020, it was reported that the global market of industrial hemp is expected to grow at an annual rate of 15.8% from 2020 to 2027, with an estimated total market value of $15.26 billion by 2027 (James, 2020). Cannabis industry in India is facing challenges of traditional banking along multiple other legal aspects (Abbott and Zack, 2018). Most of the cannabis businesses are dealt completely in cash, which leaves myriad discrepancies in banking activities and causes illegal trafficking (Hendricks, 2020). On 9 December 2020, India supported removal of cannabis from the list of deadly opioids in the Single Convention on Narcotic Drugs at the United Nations Commission (Kuppuram, 2021).

Hunter (2022) meticulously presented a case of pharmaceutical start-up in a state which legalised the recreational cannabis use. The struggles to get access to the capital and the shunning approach of banks towards cannabis businesses were the top challenges presented for the entrepreneur. It was further highlighted that cash only businesses are at higher risk of robbery. Cannabis businesses are high risk businesses as face shrinkages in case of cash becoming unusable and incurring added expense due to its cash only nature. Paying taxes and licensing fees could be challenging for cannabis businesses and hence adding to the State loss.

Fintech and Technological Possibilities in the Cannabis Sector

Fintech solutions are getting popular in many sectors worldwide have potential in the emerging licit cannabis industry (Nassiry, 2018). Avasthi and Ghosh (2019) argued that a robust initiative of cultivating Cannabis could be taken using Fintech solutions, which are widely accepted. Fintech has brought digital transformation for the Cannabis industry just like in many other sectors. Sophisticated supply chain operations can be revolutionised at distinct stage through the technological adoption ranging from Cannabis farming to the value-added products supply. KeefX, is a USA based Fintech company providing safe and effective payments and monetary transaction system, also supporting Cannabis industry (Herd, 2021). The company provides transparency for all cannabis-related operations, including flexibility of payment options as well as secure network. Another company in the USA named Bespoke Financial is offering Fin-Tech services to cannabis farmers and related businesses by providing safe and flexible financial options through their fast and reliable systems (Techcrunch.com, 2019).

Cannabinoid components are manufactured into ingestible, inhalable, and tropical products. Krause and Pullman (2020) analysed value-added producers of cannabis supply chain. They found that cannabis businesses flourish on their social capital though their human and cognitive capital could not be ignored. Value-added producers of cannabis have appeared as third group along farmers and retailers within cannabis industry, growing after the legalisation regime for cannabis recreational use. Food products like cookies and candies, with unknown dosage of cannabis for the consumers like children, are outcome of these producers, bringing them in notice of regulatory authorities. In the supply chain of cannabis industry, value-added producers operate in high supply and demand instability. Krause and Pullman (2020) argued that new 'quasi-legal' cannabis industry provides an exceptional case for supply chain research and practice, due to its vibrant and strictly regulated environment. Considering the rigorous monitoring needs of auditing, inventory management, chain of custody, cash management and tax needs in the cannabis supply chain, Cannaledger-a software system, was introduced by lawyers and accountants, to address distinctive compliance issues (Abdekalimi, 2019).

The use of financial technologies is expected to be a solution to avoid these problems and minimise the possibilities of illegal trading (Azarenkova, Shkodina, Samorodov, and Babenko, 2018). The use of cryptocurrency can be an effective solution as it curbs the obstacles in bank transactions and allows the use of seed-to-sale software for facilitating the entire process of cultivating, extracting, distributing, and retailing cannabis (Kyriazis, 2021).

The blockchain technology is capable of tracking cannabis throughout the supply chain, from seed to shelf, for growers, retailers, and consumers (Farinon et al., 2020). Custody and transactional privacy protection could allow safe and secure movement of the cannabis and related products. Advancement in cryptography could support the digital supply chain of cannabis (Leinow and Birnbaum, 2017). This could even suit over the counter sale of the related cannabis medicines assuming a transparent movement from farm to consumer. Digital sales, electronic payments and electronic stock counts could be easily met with the technological advancements, leaving little room for unlawful activity. E-prescription systems are bridging communication between prescribers and pharmacists. Digital identification especially for the team at clinics and dispensaries could ensure safety and efficiency in the cannabis industry (Farinon et al., 2020). Verification checks through the digital identity cards could ensure that cannabis products are in safe hands thereby reducing drug trafficking. Whereas schemes like loyalty card could further bring attraction to the cannabis businesses.

Peer- to- peer (P2P) payment systems have reduced transactional and intermediary costs (Fazi, 2021). According to Liu et al. (2020), future fin-tech is expected to be peer-to-peer transfer across regions. The range of P2P solutions offer individuals and corporate integrated encryption and fraud monitoring making it secure, and ideal for the cannabis industry. Start-ups like Zaver develops P2P solutions (Farinon et al., 2020). P2P loans have connected lenders to borrowers without the need for intermediary financial institutions. Some solutions even allow mobile banking without connectivity to the Internet (Farinon et al., 2020).

Cannabis Big Data (2021) provided assurance towards reliable record keeping of plants, extractions, products, and sales. The BioTrack traceability and the Hemp system offer extensive processes and reports related to compliance, taxation, quality control, as well as illegal diversion of the cannabis products (Oultram et al., 2021). It enables regulatory bodies to keep checks at the grams level of cannabis production. The technology was initially developed by the healthcare industry, to help state governments and law-enforcement agencies to prevent the use of drugs or to advance public safety and was developed as a prescribed drug and methamphetamine precursor tracking system.

Fincann™ (2022) is another entrepreneurial initiative providing financial platform to cannabis businesses, based in New York. Digital wallets are providing mediation for card networks, but repeated transaction could be caught and end up in account termination for federally illegal purchase. Cashless ATMs digitally withdraws from customer debit card against the purchase of products like cannabis, but the approach is unsafe and falls in illegal category. Fintech have the potential to fill the gap of lending platform by offering a marketplace where cannabis investors and lenders come together. Fincann™ (2022) shared three key lessons from there adaptation of fintech as 1) avoid card networks, 2) keep transparency, and 3) the fintech solution must be easy. A sustainable payment option for cannabis is PIN debit merchant account- an ATM transaction enabled by bank rather than card networks. This provides compliance for anti-money laundering by providing full transparency to bank examiners and other financial stake holders through cannabis compliant sponsor bank. PIN debit merchant is not e-commerce compliant and thus require person and card presence for verification.

Fintech application platforms introduce convenience and ease of access, and this was tested by Wambua (2022) in Nairobi, Kenya for the access of credit facilities among youth. He suggested redesigning of banking and financial institutions products and services to align with Fintech loan companies. Whereas the fintech companies need to develop responsibly and sustainably. In a study related to federal reserve bank account opening procedures Hill (2022) analysed unique financial institutions including Cannabis Credit Union, Colorado. Colorado has legalised cannabis whereas it remained illegal under federal law. Alex Mason- An attorney, commissioned the union under Colorado law and development an advanced anti-money laundering unit. Despite the growth, the industry face banking problems and lack of transparency and consistency were the key challenges.

The Safe and Fair Enforcement (SAFE) Banking Act is an immensely potential way forward for small cannabis businesses who struggle to avail services within the financial sector. Lack of capital, cash dealing, and financial security could also be addressed by a similar Act for the businesses in India, with huge potential around usefulness of cannabis. Equitable access to financial services would remain a challenge for the cannabis sector. As analysed by Packer et al., (2022) the SAFE Act has some shortfalls but could be improved to be utilised by the cannabis business holders and other stakeholders. Prevention against anti-money laundering, state-legal cannabis businesses, decriminalising cannabis at federal level, promoting research on the useful cannabis components, protection to financial institution for related activities would be some the direct benefits of such a legalisation.

Whilst discussing self-regulation in the emerging industries, Walters and Wisemen (2022) argued that federal inhibits at each stage from capital gathering to tax generation for the cannabis industry. The grey areas in the legalisation of cannabis in the states where its recreational use has been allowed, could lead to criminalisation under the federal acts internationally. They suggested 'Peer-to-Peer' sharing economy and Fintech regulatory sandboxes for the innovation space of self-regulated emerging industries.

METHODOLOGY

This study follows exploratory research approach to find out the ways for legitimate cannabis farming and production for medical purposes. Previous research has already established the medical benefits that could be attained through Cannabis compounds. The need is to find legal provisions for cannabis farming, trading, production and expanding beneficial research in the industry. Moreover, the urge of technological advancements to be tested in niche industries like the cannabis industry sector, which is been looked down upon despite of its huge hidden benefits and future potential.

The first concern for any such study, where the impression of legitimacy is not clear, is where to start safely and remain in the legal boundaries. The key concern of drug addiction associated with cannabis pushed the research first to clarify the associated addiction concerns and if there are any medical benefits associated with it. This led the researchers to seek expert opinion and through semi structured, semi formal in-depth interview with a physician. The interviewee's services within Jammu and Kashmir had been acknowledged by the Indian Medical Association. She is versatile, with various certifications and experience of serving in emergency and non-emergency situations. She holds vast experience of working with rehabilitation centres and actively monitoring drug addiction cases specifically among youth. She actively participates in free medical camps and provides voluntary support to related NGOs. The interview explored use of cannabis, its medical benefits, related drug addiction, anxiety issues and possible treatment through cannabis compounds, and possibility of Fintech solutions for the cannabis industry.

This chapter aims to find out the possibilities from the Fintech solutions to be utilised in the cannabis industry. As one of the pioneer studies, it attempts to understand stakeholders' perception about legalisation and technological advancement of the cannabis industry. Thus, the study adopted mixed methods approach by adding a quantitative survey along expert interview, to find out the answers for research questions. A quantitative research questionnaire was used to capture perceptions regarding beneficial medical use of cannabis, preference for the locally grown cannabis, purchase preferences, associated dangers regarding addiction, recreational use, and possibilities using Fintech.

The cannabis industry in Jammu and Kashmir, India which is known for cannabis production as well as its medicinal use, was investigated case study. Previous studies have struggled to gain access to the cannabis farmers and dealer considering its illegitimate face. Access to the pharmaceutical firms using farm grown cannabis in the region has enabled this study to capture and gain a deep understanding of stakeholder perception. Primary quantitative data gave the edge to the researchers to critically analyse the cannabis industry context in Jammu and Kashmir.

Jammu and Kashmir, India was selected as a context for this study not only due to the origin of first author from the area, but also considering the region as a golden opportunity for the ventures related to Cannabis industry. The region's soil is very ideal for Cannabis farming, drug addiction including cannabis is a major social issue, and the traditional routes of ayurvedic medicine has deep roots in the region. For such research where boundary of legalisation is quite blurred it is never an easy task to gain responses, as the respondents worry to be stereotyped to be involved in some dishonest activity. The research gathered survey responses from a diverse set of respondents including general youth considering the possibility of inclination towards the addiction, a neurologist considering the increased anxiety and related issues where cannabis compound usage had medical effectiveness, pharmacist to capture awareness of the cannabis compound for medical purposes, a police officer dealing with cases of illegitimate cannabis addiction, an official from the narcotics department, non-governmental medical organisations supporting the reduction of cannabis related drug addiction and a respondent from a rehabilitation organisation to capture insights from various dimensions.

A survey questionnaire was carefully developed to cover the themes of cannabis farming, production, and its use for medicinal purposes as well as to gauge stakeholders' perception about the use of fintech in the Indian cannabis industry. The respondents randomly selected for the purpose were government and regulatory bodies, pharmacists, neurologists, related research organisations, farmers, and dealers. The research obtained ethical approval from the Huddersfield Business school research committee. Confidentiality and anonymity were ensured to the participants, using participant information sheet and debriefing. Slightly different version of the questionnaire was presented to various categories of participants. The questionnaires were tested to be completed in no more than 10 minutes and each including 12-15 questions mainly against the 5-point Likert scale ranging from strongly agree to strongly disagree. Although 60 responses from range of respondent categories cannot serve for statistically rectifiable data but for an exploratory study to capture the inductive insights provided useful findings.

Findings

The study provides rare findings, as only few studies have successfully provided empirical data for the cannabis related research mainly due to legitimacy issue prevailing in the industry. Another edge this study gained is gathering empirical data from the Jammu and Kashmir, a golden cannabis Indian region. Moreover, getting hold of the data about an industry which has been labelled as illicit and understanding the perceptions in a developing context where the awareness of an advanced technological subject like Fintech was low, proved a challenge.

Cannabis has several subspecies including Cannabis Sativa which is mainly grown for the hemp fibre and is also used in drugs. The sativa plant grows in warmer environments. Data from the expert interview introduced the researcher to subspecies of cannabis and various of its uses. The first few paragraphs present the empirical qualitative data, and the rest is quantitative data. The image below is a picture of the Cannabis sativa plant

Figure 1. Cannabis Sativa Plant

In the expert interview, the medical practitioner, confirmed that

"The most common use of medical cannabis is for severe pain, nausea, vomiting due to chemotherapies, seizures, muscle spares and anxiety disorder."

The discussion with the expert led to generate understanding that use of cannabis has mostly been perceived as negative due to poor knowledge about its medical benefits, during the current century. It is a classic case of lost of indigenous knowledge. It has been found that cannabis compounds mainly comprise of tetrahydrocannabinol (THC) that has psychoactive effects that are experienced when cannabis is consumed. There are many medical shreds of evidence of usage and effectiveness in cases of chemotherapies, seizures, muscle spars and anxiety disorder. She further shared that some of the United States Food and Drug Administration (FDA) India Office authorised cannabinoid drugs are available in the market like Dronabinol and Nabilone, which is prescribed in the pill form for post-chemo nausea. She feels that the perception of side effects of these drugs is somewhat negative especially association with addiction.

Sharing her experience about the awareness about cannabis she said

"Cannabis is misunderstood legally and industrially in India"

Explaining the Narcotic Drugs and Psychotropic Substances NDPS (1985) Act in India she explained that

"Trade and Consumption of both cannabis and the bud are illegal, and anyone found with them could face up to 20 years of imprisonment and there is also a strict ban on cannabis production in India."

Describing the governmental licensing for cannabis cultivation and research she said

"Although some powers are given to the state government to grant licenses to cultivate cannabis under certain circumstances relatively few research organizations have obtained them but only two states Uttar Pradesh and Uttarakhand regions - both in northern India have received hemp cultivation licenses."

The interviewee discussed about the recent hype in news of cannabis industry, saying

"The Indian Cannabis market has gathered attention recently with various activities of NGO's, court petitions, demanding the legalization of Cannabis. The argument is that the medical benefits associated with cannabis are hard to ignore. In addition, the ideal climatic conditions for cannabis cultivation in India have the potential to boost the economy and create millions of jobs for people. A Non-Governmental Organisation is actively pursuing the agenda to legalize the use of cannabis for medical industrial purposes in India."

Indian warm weather and nourishing soil is boosting for cannabis cultivation, and it could be easily encashed to contribute for the economy and local people. We further found that some known activists are keenly following the agenda of cannabis legalisation. Such legalisation won't be easy due to some lobby groups with their vested interest in keeping the agenda hanging. It will pose a challenge to the regulatory bodies to standardise the processes and legalise the medicinal and rather recreational use.

The key issue with cannabis is its misuse and drug addiction concerns among the young generation. A general practitioner who has experience of working in the rehabilitation centres, in the interview explained that:

"Drug abuse among youths increases the risk to their wellbeing and health. Studies have shown that drug use increases the risk of mental health issues such as anxiety, depression, and psychosis. People use the drug for many reasons like they want to feel good, stop feeling bad and perform better in life or at school or work and as a human being I feel very pity for them, and it is very sad to see youth taking drugs."

Regarding mental illnesses, the interviewee further explained that:

"Anxiety disorders are the most common mental illness affecting more than 50 million adults in India above 18 years of age. Anxiety disorders are treatable if dealt seriously by a qualified psychiatrist."

As a possible measure, she added that

"THC psychoactive compounds decrease anxiety at lower doses."

She also explained that the benefits of cannabis, include the those clearly stated in the following extract from the interview

"The commonly reported benefits of Cannabis are increased sense of calmness, improved relaxation, and better sleep. It is not a full cure though instead; most people report that it helps reduce their overall stress. Cannabis is anti-anxiety that provide short term relief."

Discussing the common use of cannabis for medical relief and the need for legalisation, she acknowledged

"There is no harm in it provided it is done under governmental supervision"

She confessed little awareness of the technological advancements like Fintech and classified herself as a lay person in that perspective. The following quote clearly reveals this observation.

"Fin-Tech solutions for the Cannabis industry have proliferated as a legally emerging fastest growing industry in the nation. Digital wallets serve as a middleman between a bank account and a cannabis transaction. Some Fin-Tech solutions have proven untenable but that does not mean they don't offer important lessons for the future of cannabis payments, illegal drug trade, cultivation, manufacturing, and sale of prohibited drugs including Cannabis. Fintech can be limited and checked to a great extent. But there is still a long way to go, there are still many challenges that Fin-Tech start-ups face in India some of them are regularity and compliance laws, Indian population which still doesn't use banking and prefer cash transactions, Cyber threats, and a lack of support from the government."

When the interviewee was asked if she sees any further benefits of Fintech for the cannabis industry she responded

"Positive effects are that you can legally grow and cultivate Cannabis for scientific research and medical purposes and can do safe and secure transactions and to be very honest I did not see any negative effect in it, just make sure everything is done under strict supervision and is being properly operated."

As a final point, she shared her insight from the research and sector advancement that

"New hemp-based medicines for cancer pain management and epilepsy treatment in India are set to be available in the next year. The two new drugs are expected to be superior to the existing line of treatment. For example, Morphine is currently used for pain while it can be habit-forming but Cannabis-based drugs will not be"

There are hopes that with continued advancement in medical research, better ayurvedic products will be readily available and easily accessible even by the urban population. The above discussion unveiled various challenges including need of research, lack of awareness about Fintech, cyber threats, and regulatory challenges. Lack of awareness about Fintech in the India and so the cannabis industry of Jammu and Kashmir, pose a challenge for the potential adoption. Furthermore, risk of cyber-attacks and lack of governmental support and management makes it less attractive. In that regard, the interviewee suggested collaboration of regulatory and medical authorities to raise awareness about the cannabis drug trafficking and addiction control, its medical benefits, and technological possibilities for the industry.

Survey respondents were asked if cannabis could be used for recreational purposes. The survey found little disagreement on the usefulness of cannabis and its allowance for the recreational purposes as fifty six percent (56%) of the respondents strongly agreed for various beneficial use of cannabis including pain relief and mental relaxation. Thirty six percent (36%) of the respondents agreed, 7% opted to be neutral and 1% disagreed. These observations are presented in figure 2 below

Figure 2. Cannabis could be used for recreational purposes

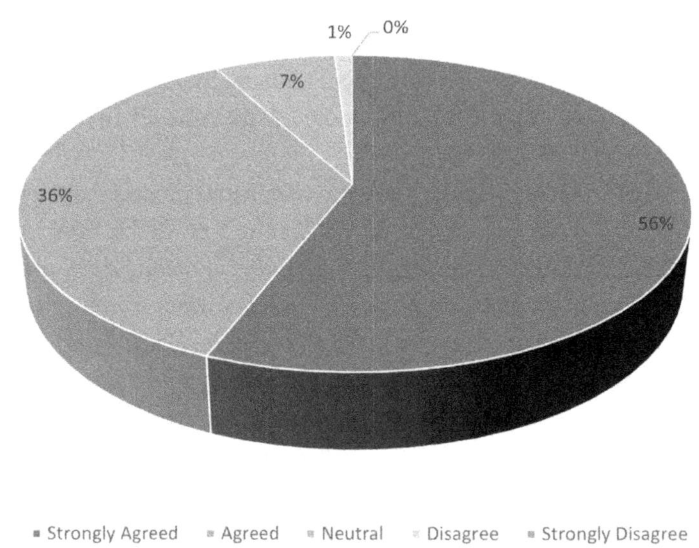

Respondents were further asked if they support the legislation of cannabis and its compounds for recreational use. A widespread consensus was found to legalise the recreational use of cannabis. Forty one percent (41%) respondents strongly agreed, 45% agreed, 7% stayed neutral, whereas 7% disagreed to legalise cannabis and related compound for recreational purposes. These observations are presented in figure 3 below

Figure 3. Support to legalise the recreational use of cannabis and its compounds

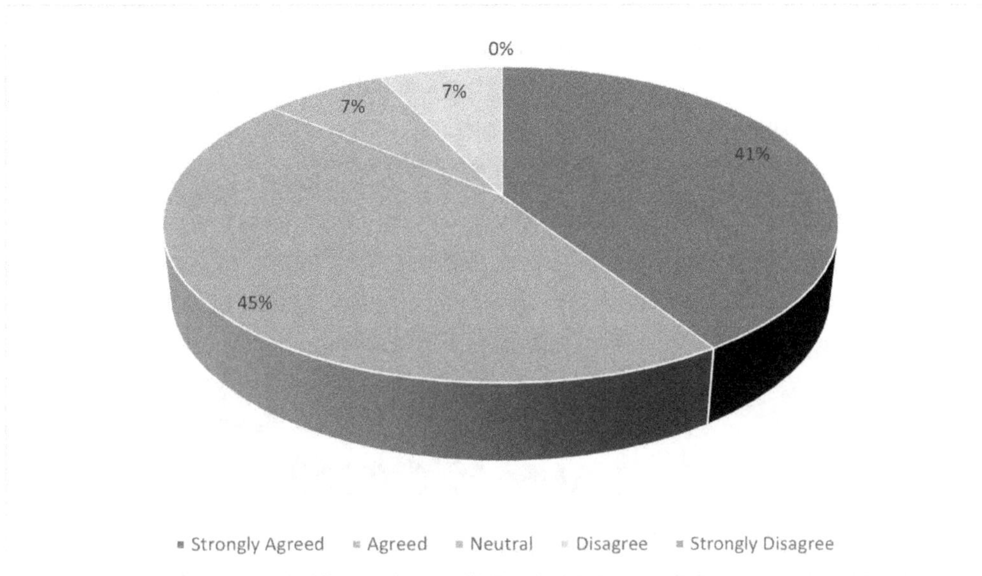

It was realized that majority was accepting the medical benefits of cannabis and was comfortable to legalise for medical purposes. Fifty percent (50%) of the respondents strongly supported the legislation of cannabis and its compounds for medical purposes. Forty three percent (43%) of the respondents agreed, and 7% opted to stay neutral about the question to legalise cannabis for medical purposes. These observations are presented in figure 4 below

Figure 4. To legalise the medical use of cannabis

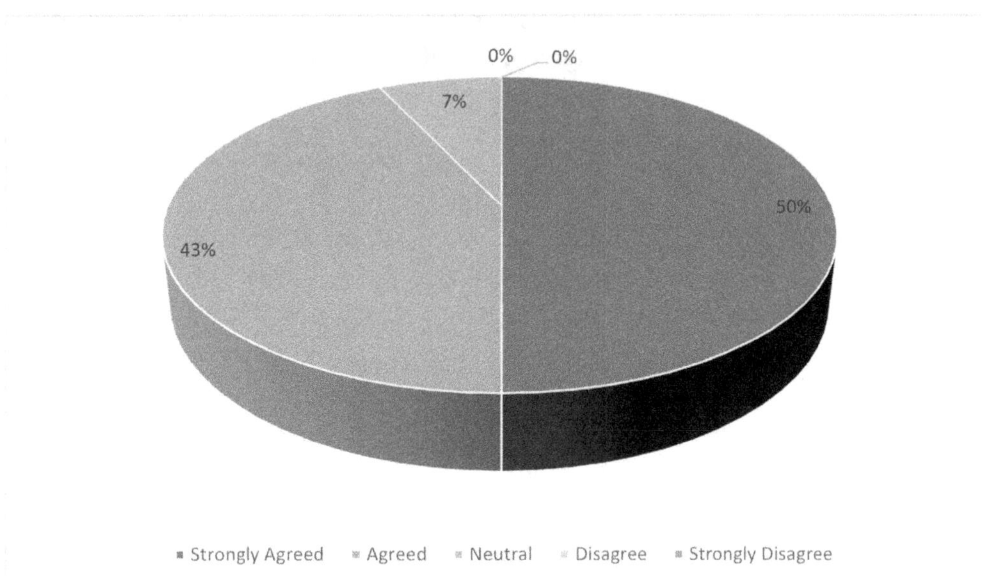

Respondents were also asked to indicate their willingness to buy cannabis-based medicine. Twenty eight percent (28%) strongly agreed, 26% agreed, 18% stayed neutral, 21% disagreed, and 7% strongly disagreed. Willingness to buy cannabis-based medicine was found among the respondents with 54% whereas 28% of the respondents were not positive to buy cannabis-based medicine. These observations are presented in figure 5 below

Figure 5. Willingness to buy cannabis-based medicine

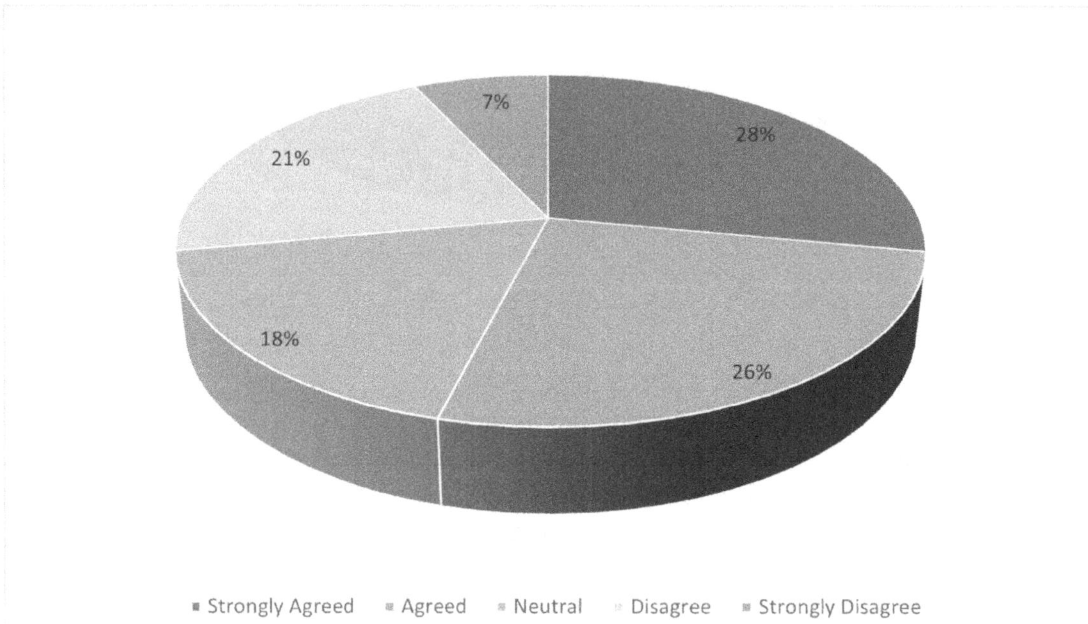

The survey respondents showed ease to purchase cannabis for medical purposes from the local farm. In response to the question of buying cannabis from the local farm for medical purposes, only 10% respondents strongly agreed, whereas 60% agreed, and 30% remained neutral. These observations are presented in figure 6 below

Figure 6. Buying cannabis from the local farm for medical purposes

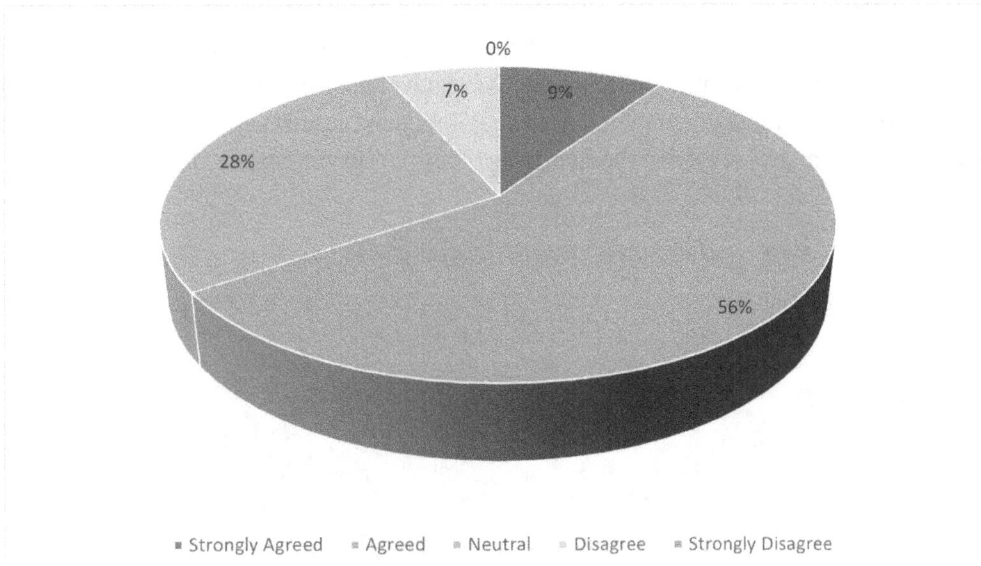

Whereas the survey respondents were more confident to buy cannabis-based medicine from pharmaceutical store rather than local farm. Exploring further when the participants were presented with an option to either buy cannabis-based medicine from local farm or authorised pharmaceutical store, 60% respondents opted for pharmacy and 35% preferred to buy it from local farm. Whereas 5% respondents were reluctant to buy cannabis-based medicine. These observations are presented in figure 7 below

Figure 7. buy cannabis-based medicine from local farm or authorised pharmaceutical store

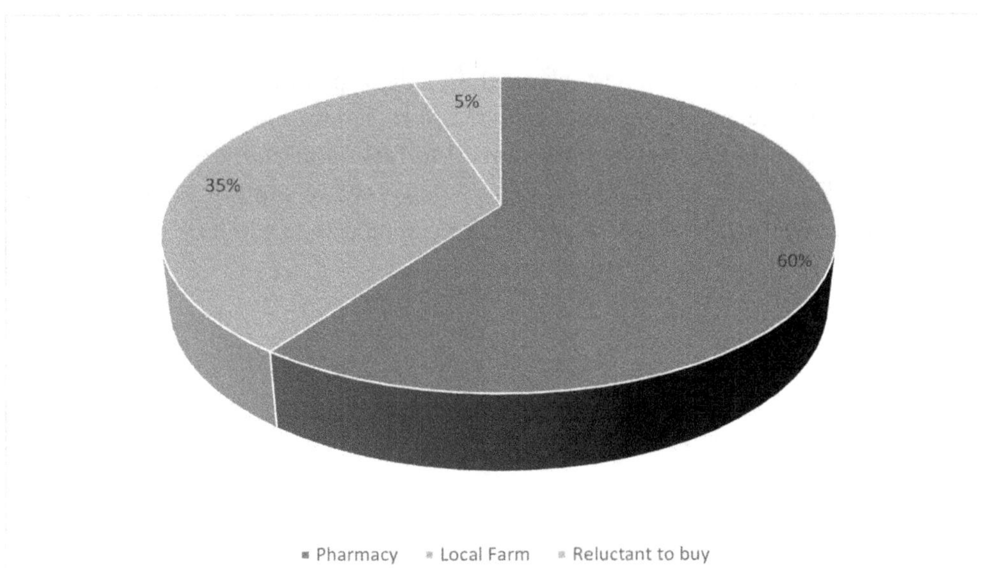

Respondents were asked if they had ever used cannabis for medical reasons. It was observed that the user might not always be sure if the medicine they are using have cannabis as an ingredient. Also, it is not necessary that the consumer might have notice if they are using cannabis-based medicine. Seventy one percent (71%) of the respondents indicated that they have never used cannabis for medical reason. Twenty percent (20%) of the respondents were aware that they had used cannabis-based medicine. Whereas 9% respondents selected 'may be' option to the question. These observations are presented in figure 8 below

Figure 8. If respondents ever used cannabis for medical reasons

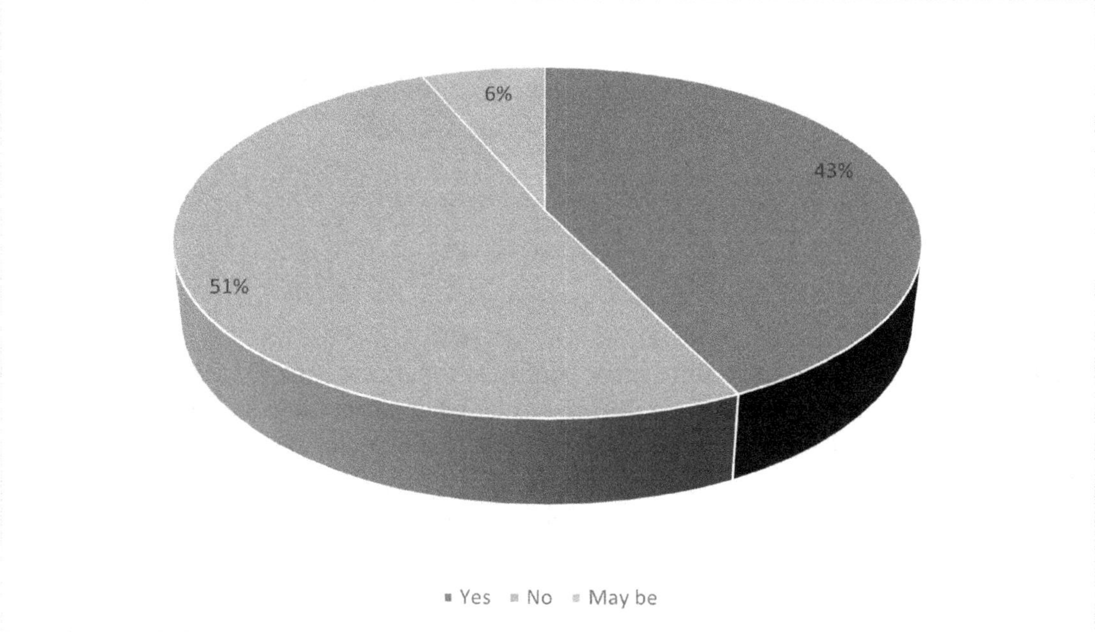

There was consensus that the awareness about the medical benefits of cannabis should be raised. Twenty five percent (25%) respondents strongly agree to raise awareness for the medical benefits of cannabis. Sixty one percent (61%) respondents agreed to raise awareness on the medical benefits of cannabis, 13% respondents opted to be neutral and 1% disagreed to support awareness about cannabis even for the medical purposes. These observations are presented in figure 9 below

Figure 9. Raise awareness for the medical benefits of cannabis

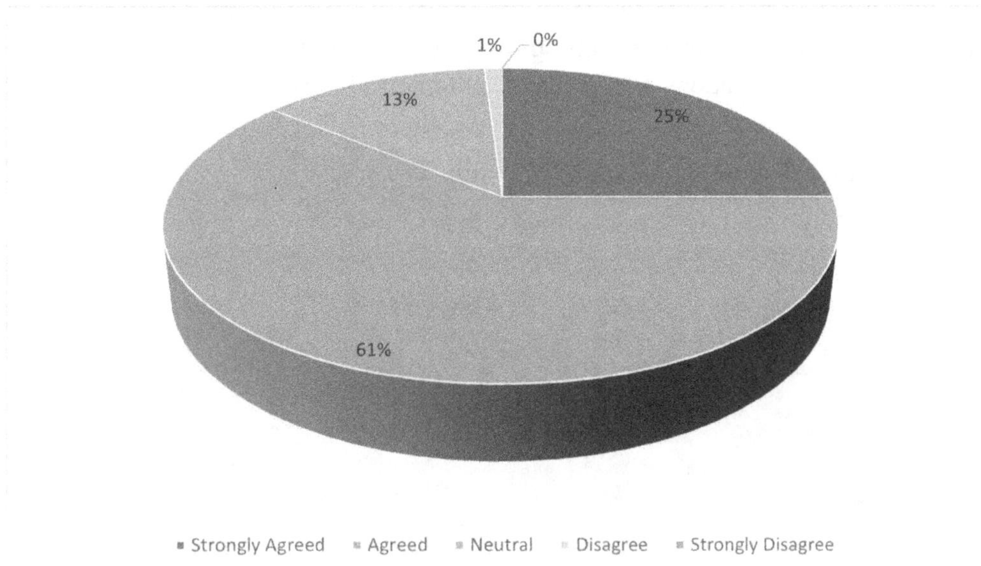

Considering high stress level in today's society and increasing anxiety disorders, participants were asked about their preference for either pharmacological medicine or cannabis-based medicine. When brought in comparison to the pharmacological medicine, cannabis-based medicine is getting little attention, which is again possible to the lack of awareness about the benefits and side effect of cannabis. Only 9% respondent marked preference for cannabis-based medicine mainly due to lack of awareness and confidence for the use of such medicine, 90% preferred pharmacological medicine and 1% remain silent. These observations are presented in figure 10 below

Figure 10. Preference for either pharmacological medicine or cannabis-based medicine

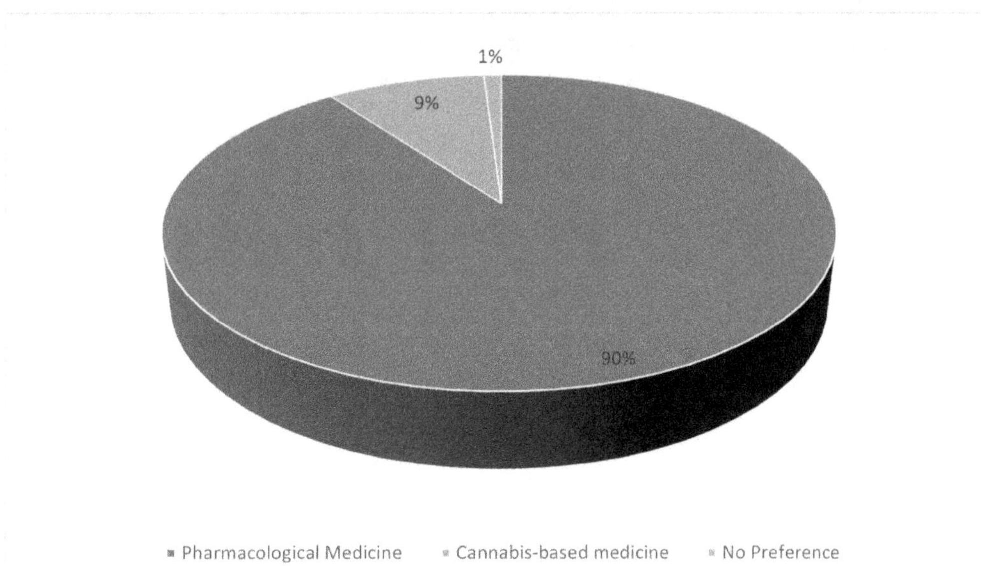

It was observed that the cannabis-based medicines are heavily perceived for side effects, without knowing the facts. When participants were asked about the possible side effects associated with the use of cannabis-based medicine, 17% respondents strongly agreed that it has side effects, 63% agreed, 20% remained neutral. These observations are presented summarised in figure 11 below

Figure 11. Possible side effects with the use of cannabis-based medicine

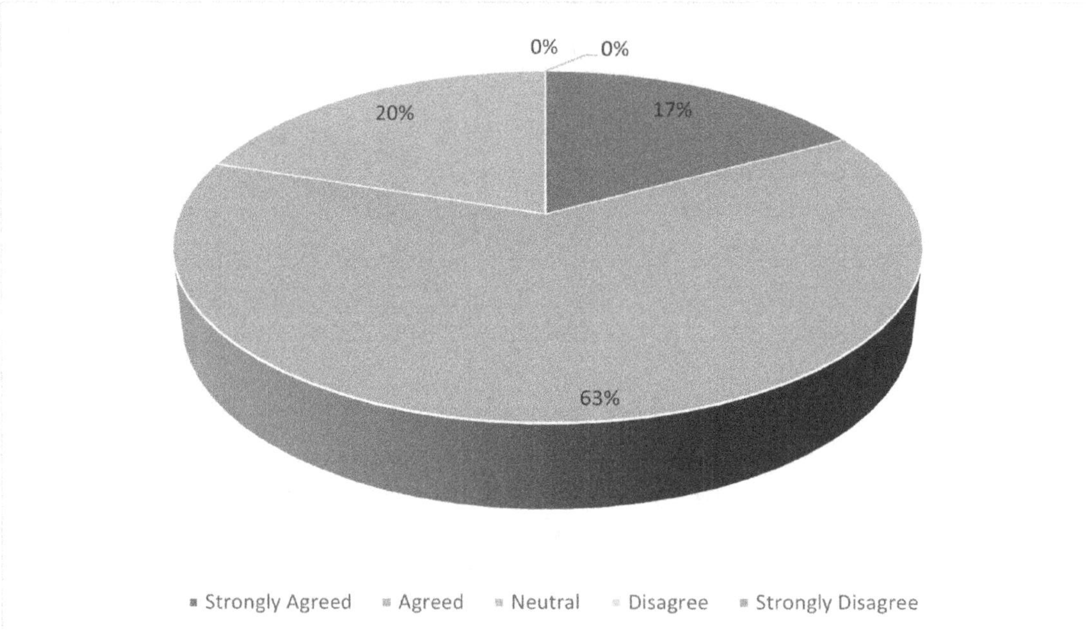

Participants awareness about Fintech and its use in various industries was also investigated by the survey. Through the survey low awareness about the advancement of Fintech was evidenced. Twelve percent (12%) respondents strongly agreed, 8% agreed, 33% stayed neutral, and 47% respondents disagreed to having awareness about Fintech. These observations are presented in figure 12 below

Figure 12. Awareness about Fintech

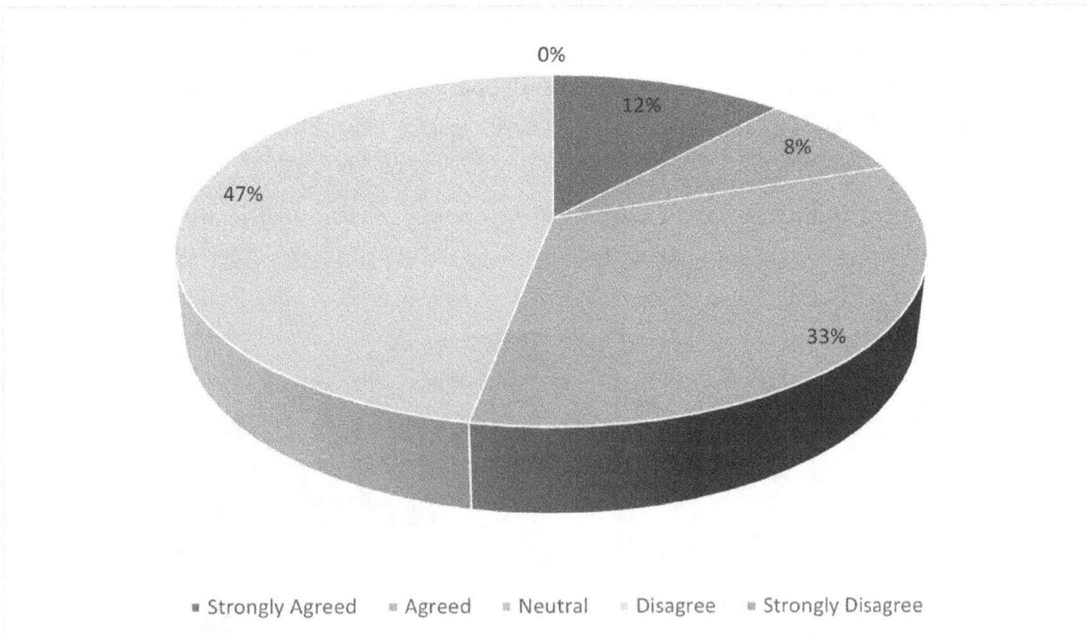

Survey participants were further asked about their perception of Fintech utilisation for drug trafficking control. Possibility of drug trafficking control was admitted by majority of the respondents. Fifty one percent (51%) respondents strongly agreed that Fintech solutions could help track activity in the cannabis sector, 8% agreed, 40% respondents marked neutral and 1% disagreed. These observations are presented in figure 13 below

Figure 13. If Fintech could be utilised for drug trafficking control

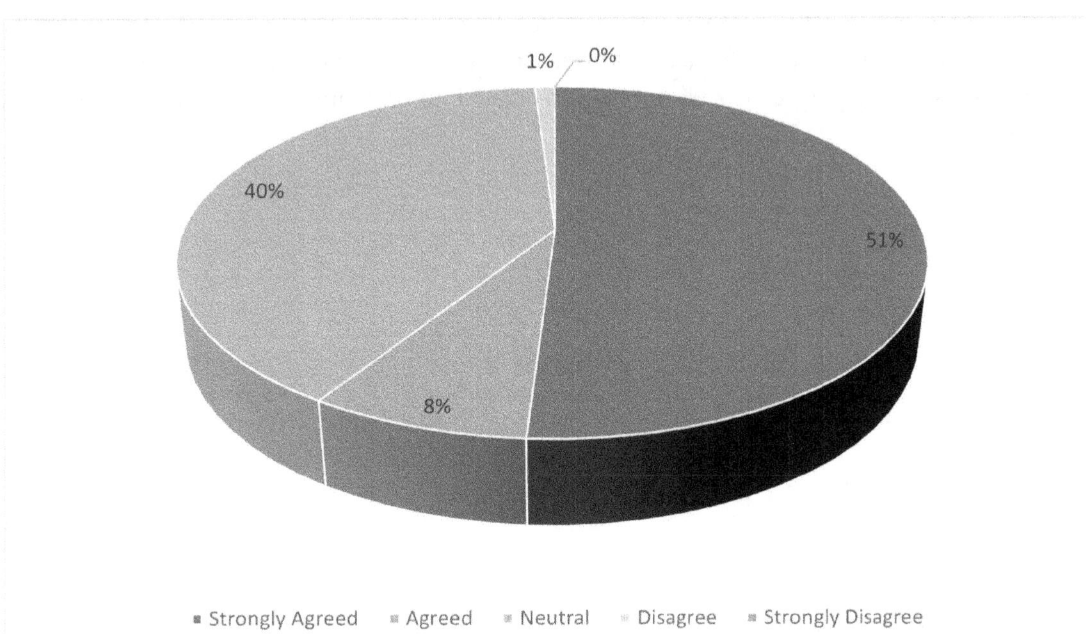

The participants were further asked if government should support the use of Fintech solutions for the control of drug trafficking. Sixty seven percent (67%), majority of the respondents were convinced that government should support Fintech use for drug trafficking control. Thirty six percent (36%) respondents strongly agreed, 31% agreed, 23% stayed neutral, and 7% strongly disagreed. These observations are presented in figure 14 below

Figure 14. If government should support Fintech for the control of drug trafficking

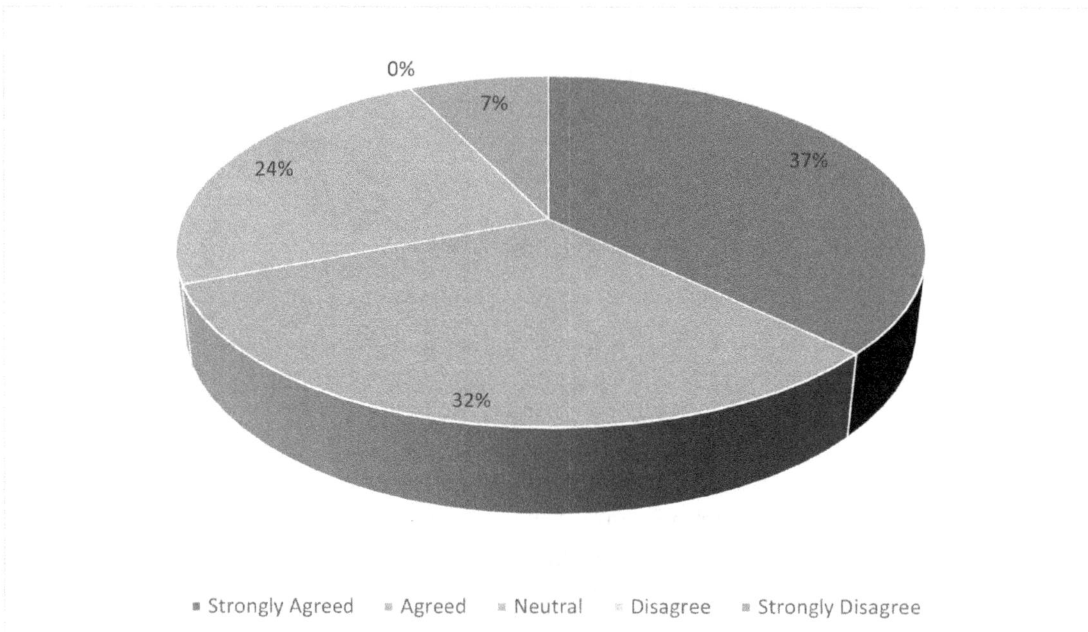

The survey asked the participants if the regulatory bodies should be using Fintech to monitor drug related activities in the country. There was immense agreement from the respondents that regulatory body should be making use of the advanced Fintech for monitoring drug related activities. Sixty percent (60%) respondents strongly agreed, 23% agreed, 7% stayed neutral, and 7% disagreed. These observations are presented in figure 15 below

Figure 15. Regulatory bodies should be using Fintech to monitor drug related activities

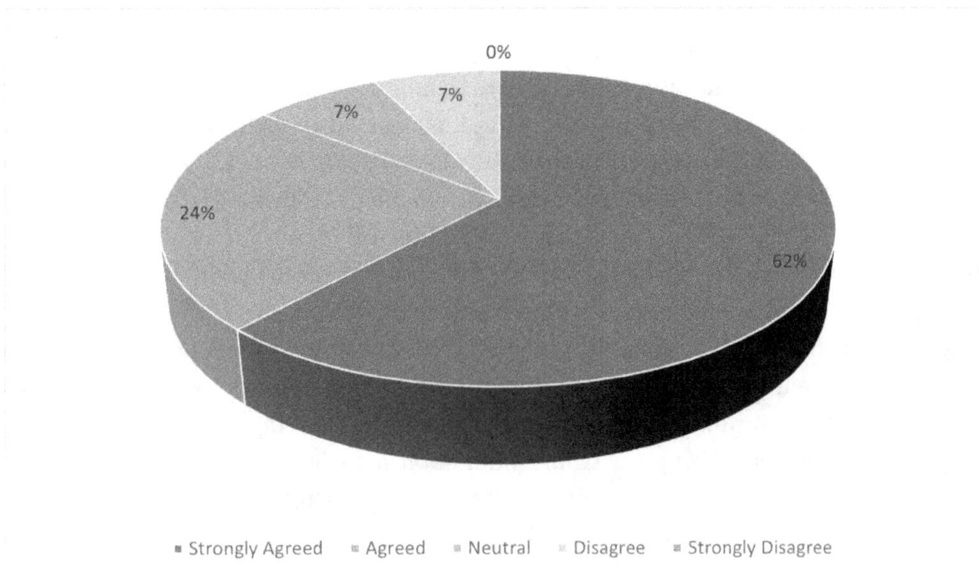

The survey participants were asked about the possibility of legal drug distribution using intelligent Fintech programs. Seventy seven percent (77%) of the majority respondents reflected positivity and hope towards the legal drug distribution system using advanced Fintech solutions. Seventy percent (70%) respondent strongly agreed, 7% agreed, 23% opted to be neutral. These observations are presented in figure 16 below

Figure 16. Possibility of legal drug distribution using intelligent Fintech programs

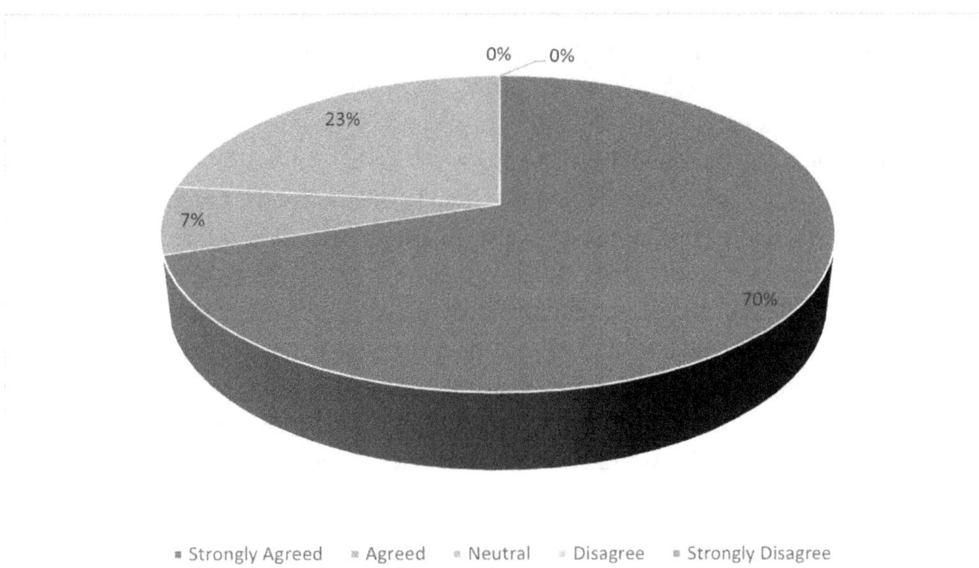

Discussion

Cannabis, also known by several popular names (marijuana, weed, marijuana, hemp, hashish and bagha) is a plant of the Cannabiaceae family. Biologically, Cannabis is part of the angiosperm plant genus which produce flower and is cultivated in various regions around the world. Cannabis currently refers to psychoactive drugs and medicines derived from the plant (Pacek, et al., 2018). Cannabis stem fibre is durable and is used for paper, rope, yarn, fabric and so cloth manufacturing. From the seeds of Cannabis, oil is extracted to produce cosmetics, soap, paints, and edible oil (Solimini, et al., 2017). It is estimated that 20,000 patients have access to the drug, which is sold not only in the form of flowers, to be smoked, but also as oil, present in cakes, chocolates, and cookies (Solimini, et al., 2017).

Promoting safe consumption of cannabis, global decriminalisation procedures need to be adopted in India as well. The developing state of the country and lack of technological adaption is proving to be a hindrance in the development of native industries like Cannabis, leaving behind the huge potential. As mentioned by the interviewee "*Cannabis is misunderstood legally and industrially in India*". A suitable environment for cannabis cultivation could serve as an opportunity for the economic and medical contribution. Moreover, the increasing mental illnesses as explained by the interviewee that "*anxiety disorders are the most common mental illness affecting more than 50 million adults in India above 18 years of age*" are anticipating demand of the medicine with less side effects and the gap could be filled with the ayurvedic medicine. Various cannabis compounds could be explored and utilised for various treatments. The interviewee shared a hopeful news that "*new hemp-based medicines for cancer pain management and epilepsy treatment in India are set to be available in the next year.*"

Cannabis farming is still illegal and restricted in India except some production for medical, industrial manufacturing and horticultural use (Kuddus et al., 2013). The interviewee further clarified this as "only two states U.P and Uttarakhand regions - both in northern India have received hemp cultivation licenses." In India, Indian National Policy on Narcotic Drugs and Psychotropic Substances allows the use of drugs based on substances present in Cannabis, if its registration is approved by the Agency, based on data that prove its safety and efficacy (Hill, 2019). Under current legislation that Indian National Policy on Narcotic Drugs and Psychotropic Substances complies with, marijuana is considered proscribed, except for medical and scientific purposes, in a controlled and supervised manner. In other words, this does not prevent research and use for therapeutic purposes, and it is even possible to register a drug based on a proscribed substance and/or plant (Pacek, et al., 2018). Indian National Policy on Narcotic Drugs and Psychotropic Substances has carried out several actions and consequently created a specific Working Group (WG) for this topic. The members of the working group have held internal meetings and with the health authorities of other countries, such as Israel, Canada, Netherlands, Chile, and the United States, in order to obtain knowledge of the regulatory framework and experiences related to the topic, to support the current discussions (Solimini, et al., 2017).

The legislation of cannabis for medicinal and therapeutic use is now at advanced stages as two bills are being processed in US Congress and of the 17 proposals on the subject, three provide for the relaxation of the rules, while 14 are trying to tighten the rules regarding usage (Boehnke, et al., 2019). The medicinal use of Cannabis is perfectly justifiable given that its use provides a more dignified human life for people who suffer from chronic diseases (Russo, 2017). With respect to the teleology of individual well-being, inscribed in norms such as protection and promotion of human dignity, as well as importance of health care for all, should guide the Indian Constitution to allow the medicinal use of substances derived from Cannabis (Balhara, et al., 2020).

India has its own stature in cannabis plant science and related pharmaceutical research (Solimini, et al., 2017). Reportedly, the Jammu and Kashmir region in India is set to be the pioneering region for cannabis-based medicine manufacturing. As the country moves towards greater liberalisation of cannabis use, in the long run, people will recognize and accept opportunities offered by the cannabis industry sector. Cannabis farmers have higher understanding about the remedial benefits of cannabis and the related benefits offered by rare home remedies long used over generations. There is a profound need to preserve that rare knowledge so the future generation can reap the wanted benefits.

The study findings confirmed that 92% of the respondents agree with the use of cannabis for recreational purposes. Whereas slightly less respondents i.e., 86% agreed to legalise the cannabis for recreational use. A past survey by Hall and Lynskey (2016) in US about legalising cannabis for recreational use found that increase in probable use in long term with reduced prices, increased new users and some types of cannabis-related harm in existing users. 93% of the respondents agreed with the legalisation of cannabis for the medical purposes. 54% of the respondents showed willingness to buy cannabis-based medicine whereas 29% showed disagreement. In response to the question of purchasing cannabis-based medicine from local farms, 70% of the respondents agreed and 30% remained neutral. But in another follow up question that required respondents to indicate whether they would buy cannabis prescription from pharmacies or the local farms, 60% indicated preference to buy from pharmacies and 35% confirmed willingness to buy from local farms. Whereas 5% remained hesitant to buy cannabis-based medicine. On the use of cannabis-based medicine, 71% of the respondents said they have never used cannabis-based medicine, 20% respondents agreed that they had used cannabis-based medicine, whereas 9% showed that they are not aware of any cannabis-based medicine available. Han, Alton, Colwill, and Jensen's (2021) found that women showed willingness to use cannabis-based medicine for medicinal purposes even in the lack of evidence for its effectiveness and safety. The study also found out that there is need to raise awareness on the medical benefits of cannabis and in that regard 86% of the respondents agreed that awareness about the medical benefits of the cannabis should be raised, whereas 13% respondents remained neutral and only 1% disagreed with the need to raise awareness on the medical benefits of cannabis. Although preference for the cannabis-based medicine remained only 9%, which is possible due to the lack of awareness towards its medical benefits. 80% of the respondents have the perception that cannabis-based medicine has side effects. A past survey by Carliner, Brown, Sarvet, and Hasin (2017) found that perception about risks associated with cannabis use has decreased since early 2000s.

The study found good scope for developments in the cannabis industry and the possibility of legalisation for medical purposes. There are many misconceptions related to the illicit use of cannabis and cannabis-based products but with the support of regulatory and health authorities through awareness campaigns and programmes, these misconceptions can be reduced. Moreover, Fintech can support safe financial transactions in the cannabis industry by controlling the illicit use of cannabis products (Fosso et al., 2020). Although Fintech and blockchain technologies are at their nascent stages and need regulatory frameworks (Fazi, 2021) especially in the developing world like India, the hopes are high, and the urge of testing is increasing. The survey findings presented above showed that only 20% of the respondents agreed on the need to raise awareness about Fintech and 41% boldly acknowledged the lack of awareness. Despite the low awareness, considering the possibilities, 59% of the respondents agreed to utilise technology to resist drug trafficking. 83% of the respondents approved that regulatory bodies should be making use of technological advancement to monitor drug trafficking. Moreover, 77% of the respondents agreed to legal drug trading using intelligent Fintech systems.

Fintech have ability to provide reliable tracking of the supply chain along secure and transparent financial transactions from procurement of raw material to the delivery of consumables to the end users (Dorfleitner & Braun, 2019). Fintech can reduce risks related to transactional transparency and sustainability, thus increasing trust among stakeholders. The Fintech technologies may also comprise PIN debit merchant account systems, card networks, traditional merchant processing for THC licensee, digital wallets, merchant processing systems and ISO certified cyber security systems (Dubey, 2019).

CONCLUSION

Modern era ventures are highly concerned with ethics, sustainability, and responsibility issues (Uecker-Mercado and Walker, 2012). It is quite an audacious agenda, to raise voice about the benefits of cannabis and demanding for its legalisation, in Indian context where drug addiction and illegal trade are a detrimental issue. Historical home remedies and traditional medicine aired this idea along a famous cultural phrase that God had made nothing but beneficial. It is highly recommended to explore the beneficial aspects and control any harmful aspects, related to cannabis. It is very important to put robust control measures for the flourishing Indian Cannabis industry. The need is to regulate the industry utilising fintech technology to keep it within the ethical, sustainable, and responsible boundaries. These efforts will pave way for the required research in the cannabis compound and the medical benefits could help deal with conditions like anxiety, cancer, neurological disorders, skin allergies etc. There is high need to legitimise and encourage cannabis farming, trade, and related manufacturing for medical purposes. This should be supported by positive awareness about the industry and assurances that illegal trade in cannabis products will be strictly controlled, and medical subsidies will be encouraged. While regularising complex cannabis industry sector social, environmental, and economic developments should be deeply considered (Fang et al., 2015). Resultant employment opportunities as a reform of the cannabis industry sector, could further boost the economy of rural Jammu and Kashmir.

The hesitation due the prohibited nature of the industry raised questions for the enquiry. Future studies could further explore expert voice from wider stakeholder groups as this study initiated with single expert interview and was limited in bringing the perspective and related presentation. Moreover, the 60 survey responses from a prespecified geographic area contribute to restricted outcomes but an imprecise result was very few disagreements. Out of 13 questions where the response was captured over the 5-point scale of strongly agreed to strongly disagreed, only 7 questions brought minority disagreements. Furthermore, future studies could explore reasons behind the perceptions related to cannabis, additional benefits and biproducts of cannabis and fintech adoption with the cannabis industry sector.

The study proposes to authorities and influential bodies to support ventures of cannabis farming and cannabis pharmaceutical compound manufacturing. Seed sourcing could be planned from local and international producers backed with research evidence related to composition and quality, further encouraging related research. Lessons could be learnt for such venturing from the Canadian research units and other international collaborations (Rotermann, 2020). Moreover, adapting Fintech advancements from US and rest of the advanced world could be useful for such venturing. For example, digital employee identity will restrict unauthorised access, e-accounting will facilitate financial transactions and other digital tools will support operations through standard operating procedures. Verification and tracking of cannabis-based products could be ensured using GPS technology. Such ventures will enhance local farming (sharma, 2020) and traditional ayurvedic medicine producers, bringing them at limelight and resulting in economic benefit. Product testing, seed quality and procedural quality assurance could be learned from developed world companies like CSIR.

REFERENCES

Abbott, B. A., & Zack, J. B. (2018). Current banking issues in the cannabis industry. *CONSUMER FIN. LQ REP*, *72*, 390–396.

Abdekalimi, D. (2019). One CPA's Journey from Auditor to Consultant and Fintech Entrepreneur. *The CPA Journal*, *89*(10), 11–11.

APSA (2019). India Cannabis Industry 2019. *APSA Seed.*

Arya, S., Ghosh, A., & Kazhungil, F. (2022). Early career psychiatrist's attitude toward medicinal and recreational cannabis legalization in India; findings from an online survey. *Journal of Substance Use*, 1–6. doi:10.1080/14659891.2022.2120424

Azarenkova, G., Shkodina, I., Samorodov, B., Babenko, M., & Onishchenko, I. (2018). The influence of financial technologies on the global financial system stability. *Investment Management & Financial Innovations*, *15*(4), 229–238. doi:10.21511/imfi.15(4).2018.19

Badiola, I., Doshi, A., & Narouze, S. (2022). Cannabis, cannabinoids, and cannabis-based medicines: Future research directions for analgesia. *Regional Anesthesia and Pain Medicine*, *47*(7), 437–444. doi:10.1136/rapm-2021-103109 PMID:35534020

Balhara, Y. P. S., Mishra, A., Sethi, H., Singh, S., & Khandelwal, S. K. (2016). Time trends of cannabis use among treatment-seeking individuals at government de-addiction centers across India over a period of 7 years. *Indian Journal of Psychological Medicine*, *38*(4), 331–335. doi:10.4103/0253-7176.185961 PMID:27570345

Balhara, Y. P. S., Parmar, A., Modak, T., & Vikram, V. (2020). From "Bhang Shops" to "Cannabis in Coffee Shops": Time to Debate the Option? *Indian Journal of Psychological Medicine*, 0253717620957501. PMID:35656417

Boehnke, K. F., Gangopadhyay, S., Clauw, D. J., & Haffajee, R. L. (2019). Qualifying conditions of medical cannabis license holders in the United States. *Health Affairs*, *38*(2), 295–302. doi:10.1377/hlthaff.2018.05266 PMID:30715980

Cannabis Big Data. (2021). Integration to BioTrackTHE. Cannabis Big Data. Accesses online at BioTrackTHC - Cannabis. *Big Data.*

Cannabis Times India, (2020, May 22). Cannabis cultivation legalized in Uttarakhand. *Cannabis times india.*

Carliner, H., Brown, Q. L., Sarvet, A. L., & Hasin, D. S. (2017). Cannabis use, attitudes, and legal status in the US: A review. *Preventive Medicine*, *104*, 13–23. doi:10.1016/j.ypmed.2017.07.008 PMID:28705601

Couch, D. (2020). *Left behind: The scale of illegal cannabis use for medicinal intent in the UK.* Centre for Medical Cannabis.

Crescioli, G., Lombardi, N., Bettiol, A., Menniti-Ippolito, F., Da Cas, R., Parrilli, M., Del Lungo, M., Gallo, E., Mugelli, A., Maggini, V., Firenzuoli, F., & Vannacci, A. (2020). Adverse events following cannabis for medical use in Tuscany: An analysis of the Italian Phytovigilance database. *British Journal of Clinical Pharmacology*, *86*(1), 106–120. doi:10.1111/bcp.14140 PMID:31656045

Decorte, T., Lenton, S., & Wilkins, C. (Eds.). (2020). *Legalizing cannabis: Experiences, lessons and scenarios*. Routledge. doi:10.4324/9780429427794

Djordjevic, N. (2021). 36 worrisome Global obesity Statistics & Facts for 2022. *MedAlertHelp.*

Dorfleitner, G., & Braun, D. (2019). Fintech, digitalization and blockchain: possible applications for green finance. In *The rise of green finance in Europe* (pp. 207–237). Palgrave Macmillan. doi:10.1007/978-3-030-22510-0_9

Drozd, M., Marzęda, P., Czarnota, J., Dobrzyński, M., Skubel, T., Dudek, I., & Rybak, N. (2022). The potential of cannabinoids in the treatment of lung cancer. *Journal of Education, Health and Sport*, *12*(8), 1100–1110. doi:10.12775/JEHS.2022.12.08.094

Dubey, V. (2019). Fin-Tech innovations in digital banking. [IJERT]. *International Journal of Engineering Research & Technology (Ahmedabad)*, *8*(10), 597–601

Fang, K., Heijungs, R., Duan, Z., & De Snoo, G. R. (2015). The environmental sustainability of nations: Benchmarking the carbon, water and land footprints against allocated planetary boundaries. *Sustainability*, *7*(8), 11285–11305. doi:10.3390u70811285

Farinon, B., Molinari, R., Costantini, L., & Merendino, N. (2020). The Seed of Industrial Hemp (Cannabis sativa L.): Nutritional Quality and Potential Functionality for Human Health and Nutrition. *Nutrients*, *12*(7), 1935. doi:10.3390/nu12071935 PMID:32610691

Fazi, A. M. (2021). *A Contextual Study of Regulatory Framework for Blockchain. Regulatory Aspects of Artificial Intelligence on Blockchain.* IGI Global. doi:10.4018/978-1-7998-7927-5.ch003

Finncann™ (2022). Fintech Solutions and Cannabis Banking: what works and what doesn't?. *Fintech Solutions and Cannabis Banking Opportunities.*

Groce, E. (2018). The health effects of cannabis and cannabinoids: The current state of evidence and recommendations for research. *Journal of Medical Regulation*, *104*(4), 32. doi:10.30770/2572-1852-104.4.32

Hall, W., & Lynskey, M. (2016). Evaluating the public health impacts of legalizing recreational cannabis use in the United States. *Addiction (Abingdon, England)*, *111*(10), 1764–1773. doi:10.1111/add.13428 PMID:27082374

Han, L., Alton, K., Colwill, A. C., Jensen, J. T., McCrimmon, S., & Darney, B. G. (2021). Willingness to use cannabis for gynecological conditions: A national survey. *Journal of Women's Health*, *30*(3), 438–444. doi:10.1089/jwh.2020.8491 PMID:33667129

HempStreet (2022). Cannabis meets Ayurveda: India's First Research to Retail Venture in the Ayurveda Cannabis Sector. *HempStreet Medicare Private Limited.*

Hendricks, B. O., II. (2020). *Cash Management Strategies in the Marijuana Industries* [Doctoral dissertation, Northcentral University, USA].

Herd, T. (2021). How KeefX Is Fueling The Growth Of The B2B Cannabis Industry. *Forbes*

Hill, J. A. (2022). Bank Access to Federal Reserve Accounts and Payment Systems. *U of Alabama Legal Studies Research Paper Forthcoming.*

Hill, K. P. (2019). Medical use of cannabis in 2019. *Jama Insights*, *322*(10), 974–975. doi:10.1001/jama.2019.11868 PMID:31397842

Hunter, M. (2022). *The High Cost of Federal Cannabis Prohibition.* Seton Hall University.

James, S. (2020, February 27). Industrial Hemp Market Size Worth $15.26 Billion by 2027. *Cision PR Newswire.*

Kavousi, P., Giamo, T., Arnold, G., Alliende, M., Huynh, E., Lea, J., Lucine, R., Tillett Miller, A., Webre, A., Yee, A., Champagne-Zamora, A., & Taylor, K. (2022). What do we know about opportunities and challenges for localities from Cannabis legalization? *The Review of Policy Research*, *39*(2), 143–169. doi:10.1111/ropr.12460

Krause, D., & Pullman, M. (2021). Fighting to survive: How supply chain managers navigate the emerging legal cannabis industry. *The Journal of Supply Chain Management*, *57*(3), 50–71. doi:10.1111/jscm.12238

Kuddus, M., Ginawi, I., & AlHazimi, A. (2013). Cannabis sativa: An ancient wild edible plant of India. *Emirates Journal of Food and Agriculture*, *25*(10), 736. doi:10.9755/ejfa.v25i10.16400

Kuppuram, G. (2021). Decriminalizing Marijuana: The Science and Social Sustainability Behind the use of Marijuana (Cannabis) in India. *Journal of the Association of Researchers*, *26*(2), 11–32.

Kyriazis, N. A. (2021). Investigating the diversifying or hedging nexus of cannabis cryptocurrencies with major digital currencies. *Decisions in Economics and Finance*, *44*(2), 845–861. doi:10.100710203-021-00356-5

Leinow, L., & Birnbaum, J. (2017). *CBD: A Patient's Guide to Medicinal Cannabis*. North Atlantic Books.

Liu, J., Li, X., & Wang, S. (2020). What have we learnt from 10 years of Fin-Tech research? a scientometric analysis. *Technological Forecasting and Social Change*, *155*, 120022. doi:10.1016/j.techfore.2020.120022

Ma, J., Lyoo, I. K., Renshaw, P. F., & Yurgelun-Todd, D. A. (2022). Effect of cannabinoids on brain metabolites: A review of animal and human studies. *Experimental and Clinical Psychopharmacology.* doi:10.1037/pha0000553 PMID:35201831

Merelli, A. (8 February 2020). India has the world's biggest cannabis industry that doesn't exist yet. *Quartz.*

Nassiry, D. (2018). *The role of fintech in unlocking green finance: Policy insights for developing countries* (ADBI Working Paper 883).

National Institute of Health. (2022). Cannabis (Marijuana) and Cannabinoids: What You Need To Know. *National Centre for complementary and integrative health.*

Oultram, J., Pegler, J., Bowser, T., Ney, L., Eamens, A., & Grof, C. (2021). Cannabis sativa: Interdisciplinary Strategies and Avenues for Medical and Commercial Progression Outside of CBD and THC. *Biomedicines*, *9*(3), 234. doi:10.3390/biomedicines9030234 PMID:33652704

Pacek, L. R., Towe, S. L., Hobkirk, A. L., Nash, D., & Goodwin, R. D. (2018). Frequency of cannabis use and medical cannabis use among persons living with HIV in the United States: Findings from a nationally representative sample. *AIDS Education and Prevention*, *30*(2), 169–181. doi:10.1521/aeap.2018.30.2.169 PMID:29688777

Packer, C., Crockett, R. A., & Dawson, D. (2022). Not a SAFE Bet: Equitable Access to Cannabis Banking, An Analysis of the SAFE Banking Act. *Ohio State Legal Studies Research Paper*, (721).

Parker, K., Di Mattia, A., Shaik, F., Cerón Ortega, J., & Whittle, R. (2019). Risk management within the cannabis industry: Building a framework for the cannabis industry. *Financial Markets, Institutions and Instruments*, *28*(1), 3–55. doi:10.1111/fmii.12104

Pedrazzi, S., Santunione, G., Mustone, M., Cannazza, G., Citti, C., Francia, E., & Allesina, G. (2021). Techno-economic study of a small scale gasifier applied to an indoor hemp farm: From energy savings to biochar effects on productivity. *Energy Conversion and Management*, *228*, 113645. doi:10.1016/j.enconman.2020.113645

Przybycień, P., Gąsior-Perczak, D., & Placha, W. (2022). Cannabinoids and PPAR Ligands: The Future in Treatment of Polycystic Ovary Syndrome Women with Obesity and Reduced Fertility. *Cells*, *11*(16), 2569. doi:10.3390/cells11162569 PMID:36010645

Rahman, A. M., Nemoto, K., Matsushima, K. I., & Uddin, S. B., & AKM, G. (2022). A History of Cannabis (Ganja) as an Economic Crop in Bangladesh from the Late 18th Century to 1989. *Tropical Agriculture and Development*, *66*(1), 21–32.

Ritter, S., Zadik-Weiss, L., Almogi-Hazan, O., & Or, R. (2020). Cannabis, One Health, and Veterinary Medicine: Cannabinoids' Role in Public Health, Food Safety, and Translational Medicine. *Rambam Maimonides Medical Journal*, *11*(1), e0006. doi:10.5041/RMMJ.10388 PMID:32017686

Rotermann, M. (2020). What has changed since cannabis was legalized. *Health Reports*, *31*(2), 11–20. PMID:32073644

Russo, E. (2005). Cannabis in India: ancient lore and modern medicine. In R. Mechoulam (Ed.), *Cannabinoids as Therapeutics. Milestones in Drug Therapy MDT.* Birkhäuser Basel. doi:10.1007/3-7643-7358-X_1

Russo, E. B. (2017). Cannabis and epilepsy: An ancient treatment returns to the fore. *Epilepsy & Behavior*, *70*, 292–297. doi:10.1016/j.yebeh.2016.09.040 PMID:27989385

Salami, S., Martinelli, F., Giovino, A., Bachari, A., Arad, N., & Mantri, N. (2020). It Is Our Turn to Get Cannabis High: Put Cannabinoids in Food and Health Baskets. *Molecules (Basel, Switzerland)*, *25*(18), 4036. doi:10.3390/molecules25184036 PMID:32899626

Sharma, A. (2020). Working with Cannabis, These Indian Hemp Startups are making high profits. *Bingedaily*.

Sharma, S., & Ravikumar, K. V. (2017). Narco-terrorism–A reat to national security. *International Research Journal on Police Science*, *3*(1), 40–45.

Sheel, A. (2021). The Wonder Resources: All Hemp, CBD, and Ayurvedic Cannabis Companies in India. *Itshemp*.

Sinha, S. and Fogla, R. (2020). India's Cannabis Market: Examining Regulatory Frameworks then and now. *Cannabis Industry Journal*.

Solimini, R., Rotolo, M.C., Pichini, S. and Pacifici, R., (2017). Neurological disorders in medical use of cannabis: an update. CNS & Neurological Disorders-Drug Targets (Formerly Current Drug Targets-CNS & Neurological Disorders), 16(5), pp.527-533.

The Financial Express. (2020). India's cannabis problem is not just about its use. *Financial Express*

The Week, (2021, Dec 14). Where is Cannabis legal?. Malta legalises the drug in in European first. Future PLC. *The Week*.

Tulsyan, A. (2022). Cannabis and the constitution:'High time for amending the NDPS act?. *ILE Human Rights Law Review*, *1*(1).

Uecker-Mercado, H., & Walker, M. (2012). The value of environmental social responsibility to facility managers: Revealing the perceptions and motives for adopting ESR. *Journal of Business Ethics*, *110*(3), 269–284. doi:10.100710551-011-1153-x

UN office on Drugs and Crime. (2021). *INDIA*. https://www.unodc.org/pdf/india/publications/south_Asia_Regional_Profile_Sept_2005/10_india.pdf

Vivek, V. (2021). Top 10 Hemp Startups in India. *Hemp Foundation*.

Walters, D., & Wiseman, H. J. (2022). Self-Regulation in the Cradle: The Role of Standards in Emerging Industries. SSRN 4226081.

Wamba, S., Kamdjoug, J. R., Bawack, R., & Keogh, J. G. (2020). Bitcoin, blockchain and Fin-Tech: A systematic review and case studies in the supply chain. *Production Planning and Control*, *31*(2-3), 115–142. doi:10.1080/09537287.2019.1631460

Wambua, F. N. (2022). *Effect of Fintech Companies on Credit Access among Youths in Nairobi County*, [Doctoral dissertation, United States International University-Africa, Africa].

Wilcox, A. (19 July, 2020). Why is Cannabis Illegal? The story of Cannabis prohibition will shock you. *Green Flower*.

Chapter 6
The Legalisation of Cannabis in South Africa:
Proposing an Economic Value Chain Model for South Africa

Ranson Sifiso Gwala
https://orcid.org/0000-0002-1545-2259
University of KwaZulu-Natal, South Africa

ABSTRACT

The recent legalisation of cannabis in South Africa has created a sizable market for the importation of cannabis products into the country. The cannabis-masterplan explains how the value creation features must be reflected in legislation. Cannabis products may already be imported with approval. This causes yet another delay and issue because it prevents the local market from being primary, secondary, and tertiary producers. Small-scale cannabis producers are a secondary segment of the value chain that can best solve this. Consequences can be anticipated from making cannabis farming the main source feeding into the value chain. The chapter suggests a value conceptual framework that creates new players, markets, and jobs for the local women and the youth, thus addressing one the sustainable developmental goals of creating employment.

INTRODUCTION

The South African authorities have long regarded cannabis as an illegal substance. Marijuana use was consequently made unlawful. Cannabis continued to be sold on the underground market despite being deemed to be illegal to grow and use. Its illegality was closely tied to the apartheid-era ban on alcoholic beverages for Africans in South Africa. Consumption acted as a form of liberation movement in addition to being a cheap way to get alcohol and drugs. Cannabis was used by Rastafarians for religious purposes even though it was illegal, which contributed to its rise in popularity. Cannabis is the most commonly used illegal substance in western nations, with 32% of young adults in the European Union and over

DOI: 10.4018/978-1-6684-6346-8.ch006

half of young adults in the USA and Canada reporting lifetime use (Skypala et al., 2022). Cannabis use is strongly associated with young people (10–24 year-olds) who are more impulsive and have poor response inhibition (Lawn et al., 2022).

BACKGROUND AND THE STUDY FOCUS (PROBLEM STATEMENT)

The history of cannabis is extensive and fascinating. Central Asia or western China were the earliest places to use cannabis. When it was added to the pharmacopoeia in 2800 BC, the first mention of its use was made. Writings by Indian Hindus, Assyrians, Greeks, and Romans claim that cannabis helps treat a variety of illnesses, including asthma, amenorrhea, depression, inflammation, pain, and loss of appetite (Ayenigbara, 2014, Acharya, 2005).The emergence of trade saw the spread of cannabis throughout the world. In Africa, the indigenous use is cited as far back as in the fourteenth (14th) century in Ethiopia (Samuel and Edward, 2015). It was exchanged as a kind of product. The Khoikhoi in South West Africa, now known as Namibia, and the former Southern Rhodesia, now known as Zimbabwe, were early populations that cultivated cannabis and traded it for a living. The use varied from the herb's traditional use among some of the sangomas (traditional healers) in the southern tip of Africa to its use as a combat herb, medicine, insecticide, anaesthetic, and recreational activity (Almqvist, 2020).

As colonisation developed in Africa starting in the 1650s, colonisers began enacting laws as they gained knowledge of local customs, laws that were designed to oppress and rule over Africans. Cannabis was a legal drug prior to the 1890s, and its primary method of use went unnoticed. Cannabis was first rightfully prohibited in numerous colonies by the Geneva Convention on Opium and Other Drugs, which was passed in 1925 (Merleaux, 2020). Many governments have continued to ban cannabis outright ever since without taking another look at other uses of cannabis that could benefit their economies. However, the United Nation's Single Convention on Narcotic Drugs of 1961 legislated cannabis use for medicinal and scientific use under Schedule1 and Schedule 4 (Collins, 2020). Regrettably individual nations fear to tread where the United Nations or the United States of America and its partners have put their regulations. African nations unfortunately continue to be conformists, and have adopted prohibitionists approach on cannabis regulations.

Figure 1. A timeline illustrating highlights from the history of the medical use of cannabis with an emphasis on the treatment of seizures and epilepsy (Source:(Friedman and Sirven, 2017)

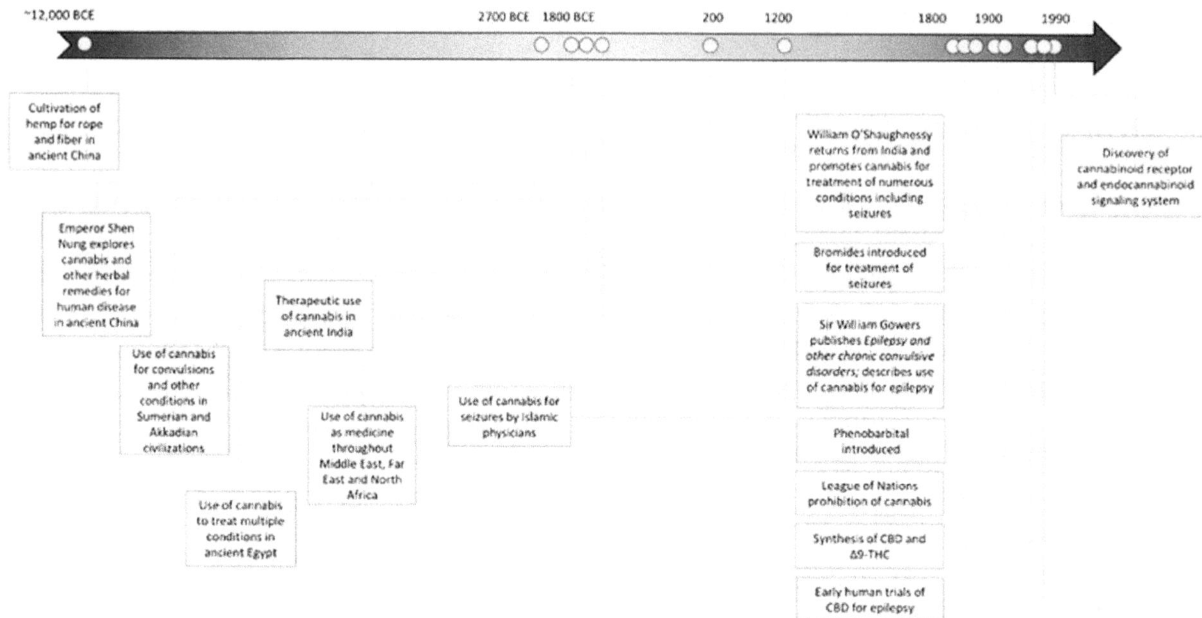

The pharmaceutical industry however has not given up in influencing changes in legislative framework (Brooks, 2018). Figure 1 depicts the history of cannabis use from 12 000 BC to the present. In order to develop a value chain that will benefit regional small cannabis growers, the study will look at literature on legalisation and value chain creation in other regions of the world. Cannabis use for medical purposes and for personal use is now legal in South Africa, however no laws governing the sale of cannabis in many forms or its commercialization have yet been passed. This is because deregulation must go through a laborious process. As a result of the South African Constitutional Court's decision in Minister of Justice v. Prince, the Constitutional Court decided in 2018 that the state should legalise cannabis.

DEFINITION OF CANNABIS

Cannabis comes in three mains strains, known as *cannabis sativa, cannabis indica* and *cannabis ruderalis*. *Cannabis sativa*, popularly known as marijuana, hemp, marihuana, ganja or *insangu* is included in the list of the five primary crop groupings, along with grains, cotton, vegetable oils, and cotton (Rupasinghe et al., 2020, Nath et al., 2022). The application of cannabis sativa is widespread and includes industries like textile technology, home furnishings, food processing, medicine, and health, among others (Crini et al., 2020). Cannabis has a wide variety of complex compounds, including lipids, flavonoids, terpenes, hydrocarbons, non-cyclic macrophenols, alkaloids, silver citrate, and cyclic cannabinol among others. Cannabis strains produce more than 500 compounds, including phytocannabinoids, terpenes and flavonoids (Radwan et al., 2021). *Cannabis indica* psychotropic originating from the harsh environments of Asia. *Cannabis ruderalis*, grows tall and is perfect for cultivating outside. These types only differ in the concentration levels of tetrahydrocannabinol (THC), which is the main cannabinoid or drug element.

Studies continue to reveal a lot that was not understood about cannabis. However, the uses of cannabis have been extensively exhausted with the medical use of cannabis being the leading topic in cannabis studies.

THE LITERATURE REVIEW

Cannabis or marijuana is a tropical plant known as ganja and sometimes hemp. It is a flowing plant that belongs to the Cannabaceae family. Its origin is in Middle Asia and has scattered to various parts of the world. Historically, cannabis has been known to be used for over four thousand years for various purposes such as animal feeds, cooking, recreation, etc (Gerra et al., 2010, Katsidoni et al., 2013, Grotenhermen, 2003). The scientific name of the plant is Cannabis sativa L. subsp. indica. The plant has male and female genders (dioecious plant). Cannabis has over 400 chemicals known as cannabinoids. Among these, tetrahydrocannabinol-THC is the most potent brain stimulant (Laohavanich, 2022). The following figure shows the chemical formula of cannabis. The banning of cannabis by many countries including South Africa was based on the stimulant effect of cannabis (Atakan, 2012). Cannabis is a complex plant with over 400 chemical entities of which more than 60 of them are cannabinoid compounds, some of them with opposing effects. Figure 2 shows the chemical formulae of significant cannabinoids found in cannabis with tetrahydrocanabiod (THC) being the main drug in cannabis.

Figure 2. The Chemical formula of cannabis product derivatives (Source: (Salami et al., 2020))

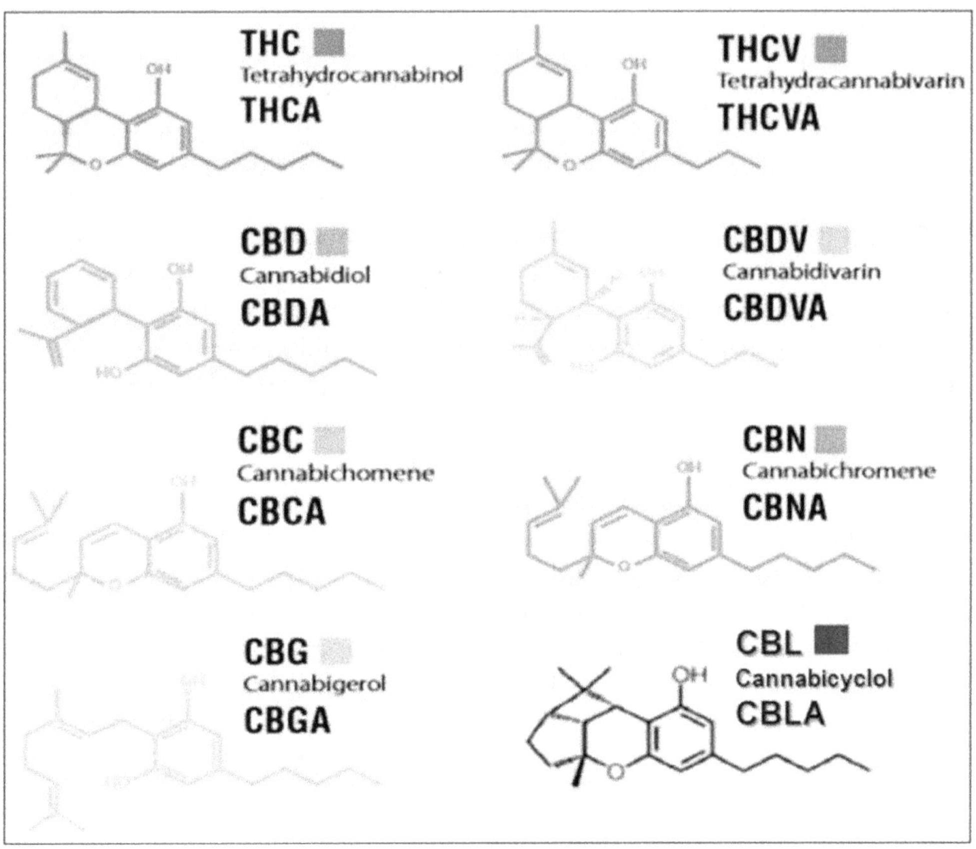

Figure 3. Mapped: The Most Common Illicit Drugs in the World (Source: The Economist and World Drug Report 2021 in (Wallach, 2017)

Cannabis is also the most widely used illicit drug in the world and its use has been associated with various mental health problems, particularly in the young (Degenhardt et al., 2010). There are many advantages of cannabis. Hemp has been identified as a potential alternative fibre source for the pulp and paper industry due to its high potential yields, resistance to disease and pests, and industrial quality (Francis, 1996). This is far better than using traditional wood which takes years to grow, it utilises vast amounts of land and water and degrades the land. Using cannabis would add much value and ensure that the environment is taken good care of. Cannabis takes one season, which is typically a few months to grow and harvest. Hemp is further promoted as a crop that could fit into farmers' rotations, improve soil conditions, and decrease the need for chemical inputs, in addition to a source of non-wood fibre (Robinson, 1996). The chapter aims to develop the proposed value chain and value add framework post the legalisation of cannabis in South Africa to benefit the rural men and women who have cultivated cannabis throughout decades if not centuries. Figure 3 shows the extent of drug use in countries in 2021. The United Nations (UN) as well as the World Health Organisation (WHO), through the United Nation's Single Convention on Narcotic Drugs of 1961 and the Geneva Convention on Opium and other Drugs of 1925, changed cannabis legislation towards stricter control or straight banning.

Figure 3 shows counties that have shown the growing use of cannabis in different countries. These countries mainly use cannabis as an herb, resin or any other type. In many of these countries cannabis is still illegal and its use is strictly forbidden although enforcement of illegality is hard to enforce.

The Road to Decriminalisation of Cannabis, the Worldwide View

Cannabis use and cultivation can be traced to 12000BC in Asia and later in China. Many countries were using cannabis for years. The fact is that no death has been directly associated with cannabis oral use for centuries (Zahra et al., 2020). The formal legalisation of cannabis started in earnest in the late 20th century (Chouvy, 2019, Small, 2017). Netherlands took a lead in ensuring that it legalises recreational cannabis opening a lot of the so called coffee shops (Hall and Weier, 2015, Bennett, 2018). Figure 4 shows the countries which by March 2021, had legalised in some form the use of cannabis in their countries. The darker shade shows countries where medical and recreational cannabis had been legalised for adult use. Whilst a slightly darker shade shows the legalisation of treatment, the so called medical use. The less darker shade shows countries where the planting and production of cannabis has been legalised, these include countries like China which is producing tons of cannabis but its use for medical and recreational purposes is illegal (Wen et al., 2022).

Figure 4. States or countries where cannabis is legal (Source: The Economist)

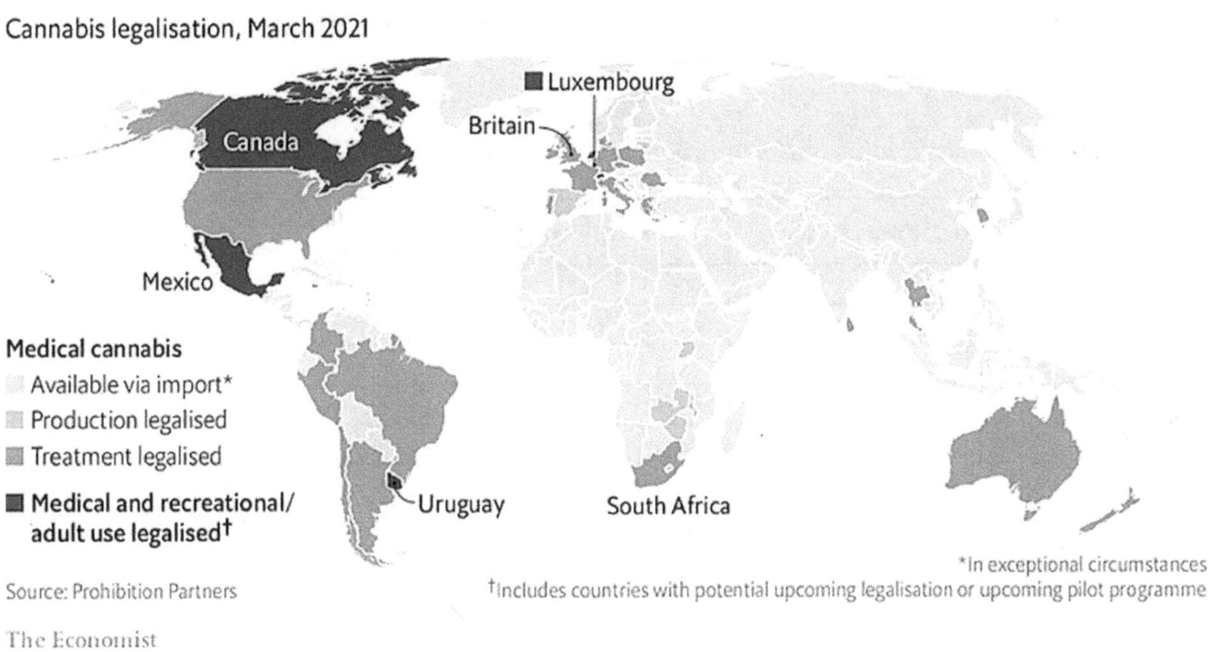

The Use of Cannabis, the Worldwide View

This section will deal with the uses of cannabis in the United States followed by China, Africa and then South Africa. The aim is to establish the already established use irrespective of legalisation in part or in full.

The Use of Cannabis in the United States

The two most popular varieties of cannabis are those produced for drug production, also known as "marijuana," and those grown for fibre and other industrial uses, also known as "hemp." (Johnson, 2014, West, 1998). Famously, hemp was the first cannabis variety grown in what would eventually become the United States (Hudak, 2020). Hemp was widely grown throughout the American colonies and the fledgling nation that resulted from them between the early seventeenth and the late nineteenth century(Crosby, 1965). Kentucky was already the top hemp producer in the country when it became a member of the union in 1792 (Johnson, 2019).

The Use of Cannabis in the China

China is the largest cannabis-growing region. The World Intellectual Property Organization reports that 306 of the 606 cannabis-related patents in existence worldwide are the work of Chinese businesses and individuals. A sizeable hemp sector has only persisted in China, the former Soviet Union, and Eastern Europe (Bhamra et al., 2021, Romero et al., 2020). In China, the average hemp cultivation area originally totalled roughly 160,000 ha in the late 1970s and early 1980s (Griffith, 2010, Clawson and Lee, 2016). The cultivated area then started to decline.

Table 1. Provincial Distribution of Hemp Production in China

Province	Fiber (×10^4ha)	Seed (×10^4ha)	Flowering Heads (×10^4ha)	Total (×10^4ha)
Shanxi	1.07	1.00	-	2.07
Heilongjiang	1.95	-	-	1.95
Yunnan	-	-	1.33	1.33
Inner Mongolia	-	0.67	-	0.67
Jilin	0.09	0.05	-	0.13
Other Regions	0.39	-	-	0.39
Total	3.50	1.72	1.33	6.54

Source: China Agricultural Research for Bast and Leaf Fibre Crops, 2020

Ancient documents and archaeological discoveries indicate that China has been growing hemp for fibre and seed for more than 6000 years (Small, 2015). Numerous hemp landraces have been established as a result of the long history of agriculture and widespread distribution of this fibre crop over various climatic regions. Figure 5 shows the sizeable number of hectares and tonnage of cannabis production in China. The intelligent use of land in China goes a long way in balancing both food production and agricultural use for other production purposes.

The Use of Cannabis in the Africa

On the African continent, cannabis is produced at the highest levels in the world. According to estimates, Africa produced 10,000 metric tons of cannabis herb in 2005, or nearly 25% of the world's total production. Of all seizures in Africa, 42% were made by South African law enforcement alone.

Figure 5. Breakdown of global cannabis herb production in 2005 (N= 42,000 metric tons) Sources UNDOC; Government Reports.

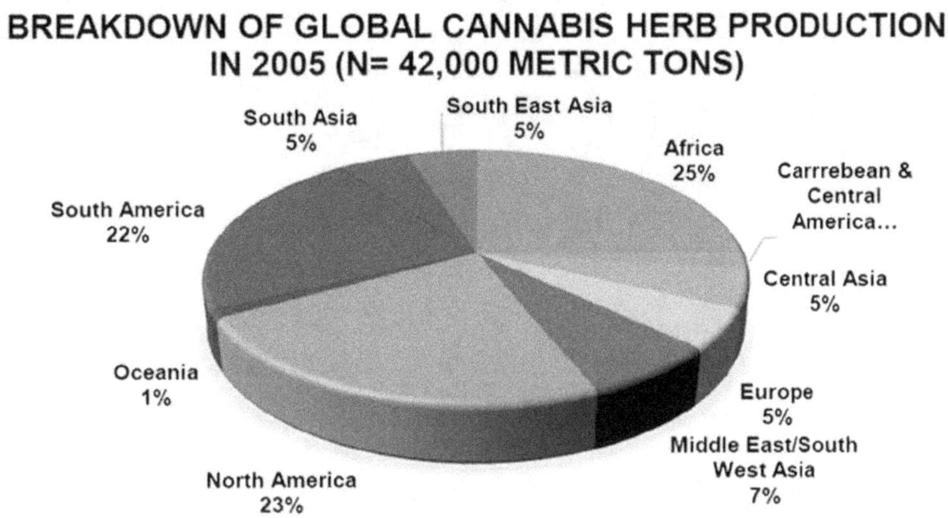

South Africa, just like a number of African countries, have planted cannabis in their backyards for years, some in forests for large scale sales. Much of African cannabis production is consumed on the continent in its simplest form (Duvall, 2019a, Ellis, 2009). An estimated 38,200,000 African adults (or 7.7 per cent of the adult population) consume the drug each year – far higher than the 3.8 per cent of cannabis users among the world population aged 15 to 64 (Kayange, 2019). Cannabis resin is also produced in large amounts on the African continent (Charitos et al., 2021). Over the period 1995 – 2005, a total of 19 out of 53 African countries reported the cultivation of cannabis on their territory (Akyeampong, 2005). Africa alone accounted for 10,500 metric tons or 25 per cent of the total.

Figure 6. The arrival of cannabis in Africa [LEFT] ; The criminalisation of cannabis in Africa [RIGHT] Source: (Duvall, 2019b)

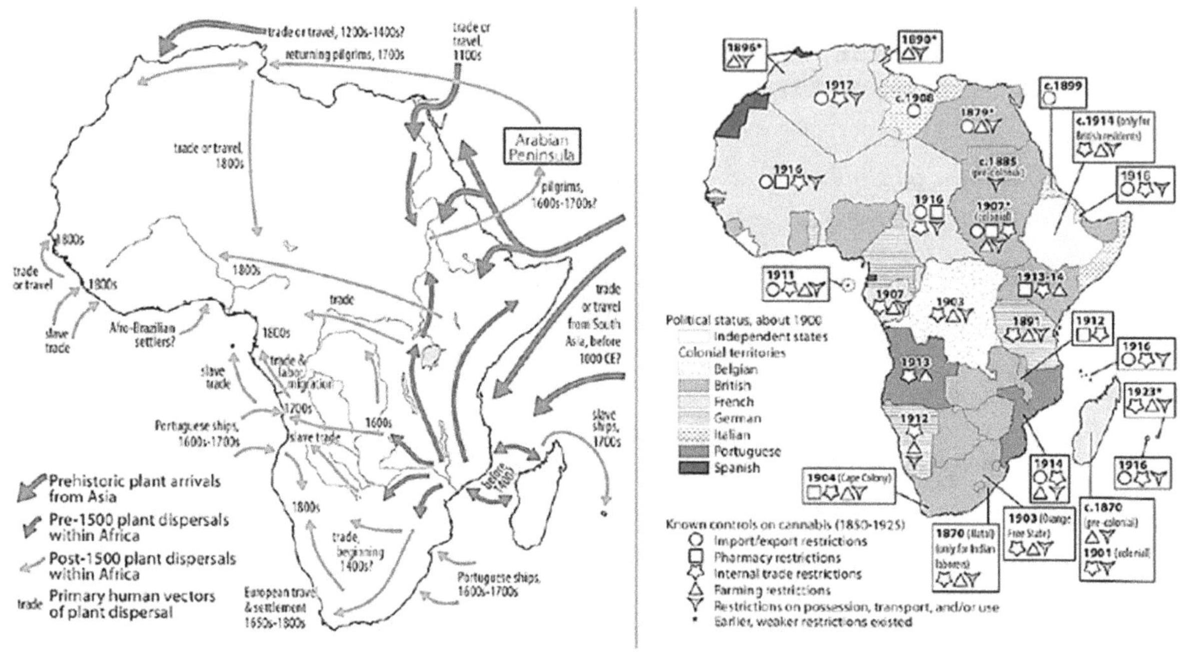

Figure 6 shows the arrival of cannabis in the 1400, and how it spread throughout Africa from the Port of Cape of Good Hope, now known as Cape Town. As easily as cannabis had spread as soon as the United Nations in 1925 passed stricter control of cannabis, the colonies soon imposed stricter controls in their colonies (Chris, 2019).

The Developing South African Cannabis Industry

The current legal framework, which was developed in accordance with the South African Cannabis Masterplan's goals to establish a sustainable cannabis market, came next. The Medical, Dental, and Pharmacy Act, which was passed in 1928, outlawed cannabis use completely in South Africa. Cannabis is prohibited under the 1937 Weeds Act as well. The Drugs and Trafficking Act of 1992, the Pharmacy Act of 1974, the Criminal Procedure Act of 1974 (which authorises searches and seizures), and the Medicines and Related Substances Act of 1965 all closely followed. These laws prohibit the manufacturing, distribution, and use of cannabis. For the sake of upholding the Constitutional Court ruling, all of these laws must be abolished.

The South African Draft Cannabis Master Plan

According to the South African Master Plan on cannabis drafted in 2021, there are nine points that highlight what the government plans to do as they roll out and legitimise the cultivation, value adding, sale of cannabis products as well as enter into the export market. However, it would seem that the government is lagging far behind as many cannabis products are now readily available in South Africa with fully fledged shops selling imported products.

Figure 7. The South African Cannabis Master Plan Framework (Source: DRDLR)

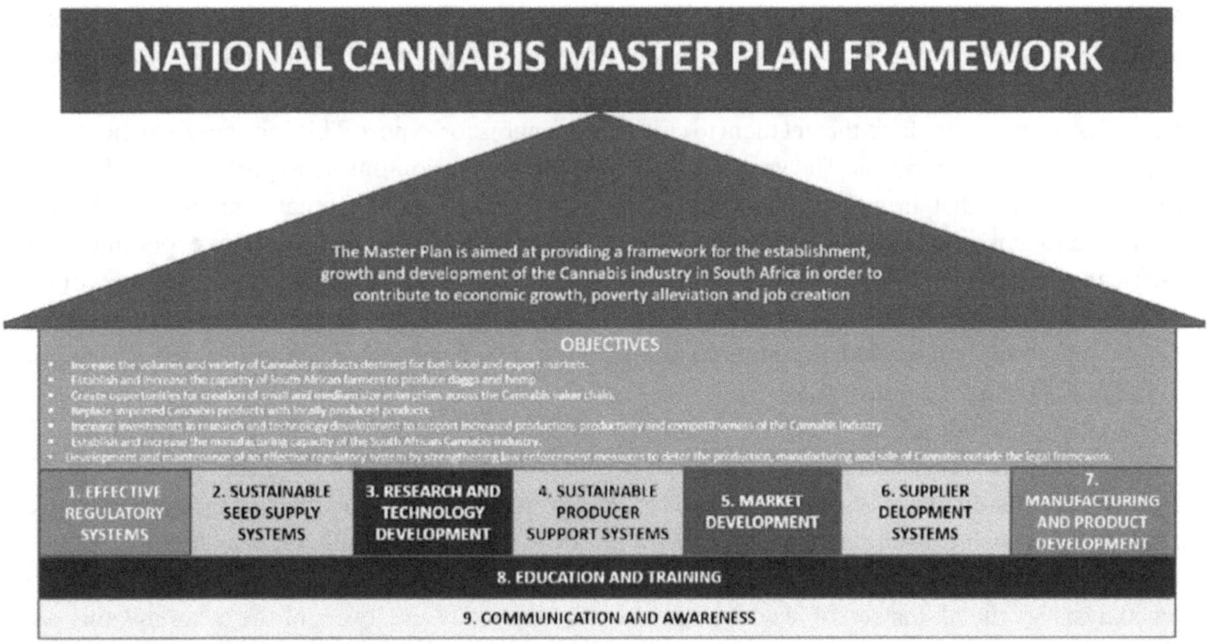

The South African government has 9 plans of relevance to this study are the following two:

i. Including indigenous dagga growers in the value chain
ii. Developing and supporting the growth and development of the manufacturing and product development capacity of the South African cannabis sector.

The South African Cannabis Masterplan Framework looks good on paper (de Wee and Asmah-Andoh, 2022). It speaks to creating an effective regulatory framework which speak to the synergy between legislations that will allow the masterplan to work. These laws must ensure that they regulate how players are going to play the game. The players, will also use the legislation weaknesses to their advantage and challenge government in pursuit of profits. The research and development could only work if it is controlled by the government entity like the CSIR working with universities in the identified province. The plans must also be regulated in favour of the weaklings in the value chain. The questions that arise as the Cannabis Masterplan Framework is still under conceptualisation are:

- Will such a policy ensure that the cannabis market favours South African development and value chain creation that will develop local economic development in favour of rural and township economy?

- Has the lack of policy development prior to the clear Masterplan already opened economic floodgates in favour of western markets?

Intention in Creating Value in the local South African Market

Cannabis legislation changes in the Global North have made it permissible for privately held businesses and publicly listed enterprises to generate profit. Through the payment of licencing fees that are too expensive for the majority of the inhabitants of the countries to afford, these firms have compensated African governments for laws that let them to cultivate cannabis for export. This is opposed to the freedom and empowerment of Africans. The western countries and Europe continue to export processed cannabis goods from Africa that are priced 100 times higher than the raw cannabis that is shipped to Africa. If citizens are to gain, this generational error cannot be permitted to continue. Multiple economic sectors in African nations have been hampered by neo-colonialism in terms of wealth creation (Arowolo and Lalude, 2022), and the recent phenomenon of land acquisition through long-term leases (i.e. land grabbing) is commonly interpreted as accumulation through dispossession, enabled through neo-colonial power (Ethiopia, 2019, Andrews, 2018).

The GDP of South Africa peaked in 1964 at 7.94% and experienced its lowest decline in 2020 at 6.43%. The fact that there was negative growth in 1983, 1985, 1992, 2009, and most recently in 2022 is notable. Events that have resulted in negative GDP growth are simply explained by economists. The global credit crunch caused the negative growth in 2009, whereas COVID-19, which is the worst decrease since 1961, caused the decline in 2020. For the legislators to make changes that have an impact, data analysis is crucial. Instead of leaving everything in the hands and levers of the economy, this paper makes the case for empowerment. The economy forgets the poor and the economically weak, the South African government must not. The value creation must be direct and enforceable (John and Ross, 2021). This should be in favour of old grannies, unemployed youth who currently have small yards of land and need the government to release land for cultivation. These people should be organised into small primary to secondary cooperatives which should form the core of the production of cannabis.

Figure 8. South Africa GDP Growth Rate 1961-2022 (Source: StatsSA)

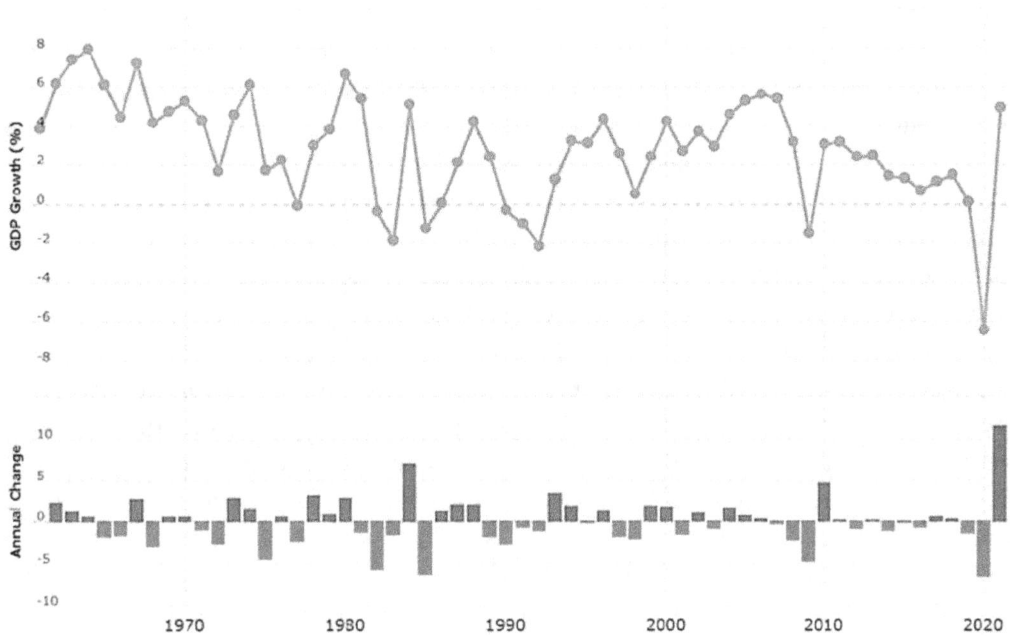

The next layer should capacitate the young in value adding and production. The formation of the state owned enterprise will ensure that the targets of ownership and supply are adhered to.

Figure 9. The South African Cannabis Model that includes small growers in the value chain. (Source: DRDLR)

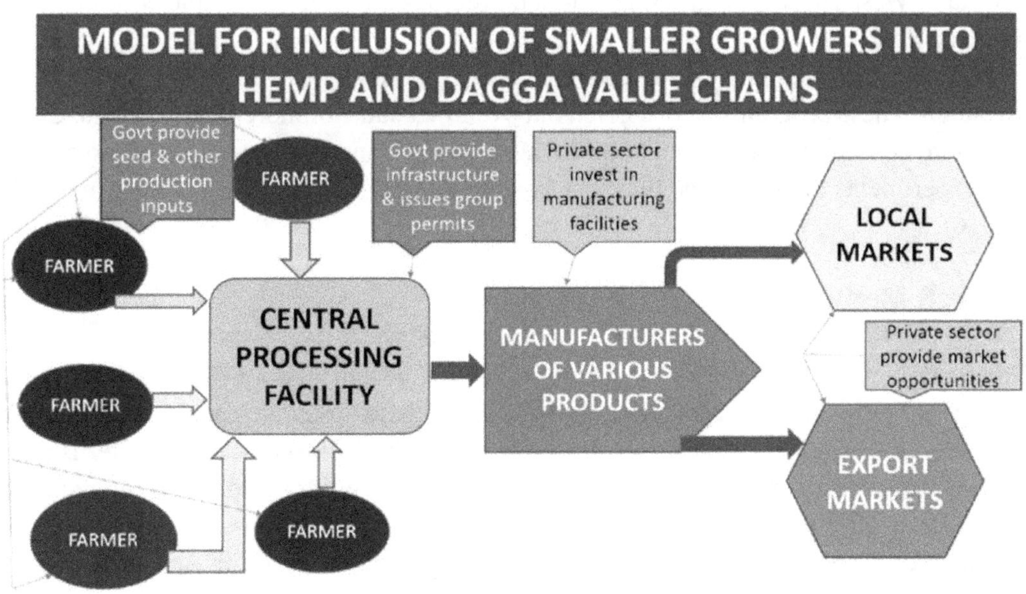

Figure 9 shows how the state plans to include small farmers in the supply chain of cannabis as the primary product that will be used in the central processing facility. It is a good intent to create a central facility, but it is problematic if farmers can just supply without authenticating the source of production or supply. In order to empower South African women, youth, and those on the economic margins, this must be done purposefully. The most economically marginalised members of society would not have been empowered if the masterplan and, finally, the legislation, failed to address it.

The sale of cannabis-related goods is now legal in South Africa. Since this market is still developing, local competitors are currently at a disadvantage. But because obtaining a licence is so expensive, global corporations control the market. Many small-scale farmers all around the nation have been grumbling that they receive no benefits from this sector. According to the Department of Agriculture Land Reform and Rural Development (DALRRD), the South African cannabis business is expected to be worth R28 billion in 2021. (Daniel, 2021). But current legislation, despite the private use of cannabis being decriminalised by the Constitutional Court (CC) in 2018, is a major hurdle in realising the economic potential of commercialisation (Dostal, 2021). There are no provisions for the commercialisation of cannabis in the Cannabis for Private Purposes Bill (Adinoff and Reiman, 2019), which needs to be approved by parliament (Aguilar et al., 2018). Industrialization is still not permitted, as noted by the Department of Trade, Industry and Competition, until changes are made to the Drugs and Drug Trafficking Act to better align it with the Medicines Act, which regulates the growth, manufacture, distribution, import, and export of medicines containing THC (DTIC).

The Production Process: Laying the Background and Preparing the Seeds

South Africa started formally growing hemp in 1999. The National Hemp Pilot Initiative was a joint effort between the Eastern Cape Provincial Department of Agriculture, the then-National Department of Agriculture, and the Department of Trade and Industry to establish the hemp industry in South Africa. According to preliminary studies by the CSIR and partners that formed the basis for this programme, the Eastern Cape, Western Cape, and KwaZulu-Natal regions all offer favourable conditions for hemp growing (Wynn, 1998).

The responsibility for breeding and agronomic research on hemp was delegated to the Agricultural Research Council. These programs were carried out over the course of more than 20 years. Commercial experiments were carried out with the help of the DAFF, ARC, and Eastern Cape Department of Agriculture. The experiments demonstrated that it is feasible to produce commercial hemp in South Africa (Coogan, 2016).

The Research Methodology

Research methodology includes the steps used to define the design, choose methodologies and strategies, process sampling, choose data gathering tools, and perform a systematic analysis of secondary data on the cannabis study topic. The descriptive research approach employed in this chapter is qualitative. The qualitative method is used in the systematic review to assess written and published records as well as theme-based scholarly publications. The qualitative technique helps in comparing South Africa's legalisation and value creation to that of other nations. The main goal of this study's use of past and present data was to perform a literature review and analyse the secondary data that had been gathered.

PRISMA protocols were employed, which are a standard protocol and an evidence-based framework for conducting comprehensive review researches.

Secondary Data

Data from several secondary sources were compiled through a desk review. Credible academic journals, books, numerous articles, periodicals, conferences, magazines, newsletters, newspapers, websites, and other sources were taken into account when examining the development of the cannabis sector. Data from up-to-date working papers, manuals, protocols, reports, statistical information, rules, regulations, and standards were also utilised in the review. Secondary data (scholarly publications) and data analysis are categories assigned to the study design (thematic analysis). Data were analysed using discourse analysis. Only 39 of the initial 161 peer-reviewed articles were kept and qualified by the exclusion criteria to serve as the analysis's starting point.

THE FINDINGS AND EMERGING THEMES AND TRENDS

Key indicators were identified under four broad themes and these are legislation framework; commercialisation; farming or cultivation and safety. Many countries that have adopted legalisation of cannabis struggle to come up with legislation that addresses some of their socio-economic challenges. (Potter et al., 2013) identified cultivation and commercialisation as key issues in the cannabis legalisation. Safety was identified as critical amongst cannabis users compared to other inhaler, medical, or recreation drugs (Chang et al., 2019). Legalisation of cannabis has been widely identified as a key factor in the safety and commercialisation of cannabis (Kepe, 2003, Manu et al., 2021, Stein, 2016, Mokwena, 2019).

Figure 10. Themes emerging from research

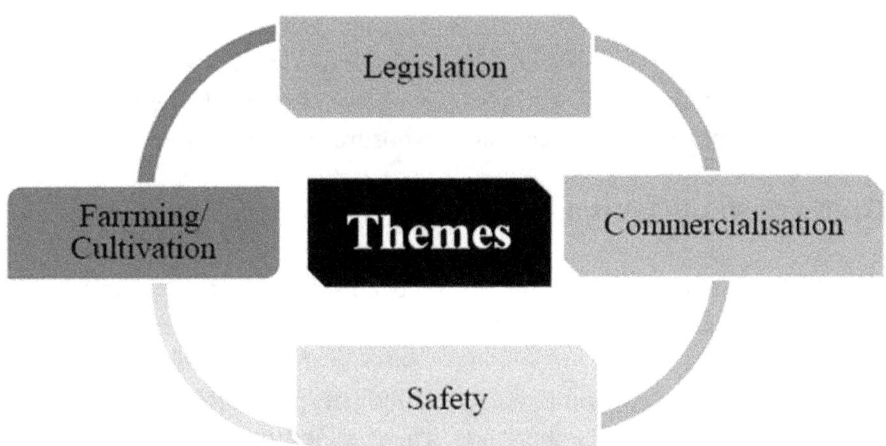

Preliminary trends from other legalised jurisdictions reveal little consensus regarding the effect of cannabis legalisation on public health and safety harms and an emerging body of evidence to support potential benefits (e.g. reductions in opioid use and overdose)

The Reliance on Foreign Investments in Developing the Cannabis Industry

Key informants (KIs) from Jamaican government agencies and domestic cannabis business owners believed that foreign investment was a crucial source of funding for legal cannabis enterprises' start-up costs (Steinberg, 2022). Local cannabis business owners gave priority to investors with the best financial standing, brand recognition, and export connections. They also took into account how closely an investor shared their vision for the company (e.g., organic cultivation, medical vs. recreational). Transfer of technological know-how and financial capital, which improved production, quality assurance, and seed-to-sale tracking, were the main advantages of working with a foreign investor (Rychert et al., 2020, Martinez et al., 2022). Some KIs raised concern regarding investors' emphasis on boosting production volume and efficiency at the expense of supporting R&D and clinical trials, investment in Jamaica's domestic cannabis industry's diversification (Rychert et al., 2021). In the US, they also grapple with national legislation as opposed to federal legislation (Chemerinsky et al., 2015). This leads to the creation of an industry within an industry. A focus on studying the effects of Western-driven policies, such as the war on drugs, high value commodity chains, is some of the challenges in establishing the local cannabis industry.

Towards a Well-Balanced Cannabis Legislation

When creating a policy, decision-makers must strike a balance between conflicting socially desirable objectives, such as protecting children from the negative effects of cannabis use by limiting their access and use, minimising the negative effects of cannabis use on adults' public health and public order, allowing adults to use cannabis for recreational purposes without state interference, and minimising the social and economic costs of the policies intended to achieve these objectives (Hall, 2020). Reforms involving "decriminalisation" have yielded conflicting outcomes (Melchior et al., 2019). Current cannabis legalisation frameworks differ greatly in their key elements. Legalisation has certain clear benefits, including as regulated usage, products, and user education; however, results are dependent on key regulatory factors, such as commercialization and policy ecologies (Budney and Borodovsky, 2017). Although significant changes in consumption have not been noticed, legalisation experiences have so far had mixed social and health effects, with some harms growing and persistent black markets. Uncertainty exists over whether legalisation lessens youth social harms or cannabis exposure (Fischer et al., 2020).

The Local Cultivation of Cannabis

The availability of "coffee shops," where cannabis has been sold to the public for personal consumption by municipal authorities under the Netherlands' drug policy since 1976, helped to encourage domestic growing. The stronger regulation of cannabis cultivation in the Netherlands appears to have had an impact on Belgium's decision to expand its cannabis industry (Decorte, 2019). In Spain, localisation is undoubtedly the model, just like in Netherlands. The availability of "coffee shops," where cannabis has been sold to the public for personal consumption by municipal authorities under the Netherlands' drug policy since 1976, helped to encourage domestic growing. The stronger regulation of cannabis cultivation in the Netherlands appears to have had an impact on Belgium's decision to expand its cannabis industry (Decorte, 2015, Belackova et al., 2015). Studies on domestic cannabis cultivation have shown repeatedly that even in an illegal context, users and growers can be part of informal networks or co-operatives of cannabis producers. South Africa can learn a lot from this model (Decorte & Pardal, 2017). When it comes to determining cannabis legislation, in the United States, the states are in charge, and they've largely chosen to permit private businesses to be in charge of the means of production and sale, albeit with various types and levels of state regulation (Larkin Jr, 2021; Gloyer, 2018). This is also a trend that is observed in South Africa and Lesotho.

The Safe Use of Cannabis Products

Marijuana usage during pregnancy may have negative effects on the foetus, including foetal growth restriction and long-term neurological repercussions (Obstetricians and Gynecologists, 2017). In several high-income nations, the legalisation of non-medical cannabis usage may increase the prevalence of cannabis use disorder (CUD) (Connor et al., 2021). Edibles were criticised for their inconsistent distribution of marijuana in the product, delayed effects, surprise highs, and unpredictable highs. No one in either region expressed concern about the negative health impacts of eating edibles (Giombi et al., 2018). The safety of marijuana products is of very high standards and it is being continuously improved. Countries and states may think about working with medical specialists to create a more appropriate standardised legal framework for safe medicinal cannabis use worldwide (Cash et al., 2020). More US 'legal' states than 'illegal' states as well as Canada reported using cannabis concentrates, vaped oils, edibles, and drinks. In both legal and illicit US countries, dried herb vaping was more prevalent than in Canada, where Canadians were more inclined to smoke dried herb with tobacco (Goodman et al., 2020).

THE PROPOSED CONCEPTUAL VALUE CHAIN

A variety of elements need to be taken into account in order to develop a well-balanced strategy for both recreational and medicinal usage. Figure 11 shows that the policy must carefully take the supply and demand of cannabis into account. It must also control cannabis abuse. For the industry to operate within the confines of the law, all of these products must be licenced and subject to strict regulation. These rules must provide for proper governmental regulation that enables both domestic and foreign players to contribute to the development of the regional economy. To expand the local market and attract local companies, the government has a vital role to play. More than a few hundreds of stores opened at the start of 2022. A quick Google search turned up around 60 stores in Durban alone, as well as 15 stores in Umhlanga, 60 outlets in Pinetown, and 12 stores in Ballito. These are businesses that deal in finished goods with added value. Over 140 stores were found within a radius of less than 100 miles. This demonstrates how cannabis sales are growing. How will local players develop to a point where they can compete with products and players from other countries? This is taking place without a clear policy being formulated and discussed with the populace. The legislation needs to acknowledge that rural people have been growing marijuana for decades. By the time a policy or legislation is in operation those who are well educated and connected would already taken advantage of the loopholes in the policy. They would have formed part of the value chain by either organising the would be recipients and lined them up as fronts for their benefit. This was seen in the implementation of Black Economic Empowerment Act (BEE) and Broad Based Black Economic Empowerment Act BBBEE in South Africa (Van de Rheede, 2020). It is also expected that this upcoming Cannabis Legislation will not escape such scrutiny and self-enrichment from estalished business. Any policy must evolve to respond to conditions on the ground. It must also pass the constitutional master and avoid the challenges as those suffered by the original BEE policy. It must however create new sustainable businesses and attrack new entrants to the domestic market thereby addressing some socio-economic challenges of the country.

Figure 11. Factors to be considered in developing a viable people driven (economic empowering) cannabis policy

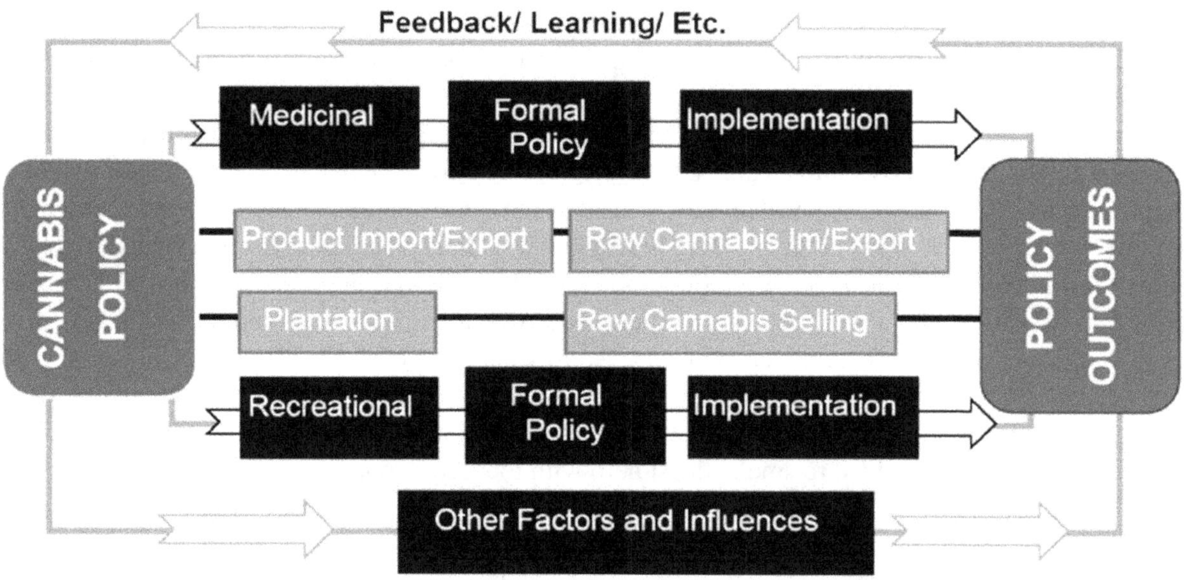

The proposed conceptual value chain is mainly targeted at regressive tendencies of underhanded corporations to either buy government favours, dictate to governments or use the legislations and courts to bulldoze and undermine the local suppliers who are small and underdeveloped. Thus creating a continuous monopoly that destroys any plans to create new and emerging farmers. This plan must be deliberate, it must be legislated and it must be government led and government supported for some time before it is allowed to be run by the dictates of the markets. The proposed conceptual value chain proposes the targeted local economic empowerment for rural communities, especially the youth and women. The women have planted cannabis for years during times of illegality. They have known the conditions under which the cannabis can be planted and produce a good yield. The formation of a primary producer cooperative which collects and sells the cannabis to all secondary producers will create value for primary producers. The secondary producer licence should also be sufficient enough to create value for the local market and export market. South Africa identifies four main production areas for cannabis development, and these are:

- Medicinal use
- Foods
- Industrial use
- Recreational use

The identified areas are well and good but the failure to acknowledge the development of products in other parts of the world and how these will impact the infant South African cannabis industry is rather short-sighted. It assumes that other players will wait for the South African legislators, let alone the South African cannabis industry development to reach its peak. This assumption is partly the basis of legislators' myopia. The South African cannabis industry will pay a huge price and country to country relations will also suffer a great knock if these relations are not well managed at the onset.

Figure 12. Proposed Conceptual Value Chain for Cannabis Production in South Africa

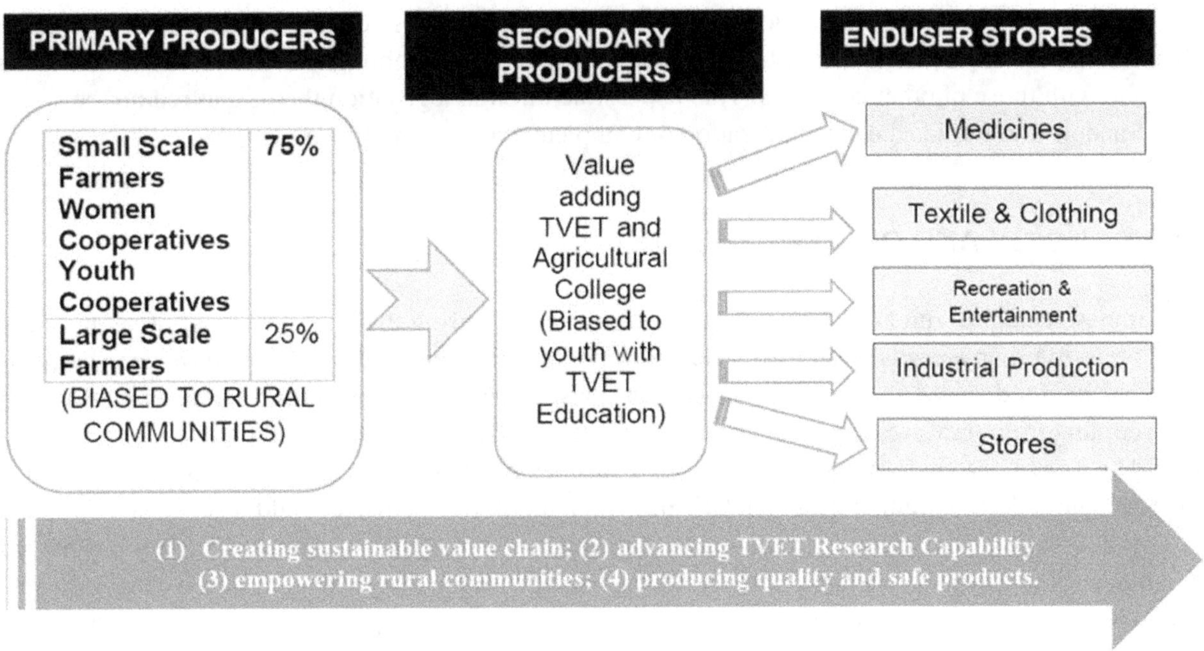

Similarly, goodwill and money thrown to people may undermine the very process, as people opted for money instead of land. Where land was returned to the people it either pay dormant or again leased back to white farmers who know how to till and farm the land. Without proper support and government backing many of these laws seemingly do not make any difference at all. The link between higher institutions of learning specifically researching the safety of products as well as the South African Bureau of Standards (SABS) should create value and make the sustainability and skilling for producers. To change the economic relations in favour of the poor, the state must be willing to legislate and empower those communities. Cannabis unlike commercial agriculture does not need a lot of care and irrigation. It needs minimal care and therefore can be planted by rural communities with minimal investment but give meaningful income thereafter.

IMPLICATIONS OF THE STUDY

Future studies must examine how much established businesses, most of which are multinationals, are benefited by the global legalisation of cannabis. Future research may compare the ways in which the government has been successful in creating new markets by utilising the blue ocean and red ocean principles. The creation of small to medium-sized businesses is essential for generating employment and finding a solution to the unemployment problem. The results of this study should contribute to a better knowledge of the regional cannabis market and how new markets may be targeted to help local businesses who are just entering the market. Legalisation should be seen as a reset button that creates new opportunities and, at the very least, increases the power of local economic actors. It also builds new value chains and gradually opens the door to international competition, enabling local markets to expand and compete with those of other countries. This is possible through legislation that is centred on the needs of the people and forbids the cannibalization or complete eradication of local markets.

CONCLUSION AND RECOMMENDATIONS

The empowerment of rural communities is very critical in ensuring that the movement of people from rural areas to urban areas is not forced. The people from rural areas and townships have been cultivating cannabis for decades under illegality. They have also been buying and selling cannabis in its rawest form coming from rural areas and neighbouring countries. Many people have been arrested as a result. It would be a great gesture for the state to release all those convicted of selling small amounts of cannabis for sustenance. As this would release a lot of space in South African jails, it would further start a process of changing legislation on cannabis illegality. However, it is critical to ensure that legislation is passed as a matter of urgency, ensuring that it does not have dire consequences on the envisaged cannabis value chain. It will undermine the very efforts of legalising cannabis. The importance of cannabis value chain creation should be to change the lives of the rural and township unemployed people. These people's lives could be changed drastically by ensuring empowering legislation. Local and provincial governments have failed because what they say has always had an element of sustaining the current economic beneficiaries and not creating another layer of beneficiaries. If the economy is to grow, it must create new markets and new role players. There can be no change, no new markets of value of governments if we still look at the current governments markets, we must create markets that create value (Kim and Mauborgne, 2015). The rural communities must continue to stay and improve their lives. The new industries must be geared at making a difference rather than enriching the already rich. The transformation mandate that is enshrined in the Constitution must become a reality (The South African government, 1996). We can only change the past through real economic transformation, and that is the only way we can make the constitution a living document.

REFERENCES

Acharya, H. J. 2005. Medicine and the recent history of marijuana. *History of medicine days,* 157.

Adinoff, B., & Reiman, A. (2019). Implementing social justice in the transition from illicit to legal cannabis. *The American Journal of Drug and Alcohol Abuse*, *45*(6), 673–688. doi:10.1080/00952990.2019.1674862 PMID:31634005

Aguilar, S., Gutiérrez, V., Sánchez, L. & Nougier, M. 2018. Medicinal cannabis policies and practices around the world. *Int Drug Policy Consort. Briefing paper*, 1-32.

Akyeampong, E. (2005). Diaspora and drug trafficking in West Africa: A case study of Ghana. *African Affairs*, *104*(416), 429–447. doi:10.1093/afraf/adi015

Almqvist, I. (2020). *Medicine of the Imagination: Dwelling in Possibility: An Impassioned Plea for Fearless Imagination*. John Hunt Publishing.

Andrews, N. (2018). Land versus livelihoods: Community perspectives on dispossession and marginalization in Ghana's mining sector. *Resources Policy*, *58*, 240–249. doi:10.1016/j.resourpol.2018.05.011

Arowolo, A. L., & Lalude, O. M. (2022). "Their Color is a Diabolic Die," Colonialism and the State of Environmental Justice in Africa. *Society & Sustainability*, *4*(2), 1–8. doi:10.38157s.v4i2.418

Atakan, Z. (2012). Cannabis, a complex plant: Different compounds and different effects on individuals. *Therapeutic Advances in Psychopharmacology*, *2*(6), 241–254. doi:10.1177/2045125312457586 PMID:23983983

Ayenigbara, G. (2014). Cannabis sativa: A plant with multiple utilities, misunderstood, and a victim of controversial hypocrisy. *Journal of Emerging Trends in Educational Research and Policy Studies*, *5*, 54–59.

Belackova, V., Maalsté, N., Zabransky, T., & Grund, J. P. (2015). "Should I Buy or Should I Grow?" How drug policy institutions and drug market transaction costs shape the decision to self-supply with cannabis in the Netherlands and the Czech Republic. *The International Journal on Drug Policy*, *26*(3), 296–310. doi:10.1016/j.drugpo.2014.12.002 PMID:25655217

Bennett, E. A. (2018). Extending ethical consumerism theory to semi-legal sectors: Insights from recreational cannabis. *Agriculture and Human Values*, *35*(2), 295–317. doi:10.100710460-017-9822-8

Bhamra, S. K., Desai, A., Imani-Berendjestanki, P., & Horgan, M. (2021). The emerging role of cannabidiol (CBD) products; a survey exploring the public's use and perceptions of CBD. *Phytotherapy Research*, *35*(10), 5734–5740. doi:10.1002/ptr.7232 PMID:34350641

Brooks, E. (2018). Using the Advocacy Coalition Framework to understand EU pharmaceutical policy. *European Journal of Public Health*, *28*(suppl_3), 11–14. doi:10.1093/eurpub/cky153 PMID:30383259

Budney, A. J., & Borodovsky, J. T. (2017). The potential impact of cannabis legalization on the development of cannabis use disorders. *Preventive Medicine*, *104*, 31–36. doi:10.1016/j.ypmed.2017.06.034 PMID:28668544

Cash, M. C., Cunnane, K., Fan, C., & Romero-Sandoval, E. A. (2020). Mapping cannabis potency in medical and recreational programs in the United States. *PLoS One*, *15*(3), e0230167. doi:10.1371/journal.pone.0230167 PMID:32214334

Chang, J. C., Tarr, J. A., Holland, C. L., De Genna, N. M., Richardson, G. A., Rodriguez, K. L., Sheeder, J., Kraemer, K. L., Day, N. L., Rubio, D., Jarlenski, M., & Arnold, R. M. (2019). Beliefs and attitudes regarding prenatal marijuana use: Perspectives of pregnant women who report use. *Drug and Alcohol Dependence, 196*, 14–20. doi:10.1016/j.drugalcdep.2018.11.028 PMID:30658220

Charitos, I. A., Gagliano-Candela, R., Santacroce, L. & Bottalico, L. 2021. The Cannabis spread throughout the continents and its therapeutic use in history. *Endocrine, Metabolic & Immune Disorders-Drug Targets (Formerly Current Drug Targets-Immune, Endocrine & Metabolic Disorders), 21,* 407-417.

Chemerinsky, E., Forman, J., Hopper, A., & Kamin, S. (2015). Cooperative federalism and marijuana regulation. *Ucla L. Rev., 62*, 74.

Chouvy, P.-A. (2019). Cannabis cultivation in the world: Heritages, trends and challenges. *EchoGéo*, (48). doi:10.4000/echogeo.17591

CHRIS. (2019). A brief agricultural history of cannabis in Africa, from prehistory to canna-colony. *EchoGéo*.

Clawson, P., & Lee, R. (2016). *The Andean cocaine industry*. Springer.

Collins, J. (2020). A brief history of cannabis and the drug conventions. *The American Journal of International Law, 114*, 279–284.

Connor, J. P., Stjepanović, D., Le Foll, B., Hoch, E., Budney, A. J., & Hall, W. D. (2021). Cannabis use and cannabis use disorder. *Nature Reviews. Disease Primers, 7*(1), 16. doi:10.103841572-021-00247-4 PMID:33627670

Coogan, C. J. (2016). *The South African hemp story: saviour crop or business as usual*. Stellenbosch University.

Crini, G., Lichtfouse, E., Chanet, G., & Morin-Crini, N. (2020). Applications of hemp in textiles, paper industry, insulation and building materials, horticulture, animal nutrition, food and beverages, nutraceuticals, cosmetics and hygiene, medicine, agrochemistry, energy production and environment: A review. *Environmental Chemistry Letters, 18*(5), 1451–1476. doi:10.100710311-020-01029-2

Crosby, A. W. (1965). *America, Russia, hemp, and Napoleon: American trade with Russia and the Baltic,* 1783-1812. Citeseer.

Daniel, L. (2021). Degrees for dagga growers and govt-supplied seeds– inside SA's Cannabis Master Plan. *Business Insider.*

De Wee, G., & Asmah-Andoh, K. (2022). Model for Overcoming Policy Analysis Limitation and Implementation Challenges: Integrative Propositional Analysis of South African National Mental Health Policy Framework and Strategic Plan 2013-2020. *International Journal of Public Administration, 45*(8), 658–674. doi:10.1080/01900692.2021.1878219

Decorte, T. (2015). Cannabis social clubs in Belgium: Organizational strengths and weaknesses, and threats to the model. *The International Journal on Drug Policy, 26*(2), 122–130. doi:10.1016/j.drugpo.2014.07.016 PMID:25179934

Decorte, T. (2019). *Characteristics of the cannabis market in Belgium. Drugs in Society*. CRC Press.

Decorte, T., & Pardal, M. (2017). *Cannabis social clubs in Europe: prospects and limits. European Drug Policies*. Routledge. doi:10.4324/9781315690384-20

Degenhardt, L., Coffey, C., Carlin, J. B., Swift, W., Moore, E., & Patton, G. C. J. T. B. J. O. P. (2010). Outcomes of occasional cannabis use in adolescence: 10-year follow-up study in Victoria, Australia. The British Journal of Psychiatry, 196, 290-295.

Dostal, H. (2021). *An Examination of Barriers that Retailers Face to Enter the Legal Cannabis Markets in California*. Northeastern University. doi:10.17760/D20412871

Duvall, C. S. (2019a). *The African roots of marijuana*. Duke University Press.

Duvall, C. S. (2019b). A brief agricultural history of cannabis in Africa, from prehistory to canna-colony. *EchoGéo*, (48). doi:10.4000/echogeo.17599

Ellis, S. (2009). West Africa's international drug trade. *African Affairs*, *108*(431), 171–196. doi:10.1093/afraf/adp017

Ethiopia, G. (2019). Illegal cannabis cultivation in the world. EchoGéo.

Fischer, B., Daldegan-Bueno, D., & Boden, J. M. (2020). Facing the option for the legalisation of cannabis use and supply in New Zealand: An overview of relevant evidence, concepts and considerations. *Drug and Alcohol Review*, *39*(5), 555–567. doi:10.1111/dar.13087 PMID:32436274

Francis, S. K. 1996. Hemp (Cannabis sativa L.) as an Alternative Fibre Source. Taylor and Francis Online.

Friedman, D., & Sirven, J. I. (2017). Historical perspective on the medical use of cannabis for epilepsy: Ancient times to the 1980s. *Epilepsy & Behavior*, *70*, 298–301. doi:10.1016/j.yebeh.2016.11.033 PMID:28089286

Gerra, G., Zaimovic, A., Gerra, M. L., Ciccocioppo, R., Cippitelli, A., Serpelloni, G. & Somaini, L. J. R. P. O. C. D. D. (2010). Pharmacology and toxicology of Cannabis derivatives and endocannabinoid agonists, *5*, 46-52.

Giombi, K. C., Kosa, K. M., Rains, C., & Cates, S. C. (2018). Consumers' Perceptions of Edible Marijuana Products for Recreational Use: Likes, Dislikes, and Reasons for Use. *Substance Use & Misuse*, *53*(4), 541–547. doi:10.1080/10826084.2017.1343353 PMID:28910182

Gloyer, G. (2018). *Bradt Travel Guides*. Bradt.

Goodman, S., Wadsworth, E., Leos-Toro, C., & Hammond, D. (2020). Prevalence and forms of cannabis use in legal vs. illegal recreational cannabis markets. *The International Journal on Drug Policy*, *76*, 102658. doi:10.1016/j.drugpo.2019.102658 PMID:31927413

Griffith, I. L. (2010). *Drugs and security in the Caribbean: Sovereignty under siege*. Penn State Press.

Grotenhermen, F. (2003). Pharmacokinetics and pharmacodynamics of cannabinoids. *Clinical Pharmacokinetics*, *42*(4), 327–360. doi:10.2165/00003088-200342040-00003 PMID:12648025

Hall, W. (2020). The costs and benefits of cannabis control policies . *Dialogues in Clinical Neuroscience, 22*(3), 281–287. doi:10.31887/DCNS.2020.22.3/whall PMID:33162771

Hall, W., & Weier, M. (2015). Assessing the public health impacts of legalizing recreational cannabis use in the USA. *Clinical Pharmacology and Therapeutics, 97*(6), 607–615. doi:10.1002/cpt.110 PMID:25777798

Hudak, J. (2020). *Marijuana: A short history*. Brookings Institution Press.

John, K., & Ross, D. G. (2021). How a firm's value capture affects value creation in its ecosystem. *Academy of Management Review*.

Johnson, N. (2019). American weed: A history of cannabis cultivation in the United States. *EchoGéo*, (48). doi:10.4000/echogeo.17650

Johnson, R. (2014). *Hemp as an agricultural commodity*. Library of Congress Washington DC Congressional Research Service.

Katsidoni, V., Kastellakis, A., & Panagis, G. (2013). Biphasic effects of Δ9-tetrahydrocannabinol on brain stimulation reward and motor activity. *The International Journal of Neuropsychopharmacology, 16*(10), 2273–2284. doi:10.1017/S1461145713000709 PMID:23830148

Kayange, G. M. (2019). *Cannabis Use and Addiction in African Communities; a Value or a Vice? Addiction in South and East Africa*. Springer.

Kepe, T. (2003). Cannabis sativa and rural livelihoods in South Africa: Politics of cultivation, trade and value in Pondoland. *Development Southern Africa, 20*(5), 605–615. doi:10.1080/0376835032000149252

Kim, W. C., & Mauborgne, R. (2015). Red ocean traps. *Harvard Business Review, 93*, 68–73.

Laohavanich, M. (2022). *Political economy of cannabis in Thailand*. Chula Medical Journal.

Larkin, P. J. Jr. (2021). Cannabis Capitalism. *Buff. L. Rev., 69*, 215.

Lawn, W., Fernandez-Vinson, N., Mokrysz, C., Hogg, G., Lees, R., Trinci, K., Petrilli, K., Borissova, A., Ofori, S., Waters, S., Michór, P., Wall, M. B., Freeman, T. P., & Curran, H. V. (2022). The CannTeen study: Verbal episodic memory, spatial working memory, and response inhibition in adolescent and adult cannabis users and age-matched controls. *Psychopharmacology, 239*(5), 1629–1641. doi:10.100700213-022-06143-3 PMID:35486121

Manu, E., Douglas, M., Ntsaba, M. J., & Tarkang, E. E. (2021). Perspectives of illicit marijuana growers and traders on commercial legalisation of marijuana in South Africa: Considerations for policy formulation. *Substance Abuse Treatment, Prevention, and Policy, 16*(1), 1–13. doi:10.118613011-021-00391-w PMID:34174921

Martinez, D. E., Pflueger, D., & Palermo, T. (2022). Accounting and the territorialization of markets: A field study of the Colorado cannabis market. *Accounting, Organizations and Society, 102*, 101351. doi:10.1016/j.aos.2022.101351

Melchior, M., Nakamura, A., Bolze, C., Hausfater, F., El Khoury, F., Mary-Krause, M., & Da Silva, M. A. (2019). Does liberalisation of cannabis policy influence levels of use in adolescents and young adults? A systematic review and meta-analysis. *BMJ Open*, *9*(7), e025880. doi:10.1136/bmjopen-2018-025880 PMID:31296507

Merleaux, A. (2020). Drugs, empire, and US foreign policy. *A Companion to US Foreign Relations: Colonial Era to the Present*, 572-595.

Mokwena, K. (2019). Social and public health implications of the legalisation of recreational cannabis: A literature review. *African Journal of Primary Health Care & Family Medicine*, *11*(1), 1–6. doi:10.4102/phcfm.v11i1.2136 PMID:31793317

Nath, M. K., Po-Dergaon, D. & Golaghat, A. (2022). Benefits of Cultivating Industrial Hemp (Cannabis sativa ssp. sativa)-A versatile plant for a sustainable future. MDPI.

ACO Obstetricians and Gynecologists (2017). Marijuana use during pregnancy and lactation. *ACOG Committee Opinion.*

Potter, G., Bouchard, M. M., & Decorte, M. T. (2013). *World wide weed: Global trends in cannabis cultivation and its control.* Ashgate Publishing, Ltd.

Radwan, M. M., Chandra, S., Gul, S., & Elsohly, M. A. (2021). Cannabinoids, phenolics, terpenes and alkaloids of cannabis. *Molecules (Basel, Switzerland)*, *26*(9), 2774. doi:10.3390/molecules26092774 PMID:34066753

Robinson, R. (1996). *The great book of hemp: the complete guide to the environmental, commercial, and medicinal uses of the world's most extraordinary plant.* Inner Traditions/Bear & Co.

Romero, P., Peris, A., Vergara, K., & Matus, J. T. (2020). Comprehending and improving cannabis specialized metabolism in the systems biology era. *Plant Science*, *298*, 110571. doi:10.1016/j.plantsci.2020.110571 PMID:32771172

Rupasinghe, H. V., Davis, A., Kumar, S. K., Murray, B., & Zheljazkov, V. D. (2020). Industrial hemp (Cannabis sativa subsp. sativa) as an emerging source for value-added functional food ingredients and nutraceuticals. *Molecules (Basel, Switzerland)*, *25*(18), 4078. doi:10.3390/molecules25184078 PMID:32906622

Rychert, M., Emanuel, M. A., & Wilkins, C. (2020). Issues in the establishment of a therapeutic cannabis market under Jamaica's dangerous drugs amendment act 2015. *The International Journal on Drug Policy*, *86*, 102945. doi:10.1016/j.drugpo.2020.102945 PMID:32947242

Rychert, M., Emanuel, M. A., & Wilkins, C. (2021). Foreign investment in emerging legal medicinal cannabis markets: The Jamaica case study. *Globalization and Health*, *17*(1), 1–11. doi:10.118612992-021-00687-3 PMID:33794932

Salami, S. A., Martinelli, F., Giovino, A., Bachari, A., Arad, N., & Mantri, N. (2020). It Is Our Turn to Get Cannabis High: Put Cannabinoids in Food and Health Baskets. *Molecules (Basel, Switzerland)*, *25*(18), 4036. doi:10.3390/molecules25184036 PMID:32899626

Samuel, A.-G. & Edward, B. 2015. The marijuana factor in a university in Ghana: A survey. *Журнал Сибирского федерального университета. Гуманитарные науки, 8*, 2162-2182.

Skypala, I. J., Jeimy, S., Brucker, H., Nayak, A. P., Decuyper, I. I., Bernstein, J. A., Connors, L., Kanani, A., Klimek, L., Lo, S. C. R., Murphy, K. R., Nanda, A., Poole, J. A., Walusiak-Skorupa, J., Sussman, G., Zeiger, J. S., Goodman, R. E., Ellis, A. K., Silvers, W. S., & Ebo, D. G. (2022). Cannabis-related allergies: An international overview and consensus recommendations. *Allergy, 77*(7), 2038–2052. doi:10.1111/all.15237 PMID:35102560

Small, E. (2015). Evolution and Classification of Cannabis sativa (Marijuana, Hemp) in Relation to Human Utilization. *Botanical Review, 81*(3), 189–294. doi:10.100712229-015-9157-3

Small, E. (2017). *Classification of Cannabis sativa L. in relation to agricultural, biotechnological, medical and recreational utilization. Cannabis sativa L.-Botany and biotechnology*. Springer.

Stein, D. J. (2016). Position statement on cannabis. *SAMJ: South African Medical Journal, 106*, 569–570. doi:10.7196/SAMJ.2016.v106i9.11222

Steinberg, J. N. (2022). *Cannabis legalization: an ethnography of the global movement and market forces*. University of Oxford.

Van De Rheede, J. (2020). The Broad-Based Black Economic Empowerment Act 53 of 2003 and the ways in which the commission of fronting practices affects the achievement of its objective. *African Journal of Democracy and Governance, 7*, 101–118.

Wallach, O. 2017. Mapped: The Most Common Illicit Drugs in the World. Available: https://www.visualcapitalist.com/mapped-the-most-common-illicit-drugs-in-the-world/.

Wen, J., Kozak, M., & Ying, T. (2022). Cannabis tourists' perceived constraints to engaging in commercial cannabis tourism overseas: A comparison of first-time and repeat tourists. *Asia Pacific Journal of Marketing and Logistics*. doi:10.1108/APJML-06-2021-0411

West, D. P. (1998). *Hemp & Marijuana: Myths and Realities*. The Council.

Wynn, J. (1998). South Africa Hemp Feasibility Report. Terraforms.

Zahra, E., Darke, S., Degenhardt, L., & Campbell, G. (2020). Rates, characteristics and manner of cannabis-related deaths in Australia 2000–2018. *Drug and Alcohol Dependence, 212*, 108028. doi:10.1016/j.drugalcdep.2020.108028 PMID:32370933

Chapter 7
The Role of the South African Government in Advancing the Cannabis Industry to Assist the Ailing Economy and Improve Unemployment

Jacqueline Grant
https://orcid.org/0000-0003-3956-8595
University of KwaZulu-Natal, South Africa

ABSTRACT

The cannabis industry, although shrouded with controversy due to stigmatization, has the potential to substantially enhance the economies of countries and assist with alleviating unemployment. The industry is projected to be worth some two hundred and seventy-two billion dollars by 2028. Besides the commonly understood medicinal properties, the plant has broad applications for use in construction, food products, toiletries, paper, and furniture. Following the devastation of the coronavirus pandemic and the looting in July 2021, the South African government needs to pursue alternative revenue streams. Public debt is mounting, unemployment figures continue to rise, and the economy is strained. This chapter thus seeks to offer insight into the contribution that the cannabis industry could provide in assisting the ailing economy and in alleviating unemployment.

INTRODUCTION

The cannabis industry is shrouded by controversy with many political and religious leaders decrying its use on moral grounds (Duvall, 2019; Kafeero, 2021). Despite growing evidence of the significance of this industry as a major contributor to the economy (Kane, 2020; Davids, 2021; Kafeero, 2021), the plant remains highly stigmatized throughout Africa with many leaders believing that a more liberal approach will result in increased addiction and crime (Mukeredzi, 2021).

DOI: 10.4018/978-1-6684-6346-8.ch007

However, cannabis has a much broader application than the commonly known medicinal or recreational drug use. Research reveals some fifty thousand industrial purposes, including paper, cardboard, construction, and textile uses (Parker, DiMattia, Shaik, Ortega, & Whittle, 2019; Oduor, 2021).

The Covid-19 pandemic created an economic crisis of catastrophic proportions on a global scale. Millions of people are without work and governments are seeking new sources of revenue and job creation (Kane, 2020; Davids, 2021; Kafeero, 2021; Manu, Mbuyiselo, Mohlomi, & Tarkang, 2021). The cannabis industry has been identified as one such avenue (Kane, 2020; Davids, 2021; Kafeero, 2021). In South Africa, the unveiling of the *Cannabis Master Plan* substantiates the importance of legalizing the industry to improve the ailing economy (Businesstech, 2021).

This chapter thus seeks to identify the progress made by the South African government as leaders of the nation to advance the industry for the economic benefit of the country and in an attempt to alleviate unemployment.

BACKGROUND

The Cannabis Industry: Legalization, Growth, and Expansion

A Western Experience

Kane (2020) likens the legalization of the cannabis industry to the end of prohibition in America almost a century ago, stating that the industry has a significant role to play in creating federal income streams and alleviating unemployment. The United States federal government lost an estimated eleven billion dollars in tax revenue from 1920 to 1933 due to prohibition. The ending of the nationwide prohibition in February 1933 was aimed at creating much-needed government revenue (Boudreaux, 2022) and decreasing unemployment (Kane, 2020). Kane (2020 argues that legalizing cannabis on a national scale in the United States could see more than one hundred and twenty-eight billion dollars being generated in tax revenue and approximately one million six hundred thousand new jobs being created.

The Influence on Africa

Advancements in the legalization of the cannabis industry in Western economies have influenced major reforms in decriminalizing the industry on the African Continent (Kafeero, 2021). Africa has seen a progressive movement towards the liberalization of the cannabis industry. This is evidenced by the fact that some twenty-two countries have reportedly taken steps toward policy reforms in this regard (Duvall, 2019; Kafeero, 2021; Oduor, 2021). Figure 1 represents the progress toward liberalisation from 2010 to 2019.

Figure 1. Actions taken towards cannabis liberalization (Duvall, 2019)

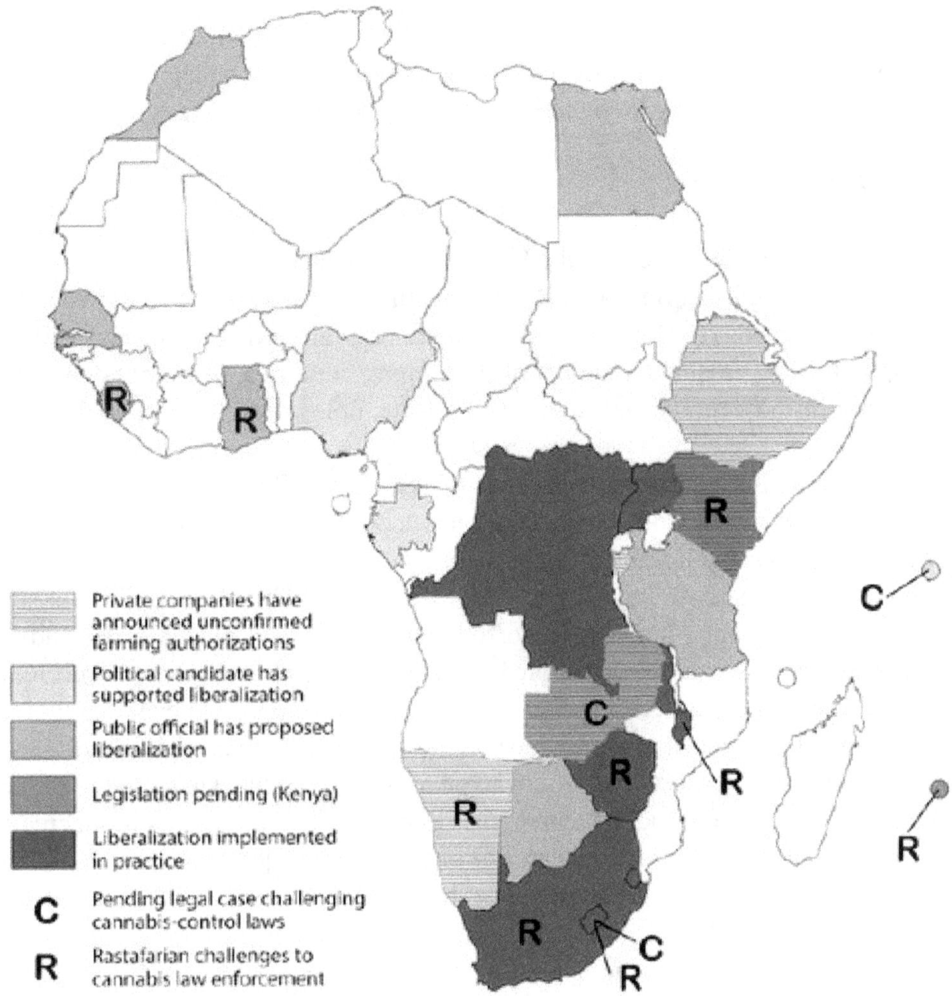

These policy reforms came about in response to the fact that global Northern countries are benefitting from liberalization (Duvall, 2019; Kafeero, 2021). In addition, traditional agricultural crops such as maize, cocoa, and cotton are highly susceptible to market fluctuations (Mukeredzi, 2021). Decriminalizing cannabis in African countries could pave the way for additional, profitable income to be generated while aiding the unemployment situation (Kafeero, 2021; Mukeredzi, 2021). Multinational firms have set up cannabis farms within Lesotho and the Democratic Republic of Congo (Duvall, 2019; Kafeero, 2021). Policy changes in Africa are needed to open pathways for foreign income that is vital to boost stagnating economies (Rusenga, Klantschnig, Carrier, & Howell, 2022).

South Africa, however, seems to be lagging behind. (Davids, 2021; Maposa, 2021). Dr Nqobile Bundwini from the University of Cape Town researched de-stigmatizing the cannabis industry given the significant economic benefit it can offer. Bundwini's research (Davids, 2021), supports Kane's (2020) view that the industry has a vital role to play in achieving economic growth (Kane, 2020; Davids, 2021), going as far as to state that the industry has the capacity to bring South Africa back from the cusp of economic ruin. This is only achievable, however, if the cannabis industry is de-stigmatized to attract investors. Bundwini (Davids, 2021), emphasizes that South Africa remains one of the largest exporters of cannabis and that the industry offers possibilities for economic growth. The researcher warns that if South Africa does not maximise this potential, Western countries will do so, ultimately resulting in the South African market being run by foreigners (Kedem, 2019; Davids, 2021).

The South African Context

The significance of this in the context of the South African economy cannot be overstated. South Africa is deemed to be a second-world country as it is neither a first-world nor a third-world country but a combination of both (Bakari, 2017). The country boasts a solid infrastructure and a wealth of natural resources. Despite this, it remains on the list of developing countries, primarily due to the social and economic disparity in the country and high levels of unemployment (Bakari, 2017; Government of South Africa, 2020).

The legacy of corruption, government bailouts of Eskom and South African Airways, the increasing public wage bill, and a (pre-Coronavirus) national debt of 67.5% derailed investor confidence and resulted in Moody's (being the last of the three main credit rating agencies to do so) downgrading the country to junk status in April 2020 (African News Agency, 2020; Stoddard, 2020). The downgrade essentially questions the country's ability to borrow and honour debt repayments, It adversely affects foreign investment, which is vital for developing countries such as South Africa. The credit rating thus affects the overall economic prosperity of the country as it is ultimately an evaluation of the economy, fiscal policies, political situation, and governance of the country (Zikalala, Mutambara, & Mthuli, 2020).

The country's downgrade affected all South African banks' ratings, which led to higher borrowing costs for organizations, the state, and the man in the street (Chen, 2020). In addition, credit to entrepreneurs is affected, which in turn impacts negatively on capacitating job creation. As South Africa does not have sufficient savings to meet its obligations, it has to borrow from global capital markets (African News Agency, 2020; Chen, 2020).

The downgrade took place near the beginning of South Africa's level five lockdown, which was implemented in an attempt to curb the spread of the Coronavirus. The timing could not be worse from an economic point of view. The additional burden of economic and social relief required by businesses and individuals amid the pandemic placed more pressure on an economy already under severe strain (Stoddard, 2020). In July 2020, the World Bank loaned South Africa $4.3 billion to facilitate job creation and aid businesses impacted by the pandemic. In April 2021, the country received $1 billion from the New Development Bank. In addition, South African banks have increased their holding of government debt. Overall, government debt has increased by R1,8 trillion in the last five years (Felix, 2022)

Now some two years later, the country has experienced interest rate hikes and the devastation of the looting that took place in July 2021 (Mthuli, Singh, & Reddy, 2022; Trading Economics, 2022). The government, in their role as leaders of the country, needs to urgently focus on rebuilding the economy and alleviating unemployment which in the last quarter of 2021 hit a record high of almost thirty-five per cent (Trading Economics, 2022).

Moreover, the country's structural capacity for growth is on a downward trajectory (Fedderke, 2021) primarily because of the three major macroeconomic problems, namely, increasing inflation, severe unemployment levels and poor economic growth (Sheefeni, 2022). This, coupled with its poor resilience to external shocks, essentially points toward an economy in stagflation – that is where inflation exists although economic growth is limited (Duvenage, 2021; Fedderke, 2021).

The dire state of the economy calls for the South African government to advance the cannabis industry. To this end, the next section offers a critical analysis of the present literature to uncover the existing scholarship about the cannabis industry and its potential contribution to the economy and employment.

THE ROLE OF THE GOVERNMENT IN ADVANCING THE CANNABIS INDUSTRY IN SOUTH AFRICA

Leadership Role

The concept of leadership has been widely discussed amongst academics and in various fields yet remains an overlooked area of research in the spheres of political science and public administration (Mthuli, Singh, & Reddy, 2022). There has been no consensus on a single definition for this phenomenon. However, several scholars agree that leadership involves the ability to influence (Ali, Tao, Shaikh, & Sajid, 2017; Iszatt-White & Saunders, 2017). In the context of this study, the South African government are the political and public *leaders* who can exert *influence*. This is significant in the context of the government's role in advancing the cannabis industry to alleviate unemployment and improve the economy as highlighted in the preceding section (Kane, 2020; Davids, 2021).

Ali et al. (2017) offer that *political* leadership centres around ensuring the welfare of the state and its citizens. This is expanded upon by Pichler (2018), who identifies three major functions (roles) of political leaders. These are: identifying the most urgent issues; devising an action plan; and mobilizing for action. Political leaders have the authority and resources to forge robust, sustainable relations with their stakeholders to bring about meaningful change (Ali, Tao, Shaikh, & Sajid, 2017).

It can therefore be argued that government as political leadership has a role to collaborate with stakeholders in achieving economic development and sustainability. In other words, the government needs to ensure the collective effectiveness of the economy in sustaining the people of the country (Ali, Tao, Shaikh, & Sajid, 2017). In a report prepared by the South African National Treasury in 2019, concern was raised about South Africa's economic situation. The report highlighted that economic growth has stagnated, unemployment is increasing, and inequality remains high (National Treasury, 2019). The National Treasury called for short-term relief and long-term sustainable measures to support economic growth (National Treasury, 2019). To this end, the government needs to:

- identify the urgent issues – namely unemployment and the ailing economy;
- formulate an action plan (which, for the purposes of this chapter, is limited to the facilitation of the advancement of the cannabis industry);
- mobilize for action

(Pichler, 2018).

The Potential of the Cannabis Industry and the role of the South African Government as Leadership in Advancing the Industry

The cannabis industry is much broader than commonly understood – this is demonstrated in figure 2 below.

Figure 2. Potential uses of Cannabis (Parker, DiMattia, Shaik, Ortega, & Whittle, 2019)

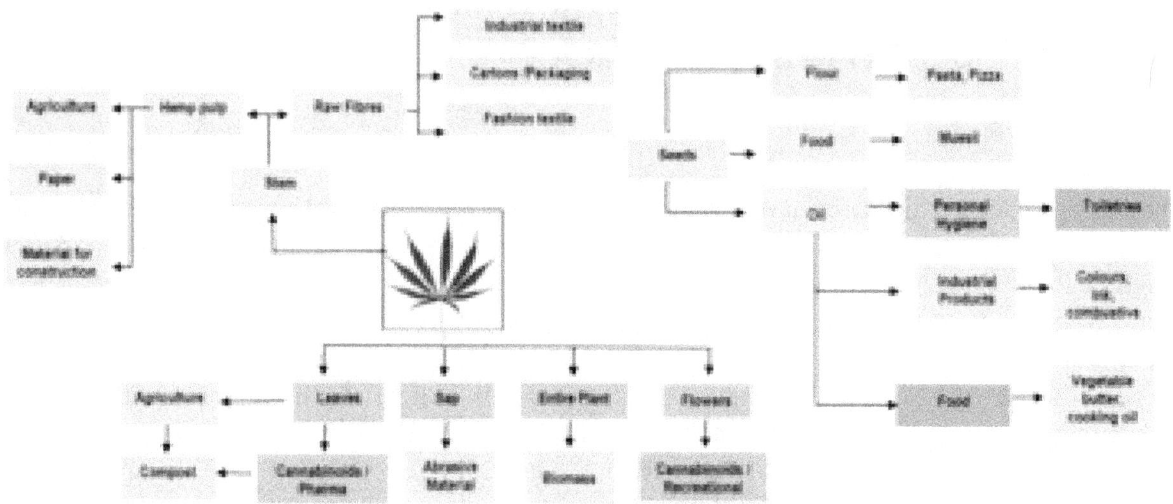

Besides recreational and medicinal uses, industrial applications in the building and furniture industry offer environmentally sustainable alternatives in these sectors (Chouvy, 2019; Sorrentino, 2021). In fact, the cannabis Sativa plant has demonstrated over fifty thousand industrial purposes, including paper, cardboard, and medicinal uses (Parker, DiMattia, Shaik, Ortega, & Whittle, 2019; Oduor, 2021).

Parts of the stem can be used in the textile industry while the flowers and roots have significant applications in the pharmaceutical and para-pharmaceutical environments (Sorrentino, 2021). The worldwide market for medicinal marijuana is approximately one hundred and fifty billion dollars and could potentially be worth two hundred and seventy-two billion dollars by 2028 (Manu, Mbuyiselo, Mohlomi & Tarkang, 2021). In 2019, Africa reportedly supplied eleven per cent of the global market, representing an amount exceeding thirty-seven billion dollars (Mukeredzi, 2021; Oduor, 2021). The South African cannabis industry is estimated at some twenty-eight billion rands (Businesstech, 2021; Davids, 2021).

In addition, hemp, which is a strain of cannabis, is a plant that can be used in the agri-food industry. The seeds of the plant can be used in the production of flour, pasta, pastry, and oil (Parker, DiMattia, Shaik, Ortega, & Whittle, 2019; Sorrentino, 2021). This is significant in light of the world food insecurity problem, where more than eight hundred million people do not have enough food daily (World Wildlife Fund, 2017). From a South African perspective, just under twenty-four percent of the population is affected by moderate to severe food insecurity and some fifteen percent of the people suffer from severe food insecurity (Statistics South Africa, 2022).

It is evident from the above that the cannabis industry has great potential from an economic perspective and in terms of alleviating poverty and hunger (Parker, DiMattia, Shaik, Ortega, & Whittle, 2019; Sorrentino, 2021) which are associated with unemployment. South Africa has a major housing shortage with millions of people living in informal settlements (Marutlulle, 2021). Using cannabis in construction offers an environmentally friendly alternative to addressing this crisis (Chouvy, 2019; Sorrentino, 2021).

Other African countries such as Lesotho, Zambia, and Zimbabwe have recognised the economic advantages brought about by the commercialisation of cannabis, decriminalizing commercial use and export of the product. Morocco has recently followed suit, permitting the use of cannabis for medicinal and industrial purposes while Rwanda has legalised the processing and manufacturing of marijuana for medicinal purposes (Oduor, 2021). The Ugandan government invested more than two hundred and sixty-four thousand dollars to secure high-quality cannabis seeds in 2019 (Mukeredzi, 2021). They also secured buyers from Germany and Canada after getting approval from the European Union in 2019 (Oduor, 2021). Malawi has also recently legalized the commercial cultivation and trade of marijuana (Manu, Mbuyiselo, Mohlomi, & Tarkang, 2021).

Arguments for decriminalizing the industry and implementing proper control and regulation include that a formalised, regulated industry would generate additional tax revenue, which in turn, would stimulate the economy. The illegal cannabis industry is flourishing in Africa and efforts at prohibiting the drug trade have proved futile (Kafeero, 2021; Manu, Mbuyiselo, Mohlomi, & Tarkang, 2021; Mukeredzi, 2021). Governments are essentially losing out on much-needed revenue from taxes and licence fees (Kafeero, 2021; Mukeredzi, 2021) that can be used to introduce reforms to alleviate unemployment (National Treasury, 2019). Improvements in the regulatory and legal arenas will facilitate investment into the industry in Africa, where labour is inexpensive and the land and climate are conducive to cannabis cultivation (Kedem, 2019; Kafeero, 2021).

Despite the moves made by other African countries and evidence to support the positive impact the industry could have on the economy (Davids, 2021; Kane, 2020; Manu, Mbuyiselo, Mohlomi, & Tarkang, 2021; Oduor, 2021), the South African government has only permitted the use of marijuana (cannabis) for medicinal and personal recreational use within private homes since 2018 (Duvall, 2019) Experts aver that South Africa could house the continent's largest medicinal cannabis market with a projected value of six hundred and sixty-seven million dollars (Kedem, 2019). The cultivation and trading of marijuana for commercial purposes remains prohibited in the country (Manu, Mbuyiselo, Mohlomi, & Tarkang, 2021; Mukeredzi, 2021; Oduor, 2021).

Government is, however, investigating proposals for the commercialisation of cannabis (Businesstech, 2021; Oduor, 2021; Mukeredzi, 2021). This relates to the role of the leadership (being the Department of Agriculture, Land Reform and Rural Development as the ministry responsible) to facilitate the advancement of this industry. Moreover, in terms of the function and role of political leaders, as identified by Pichler (2018), it can be argued that the South African government has identified the urgent need to address the ailing economy and unemployment. This is true in its acknowledgement of the positive impact that the cannabis industry can have on the economy and job creation. (Businesstech, 2021; Davids, 2021; Manu, Mbuyiselo, Mohlomi, & Tarkang, 2021; Mukeredzi, 2021).

The Department of Agriculture, Land Reform and Rural Development presented its *Cannabis Master Plan*, (depicted here below in Figure 3) to parliament in August 2021, emphasising the significance the industry would have on the development of Small, Medium and Micro Enterprises (SMMEs) as well as on domestic and foreign investment.

Figure 3. National Cannabis Master Plan Framework (Businesstech, 2021)

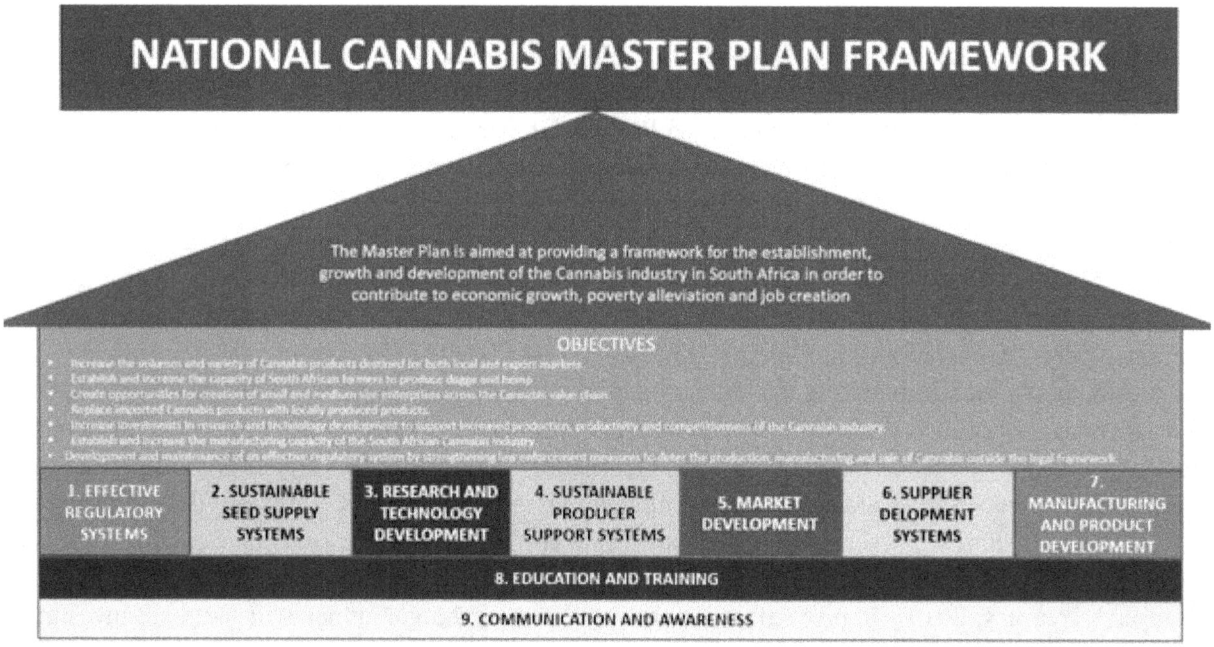

From a job creation perspective, the industry has the potential to generate between ten and twenty-five thousand new jobs (Businesstech, 2021; Maposa, 2021). In addition, as South Africa is the most industrialised country on the continent, it is well poised to establish itself as a serious player in the market, with a substantial competitive advantage for a domestic market estimated at two billion dollars (Kafeero, 2021).

The Department highlighted, however, that before accessing the value evident in the cannabis industry, the government needs to resolve issues such as industry regulations, the manner and place in which seeds will be distributed, and education programmes (Businesstech, 2021). The stigma associated with cannabis on moral, health and religious grounds (Davids, 2021; Mukeredzi, 2021; Oduor, 2021) needs to be addressed. Educational reforms regarding the uses and effects of cannabis are required to attract investors. Collaboration between industry stakeholders is another significant requirement for the plan to yield success (Davids, 2021).

The first pillar of the master plan focuses on effective regulatory systems. Here the role of the government is to revise legislation that is causing barriers to commercialization (Businesstech, 2021; Davids, 2021). It is significant to note, however, that the regulatory process should not be overly cumbersome as this may in fact deter investors and cause delays. A case in point is the granting of a *Cannabis Cultivation License* to the *House of Hemp* for medicinal marijuana. The process reportedly took seven years to meet legislative and other requirements such as quality standards (South African Food Review, 2019). Government, therefore, needs to make the process as expedient as possible by instituting pro-business legislation, should it wish to tap into the value offered by the cannabis industry (Kedem, 2019; Businesstech, 2021) in order to meet the urgent need of addressing unemployment and improving the economy.

The next pillar centres around creating a sustainable seed supply system. To this end, all organisations involved in the growing and sale of cannabis seeds must be properly registered and must have the required permits (Businesstech, 2021).

In other African countries, governments have instituted expensive licensing systems in a bid to regulate the industry. This could in fact result in unintended consequences where small farmers will be marginalized and unable to participate in the market (Manu, Mbuyiselo, Mohlomi, & Tarkang, 2021; Mukeredzi, 2021). Moreover, as most of the licences are held by international organisations (Duvall, 2019; Kafeero, 2021; Mukeredzi, 2021), profits from the industry are channelled offshore (Mukeredzi, 2021). The leaders of South Africa, need to ensure that the livelihoods of rural communities are considered in developing these types of regulations (Maposa, 2021; Manu, Mbuyiselo, Mohlomi, & Tarkang, 2021).

The Department proposes a certification system to ensure that the seeds meet quality standards and that import and export controls for the seed must be implemented (Businesstech, 2021). The government needs to engage and collaborate with relevant departments (Ali, Tao, Shaikh, & Sajid, 2017) (for example the Departments of Agriculture and Excise) to formalise these proposals in order to advance the cannabis industry in South Africa.

Research and development is another important area (Businesstech, 2021) as very little is known about the industry (Kedem, 2019; Davids, 2021). The government needs to spearhead research into various cultivation and technologies across the entire value chain for the growth and production of cannabis and related products (Businesstech, 2021). According to Kedem, (2019), many investors are seeking to inject funds into the African market but Africa needs to display the capability to produce quality cannabis locally, before capitalising on the export market.

The fourth pillar is aimed at mobilising and supporting farmers to partake in this value chain (Businesstech, 2021). To this end, the government needs to ensure that farmers have access to the latest technology such as automated irrigation systems and greenhouses (Mukeredzi, 2021) and needs to look at funding farmers in this regard (Businesstech, 2021). Moreover, the current illicit farming operations need to be incorporated into a formal system so that local producers are protected and supported (Kedem, 2019; Businesstech, 2021; Manu, Mbuyiselo, Mohlomi, & Tarkang, 2021). This pillar is closely aligned with the sixth element of the plan, being supplier development, which calls for the inclusion of indigenous and small-scale farmers (Businesstech, 2021)

The fifth pillar revolves around enabling domestic and international markets for South African cannabis products as well as the necessary infrastructural support such as processing plants and storage (Businesstech, 2021). As the market is still in its infancy and elements of the supply chain need to be established, there are challenges in developing the market (Kedem, 2019). The Department also proposes that government assist poorer farmers through government procurement of cannabis products and incentive programmes (Businesstech, 2021).

The seventh pillar centres on manufacturing and product development, which requires investment from the government and the private sector (Businesstech, 2021).

The foundational aspects of the master plan are education and communication. The Department proposes implementing formal and informal training courses throughout the value chain and in secondary and tertiary education curricula (Businesstech, 2021). From a communication aspect, the de-stigmatization of the industry is essential (Businesstech, 2021; Davids, 2021). The facets of education and communication are particularly significant in light of the fact that there is insufficient knowledge about the industry by most governments in Africa (Kangethe, 2022).

Discussion

While the above is certainly indicative that the leadership of the country has formulated a plan to tackle the urgent need to reduce unemployment and assist the economy, it is the third function of political leaders as identified by Pichler (2018) that is the most important – that is to act. The delays in finalising the master plan are impinging on the commercialisation (Maposa, 2021) of an industry that has been established as having a significant positive impact on rural livelihoods and the country in general (Businesstech, 2021; Davids, 2021; Manu, Mbuyiselo, Mohlomi, & Tarkang, 2021).

There has been some progress to date, which the co-founder and Chief Executive Officer of the *Africa Cannabis Advisory Group*, Sibusiso Xaba, avers as significant, particularly given that South Africa has the potential to have the largest market by revenue in Africa (Kangethe, 2022). However, the slow pace at which regulations are being opened up impedes being able to fully capitalise on the economic benefits of the cannabis industry. Improved coordination between the Departments of Trade and Industry), Agriculture and Fisheries and the South African Health Products Regulatory Authority is required (Faku, 2021).

The unemployment rate remains stubbornly high and had been on the increase before the crisis brought about by the Covid-19 pandemic (Government of South Africa, 2020). The economy has also been hit by a slew of downgrades driving up the cost of obtaining funding for critical government projects (African News Agency, 2020; Government of South Africa, 2020; Stoddard, 2020). In addition, the economy has seen significant job losses or redundancies across various industries (Government of South Africa, 2020), with over six hundred thousand jobs being lost in the third quarter of 2021 alone (Statistics South Africa, 2021).

The current circumstance presents an opportunity to build a better, more inclusive economy that benefits all South Africans. This is a chance to break with the past of low and declining growth, falling per capita incomes, poor investment, and high and deeply entrenched levels of inequality, poverty, and unemployment (Government of South Africa, 2020; Ede & Jili, 2021).

One such opportunity lies in the *Cannabis Master Plan*. President Ramaphosa confirmed the government's plan to facilitate the advancement of the cannabis and hemp industry in his state of the nation address in February 2022 (Vanek, 2022). It is significant to note that the decision to formalise a national strategy for the commercialization of cannabis in the country was made in July 2019 but the plan was only presented in late August of 2021. This is indicative of the government's ongoing challenge with policy coordination. In addition, the call for hemp licencing applications could in fact be premature given that the master plan lacks an all-encompassing framework to develop this sector of the economy (Maposa, 2021).

As highlighted earlier the triple challenge of inequality, unemployment, and poverty are chronic problems in South Africa. Over time, low levels of investment and development have exacerbated these issues. Prior to the impact of Covid-19 on the economy, South Africa saw two consecutive quarters of negative growth (Mputing, 2020; South African Government News Agency, 2020; Duvenage, 2021; Fedderke, 2021).

Of critical importance in the implementation of the master plan and steps taken towards liberalization of the cannabis industry is that the livelihoods of smaller, indigenous farmers need to be protected (Manu, Mbuyiselo, Mohlomi, & Tarkang, 2021; Waetjen, 2022). This is particularly important to prevent widening the inequality, unemployment, and poverty gap prevalent in the country. Concerns regarding the so-called "corporate capture" of the industry have been raised whereby local communities who are essentially responsible for developing the country's cannabis industry are at risk of being marginalised (Clark, 2019; Waetjen, 2022).

Small-scale growers do not have the resources that major commercial operations have. The gateway to South Africa's legal cannabis trade is through obtaining a license from the South African Health Products Regulatory Authority for medical marijuana cultivation (Clark, 2019). This is costly and overlooks the myriad of other (industrial) uses for the plant, which in themselves offer employment opportunities, alternatives for textile, paper and construction resources and thus the development of new business opportunities in the country (Sorrentino, 2021).

Community leaders in Pondoland, in the Eastern Cape, that are dependent on the still illicit cultivation of marijuana, have expressed their discontent at not being properly informed about the legal changes affecting their livelihoods (Clark, 2019). This is despite the establishment of a steering committee by the Premier to develop local standards in collaboration with the private sector that will be presented at a national level as a workable model (Clark, 2019).

In addition, the Eastern Cape provincial government has approved the establishment of a cannabis college. This is a bid to facilitate the advancement of the industry and remove the stigma associated with cannabis. Moreover, the Department of Rural Development and Agrarian Reform has confirmed that Canadian investors have expressed interest in setting up processing plants in South Africa and have committed to training farmers in growing and processing cannabis. However, the investors are awaiting the implementation of the correct legal framework to facilitate this (Matavire, 2020). Yet, despite these advancements, cannabis cultivation for non-medicinal commercial use remains illegal (Manu, Mbuyiselo, Mohlomi, & Tarkang, 2021; Mukeredzi, 2021; Oduor, 2021). This supports Maposa's (2021) view that the master plan lacks a comprehensive framework to develop the cannabis industry in South Africa and underscores the need for collaboration and coordination between departments (Faku, 2021).

The industry is new. Significant investment in irrigation, improved farming techniques, skilled pharmacists for medical research, security and skilled administrators that can navigate through the regulatory red tape on a domestic and international level is required (Clark, 2019). This will harness the capacity for mass-scale operations. Moreover, the supply chain is not fully developed (Kangethe, 2022). These challenges need to be addressed through collaboration and engagement with all stakeholders in the value chain being local and national government, farmers, investors, and the private sector (Ali, Tao, Shaikh, & Sajid, 2017).

It can be argued, notwithstanding the government's intentions in terms of the master plan detailed above, without a concrete, definitive and measurable action plan it remains just a proposal (Maposa, 2021). While it is still early days, the government's record of accomplishment in dealing swiftly with issues is poor as evidenced in the annual reports of the country's Auditor-General and the poor service delivery issues prevalent in local governments (Mthuli, Singh, & Reddy, 2022). The state of Eskom and South African Airways are but two examples (African News Agency, 2020; Stoddard, 2020). Another case in point is the government's response to the poor economic growth and socio-economic difficulties brought about by the Covid-19 pandemic – namely the *Economic Reconstruction and Recovery Plan* presented by President Cyril Ramaphosa in October 2020. The plan encompasses a broad spectrum of initiatives to stimulate the economy (Government of South Africa, 2020; Mputing, 2020). However, critics attest that is not a plan but a document containing a large number of priorities that have no strategic direction since it provides a myriad of possibilities without discerning the best course of action and in which order of priority (Bernstein, 2022). This again points to the need for government to act and mobilise its resources effectively to achieve the objectives of the *Economic Reconstruction and Recovery*

Plan (Pichler, 2018). While the government attests to progress being made in just eight months of the plan's release, (South African Government News Agency, 2021), increased load shedding and decreasing consumer and investor confidence seem to be the order of the day (Bernstein, 2022). In a similar vein, the *National Cannabis Master Plan* will remain a theoretical proposal to solve a dire situation should the government not act swiftly and purposefully.

CONCLUSION

The benefits of the cannabis industry to the South African economy and its potential role in alleviating the burden of employment have been well documented. Moreover, the plant has numerous other applications besides the commonly understood medical use. Cannabis offers many sustainable alternatives in industrial applications to the construction, printing, and textile industries to name a few. The use of the plant to manufacture flour, pasta, and oil in a world where food insecurity and hunger are rife cannot be over-estimated. More research into these applications and the potential areas of business development needs to be carried out, particularly in light of the potential to alleviate unemployment and provide housing (Misselhorn & Hendriks, 2017; Kedem, 2019; Parker, DiMattia, Shaik, Ortega, & Whittle, 2019; Businesstech, 2021; Davids, 2021; Kafeero, 2021; Manu, Mbuyiselo, Mohlomi, & Tarkang, 2021; Mukeredzi, 2021; Oduor, 2021)

The South African government as the leader of the nation has a duty and responsibility to ensure the economic welfare of its citizens. (Ali, Tao, Shaikh, & Sajid, 2017; Pichler, 2018) To this end, the government, having recognised the urgent need (Pichler, 2018) to address the poor economy and unemployment (National Treasury, 2019; South African Government News Agency, 2020), and having received a proposal from the Department of Agriculture, Land Reform and Rural Development (Businesstech, 2021) needs to mobilise to act (Pichler, 2018). This entails collaboration (Ali, Tao, Shaikh, & Sajid, 2017) with relevant stakeholders to de-stigmatize the industry (Davids, 2021), and attract investors (Kedem, 2019; Businesstech, 2021) and to streamline regulations and processes. Efforts should be coordinated in a cohesive manner. In addition, the livelihoods of smaller, indigenous farmers need to be protected. These actions will allow South Africa to tap into the value that this industry offers. In this way, the government will be taking concrete steps in fulfilling its mandate to address the urgent issue of unemployment and assist the ailing economy (Businesstech, 2021; Davids, 2021; Manu, Mbuyiselo, Mohlomi, & Tarkang, 2021; Maposa, 2021; Mukeredzi, 2021; Vanek, 2022).

REFERENCES

African News Agency. (2020, February 24). *Tito Mboweni called on to prevent downgrade to junk status, tackle unemployment.* IOL: https://www.iol.co.za/news/politics/tito-mboweni-called-on-to-prevent-downgrade-to-junk-status-tackle-unemployment-43386
368

Ali, M., Tao, L., Shaikh, A. A., & Sajid, M. (2017). The political leadership and corporate governance: An analysis of leadership theories and its influence. *International Journal of Basic and Applied Sciences*, *6*(3), 45–50. doi:10.14419/ijbas.v6i3.7706

Bakari, S. (2017, August 11). *Why is South Africa Still a Developing Country?* Ideas. https://ideas.repec.org/p/pra/mprapa/80763.html

Bernstein, A. (2022, February 7). Ramaphosa's economic reconstruction and recovery plan is a mess – time to throw the baby out with the bathwater. *Daily Maverick*. https://www.dailymaverick.co.za/article/2022-02-07-ramaphosas-economic-reconstruction-and-recovery-plan-is-a-mess-time-to-throw-the-baby-out-with-the-bathwater/

Boudreaux, D. J. (2022, November 11). *Alcohol, Prohibition, and the Revenuers*. Foundation for Economic Education. https://fee.org/articles/alcohol-prohibition-and-the-revenuers/

Businesstech. (2021, August 26). *South Africa's master plan for cannabis: rules, regulations, and adding it to the school curriculum*. Businesstech. https://businesstech.co.za/news/business/516152/south-africas-master-plan-for-cannabis-rules-regulations-and-adding-it-to-the-school-curriculum/

Chen, J. (2020, January 19). Investopedia: Sovereign Credit Rating. *Investopedia*. https://www.investopedia.com/terms/s/sovereign-credit-rating.asp

Chouvy, P.-A. (2019). Cannabis cultivation in the world: Heritages, trends and challenges. *EchoGéo*, (48), 1–20. doi:10.4000/echogeo.17591

Clark, C. (2019, October 14). "People feel betrayed": small-scale dagga growers fear exclusion from legal trade. *GroundUp*. https://www.groundup.org.za/article/people-feel-betrayed-small-scale-dagga-growers-fear-exclusion-legal-trade/

Davids, N. (2021, December 21). Destigmatise SA's multibillion-rand cannabis sector to achieve economic growth. *University of Cape Town News*. https://www.news.uct.ac.za/article/-2021-12-02-destigmatise-sas-multibillion-rand-cannabis-sector-to-achieve-economic-growth

Duvall, C. S. (2019, July 13). A brief agricultural history of cannabis in Africa, from prehistory to canna-colony. EchoGéo. doi:10.4000/echogeo.17599

Duvenage, A. (2021, November 26). The outlook for 2022. *Finweek*: https://ukzn.idm.oclc.org/login?url=https://search.ebscohost.com/login.aspx?direct=true&db=bth&AN=153857239&site=ehost-live&scope=site

Ede, C. I., & Jili, N. (2021). Microscopic Examination of the New South African Economic Reconstruction and Post-Pandemic Recovery Plan. *Journal of Political Science and International Relations*, *4*(2), 56–65. doi:10.11648/j.jpsir.20210402.15

Faku, D. (2021, August 22). *Regulatory certainty needed for dope exports to gain momentum*. IOL. https://www.iol.co.za/business-report/companies/regulatory-certainty-needed-for-dope-exports-to-gain-momentum-dcca7629-4273-47a5-a565-3c4d0d1b252f

Fedderke, J. W. (2021, July 29). *Identifying Steady-State Growth and Inflation in the South African Economy, 1960-2020.* South African Reserve Bank. https://www.resbank.co.za/en/home/publications/publication-detail-pages/working-papers/2021/IdentifyingSteadyStateGrowthandInflationintheSouth-AfricanEconomy1960-2020

Felix, J. (2022, April 17). In just five years, SA has borrowed R1.8 trillion from investors - Enoch Godongwana. *News 24.* https://www.news24.com/news24/southafrica/news/in-just-five-years-sa-has-borrowed-r18-trillion-from-investors-enoch-godongwana-20220417

Government of South Africa. (2020). *South African Economic Reconstruction and Recovery Plan.* Government of South Africa: https://www.gov.za/sites/default/files/gcis_document/202010/south-african-economic-reconstruction-and-recovery-plan.pdf

Iszatt-White, M., & Saunders, C. (2017). *Leadership* (2nd ed.). Oxforfd University Press.

Kafeero, S. (2021, July 2). Business is starting to trump morality in Africa's cannabis industry. *Quartz Africa Weekly.* https://qz.com/africa/2028012/africas-cannabis-industry-is-set-to-boom-due-to-legalization/

Kane, K. (2020, May 26). Cannabis Legalization Is Key To Economic Recovery, Much Like Ending Alcohol Prohibition Helped Us Out Of The Great Depression. *Forbes.* https://www.forbes.com/sites/kriskrane/2020/05/26/cannabis-legalization-is-key-to-economic-recovery-much-like-ending-alcohol-prohibition-helped-us-out-of-the-great-depression/?sh=20d927353241

Kangethe, J. (2022, January 15). Africa's Cannabis Market to Hit U.S.$7.1 Billion By 2023. *All Africa.* https://allafrica.com/stories/202201150144.html#:~:text=According%20to%20Phobition%20Partners%2C%20a,the%20world's%20most%20cultivated%20drug

Kedem, S. (2019, July 10). *Africa's budding cannabis market.* African Business. https://african.business/2019/07/trade-investment/africas-budding-cannabis-market/

Manu, E., Mbuyiselo, D., Mohlomi, J. N., & Tarkang, E. E. (2021). Perspectives of illicit marijuana growers and traders on commercial legalisation of marijuana in South Africa: Considerations for policy formulation. *Substance Abuse Treatment, Prevention, and Policy, 16*(1), 1–13. doi:10.118613011-021-00391-w PMID:34174921

Maposa, S. (2021, December 22). The complexities of SA's cannabis policy - more integration needed. News 24. https://www.news24.com/news24/columnists/guestcolumn/opinion-siseko-maposa-the-complexities-of-sas-cannabis-policy-more-integration-needed-20211222

Marutlulle, N. K. (2021). A critical analysis of housing inadequacy in South Africa and its ramifications. *Africa's Public Service Delivery and Performance Review, 9*(1). doi:10.4102/apsdpr.v9i1.372

Matavire, M. (2020, February 2020). *Eastern Cape government approves setting up of a cannabis college.* City Press. https://www.news24.com/citypress/business/eastern-cape-government-approves-setting-up-of-a-cannabis-college-20200207#:~:text=a%20cannabis%20college-,In%20a%20move%20to%20develop%2C%20commercialise%20and%20remove%20stigma%20associated,up%20of%20a%20cannabi

Misselhorn, A., & Hendriks, S. (2017). A systematic review of sub-national food insecurity research in South Africa: Missed opportunities for policy insights. *PLoS One*, *12*(8), 1–32. https://journals.plos.org/plosone/article?id=10.1371/journal.pone.0182399. doi:10.1371/journal.pone.0182399 PMID:28829787

Mputing, A. (2020, October 19). *President Ramaphosa Delivers Economic Recovery Plan to Joint Sitting of Parliament.* Parliament of the Republic of South Africa. https://www.parliament.gov.za/news/president-ramaphosa-delivers-economic-recovery-plan-joint-sitting-parliament

Mthuli, S. A., Singh, N., & Reddy, P. S. (2022). Political leadership for improved performance in South Africa: Towards Inspirational and Transformational Leaders. In C. Jones, P. Pillay, P. S. Reddy, & S. I. Zondi (Eds.), *Lessons from Political Leadership in Africa* (pp. 16–31). Cambridge Scholars Publishing.

Mukeredzi, T. (2021, May 13). *Africa Needs Cannabis to Spark Economic Growth.* Foreign Policy. https://foreignpolicy.com/2021/05/13/africa-cannabis-marijuana-legalization-economy-growth/

National Treasury. (2019). *Economic transformation, inclusive growth, and competitiveness: Towards an Economic Strategy for South Africa.* National Treasury. https://www.treasury.gov.za/comm_media/press/2019/towards%20an%20economic%20strategy%20for%20sa.pdf

Oduor, M. (2021, May 27). Morocco joins growing list of African countries to legalize cannabis. *Africa News.* https://www.africanews.com/2021/05/27/morocco-joins-growing-list-of-african-countries-to-legalize-cannabis//

Parker, K., DiMattia, A., Shaik, F., Ortega, J. C., & Whittle, R. (2019). Risk management within the cannabis industry: Building a framework for the cannabis industry. *Financial Markets, Institutions and Instruments*, *28*(1), 3–55. doi:10.1111/fmii.12104

Pichler, D. M. (2018). *Political Leadership in Urban Governance: a determinant factor for transformative innovation?* [Masters Thesis, Erasmus University, Rotterdam, the Netherlands].

Reuters. (2022, March 22). South Africa's unemployment rate hits new record high in Q4 2021. *Reuters.* https://www.reuters.com/world/africa/south-africas-unemployment-rate-hits-new-record-high-q4-2021-2022-03-29/

Rusenga, C., Klantschnig, G., Carrier, N., & Howell, S. (2022, May 30). Cannabis policy changes in Africa are welcome. But small producers are the losers. *The Conversation.* https://theconversation.com/cannabis-policy-changes-in-africa-are-welcome-but-small-producers-are-the-losers-179681

Sheefeni, J. P. (2022, June 2). South Africa's economy has taken some heavy body blows: can it recover? *The Conversation*. https://theconversation.com/south-africas-economy-has-taken-some-heavy-body-blows-can-it-recover-183165

Sorrentino, G. (2021). Introduction to emerging industrial applications of cannabis (cannabis sativa l.). *Rendiconti Lincei. Scienze Fisiche e Naturali*, *32*(2), 233–243. https://link.springer.com/article/10.1007/s12210-021-00979-1. doi:10.100712210-021-00979-1 PMID:33777341

South African Food Review. (2019, November 4). *Afriplex aligned with prized cannabis cultivation license*. South African Food Review. https://ukzn.idm.oclc.org/login?url=https://search.ebscohost.com/login.aspx?direct=true&db=bth&AN=135842391&site=ehost-live&scope=site

South African Government News Agency. (2020, November 18). Economic Recovery Plan: The key to unlocking SA's growth. *South African Government News Agency*. https://www.sanews.gov.za/south-africa/economic-recovery-plan-key-unlocking-sas-growth

South African Government News Agency. (2021, June 11). Progress made in implementing economic recovery plan. *South African Government News Agency*. https://www.sanews.gov.za/south-africa/progress-made-implementing-economic-recovery-plan

Statistics South Africa. (2021, November 30). The South African economy sheds more than half a million jobs in the 3rd quarter of 2021. *Statistics South Africa*. https://www.statssa.gov.za/?p=14922

Statistics South Africa. (2022, March 31). Measuring Food Security in South Africa: Applying the Food Insecurity Experience Scale. *Pretoria: Statistics South Africa*. https://www.statssa.gov.za/?p=15273

Stoddard, E. (2020, March 15). Moody's dispenses with SA's investment-grade fiction, the descent into junk is complete. *Daily Maverick*. https://www.dailymaverick.co.za/article/2020-03-28-moodys-dispenses-with-sas-investment-grade-fiction-the-descent-into-junk-is-complete/

Trading Economics. (2022). South Africa's unemployment rate. *Trading Economics*. https://tradingeconomics.com/south-africa/unemployment-rate

Vanek, M. (2022, February 10). *South Africa Looks to Cannabis, Hemp Industry to Create Jobs*. Bloomberg. https://ukzn.idm.oclc.org/login?url=https://search.ebscohost.com/login.aspx?direct=true&db=bth&AN=155177988&site=ehost-live&scope=site

Waetjen, T. (2022). South Africa's Century of Cannabis Politics, 1922–2022. *South African Historical Journal*, 1–5. doi:10.1080/02582473.2022.2128274

World Wildlife Fund. (2017). *Food Loss and Waste: Facts and Futures*. World Wildlife Fund.

Zikalala, S., Mutambara, E., & Mthuli, S. A. (2020). The Influence of Credit Rating Agencies on State Governance: The case of South Africa. *Gender & Behaviour*, *18*(4), 16732–16752.

Chapter 8
Empowering South African Rural Stakeholders to Participate in the Legal Cannabis Market:
A Sustainable Livelihoods Approach

Tshililo Ruddy Farisani
https://orcid.org/0000-0002-8486-6965
University of KwaZulu-Natal, South Africa

ABSTRACT

The chapter aimed to contribute to the understanding of the roles of the cannabis industry's stakeholders/transforming structures/institutions to empower and sustain local rural SMMEs in SA. The lesson learned from the literature reviewed in this chapter is that local stakeholders/institutions/transforming structures can either play a positive role or be a negative force in the empowerment and sustainability (using available resources/assets) of the cannabis-related SMMEs. It is therefore concluded that for South African cannabis stakeholders to effectively empower and sustain (using their resources) local rural SMMEs, they ought to embrace cannabis-related SMMEs' local values and assumptions alongside their regulations and laws. The contribution of this chapter is in the process of how key local rural-based institutions/stakeholders/structures can effectively use their resources/assets, rules, regulations, local values, and assumptions to transform each other positively in pursuit of cannabis-related SMME's empowerment and sustainability in SA.

INTRODUCTION

The past two decades have seen the greatest world shift in the cannabis market (Donnan et al., 2022; Burdette et al., 2018; and Carliner, 2017). Firth et al. (2022) affirm and point out that several countries in the world (especially the United States of America) have changed their cannabis-related laws and policies. They have changed their cannabis-related laws and policies from criminalizing cannabis to accepting cannabis production and sale with differing regulations. Firth et al. (2022) further assert that

DOI: 10.4018/978-1-6684-6346-8.ch008

"the approach is to increase cannabis outlet licensure and employment for low income and BIPOC communities" (p.1) i.e to encourage Black, Indigenous, and People of Colour (BIPOC) to start licensed small, medium, and micro enterprises (SMMEs) that will create jobs and grow the local economy. Despite South Africa's highest court (the Constitutional Court) legalizing, in 2018, the use and sale of cannabis (with conditions), South African SMMEs and related stakeholders remain a novice in the race to use legal cannabis sales to create jobs and sustain livelihoods for the marginalised (Page et al., 2020). Viviers et al. (2022) corroborate and encourage more research; stating, "to date, no data of this kind exist in South Africa specifically relating to cannabis-based medicinal, recreational, or complementary products" (p.1).

Despite the cannabis legalization in SA, most citizens still view cannabis as an illegal drug because of lack of access to reliable data (Mokwena, 2019). Thus, cannabis continued to be associated with substance abuse and not as a potential product within the SMME owners reach to make a legal livelihood for themselves. Riley et al. (2020) also corroborate Viviers et al. (2022) and add that there is a global lack of research and therefore understanding of how cannabis can be used for trading purposes i.e. how Small Medium and Micro Enterprises (SMMEs) can participate legally in growing the acceptable quality, process it, package it, and distribute it to customers for their medicinal, recreational or complementary needs. As Firth et al. (2022) point out, marginalised communities stand a good chance to benefit from the cannabis trade. In South Africa, most marginalised people live in rural areas (governed by Local Government) throughout the country. Rural communities in South Africa are, therefore, natural potential traders and targets for the legal cannabis trade, not only because they need financial capital the most, but because they have been doing it illegally for years. Smart (2017) asserts that growing cannabis in rural areas reduce the costs associated with cannabis sale and therefore direct benefit to rural SMMEs.

In this chapter, different aspects of the Sustainable Livelihoods Framework (see fig 1) and institutional theory (see table 1) are used to suggest a model. A model that local stakeholders can use to participate in empowering local rural potential cannabis traders. Sustainable Livelihoods Framework (SLF) is crucial in this chapter due to its ability to examine the roles of institutions in sustaining livelihoods in rural areas using SMMEs (Smyth and Vanclay, 2017). In addition, Institutional Theory will assist in understanding the policies, laws and culture of the relevant rural SMME stakeholder institutions (Scott, 2013). Policies, laws and culture of relevant rural SMME stakeholder institutions are crucial in understanding the processes involved in supporting potential rural SMMEs in the legal cannabis market.

Relevant South African key rural stakeholders to be discussed in this chapter are Local Government (LG), Tax Authority, Insurance, Banking Industry, Department of Police, Department of Health, Non-Governmental Organizations (NGOs) (this includes rural-based agricultural and religious organizations amongst other local organizations interested in the sustainability of local rural livelihoods) and the Traditional Authority. These are key institutions in assisting potential local rural cannabis SMME owners with critical assets (see Figures 1 and 2). Critical assets in the production and sale of legal cannabis products to relevant customers for their medicinal, recreational or complementary needs. What follows is the background on the cannabis industry and related stakeholders globally.

BACKGROUND OF GLOBAL CANNABIS LEGALIZATION

In this section, a review on the background of cannabis industry legalization globally and in SA is presented first. Then the review on challenges to the Cannabis industry due to different roles of relevant local stakeholders through the institutional theory lenses and the Sustainable Livelihood Approach.

Cannabis Industry Legalization

Aizpurua-Olaizola et al. (2014) point out that Cannabis products have been used by different communities in various locations for differing purposes for thousands of years. Duvall (2017) agree and trace the production and use of cannabis to the early 1500. Duvall (2017) asserts that cannabis production was introduced in Asia and shortly after to eastern African and then slowly into the entire continent ever since. Duvall (2017) further suggest that cannabis use and production was transferred to the western world as a result of slavery practice i.e enslaved Africans later introduced cannabis use and production on arrival as slaves in the western nations such as USA.

Pourseyed-Lazarjani et al. (2020) corroborate and state, "cannabis has been used for its therapeutic properties for thousands of years and it was introduced in western medicine in the nineteenth century until its prohibition in the US from the mid-1930s" (p.1). Gieringer (1999) affirms the prohibition in the United States of America (USA) and points to the U.S Marijuana Tax Act of 1937 and the U.S Substance Control Act of 1970. Such prohibition effectively forced cannabis-related businesses to operate illegally and halted open collaborations and innovation on the use of cannabis products.

However, Hartman (2021) argues that the reforms on the prohibition of cannabis started between 1960 and 1970 due to the medical needs of different communities in the USA. Cannabis products were increasingly being considered legitimate medicine to effectively fight anxiety and chronic pain. Nevertheless, Dufton (2017) points out that such favourable cannabis views did not last and that many states in the USA passed laws and policies that classified cannabis as an illegal drug or substance shortly after the 80s. Such wave of banning continued until the mid-90s when the state of California passed favourable laws for cannabis production and consumption. Kavousi et al. (2022) validates and posit that such back and forth in legalization and criminalization of cannabis production and consumption continued under different USA administrations in different states. Bridgeman and Abazia (2017) support Kavousi et al. (2022) and assert that the reforms started to intensify when other states became aware of the medical data associated with cannabis use for medicinal purposes. Such reforms between states were kickstarted by New York in 2017 when it effectively allowed opioid patients to replace opiates with cannabis. In addition to the increase of medical cannabis legalization in different states, cannabis for recreational purposes was also made legal in 2012 starting in Colorado and Washington state to 18 other different states (Leins & Alas, 2021). Such legalization allowed different businesses to scale their operations legally around the USA i.e. legalization allowed different local and rural people in different states to have access to land and other assets needed in the production and sale of cannabis for medical, recreational or complementary purposes (Valachovic et al., 2019).

However, in South Africa, the cannabis industry is still in its infancy because it only became legal after the 2018 constitutional court judgement (Riley et al., 2020). Riley et al. (2020) point out that before 2018, cannabis production and sale had been prohibited by law from as early as 1929 in SA. Mokwena (2019) affirms and states that "after a history of cannabis being outlawed for centuries, the Constitutional Court of South Africa ruled in favour of the legalisation of recreational cannabis in September 2018" (p.1). However, unlike in the USA, there is very little literature in SA concerning cannabis production, sale or the legalization process between 1929 and now i.e. there is a gap of knowledge concerning the stakeholders and processes that were followed by the cannabis producers and consumers in SA. Viviers et al. (2022) corroborate and encourage more research to inform SA future studies in cannabis production and consumption for medicinal, recreational, or complementary purposes.

Mokwena (2019) points out that despite cannabis legalization in SA following the constitutional court's judgement, many institutions still stand opposed to cannabis production and sale. According to Mokwena (2019), the reason behind the opposition is that "many South Africans, as well as government departments, view this ruling as a direct barrier to the goal of promoting health and well-being of the citizens " (p.1). The South African Department of Health is on record concerning its opposition citing the perceived health related disadvantages associated with cannabis use. Payan et al. (2021) corroborate the opposition to the production and sale of cannabis-related products by government and other non-governmental institutions or local stakeholders using any powers or leverage they have at their disposal. Lux (2019) affirms pointing out that those in government leadership positions have been known to use police power, tax rules or land sale or lease to effectively oppose the production and sale of cannabis-related products. Such use of authority by government institutions and its leadership impact SMMEs negatively and effectively slow cannabis industry growth to the point that it is unable to sustain itself and cannabis industry-related local livelihoods. Smyth and Vanclay (2017) affirm pointing out that institutions are vital in transforming or sustaining local livelihoods. According to Smyth and Vanclay (2017), this (transforming impact of institutions/structures) is consistent with the Sustainable Livelihoods Framework's (see figure 1) transforming structures and process aspect. Kavousi et al. (2022) corroborate and state that "A locality with legalized cannabis typically sees agricultural sector expansion, with growth in sales of farm supplies, generators, soil, and hardware, and investment in agricultural technology, research, and development" (p.147). The position of relevant local and national institutions with local presence is therefore crucial in transforming and sustaining (using their assets) livelihoods through SMMEs. What follows is the review of challenges that Institutions and related stakeholders impose on cannabis-related SMMEs and cannabis industry-related livelihoods.

Institutional Challenges to Cannabis Industry related SMMEs and Rural Livelihoods

As already argued above, the collective power of government institutions and other relevant stakeholders in a locality can, effectively, either positively transform or destroy the cannabis industry through SMMEs. This subsection provides background on how key institutions have effectively used their rules, regulations, values and assumptions to influence and deny cannabis-related SMMEs an opportunity to sustain themselves and local livelihoods. This approach is consistent with regulative and socio-cognitive elements of Institutional Theory (see table 1).

Table 1. Comparison between regulative, normative and cultural-cognitive elements of Institutional Theory

Element	Regulative	Normative	Cognitive
Legitimacy	Legal systems	Moral and ethical systems	Cultural systems
Central Rudiments	Policies, legislation, and rules	Work role, habits and norms	Values, beliefs and assumptions
System Transformation Drivers	Legal obligation	Moral obligation	Transformation values are internalized
System Transformation Sustainers	Fear and coercion	Duty and responsibility	Social identity and personal desire
Behavioural Reasoning	Have to	Ought to	Want to

Source: (Adopted from Palthe, 2014)

According to Palthe (2014), the Regulative element's focus is on institutional policies, rules and regulations while the socio-cognitive element focuses on institutional values, beliefs and assumptions. Institutions to be discussed concerning regulative and socio-cognitive elements in this subsection are: Local Government, Tax Authority, Insurance, Banking Industry, Department of Police, Department of Health, Non-Governmental Organizations and the Traditional Authority.

Local Government

Kavousi et al. (2022) highlight the importance of LG amongst other local rural stakeholders by pointing out that "this is where the rubber hits the road for stakeholders" (p.144). Kavousi et al. (2022) go on to clarify the importance of LG in a locality by elaborating on how the it may use its power to shape local livelihood strategies. They elaborated in this way: "local governments increasingly are using land use and police power authority, taxation, investment, and programming to shape how their residents engage with cannabis" (p.144).

Leins and Alas (2021) corroborate Kavousi et al. (2022) and point to a cannabis legalization wave that started locally in California and soon enveloped states and most parts of the USA. LG authorities are therefore always ensuring they listen to what their constituencies want and act accordingly. More often, such LG constituencies' thinking concerning cannabis legalization, production and sale may be changed repeatedly. Such changes often affect cannabis businesses and the livelihoods or jobs that the cannabis industry creates in that locality. Carnevale et al. (2017) affirm and point to instances where a local referendum was used to change local cannabis governing policies and rules. Such changes impact cannabis-related SMMEs directly. Mokwena (2019) also affirm citing that in South Africa "the legalisation of cannabis was driven by grassroots movements" (p.1) i.e. starting in local or rural areas and continuing to envelop the whole country. Grassroots movements change LG authorities through the ballot box and therefore the LG often listens to the loudest voices (Lux, 2019). The LG listens to the loudest voices because of their perceived power to keep them in their positions or take them out without fully considering the views of cannabis-related local rural SMMEs that sustain local livelihoods. Such turn of events often shadows the cannabis-related SMME values, believe or their assumptions on what is best for their businesses and local livelihoods. As already mentioned above, tax can be used by LG or the national government to impact the local cannabis industry negatively or positively.

Tax Authority

According to Bhattarai (2021), the USA legal cannabis industry has been growing steadily and in 2020 it was estimated at USD 19 Billion. All such traceable revenue was subjected to local taxes and boosted relevant local economies. Johns (2015) corroborates and cited the Colorado LG authorities who pointed out that their decision to legalize cannabis production and sale was motivated by their aim to increase local tax revenue and local economic development. Kavousi et al. (2022) affirm and assert that "these tax regimes can benefit localities" (p.146).

Riley et al. (2020) validate Kavousi et al. (2022) and elaborate on how South African local economies may gain from legalized cannabis production and sale. Riley et al. (2020) point out that like in other states where cannabis has been legalized, the legalized cannabis industry in SA will also increase the amount that local rural tax authorities collect but also directly impact consumers positively. Riley et al. (2020)

argue that consumers benefit because "the price of cannabis is likely to decrease since legalization would result in eliminating the risk associated with buying and selling cannabis" (p.124).

Mallinson et al. (2020) pointed out that cannabis industry-related SMMEs still face much difficulty and exclusion from local and national tax authorities. Mallinson et al. (2020) argue that such difficulty remains even in many states that legalized cannabis a long time ago. Mallinson et al. (2020) point to the lack of federal bankruptcy protections and federal tax incentives in the USA. Kavousi et al. (2022) affirm and point to cases where local authorities use tax regulations to communicate their disapproval and to destabilize the cannabis industry with unreasonable taxes to local cannabis-related SMMEs. When tax regulations are used by local authorities to limit or destroy the cannabis industry and related SMMEs it does not go unnoticed by business insurers.

Insurance Industry

Wright (2020) argues that the behaviour of local government and authorities concerning the local cannabis industry influence how they value cannabis-related SMMEs. Polson & Petersen-Rockney (2019) corroborates and add pointing out that negative laws toward the local cannabis industry would lead to insurance considering their business interest also i.e. whether it would bring them value to avail insurance to industry bound to fail due to lack of key stakeholders' support within the locality. Karch (2021) affirms and asserts that the support of key stakeholders such as local government and tax authorities is needed to ensure that insurers do not categorize cannabis-related SMMEs as an investment risk. Mallinson et al. (2020) also agree with Karch (2021) and add that such a lack of support from key stakeholders not only impacts cannabis-related SMMEs but the local community who need local jobs. Such lack of support also extends into the banking industry.

Banking Industry

According to Mallinson et al. (2020), there is still a high percentage (more than 99%) of USA banks that still refuse to do business with cannabis-related producers and operators. Martiroysan (2017) corroborates and points out that the banks' behaviour is caused by the fact that despite many states legalizing cannabis production and sale, federal laws have not. Most banks would rather be safe on the federal law requirements rather than obey state laws and risk their operations in other states that have not legalized cannabis production and sale. Plakias et al. (2021) validate and add that such federal laws and the banking industry cause direct financial challenges. Cause direct financial challenges to the cannabis industry, the local economy and therefore the sustainability of local livelihoods. The sustainability of local livelihoods is directly impacted because the local economy cannot create jobs if it is experiencing direct financial shortfalls.

Schulz (2019) also supports Plakias et al. (2021) pointing out that the legal cannabis industry in states like Washington, Colorado and California sustained 12 full-time jobs for every 1 million dollars they received in revenue. Fersko (2018) argue that such sustainability of livelihoods by the cannabis industry in the states of Washington, Colorado and California could not have been achieved without the full support of banks and business licensing authorities. Mallinson et al. (2020) affirm, pointing out that without the support of local banks and business licensing authorities, the cannabis industry becomes a cash-based industry without any real prospect of growth or sustainability of local jobs. Operating without a license invite local and federal police to such cannabis industry operations.

Department of Police

Fersko (2018) point out that even in states (inside the USA) that legalize cannabis, local police are helpless when federal police decide to enforce federal laws that criminalize cannabis operations. Payan et al. (2021) corroborate and add that it is not only the federal police but also the local police that cannabis industry-related SMMEs around the globe had to contend with. Payan et al. (2021) point out that LG authorities against the cannabis industry have also used police to weaken or destroy the local cannabis industry operations. Martiroysan (2017) affirm and asserts that such fear of local or federal police departments has forced many cannabis-related SMMEs into hiding and to operate illegally. Such illegal operations are often unregulated and may sell cannabis that has not gone through good manufacturing practice and thereby inviting the wrath of the department of health to their operations.

Department of Health (DoH)

Viviers et al. (2022) elaborated on the need for safety measures to protect medical cannabis consumers. Viviers et al. (2022) further state that such safety measures are only achieved "through good manufacturing practice (GMP) and quality control of the final products" (p.1). Romano and Hazekamp (2013) corroborate, citing the rising popularity of medical cannabis amongst self-medicating patients. Pourseyed-Lazarjani et al. (2020) affirm and add that "because consumers have limited means to analyse the chemical composition of the cannabis products, consumers may be inadvertently purchasing products with undesired properties given that different cannabinoids produce different effects" (p.2).

Nevertheless, Viviers et al. (2021) point out that legalized cannabis products are safe, and the efficacy and measures are regulated by several organizations including World Health Organizations (WHO) and pharmaceutical industries. Therefore, without the support of DoH, licensing authorities and other key stakeholders mentioned above, the cannabis industry becomes a danger to its consumers due to unregulated final products sold to patients. Local NGOs (from agricultural and other related industries) are therefore key in ensuring that the cannabis industry produces acceptable quality (according to DoH guidelines) at affordable prices for both medicinal, recreational or complementary use in the formal and informal markets that are yet to be licensed.

Non-Governmental Organizations (NGOs)

As already quoted above, Mokwena (2019) attributed the successful legalization of cannabis in SA and other countries around the globe to grassroots movements. Such movements include partnerships between different NGOs that have some issues or concerns that are common. While such NGOs might not necessarily agree on all matters, they must act together to achieve common goals. As already discussed above, the literature on cannabis point to different views amongst key stakeholders and communities concerning the legalization, production and sale of cannabis for medical, recreational or complementary purposes.

Therefore, NGOs fighting drug abuse in their communities would naturally fight the legalization of cannabis in all its forms unless educated otherwise (Johns, 2015; and Hurd et al., 2014). LaChance (2019) corroborates pointing out that agricultural NGOs might be concerned about water use of the new crops that have never been produced in the area and how that might affect their existing crops or those of their stakeholders. Other religious NGOs or groups might view cannabis products or their producers in a negative light (Polson & Peterson-Rockney, 2019). On the other hand, NGOs fighting for sustainable livelihoods will likely welcome any new investments and new business establishments that would create more jobs (Bartlett, 2021; Hodgson, 2021; Rosario, 2021; and Gurewitz, 2019). Again, knowledgeable tourism promoting NGOs would naturally want cannabis production in their areas to attract more tourism that comes with new cannabis production sites (Crowder, 2020). Therefore, all these competing voices in the form of NGOs need proper education and leadership. Proper education on how all NGOs can coexist in harmony. Such coexistence in harmony needs leadership that can rise above local politics. Thus, locally respected leadership is needed. Farisani (2022) point out that in rural areas, such leadership seen to be above politics would be in the form of rural Traditional Authority.

Rural Traditional Authority

Farisani (2022) argues that Rural Traditional Authority is not only respected but has been very successful in resolving disputes in South African rural areas. Rural Traditional Authority leaders are elders of the local community and are respected by all stakeholders. Local stakeholders respect such leadership not only because of the shared beliefs and assumptions but because they bring value (Smyth and Vanclay, 2017). Such value come in different assets to different groups. Different assets such as social, financial, human, natural and physical. That is primarily because all stakeholders mentioned above know they need to work with Traditional Authority to effectively advertise and distribute their services or products in rural areas. Examples of assets that stakeholders mentioned in this article need from rural areas include but are not limited to rural land (natural resource/asset) and congregated communities called by traditional leaders (social resource/asset) and local rural knowledge (human capital) about the community. Thus, traditional authorities are crucial in creating a harmony that will enable all stakeholders to come together in rural areas to learn about the benefits of cannabis production and sale. Benefits that will avail assets to enrich all and not just a few amongst the stakeholders. Such an approach (to benefit all) is consistent with how Palthe (2014) present Institutional Theory's cultural Cognitive element (see table 1). The next section reviews the sustainable livelihood framework and approach to sustaining livelihoods through cannabis-related SMMEs as strategies.

Sustainable Livelihood Framework and Approach to sustaining local livelihoods

Smyth and Vanclay (2017) assert that the sustainable Livelihood Framework (see figure 1) offers the best approach to guiding institutions to sustain local rural livelihoods. In elaborating further, Smyth and Vanclay (2017) state "in its simplest form, the framework views people as operating in a context of vulnerability. Within this context, they have access to certain assets or poverty-reducing factors. These gain their meaning and value through the prevailing social, institutional and organizational environment. This environment also influences the livelihood strategies – ways of combining and using assets – that are open to people in pursuit of beneficial livelihood outcomes that meet their livelihood objectives" (p.68). Thus, institutions that are for or against local livelihood strategies (including SMMEs) have the power to avail or block assets that are crucial in sustaining local livelihoods. Nair (2012) corroborates and points out that the environment in which sustainable livelihoods thrive is dependent on all local stakeholders/institutions. Thus, local stakeholders and institutional processes are crucial in availing assets for the sustainability of local rural livelihoods. What follows is the review of the assets that cannabis-related local rural SMMEs avail and need in line with sustainable livelihoods Framework's livelihood asset base and transforming structures and processes to sustain local rural livelihoods (see figure 1 below).

Figure 1. The sustainable livelihoods framework.

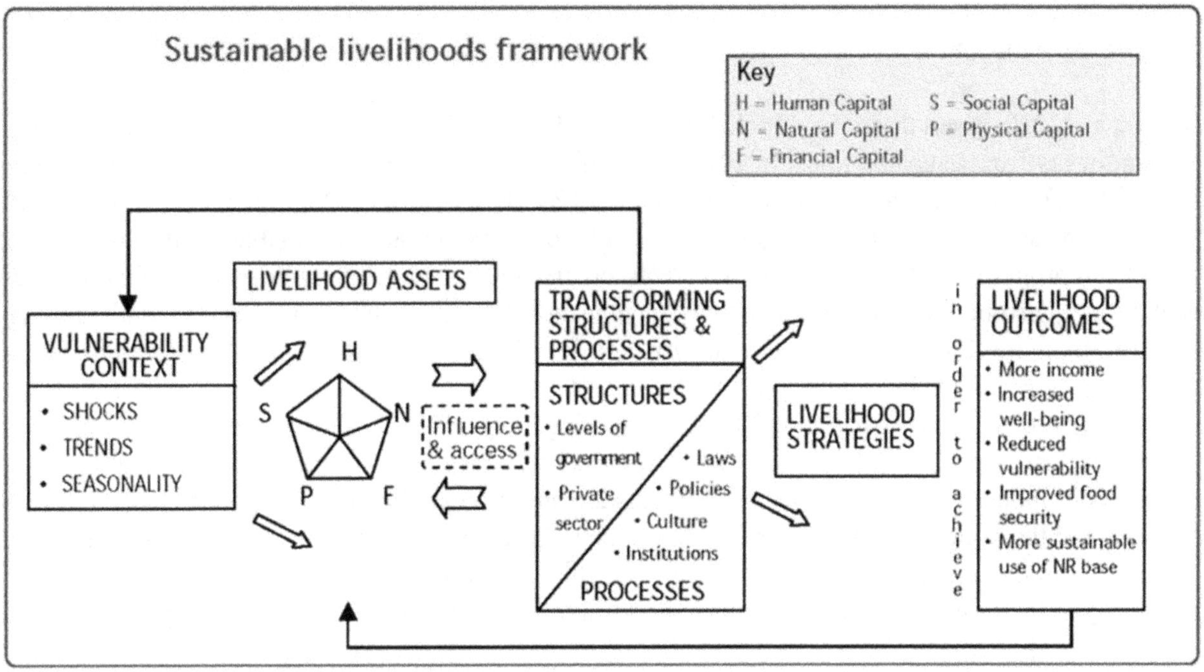

Human Assets

According to Schulz (2019) and Murphy (2019); the literature is inundated with statistics showing the human assets that cannabis-related SMMEs can be involved in rural areas. Rural areas often face the challenge of retaining skilled labourers as skilled labourers emigrate to urban areas. Cannabis production and sale from rural areas is therefore crucial to creating and sustaining livelihoods in rural areas. Schulz (2019) validates and asserts that cannabis-related SMMEs can create between 121 000 and 150 000 new sustainable rural jobs in one country in a year. Murphy (2019) put his estimation to about 211 000 sustainable jobs. Nobile (2020) corroborates citing the 68% growth of cannabis-related SMMEs in the USA between 2018 and 2019.While such data is not available in South Africa due to the fact that cannabis trade has just been legalized, the impact to job creation and livelihoods may be reasonably expected to be similar to those in rural areas in the USA. Ganjier (2021) affirm such expectation highlighting the growing demand for formal education and certificates needed to work in the rural legal cannabis industry in the USA.

Moreover, different scholars have provided evidence that not only do cannabis-related SMMEs create sustainable jobs but that they pay well above average too (Wilson et al., 2019; Valachovic et al., 2019). Farisani (2022) has pointed out that because unemployment is rife in rural areas, sustainable rural jobs are crucial not only for rural dwellers and prospective employers but for the overall rural local economies too.

Wilson et al. (2019) affirm and recommend that cannabis-related SMMEs should source their employees locally to boost local economies. Thus, LG and other local institutions need to work together to grow the local cannabis industry to create much-needed jobs and grow the local rural economy. A thriving local economy with low unemployment avails many financial assets to other local crucial programmes and projects for the benefit of all (Scarboro & Bishop-Henchman, 2016).

Financial Assets

Riley et al. (2020) assert that "after legalizing cannabis in 2014, Colorado started collecting a substantial amount of tax from cannabis sales: in 2015, $113 million was collected in retail cannabis tax revenue – twice the amount collected from alcohol taxes" (p.124). Riley et al. (2020) argue that such a tax collection increase can assist the local government in its efforts to create sustainable local jobs and fund other local programmes that would not have been otherwise funded due to budget constraints. Kavousi et al. (2022) corroborate and assert that "the cannabis industry's economic impact is large and growing" (p.146). Bhattarai (2021) affirms and points to the USD 21 Billion that the legal cannabis industry was able to inject into the USA economy in 2020 alone.

Murphy (2019) echoes Bhattarai (2021) highlighting the growth trajectory of the cannabis industry. The growth trajectory exploded in just two years to almost 100% growth in other states that legalized the cannabis industry earlier such as Colorado. As already discussed above, Institutions like the tax authorities and the police department's processes impact the growth of the cannabis industry. The impact by such institutions may be positive or negative on the growth of the cannabis industry and ultimately the ability of the cannabis-related SMMEs to contribute to the local financial assets and physical assets.

Physical Assets

Polson and Peterson-Rockney (2019) point out that in regions where the cannabis industry is legalized, there has been an expansion in agricultural equipment manufacturing and other physical assets. Meehan et al. (2020) corroborate and assert that there is a direct relationship between the Colorado cannabis legalization process and the increase in the physical assets in the tourism and hospitality industries in Colorado state between 2011-2015. Meehan et al. (2020) further elaborate that such an increase and upgrade in the physical assets was made possible by the increase in cannabis tourism-related activities and generated USD 23 million in revenue between 2011-2015. Such revenue makes it possible for hotel owners to either increase their properties or renovate existing structures while LG can use local taxes from such revenues to upgrade roads and other public physical assets.

Social Assets

Keul and Eisenhauer (2019) posit that the legalized cannabis industry-related SMMEs have social roles to play (Social roles in entertainment and community building). Such social roles are to act as social catalysts in regions and states that have legalized cannabis production and sale. Butsic et al. (2017) corroborate, citing the ability of the cannabis industry to add to a region's social assets where it has proven to create prestigious markets for local SMMEs. Owens (2019) points out that prestigious markets are created in areas where cannabis production and sale are legalized due to the related trades in the manufacturing of farm supplies, hardware and investment in agricultural technologies. Kavousi et al. (2022)

affirm pointing out that when new workers in such production of farm supplies, hardware and investment in agricultural technologies arrive, they will "need places to shop, eat, and recreate" (p.148).

Polson and Peterson-Rockney (2019) point out that local stakeholders and key institutions such as religious organizations will need to lead in the integration of such new workers in the community. Polson and Peterson-Rockney (2019) elaborate further to explain that anti-cannabis stigma may cause the locals to see cannabis workers as dirty or unholy and therefore side-line them on key social platforms.

Traditional Authorities are equally important (in fighting anti-cannabis stigma) in the South African context due to their influence on rural communities. Farisani (2022) highlight and point out why traditional authorities have tremendous social influence in rural areas. Farisani (2022) point out that such social influence is sustained and has to do with the legal power (guaranteed in the SA constitution) and the traditional laws. SA traditional authorities are the real owners (e.g. in rural KwaZulu-Natal) of public rural natural assets such as land and the communities need special permission from the traditional authorities to use land.

Natural Assets

A close examination of the Sustainable Livelihoods Framework (see figure 1) reveals that Natural assets are key to livelihood strategies that rural people choose. Those who cultivate or own cannabis-related SMMEs need natural assets such as water and land to successfully carry out their trade. As already mentioned, and cited, Kavousi et al. (2022) and Farisani (2022) point to the influence and legal power that LG and Traditional Authorities have in shaping cannabis-related SMMEs use of natural assets. Without water and land, the cannabis industry cannot exist and therefore cooperation between relevant stakeholders is key. It is key in the cannabis production and sustainability of local livelihoods through SMMEs as strategies.

EMPOWERING SOUTH AFRICAN RURAL STAKEHOLDERS TO PARTICIPATE IN THE LEGAL CANNABIS MARKET

The process of empowering SA stakeholders in the cannabis industry to participate in the production and sale of legal cannabis products is important. It is important because key stakeholders (i.e. transforming structures. See figure 1 and 2) have the authority and assets to assist or to hinder the cannabis industry's potential to sustain local livelihoods. Thus, such key stakeholders need to be guided on the proper use of authority and assets to empower local SMMEs and in so doing sustain livelihoods. This subsection borrows from different aspects of Institutional Theory and Sustainable Livelihoods Framework and Approach to guide relevant stakeholders. To guide relevant stakeholders on how to use their authority and assets to support each other in the production and sale of cannabis products i.e. how key SA rural-based institutions can effectively use their rules, regulations, values and assumptions to transform each other positively in pursuit of cannabis industry sustainability. LG is the first key stakeholder/institution to be discussed.

Local Government in South Africa

As already mentioned above, Kavousi et al. (2022) elaborated in detail on the importance of LG in a region by elaborating on how the local government may use its power to shape local livelihood strategies. Kavousi et al. (2022) specifically point out that "local governments increasingly are using land use and police power authority, taxation, investment, and programming to shape how their residents engage with cannabis" (p.144). From the Sustainable Livelihood Framework's (SLF) perspective, it can be said that Local Governments are drawing from both the livelihood resource/asset base (e.g. land) and the transforming structures and processes (e.g. police or taxation structures) of the SLF to dictate livelihood outcomes (see figure 2).

Therefore, SA LG (also known as local municipalities) may also learn from such an approach (SLF) and apply it to lead local stakeholders. To lead local stakeholders in empowering and sustaining the cannabis industry rather than destroying it. LG have the authority to use the human assets employed in the local offices of every department (e.g. police and taxation structures) in the country to teach and explain the benefits of the cannabis industry to the local population. Similarly, they may use their power to distribute water to ensure that there is enough water to avoid conflicts (as referred above concerning LaChance, 2019's assertion) between agricultural groups that feel threatened by the new cannabis growers/cultivators in the region.

Thus, LG as a transforming structure has the authority and assets to influence the local stakeholders. To influence the local stakeholders to value local cannabis-related SMMEs and in so doing sustain local livelihoods. Meehan et al., (2020) corroborate pointing to the increased value to all local stakeholders due to the cannabis industry's impact on local physical assets in the tourism and hospitality industries. Such an approach is not only in line with SLA but consistent with both Institutional Theory's cultural cognitive element. It is in line with SLA due to the assets/asset aspect (see fig 1 and 2) and consistent with Institutional Theory's cultural cognitive element in changing behavioural reasoning. Changing behavioural reasoning of all local stakeholders from *having to wanting to* coexist with the cannabis-related SMMEs (see table 1).

Tax Authority (known as South African Revenue Services)

Johns (2015) points out that the Colorado LG authorities' decision to legalize cannabis production and sale was motivated by their aim to increase local tax revenue and local livelihoods. Riley et al. (2020) corroborate and assert that legalized cannabis industry in SA has the potential to increase the amount that local rural tax authorities collect and in so doing sustain local livelihoods. Sustain local livelihoods through job creation in critical new projects to rebuild or upgrade local physical assets that might have been damaged as a result of seasonal floods (see figure 2 for the flow of financial assets into transforming structures and vulnerability context).

As Mallinson et al. (2020) point out, tax authorities are often slow to transform their rules and regulations to enable cannabis-related SMMEs to trade legally. South African Revenue Services (SARS) will therefore do well to ensure that the transformation of its laws to accommodate cannabis-related SMMEs are effected immediately i.e. the regulations and laws are changed to ensure cannabis-related SMMEs are protected from bankruptcy protections and tax incentives just like any other SMMEs in SA. Such an approach is consistent with SLF/SLA and Institutional Theory's regulative element i.e. the SARS new approach would avail financial assets to cannabis-related SMMEs and ensure that they are protected by the laws of the land. Such protection also impacts the cannabis-related SMME relationship with the insurance industry.

Insurance Industry in South Africa

As Karch's (2021) viewpoint has already been elaborated upon above, the support of key stakeholders such as local government and tax authorities is needed to ensure that insurers do not categorize cannabis-related SMMEs as investment risk. Like any other business, SA cannabis-related SMMEs need insurance to protect them and ensure they can survive unforeseen circumstances financially. Thus, a cordial relationship between SA insurance industries (as a transforming structure) and SA legal cannabis-related SMMEs is in the best interest of the local economies and local livelihood outcomes (see figure 2). Such a relationship also extends into the banking industry. It extends into the banking industry because both the cannabis industry's assets and the assets of the workers in such industries will need to be legally protected.

The Banking Industry in South Africa

According to Fersko (2018), the local banks' good relations were responsible for the sustainability of rural livelihoods through the cannabis industry in the states of Washington, Colorado and California. Similarly, SA banks will need to support the local cannabis industry the same way they support other SMMEs in the region to allow the industry to sustain local livelihoods. Allowing cannabis-related SMMEs and their employees to open local businesses and personal accounts without hiding their affiliations with the cannabis industry would be a step in the right direction. Such an approach avails financial assets (especially loans during vulnerability contexts such as the current Ukraine conflict or Covid 19 related economic challenges), sustains the cannabis industry and brings local value to both the legal cannabis-related SMMEs and their employees (see figure 2). Schulz (2019) and Plakias et al. (2021) corroborate citing the flow of good relations between the banking industry and local SMMEs into the local revenue collection. Mallinson et al. (2020) affirm pointing out that such good relations flow into the local relationships between the legal cannabis industry and the local police.

Department of police in South Africa

The South African Police Service (SAPS) and other local municipality police are responsible for enforcing local laws i.e. they are responsible for ensuring only legally recognized businesses with relevant licences operate throughout SA. Thus, there is naturally a good relationship between the police and the cannabis-related SMMEs if they obey SARS and the banking industry regulations. The good relationship is sustained because the police would not treat the legal cannabis-related SMMEs in the same way they treat illegal cannabis operators or illegal drug dealers (Martiroysan, 2017). Such illegal businesses or dealers can easily do money laundering and disobey other financial regulations because they are mostly cash-based and do not pay their taxes (Mallinson et al.,2020).

Therefore, SAPS and the local metropolitan police ought to support and encourage the legal cannabis industry to register their businesses without any fear of arrest because they benefit from such dispensation i.e. they will be able to use their human assets and financial assets to fight other serious crimes instead of regulating the cannabis industry's subjection to licensing, banking and SARS regulations (see figure 2 for the interdependent relationship between transforming structures and resource/assets). Such effort from the local police would also benefit the local cannabis consumers and the DoH efforts to ensure safety measures and controls are observed by the legal cannabis traders.

Department of Health in South Africa

As already stated above, Viviers et al. (2022) advocated for safety measures to protect medical cannabis consumers in SA. Viviers et al. (2022) further state that such safety measures are only achieved "through Good Manufacturing Practice (GMP) and quality control of the final products" (p.1). South African DoH-related stakeholders/institutions such as pharmacies and other retailers of medical cannabis will need to participate in the empowerment of cannabis-related SMMEs. They will need to participate in the empowerment of cannabis-related SMMEs to ensure adherence to good manufacturing practices and quality control at every stage of cannabis production and sale. Adherence to good manufacturing practice and quality control at every stage of cannabis production and sale by related SMMEs is crucial for their sustainability. Relevant local NGOs will also be needed to empower the cannabis-related SMMEs with their human (skills), physical (buildings or machinery) and social assets (weekly or monthly meetings with their stakeholders) in their quest to grow their businesses and sustain local livelihoods.

Non-Governmental Organizations in South Africa

Like the cannabis-related SMMEs, the South African local-based NGOs advocating for sustainable local livelihoods are equally interested in local economic development and job creation (Farisani 2022, Bartlett, 2021; Hodgson, 2021; Rosario, 2021; and Gurewitz, 2019). Therefore, there is a need for relevant local NGOs to play their part in resolving disputes. Resolving disputes between local SMMEs, agricultural groups and other institutions that view new legal local cannabis-related SMMEs in a negative light (LaChance, 2019). Such local NGOs may assist by using their social assets (weekly or monthly meetings with their stakeholders) with the locals to teach them the benefits of the legalized cannabis industry i.e. benefits of the local legalized cannabis industry on their sustainable livelihood outcomes (see figures 1 and 2). Owens (2019) corroborates pointing to tangible benefits of legalized cannabis industry such as the creation of local prestigious markets in the manufacturing of farm supplies, hardware and investment in agricultural technologies. However, NGOs will also need the support of the local Traditional Authority in teaching the locals about the benefits of cannabis-related production and sale in the region.

Traditional Authorities in South Africa

Farisani (2022) point out that Local Traditional Authorities' role in empowering relevant stakeholders in empowering rural SMMEs and relevant stakeholders goes beyond availing assets. Go beyond availing natural (rural land) and social assets (platform in the village traditional meetings) into assisting with human assets (i.e. their unique approach to resolving local rural disputes between stakeholders/institutions). Traditional Authorities are the only institution that can be trusted by the locals if key government institutions like the LG fail to convince the rural communities that the cannabis industry is good for their rural economy and job creation. Traditional Authorities are well positioned to convince the locals that new cannabis-related SMMEs resonate with local values and their local assumptions about sustainable rural livelihoods. Smyth and Vanclay (2017) affirm and point out that local stakeholders respect such leadership not only because of the shared beliefs and assumptions but because they bring value to all of them. Such respect and trust are key in the empowering process (through transforming structures/institutions) needed in the SLA to achieve desired livelihood strategy outcomes. Thus, Traditional Authorities are key transforming structures/institutions in the empowering of local rural stakeholders to participate in sustaining rural cannabis-related SMMEs and livelihoods (see figure 2 below).

Figure 2. A proposed model (adapted from SLF) for empowering rural stakeholders to sustain livelihoods through Cannabis related SMMEs.

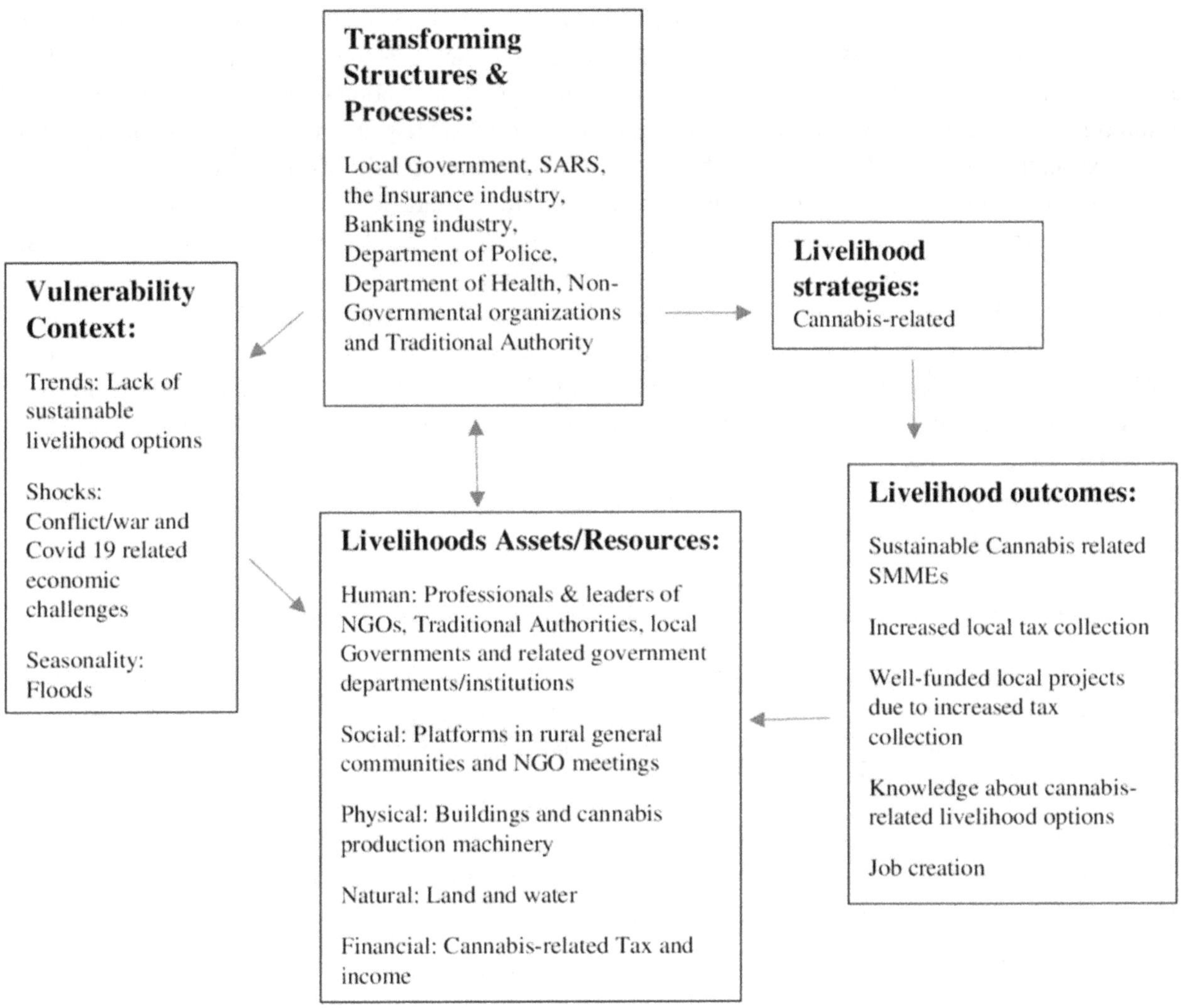

CONCLUSION

This chapter reviewed the cannabis industry-related literature with the aim to contribute to the understanding of the roles of the cannabis industry's stakeholders in SA. The roles that local stakeholders play and how they use their assets to either derail or empower the local rural cannabis-related SMMEs. To achieve the aim of the study; the background on the cannabis industry legalization in SA and internationally was reviewed first. Secondly, the challenges due to roles played by stakeholders were reviewed through the lenses of the Institutional Theory (regulative and socio-cultural cognitive elements, see table 1) and the Sustainable Livelihoods Framework (assets and transforming structures and processes, see figure 1). And lastly, suggestions were discussed based on the literature review on how to guide SA relevant stakeholders to participate in empowering cannabis-related SMMEs. To participate in the empowering and sustaining of cannabis-related SMMEs by learning from different aspects of Institutional Theory and Sustainable Livelihoods Framework and Approach.

The lessons learned from the literature reviewed in this chapter is that local stakeholders can either play a positive role or be a negative force in the empowerment and sustainability (using available assets) of the cannabis-related SMMEs i.e. Such local stakeholders achieve their intentions (using available assets, see figures 1 and 2 for assets/asset base) through regulations and laws or choose local values and assumptions (see table 1) to empower and sustain local rural SMMEs. It is therefore concluded that for South African cannabis stakeholders to effectively empower and sustain (using their assets) local rural SMMEs, they ought to embrace local values and assumptions alongside their regulations and laws.

The contribution of this chapter is in the process (see figure 2) of how key SA local rural-based stakeholders can effectively use their assets, rules, regulations, local values and assumptions to transform each other positively in pursuit of cannabis-related SMMEs' empowerment and sustainability in SA.

The limitation in this chapter is born out of the limited research done concerning cannabis-related SMMEs in South Africa and globally. Hence this chapter's contribution to this field. There is a need for future research on the roles of individual rural local leaders in the planning, implementation, monitoring and evaluation of the regulations and laws that increase the local value of cannabis-related products produced by rural SMMEs.

REFERENCES

Aizpurua-Olaizola, O., Omar, J., Navarro, P., Olivares, M., Etxebarria, N., & Usobiaga, A. (2014). Identification and quantification of cannabinoids in Cannabis sativa L. plants by high-performance liquid chromatography-mass spectrometry. *Analytical and Bioanalytical Chemistry*, *406*(29), 7549–7560. doi:10.100700216-014-8177-x PMID:25338935

Bartlett, J. (2021,May 11). Smokescreen. *The Boston Business Journal*. https://www.bizjournals.com/boston/ news/2021/05/11/smokescreen-a-lack-of-transparency-in-the-money-c.html

Bhattarai, A. (2021, July 24). Greener pastures: Marijuana jobs are becoming a refuge for retail and restaurant workers. *Washington Post*. https://www.washingtonpost.com/business/2021/07/24/marijuana-dispensaries-jobs/

Bridgeman, M. B., & Abazia, D. T. (2017). Medicinal cannabis: History, pharmacology, and implications for the acute care setting. *P&T*, *42*(3), 180. PMID:28250701

Burdette, A. M., Webb, N. S., Hill, T. D., Haynes, S. H., & Ford, J. A. (2018). Religious involvement and marijuana use for medical and recreational purposes. *Journal of drug issues*, *48*(3), 421-434. https:// doi/pdf/ doi:10.1177/0022042618770393

Butsic, V., Schwab, B., Baumann, M., & Brenner, J. C. (2017). Inside the Emerald Triangle: Modelling the placement and size of cannabis production in Humboldt County, CA USA. *Ecological Economics, 142*, 70–80. doi:10.1016/j.ecolecon.2017.06.013

Carliner, H., Mauro, P. M., Brown, Q. L., Shmulewitz, D., Rahim-Juwel, R., Sarvet, A. L., & Hasin, D. S. (2017). The widening gender gap in marijuana use prevalence in the US during a period of economic change, 2002–2014. *Drug and Alcohol Dependence, 170*, 51–58. doi:10.1016/j.drugalcdep.2016.10.042 PMID:27875801

Carnevale, J. T., Kagan, R., Murphy, P. J., & Esrick, J. (2017). A practical framework for regulating for-profit recreational marijuana in US states: Lessons from Colorado and Washington. *The International Journal on Drug Policy, 42*, 71–85. doi:10.1016/j.drugpo.2017.03.001 PMID:28366598

Crowder, M. (2020, June 22). New appellations would celebrate individual terroir of cannabis strains. *San Francisco Chronicle*. https://www.sfchronicle.com/bayarea/article/New-appellations -would-celebrate-individual-15587030.php

Department For International Development. (1999). *Sustainable livelihoods guidance sheets 1-2*. DFID.

Donnan, J., Shogan, O., Bishop, L., Swab, M., & Najafizada, M. (2022). Characteristics that influence purchase choice for cannabis products: a systematic review. *Journal of cannabis research, 4*(1), 1-27. https:// doi:10.1186/s42238-022-00117-0

Dufton, E. (2017). *Grassroots*. Basic Books.

Duvall, C. S. (2017). Cannabis and tobacco in precolonial and colonial Africa. In Oxford Research Encyclopedia of African History. doi:10.1093/acrefore/9780190277734.013.44

Farisani, T. R. (2022). The impact of social and institutional networks in sustaining South African rural small, medium and micro enterprises during the crisis. *Acta Commercii, 22*(1), a1007. doi:10.4102/ac.v22i1.1007

Fersko, J. (2018, May). The business of marijuana. *ACREL News & Notes*. https://cdn.ymaws.com/acrel.site-ym. com/resource/resmgr/news_and_notes/May/2018-05_Fersko_-_Cannabis_Ar.pdf

Firth, C. L., Warren, K. M., Perez, L., Kilmer, B., Shih, R. A., Tucker, J. S., D'Amico, E. J., & Pedersen, E. R. (2022). Licensed and unlicensed cannabis outlets in Los Angeles County: The potential implications of location for social equity. *Journal of Cannabis Research, 4*(1), 1–7. doi:10.118642238-022-00120-5 PMID:35410443

Ganjier. (2021). Become a master of cannabis service: Cannabis sommelier certification. *Ganjier*. https://www.ganjier.com/ certified-ganjier-cannabis/

Gieringer, D. (1999). The forgotten origins of cannabis prohibition in California. *Contemporary Drug Problems, 26*(2), 237–288. doi:10.1177/009145099902600204

Gurewitz, H., Petrillo, M. A., Scott, T., McDonald, B., Weir, A., & Pickman, H. (2019). *Mendocino county 2018–2019 economic assessment*. EDFC.

Hartman, M. (2021). Cannabis overview. *National Conference of State Legislators*. https://www.ncsl.org/research/ civil-and-criminal-justice/marijuana-overview.aspx

Hodgson, M. (2021, April 16). Santa Barbara County supervisors spend cannabis tax funds on expansion requests. *Lompoc Record*. https://lompocrecord.com/news/local/govt-and-politics/santa-barbara-county-supervisors-spend-cannabis-tax-funds-on-expan sion-requests/article_42d8c7a1-110f-5479-86f7-391e0 a5cbd39.html

Hurd, Y. L., Michaelides, M., Miller, M. L., & Jutras-Aswad, D. (2014). Trajectory of adolescent cannabis use on addiction vulnerability. *Neuropharmacology*, *76*, 416–424. doi:10.1016/j.neuropharm.2013.07.028 PMID:23954491

Johns, T. (2015). Managing a policy experiment: Adopting and implementing recreational marijuana policies in Colorado. *State & Local Government Review*, *47*(3), 193–204. doi:10.1177/0160323X15612149

Karch, A. (2021). Filling a vacuum: Subnational governance amid national government inaction. *State & Local Government Review*, *52*(4), 232–240. doi:10.1177/0160323X21999585

Kavousi, P., Giamo, T., Arnold, G., Alliende, M., Huynh, E., Lea, J., Lucine, R., Tillett Miller, A., Webre, A., Yee, A., Champagne-Zamora, A., & Taylor, K. (2022). What do we know about opportunities and challenges for localities from Cannabis legalization? *The Review of Policy Research*, *39*(2), 143–169. doi:10.1111/ropr.12460

Keul, A., & Eisenhauer, B. (2019). Making the high country: Cannabistourism in Colorado, USA. *Annals of Leisure Research*, *22*(2), 140–160. doi:10.1080/11745398.2018.1435291

LaChance, J. (2019). We can't just be a county that supports inebriants: Voices of the non-cannabis agricultural community. *California Agriculture*, *73*(3), 169–176. doi:10.3733/ca.2019a0016

Leins, C., & Alas, H. (2021, June 30). States where recreational marijuana is legal. *U. S. News and World Report*. https://www.usnews.com/news/best-states/slideshows/where-is-pot-legal

Long, A. (2020, November 17). Colorado's summer cannabis sales thrive despite the collapse of the state's tourism industry. *MJBizDaily*. https://Mjbizdaily.Com/Colorado-Summer-Cannabis-Sales-Thrive -Despite-Tourism-Slowd own/

Lux, T. (2019). The California cannabis industry. *Journal of Business Entrepreneurship and Law, 13*, 209–244. https://doi/pdf/ doi:10.1177/0276146716655848

Mallinson, D., & Hannah, A. L. (2020). Policy and political learning: The development of medical cannabis policies in the states. *Publius: The Journal of Federalism, 50*(3), 344–369. doi: us/pjaa006 doi:10.1093/publi

Mallinson, D. J., Hannah, A. L., & Cunningham, G. (2020). The consequences of fickle federal policy: Administrative hurdles for state cannabis policies. *State & Local Government Review*, *52*(4), 241–254. doi:10.1177/0160323X20984540

Martiroysan, S. (2017). The Decriminalization of Recreational Cannabis in California: Commercial Cultivation Could Cost Growers an Arm, a Leg, and Their Freedom. *San Joaquin Agricultural Law Review*, *27*(2), 187–208.

Meehan, B., Rusko, C., & Frank Stephenson, E. (2020). (Pot)heads in beds: The effect of marijuana legalization on hotel occupancy in Colorado and Washington. *The Journal of Regional Analysis & Policy*, *50*(1), 46–53.

Mokwena, K. (2019). Social and public health implications of the legalisation of recreational cannabis: A literature review. *African Journal of Primary Health Care & Family Medicine*, *11*(1), 1–6. doi:10.4102/phcfm.v11i1.2136 PMID:31793317

Murphy, K. (2019, May 20). Cannabis is becoming a huge job creator. *Forbes*. https://www.forbes.com/sites/kevinmurphy/2019/05/20/cannabis-is-becoming-a-huge-job-creator/

Nair, T. (2012). Understanding livelihoods: A review of major debates. In S. Vipin (Ed.), *State of India's livelihoods report* (pp. 1–12). ACCESS Development Services.

Nobile, J. (2020, February 11). Report: Cannabis job growth projected to outpace all other fast-growing industries. *Crain's Cleveland Business*. https://www.crainscleveland.com/jeremy-nobile-blog/report-cannabis-job-growth-projected-outpace-all-other-fast-growing-industries

Owens, B. (2019). The professionalization of cannabis growing. *Nature*, *572*(7771), S10–S11. doi:10.1038/d41586-019-02527-2 PMID:31462785

Page, R. L. II, Allen, L. A., Kloner, R. A., Carriker, C. R., Martel, C., Morris, A. A., Piano, M. R., Rana, J. S., & Saucedo, J. F. (2020). Medical marijuana, recreational cannabis, and cardiovascular health: A scientific statement from the American Heart Association. *Circulation*, *142*(10), e131–e152. doi:10.1161/CIR.0000000000000883 PMID:32752884

Palthe, J. (2014). Regulative, normative, and cognitive elements of organizations: Implications for managing change. *Management and Organizational Studies*, *1*(2), 59–66. doi:10.5430/mos.v1n2p59

Payan, D., Brown, P., & Song, A. (2021). County-level recreational marijuana policies and local policy changes in Colorado and Washington State (2012–2019). *The Milbank Quarterly*, *99*(4), 1132–1161. Advance online publication. doi:10.1111/1468-0009.12535 PMID:34407252

Plakias, Z., Jodlowski, M., Giamo, T., Kavousi, P., & Taylor, K. (2021). Pot of money: Characterizing agricultural lending and banking in the California cannabis industry. *Agricultural Finance Review*, *82*(2), 214–246. doi:10.1108/AFR-06-2021-0075

Polson, M., & Petersen-Rockney, M. (2019). Cannabis farmers or criminals? Enforcement-first approaches fuel disparity and hinder regulation. *California Agriculture, 73*(3), 185–193. 0017 doi:10.3733/ca.2019a

Pourseyed Lazarjani, M., Torres, S., Hooker, T., Fowlie, C., Young, O., & Seyfoddin, A. (2020). Methods for quantification of cannabinoids: A narrative review. *Journal of Cannabis Research*, *2*(1), 1–10. doi:10.118642238-020-00040-2 PMID:33526084

Riley, S., Vellios, N., & van Walbeek, C. (2020). An economic analysis of the demand for cannabis: Some results from South Africa. *Drugs Education Prevention & Policy*, *27*(2), 123–130. doi:10.1080/09687637.2019.1581139

Romano, L. L., & Hazekamp, A. (2013). Cannabis oil: Chemical evaluation of an upcoming cannabis-based medicine. *Cannabinoids*, *1*(1), 1–11.

Rosario, J. (2021, July 13). City council members agree on even split of Jersey City cannabis tax revenue between schools, social programs. *The Jersey Journal.* https://www.nj.com/hudson/2021/07/city-council-member-agree-on-even-split-of-jersey-city-cannabis-tax-revenue-between-sc hool

Scarboro, M., & Bishop-Henchman, J. (2016). Marijuana legalization and taxes: Lessons for other states from Colorado and Washington. *Tax foundation.* https://taxfoundation.org/marijuana-taxes-lessons-colorado-w ashington/#_ftnref1

Schulz, L. (2019, April 25). The economic impact of developing the adult-use cannabis industry in New York. *Rockefeller Institute of Government*. https://rockinst.org/issue-area/the-economic-impact-of-devel oping -the-adult-use-cannabis-industry-in-new-york/

Scott, W. R. (2013). *Institutions and organizations: Ideas, interests, and identities*. Sage publications.

Smyth, E., & Vanclay, F. (2017). The Social Framework for Projects: a conceptual but practical model to assist in assessing, planning and managing the social impacts of projects. *Impact Assessment and Project Appraisal, 35*(1), 65-80. doi:10.1080/14615517.2016.1271539

Valachovic, Y., Quinn-Davidson, L., Stackhouse, J., & Butsic, V. (2019). Perceptions of cannabis among Humboldt County timberland and ranchland owners. *California Agriculture*, *73*(3), 161–168. doi:10.3733/ca.2019a0010

Viviers, H. J., Petzer, A., & Gordon, R. (2022). An assessment of solvent residue contaminants related to cannabis-based products in the South African market. *Journal of cannabis research, 4*(1), 1-10. doi:10.1186/s42238-022-00130-3

Wilson, S., Bodwitch, H., Carah, J., Daane, K., Getz, C., Grantham, T., & Butsic, V. (2019). First known survey of cannabis production practices in California. *California Agriculture*, *73*(3), 119–127. doi:10.3733/ca.2019a0015

Wright, A. (2020, November 6). What if I build a cannabis business and no one will insure it? *Risk and Insurance.* https://riskandinsurance.com/what-if-i-build-a-cannabis-busi ness-and-no-one-will-insure-it/

Chapter 9
Analysis of Lessons That Can Be Learnt by South African Government Leaders in Their Role in Advancements Within the Cannabis Industry of South Africa

Thulile Purity Dali
University of KwaZulu-Natal, South Africa

ABSTRACT

Government leaders have a key role to play in leading a diverse economy towards alleviation of poverty. Throughout the years cannabis has contributed to improved livelihoods for several years even with strong legislative policies that prevented its cultivation (Nkosi, 2021). In efforts to grow its economy, South Africa has joined many countries in changing its legislative policies to allow for legalization of hemp and cannabis under certain conditions. This chapter provides an analysis of the lessons that can be learnt by South African government leaders from the cannabis industry and their role in advancements within the cannabis industry of South Africa.

INTRODUCTION

The cannabis industry has seen transformation since its legalization by many countries including South Africa. The race to achieve economic growth in the cannabis industry is strong, according to the research from the leading market research company (IMARC) group medical cannabis market was worth $7.8 billion (~R117.5 billion) in 2020 with a 15.3% projected growth in 2026 (IMARC CANNABIS - Zoeken, 2020). Whilst many countries have progressively embraced the economic growth and benefits from this industry South Africa's progress has fallen behind. Recent events such as the COVID19 pandemic, Rus-

DOI: 10.4018/978-1-6684-6346-8.ch009

sian invasion of Ukraine (Team, 2022), July 2021 unrest in KwaZulu Natal and Gauteng (ACCORD, 2021) and the recent floods in KwaZulu Natal (South Africa: Floods and Landslides - Apr 2022, 2022) weigh unfavorably on South Africa's bottom line.

In his 2022 state of the nation address South African president Cyril Ramaphosa announced government's strategic plan for expansion through the industrialization and commercialization of hemp and Cannabis which is estimated at approximately R28 billion, with a potential of 130,000 new jobs (State of the Nation Address 2022 I South African Government, n.d). South Africa's cannabis strategy is detailed in the Cannabis master plan which was compiled in 2021. Success in the implementation of this strategy requires leadership to ensure strategic integration of functional strategies linked to the overall strategy with coherence of unified and mutually supportive policies and practices.

Literature has a lot of theories on government leadership roles. This chapter focuses on the six important leadership roles described by Stiglitz. These six important roles are unpacked in this chapter in relation to the cannabis industry and they include promoting education, promoting technology, supporting the financial sector, investing in infrastructure, preventing environmental degradation, and lastly creating and maintaining a social safety net (Stiglitz, 1997). In understanding its role in advancing the cannabis industry, South African government leaders can ensure improved delivery of the National cannabis master plan through the implementation of learnings gathered from countries that are ahead in their execution plans. This chapter also covers lessons derived from the current challenges described in the National cannabis master plan for South Africa with the intention to provide a broader spectrum of lessons that can reduced the challenges within South Africa. The academic value and intention of this chapter is to extend on currently available literature in providing an analysis of lesson's that can be learnt by South African government leaders on their role towards advancements within the Cannabis industry in South Africa.

Research Philosophy

In unpacking the lessons that can be learnt by South African government leaders on their role towards advancements within the Cannabis industry in South Africa. This chapter adopts a qualitative method of research philosophy which focuses on generation of non-numerical data for understanding beliefs, experiences, and behaviors using available literature sources (Kalra et al., 2013).

Data Collection

The data collection method for this chapter is qualitative. Historical and recent research events from the literature are used to create a framework for addressing the lesson's that can be learnt by South African government leaders on their role towards advancements within the Cannabis industry in South Africa. The method for analyzing the data involved a content analysis based on grounded theory to identify differences and similarities on available literature.

Background of the Study

"Cannabis the plant that produces hemp as well as hashish, is now known primarily as one of the leading psychoactive plants in the world use following, tobacco and alcohol in popularity" (Schultes, 1974). Cannabis was cultivated for fibre food medicine thousands of years ago before it became the 'superstar;

of the drop culture (Schultes, 1974). Cannabis is one of man's oldest plants with its popularity in the psychoactive plants (Schultes 1974). Produced from sativa plant, cannabis is available in three forms which include herbal cannabis, cannabis resin and cannabis oil. The herbal cannabis comes from dried leaves and flowering tops and is often referred to as dagga, weed amongst other names whilst the cannabis resin is the pressed secretions of the plant and cannabis oil is an extraction of active ingredients of the plant (United nations office on drugs and crime, n.d.). The history of cannabis in South Africa dates back into many centuries ago. The benefits of this plant were first adopted by the Khoikhoi nations as an intoxicant and herbal remedy. In 1928 through the medical, dental and pharmacy act no.13 of 1928 cannabis was regarded as illegal in South Africa, however, post the law coming into effect media has continued to report multiple arrest made from illegal possession of this plant. In 2004 Interpol recorded South Africa as the fourth cannabis producer in the world and estimated between 1000 to 1200 hectares of land used to grow the plant (Perkel, 2004). People have continued to feed their families throughout history through the cannabis industry and whilst South Africa has made bold announcements to capitalize its efforts in this sector knowledge of this industry is limited. With some countries already ahead of South Africa this chapter aims to review lessons that the government leaders in South Africa can learn about advancing this industry.

This chapter aims to answer the following research questions:

§ What role does South African government leaders play in advancing the Cannabis Industry?
§ What are the advancements in the cannabis industry?
§ What lessons can the government leaders in South Africa learn about the cannabis industry from countries who are ahead of this transformation?

The objectives of this chapter are:

§ To establish the role of government leaders in driving strategies within the cannabis industry.
§ To determine the lessons that South African leaders can learn on the cannabis industry from other countries.
§ To contribute to the limited literature available on the advancements of the cannabis industry.

THE ROLE OF SOUTH AFRICAN GOVERNMENT LEADERS IN ADVANCING THE CANNABIS INDUSTRY

The South African government leaders play a key role in improving the livelihoods of South African's. There are various theories and literature available on the role of governments, in this chapter the six important roles for economic development are reviewed (Stiglitz,1997). These six important roles include promoting education, promoting technology, supporting the financial sector, investing in infrastructure, preventing environmental degradation, and lastly creating and maintaining a social safety net (Stiglitz,1997). The following provides a breakdown on these six key roles in relations to the cannabis industry.

Role of Government in Promoting Education

The intellectual roots of different scholars have distinguished between three types of learnings that need to occur during the process of policy diffusion these include, political, instrumental, and social learnings (Mallinson, 2020). Instrumental learning occurs from observations of policy experimentations in other states, this allows legislators to adopt learnings into their own frameworks. This is key for the South African cannabis legislators and is covered in the master plan as the plan details a balance of learnings drawn from countries outside and within the African continent.

Another important area of learning is social learning which focuses on the social constructs of the policy scope, goals, and problems (Mallinson, 2020). The confidence of society in government leadership has declined drastically over the past years, this has been further exacerbated by the current economical constraints affecting the livelihoods of many and demonstrated through the increased frequency in public protest. A stable society is built on an educational foundation. The gain of knowledge from education extends to other members of society and ultimately to the positive transformation of the country. It is important for government to ensure knowledge of cannabis is extended to schools, universities and ultimately society. This will aid school prevention programs that discourage the additive uses of this illicit drug and encourage social cohesion for driving the cannabis strategy.

A study conducted on Australian university students on their knowledge of cannabis showed that whilst students recognized the medical use of cannabis their knowledge was limited (Felnhofer et al., 2021). Therefore, to aid the government plans announced in the 2022 state of the nation address for growing this sector, government can expand the knowledge about cannabis through research centers and other education facilities.

The South Africa's cannabis master plan has a detailed educational framework with identified training needs which it aims to deliver though the Department of Education both basic and higher. The formation of the cannabis institute as South Africa's first online Agri SETA accredited cannabis school is testament to government plans of realizing expansion in building and offering a wide range of courses to educate learners on the cannabis value chain ("National Certificate in Plant Production – Cannabis & Hemp I AgriColleges International," 2022). Whilst the integration of cannabis into school curriculum is important in establishing an educational framework, training that supports this industry should not exclude the importance and value that can be derived from programs that create awareness and education for society outside the institutional walls.

According to the Cannabis master plan, government has plans to communicate to the public through information sharing and awareness programs key messaging that addresses negative perceptions of hemp and cannabis and the government regulations matters. Lastly Political learnings which focuses on policy processes are key in driving the implementation of the cannabis master plan. The first challenge listed in the cannabis master plan is that of legislation restrictions. Although the inter-departmental committee that guides the development of national cannabis as detailed in the cannabis master is a multidisciplinary team government should not neglect its own accountability by having high reliance on the committee. This makes political learning on policy awareness a key deliverable in promoting education within the cannabis industry even more so with the provincial cannabis committee forming part of the implementation and monitoring structures.

Role of Government in Promoting Technology

Cannabis industry discussions often focus on the legalization and the market potential of this industry, another corollary of interest in advancing this industry is technology. The white paper on science and technology was introduced in 1996 by the Department of science and innovation aimed at a set of policies on the government sector (Constitution of the Republic of South Africa, 1996 » Department of Science and Technology » Draft White Paper on Science, Technology, and Innovation, n.d.). With technology said to replace more than half of today's jobs within the next 35 years it is critical that government plans for economic transformation taking the impact of technology into consideration.

For the cannabis industry it is of importance that government understand its role of using technology to promote economic growth, job creation and socio- economic reform. Legalization of cannabis market from various countries in the world is exploding and requiring technological advancements to maximize its supply chain from crop management to distribution.

Blockchain, access control, artificial intelligence and internet of things technology are some of the four technologies explored throughout the world in the cannabis industry (Astran, 2021). Block chain technology addresses the issues around polices that pose a challenge to cannabis companies working with banks this technology is employed for cryptocurrency payments and transactions tracking with the intention of having a secure monitoring system for growing and shipping cannabis and its product. Access control is employed within this industry to ensure traditional protections and insurance as it is regarded as a high-risk industry due to the nature of its products. Artificial Intelligence advances in the cannabis industry helps to optimize growing processes from environmental changes and in delivery of the plants effectively and efficiently. "Internet of Things" technologies, which includes humidity sensors, lighting cycles etc. are used for growing operations to manipulate the environment for conducive cannabis growing (IoT in Cannabis Farming, 2021).

Role of Government in Supporting the Financial Sector

The South African cannabis master plan acknowledges the need to offer financial support to farmers in the form of funding loans and blended funding offerings without details of where and which institutions will offer this support. Cannabis related businesses continue to struggle with bank depositary and other financial support from banking facilities. This then results in high amounts of cash dealings which pose a risk of robberies and introduces other crimes relating to cash such as money laundering and loss of taxes.

The US Drug Enforcement Administration (DEA) in the United States lists marijuana as a schedule 1 drug which is in the same category as heroin (Lopez, 2016). There are numerous differing views on the accuracy of listing marijuana as a schedule 1 drug and this then disqualifies the business participation of this product in the banking systems which promotes cash transactions and results in a loss of government taxes.

Revenue generation through cannabis taxes is how government can drive economic growth, however if banking facilities do not extend their support to the cannabis business sector, businesses will evade paying taxes on their true revenue generated. As the brain of the economy government's role in this sector is in the deployment of resources in the most efficient and effective way and the banking sector should also form part of the different committees detailed in the South African cannabis master plan. As policies and legislation drivers' government leaders need to integrate the details of the policies and legislations, they implement to safeguard against loss of tax revenue.

Role of Government in Investing in Infrastructure

The expansion into the industrialization and commercialization of cannabis requires infrastructure investments in the form of manufacturing plants. The South African cannabis master plan details the need for investments from different sectors including both private and public sector in establishing these manufacturing plants. South Africa has a long history of foreign direct investment. In a country that is grappling challenges that are threating the economic growth, foreign investments during economic downturn becomes an area of vulnerability for the country's economy .As government continues to partake in initiatives to attract foreign investments the long-term effects of some key aspects of the relationship drivers between investment and economic growth decisions should not go undetected (SAIIA, 2022).The role of government leaders is to strategically channel investments and safeguard through the application of policies and legislations against any economic, political and social threats as the country transitions from illegal to legal cannabis markets.

Role of Government in Preventing Environmental Degradation

There is a limitation in scientific studies that inform the understanding on the linkages between cannabis and environmental degradation. In-door, greenhouse and outdoor are the three typologies of legal cannabis cultivation systems (Wartenberg et al., 2021). The environmental impacts from these three modes of cannabis cultivation vary and its of importance that these impacts are understood as a way of supporting sustainable development.

Sustainable development is development that ensures the future generations needs are met by ensuring that the current developments do not compromise the future which is the opposite of traditional development which was material based economic growth focused on development initiatives aimed at addressing poverty alleviation, inequality, and sickness (21, 2016). The direct and indirect effects of cannabis cultivation and production on the ecosystem need to be understood as the world continues to fight climate change.

The subject of climate change has gained a lot of popularity because of the recent weather destructions it is therefore pertinent that government leaders safeguard the environment from any forms of degradation that can arise from cannabis. Land used for cultivation and production, water usage and pollution, energy usage and air pollution are amongst the key areas that require cannabis policy revisions. To manage the negative environmental impacts of growing cannabis in environmentally sensitive areas requires land use strategies as a way of incorporating policies that promote wildlife conscious farming practices.

The challenge however arises from already established sites and new applications in areas that pose a risk to the survival of the ecosystem as result of cannabis activities. In overcoming this challenge government can investigate implementing site relocation initiatives that provide affected stakeholders with incentives to move their cannabis activities to areas with low risk, this initiative was conducted by Humboldt County based in the State of California (Bodwitch et al., 2021). As part of the cannabis master plan South African government leaders should also review zoning policies and other best practices that safeguard the use of land from cannabis activities.

According to Butsic, (2016) cannabis accounts for a small portion of water usage footprint when compared to other crops however the expansion of this industry will result in an increased water usage. With South Africa's projected freshwater availability of less than 1000m3 per capita by the year 2025 water scarcity is fast becoming a reality for South Africa. To alleviate further strain to the countries water capacity government policies on cannabis should address efficient water management practices for cannabis activities.

Another key consideration for environmental impacts is pesticides. Pesticides are used in agriculture as a means of protecting plants from pests. In relation to cannabis plants human exposure because of pesticide residue must be understood and well-regulated as part of government policies for this industry. California is an example of a stated that has adopted robust pesticide testing in legal cannabis to curb against amongst other human exposure (Seltenrich, 2019). It is the role of government to ensure that pesticides and their effects are understood beyond agricultural activities and human exposure.

One cannot review environmental impacts without the consideration of energy consumption. South Africa's energy crisis has resulted in long hours of loadshedding as its power supply utility Eskom has failed to consistently meet the countries demands (Tandwa, 2022). In realizing growth expectations from this market as set by the cannabis master plan, energy consumption from the different cannabis activities must be understood and energy plans put in place to avoid causing further strain on the countries power supply. Best practice such as efficient energy saving lighting, renewable energy and setting up policies that encourage energy efficiency should form part of the south African governments plan for expansion of this market.

Air and water pollution are key environmental impacts considerations that must form part of government sustainable development plans for cannabis expansion. Regulations and policies of safeguarding the environment should be informed by amongst other science-based studies. The considerations highlighted are amongst the key considerations for safeguarding against environmental depletion and promoting sustainable development for the cannabis market. For government as policies makers whilst it's important to ensure policies are robust in discouraging environmental depletions, government should safeguard against environmental tradeoffs. These tradeoffs can result in a shift between the three cannabis typologies which are In-door, greenhouse and outdoor.

Role of Government in Creating and Maintaining a Social Safety Net

The creation of safety nets includes access to health facilities and improved standards of living. Government plays a key role in ensuring this and relies on income generated from different revenue streams to accomplish this. Whilst this responsibility does not solely rest on government leaders, they drive the policies that allow accessibility to trade in the markets were the social safety nets can be realized (Stiglitz,1997). One area where government can generate revenue to build better safety nets is through the job creations and taxes from the cannabis industry.

Lessons that Government Leaders in South Africa can learn about the Cannabis Industry

The Cannabis master plan for South Africa describes various challenges facing the cannabis industry. These challenges include legislative restrictions, lack of formal seed supply systems, high entry barriers, negativity of public perceptions, manufacturing capacity constraints, limitations within the research and technology development programs for cannabis, growing of illegal products, market challenges and threats because of market dominance from large scale corporations and pharmacy groups (Burkhardt, 2021). With various countries such as Mexico, Canada, Spain, USA, China, Portugal Mexico, and other countries in the African continent such as Nigeria, Ethiopia, Egypt, DRC, Tanzania, Kenya, and Lesotho already established as major cannabis producers South Africa can already take learnings from these countries in overcoming the challenges within this industry. In this section of this chapter lessons learnt are presented for each of the challenges described in the South African Cannabis master plan 2021.

Legislative Restrictions

To effectively deliver on the cannabis master plan South African government leaders need to continuously gauge for legislative opportunities. Age restrictions on sale of recreational cannabis, the role of municipalities, defined recreational cannabis sales and limits on quantity of possession are some of the legislative restrictions passed by the government of Ontario in various cannabis legislations (Farag, n.d.). These restrictions are backed by various studies that have already been conducted for example BMC Public Health defines the minimum legal age of cannabis consumption for non-medical purposes as age 19 based on studies conducted on the long-term health effects of cannabis use at an early age (Nguyen et al., 2022).

Another issue which has been an oversight in many countries is the readiness position of municipalities when it comes to delivering on the expectations of enforcing legislation on cannabis legalization (Caulkins & Kilborn, 2019). From reviewed literature sources it is evident that the restrictions mentioned have sparked debates globally within the cannabis industry with many opposing views on the conclusions drawn from the various studies conducted. South Africa has an advantage of building its legislative frameworks on successful and proven theories whilst improving on the areas that have either failed or proven to be least successful.

Lack of Formal Seed Supply Systems

The Netherlands, United Kingdom, Spain, and other countries with less restrictions on cannabis laws have established seed banks that provide variations of cannabis seeds to suit different uses (Miller, 2022). Whilst the establishment of seed banks ensures sustainable seed supply if not well regulated it can be prone to vulnerabilities such as compromised quality of seeds. Achievement of a formal cannabis seed supply system according to the South African cannabis master plan requires the formal registration of certified organizations and persons who cultivate these seeds (Daniel, 2021). South African government plans to offer various streams of support to farmers as a way of encouraging their participation in the cannabis value chain. A well-regulated seed bank may be an option that the South African government can explore in establishing a more formalized cannabis seed supply system.

High Entry Barriers

According to a study conducted in California the inability of overcoming barriers in securing their legitimacy for participating in the cannabis industry has resulted in many farmers not adhering to the countries licensing legislations (Bodwitch et al., 2021). Barriers that affect the transformation of cannabis from an illegal drug to an agricultural product are financial, administrative, and psychological (Bodwitch et al., 2021). Barriers form an integral part towards the protection of the legal markets however a fair reduction is necessary to discourage further expansions within the black market. South African government leaders must ensure that their support structures are not only limited to financial support but should also cover administrative and psychological support as both bear financial implications.

Psychological support is inclusive of the psychological costs that occur because of non-compliance in engaging in illicit activities. Government outreach programs are imperative in the initial stages in building trust relationships between government and farmers and other key stakeholders. Critical in these outreach programs is the demonstration that small scale farmers can succeed in regulated markets. In absence of government outreach programs experience exchange from a system of "neighbor to neighbor" information exchange becomes an impactful source of information sharing especially in rural areas (Hansen et al., 2020). These outreach programs help in managing the universal fears which translates into psychological costs due to cascading regulatory requirements from regulatory interactions (Bodwitch et al., 2021).

The cannabis master plan does not provide the details of the support programs however structures that are responsible for the guidance and monitoring of the implementation of the master plan are provided. It's important that South Africa makes use of the government outreach programs in building trust with the communities as the "neighbor to neighbor" information exchange system may not be effective in translating government legislations and regulation requirements or be kept fully abreast with changes.

Legalization

Cannabis legalization is a contentious issue, the current dilemma faced by many countries on the legalization of cannabis is found in the validity of the arguments presented by various parties both with opposing and supporting views on the topic. The cannabis policy reformed has been affected by the recent court rulings in many countries. As an example, the constitutional court of Georgia in December 2016 made an amendment that imprisonment of small amounts of cannabis, its purchase, retention, and production for personal use was unconstitutional ("Norms Envisaging Imprisonment for Marijuana Use Now Null and Void in Georgia," n.d.-b). In July 2018 the use and possession of cannabis was legalized in Georgia, but penalties imposed for cultivation and sale (Roberts, 2018).

For South Africa, in 2017 the Department of health introduced a licensing framework for domestic, cultivation and manufacture of medical cannabis. In 2018 the private use and cultivation of cannabis was decriminalized by the constitutional court. In 2019 a notice that excludes certain preparations containing cannabidiol from the operations of certain provisions of medicine and related substances act was published by minster of health. In 2019 the South African cabinet appointed the minister of agriculture, land reform and rural development as governor for the national strategy for industrialization and commercialization of cannabis aimed at improved economic growth. In 2020 a draft bill was published for public comment by the South African parliament portfolio committee. The proposed bill covers cannabis possession rules for people who want to cultivate the plant at home. The bill makes provision for commercial activities, cultivation for religious and cultural purposes and lastly the right to privacy for medical use of cannabis (Cannabis for Private Purposes Bill B19-2020 | South African Government, n.d.)

The drugs and drug trafficking Act 140 of 1992 and the medicines & related substances control Act are the two pieces of legislation that regulate cannabis in South Africa. What is evident from the cannabis master plan for South Africa is the much-needed policies and legislation for the commercialization of cannabis. The legislative hurdles in the South African Cannabis industry results in some exclusions especially for small scale farmers from an industry with a potential to thrive.

Negativity of Public Perceptions

The public debate on the drug policy for cannabis ranges between perceived and actual benefits and the opposing views that are concerned with avoiding health and social harms. The risk of addiction has greatly influenced the stringent measures put on the cannabis industry and whilst countries relax legislation it is of great importance that control measures are put in place to deal with the risk of addiction. In the United States a single pharmacy in West Virginia reported above board sales of 9 million opioid pills over a period of two years bearing testament to the high consumption rates of cannabis (Foley, 2022).

In the South African cannabis master plan, negative perceptions arising from the public is acknowledged as one of the challenges facing the cannabis industry (Burkhardt, 2021). Public perceptions for the use of cannabis range between social problems, spiritual attributes, health benefits and denial of negative health consequences (Ntsaba, 2016). The opposing perceptions of cannabis legalization associated with social problems are mostly based on the concern around cannabis consumption in youth and students (Kafeero, 2022).

Traditional and spiritual healing is often founded on a belief system that emanates from experiences based on indigenous cultures. The history of cannabis as a spiritual plant is deeply rooted in Hinduism, Islam, Rastafarianism, and indigenous traditions in Asia and Africa (Heide et al., 2021).The characteristics of cannabis as an entheogen that expands consciousness and increases spiritual growth is evident in its current increased use in practices such as yoga, meditation, and mindfulness (Ferrara, 2021). The perceptions of the public when it comes to the spiritual use of cannabis boarders on the thin line between spiritual use versus pleasure.

There are many conflicting views on the health risks associated with the use of cannabis, whilst some views are opposed to medical use of cannabis others support the use of the plant. Heart rate and blood pressure are cited as some of the symptoms relating to the cannabis use which influences the risk perceptions (Greydanus et al., 2013). Other studies refer to long term mental effects which can also be difficult to establish due to factors that are not related to cannabis use (Volkow et al., 2014).

The dilemma that is facing many countries is that declining risk perceptions are resulting in increased availability which will inevitability lead to increased use of cannabis in adolescences. With the average age ranging between 12-15 years for the first use of cannabis in some countries the growing public concerns is based on the related harmful effects of this plant within this age group (Johnston, 2016). The effect of COVID19 on people's mental health has been on the rise since the start of the pandemic and has influence the use of cannabis. A study conducted by Lancet in October 2021 reported addition of 53.2 million cases of depression and 76.2 million cases of anxiety during the pandemic (Santomauro, 2021), a correlation between the growing cases of depression and anxiety and the projected annual growth rate of 26.6% for the global cannabis industry can be made (Ï,§ PR Newswire. "Medical Cannabis Market Is Estimated to Rise at a CAGR of 26.6% During the Forecast Period, Observes TMR Study." - Zoeken, n.d). As the medical use and perceptions around cannabis continue to evolve, there are studies that show that cannabis has been successful in treating certain conditions, its effectiveness in medicine was seen in its inclusion as part of the plant's trials conducted during COVID19 in South Africa in the fight against the coronavirus (Khalsa et al., 2021).

We are living in a digital age where the growing use of social media has taken over the world. The liberal data policy for platforms such as twitter has given rise to its use in academic research (Zimmer & Proferes, 2014). In addressing public perceptions, the Canadian government has used social media platforms to share information and gather data from the public around its cannabis policies (Aversa et al.,

2021). Whilst there are heavy social media regulations on cannabis, South African government leaders can also make use of social media platforms to educate and share information as a way of influencing a positive shift in the current stereotypes associated with the use of cannabis.

Manufacturing of Cannabis

The cannabis master plan for South Africa identifies infrastructure investments and incentive programs as some of the key intervention's measures for manufacturing and product development. Some of the other capacity constraints that South African government should address regarding manufacturing is the high level of skills required in this sector which can be done through skills development programs (De Gobbi, 2022). The monitoring of compliance for cannabis manufacture through the entire supply chain is a challenge that government leaders need to address. The South African health products regulatory authority (SAHPRA) details the use of standard operating procedures to be developed for the production activities related to cannabis as part of the guidelines for cultivation of cannabis and manufacturing of cannabis related pharmaceutical production for medicinal and research purposes (Department of Health, 2022). The South African government leaders need to ensure that documented standard guidelines are in place for the different cannabis activities as per legislation and compliance is driven as part of robust audit programs.

LIMITATIONS WITHIN RESEARCH AND TECHNOLOGY DEVELOPMENT PROGRAMS FOR CANNABIS ADVANCEMENTS

The Cannabis industry discussions often focus on the legalization and the market potential of this industry, another corollary of interest in advancing this industry is technology (CNBS, 2019). With increase in its legalization from various countries in the world the cannabis market is exploding and requiring technological advancements to maximize its supply chain from crop management to distribution. Breeding on new cultivators, product development and technology adoption are the three focus areas for the research and technology development programs described in the master cannabis plan for South Africa.

Growing of Illegal Products

Supply shortages in countries such as California and Canada because of red tape in the form of fees and stringent environmental laws has pushed consumers to black markets whilst markets such as Colorado which have less limitations on licensing limits encountered oversupply (Meadows, 2019). Amongst other issues arising from illegal growing of cannabis is the ecological catastrophes which include but not limited to environmental contamination and hazardous waste resulting from illegal cannabis cultivation sites (Vasic, 2020). Further degradations of landscapes are caused by harsh chemicals used by illegal growers (Vasic, 2020). Legalization does not address the growing black market and South African government leaders should aim for a balance legislative compliance program in discouraging illegal growing (Meadows, 2019).

Market Dominance from Large Scale Corporations and Pharmacy Groups

By the year 2024 the global cannabis market is expected to be worth 103 billion dollars of this projected growth Europe and North America are expected to have the largest market share value accounting to 39.1 and 37.9 billion dollars respectively (Content, 2022). If legalization is well implemented for both medical and recreational use the combined project growth from nine African continent countries is estimated to be 7.1 billion dollars by the year 2023 which is a small fraction of the global growth projections within this market (Content, 2022). The recognition of medical benefits and application of marijuana are the drivers of cannabis industry growth in the Europe markets which has led to an increase in the variety of products for medical use. Dominance of the cannabis market by large scale corporations can result from market entry barriers that make it difficult for small scale participation in the market. Dominance prevents effective competition by affording power to a selected group over another (McMahon, 2018).

Market dynamics have an impact on supply and demand through the way they influence pricing signals. With the projected growth of the cannabis industry, it is imperative that market dynamics are well understood by South African governments leaders in realizing the successful implementation of the cannabis master plan. One of the key successors of the cannabis market in Europe is the strict regulation structures that govern entries into this market, these regulations are subjected to periodical reviews as a way of ensuring compliance and relevance. South African government leaders should also adopt similar controls measures to protect its market share and realize economic growth with this industry.

State of the Medical and Scientific Information

The state of medical and scientific information is another area where South Africa can take learnings from. There are several chemical compounds within the cannabis plant. Some of these compounds produce feelings of relief and health improvements that cover a range of illnesses. The best studied compounds are THC and CBD (cannabidiol), cannabidiol has its own properties which are still being discovered. It is therefore important to understand the effects of the different compounds at different concentrations. Canada the first G7 country to legalize cannabis for adult use through two-phase regulations roll out process the legal framework (Pusiak et al., 2021). Through its quality control and quality assurance measures Canada ensures safe cannabis is supplied to their customers this measure also includes labeling of the THC and CBD content per product.

CONCLUSION

The state as a regulator and state as an enabler are the two different positions for the South African government leaders. As a regulator the key responsibilities of government leaders is to ensure the development and design of systematic rules that resolve conflicts that safeguard individuals and different organization bodies (Otobo, 1997:44). As an enabler government supports private sector development (Otobo, 1997:1). The ideal state of policies is that they need to capture the benefits of a legally regulated market for cannabis whilst avoiding over-commercialization. Some of the vulnerabilities which can hinder the successful implementation of the National cannabis master plan for South Africa have already been experienced in varying degrees by different countries who are ahead in this market. These vulnerabilities present themselves as learnings and whilst effective solutions have not been established in all areas there is several lessons that can be derived. This chapter covered an analysis of lesson's that can be learnt by South African government leaders in their role in advancements within the Cannabis industry of South Africa. From the various sources of literature consulted in this chapter it is evident that revised policy thinking is still required around the cannabis market framework.

REFERENCES

BBC Visual Journalism Team. (2022, November 14). Ukraine in maps: Tracking the war with Russia. *BBC News*. https://www.bbc.com/news/world-europe-60506682

ACCORD. (2021, December 10). The July 2021 Protests and Socio-political Unrest in South Africa. *ACCORD*. https://www.accord.org.za/conflict-trends/the-july-2021-protests-and-socio-political-unrest-in-south-africa/

Agenda.GE. (2016). Norms envisaging imprisonment for marijuana use now null and void in Georgia. *Agenda.Ge*. https://agenda.ge/en/news/2016/3159

AgriColleges International. (2022, August 24). National Certificate in Plant Production – Cannabis & Hemp. *Agricolleges*. https://agricolleges.com/national-certificate-in-plant-production-cannabis-hemp/

Astran, J. (2021, March 17). How Can Blockchain Technology Help The Cannabis Industry? *HealthMed*. https://healthmed.org/how-can-blockchain-technology-help-the-cannabis-industry/

Aversa, J., Jacobson, J., Hernandez, T., Cleave, E., Macdonald, M., & Dizonno, S. (2021). The social media response to the rollout of legalized cannabis retail in Ontario, Canada. *Journal of Retailing and Consumer Services*, *61*, 102580. https://doi.org/10.1016/j.jretconser.2021.102580

Bodwitch, H., Polson, M., Biber, E., Hickey, G. M., & Butsic, V. (2021). Why comply? Farmer motivations and barriers in cannabis agriculture. *Journal of Rural Studies*, *86*, 155–170. https://doi.org/10.1016/j.jrurstud.2021.05.006

Burkhardt, P. (2021, August 26). Govt unveils master plan for R28bn dagga industry. *News 24*. https://www.news24.com/fin24/economy/govt-unveils-master-plan-for-r28bn-dagga-industry-20210826

Butsic, V. (2016, March 18). Cannabis (Cannabis sativa or C. indica) agriculture and the environment: a systematic, spatially-explicit survey and potential impacts. *IOPscience*. https://iopscience.iop.org/article/10.1088/1748-9326/11/4/044023/meta

Cannabis for Private Purposes Bill B19-2020. (2020). South African Government. https://www.gov.za/documents/cannabis-private-purposes-bill-b19-2020-1-sep-2020-0000

Caulkins, J. P., & Kilborn, M. L. (2019). Cannabis legalization, regulation, & control: A review of key challenges for local, state, and provincial officials. *The American Journal of Drug and Alcohol Abuse*, *45*(6), 689–697. https://doi.org/10.1080/00952990.2019.1611840

CNBS. (2019, February 7). Cannabis Technology: The Evolution of an Industry. *CNBS*. https://www.cnbs.org/cannabis-101/cannabis-technology/

Constitution of the Republic of South Africa. (2018). *Draft White Paper on Science, Technology and Innovation*. Green Gazzette. https://www.greengazette.co.za/notices/constitution-of-the-republic-of-south-africa-1996-department-of-science-and-technology-draft-white-paper-on-science-technology-and-innovation_20180914-GGN-41909-00954

Content, S. (2022, April 12). Catching the Growth of the Cannabis Industry. *Visual Capitalist*. https://www.visualcapitalist.com/sp/catching-the-growth-of-the-cannabis-industry/

Daniel, L. (2021, August 25). Degrees for dagga growers and govt-supplied seeds – inside SA's Cannabis Master Plan. *Business Insider*. https://www.businessinsider.co.za/south-africa-cannabis-master-plan-for-growers-2021-8

De Gobbi, M. S. (2022). Exploring decent work in the pharmaceutical industry: job creation in the production of medical cannabis in Lesotho and Zimbabwe. *International Labour Office*. doi:10.54394/isri3535

Department of Health. (2022, November 30). SAHPRA - South African Health Products Regulatory Authority. *SAHPRA*. https://www.sahpra.org.za/

Farag, R. (n.d.). Provincial Cannabis Legislation, Regulation, and Licensing: Its Effectiveness and Impacts on Municipalities in Ontario. *Scholarship at UWindsor*. https://scholar.uwindsor.ca/major-papers/211/

Felnhofer, A., Kothgassner, O. D., Stoll, A., & Klier, C. (2021). Knowledge about and attitudes towards medical cannabis among Austrian university students. *Complementary Therapies in Medicine*, *58*, 102700. https://doi.org/10.1016/j.ctim.2021.102700

Ferrara, M. S. (2021). Peak-experience and the entheogenic use of cannabis in world religions. *Journal of Psychedelic Studies*, *4*(3), 179–191. https://doi.org/10.1556/2054.2020.00122

Foley, K. E. (2022, July 21). Drug wholesalers shipped 9 million pain pills over two years to a single West Virginia pharmacy. *Quartz*. https://qz.com/866771/drug-wholesalers-shipped-9-million-opioid-painkillers-over-two-years-to-a-single-west-virginia-pharmacy

Greydanus, D. E., Hawver, E. K., Greydanus, M. M., & Merrick, J. (2013). Marijuana: Current Concepts. *Frontiers in Public Health, 1*. doi:10.3389/fpubh.2013.00042

Hansen, E. M. Ø. (2020). The role of experience exchange groups in farmers' practice transitions: The case of reduced tillage in Danish conventional farming. *Roskilde Universitets Forskningsportal*. https://forskning.ruc.dk/da/publications/the-role-of-experience-exchange-groups-in-farmers-practice-transi

Heide, F. J., Chang, T., Porter, N., Edelson, E., & Walloch, J. C. (2021). Spiritual Benefit from Cannabis. *Journal of Psychoactive Drugs*, *54*(2), 149–157. https://doi.org/10.1080/02791072.2021.1941443

Johnston, L. D. (2016, January 31). Monitoring the Future National Survey Results on Drug Use, 1975-2015: Overview, Key Findings on Adolescent Drug Use. *Institute for Social Research*. https://eric.ed.gov/?id=ED578539

Kafeero, S. (2022, July 20). Business is starting to trump morality in Africa's cannabis industry. *Quartz*. https://qz.com/africa/2028012/africas-cannabis-industry-is-set-to-boom-due-to-legalization

Kalra, S., Pathak, V., & Jena, B. (2013). Qualitative research. *Perspectives in Clinical Research*, *4*(3), 192. https://doi.org/10.4103/2229-3485.115389

Khalsa, J. H., Maggirwar, S. B., & Bunt, G. (2021). Cannabis/Cannabinoids for Treating COVID-19 Associated Neuropsychiatric Complications. *Journal of Neuroimmune Pharmacology*, *16*(4), 718–721. https://doi.org/10.1007/s11481-021-10013-8

Lopez, G. (2016, August 11). The federal drug scheduling system, explained. *Vox*. https://www.vox.com/2014/9/25/6842187/drug-schedule-list-marijuana

Mallinson, D. J. (2020). Policy Diffusion Results: A New Database for Systematic Review and Meta-Analysis. *State & Local Government Review*, *52*(1), 18–27. https://doi.org/10.1177/0160323x20965682

McMahon, P. (2018, July 2). Market Dominance. *McMahon Legal*. https://mcmahonsolicitors.ie/market-dominance

Meadows, W. J. (2019). Cannabis Legalization: Dealing with the Black Market. *Electronic Journal*. doi:10.2139/ssrn.3454635

Miller, A. (2022). Top-rated Reputable Cannabis Seed Companies that Ship to USA *The Sacramento Bee*. https://www.sacbee.com/news/california/california

Nguyen, H. V. (2020, May 14). Too young for Cannabis? Choice of minimum legal age for legalized non-medical Cannabis in Canada - BMC Public Health. *BioMed Central*. https://bmcpublichealth.biomedcentral.com/articles/10.1186/s12889-020-08639-z

Nkosi, P. I. (2021). Dagga and Data: Cannabis, Race, and Policing in Midcentury South Africa, 1932–1960. *The Social History of Alcohol and Drugs*, *35*(2), 232–259. https://doi.org/10.1086/716209

Ntsaba, J. M. M. E. (2016, February 2). Perceptions of marijuana use: Chronicles of marijuana smokers from two marijuana-Growing communities in South Africa. *IDEAS*. https://ideas.repec.org/a/apb/jahmss/2016p82-91.html

Otobo, E. E. 1997. The civil service and the private sector in Africa: From relationship of "conflict" to complimentarity. *DPMN Bulletin*. http://www.dpmf.org/civil-service-conflict-ejeviome. html

Perkel, C. (2005). Cannabis - the debate continues: a South African perspective: original article. *The African Journal of Psychiatry*, *8*(1). https://doi.org/10.4314/ajpsy.v8i1.30181

PR Newswire. (2020).. Medical Cannabis Market is Estimated to Rise at a CAGR of 26.6% during the Forecast Period, observes TMR Study. *Zoeken*. https://www.bing.com/search?q=%EF%82%A7+PR+Newswire.+&qout;Medical+Cannabis+Market+is+Estimated+to+Rise+at+a+CAGR+of+26.6%+during+the+Forecast+Period,+observes+TMR+Study.&qout

Pusiak, R. J., Cox, C., & Harris, C. S. (2021). Growing pains: An overview of cannabis quality control and quality assurance in Canada. *The International Journal on Drug Policy*, *93*, 103111. https://doi.org/10.1016/j.drugpo.2021.103111

Roberts, C. (2018, July 31). Georgia's High Court Removes Marijuana Possession Penalties. *Marijuana Moment*. https://www.marijuanamoment.net/georgias-high-court-removes-marijuana-possession-penalties/

SAIIA. (2022, August 16). The Dark Side of Foreign Direct Investment: A South African Perspective. *SAIIA*. https://saiia.org.za/research/the-dark-side-of-foreign-direct-investment-a-south-african-perspective/

Santomauro, D. F. (2021, November 6). Global prevalence and burden of depressive and anxiety disorders in 204 countries and territories in 2020 due to the COVID-19 pandemic. *The Lancet*. https://www.thelancet.com/journals/lancet/article/PIIS0140-6736(21)02143-7/fulltext

Schultes, R. E. (1974, February 28). Details - Cannabis: an Example of Taxonomic Neglect. *Biodiversity Heritage Library*. https://www.biodiversitylibrary.org/part/168565

Seltenrich, N. (2019). Into the Weeds: Regulating Pesticides in Cannabis. *Environmental Health Perspectives*, *127*(4), 042001. https://doi.org/10.1289/ehp5265

ReliefWeb. (2022). South Africa. Floods and Landslides - Apr 2022. *ReliefWeb*. https://reliefweb.int/disaster/fl-2022-000201-zaf

South African Government. (2022). *State of the Nation Address*. South African Government. https://www.gov.za/SONA2022

Stiglitz, J. (1997). Reflections on the Natural Rate Hypothesis. *Journal of Economic Perspectives, 11*(1), 3–10. .3 doi:10.1257/jep.11.1

Tandwa, L. (2022, September 18). Eskom warns of higher stages of load-shedding as it scrambles to procure power. *The Mail & Guardian*. https://mg.co.za/news/2022-09-18-eskom-warns-of-higher-stages-of-load-shedding-as-it-scrambles-to-procure-power/

Thingstel. (2021, April 29). IoT in Cannabis Farming *Thingstel*. https://www.thingstel.com/blog/iot-in-cannabis-farming/

United Nations Office on Drugs and Crime. (n.d.). *United Nations: Office on Drugs and Crime*. UN. https://www.unodc.org

Vasic, A. (2020, March 10). Illegal Cannabis Grows Trigger a Chain of Environmental Disasters on Public Lands. *Greencamp*. https://greencamp.com/illegal-cannabis-grows/

Volkow, N. D., Baler, R. D., Compton, W. M., & Weiss, S. R. (2014). Adverse Health Effects of Marijuana Use. *The New England Journal of Medicine*, *370*(23), 2219–2227. https://doi.org/10.1056/nejmra1402309

Wartenberg, A. C., Holden, P. A., Bodwitch, H., Parker-Shames, P., Novotny, T., Harmon, T. C., Hart, S. C., Beutel, M., Gilmore, M., Hoh, E., & Butsic, V. (2021). Cannabis and the Environment: What Science Tells Us and What We Still Need to Know. *Environmental Science &Amp; Technology Letters*, *8*(2), 98–107. doi:10.1021/acs.estlett.0c00844

Zimmer, M., & Proferes, N. J. (2014). A topology of Twitter research: disciplines, methods, and ethics. *Aslib Journal of Information Management*, *66*(3), 250–261. doi:10.1108/ajim-09-2013-0083

Chapter 10
Addressing the Cannabis Stigmas: South African Perspective

Nkhensani Angelic Maluleke
University of KwaZulu-Natal, South Africa

ABSTRACT

There is a confusion leading to the stigmatization of cannabis topics. Cannabis is referred to as 'marijuana', weed, and dagga, among other names depending on the adjoining audience. Consumption of cannabis leads to social devaluation of the user within communities. The cannabis industry is known for being illegal, scheduled as an illicit drug, and associated with brain damage leading to criminal activities. There is zero to less information available for the public regarding the topic. Cannabis use is associated with negativity arising from the consequences of substance abuse. The researcher followed the commonly practiced stigmas toward cannabis. The stigmas accumulate from the familiarity of the topic following the media, word of mouth, and local experience. all of which affect the uneasiness and discrimination of users. RSA policies were used as a guide in addressing the cannabis stigmas. The names: cannabis, marijuana, dagga, etc. were clarified. The chapter aims to address the stigma by giving insights into the legislation, medical cannabis, and clarifying the commonly identified stigmas.

KEY ISSUES

The following issues will be covered in this chapter

- Introduction: what are the stigmas around the topic
- Is cannabis unhealthy: Medical perspective
- Is cannabis legal: Legislation perspective
- General discussion: other stigmas
- Possibility: Future without cannabis stigma

DOI: 10.4018/978-1-6684-6346-8.ch010

INTRODUCTION

The normal state of Cannabis is illegal unless the use is justified. There is a lot of confusion leading to the stigmatization of adjoining Cannabis. The conversation around the "cannabis" topic is not so easy to strike, definitely not around children and not even health practitioners. The term cannabis tends to automatically echo marijuana in the conversation of many people. Cannabis is a term used to describe a plant. Today cannabis is referred to as 'marijuana', weed, and dagga among other names depending on the adjoining audience. First and foremost, it is important to note that cannabis is not marijuana/dagga/weed. Cannabis remains the plant that has the ability to produce a variety of cannabis plants just like many other plants.

Cannabis has descendants and it can be used in different ways. The cannabis industry is on the rise throughout the world [United Nations Office on Drugs and Crime (UNODC, 2022)]. From the 1970s cannabis became illegal in most countries up until the 21st century (Payan, Brown, & Song, 2021, p. 1149). In South Africa, a person found in possession of any raw cannabis species anywhere would be jailed (Perkel, 2005; National Prosecuting Authority, 2015), this was supported by parliament decisions through the medicines act and Drug act (Medicine and Related Substances Control act 101 of 1965 section 22a & Drugs and Drug trafficking act 140 Of 1992 section 4b) (Lubaale & Mavundla, 2019). On the other hand, Citizens were encouraged to report any illegal possession of raw cannabis of any form. This elevated an adverse impact on how the world views cannabis in the current age. The passage below aims to acknowledge the stigmas entangled.

To date, the cannabis industry is known for being illegal, classified as an illicit drug, associated with brain damage or increased productivity, and influencing criminal activities (UNODC, 2022). Common concerns discovered from cannabis legalization globally are public health, crime, illicit market, accidents, and the economy (Light, Orens, Rowberry, & Saloga, 2016; Farmer, Monfort, & Woods, 2022; UNODC, 2022). These concerns influence the stigmatisation of the industry, as a result, the address below will cover the concerns.

There is zero to less information available for the public regarding the topic, the information is not easily accessible, and the world is filled with different perceptions around the topic. The government of South Africa has developed policies, collaborated with United Nations (INCB), and employed a regulating body (SAHPRA) to regulate the cannabis industry. South African policies were used as a guide in addressing the cannabis stigmas. This chapter aims to address the stigma by giving insights into the legislation on cannabis and clarifying the commonly identified concerns about cannabis.

Cannabis Stigma

Stigma is a concept that encompasses the attitudes and behaviour of an individual or group towards anything controversial to a shared belief (Ahern, Stuber, & Galea, 2007). According to Goffman, Shared belief refers to standards, culture, as well as anything categorised as normal ("norms") by a social unit (Goffman, 1963). Stigmatization is defined as "*a process that happens as a result of the social construction of identity, whereby people who don't fit the stereotype of being "normal" are susceptible to criticism from others*" (Skliamis, Korf, & Benschop, 2020, p. 4). Communities form their own beliefs and societal norms based on their encounters, religion, and culture, as a result, the perceived stigmas cannot be generalized (Goffman, 1963). Stigma is said to arise when there is a perceived characteristic that is conflicting with a set societal norm leading to uneasiness and discrimination. Consumption of cannabis results in the social devaluation of the user in society, Therefore, stigmas differ depending on the discrediting audience (Skliamis, Korf, & Benschop, 2020).

Cannabis use is associated with negativity arising from the consequences of cannabis substance abuse (Ventura, Carrara, & Fernandes, 2022). Out of curiosity, the researcher followed the commonly practised stigmas toward cannabis. The stigmas below accumulate from the familiarity of the topic from early 2000 following the media, word of mouth, and local experience.

BACKGROUND

The cannabis industry is associated with negativity in a global society. The cannabis industry refers to participants involved in the cannabis plant. These are cannabis growers, producers, manufacturers, governing bodies, standards officials, researchers, and consumers. The stigmas are *cannabis is unhealthy, illegal, and has bad consequences* as expressed by some healthcare practitioners, parents/guardians, law enforcement, and some researchers. The severity of stigma depends on the area, environmental conditions, and audience.

Yury Fedotov advised in the preface of the World Drug Report that the consequences of intoxicated individuals may result in permanent circumstances such as death through an accident, contribute to crime, and degrade economic and social development. Individuals and families that have suffered any aftereffects will automatically have a bad perception towards cannabis without understanding that there are various cannabinoids apart from the ones with high THC content. Marijuana has gained a bad reputation in society; it is listed as an illicit drug together with heroin and cocaine. Illicit drugs contribute to bringing misery to thousands of families worldwide (UNODC, 2012)

The stigmatization of cannabis has evolved positively considering the increase in the number of users globally. Over the past decade, the use of cannabis increased as reported in the World Drug report which is published annually (UNODC, 2022). Research done during the covid-19 pandemic discovered that parents of the 21st century are more relaxed towards the recreational use of cannabis compared to the parents in the previous generation (Bjorgan & Jimenez, 2022). Below are global trends which are primarily influenced by the World Drug Report, the reports gather information from over 100 countries working together with the international institution under the United Nations Office on Drugs and Crime (UNODC).

GLOBAL TRENDS

The Global trends on cannabis reported an increase in cannabis herb trafficking and an increase in the consumption of medical cannabis production. There is an increase in usage as well as cultivation of the cannabis plant as per the United Nations report of 2022 (UNODC, 2022). Following are stigmas associated with cannabis relatable in SA, however, experienced by other countries.

Cannabis affects driving ability; there is a link between car fatalities and drivers who consume cannabis THC/marijuana. High THC content cannabis reduces driving capacity (Farmer, Monfort, & Woods, 2022). This was recorded by testing drivers who were involved in car accidents (Destrebecq, 2007). The department of transport and a research Company by the name CSIR in South Africa conducted a test on 400 professional drivers. The tests were conducted on various national roads and 60 drivers tested positive for cannabis. In many countries, drivers involved in fatal accidents commonly test positive for cannabis THC, and alcohol (Perkel, 2005). A study conducted in the United States between 2009-2019 indicates an increase in injuries from accidents as well as an increase in fatal crash rates in drivers who tested positive for THC (Farmer, Monfort, & Woods, 2022). Studies advise that cannabis has a lesser effect compared to alcohol, however, the consumption of both alcohol and cannabis at the same time is much more dangerous and it is highly discouraged among drivers (UNODC, 2016).

Negative influence towards the youth; globally, the consumption of marijuana among youth keeps on increasing as recorded by Destrebecq (2007), UNODC (2012, 2016), and UNODC (2022). In the year 2005, 139 Teenagers admitted to Durban hospital in the trauma ward tested positive for THC (Perkel, 2005). As of 2020, reports indicate an increase in hospital admissions of cannabis-related cases among youth (UNODC, 2022). Cannabis herbs are said to be the most affordable and accessible to the majority of adolescents (Bjorgan & Jimenez, 2022). This contributes to the increase in cannabis consumption by the youth.

The effects of cannabis use on the brain stigma; Scientists have indicated that the THC content may cause harm to the developing brain (Perkel, 2005). The brain develops from the beginning of life to about the early twenties and varies from person to person. Studies on the effects of Marijuana among youth indicate negative effects on cognitive functions, IQ, memory, and brain retention (Bjorgan & Jimenez, 2022). Furthermore, teenage pregnancy and school dropout are linked to the increase in alcohol and illicit drug consumption, which results in demonizing cannabis (Bjorgan & Jimenez, 2022; Manu, Douglas, Ntsaba, & Tarkang, 2021).

Influence on the market; worldwide there is a concern of cannabis negatively influences the market through an increase in the illicit market (UNODC, 2022). The perception was that cannabis for recreation will replace alcohol and cigarettes and decrease the market (UNODC, 2012). The tax rates on alcohol and cigarettes are normally higher compared to other products, and tax contributes to the state funds (Light, Orens, Rowberry, & Saloga, 2016). The cannabis market on its own has increased and the industry is generating income, however, sales of Tobacco cigarettes have decreased (UNODC, 2022).

A study was conducted in the Eastern Cape province of South Africa, to harness the perspective of illicit marijuana growers and traders concerning the legalization of commercial marijuana. The study reveals that some growers and traders rely on selling without lawful permission (committing a crime) to make a living (Manu, Douglas, Ntsaba, & Tarkang, 2021). Although there is a valid reason such as lack of employment, this proves that the level of desperation to generate income is high, therefore, highly possible for the traders to sell to teenagers. As a result, teenagers are seen intoxicated or under the influence of substances on many occasions within communities.

Cannabis use influences levels of crime (Kitchen, Kabba, & Sekamatte, 2022). First, the Illicit market of cannabis has been noted to be a challenge in many countries. The records vary and they are estimated. These allegations are linked to the increase in the recreational use of cannabis, popularly consumed by smoking (UNODC, 2022). Secondly, Criminal activities such as violence and property crimes have been noted as concerns. UNODC report stated that there are no clear changes in crime rates (UNODC, 2022).

Studies predict that the use of cannabinoids is addictive and releases chemicals that contribute to psychoactive effects (Chakravarti, Ravi, & Ganju, 2014). Substances dependence may encourage the user to attain substances at any cost including criminal activities. For example, breaking in properties in order to attain currency to purchase substances. An increase in break-ins to cannabis dispensaries has been noted in low-income neighbourhoods (UNODC, 2022). SAHPRA has a security requirement for businesses dealing with cannabis (SAHPRA, 2020).

Generally, the use of substances does not have an impact on crime levels, however, the abuse of substances could lead the users to various activities. Note, reaction differs from person to person and can be relatable to the effects of alcohol, (Ventura, Carrara, & Fernandes, 2022). The perception of cannabis is demarcated by the heavy smokers and mischievous users of the marijuana drug. Nevertheless, other useful arrays can be beneficial from cannabis

MEDICAL CONTEXT

Cannabinoid is a biological term used to describe active constituents of cannabis composites (Fishera, Moorec, & Fogartyd, 2020). Cannabinoids consist of active cannabinoid receptors, receptor one and receptor two. Society including some medical practitioners believes cannabis is unhealthy and has long-term consequences, Adebisi & Olaoye, (2022) discusses medical benefits and possible roles that African pharmacists can play in advancing medicinal cannabis. The below passage discusses cannabis stigma from the medical perspective, learning about medical cannabis and why it is used for medicinal purposes and answering the question: Is cannabis unhealthy?

What is medical cannabis? Fishera, et al., (2020) used the word "Medicinal Cannabis", it is a term used for products that are administrated for medical purposes. These products contain cannabinoids, including extracts from cannabis plants and synthetic cannabinoids. Cannabinoids are exerted into the human body to affect cell function through interactions with coupled cannabinoids receptors, type 1, and type 2 (Kovalchuk & Kovalchuk, 2020)

The primary symptom of cannabis usage in the health segment is pain (Pratt, Adrienne, & Thuku, 2019). This is because many illnesses, including HIV/AIDS, cancer, TB, and flu, have painful symptoms. According to research done by Fishera, Moorec, & Fogarty, (2020) on pain, people who used cannabis to relieve pain after stopping their medicine reported excellent outcomes including pain after surgical procedures to treat cancer (chemotherapy).

In accumulation, cannabis is also widely utilized in psychiatric wards to address diseases connected with mental health such as sleep problems (Datta, et al., 2021). The government is advised to do a study on the cannabis sector, particularly cannabis products, and to familiarize all residents with the industry by raising awareness about the benefits offered by the industry. Mujuru and Sekhejane (2014) have observed that illegal cannabis "marijuana" usage has been rising in the present generation (Mujuru & Sekhejane, 2014).

Medicinal cannabis is legal in most countries, However, the legality of cannabis in South Africa is debatable and there are uncertainties entangled. Medical cannabis goes beyond pharmaceutical, lab-tested, and "clinically proven" products in South Africa. This is due to what is referred to as "African medicines", there are many people who grew up under the care of African medicines of which cannabis products are one of them. Cannabis product refers to all containing cannabinoids prepared to be administrated by human beings or animals (Republic of South Africa, 2020). There are various methods of administrating cannabinoids in the human body, this includes smoking, being taken orally for ingestion, placed under the tongue, injecting through the rectum, smoked, inhaled (steaming), sublingually, and rubbing onto the skin (Whiting, et al., 2015) (Freeman, Hindocha, Green, & Bloomfield, 2019).

A pharmacy practice-based research study done by two Nigerian lecturers confirms that there is a knowledge gap among health professionals that needs to be filled when it comes to the risk and benefits of cannabis. The two lecturers are qualified pharmacists and highly aware of everyday discussions around the topic within their field. Breaches were discovered based on the African perspective of medical cannabis. The emphasis remains that the study on the cannabis paradigm should not be generalized (Adebisi & Olaoye, 2022).

The purpose of the study was to maximize the use of cannabis in Africa, despite the perception of the potential aggressive use of recreational cannabis. Cannabis can be used to aid many health conditions in people's lives. Various cannabis plants contain over 450 active constituents and more than 60 exclusive cannabinoids (Adebisi & Olaoye, 2022).

About the Medical Cannabis

Cannabinoids originate from cannabigerolic acid (CBGA) (Kovalchuk & Kovalchuk, 2020). Four major cannabinoids are currently researched for medicinal purposes.

1. Cannabigerol (CBG) – is known for the treatment of depression in psychiatric institutions. Support in sleeplessness as well. CBG is obtained from direct heat or light including sunlight.
2. Tetra hydro cannabinolic acid (THCA) – is known for promoting high effects however it is also known for inducing relaxation of the body and mind. responsible for anti-anxiety and pain
3. Cannabidiolic acid (CBDA) – is known for curing various pain including the one induced by chemotherapy
4. Cannabichromene acid (CBCA) – is known for anti-inflammation widely used during chemotherapy and radiation it also cures acne

THCA, CBDA, and CBCA undergo heat-induced decarboxylation process separately which converts them into active compounds known as tetra hydro cannabinol (THC). cannabidiol (CBD), and cannabichromene. Further exposure to THCA can result in conversion to Cannabinolic acid (CBNA) therefore THC converts into Cannabinol (CBN) – known for supporting bone cells and effective sleep aid. (Kovalchuk & Kovalchuk, 2020)

Cannabinoids' mode of action depends on their neuromodulator activity through retrograde neurotransmission and binding to the two main types of receptors - CB1 and CB2 receptors. The two receptors allocate the cannabinoids into the central nervous system and then further allocate them in various extra-neural tissues bordering the nerve terminals. (Datta, et al., 2021)

Cannabinoids can be derived from various sources, which regulate differently, as a result, the cannabinoids signal pathways to the host physiological system and locate different tumour cell types (Kovalchuk & Kovalchuk, 2020). An individual needs to understand cannabinoid types of receptors that are being activated by receiving cannabinoids. (Chakravarti, Ravi, & Ganju, 2014)

Many researchers have classified cannabis into two groups: hemp and marijuana. Hemp has a variety of CBDs and marijuana is the one with high THC content. Depending on the country of residence, cannabis with a THC content of 0.3 per cent or less is referred to as hemp and is regarded as lawful. Whereas cannabis with a THC content of 0.3 per cent or more, is commonly known as marijuana and is prohibited in public spaces (SAHPRA, 2019).

The most dominant cannabinoid in hemp is CBD and marijuana is dominated by THC cannabinoid. The significant variance is in CBD and THC content. The leaves of the two (marijuana and hemp) looks almost the same. It is difficult to differentiate them by just observing with the naked eye. That is one of the reasons they both became illegal at the same time. Conversely, Hemp is grown specifically for industrial and medicinal use. Marijuana works for both medicinal and recreational use.

When THC is administrated, it influences the cannabinoid receptors in the central nervous system including the brain and immune system and produces intoxicating effects. However, due to genetic variation from one person to another, it is not possible to generalize the response of an individual without an experiment.

Following the old cures for many diseases, medical study has discovered the advantages of cannabis lineage (Datta, et al., 2021). Medical cannabis is used to treat cancer treatment or radiation-related nausea, loss of appetite, muscular spasticity, lack of sleep, and other conditions (Savundranayagam & Sager, 2021). To treat chronic diseases, cannabis African medicine products can be used instead of other prescribed medications.

In studies where compounds were analysed, it was shown that while healthy tissues are shielded from apoptosis, cannabinoid receptors exhibit particular cytotoxicity that acts against tumour cells (Datta, et al., 2021). Studies on cancer cell lines were conducted and cannabinoids have been shown to be a powerful anticancer fighter for tumour xenografts. Some tumour cells were shown to exhibit quantity-limit resistance to the chemotherapy treatment (Bogdanovic, Borisev, & Mrdjanovic, 2017).

Cannabinoids generated from the cannabis plant are what make up medical cannabis products effective (Freeman, Hindocha, Green, & Bloomfield, 2019). The health quality controller and good manufacturing practices should be in place to certify products as being of high quality. Products come in a variety of forms, including prescription doses in the form of pills or supplements, oils, edibles, lotions/creams, tea, liquids, or dried blooming buds that are occasionally offered in granular form. These products are produced in accordance with the recommended level of standardized cannabinoids content (SAHPRA, 2020)

On the other side, cannabis is sometimes misused to treat ailments including headaches, stress, sleeplessness, etc (Business Tech, 2022). In Africa, some people attempt to create their own homemade treatments/medicine by smoking, boiling, inhaling, and ingesting cannabis herbs. Such practices are done in an effort to heal various diseases and disorders. The problem lies in the fact that the content composition is unknown, and it can only be determined through laboratory tests. The above-mentioned practices have resulted in many people being admitted to hospitals due to abuse and addiction. 2019 (Freeman, Hindocha, Green, & Bloomfield, 2019). Germany reported an increase in cannabis-related hospital admissions with high dependence syndrome (UNODC, 2022).

Africans (specifically black Africans) acknowledge the presence of conventional healers. These include religious healers, traditional healers, and herbalists. These healers issue a prescription to their patients to use cannabis products. However, for safety and effectiveness, the Medical Innovation Bill,(2014) states that a prescription is to be written by a licensed professional. In most cases, the prescription contains a non-psychoactive cannabinoid. Furthermore, regulating body recommends necessary medical tests taken to account and ensure the treatment is effective before ingesting cannabis products (SAHPRA, 2020).

In general, hemp produces products filled with nutrients that are good for the health of an individual (Callaway, 2004). Hemp has been recorded as a source of protein and fatty acids (Rupasinghe, Davis, Kumar, & Murray, 2020). Hemp can be in a form of raw seed, cooked or pressed to form other products (Callaway, 2004). Products such as hemp juice, Maltos-cannabis, hemp milk, hemp oil, hemp protein, and of course medicinal drugs made from various CBDs. These products are believed to offer much relief to the overall health sector (Rupasinghe, Davis, Kumar, & Murray, 2020, pp. 9-14).

In a study conducted to determine the seed chemical composition of hemp farming in Quebec, the study examines protein concentration and fatty acids, it was concluded that the hemp seed grown in the area of the research (Canada), is a balanced diet Product (Vonapartis, Aubin, Seguin, & Mustafa, 2015). A recent study suggests advances in science be made to include industrial hemp in food ingredients and nutraceuticals to aid functional food (Rupasinghe, Davis, Kumar, & Murray, 2020). The medication's content and nutritional information should be made clear, together with the product's adverse effects must be conversed.

Side effects of cannabis use include dizziness, short-term memory loss, severe anxiety, drowsiness, and psychosis (Datta, et al., 2021). It is recommended the drivers wait a minimum of 4 hours after consumption and observe any possible side effects. Poor HIV/Aids management has been reported among illicit drug users, and users' maladministration of chronic medications (Castro-Granell, Garin, & Jaen, 2021). Individuals have been advised to keep a record of any symptoms and disclose them to a healthcare practitioner of reach.

Is cannabis unhealthy? No, however, cannabis should be consumed with the right intentions. Anything can cause harm if not administered with caution. The stigma is highly likely to be caused by a lack of knowledge regarding the chemical composition of the cannabis product at hand especially the THC content and cannabinoid composition. Knowledge about the product at hand is firmly advised. People should refrain from demonizing the term "cannabis" based on one of four major cannabinoids for the sake of the health benefits contained. Traditional doctors are not trained in cutting-edge science, therefore, the administration of cannabis products in an attempt to cure certain diseases may result in undesirable situations.

LEGISLATION PERSPECTIVE

Is cannabis legal? To date, there is confusion when it comes to the legal status of the topic. The stigma is *cannabis is illegal*. The legal status of cannabis differs from one country to another. The clarity below is in accordance with the Republic of South Africa 2021. In the ancient ages, Cannabis was just another plant, used for industrial, medicinal, and recreational.

To start, it is significant to introduce "marijuana/dagga" among other terms used to denote cannabis: Tetra Hydro Cannabinoid (THC). Dagga is another name for the high THC content, cannabis Sativa plant also known as Ganja, Grass, Hash, holy herb, Joint, Pot, Weed, Marijuana, etc. This emanates from the cannabis Sativa species widely used as intoxicated stimulation. It gives the famously known *high effects* experience (Datta, et al., 2021). The United States has listed Marijuana as a schedule 1 drug. High stimulation from THC is said to be a root cause of various crimes in the communities (UNODC, 2022). In 2005, Charles Perkel reported above one-quarter number of 1050 convicted persons were found to have THC content in their bodies. Tests were conducted in various SA police stations in the year 2000, Of which 26,9% of prisoners were from Cape Town and 44,4% in Durban (Perkel, 2005).

The possession of cannabis is legal however, there is a quantity limit (Republic of South Africa, 2020). Cannabis dagga as referred to by the government gazette of drugs and drug trafficking act No. 140 of 1992, has been mentioned under a schedule of undesirable dependence-producing substances (Republic of South Africa, 1992, p. 67). .

Schedule 1 drugs are characterized by a lack of accepted safety, has a high potential for substance abuse, and are not used for any medical treatment in the *United State* of America (Anderson, 2022). This means that no prescription is permissible to be issued by a health practitioner to patients. RSA partake in the United Nations on Narcotic drugs (1961) which is an International Narcotics Control

Board (INCB). According to the INCB, Cannabis marijuana is categorized as schedule 1 and schedule 4 subject to special restrictions.

Special restrictions include the content level of THC among other levels of cannabinoids. Please bear in mind that Marijuana (high in THC content) hails from Cannabis, it is not Cannabis. For this clarification, Marijuana is defined as dried leaves looking green to light brown in colour sometimes combined with stems, seeds, and flowers. Categorization of marijuana as schedule one only means that it is a dangerous substance and not acceptable by law.

Through the internet, movies, and all things media the world is connected and exposed to almost everything, the good, and the bad. Countries have developed and implemented measures to control the use of substances in order to mitigate social risk and abuse. However, through information transfer, migration, and emigration the rules are likely to be compared and sometimes misdirected leading to confusion. The schedule 1 drug status was adopted by many countries and marijuana was banned completely.

The public made an appeal for marijuana to be removed as a Schedule I drug due to the health benefits that it offers (Lubaale & Mavundla, 2019). And that is when the INCB scheduled cannabis as level 4 with special conditions. The scheduling of cannabis varies from country to country (UNODC, 2022). There are amendments witnessed with regard to the policies pertaining to the subject (Lubaale & Mavundla, 2019). Policies get misinterpreted easily throughout the world; this is due to high interest in the topic. In South Africa, dagga is listed as a drug (Republic of South Africa, 2017). However, dagga, also known as marijuana, is a member of the cannabis plant.

Guidelines stipulated (policies) should be read in context with the topic in cases where the policy just mentions the term "cannabis" without specifying which one. For example, under the drug trafficking act of 1992, the policy is addressing cannabis for recreational use, in some pages of the policy, there is the stand-alone term cannabis while on some pages it classifies cannabis-dagga (marijuana). The same applies to the SAHPRA regulative body. Cannabis has various products, and different methods of applications and can be used for different purposes.

The Republic of South Africa is a constitutional state whereby customary law and religious personal law apply. The government together with a regulatory body made measures to mitigate the risk of misuse in order to protect the citizen's well-being. The table below summarises the current regulatory status of cannabis in SA.

Table 1. Overview of cannabis regulations in South Africa.

Cannabis use	Regulatory
Medicinal Cannabis Legislation	Medicines and Related Substances Act (Act 101 of 1965)
Recreational Cannabis Legislation	Cannabis for Private Purposes Bill, 2020
Recreational Cannabis Legal status: Illegal	Decriminalized (Confined to private settings to which the public does not have access as of right.)
Medicinal Cannabis Legal status:	Legal for all purposes
Penalties for cannabis possession for personal use	Public consumption is liable to a fine or between two and fifteen years of imprisonment.
Regulatory body	South African Health Products Authority (SAHPRA)

The legality of the topic is subject to limitations, sometimes known as terms and conditions. Before the year 2019, in South Africa possession of marijuana meant imprisonment between 0 to 15 years depending on the quantity. The government (of RSA) together with researchers began to investigate the topic and in 2014 completed the research and announced the results in a form of a policy. The policy document was released as "The Medical Innovation bill". Various citizens contested against the bill in magistrate court demanding freedom to practice their religion and beliefs (National Prosecuting Authority, 2015; Lubaale & Mavundla, 2019).

In response, the government gave other citizens affected to submit their input online for review. Even though not everyone had access to technology, the inputs were to be submitted through the government's website. In 2019 the policy was developed and published as Cannabis for private purpose bill, (2020). There are few disputes with the current policy (Lubaale & Mavundla, 2019), however, until the final review is released the statutes of the current bill remains effective (Republic of South Africa, 2020).

The medical innovation bill is intended for the department of health service and public use. The purpose of the bill is to enable innovations in medical treatments and the legalization of cannabinoids for medical purposes for the benefit of commercial and industrial use (Medical Innovation Bill, 2014). The bill provides clearance to the medical practitioner and encourages responsible innovation in medical treatment. Support best practices and regulate the use of cannabinoids.

South Africa has employed a regulatory body known as SAHPRA (South Africa Health Products Regulatory Authority). SAHPRA regulates all health products. This means that all cannabis medications have to undergo this regulatory body before they can be available for public consumption. SAHPRA ensures the THC content of all cannabinoids complies with the maximum content stipulated by the medical innovation bill. The regulatory body monitors the cultivation of cannabis and is responsible for issuing a cultivator's license for medical purposes.

Manufacturing of medical cannabis is to be monitored by SAHPRA, whereby monitoring and evaluation of production take place. They are responsible for inspecting and then registering medical products such as complementary medicines, medical devices, and vitro diagnostics. The objective is to ensure the safety, efficiency, and quality of the product. Manufacturers, distributors, and wholesalers are bound by law to obtain a license and permit from SAHPRA. For both human and animal health products.

SAHPRA and the department of health assess the benefits and risks of the products and categorize the product according to the suitable scheduling of substances. Scheduling assists in controlled substances. The scheduling process of medicines is on the basis of their Active Pharmaceutical Ingredients (APIs) (SAHPRA, 2019). Scheduling in this context refers to the categorization of substance for the following reasons:

- Compliance with international drug control conventions
- Protect patients against harmful medicines
- Meet medical needs through appropriate levels of control
- Resolution and policy with the International Narcotics Control Board (INCB)
- National policy implementation and amendments (Drugs and Drug Trafficking Act No. 140 of 1992, Prevention and Treatment of Drug Dependency Act No. 20 of 1992, and the Criminal procedure Act No. 51 of 1977

The scheduling of Cannabis according to SAHPRA is influenced by the safety of the cannabinoids content. THC and CBD are listed as substances in the Medicines and Related Substances act 1965, act

101 (Republic of South Africa, 2017). The medicines and related substances act stipulated the parent's name of the substance, scheduling, and the level of substance administrator according to the Health Professional Council of South Africa. Cannabis: "dagga" plant including products is schedule 7 except for processed hemp fibre which contains 0.1 per cent of THC.

According to the substance act products containing 0.01 THC are exempted from schedule 7. These are all products manufactured from processed cannabis, which does not contain whole cannabis seeds and is not suitable for smoking, ingestion, or inhaling purposes. Alternatively, the products are labelled "not for internal human use". Products made from processed cannabis seed must contain less or equal to 10 milligrams per kg. Processed products refer to chemical, mechanical, or other artificial means excluding natural decay. (Republic of South Africa, 2017)

The scheduling of substances is approved by the minister of health upon the recommendation of the regulatory body, SAHPRA. Schedules and Acts are published in the Government Gazette. Amendments notices and regulations are published in the Government Gazette and SAHPRA website. The supply, sale, and administration of scheduled substances is in accordance with the Medicines and Related Substance act No 101 of 1965, the legal framework for scheduling and regulations control.

According to the department of health, all medicines are subjected to the scheduling process through SAHPRA. Scheduling allows for various regulatory controls to be applied to substances. The main goal is the safety of products concerning one of eight therapeutic Schedules. Cannabis has been listed more than once in different scheduling levels, this is due to its various therapeutic use as indicated by the usage indication, depending on the dosage form, mode of administration, strength, dose, duration, or a combination of these variables (SAHPRA, 2019, p. 4; SAHPRA, 2020). The below table is a clarification of the scheduling of substances

Table 2. Schedule framework, adapted from (SAHPRA, 2019) and (Republic of South Africa, 2017)

Scheduling Framework	
Schedule 0	Available through general sales retailers
Schedule 1	Available at pharmacy over-the-counter product
Schedule 2	Pharmacist prescription product
Schedule 3	Prescription-only medicines
Schedule 4	Authorized prescriber, level of profession differs, specified by the health profession Council
Schedule 5&6	
Schedule 7	Prohibited substances, special permit required
Schedule 8	Limited use, special permits

As part of the INCB, it is required that the participating country define the type of cannabis permissible for cultivation. The country is to define the procedures for scheduling, registration, and licensing qualifying products. And the control system used by the country to control medical cannabis cultivation should be well-defined. The country of RSA has established a regulatory framework that supports medical cannabis and general research on the topic. The research assists with the improvement of the regulatory procedure and framework.

Cannabis is controlled internationally in line with the 1961 single conversion of the United Nations. However, the legal status of Cannabis in South Africa is as follows (SAHPRA, 2019):

- Schedule 7: cannabis, the whole plant, and part of.
- Schedule 6: tetrahydrocannabinol (THC) for therapeutic use as prescribed by a professionally registered medical practitioner
- Schedule 4: cannabidiol (CBD) for therapeutic use by an authorised prescriber
- Schedule 0: CBD as a supplement, subject to a limited dose.

Synthetic cannabinoids are also recognized and scheduled accordingly. Synthetic cannabinoids are substances with cannabis and related effects chemicals (Republic of South Africa, 2017).

Cannabis for medicinal use is a pharmaceutical cannabis product registered by SAHPRA. In the year 2020, the contradiction of the law was made clear by the release of cannabis for private purpose bill. The bill was issued to the department of justice and correctional services to regulate cannabis use and amend provisions of certain laws.

The cannabis for private purpose bill respects the right to privacy for adults however they regulate the amount of cannabis to be possessed. Adults are also allowed to cultivate a specified amount and possess cannabis plant materials. However, adults must ensure children do not have access to cannabis material, to protect children against the harm of cannabis. The bill provides guidelines for the penalty of a person arrested for misuse or possession of more than the stipulated quantity of cannabis (Republic of South Africa, 2020, p. 2).

Licensed manufacturers are allowed to dispatch herbal cannabis products which are lab tested, free of contaminants, and contains accepted level of cannabinoids. Cannabis products that are not yet registered but authorized by registered medical practitioners can be obtained under section 21 of the Medicines Act. Authorization of products is motivated by the severity of illness with evidence that supports the patient's need for such products. (SAHPRA, 2019, p. 11)

Licensing of cannabis is to be applied through SAHPRA. The approval is subject to the integrity of the business representative, security of the premises, and special requirement pertaining to staff working with cannabis products and cultivation. There are stipulated security measures that need to be in place surrounding cannabis. Workers should undergo training as specified by the regulating body. If conditions are compromised (such as security breach, staff reshuffling, business relocation or suspension) the business representative should report the incident and have the license suspended until the restoration of the accepted conditions.

In summary, all cannabis use is legal but subject to conditions. Conditions for recreational includes administration in a private space and for a person above the age of 18 years. Transportation and possession should be within the stipulated quantity. Citizens will be charged if found in possession of more than the stipulated weight. Medical use of cannabis raw herbs is subject to authorisation subsequent to supporting evidence which includes dosage quantity, method of administration, duration of treatment, and monitoring of patient technique. In case the patient is under 18 years, informed consent by a parent or legal representative is required. The legislation is subject to amendments, therefore, requires a continuous learning of the current and unlearning of the outdated regulations.

DISCUSSIONS

The cannabis industry is the fastest-growing industry worldwide. Rising popularity among all ages among the population. Continuing with the topic, it is important to recall that cannabis is the umbrella of many other products, and the famous product is "marijuana." However, marijuana is not the topic, the topic aims to address the stigmas around the cannabis industry. The aim is to facilitate another perspective in the direction of the cannabis industry.

Commercial farming of cannabis is allowed provided the farmer has obtained a license from the regulating body (SAHPRA, 2020). Retailers, importers, exporters, manufacturers, distributors, and cultivators in the cannabis market should have a license and permit to acquire or supply THC-containing products according to the medicines act (SAHPRA, 2020). Recall, Cannabis has been authorized for medical purposes since 2014 (Medical Innovation Bill, 2014), and as of 2019 people are now allowed to grow the plants in their private space (Cannabis for private purpose bill, 2020). Retailers have to apply for a distribution and transportation license (SAHPRA, 2020).

Over 100 different cannabinoids have been identified in the cannabis Sativa plant (Bogdanovic, Borisev, & Mrdjanovic, 2017). Cannabis is used for varied reasons, however, due to the normalized illicit status. Consumers need to justify their reasons for using cannabis to be accepted by their relative communities. Cannabis users experience social stigmatization of discrimination, perceived devaluation, and alienation (Skliamis, Korf, & Benschop, 2020). Depending on the audience, the user experience discrimination simply by disclosing that they use cannabis. The user is then expected to give an explanation in order to earn social value and acceptance.

Stigmatization of cannabis can sometimes be gender-based, when a woman consumes cannabis, society perceives the woman as being rebellious. As a result, cannabis user prefers not to disclose their usage status for fear of embarrassment or losing their social status. The stigmatization is also influenced by several religious beliefs; some beliefs disapprove of recreational cannabis use (Skliamis, Korf, & Benschop, 2020). As a result, users suffer internalized guilt and perceive social rejection (Ventura, Carrara, & Fernandes, 2022). It is at the heart of this chapter to bring awareness to reduce stigmatization so that people can be honest and also easily get help should there be a need such as addiction rehabilitation.

Recreational use of marijuana may result in a generation that considers the entire cannabis industry immoral. People indulge in the cannabis-Tetra hydro cannabinoid in various forms (space cookies, smoking, etc.) to experience the psychoactive "high" reaction. Marijuana substance abuse is at most through smoking, as marijuana, is often referred to as a "holy herb." On the perception of marijuana being better than a tobacco cigarette, the perception is supported by a statement such as "cannabis *is pure plant leaves crushed mechanically, there are no processes interrupting its natural form apart from leaves being crushed*. When cannabis leaves are burnt, they produce over 4000 chemicals therefore, when smoked all the chemicals go to the lungs which causes danger to the physical health of the human body. Smoking during pregnancy is discouraged (Perkel, 2005; Datta, et al., 2021).

The government has put measures in place to regulate the cannabis industry as a whole. However, the chapter cannot be concluded without acknowledging the last and sensitive political stigma. This stigma has become the norm in South Africa, corruption. Substance abuse is commonly linked with corruption within the justice system of the country. The governments are blamed for the weak justice system, which is also said to be the enabler of illicit use. The assumption is that the Government of the Republic of South Africa pays law enforcement labours low salaries, as a result, labours take bribes and compromise the controlling measures for drugs and related substances. The above paragraph is a highly sensitive topic and hopefully, future researchers will look deep into the matter.

Substance abuse is a stand-alone topic which requires systematic intervention. The aim is for readers to have enlightened perspectives, be open-minded in the communities of residence. Knowledge about the topic will enable parents and caregivers to raise a well-informed future generation and enable the government in formulating more preventative measures instead of policies. The study's objectives are to provide better treatments and precisely define negative effects, to ensure safe administration. It is recommended to follow the latest research pertaining to the above findings.

Possibility

Imagine a future without cannabis stigma. Today you can find hemp in everything from pasta and iced tea to personal care products, nutritional supplements, building materials, and clothes. The population will gain from the cannabis sector by growing the economy. The more citizens accept cannabis products, the greater the demand will be, creating more employment prospects for the unemployed. According to records (Trading Economics, 2022), South Africa possesses a high unemployment rate in African countries. With an active cannabis industry market, many citizens will be allocated work in cultivation, distribution, testing labs, and retail. These will also add to the possibility of an increase in local pharmaceutical industries.

The unemployment rate will decrease, and as a result income tax will rise. Light, Orens, Rowberry, and Clinton came to the conclusion that the legalization of cannabis had a favourable influence on the economy and noted that medical cannabis production was among the industries in Colorado that paid the most in taxes (Light, Orens, Rowberry, & Saloga, 2016). The government will earn more money as a result, and significantly, the quality of services provided by the government will increase.

Citizens will highly benefit from knowing more about the subject. Many people are suffering due to a lack of knowledge. The Department of Education should incorporate lessons on the cannabis sector into its syllabus along with actual clinic teaching in hospitals, clinics, and medical schools. The policies should also be part of the school syllabus especially concerning issues that appear every day on television.

It is important to note that there is a variety of cannabis plants, and the plant can be genetically modified to allow for the desired standards. The chemical composition of the plant highly depends on the environmental conditions, tools used, watering, and the type of lighting, soil, and fertilizers. As a result, the final outcome of the plant will determine the usage of the plant, medicinal or recreational. Cannabis comprises wide-scope production which can positively benefit the economy.

CONCLUSION

The cannabis plant receives various perceptions from different communities. Perceptions are motivated by the background factors such as economic status, level of education, personal experience concerning the topic, and knowledge of the topic. The common perception relative to the researcher was addressed. RSA regulation has been used as a point of reference to clarify some of the stigmas according to relativeness.

Stigmatization is the judgement of others who do not conform to the social standards of a particular community. Factors leading to the stigmas were investigated for a better approach when addressing the stigma. It was discovered that the majority of the perceptions from various communities arise from the view of cannabis as an intoxicating drug. The UNODC categorized cannabis marijuana as a drug and it is part of the 1992 Drugs and Drugs Trafficking Act No. 140. It is a fact that marijuana tops the list of abused drugs and related substances.

SA collaborate with the INCB, the adjoining board of participating countries that stands to regulate and control sedatives on the global level. RSA uses the Medical Innovation Bill (2014), cannabis for private use purposes (2020), and Medicine and Related substance act 1965, amended in 2017. The RSA department of health has employed a regulating body, SAHPRA, to control the production of medical products including cannabis and related products and issuing of licenses for cultivation and distribution.

Various cannabinoids support the health of humans and animals. There are several ways of administering cannabis products to the human body for various reasons. The cannabinoids give different side effects, and individual response varies. Adults are free to use a partial dose of any cannabis product of choice in private spaces. The abuse of marijuana in various communities is the problem. It would be beneficial for communities to address substance abuse which is common and unfruitful. Cannabis is not marijuana; marijuana is one of the descendent of the cannabis plants.

REFERENCES

Adebisi, Y. A., & Olaoye, D. Q. (2022). Medical Use of Cannabis in Africa: The Pharmacists' Perspective. *Innovations in Pharmacy*, *13*(1), 8. doi:10.24926/iip.v13i1.4430 PMID:36304681

Ahern, J., Stuber, J., & Galea, S. (2007). Stigma, discrimination and the health of illicit drug users. *Drug and Alcohol Dependence*, *88*(2-3), 188–196. doi:10.1016/j.drugalcdep.2006.10.014 PMID:17118578

Anderson, L. (2022, February 7). *Articles: List of Schedule 1 Drugs*. Drugs.com: https://www.drugs.com/article/csa-schedule-1.html

Bjorgan, Y., & Jimenez, S. (2022, January 1). *Effects of Recreational Marijuana Use in Adolescents*. [Thesis, Bethel University, USA]. Electronic Thesis and Dissertations, 1-64.

Bogdanovic, V., Borisev, I., & Mrdjanovic, J. (2017). A review of the Therapeutic antitumor potential of cannabinoids. *Journal of Alternative and Complementary Medicine (New York, N.Y.)*, *23*(11), 831–836. doi:10.1089/acm.2017.0016 PMID:28799775

Business Tech. (2022, April 19). South Africa is looking at legalising medical marijuana – here's how it will work. *Business Tech*. https://businesstech.co.za/news/lifestyle/578102/south-africa-is-looking-at-legalising-medical-marijuana-heres-how-it-will-work/

Callaway, J. (2004). Hempseed as a Nutritional Resource: An overview. *Euphytica*, *140*(1-2), 65–72. https://link.springer.com/content/pdf/10.1007/s10681-004-4811-6.pdf. doi:10.100710681-004-4811-6

Castro-Granell, V., Garin, N., & Jaen, A. (2021). Prevalence, beliefs and impact of drug-drug Interactions illicit drugs-antiretroviral therapy in people living with HIV in Spain. *PLoS One*, *16*(11), 1–19. doi:10.1371/journal.pone.0260334 PMID:34797882

Chakravarti, B., Ravi, J., & Ganju, R. (2014). Cannabinoids as therapeutic agents in cancer: Current status and future implications. *Oncotarget*, *5*(15), 5852–5872. doi:10.18632/oncotarget.2233 PMID:25115386

Datta, S., Ramamurthy, P., Anand, U., Singh, S., Singh, A., Dhanjal, D., Dhaka, V., Kumar, S., Kapoor, D., Nandy, S., Kumar, M., Koshy, E. P., Dey, A., Prośków, J., & Singh, J. (2021). Wonder or evil?: Multifaceted health hazards and health benefits of Cannabis sativa and its phytochemicals. *Saudi Journal of Biological Sciences*, *28*(1), 7290–7313. doi:10.1016/j.sjbs.2021.08.036 PMID:34867033

Destrebecq, D. (2007). *Cannibis in Africa; An Overview*. UNODC.

Farmer, C., Monfort, S., & Woods, A. (2022). Changes in Traffic Crash Rates After Legalization of Marijuana: Results by Crash Severity. *Journal of Studies on Alcohol and Drugs*, *83*(4), 494–501. doi:10.15288/jsad.2022.83.494 PMID:35838426

Fishera, E., Moorec, R. A., & Fogartyd, A. E. (2020). Cannabinoids, cannabis, and cannabis-based medicine for pain management: A systematicreview of randomised controlled trials. *International Association for the Study of Pain*, *00*(00), 1–22. doi:10.1097/j.pain.0000000000001929

Freeman, T. P., Hindocha, C., Green, S. F., & Bloomfield, M. A. (2019). Medicinal use of cannabis based products and cannabinoids. *BMJ (Clinical Research Ed.)*, *365*(1141), 1–7. doi:10.1136/bmj.l1141 PMID:30948383

Goffman, E. (1963). *Stigma: Notes on the Management of a Spoiled Identity*. Penguin Group.

Kitchen, C., Kabba, J. A., & Sekamatte, T. (2022). Perceptions of Cannabis in sub-Saharan Africa: Findings from a general population survey in six African countries with different Cannabis policies. Research Square, *1*, 1-14. doi:10.21203/rs.3.rs-1241985/v1

Kovalchuk, O., & Kovalchuk, I. (2020). Cannabinoids as anticancer therapeutic agents. *Cell Cycle (Georgetown, Tex.)*, *19*(9), 961–989. doi:10.1080/15384101.2020.1742952 PMID:32249682

Light, M., Orens, A., Rowberry, J., & Saloga, W. C. (2016). *The Economic Impact of Marijuana Legalization in Colorado*. Market Intelligence.

Lubaale, E., & Mavundla, S. (2019). Decriminalisation of Cannabis for Personal use in South Africa. *African Himan Rights Law Journal*, 819-842.

Manu, E., Douglas, M., Ntsaba, M., & Tarkang, E. (2021). Perspectives of illicit marijuana growers and Traders on Commercial legalisation of Marijuana in south Africa: Considerations for policy formulation. *Substance Abuse Treatment, Prevention, and Policy*, *15*(54), 54. doi:10.118613011-021-00391-w PMID:34174921

Medical Innovation Bill. (2014, February 19). Republic of South Africa: Medical Innovation Bill. *Pretoria: Government Gazette No 37349*.

Mujuru, M., & Sekhejane, P. (2014). Legalising Cannabis for Cancer: Benefits of Indigenous Cannabis Therapeutics (Briefing NO 110 ed.). Pretoria: Africa Institute Of South Africa.

National Prosecuting Authority. (2015, January 29). *The National Prosecution Authority of South Africa Annual Report 2014/2015*National Prosecution Authority of South Africa. https://www.npa.gov.za/sites/default/files/annual-reports/Annual%20Report%202014%20-%202015.pdf

Payan, D., Brown, P., & Song, A. (2021). County-Level Recreational Marijuana Policies and Local Policy Changes in Colorado and Washington State (2012-2019). *The Milbank Quarterly*, *99*(4), 1132–1161. doi:10.1111/1468-0009.12535 PMID:34407252

Perkel, C. (2005, February). Cannabis- the debate continues: A South African perspective. *South African Psychiatry Review*, *8*, 25–30.

Pratt, M. A. S., & Thuku, M. (2019). Benefits and harms of medical cannabis: A scoping review of systematic reviews. *Systematic Reviews*, *8*(320), 1–35. doi:10.118613643-019-1243-x PMID:31823819

Republic of South Africa. (1992, July 15). Drugs and Drugs Trafficking Act No. 140 of 1992. *Cape Town: Government Gazette* .

Republic of South Africa. (2017, May 26). Medicines and Related Substance Act, 1965. *Pretoria: Government Gazette*.

Republic of South Africa. (2020, August 07). Cannabis for Private Purpose Bill. *Cape Town: Government Gazette No. 43595*.

Rupasinghe, H. P., Davis, A., Kumar, S., Murray, B., & Zheljazkov, V. D. (2020). Industrial Hemp (Cannabis sativa subsp. sativa) as an Emerging Source for Value-Added Functional Food Ingredients and Nutraceuticals. *Molecules (Basel, Switzerland)*, *25*(4078), 1–24. doi:10.3390/molecules25184078 PMID:32906622

SAHPRA. (2019, September 04). Medicinal and Research for Medicinal and Research Purposes. *Sahpra*. https://www.sahpra.org.za/wp-content/uploads/2019/09/SAHPRA-Medicinal-Cannabis-Update_Presentation-to-PC_04Sept2019_Final.pdf

SAHPRA. (2020, January 01). Cannabis and Related Substances. *Sahpra*. https://www.sahpra.org.za/wp-content/uploads/2020/01/Cannabis_and_related_substances_A5_final-1.pdf

Savundranayagam, M. Y., & Sager, Z. S. (2021). The Experiences, Benefits, and Harms of Cannabis Use in Later Life. *Clinical Gerontologist*, *44*(1), 1–2. doi:10.1080/07317115.2020.1855131 PMID:33357131

Skliamis, K., Korf, A., & Benschop, D. (2020). Cannabis users and stigma: A comparison of uses from European countries with different cannibis policies. *European Journal of Criminology*, 1–18.

Trading Economics. (2022, November 04). *Unemployment Rate*. Trading Economics. https://tradingeconomics.com/country-list/unemployment-rate?continent=africa

UNODC. (2012). *World Drug Report* . United Nations publication.

UNODC. (2016). *World Drug Report.* United Nations publication.

UNODC. (2022, June 01). United Nations Office on Drugs and Crime: World Drug Report part 3. *Drug Market Trends: Cannabis + Opiods.* https://www.unodc.org/res/wdr2022/MS/WDR22_Booklet_3.pdf

Ventura, C., Carrara, B., & Fernandes, R. (2022). General Beliefs About Illicit Drug Use and Stigma: Perspective of People Who Use Illicit Drugs. *Community Mental Health Journal (2022) 58,*1346–1353. doi:10.1007/s10597-022-00944-8

Vonapartis, E., Aubin, M., Seguin, P., Mustafa, A., & Charron, J.-B. (2015). Seed composition of ten industrial hemp cultivars approved for. *Journal of Food Composition and Analysis*, *39*, 8–12. doi:10.1016/j.jfca.2014.11.004

Whiting, P., Wolff, R. D., Keurentjes, J., Lang, S., Misso, K., Ryder, S., & Kleijnen, J. (2015). Cannabinoids for Medical Use: A Systematic Review and Meta-analysis. *Journal of the American Medical Association*, *1*(24), 2456–2473. doi:10.1001/jama.2015.6358 PMID:26103030

KEY TERMS AND DEFINITIONS

Cannabinoids: are the active constituent found in the cannabis plant (Fishera, Moorec, & Fogartyd, 2020)

Cannabis Products: are anything made from the cannabis plant or synthetic cannabis composites (Freeman, Hindocha, Green, & Bloomfield, 2019)

Cannabis Stigma: refers to the perceptions of the cannabis topic

Cannabis: is a genus type of flowering plant (Datta, et al., 2021).

CBD: refers to Cannabidiol, a constituent of cannabis widely used for medicinal cannabis (Fishera, Moorec, & Fogartyd, 2020)

Hemp: is a type of cannabis plant which contains low THC composites (Callaway, 2004).

INCB: *stands for* International Narcotics Control Board

Marijuana: is a cannabis descendant plant that carries high content of THC, also known as Ganja, Grass, Hash, holy herb, Joint, Pot, Weed, etc. (UNODC, 2012)

Medicinal cannabis: refers to products made from cannabis extracts, plants, or even synthetic cannabis for medical purposes (Castro-Granell, Garin, & Jaen, 2021).

SAHPRA (South African Health Product Regulatory Authority): is a regulatory body appointed by the department of health of the Republic of South Africa (SAHPRA, 2020)

Stigma: refers to discrediting attributes influenced by the societal identity (Goffman, 1963)

Tetra-Hydro Cannabinol (THC): is a type of cannabinoid that contains high stimulation constituents known as "high effects", hail from the Cannabis Sativa plant (Skliamis, Korf, & Benschop, 2020).

UNODC: *stands for* United Nations Office on Drugs and Crime

Chapter 11
The Role of Supply Chain Technology in the Growth of the Cannabis Industry

Thokozani Patmond Mbhele
University of KwaZulu-Natal, South Africa

Ncube Eric
University of KwaZulu-Natal, South Africa

ABSTRACT

Technological innovations seem to contribute to improving lifestyles, a better allocation of resources, and ensuring intensive economic growth. The purpose is to cogitate on the essence of technological transformation and encapsulate the value propositions of innovation activities to improve the producer value and socio-economic growth. The first objective is to establish the role of technology and innovations in the development of the cannabis and hemp industry. Then, to analyse how supply chain technology influences the socio-economic growth of the cannabis industry. This chapter uses the systematic literature review method and synthesizes the existing conceptual approaches in the industry. The study embodied the review protocol, identified the inclusion exclusion criteria for relevant publications, performed an in-depth search for studies, and is followed by a critical appraisal, data extraction, and a synthesis of past findings. The study reveals that the role of technology and innovation invigorates the propensity to innovativeness in the cannabis industry to generate new ideas and operations methods.

INTRODUCTION

The innovative technology is increasingly becoming an essential innovative tool for embedding innovative production, Omni-distribution, and digital marketing of cannabis, the business of hemp, and services to medicinal and recreational industries in the context of developing countries, South Africa in particular. The strategic economic recovery framework allows industries such as cannabis and hemp products to explore innovative ways of developing the cannabis and hemp industry. The chapter focuses

DOI: 10.4018/978-1-6684-6346-8.ch011

on technology's role in innovating the cannabis industry, and the systematic literature review method is germane to the essential research approach to apprise succinctly systematic discovery. The chapter uses the name cannabis, also known as "marijuana", colloquially, as an annual flowering plant from the family Cannabaceae, native to Central Asia and the Indian subcontinent. South Africa generally uses the street name "dagga" which consists of the Cannabis Sativa plant's dry leaves. In South Africa much of the dagga on the streets gets sold in small plastic bank bags, generally, a small quantity called an arm or finger, a cob, usually about 6 – 10 fingers' worth, or a brick, which is a compressed block. It is reasonably inexpensive, the price depends on the quality and is grown in many backyards as well as in Kwa-Zulu Natal, South-Eastern Cape, Swaziland, and the Drakensberg region. In this regard, the conjoint of legal and illegal cannabis activities are germane to reformed policy decision-making because dagga as it is known, grows prolifically in sometimes very poor and mountainous soil and yields very lucrative cash crops to sometimes extremely financial distress rural villages. Cultivation, manufacture, distribution, import, and export of tetrahydrocannabinol - containing medicines or CBD-containing products would require a license issued by the South African Health Products Regulatory Authority, Sec 22C of the Medicines Act. In addition to a license, manufacture, import, and export of THC-containing products for medical use require a permit issued by the Director-General of Health, in terms of section 22A (9) of the Medicines Act Mcata-Mhlauli, Ndukwana, Mosehla and Christians, 2021).

GLOBAL CANNABIS CONTEXT

Cannabis as a precious and lucrative plant has psychoactive (affecting the mind) properties and is used for industrial, recreational, and medical purposes. Jelsma, et al., (2021) focused on the three most common species Cannabis sativa, Cannabis indica, and Cannabis ruderalis. Cannabis sativa has non-psychoactive and grows in hotter climates with longer daylight and lots of sunshine usually in countries near the equator, such as Colombia, Mexico, and Thailand. Sativa reflects an energizing or uplifting effect consumption due to its primary psychoactive compound known as tetrahydrocannabinol (THC). Secondly, cannabis Indica psychoactive originally hails from the environmentally hostile Hindu Kush mountains in Central Asia. Nowadays, it is generally found in countries 30 degrees north of the equator, such as Afghanistan, Turkey, and Morocco (Silvaggio, 2018). The buds of indica are more compact and shorter than those of Sativa. The buds look tangibly fuller and firmer with purple, indica has a muscle-relaxing and sedating effect. Finally, cannabis ruderalis, which originated in Russia generally grow two feet high with shorter leaf fingers making it ideal for growing outdoors. Ruderalis is ready to harvest 10 weeks after seeding (Bennett, 2018). Ruderalis is less psychoactive and thus it is not used for recreational purposes. Instead, Cannabis ruderalis wild strains are used to create hybrid species.

The chapter focuses on both cannabis and hemp, and hemp is the English vernacular name historically given to Cannabis sativa. Nowadays, crops are explicitly grown for purposes other than psychoactive ones, such as clothing fibre, paper, fuel, building material from the fibre, or food and oil from the seeds. Cannabis and hemp crop regulation programs should be embedded within regional, national, and local agricultural strategies (FAO, 2010). In that regard, national laws legally regulating psycho activity-related Cannabis can be reformed to economically empower populations living in poverty situations and give everyone a chance to live in dignity.

RESEARCH PROBLEM

The economic empowerment and transformation can be untangled through regulatory reform, complying with Occupational Safety and Health Administration (OSHA) standards, and adapting the Drugs and Drug Trafficking Act and SAHPRA: Sec 22C of the Medicines Act best practices to the cannabis industry. In 2018, South Africa's Constitutional Court issued a ruling that effectively decriminalized cannabis, ordering that it should be legal for adults to grow and smoke cannabis in the privacy of their own homes. It denotes that "cannabis cultivated in a private place may only be used by the grower/cultivator, and it is illegal to supply it to anyone else" (Minister of Justice and Correctional Services, 2020). That has created a strong home-cultivation market in South Africa, where there is wide access to homegrown cannabis and no criminal penalties for consumption or personal use. The illegal sales policy seems to prevent South Africa from developing an innovative systemic distribution model procrastinating the country from entering the high-THC global cannabis market. Promulgation of cannabis still depicts cannabis as a prohibited drug in terms of the Drugs and Drug Trafficking Act until the possession and use by an adult person in private/industrialisation is permitted by law. However, there are plausible arguments why policy and regulatory reforms could positively influence the growth of the cannabis industry. It reflects a propensity to innovate the technological and digital industry, invigorate systemic productivity in cultivation, manufacture, distribution, marketing, and trade for in-sync supply chain networks, and allow economies of scale and better information exchange. The domino effect on marijuana production allows for new careers further up the learning curve (greatest skills in horticulture, farming, technology, and new products) and creates employment opportunities. South Africa's capital base, spare capacity in several value-adding opportunities from industrial hemp feedstock, higher labour productivity and skills profile, stronger domestic markets, and a more health- and environment-conscious consumer base, all back the idea of exploiting downstream industrial hemp production opportunities in South Africa. The main aim of the chapter is to prioritize the role of innovative technologies, encapsulate a value-adding approach to digital transformation and establish operable supply chain technologies to improve the socio-economic growth of the cannabis industry.

BACKGROUND

In Sub-Saharan Africa, Ghana and Malawi legalised cannabis for medicinal and industrial purposes in March 2020, joining Lesotho, South Africa, Zimbabwe, and Zambia. Rwanda followed in October 2020, announcing talks with four European and North American companies about growing and processing cannabis for export to meet rising pharmaceutical demand. All cannabis produced would be strictly for export and the domestic ban would remain despite the new policy allowing its production (Uwiringiyimana, 2020). Except for South Africa, the legalisation of cannabis in SSA countries is limited to medicinal and industrial use solely for export purposes, and with the intent to sell the licenses to mainly European and North American companies. The licensing processes are often rather opaque and formal regulations lacking or published after the fact, for instance in the Democratic Republic of the Congo (DRC) and Uganda, where foreign companies managed to acquire licenses (Duvall, 2019).

South Africa authorised marijuana for medicinal use in 2017 and is currently the only African country that was forced to permit the recreational use of cannabis, or dagga, by a ruling of the Constitutional Court through constitutional judgment. In September 2018, the Court decriminalised the use, possession, and cultivation of cannabis by an adult for their consumption in private (Zondo, 2018). The Court left it to parliament within 24 months to address the constitutional shortcomings in the Drugs Act and Medicines Act. However, the draft Cannabis for Private Purposes Bill, tabled in September 2020, does not take into account the existence of a subsistence economy for more than 200 years, with many small-scale farmers relying on cannabis for their livelihood. Much of this production is in the Mpondoland region of the Eastern Cape, Drakensburg, Bergville region of the KwaZulu Natal, and a few of South Africa's least developed rural regions where public services are scant and cannabis is grown, mainly by women, as the cash crop (Nyembezi, 2020). Despite recent developments toward the liberalisation of cannabis in South Africa, there is little hope among farmers – to the extent that they are even aware of these changes – that the policy will benefit them (Harper, 2020). Instead, growers see the playing field tilted towards big companies and foreign investors with the capital and political connections to apply for licenses. As one farmer states: *'Our people feel betrayed, because all of the licenses are being issued to companies from elsewhere, while we who have been growing this plant here for generations, who have the skills, who know, who have the land, are still being criminalised'* (Kay, Jelsma, and Bewley-Taylor, 2020).

ROLE OF TECHNOLOGY

The comprehensive innovative technology for agri-business serves large-scale farming for significant sustainability while smallholder/small-scale farming epitomises the dearth of a complete set digital service cycle for sustainability. In most developing countries, Mushi, Serugendo, and Burgi (2022) allude to the Tanzania case where digital technology and services respond to a challenge at a particular stage of the farming process or to a specific value chain. Initially, the United Nations (2021) asserted that the application of digital technologies in agriculture has the propensity to mitigate poverty and hunger from a constantly growing population -(from 2019 to 2050 the population will increase by 2 billion people). The digitization in the cannabis and hemp industry is expected to change the way society performs its social-economic activities. The increased interconnectivity through the internet, the internet of things, big data, and affordable digital devices create a global digital ecosystem (Jorge-Vázquez, Chivite-Cebolla, and Salinas-Ramos, 2021). Digitization is increasingly becoming an essential tool for the production of cannabis, the business of hemp, and services to medicinal and recreational industries for recovery of the society from the unexpected novel coronavirus pandemic that has brought a devastating impact on the social, economic, and environmental aspects (Mohapatra, Tripathy, Singhal and Saha, 2021). Digital technology in cannabis business farming derives knowledge from environmental science, remote sensing, geographical positioning systems (GIS), crop and soil science, and global positioning systems (GPS) (Sarker, Islam, Ali, Islam, Salam, Hasan Mahmud, 2019). Industry 4.0 has entrenched an agri-business management system allowing modern technologies such as artificial intelligence (AI), sensors, the Internet of Things (IoT), satellite images to collect data, big data, and machine learning, contributing to higher productivity and profitability in this sector (Saiz-Rubio and Rovira-Más, 2020). Modern technologies allow small-scale farmers including cannabis farmers and processors, different approaches to enable digital technology to augment productivity and create sustainable income.

THEORETICAL FRAMEWORK

The resource-based view has the integrating foundation for strategic management and other multi-discipline research (Collins, 2021). The theory focuses on the relationship which exists between a firm's resources, capabilities, and competitive advantage (Hart, 1995; Kellermanns, Walter, Crook, Kemmerer, and Narayanan, 2016). The central point of the resource-based view is the fact "that organisational advantages are enhanced to the extent that an organisation possesses strategic resources" (Kellermanns, et al., 2016, pp. 26–48). It generates a sustainable competitive advantage for both start-up performance and long-term growth stemming from the firm's entrepreneurial knowledge. The resource-based view of urban and rural entrepreneurial ecosystems can identify and distribute scarce resources within the ecosystem to maintain a competitive advantage over its competitors (Rashid and Ratten 2021), underpinned by regulatory, policy, and innovative enterprise development and industrial ecosystem partners such as government organs, venture capitals, researchers and corporate investors. Contingency theory proposes that firms must establish control systems suitable for situational factors, such as their environment, technology, and size, to improve performance (Otley, 1980). It stresses that cannabis firm producers must understand the scale, size, regulatory, innovative, and digital market environment inspired by digital transformation. The higher the institutional support, the more likely cannabis entrepreneurs are to dedicate resources to innovative, proactive, and risk-taking activities.

The institutional theory holds that the success of enterprise innovation depends on both the internal resources and the external institutional environment (Lee and Yoo, 2019). Through the promotion of industry-university–research alliances between research institutions and new enterprises, formal institutional support can provide innovation resources and environments, to improve the success rate of product or technological innovation and the innovation performance of new ventures (Yang and Yu, 2022). Entrepreneurial orientation emphasizes that enterprises take innovation as the core, actively integrate resources, and boldly carry out innovative attempts and risks to obtain market initiatives (Kurtulmu¸s, Katrinli, and Warner, 2020). The resource-based theory stresses that competitive advantage comes from the possession of valuable and scarce resources (Barney, 1991). Entrepreneurial innovation can be viewed as a critical resource, a type of knowledgeable innovative value guiding the pursuit of performance excellence (Ince, Imamoglu, and Karakose, 2021). Cannabis growers can grow by enhancing competitiveness through innovations and digital transformation. This chapter provides empirical evidence on which innovation activities seem to improve the cannabis producer value and model the nature of cannabis and hemp products guided by alertness on resource based-approach from the institutional view of innovativeness and cannabis situational-based analysis of cannabis and hemp environment, appropriateness of scale, technology, and digital orientation.

DIGITAL TECHNOLOGY MANAGEMENT

Internet of Things (IoT) in agriculture farming uses sensors and devices used to collect data from the field for easy monitoring of the crops and other digital tools to collect essential data for profitable decision-making in farming (Saiz-Rubio and Rovira-Más, 2020). The sensors are mounted in the mobile farm machinery or fixed in the field, such as a local weather station. Digital systemic data management in the cannabis industry requires IoT devices to generate meaningful information for cultivation and production in the cannabis and hemp industries. Effective digital information management facilitates the collection, storing, analysis, and manipulation of data in the precision and smart growing of cannabis crops. Cannabis cultivators can extract information such as field maps to determine crop and field conditions necessary for actions related to minimal use of resources, compliance with standards, and quality of agriculture production. The systems manage field operations based on data acquired and processed automatically for planning, monitoring, supporting decision-making, and keeping valuable records (Köksal and Tekinerdogan, 2019). Hrustek (2020), mentioned that digital management systems record critical information, including "harvests and yields, profits and losses, farm task scheduling, weather prediction, soil nutrients transport and field mapping. Digital supply chain management provides real-time data for warning, and financial management and integrates other actors such as input suppliers, product distributors, and demand planners (market intelligence).

DIGITAL TRANSFORMATION TECHNOLOGY

Transformations succeed when they are incremental, cost-effective, and sustainable. That means focusing on outcomes: new cannabis products, improved processes, building growers' capabilities, innovative business value, and buy-in for the digital transformation. Introducing mobile applications, artificial intelligence (Al), cloud computing, analytics, chatbots, and other digital services augments the existing business and changes the trajectory of the cannabis industry. Digital transformation presents enormous opportunities for cannabis businesses, as well as for government and public organizations to infuse innovation, embrace technological disruption, constant change, and rapid development for competitive advantage. Digitization is the first step in digital transformation, which must occur before digital industrial disruptive technology such as blockchain. Digital currency/payments, land registration, identity management, notarization, supply chain traceability, healthcare, education, corporate registration, data management, auditing, energy market, taxation, voting, and legal entity management are some areas where blockchain is currently being tested for public services. Blockchain is part of distributed ledger technologies that give users confidence that archived information without being tampered with (Beck et al., 2018). The main difference between blockchain and DLT is that the latter is a technology for the management of a distributed database, whereas the former is a confidence-building technology through the means of consensus mechanisms and a sequential registry of information in a chain-type formation. Furthermore, blockchains can confirm the genuineness of a transaction but whether a given input in a transaction is genuine or the transaction rules are fairly established is beyond the technical scope of blockchains. The urban club model is better suited by blockchain to re-establish the importance of trust and legitimacy, to allow transparency, integrity, and traceability of data to the authenticity of the information, and to reduce transaction costs and enhance the efficiency of the cannabis services cycle. However, rural native cannabis growers with the necessary digital infrastructure can emulate the benefits of the cannabis services cycle, authentic information and knowledge exchange, and transactional processes and costs.

KNOWLEDGE AND INFORMATION SERVICES

The lack of information and knowledge sharing has become critical for cannabis cultivators where smallholders have to rely on friends, family, and experience, resulting in low production (Consolata, 2017). Access to data in a complete farming cycle for rural cannabis growers, from preparations for quality crops, design for specifications inputs, credible finance systems, well-measured harvesting schedules, and market intelligence of the products, creates high value in the commercialization of smallholder growers for cannabis and hemp products. Ali, Durrani, Naeem, Riaz, and Shahid (2016), focussed on Pakistan for the critical information needs of farmers and developed a digital solution to deliver weather forecasts, pesticides, and fertilizer information. Behera, Das, Jishnu, Behera, Behera and Jena (2015) had the lenses on India on e-agriculture initiatives that emphasize disseminating information to most rural smallholder farmers through information and communication technology (ICT), including management information systems, knowledge management systems and expert systems. Sanga, Tumbo and Mlozi (2014), developed an information dissemination system to enable smallholder farmers to access critical farming information and knowledge from experts, bridging the gap between extension services through ICT. Scientists and organizations have developed mobile applications to disseminate different crop and livestock information. FAO (2021) entrenched in Kenya Agricultural and Livestock Research Organization (KALRO) produced more than fourteen mobile applications for crops and livestock to help farmers access information and adopt modern farming techniques for increased production.

The cannabis and hemp small-scale growers are confronted with the challenge of legitimate local and global market access for produce and processed products. USAID (2021), alludes to notorious intermediaries who coerce farmers to sell their produce at a low price, resulting in poor sustainable production. The government reforms in policy-making seem to enhance accessibility to market information and better participation in the mainstream cannabis and hemp marketplace. Behera, Das, Jishnu, Behera, Behera and Jena (2015) applauded better market accessibility in India as the critical aspect of e-agriculture initiatives where rural cannabis and hemp growers are in sync with the market and absorb fair prices for improved income and sustainable life-changing experience for native growers. Hamill (2017) averred on ICT cases in Africa including "eSoko" in Ghana, "Tru Trade" in Uganda. "Farming" in Kenya, Ghana, and Tanzania as the innovative programs for market accessibility ameliorating the challenge of concealed market information and lack of fair price for small scale farmers of products. These innovative technological developments provide a promising trajectory underpinned by the advent of industry 4.0 to improve the digital set of the service cycle for sustainable production of cannabis and quality hemp-related products. Furthermore, ICT infrastructure and resource sustainability are fundamental components for long-term production and profitability for cannabis growers (Aguirre-Villegas and Larson, 2017) especially, in the digital cannabis transformation industry.

METHODOLOGY

The research design is an instrument used by a scholar to assess how the data should be gathered, overseen, and analyzed to conclude (Sileyew, 2019). The research design is categorized as secondary data (scholarly articles and published documents) and analysing of the existing data (thematic analysis). Research methodology incorporates the systematic techniques that are used to identify the design, select approaches and strategies, process sampling, data collection instruments, and systematic analysis of secondary data about a particular cannabis research phenomenon. The descriptive research approach in this chapter uses a qualitative method. The qualitative method intends to inductively scrutinize written and published documents and review theme-based scholarly articles in the systemic review (Creswell, 2014). The qualitative approach assists with 'how' and 'why' questions on innovations for the cannabis industry (Myers, Well and Lorch, 2016:4). Ontology refers to "the nature of our beliefs about reality"

(Bryman, 2021, p. 349) with assumptions about the reality of the role of technology innovation in the cannabis industry. An interpretive philosophy of social research leans toward the qualitative and it apprises on multiple realities that exist, thus truth and reality are shaped (Guba & Lincoln, 2005, p. 204). The real aim of interpretive research is to discover and unpack 'real truths' that exist about the role of innovation and digital transformation in the context of the cannabis industry (Saunders, Lewis, & Thornhill, 2019, p. 108).

The Preferred Reporting Items for Systematic reviews and Meta-Analyses (PRISMA) statement, published in 2009, was designed to help systematic reviewers transparently report why the review was done, what the authors did, and what they found. The PRISMA 2020 statement replaces the 2009 statement and includes new reporting guidance that reflects advances in methods to identify, select, appraise, and synthesise studies. The structure and presentation of the items have been modified to facilitate implementation in this chapter. The study used PRISMA guidelines in this study (McKenzie, Bossuyt, Boutron, Hoffmann and Mulrow, 2021), which is a standard protocol and an evidence-based framework for doing systematic review studies. The systematic literature review assists to map out the existing conceptual approaches toward innovative technology in the cannabis industry in different disciplines and synthesize them into a comprehensive conceptual framework for the study. A systematic review extensively scans pertinent reports and articles published on the subject to find the answers to defined research questions, and to that end uses various inclusion and exclusion criteria to identify the articles to be included in the review, and then synthesize the findings. The first phase developed the review protocol. The second phase identified the inclusion and exclusion criteria for relevant publications. The third phase performed an in-depth search for studies, followed by a critical appraisal, data extraction, and a synthesis of past findings. Studies were eligible for inclusion if they were focused on the topic of how innovation can provide business value in the cannabis industry.

THE REVIEW PROTOCOL

In particular, the use of Google Scholar allowed for gathering reliable information from one location, along with using the institution's digital library databases such as World Share Management system modules from the University of KwaZulu Natal. An extensive literature search based was conducted on a complex query in the Web of Science (WoS), Multidisciplinary Digital Publishing Institute (MDPI) (from Journal of Sustainability), Elsevier publishing – ScienceDirect on Social Science and Humanities, and related databases (Scopus, Google Scholar, and Research Gate). The aim was to find and review the latest literature in digital technology and sustainable cannabis and hemp production, distribution and market intelligence, resilience to small-scale farmers, and the role of the mainstream market and government policy and regulatory reforms. The researchers combined the following keywords using the AND" and "OR" and parentheses during the search: "Innovation, digital technology and/or transformation, ICT services, Data management, Cannabis and Hemp growers and/or processers, IoT, AI, blockchain, Big Data, government policy and/or regulations reforms, ICT services, and small/large scale farming". However, the search string could not yield good results for the SAHPRA database including the Drugs and Drug Trafficking Act and Medicines Act due to the lack of symbiotic reforms amongst organs of the state and infant level of government legislative reforms in the cannabis and hemp industry in most developing countries. The search was conducted in May and July 2022, obtained, and imported a total number of approximately 300 articles.

THE INCLUSION AND EXCLUSION CRITERIA

The researchers applied exclusion criteria to the obtained results to identify relevant papers in digital technology/transformation, Cannabis and Hemp growers and/or processers, government policy and/or regulations reforms, ICT services cycle, and small/large scale farming. The restriction on the obtained results to the year of publication from 2017 to 2022 to get the latest articles in the subject area. The duplicated papers were filtered out duplicated papers using manual screening and abstract scanning, articles without full text, and not written in English. The inclusion criteria were as follows: "Innovation, digital technology and/or transformation, Cannabis and Hemp growers and/or processers, government policy and/or regulations reforms, and small/large scale farming. Finally, the researchers selected a total of 45 articles: 39 articles on global literature (24 for recent digital technology and/or transformation, Cannabis and Hemp growers and/or processers, government policy and/or regulations reforms, and small/large scale farming) and 15 for the African continent cases while 6 were global reports. In this search, the researchers did not limit the literature by the year of publication to obtain more detailed background information on cannabis and hemp relating to small and large scales farmers/producers using innovative technology services. The researchers obtained 8 reports from local repositories for analysis "Innovation" AND "Cannabis and Hemp growers and/or processers" AND "government policy and/or regulations reforms" OR "small/large scale farming" AND "South Africa". The following figure 1 depict the reviewed literature under PRISMA guideline such as Search Category Identification, Screening, and Included general literature and reports.

Figure 1. Thematic Map

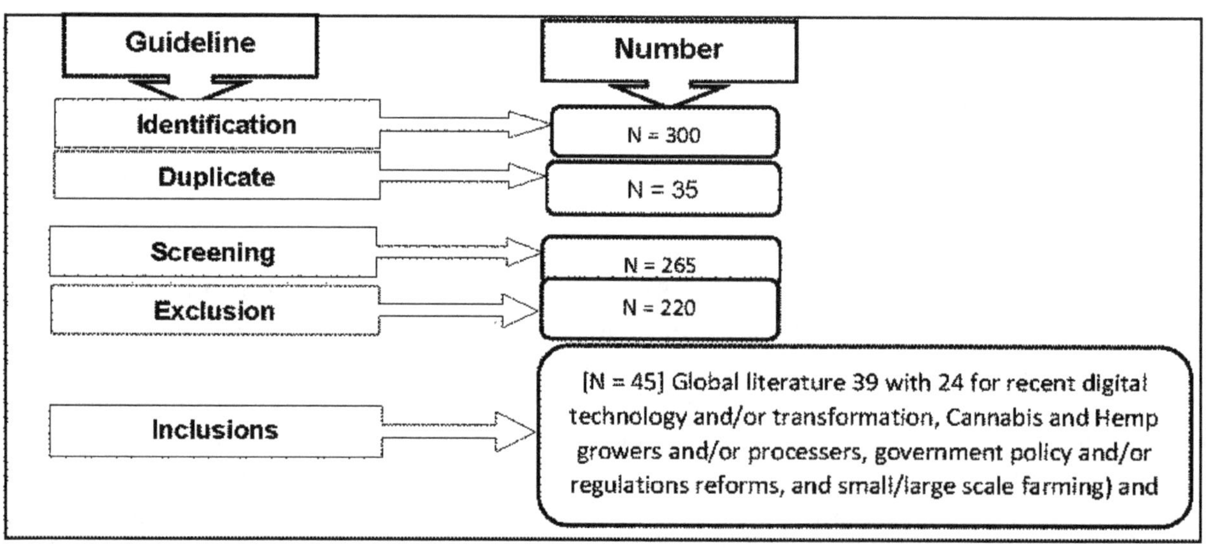

Records identified from databases (N = 300); Duplicate removed (N = 35); Records screened (N = 265); Records excluded (N = 220) the context is highly embedded on large scale and incompatible skewed industries; Studies included in the review (N = 45) [Global literature 39 with 24 for recent digital technology and/or transformation, Cannabis and Hemp growers and/or processers, government policy and/or regulations reforms, and small/large scale farming) and 15 for the South Africa and African continent cases while 6 were global and 8 SA reports].

ANALYSIS

Synthesize findings and categorize studies based on their scope, an analysis of the different research streams was performed. the first step was to search and identify the main concepts from each study, using the authors' original terms. The authors contextualised factors surrounding the study (industry, economies, firm size). The following reflects the themes - "Innovation, digital technology and/or transformation, cannabis and hemp growers and/or processers, government policy and/or regulations reforms, and small/large scale farming".

Theme 1: Innovation

The Department of Health and the SAHPRA may permit the cultivation of cannabis solely for medicinal and research purposes and for selling the resulting innovative products on the global market. South Africa's Constitutional Court ruling infers that cannabis cultivated in a private place may only be used by the grower/cultivator, and it is illegal to supply it to anyone else (Minister of Justice and Correctional Services, 2020). The innovativeness in the cannabis industry invigorates openness to new ideas and the willingness of cannabis firms to adopt new ideas for exploitation. Innovation allows cannabis cultivators to successfully enter newly reformed markets and establish barriers to entry from illegal growers and nonaccredited competitors. Innovations have a propensity for a priori propositions with a heterodox model including developing more efficient supply chain production methods and new digital services or products (Yoo et al. 2019), implementing more productive organisational structures, acquiring new resources, and entering new markets (Schumpeter, 1942; Ryu and Won, 2022). The innovation is apropos of operational efficiency, indicating the extent to which cannabis growers can optimize outputs at a given input level to entrench market value propositions. Operational innovation means "the degree to which firms maximise their outputs under the given input level and is evaluated by adopting data envelopment analysis" (Ryu and Won, 2022, pp.1-18). Yoo et al. (2019) opined that cannabis growers can reduce operating costs through efficient supply chain production technology through research and development investment while launching new cannabis and hemp products to increase stock prices. Rubera and Kirca (2017) analysed the effect of innovation and customer satisfaction on firm value and measured innovation with the number of new products. Lee (2020) measured innovation as the number of patents and analysed its relationship with the firm value. Arguably, the author revealed that patents are weakly associated with firm value, while research and development are related to increased firm value. Park et al. (2021) further argued that research and development expenses negatively affect firm value in the growth stage for small-scale cannabis firms, and research and development expenses at the mature stage are positively related to cannabis large-scale firm value.

Theme 2: Digital Technology and Transformation

Internet of Things in agriculture farming uses sensors and devices used to collect data from the field for easy monitoring of the crops and other digital tools to collect essential data for profitable decision-making in farming (Saiz-Rubio and Rovira-Más, 2020). The sensors are mounted in the mobile farm machinery or fixed in the field, such as a local weather station. Kilin, Pini, Kasparian, Gros and Wolf (2019), indicated a network of automated stations in the vineyards to detect areas affected by pathogens for site-specific application of pesticides. The stations collect real-time data such as airborne particles, temperature and relative humidity of the air and soil, solar irradiance, spores, and leaf humidity. Artificial Intelligence (AI) is then used to analyze the Spatio-temporal heterogeneity data based on optical particle counters (OPC) to identify areas affected by the pathogen (Plasmopara viticola) (Kilin, Pini, Kasparian, Gros and Wolf, 2019). The results allow farmers to apply pesticides in specific field zones leading to cost-effective, healthy products and environmentally friendly farming practices. Saiz-Rubio and Rovira-Más (2020), classified sensors into three: remote sensing, aircraft, and proximal sensing. Remote sensing, most often satellites, has been an essential tool for collecting field data in smart farming and it is cost-effective for the rural cannabis framing service cycle. Theoretically, by creating an autonomous, transparent, and secure distributed system, blockchain may enable the removal of intermediaries in public management as trustees replacing them with an algorithmic confidence system (De Filippi et al., 2020). In that regard, two diverging views appear in the literature. The first view is that blockchain allows transparency, integrity, and traceability of data to authenticate the information, thereby reducing the transaction costs and enhancing the efficiency of the cannabis services cycle (Beck et al., 2018; Ziolkowski, Miscione, and Schwabe, 2020). The second view, on the other hand, perceives blockchain as a disruptive technology that allows permission-less transactions in a truly decentralized manner (Pierre and Peters, 2000; Miscione, Ziolkowski, Zavolokina, and Schwabe, 2018). The morass bedevilling of the technology is that blockchain as a technology re-establishes the importance of trust and legitimacy in the initial policy and system design phase instead of the implementation. In both permissioned and permissionless blockchains, the rules of transactions are set at the design phase, and once a decision is made a change in the system requires the consent of authorized users (Ziolkowski, Miscione, and Schwabe, 2020).

Theme 3: Cannabis and hemp growers and processors

Meanwhile, urban entrepreneurs in South Africa have the chance to set up *'grower clubs'* that provide a service to grow, dry, and deliver cannabis for urban consumers who lack the space and/or knowledge to do so, (BusinessTech, 2020). In this *'grow club model'* the cannabis plant is owned by club members, who buy their seeds, while the cultivation and processing are outsourced to the club, at a fixed price and provide the opportunity to participate meaningfully in the cannabis value chain (Smit, 2021). In theory, if allowed, the model could be open to rural growers (Kay, Jelsma, and Bewley-Taylor, 2020), but it is hard to imagine how a decades-old model of traditional family-based growing communities can adapt to and overcome the multiple obstacles (BusinessTech, 2020), such as the logistics to deliver the cannabis from remote rural areas, and the cultural, socio-economic and legal aspects of a very different production model based in a dynamic urban setting (Seddon and Floodgate, 2020; German, Bonanno, Foster and Cotula, 2020). In practice, the innovative urban cannabis production model seems to supersede legacy rural cultivation and distribution to yield adequate protection and remuneration. The cannabis that has become legal in Africa is not the cannabis that has benefitted African farmers (Duvall, 2019). Fair or just trade seeks to redress these global inequalities by granting producers of products such as bananas, cotton, or cut flowers better opportunities to markets and consumers, predominantly in wealthy countries (Bennett, 2019). It remains an open question to what extent such a model can serve the socio-economic needs and interests of small-scale and traditional cannabis farmers. Fair Trade markets for products like bananas, cocoa, and coffee, have provided small producers with certification that has enabled them to maintain a foothold in these global markets (Kay, Jelsma and Bewley-Taylor, 2020). The crystallised model of "fair trade (non-capitalised) or fairer trade or just trade is used to imply the embedding of principles of social justice and sustainable development within cannabis policy-making and markets rather than compliance with the standards defined by the World Fair Trade Organistion" (Seddon and Floodgate, 2020; Jelsma, Blickman, Kay, Metaal, Martínez and Putri, 2021).

Both large and small scales growers of cannabis can develop mobile and online services that allow access to various services such as weather information, farming information and knowledge, market information, distribution, environmental compliance, policy and regulations, and reliable buyers for their products (Barakabitze, Kitindi, Sanga, Shabani, Philipo, Kibirige, 2015; Misaki, Apiola, Gaiani, 2016). In the same viewpoint, Boyera and Grewal (2020), and Gray et al. (2018), asserted that digital technology could help cannabis farmers access essential services and improve productivity. Developing comprehensive digital technology innovations addresses the conundrum of rural economic exclusion especially the native productivity cannabis growers in rural areas such as KwaZulu Natal and Eastern Cape regions the required access to credit, advanced farming knowledge, crucial farm inputs, designed government services, and control, and the lucrative market for cannabis and hemp products (Rutsaert, Chamberlin, Oluoch, Kitoto and Donovan, 2021).

Theme 4: Government policy and regulations Reforms,

To ensure the availability of standardised quality-assured locally grown Cannabis for the manufacture of suitable pharmaceutical products, the Department of Health and the SAHPRA may permit the cultivation of Cannabis solely for medicinal and research purposes. SAHPRA is tasked with regulating (monitoring, evaluating, investigating, inspecting, and registering) all health products and clinical trials in South Africa. Health products include complementary medicines, medical devices, and in vitro diagnostics (IVDs). SAHPRA also has the responsibility of overseeing radiation control in South Africa. SAHPRA's mandate is outlined in the Medicines and Related Substances Act (Act 101 of 1965 as amended) as well as the Hazardous Substances Act (Act No 15 of 1973). SAHPRA has three pillars to ensure that medicines, medical devices, and meet the requisite standards to protect the health and well-being of South Africans: Safety, Efficacy, and Quality. This framework, developed in consultation with the Department of Agriculture, Land Reform and Rural Development, is intended to control the cultivation, production, and manufacturing of Cannabis-containing products intended for medicinal use in South Africa (Semete-Makokotlela, 2017). Licensed domestic cultivation of Cannabis for medicinal use is aimed at ensuring sufficient local supply for medical, scientific, and clinical research purposes and the implementation of control measures necessary to prevent diversion and misuse, as well as to ensure patient safety. In addition, the Medicines Act allows SAHPRA to issue a license to manufacture either a medicine or a Scheduled substance (Active Pharmaceutical Ingredient). Section 22C(1)(b) of the Medicines Act enables the cultivation and manufacture of Scheduled substances and ensures the required oversight of SAHPRA in regulating these activities (GMP (2010)). This provision allows SAHPRA to license cultivators of Cannabis for medicinal use and enables regulatory oversight in a way that is compliant with South Africa's international obligations. Permits will be managed fairly, relative to the expected usage in the country to prevent the accumulation of Cannabis or Cannabis products. SAHPRA, together with the Department of Health, will order the seizure and destruction of any Cannabis produced by a license holder when the quantity conditions of the license are not adhered to (GMP (2010), Semete-Makokotlela, 2017).

THEORETICAL FRAMEWORK FINDINGS

In the context of the cannabis industry, the resource-based approach is critical in assisting cannabis growers to learn to develop structures and systemic models to diffuse digital transformation for themselves to become more digital adaptive, innovative, and responsive to changes in the cannabis business environment. The cannabis industry's growth can be underpinned by regulatory, policy, and innovative enterprise development and industrial ecosystem partners such as government organs, venture capitalists, researchers, and corporate investors. The resource-based theory further acknowledges limited organizations' resources need, and cannabis growers need to continuously negotiate and interact with the external environment to obtain knowledge, technology, funds, and other resources needed for innovation. While contingency theory reveals that cannabis producers must understand the scale, size, regulatory, innovative, and digital market environment inspired by digital transformation. The institutional theory advocates internal resources and the external institutional environment and through the promotion of industry-university–research alliances between research institutions and new enterprises, formal institutional support can provide innovative resources and environments for continuous growth and sustainable development of the cannabis industry. The theoretical framework recommends that the internal resources and the external institutional environment are critical factors to shape the better utilization of resources, integrating capabilities, establishing control systems suitable for situational factors, and building competitive advantages such as market environment and digital technology.

DISCUSSION FINDINGS

The innovative technology is increasingly becoming an essential innovative tool for embedding innovative production, Omni-distribution, and digital marketing of cannabis, the business of hemp, and services to medicinal and recreational industries in the context of developing countries, South Africa in particular. Innovation propositions introduce new cannabis products and services that enrich the lives of individuals both nationally and internationally with significant economic growth by providing cost competitiveness and attracting investment in the cannabis industry. South Africa promotes cannabis and hemp farming and distribution abilities within the auspices of the legislative framework to ensure the availability of standardised quality-assured locally grown cannabis for the manufacture of suitable medicinal products. The study findings infer that innovativeness in the cannabis industry seems to generate new ideas for a reformed market to develop new operations methods through digital services to entrench market value propositions. The cannabis industry needs to invest in research and development to increase the firm market value and propensity to transit to mainstream business.

Digital Technology transformation relies on industry 4.0 advent concepts where artificial intelligence allows for cost-effective, healthy products and environmentally friendly farming practices. It has been an essential tool for collecting field data in smart farming and it is cost-effective for the rural cannabis framing service cycle. Internet of Things **in** agriculture farming and cannabis growers uses sensors and devices to collect data from the field for easy monitoring of the crops and other digital tools to collect essential data for profitable decision-making in farming. The sensors are mounted in the mobile farm machinery or fixed in the field, such as a local weather station. The study found that blockchain tentatively seems to create an autonomous, transparent, and secure distributed system that enables the removal of intermediaries in public management as trustees replace them with an algorithmic confidence system. In that regard, blockchain allows transparency, integrity, and traceability of data to authenticate the information, thereby reducing transaction costs and enhancing the efficiency of the cannabis services cycle. Blockchain as a disruptive technology allows permission-less transactions in a truly decentralized manner for the cannabis industry.

Although urban growers rely on grow club model where the cannabis plant is owned by club members, who buy their seeds, the cultivation and processing are outsourced to the club, at a fixed price and provide the opportunity to participate meaningfully in the cannabis value chain, the rural growers are depicting dearth in innovativeness. The innovative urban cannabis production model seems to supersede legacy rural cultivation and distribution to yield adequate protection and remuneration. The cannabis that has become legal in Africa is not the cannabis that has benefitted African farmers. A model can serve the socio-economic needs and interests of small-scale and traditional cannabis farmers. Fair Trade markets for products like bananas, cocoa, and coffee, have provided small producers with certification that has enabled them to maintain a foothold in these global markets. Both large and small-scale growers of cannabis can develop mobile and online services that allow access to various services such as weather information, farming information and knowledge, market information, distribution, environmental compliance, policy and regulations, and reliable buyers for their products. The study further observed that regions required access to credit, advanced farming knowledge, crucial farm inputs, designed government services and control, and the lucrative market for cannabis and hemp products.

The study further observed that the tentative provision by SAHPRA to license cultivators of Cannabis for medicinal use and enables regulatory oversight in a way that is compliant with South Africa's international obligations doesn't qualify the desired socio-economic growth and interests of small-scale and traditional cannabis farmers. Fairtrade market principles for cannabis products are not congruent with permits managed fairly, relative to the expected usage in the country to prevent the accumulation of Cannabis or Cannabis products. SAHPRA, together with the Department of Health, will order the seizure and destruction of any Cannabis produced by a license holder when the quantity conditions of the license are showing defects or lack of adherence to regulatory and quality specifications.

DATA QUALITY CONTROL

Quality in any research study is important, especially in the qualitative method, and it ensures that the findings are credible and trustworthy. Trustworthiness - Stahl, and King (2020, p. 28) found that according to Lincoln and Guba (1981, p. 34), the real value and essence of a study can be examined by understanding its trustworthiness to ensure the quality of the systematic research findings. Saunders et al., (2019, p. 6) assert that developing credibility in the study ensures transparency and the creation of rich data being produced. The study attempts to promote credibility through the various processes of triangulation. Several sources of information for data triangulation used a complex query in the Web of Science (WoS), Multidisciplinary Digital Publishing Institute (MDPI) (from Journal of Sustainability), Elsevier publishing – ScienceDirect on Social Science and Humanities, and related databases (Scopus, Google Scholar, and Research Gate). The essential systematic literature review procedure from the

PRISMA guideline was used to establish identifiable patterns. Theoretical triangulation was used on multiple theoretical orientations such as contingency, resource-based view, and institutional theories to understand findings and direct the research. The dependability has ensured that the study is consistent and reliable in all contexts if it has to be repeated in different contexts with the same research methods. Conformability ensured that the findings are reflecting the data received from the inclusion cohort of scholarly and published sources rather than the perspectives of the researchers. The scientific rigorous criteria provided a measure of the extent to which a publication would make a valuable contribution to the review. Around 220 papers were excluded, leaving 45 papers for data extraction and synthesis. The coding as per area of focus allowed a categorization to be constructed by identifying the main research areas and enabling the extraction of the details needed to answer each of the posed research questions.

CONCLUSIONS AND RECOMMENDATIONS

Cannabis producers embrace the medium and long-term impact of new digital technologies on their business model. The COVID-19 pandemic has led companies to seek and establish contact with the customer as business-to-customer extending to customer-to-customer digital commerce. The creation of direct e-commerce facilitates the development of the cannabis club. However, online shoppers in the urban areas have been acquainted with digital transformation before the cannabis industry, while the rural cannabis producer is attempting entry to narrow the gap by committing limited investments in information and communication technology intelligence and infrastructure. From the broader supply chain perspective, the strategic investment in digital asset management (DAM) initiative should formalize digital information on cannabis and hemp logistical and packaging aspects for better quality products and marketing intelligence and positioning. The digital technologies strengthen supply chain relationships through strategic Omni-channels distribution, using satellite shops, accredited restaurants, and social commerce influencers, and further entrenching B2B and C2C translating into a customer-oriented social environment through cannabis social networks. The strategic supply chain operations of cannabis producers enhance market intelligence for positioning, strengthen omnichannel perspective, and improve digital data management as the form of integration between e-commerce and social networking. In addition to the effect of operational innovation, digital innovation is positively related to the firm's future value at every stage of its life cycle for the cannabis industry, signifying that the firm's sustainability is associated with technical and digital innovation rather than scale innovation (Ryu and Won, 2022). The essence of technology and innovation is recommended for invigorating the propensity to innovativeness in the cannabis industry. The generation of new ideas and the development of new operations methods can transform the cannabis industry from the poor socioeconomic challenge. The United Nations (2021) asserted that the application of digital technologies in agriculture has the propensity to mitigate poverty and hunger from the constantly growing population. Digitization in the cannabis and hemp industry is recommended for changing the way society performs its social-economic activities. The innovative urban cannabis production model seems to supersede legacy rural cultivation and distribution to yield adequate protection and remuneration. SAHPRA licenses cultivators of Cannabis for medicinal use and enables regulatory oversight in South Africa but there is no congruence with permits to manage fairly the expectation of cannabis growers.

FUTURE RESEARCH DIRECTIONS

It is essential for cannabis producers to develop innovatively and relevant trade marketing and shopper and consumer marketing processes most suitable for the nature of the cannabis industry underpinned by the digital transformation in the marketing. The cannabis producers must explore legitimate supply chain collaborative networks through tasting evenings, train the legal and accredited sales network partner, and coordinate engaging dialogue with extended supply chain members to overcome any reticence regarding the (prospective) value of creating digital technology communication and the cannabis marketplace. The provision of licenses by SAHPRA to cultivators of cannabis for medicinal use and exercising regulatory oversight should interrogate to develop better practices and quality products.

REFERENCES

Aguirre-Villegas, H. A., & Larson, R. A. (2017). Evaluating greenhouse gas emissions from dairy manure management practices using survey data and lifecycle tools. *Journal of Cleaner Production*, *143*, 169–179.

Ali, S., Durrani, H., Naeem, M., Riaz, W., & Shahid, S. (2016). Supporting Pakistani farmers through digital means: An exploratory study. *In Proceedings of the 2016 CHI Conference Extended Abstracts on Human Factors in Computing Systems*. CHI.

Barakabitze, A. A., Kitindi, E. J., Sanga, C., Shabani, A., Philipo, J., & Kibirige, G. (2015). New technologies for disseminating and communicating agriculture knowledge and information: Challenges for agricultural research institutes in Tanzania. *The Electronic Journal on Information Systems in Developing Countries*, *70*, 1–22.

Barney, J. (1991). Firm resources and sustained competitive advantage. *Journal of Management*, *17*, 99–120.

Beck, R., Müller-Bloch, C., & King, J. L. (2018). Governance in the blockchain economy: A framework and research agenda. *Journal of the Association for Information Systems*, *19*(10), 1020–1034. doi:10.17705/1jais.00518

Behera, B. S., Das, T. K., Jishnu, K. J., Behera, R. A., Behera, A. C., & Jena, S. (2015). E-governance mediated agriculture for sustainable life in India. *Procedia Computer Science*, *48*, 623–629.

Bennett, E. A. (2018, August 4). Extending ethical consumerism theory to semi-legal sectors: Insights from recreational cannabis. *Agriculture and Human Values*, *35*(2), 295–317. doi:10.1007/ s10460-017-9822-8 85

Bennett, E. A. (2019, April 14). Passing on pot: When environmental organizations disengage from political consumerism in highly stigmatized sectors. *Environmental Politics*, 1–28. doi:10.1080/09644016.2019.1654237

Boyera, S., & Grewal, A. A. (2020). Generic Template for Farmer Profiling. SBC4D.

Bryman, A. (2021). *Social research methods* (6th ed.). Oxford University Press.

BusinessTech. (2020, July 3). South Africans are setting up 'cannabis clubs' across the country – are they legal? *Business Tech.* https://businesstech. co.za/news/lifestyle/434401/south-africans-aresetting-up-cannabis-clubs-across-the-countryare-they -legal/

Collins, C. J. (2021). Expanding the resource based view model of strategic human resource management. *International Journal of Human Resource Management*, *32*, 331–358.

Consolata, A. (2017). Urban agriculture and the use of ICTS in accessing and disseminating livestock husbandry information in Urban areas of Tanzania. A review of related literature. *Libr. Philos. Pract.*, *1*, 1–38.

Creswell, J. W. (2014). *Research Design: Qualitative, Quantitative and Mixed Methods Approaches* (4th ed.). Sage.

Dai, Y., Byun, G., & Ding, F. (2019). The Direct and Indirect Impact of Gender Diversity in New Venture Teams on Innovation Performance. *Entrepreneurship Theory and Practice*, *43*, 505–528.

de Filippi, P., Mannan, M., & Reijers, W. (2020, June 17). Blockchain as a confidence machine: The problem of trust & challenges of governance. *Technology in Society*, *62*, 101284. doi:10.1016/j.techsoc.2020.101284

Duvall, C. S. (2019). A brief agricultural history of cannabis in Africa, from prehistory to cannacolony. *EchoGéo.* http://journals.openedition.org/ echogeo/17599

FAO. (2010). *Linking People, Places and Products, A guide for promoting quality linked to geographical origin and sustainable geographical indications.* Food and Agriculture Organization (FAO). https://www.fao.org/3/i1760e/i1760e.pdf

FAO. (2021, November 7). *KARLO Launches 14 Mobile Apps to Transform Agriculture|E-Agriculture.* FAO. https://www.fao.org/eagriculture/news/karlo-launches-14-mobile-apps-transform-agriculture

German, L. A., Bonanno, A. M., Foster, L. C., & Cotula, L. (2020, May 8). Inclusive business" in agriculture: Evidence from the evolution of agricultural value chains. *World Development*, *134*, 2. doi:10.1016/j.worlddev.2020.105018

GMP. (2010, November 5) Guide to Good Manufacturing Practice (GMP) for Medicines in South Africa. *SAHPRA.* https://www.mccza.com/Publications/Index/1

Gray, B., Babcock, L., Tobias, L., McCord, M., Herrera, A., & Cadavid, R. (2018). *Digital Farmer Profiles: Reimagining Smallholder Agriculture.* USAID.

Guba, E. G., & Lincoln, Y. S. (1981). *Effective evaluation: Improving the usefulness of evaluation results through responsive and naturalistic approaches.* Jossey-Bass.

Guba, E. G., & Lincoln, Y. S. (2005). Paradigmatic controversies, contradictions, and emerging confluences. In N. K. Denzin & Y. S. Lincoln (Eds.), *The Sage handbook of qualitative research* (pp. 191–215). Sage.

Hamill, S. (2017). Strengthening Agricultural Market Access with ICT. In *ICT in Agriculture (Updated Edition): Connecting Smallholders to Knowledge, Networks, and Institutions* (pp. 225–265). The World Bank.

Harper, P. (2020). Cannabis Bill carries harsh penalties. *Mail & Guardian*. https:// mg.co.za/news/2020-08-14-cannabis-bill-carriesharsh -penalties/

Hart, S. L. (1995). A natural-resource-based view of the firm. *Academy of Management Review*, *20*, 986–1014.

Hrustek, L. (2020). Sustainability driven by agriculture through digital transformation. *Sustainability*, *12*, 8596.

Ince, H., Imamoglu, S. Z., & Karakose, M. A. (2021). Entrepreneurial orientation, social capital, and firm performance: The mediating role of innovation performance. *International Journal of Entrepreneurship and Innovation*, 683199960.

Jelsma, M., Blickman, T., Kay, S., Metaal, P., Martínez, N., & Putri, D. (2021). *A Sustainable Future for Cannabis Farmers: 'Alternative Development' Opportunities in the Legal Cannabis Market*. Transnational Institute.

Jorge-Vázquez, J., Chivite-Cebolla, M. P., & Salinas-Ramos, F. (2021). The digitalization of the European agri-food cooperative sector. Determining factors to embrace information and communication technologies. *Agriculture*, *11*, 514.

Kay, S., Jelsma, M., & Bewley-Taylor, D. (2020, November 12). Fair Trade cannabis: A road map for meeting the socio-economic needs and interests of small and traditional growers. *Journal of Fair Trade*, *2*(1), 27–34. https://cronfa.swansea.ac.uk/Record/ cronfa55853/Download/55853__19169__7b6666c 67e5b47758f48e0f6e9656a0e.pdf

Kellermanns, F., Walter, J., Crook, T. R., Kemmerer, B., & Narayanan, V. (2016). The resource-based view in entrepreneurship: A content analytical comparison of researchers' and entrepreneurs' views. *Journal of Small Business Management*, *54*, 26–48.

Kilin, V., Pini, V., Kasparian, J., Gros, S., & Wolf, J.-P. (2019). Real-time and spatially resolved assessment of pathogens in crops for site specific pesticide reduction strategies. *BIO Web Conf.* EcoSciences. 10.1051/bioconf/20191501019

Köksal, Ö., & Tekinerdogan, B. (2019). Architecture design approach for IoT-based farm management information systems. *Precision Agriculture*, *20*, 926–958.

Kurtulmu¸s, B. E., Katrinli, A., & Warner, B. (2020). International Entrepreneurial Orientation and Performance of SMEs: The Mediating Role of Informal Institutional Framework. *SAGE Open*, *10*, 1–9.

Lee, J. (2020). Do patents lead to an increase in firm value? Evidence from Korea. *KDI J. Econ. Policy*, *42*, 33–52.

Lee, K., & Yoo, J. (2019). How does open innovation lead competitive advantage? A dynamic capability view perspective. *PLoS One*, *14*, e0223405. PMID:31747414

Mcata-Mhlauli, N., Ndukwana, T., Mosehla, S. & Christians, G. (2021 July 12). *Briefing to Portfolio Committee on Justice and Correctional Services on Cannabis for Private Purpose Bill.* Pretoria: Department of Trade, Industry and Competition (DTIC).

McKenzie, M., Bossuyt, P., Boutron, I., Hoffmann, T., & Mulrow, C. (2021). The PRISMA 2020 statement: An updated guideline for reporting systematic reviews. *BMJ (Clinical Research Ed.), 372*(7), 1. PMID:33782057

Minister of Justice and Correctional Services. (2020). Cannabis for Private Purposes Bill, Republic of South Africa. *Government Gazette No. 43595.* https://static.pmg.org.za/B19-2020_ Cannabis_for_Private_Pur poses6591.pdf

Minister of Justice and Correctional Services. (2020) Cannabis for Private Purposes Bill, Republic of South Africa. *Government Gazette No. 43595.*

Misaki, E., Apiola, M., & Gaiani, S. (2016). Technology for small scale farmers in Tanzania: A design science research approach. *The Electronic Journal on Information Systems in Developing Countries, 74*, 1–15.

Miscione, G., Ziolkowski, R., Zavolokina, L., & Schwabe, G. (2018, March 23). *Tribal governance: The business of blockchain authentication.* Scholar Space. http://hdl.handle.net/10125/50455

Mohapatra, B., Tripathy, S., Singhal, D., & Saha, R. (2021). Significance of digital technology in manufacturing sectors: Examination of key factors during COVID-19. *Research in Transportation Economics*, 101134.

Mushi, G. E., Di Marzo Serugendo, G., & Burgi, P. Y. (2022, November 16). Digital Technology and Services for Sustainable Agriculture in Tanzania: A Literature Review. *Sustainability, 14*, 2415.

Myers, J., Well, A., & Lorch, R. (2016). *Research design and statistical analysis.* Routledge.

Nyembezi, N. (2020, October 10). amaMpondo traditional leaders reject Private Use Cannabis Bill. *SABC News.* https://www.sabcnews.com/sabcnews/ amampondo-traditional-lea ders-reject-privateuse-cannabis-bill/

Park, S., Choi, H., & Kang, R. (2021). A study on the value relevance and accounting policy of R&D expenditures in accordance with firms' life cycle stages. *Korea Inter. Account. Rev., 96*, 73–92.

Pierre, J., & Peters, B. G. (2000). Governance, politics and the state. Macmillan Education UK.

Rashid, S., & Ratten, V. (2021). Entrepreneurial ecosystems during COVID-19: The survival of small businesses using dynamic capabilities. *World Journal of Entrepreneurship, Management and Sustainable Development, 17*, 457–476.

Rubera, G., & Kirca, A. (2017). You gotta serve somebody: The effects of firm innovation on customer satisfaction and firm value. *Journal Academic Markerting. Science, 45*, 741–761.

Rutsaert, P., Chamberlin, J., Oluoch, K. O., Kitoto, V. O., & Donovan, J. (2021). The geography of agricultural input markets in rural Tanzania. *Food Security, 13*, 1379–1391. PMID:34976233

Ryu, S. L., & Won, J. (2022, April 22). The Value Relevance of Operational Innovation: Insights from the Perspective of Firm Life Cycle. *Sustainability*, *14*, 2058.

Saiz-Rubio, V., & Rovira-Más, F. (2020). From smart farming towards agriculture 5.0: A review on crop data management. [CrossRef]. *Agronomy (Basel)*, *10*, 207.

Sanga, C. A., Tumbo, S. D., & Mlozi, M. R. S. (2014). System Design and ICT Adoption in Agricultural Extension Services Delivery in Tanzania. In *Technology Development and Platform Enhancements for Successful Global E-Government Design* (p. 25). IGI Global.

Sarker, N. I., Islam, S., Ali, A., Islam, S., Salam, A., & Hasan Mahmud, S. M. (2019). Promoting digital agriculture through big data for sustainable farm management. *International Journal of Innovation and Applied Studies*, *25*, 1235–1240.

Saunders, M., Lewis, P., & Thornhill, A. (2019). *Research methods for business students* (8th ed.). Pearson.

Schumpeter, J. A. (1942). *Capitalism, Socialism and Democracy*. Harper Collins.

Seddon, T., & Floodgate, W. (2020). *Regulating Cannabis: A Global Review and Future Directions*. Palgrave Macmillan.

Semete-Makokotlela, B. (2017, September 17). Cultivation of Cannabis for medicinal use, Cannabis, Pretoria, South African Health Products Regulatory Authority. *Pharmacy and Therapeutics.*

Sileyew, K. (2019, January 06). *Research Design and Methodology*. InTechOpen. https://www.intechopen.com/online-first/research-design-and-methodology

Silvaggio, T. (2018). Environmental Consequences of Prohibition: Lessons from California. *International Cannabis Policy Conference organized*. FAAT.

Smit, S. (2021, February 2). Haze Club case: Cannabis grow clubs allow people to access their rights. *Mail & Guardian,* https://mg.co.za/ business/2021-02-02-haze-club-case-cannabi s grow-clubs-allow-people-to-access-th

Stahl, N. A., & King, J. R. (2020, September 16). Expanding Approaches for Research: Understanding and Using Trustworthiness in Qualitative Research. *Journal of Developmental Education*, *44*, 1–5.

The Medicines and Related Substances Act, 1965 (Act 101 of 1965) as amended. http://www.SAHPRAza.com/Publications/Index/9

United Nations. (2021, October 4). *Growing at a Slower Pace, World Population Is Expected to Reach 9.7 Billion in 2050 and Could Peak at Nearly 11 Billion around 2100*: UN Report. https://www.un.org/sustainabledevelopment/blog/2019/06/growi ng-ata-slower-pace-world-population-is-expected-to-reach-9-7 -billion-in-2050-and-could-peak-at-nearly-11-billion-around- 2100

United Nations Office on Drugs and Crime (2018, October12). World Drug Report 2018. Booklet 2. *UNODC*. unodc.org/ wdr2018/prelaunch/WDR18_Booklet_2_GLOBAL.pdf

United Nations Office on Drugs and Crime (2018, October 31). World Drug Report 2018. Booklet 5. *UNODC*. unodc.org/ wdr2018/prelaunch/WDR18_Booklet_5_WOMEN.pdf

USAID. (2021, October 28). *Using ICT to Enhance Marketing for Small Agricultural Producers*. USAID. https://agrilinks.org/sites/default/ files/resource/files/Using_ICT_to_Enhance_Marketing_for_Small_Agricultural_Producers.pdf

Uwiringiyimana, C. (2020, October 14). Rwanda is in talks with EU, and U.S. firms to produce cannabis for export. *Reuters*. https://www.reuters.com/ article/us-Rwanda-drugs/Rwanda-in-talks-with-u-s-firms-to-produce-cannabis-for-exportidUKKBN26Z239

Yang, J., & Yu, M. (2022). The Influence of Institutional Support on the Innovation Performance of New Ventures: The Mediating Mechanism of Entrepreneurial Orientation. *Sustainability*, *14*(4), 2212. doi:10.3390u14042212

Yoo, J., Lee, S., & Park, S. (2019). The effect of firm life cycle on the relationship between R&D expenditures and future performance, earnings uncertainty, and sustainable growth. *Sustainability*, *11*, 2371.

Ziolkowski, R., Miscione, G., & Schwabe, G. (2020). Decision problems in Blockchain governance: Old wine in new bottles or walking in someone Else's shoes? *Journal of Management Information Systems*, *37*(2), 316–348. doi:10.1080/07421222.2020.1759974

Zondo, A.C.J. (2018, September 18). *Minister of Justice and Constitutional Development and Others v Prince* [and Others] ZACC 30 [court decision]. Constitutional Court of South Africa, Case CCT 108/17, http://www.saflii.org/za/cases/ ZACC/2018/30.html.

Chapter 12
The Legalisation of Cannabis:
Prevailing Challenges and Benefits for the South African Society

Manono Malusi Luthuli
Independent Researcher, South Africa

Njabulo Khumalo
Independent Researcher, South Africa

ABSTRACT

In recent years, cannabis has been one of the substances that many countries around the world have taken or are taking steps to legalise for certain kinds of consumption. In some countries, it is only legal in certain parts and still illegal in others. There is literature to suggest that idea of legalising cannabis tends to divide opinion with some people being for its legalisation and others being against it. The reason for the division of opinion regarding the legalisation of cannabis can be traced back to the many challenges and benefits that stem from cannabis being legal in any given society. There is sparse literature addressing the contextual dynamics of these resulting challenges and benefits. In this chapter, the authors present a commentary of some of the challenges and benefits that may result from the legalisation of cannabis in South Africa.

INTRODUCTION

There is evidence to suggest that the legalisation of Cannabis has resulted in improved public health outcomes for illnesses such as Psychosis, Schizophrenia, substance abuse disorder and their comorbidity in many populations across the globe (Bachhuber, Saloner, Cunningham, & Barry, 2014; Batall, Janssen, Gangadin & Bossong, 2019). Furthermore, the legalisation of Cannabis has been found to lead to increased tax revenue which can be funnelled into cash-strapped sectors and reduced burden on state criminal justice systems as there are significantly lower Cannabis related arrests (Colorado Department of Revenue, 2018). It is also important to note that this also presents unique challenges for tax regulation

DOI: 10.4018/978-1-6684-6346-8.ch012

and compliance as there is an increased burden on authorities to ensure that all Cannabis businesses are appropriately registered and compliant with the relevant laws (Childs & Stevens, 2021).

However, on another hand it is crucial to look at the challenges of such legalisation of Cannabis use in South Africa. Cannabis is widely known to be Africa's most used illegal substance but since the beginning of the new millennium, African countries have taken steps to reform policies and laws to align with global standards - South Africa and Seychelles have emerged to be at the forefront of this reform (Kitchen, Kabba, & Fang, 2022). The existence of legitimate Cannabis businesses presents various challenges and benefits not only for the people who own them, but for society at large. There is sparse literature that describes the prevailing challenges and benefits that stem from the legalisation of Cannabis in South Africa and since the Cannabis industry is growing in this region, there is a need for further research into this area. This commentary will provide more insights on the challenges and follows with benefits of Cannabis use.

A BRIEF HISTORY AND STATUS QUO OF CANNABIS AND RELATED CHALLENGES IN SOUTH AFRICA

Cannabis can be defined as a general term used to describe the many psychoactive variations of the Cannabis Sativa plant (Khalid, Zaidi and Ahmad, 2014). This plant contains two key components, Cannabidiol (CBD) and Tetrahydrocannabinol (THC), which induce psychoactive response when they come into contact with the human brain's Cannabidoid receptors (Stahl, 2013). The use of Cannabis in South Africa dates back thousands of years to pre-colonial times whereby indigenous South Africans known as the Khoi people/tribe referred to it as 'dachah' – a term from which the Afrikaans word 'Dagga' would later be derived (Theron, 1974; Paterson, 2009). The use of Cannabis for medical and recreational purposes can be seen as an ancient custom among many different tribes or ethnic groups in South Africa such as the Khoi, the San, the Sotho, the Nguni and the Zulu (Theron, 1974; Burchell, 2016; Crampton, 2015).

The precise use and social standards with regards to Cannabis differed from one ethnic group to the next as the Zulus were known to smoke it to reduce fear in their warriors before a war and the Nguniwere known to use it solely as a tool for socialising and relaxing (Theron, 1974; Paterson, 2009). Cannabis continued to be a socially acceptable and legal substance for centuries after the first white settlers arrived in South Africa and it was traded freely throughout the country as there were no laws governing it (Crampton, 2015). White settlers initially had positive views of Cannabis and they were known to smoke it for recreational purposes too (Paterson, 2009).

It was only in the early 20th century that public debates, led by civil society and religious groups, about the links between cannabis and public disorder as well as crime started to be made (Chanock, 2001). Thereafter, a sense of moral panic ensued among the presiding government, leading to the formation of the Customs and Excise Duties Amendment Act 35 of 1922, which forbade the use and possession of 'habit forming drugs' namely Cocaine, Heroin, Morphine, Opium, Cannabis and other synthetic substances (Kemp, 2015; Theron, 1974). Subsequent legislation regarding Cannabis prohibited cultivation, gave Police the power to detain offenders and set guidelines for punitive measures that Magistrates could implement against offenders (Crampton, 2015). It is important to note that there was legislation, the Medicines and Related Substances Act of 1965, that allowed medical practitioners to apply to the Medicines Control Council for permission to prescribe unregistered medicines such as Cannabis to their patients (Theron, 1974; Paterson, 2009).

From the 1990s, South Africa has experienced a steady increase in the accessibility and usage of illegal substances such as amphetamines, ecstasy, LSD, heroin, cocaine, and Cannabis (Atkins & Catholic Institute for International Relations, 1997). The usage and abuse of these substances can be attributed to many factors such as the rise in legal and illegal migration of people, unemployment, peer pressure among adolescents and young adults, reduced local and provincial border control resulting from a collapse of the apartheid regime, social and political liberation which enabled new trends and lifestyles as people were now free to partake in a greater variety of recreational activities such as travelling to parties anywhere in the country and until any time of day (United Nations, 1999).

Amid growing international scrutiny, in 2017 the South African Medical Controls Council moved Cannabidiol from schedule 7 (illegal) substance to a schedule 4 substance – effectively changing its status from an illicit substance to a prescription medication (Medicine Controls Council, 2017). Cannabidiol's schedule 4 status could only be valid provided it was in Cannabidiol preparations that were regarded as unscheduled and for this to be the case, the following two conditions had to be met:

1. The preparation's total quantity does not exceed 600 milligrams per sales package wherein the daily dosage is limited to 20 milligrams, so as to ensure that risk to a patient's health is kept to a minimum.
2. Preparations are strictly made up of only processed products constructed from raw cannabis plant materials thus ensuring that only the plant's naturally occurring level of cannabinoids are found in the product. Lastly, in all products, contents of THC and CBD may not be more than 0.001% and 0.0075% respectively (Republic of South Africa, 2020)

Also in the year 2017, the MCC had THC as a schedule 7 substance and it was kept this way for the most part but there was a change that meant that when THC is employed for therapeutic purposes, it is deemed as a schedule 6 substance (MCC, 2017). Schedule 6 substances are moderately to highly addictive substances that can only be dispensed with a prescription from a licensed medical practitioner who will be responsible for the close supervision of recipients (South African Health Products Regulatory Authority, 2020). All of these amendments were made with a view to aligning South Africa's Cannabis regulation with international standards and legislation, such as the World Health Organisation's (WHO) technical guidelines for establishing the safety and quality of herbal medications, of which medicinal Cannabis is a part (Viviers, Petzer, & Gordon, 2021). These guidelines operate under the remit of ensuring that the quality of herbal medicines and Cannabis is of a high standard as this has a direct impact on their efficacy and safety (World Health Organisation, 2007).

In terms of personal and recreational use, the year 2017 also marked the legalisation of Cannabis for cultivation and use by adults in the privacy of their own homes (Dippenaar, 2017). However, the buying and selling of Cannabis and being in possession of it outside of your home remained illegal (Dippenaar, 2017). In 2021, further developments in Cannabis legislation were made as it became legal to possess Cannabis in public as long as it is for personal consumption on private property (Law for All, 2021). The latest data suggests that a lot of South Africans are consuming cannabis as 41,5% of patients in rehabilitation centres for drug related treatment reported using Cannabis (Dada, Harker, Erasmus, Lucas, Parry, 2022).

Cannabis was initially made illegal in South Africa because of its links to behaviour associated with public disorder and minor crimes (Weihrauch, 2021). It is therefore important for scholars to continuously review and assess prevailing challenges and benefits arising from the legalisation of cannabis in

South Africa so as to ensure that if the issues that led to it being banned re-occur, they can be identified and addressed early.

Possible Challenges for People's Health

With an estimated population of 60,14 million people, South Africa has a vast and diverse health profile with diseases such as Hypertension, Tuberculosis (TB) and HIV leading the way in terms of the nation's burden of disease (Statistics South Africa, 2022). As the average life expectancy at birth is at 64,8 and 71,3 for males and females respectively, the country has comparatively poor public health outcomes as a result of significant mortality caused by HIV and TB (Statistics South Africa, 2022). There are also significant disparities in socio-economic status, with the unemployment rate above 35% and many South African's living in poverty (Statistics South Africa, 2022), that also contribute significantly to the relatively low life expectancy at birth. Empirical data from the Organisation for Economic Co-operation and Development (OECD) indicates that differences standards in clinical care, differences in population health, readiness of healthcare systems, quality of reporting structures and overall socio-economic status are key components of determining the extent to which burden of disease is known to result in mortality (OECD, 2021).

As Cannabis is a substance that human beings can consume, like many others, it has a broad range of impacts on the human body which tend to fluctuate between being both benign and malign (Hall, Leung, Lynskey, 2020; Abrams, 2018). With a wide range of known psychological and physical effects, it is important to consider the implications that legalising Cannabis will have on the health of South Africans at large. While a lot of people often report pleasant feelings and experiences from consuming Cannabis, these are not common for all individuals as different bodies are prone to having different reactions (Hall et al, 2020). Cannabis is known to make some people feel anxious, scared, and panicked – this usually happens when one consumes doses that are too large, when the Cannabis consumed has a high level of potency, or if the Cannabis is consumed by someone whose body is not used to inhibiting a substance of its kind (Mizzi, 2022).

The more pleasant broad physical and psychological effects that result from Cannabis consumption are sensory variations, muscle relaxation, heightened sensory sensitivity, mild euphoria (Abrams, 2018). The wide range of possible effects is caused by the variability of the strains of Cannabis plants and as each plant has different levels of concentration and thus potency (Mizzi, 2022). The role of human body variability also plays an important part in determining broadening the range of effects brought about by Cannabis consumption as different people have different tolerance levels – two people can smoke the same 'joint' and experience completely different effects (Hall et al, 2020).

It is important to understand that the physical and psychological effects of Cannabis are caused by two key compounds contained in the plant; Cannabidiol (CBD) and Tetrahydrocannabinol (THC) (Dupperouzel, Granja, Pacheco-Colon, Gonzalez, 2019; Hall et al, 2020; Mizzi, 2022). Both these compounds affect the body primarily through the brain and the central nervous system. THC is known to be responsible for inducing a lot of the mental effects such as inducing a pleasant sensory stimulation commonly referred to as a 'high' (Hall et al, 2020; Mizzi, 2022). On the other hand, CBD is known to also have some positive effects that can counter and moderate the 'high' caused by CBD as well as reduce anxiety to make on feel a sense of calm (Hall et al, 2020; Mizzi, 2022). The diagram below, figure 1, provides a visual summary of the commonly known effects on the human body.

Figure 1. Effects of THC and CBD (source: Mizzi, 2022)

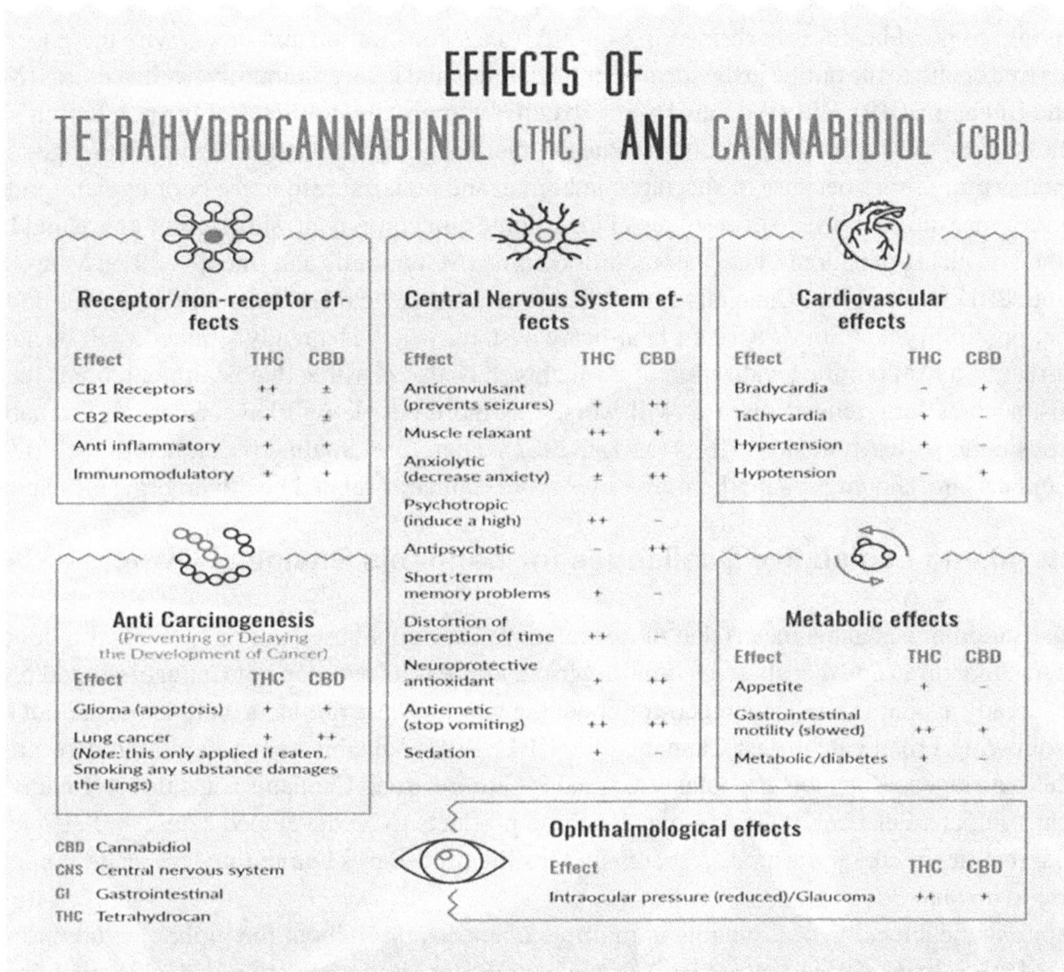

The threats posed by Cannabis to human health are significantly milder compared to other psychoactive substances that are commonly consumed by South Africans, such as alcohol and cigarettes (Hall, 2020). Moreover, much like alcohol and cigarettes, if Cannabis is consumed excessively, it can begin to pose a threat to one's health in the short and long term (Duperrouzel, Granja, Pacheco-Colón and Gonzalez, 2019). In the short term, Cannabis has been found to affect the respiratory system by predisposing one to bronchitis and other lung related illness (Mizzi, 2022). Some people also report short-term memory loss and mild cases of hallucination (Hall et al, 2020). In the long term, excessive consumers of Cannabis are at greater risk of addiction and chronic psychosis disorders such as schizophrenia (Duperrouzel et al, 2019; Hall et al, 2020). Individuals below 21 years of age are particularly in danger of becoming schizophrenic if they consume too much Cannabis as their pre-frontal cortices are not yet mature enough to withstand the psychotropic effects of Cannabis (Leadbeater, Ames, Linden-Carmichael, 2019; Hall et al 2020). For this reason, the South African government should strongly consider making Cannabis exclusively available for legal purchase only to individuals over the age of 21. The legalisation of Cannabis will mean that it is readily available for more South Africans, and this could result in more people being placed at risk of suffering some of the subsequent malign health effects.

The right to good health is enshrined in South Africa's constitution and this is why the government provides free health to the public in the form of public clinics and local community health centres (Maphumulo and Bhengu, 2019). With the state having to care for approximately 71% of the population's health (Statistics South Africa, 2022), the country's health facilities are overwhelmed with challenges such as prolonged waiting times because of shortages in human and material resources, poor hygiene and infection control measures, shortage of resources in medicine and equipment, shortage of space and beds to accommodate influx of patients, and poor record-keeping (Maphumulo and Bhengu, 2019; Munyewende and Nunu, 2017). Given that Cannabis can cause some adverse health effects on the human body, it is a distinct possibility that South Africa's healthcare system, which is already strained, will be stretched even further as a result of the legalisation of Cannabis. It is also possible that health outcomes for South Africans, such as lung related disease, will worsen as more people will have access to Cannabis and thus exposure to its harmful side effects (Mizzi, 2022). Therefore, South African health facilities, both public and private, should prepare themselves for more Cannabis related health emergencies and cases.

Structural and Legislative Challenges for Cannabis Business Owners

The legalisation of Cannabis means that more and more Cannabis-based pharmacological products can now be manufactured and distributed in South Africa. There is a vast scope of Cannabis-based products that are already available on the market throughout the world. These products include but are not limited to the following broad categories: Cannabis oil (CBD Oil), Cannabis beauty and skin care products, Cannabis beverages,, Cannabis chocolates, Cannabis Gummies and Cannabis Capsules (Nguyen, Wong, Delucchi, Halpern-Felsher, 2022). In order for these products to be developed safely and efficiently, it is crucial that they undergo rigorous research and testing procedures before they are made available for purchase to anyone.

Despite the legalisation of Cannabis in multiple countries throughout the globe, including many in Africa and sub-saharan Africa, there are still obstacles with regards to conducting Cannabis related research for the purposes of product development (Todd, 2018). The barriers to conducting Cannabis research are mainly due to laws that, despite its legalisation, still recognise Cannabis as a drug and therefore prohibit it from clinical and observational studies – Canada is a prime example of such a country (Rueda, Limanto, Chaiton, 2022). It is crucial that Cannabis products undergo the relevant level of research so as to ensure that they are manufactured in the appropriate manner and with the proper ingredients, so as to minimise harmful effects for those who consume them (Rueda et al, 2022). Research will also ensure that all products are manufactured according to industry standards for Research and Development, thereby propagating standard operating procedures that facilitate consistent quality products (Todd, 2018).

Internationally, one of the obstacles to Cannabis research and development are some of the international drug control laws which can still be viewed as limiting and outdated for the contemporary human rights and public health landscape (Rueda et al, 2022). An example of this is the UN's restrictive treaty known as the 1961 Single Convention on Narcotic Drugs, the 1971 Convention on Psychotropic Substances, and the 1988 Convention Against Illicit Traffic in Narcotic Drugs and Psychotropic (Sinha, 2001). These treaties form part of a wider legislation known as the International Drug Control Convention (IDCC) which is a legal framework that regulates products, fungi and plants that can be used in the pharmaceutical industry (Bewley-Taylor and Jelsma, 2011). Although the IDCC allows for the Cannabis plant to be cultivated, processed and researched under certain terms and conditions, there are still some limitations in terms of the parts of the Cannabis plant that can be used, purposes the final products can be used for as well as the chemical elements allowed in the final product (Rueda et al, 2022). Several clear exemptions to the 1961 Convention on Narcotic Drugs allow countries to implement hemp policies and regulations that exempt Cannabis from the IDCC (Bewley-Taylor and Jelsma, 2001). The most prominent ones are, exemptions by intended purpose of use:

- General exemption by purpose. This is reflected in Article 2(9) of the 1961 Convention, which states that countries "are not required to apply the provisions of this Convention to drugs commonly used in industry for purposes other than medical or scientific" and Article 4(b) of the 1971 Convention. In other words, it is legal for such substances to be used to manufacture non-psychotropic products.
- Full exemption for the whole Cannabis plant. The entire plant is exempt from the convention when it is used for horticurltural and/or industrial purposes.

There is also exemption by the physical parts of the Cannabis plant (Bewley-Taylor and Jelsma, 2001):

- No matter what the "purpose" of use is, the 1961 Convention explicitly exempts Cannabis seeds, fibers (Article 28(2)), and "leaves not accompanied by the tops" (Article 1(b)).
- As explained in the official explanation of the Convention, all parts of the Cannabis plant other than "fruiting or flowering tops" are excluded from the Convention if used for industrial purposes for nonmedical purposes.

After growing calls for policy reform from numerous countries across the globe, the WHO has undertaken to review and update the positioning of Cannabis in the IDCC (Rueda et al, 2022). It is clear that the aim of these calls is to further clarify the terms and conditions under which hemp and Cannabis products are exempt from the provisions and conventions of the IDCC. With an increasing number of countries legalising Cannabis for various uses and the growth of the Cannabis production industry, there is a clear paradigm shift with regards to the placement of Cannabis in society and the economy (Rueda et al, 2022). It is therefore necessary that the UN drug control mechanisms modernise their policies so as to avoid stifling international relations and the growth of global markets and economies.

Acquiring the relevant licensing to grow hemp in South Africa needs is a process bound by legal rules and regulations. To grow Cannabis one first needs to purchase a hemp permit from the South African Health Products Regulatory Authority (SAHPRA) and it costs nine hundred and two rands or about fifty five American Dollars (Vayej and De Lange, 2021). Hemp is the species of plant from which Cannabis is derived. It is still illegal to sell Cannabis for recreational use therefore the only permit available to sell Cannabis is for medicinal or industrial use (Law for All, 2021). Existing legislation does not allow SAHPRA to issue to grow Cannabis for non-medical commercial purposes (Vayej and De Lange, 2021). SAHPRA does however provide licenses for the cultivation of Cannabis for medical research purposes but the process of applying and obtaining such a license is an extremely rigorous and timeous one (Vayej and De Lange, 201).

Another possible challenge stemming from the legislation of Cannabis is that illegal growers earning a living through the illicit trade and informal economy, may begin to be marginalised amid an increase in the number legal Cannabis enterprises (Keenan, 2019). This is a distinct possibility as people who previously purchased from these illegal sellers may decide to grow their own Cannabis as the law now permits them to do so. Efforts need to be made to streamline and legalise small-scale growers as there is evidence to suggest that these are pillars of small-town economies that people rely on to survive (Keenan, 2019).

Possibility of Increased Social Ills

South Africa is already overburdened with alcohol and drug abuse, and it continues to be on the increase (Lesch and Adams, 2016). Despite having legislations that criminalise the trade of many drugs in place, people still find ways to purchase and sell drugs on a large scale throughout the country (Mbandlwa and Dorosamy, 2020).

It is widely acknowledged that the psychoactive properties of Cannabis are appealing to drug users who enjoy the 'high' that comes with consumption and now that it is legal to grow your own Cannabis, it is thus plausible that these Cannabis users will also start to farm their own gardens so they can get 'high' (Potter, Barratt, Malm, Bouchard, Blok, Christensen, Decorte, Frank, Hakkarainen, Klein, Lenton, Perala, Werse, & Wouters, 2016).. It will be difficult to police how much Cannabis people consume in private hence some people could end up consuming it excessively to the point where they can be classified as abusing the drug. While there may be limits to the amount of Cannabis one can grow, in reality, it could be argued that it is almost impossible to regulate how much an individual consumes, especially since it is now legal to consume it on private property (Potter et al, 2016).

The people growing and consuming Cannabis on private property may also have access to vehicles they can drive on public roads. Alcohol and Cannabis have been found to be the most recurringly detected substances in fatally injured drivers from car accidents (Thomas, Berning, Darrah, Graham, Blomberg, Griggs, Crandall, Schulman, Kozar, Neavyn, and Cunningham, 2020). The use of alcohol breathalysers at Police roadblocks is one means of deterring and potentially prosecuting drunk drivers. Currently, there is no preliminary means of determining Cannabis intoxication that exists, and therefore, prosecuting people who drive under the influence of Cannabis is and will remain a challenge for law enforcement officers (Liebenberg, Du toit-Prinsloo, Saayman, Steenkamp, 2019). Members of the public are also aware of this so it will also be difficult to deter them from driving under the influence of Cannabis . As a result, the legalisation of Cannabis in South Africa may lead to more drivers under the influence of Cannabis on the road and thus an increase in car accidents. South African traffic law enforcement needs to look into finding a tool, similar to an alcohol breathalyser, to make preliminary determination of Cannabis intoxication in motor vehicle drivers (Liebenberg et al, 2019; Mokwena, 2019).

There is evidence to show that certain strains of the Cannabis plant can be addictive for certain people and certain body types are genetically predisposed to addiction anyway (Hall et al, 2020; Duperrouzel et al, 2020). Addiction can be managed and cured through rehabilitation centres but unfortunately South Africa is facing a shortage of these establishments (Fokazi, 2015). South Africa only has one rehabilitation centre available for every eighteen drug users, whereas more developed nations such as Australia have one centre available for every three drug users (Fokazi, 2015). Therefore, legalising Cannabis for private consumptions opens the country's residents up to more risk of addiction while there aren't sufficient rehabilitation centres available. The government should thus look into developing more rehabilitation centres so as to mitigate this potential risk.

A BRIEF INTRODUCTION OF POTENTIAL BENEFITS FROM THE LEGALISATION OF CANNABIS IN SOUTH AFRICA

Taylor (2020) found that there are countries like the United States of America (USA) who have not nationally legalised Cannabis as it is still illegal in some states. Many other countries have fully legalised the use of Cannabis and data from these countries suggests that legalisation of Cannabis brings potential for new and improved tax revenue streams for the state (Hajizadeh, 2016; Taylor, 2020).

Hall and Lynskey (2016) discuss that there will come a time whereby the consumption of Cannabis for the recreational purposes will increase, however, when that time is, is uncertain. Furthermore, it will be difficult to monitor Cannabis consumption in private homes and whether people are selling it (Hall and Lynskey, 2016). On the other hand, it will be important to monitor Cannabis related harms including injuries, addiction treatment and minors use as well as criminal justice system. Mafolo (2019) reveals that it is scientifically proven that there is no harm to legalized Cannabis. The fact is that Cannabis have no causes of aggressive or violent behaviour after consumption, unlike other drugs (Nel, 2018). The sections below explore the benefits associates with the legalisation of Cannabis.

Possible Benefits for People's Health and Security

Maslow's hierarchy of needs puts forward the proposition that human beings have five basic needs; physiological needs, safety needs, social needs, esteem needs and self-actualization needs (Mcleod, 2007). This hierarchy (see figure 2 below) suggests that one needs to satisfy the lower level needs before being able to move to the next higher level (Mcleod, 2007). When the president of South Africa, President Cyril Ramaposa announced in his State of Nation Address that Cannabis is now legal in South Africa, this presented more opportunities of employment for South Africans and an increased growth potential in the nation's economy. As seen in figure 2 below, employment opportunity can fulfil all the needs across the hierarchy as money earned enables one to purchase food and clothing for physiological needs; shelter can be purchased or rented for safety needs; friendships formed in the workplace can satisfy love and belonging needs; employment status and recognition from the employer can fulfil esteem needs; and the growth and development gained in the workplace can facilitate self-actualisation.

Figure 2. Maslow's Hierarchy of Needs (Source: McLeod, 2007)

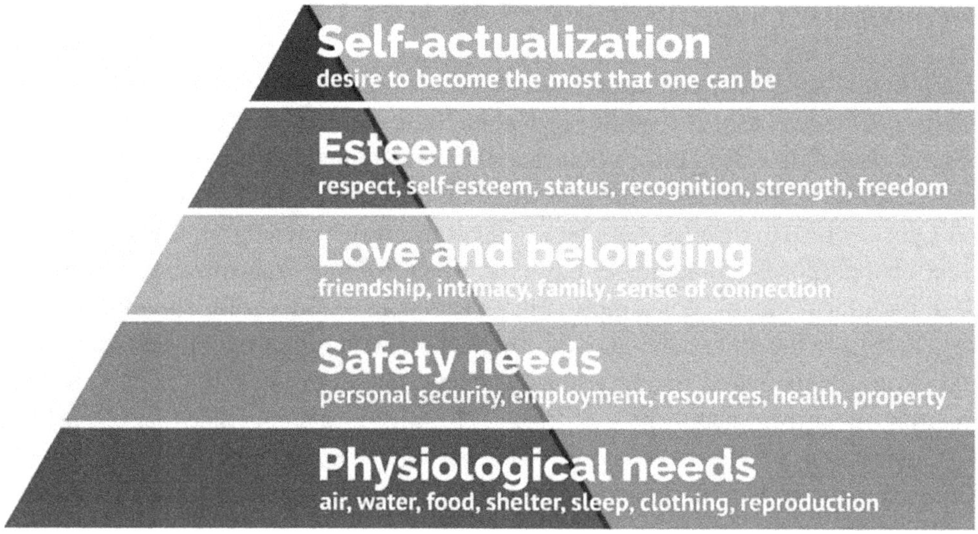

Settas (2021) indicated that for the sale of Cannabis to be legalized, it can be huge benefit for people with chronic pain, assist people with anxiety and provide treatment of cancer. Other scholars like Liput, Hammel, Stinchcom and Nixon (2013) discovered that the use of Cannabis like marijuana helps to reduce brain damage caused by consumption of alcohol. Settas (2021) believes that there is gap in literature and research, trials and treatments in medical fields from the damage done by the alcohol abuse in the brain. Therefore, there is a need for scholars to research more on how Cannabis can assist South Africa from damages done by consumption of alcohol. Many people have viewed Cannabis as a want but there is evidence to suggest that for some people, like those with health challenges that can be addressed by using Cannabis, it can be a legitimate need for the human body (Liput et al, 2013).

Different products developed from Cannabis which are needs from a physiological point of view such as to eat, drink, steam and inhale. Hajizadeh (2016) reveals that marijuana helps reduce the severity of diseases like inflammatory bowel and manages symptoms of chemotherapy and epilepsy in children. Cannabis is scientifically proven to assists damage in the brain caused by alcohol abuse. Further it is also proven that Cannabis has no effects which can cause aggressiveness. Cannabis has the potential to significantly reduce the number of people that are in hospitals due to sickness, and other diseases because of its soothing and symptom reducing characteristics. People who use Cannabis can also save a lot money which would have used buying medicines and treatments since Cannabis manages number of symptoms related to various health conditions.

According to Rensburg, Blockman, Moodley and Wilmshurst (2020) medical cannabis is still in its beginning with an aim of ensuring the good quality of product produced. However, there is still a lack of consistency and risks is since there are number of drugs used with no clear data guide tools (Rensburg et al, 2020). It is important to note that researchers and policy makers in South Africa considering conducting research into medical Cannabis treatment for patients with chemotherapy-induced nausea and vomiting even though the cost will be very high for this kind of treatment (Rensburg et al, 2020).

Social, Esteem and Self-Actualization Opportunities for Society

Legalising the use of Cannabis in South Africa can assist in reducing the consumption of alcohol and other drugs. Rees and Sabia (2019) revealed that countries like Washington State, USA, there is 9% decrease on consumption of drugs in high-school students ever since the Cannabis was legalized. South African young and old people in their gatherings can celebrate and socialise by using Cannabis and reduce the consumption of alcohol and other addictive drugs. Benefits from those social gatherings is that using Cannabis can cause people to be calm and not violent to each other which can lead people from being hospitalized due to fights caused by alcohol and drugs. By observation, that many countries still not sure about the medical advantages of Cannabis and this can be a great opportunity for the researchers and scholars to further provides findings and recommendation from their research. The existing literature on Cannabis is that in a small amount it carries a no harmful side effect compare to other drugs like alcohol which was legalized long time (Nel, 2018, in Setta, 2021).

South Africans are now allowed to consider Cannabis business through planting, growing and using Cannabis in their own spaces (Nel, 2018). This is a great opportunity for educated and non-educated people to have their own businesses which are newly legalized in South Africa. The use of Cannabis products in South Africa will be of huge benefits from both informal and formal sectors and can further provide an opportunity of the medicinal use in low-income families and villages who are far from hospitals (Global Commission on Drug Policy, 2019). Opportunities for South African business owners lies also on establishing rehabilitations centres to assist the drug addicts and alcoholics. This means that people from various sectors can now shift their minds to Cannabis business which is newly legalized. The legalisation of Cannabis has developed an opportunity for investments from anyone who is interested regardless of whether they have any pre-existing qualifications.

Economic and Employment Contributions from the Legalisation of Cannabis

Hajizadeh (2016) viewed that South Africa's economy will improve since there will be a new legal market on Cannabis which is regarded as a general product that going to contribute on taxation as a sin tax. Riley et al, (2019) viewed that the contribution to the economy can improved through selling Cannabis with similar value to that of the cigarate in South Africa and the state can use the model for benchmarking. This can produce three forms of taxes such as value added tax which is abbreviated as VAT, sin taxes and export taxes.

Taylor (2020) emphasises that Cannabis is an agricultural product which has a full production cycle from planting, cultivation, packaging, distribution and then sale. In his research he reveals that in Colorado, 27 000 occupational licenses and new tax numbers were supplied to people employed in the Cannabis market. Without this act, the country would have experienced less reduction in unemployment rates and thus a reduced amount of government tax revenue. Taylor (2020) suggests that South Africa could implement a licensing fee system for employers, whereby both the employer and the employee pay a licence fee to the government or the employer only pays a licence fee (similar to the unemployment insurance fund contributions and skills development levies determined based on salary, for instance).

Figure 3. Cannabis job creation in the USA by sector (Mafolo, 2019)

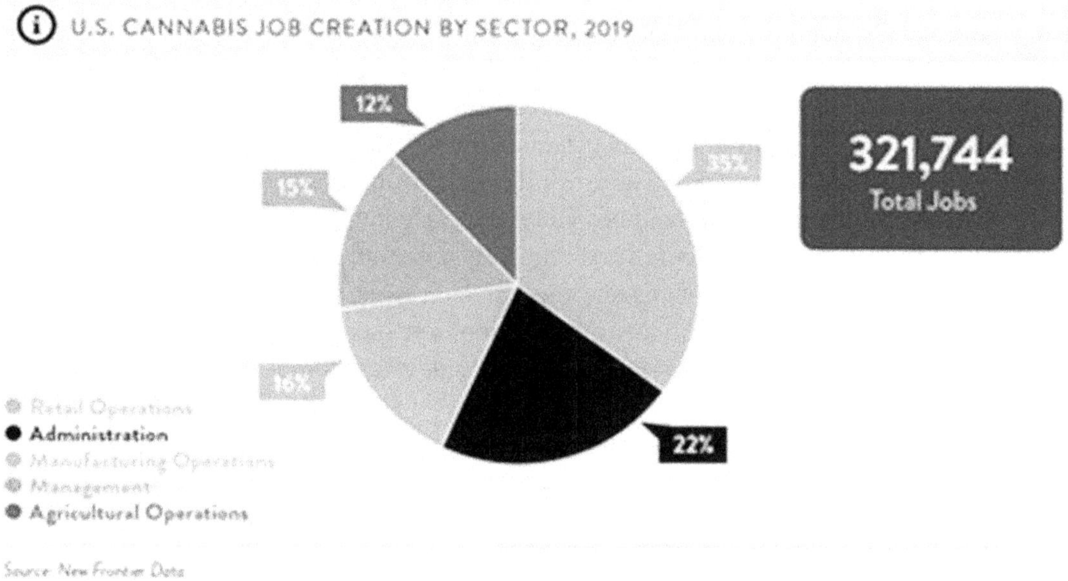

According to Mafolo (2019) in the USA, there are about 321 744 jobs created in the Cannabis industry, the bulk of which fall under retail operation. In African countries in the year 2017, Cannabis for medical use was legalized in Lesotho followed by Zimbabwe only for medical and research purposes, then South Africa for the private use in 2018 (Mokwena, 2019). The challenge is still in the unemployment rate which is still not dropping, especially in South Africa, however, the data in figure 3 above suggests that there will more job opportunities after legalising Cannabis for both low-skilled and high-skilled employees. The Cannabis industry will need people from management, administrative, manufacturing, agricultural, operational and retail people (Mafolo, 2019).

CONCLUSION

This chapter presents a commentary which discusses some of the potential implications resulting from the legalisation of the use of Cannabis products in South Africa. This chapter will not only be beneficial to South Africa but to other countries that have already legalised and also to those which are still in the process or consideration. It is imperative to look at both challenges and benefits before criticising or endorsing the legalisation of Cannabis products. The information discussed in this chapter stands to be useful for the general public, policy makers, law makers, politicians, researchers, students, members of government and Cannabis business owners as it provides insights into what can be expected as a result of the legalisation of Cannabis in South Africa.

REFERENCES

Abrams, D. I. (2018). The therapeutic effects of Cannabis and cannabinoids: An update from the National Academies of Sciences, Engineering and Medicine report. *European Journal of Internal Medicine, 49*, 7–11. doi:10.1016/j.ejim.2018.01.003 PMID:29325791

Atkins, A., & Catholic Institute for International Relations. (1997). *The illegal drugs trade and development in South Africa: Some observations.* Catholic Institute for International Relations.

Bachhuber, M. A., Saloner, B., Cunningham, C. O., & Barry, C. L. (2014). Medical Cannabis laws and opioid analgesic overdose mortality in the United States, 1999-2010. *JAMA Internal Medicine, 174*(10), 1668–1673. doi:10.1001/jamainternmed.2014.4005 PMID:25154332

Bewley-Taylor, D., & Jelsma, M. (2011). Fifty years of the 1961 Single Convention on Narcotic Drugs: A reinterpretation. *Series on legislative reform of drug policies, 12*, 1-20.

Burchell, J. (2016). *Principles of Criminal Law* (5th ed.). Juta & Co Ltd.

Chanock, M. (2001). *The making of South African legal culture 1902-1936: Fear, favour and prejudice.* Cambridge University Press. doi:10.1017/CBO9780511495403

Childs, J., & Stevens, J. (2021). A cannabis pricing mistake from California to Canada: Government can't tax cannabis optimally. *Applied Economics Letters, 28*(9), 779–783. doi:10.1080/13504851.2020.1781764

Crampton, H. (2015). Dagga: A short history. Johannesburg: Jacana Media (Pty) Ltd.

Dada, S., Harker, N., Erasmus, J., Lucas, W., Parry, C. (2022). *South African Community Epidemiology Network on Drug Use (SACENDU): Research Update (Phase 50).* SACDU.

Dippenaar, S. (2017). A joint account – just how legal is marijuana following the High Court ruling?
Duperrouzel, J. C., Granja, K., Pacheco-Colón, I., & Gonzalez, R. (2020). Adverse effects of Cannabis use on neurocognitive functioning: A systematic review of meta-analytic studies. *Journal of Dual Diagnosis, 16*(1), 43–57. PMID:28129086

Fokazi, S. (2015). *Marijuana risks adding to social woes.* The Eastern Star.

Global Commission on Drug Policy (2019). *Classification of Psychoactive Substances: When Science Was Left Behind.* GCDP.

Government Communication and Information System (2015). *Media Briefing on Operation Fiela by Inter-Ministerial Committee on Migration.* GCIS.

Hajizadeh, M. (2016). Legalising and Regulating Marijuana in Canada: Review of Potential Economic, Social, and Health Impacts. [Online]. *International Journal of Health Policy and Management, 5*(8), 453–456. doi:10.15171/ijhpm.2016.63 PMID:27694657

Hall, W., Leung, J., & Lynskey, M. (2020). The effects of Cannabis use on the development of adolescents and young adults. *Annual Review of Developmental Psychology, 2*(1), 461–483. doi:10.1146/annurev-devpsych-040320-084904

Hall, W., & Lynskey, M. (2016). Evaluating the public health impacts of legalizing recreational Cannabis use in the United States. *Addiction (Abingdon, England)*, *111*(10), 1764–1773. doi:10.1111/add.13428 PMID:27082374

Kemp, G. (Ed.). (2015). *Criminal Law in South Africa*. Oxford University Press, Southern Africa.

Khalid, S., Zaidi, W., & Ahmad, F. (2014). Evaluation of the awareness and perception of professional students in medicine, business and law schools of Karachi, regarding the use of (recreational) cannabis. *JPMA. The Journal of the Pakistan Medical Association*, *64*(9), 1025–1030. PMID:25823182

Law for All. (2021). What You Need to Know About the Legalisation of Dagga in South Africa. *Law for All.*

Leadbeater, B. J., Ames, M. E., & Linden-Carmichael, A. N. (2019). Age-varying effects of Cannabis use frequency and disorder on symptoms of psychosis, depression and anxiety in adolescents and adults. *Addiction (Abingdon, England)*, *114*(2), 278–293. doi:10.1111/add.14459 PMID:30276906

Lesch, E., & Adams, A. R. (2016). Couples living with and around alcohol abuse: A study of a farm-worker community in the Cape Winelands, South Africa. *Social Science & Medicine*, *156*, 167–174. doi:10.1016/j.socscimed.2016.03.030 PMID:27043369

Liebenberg, J., du Toit-Prinsloo, L., Saayman, G., & Steenkamp, V. (2019). Drugged driving in South Africa: An urgent need for review and reform. *SA Crime Quarterly*, (67), 7–18. doi:10.17159/2413-3108/2019/i67a4951

Liput, D., Hammell, D., Stinchcomb, A., & Nixon, K. (2013). Transdermal delivery of cannabidiol attenuates binge alcohol-induced neurodegeneration in a rodent model of an alcohol use disorder. [Online]. *Pharmacology, Biochemistry, and Behavior*, *111*, 120–127. doi:10.1016/j.pbb.2013.08.013 PMID:24012796

Mafolo, K. (2019). *Cannabis can create jobs and grow the economy new report argues* [Online]. Daily Maverick.

Mbandlwa, Z., & Dorasamy, N. (2020). The impact of substance abuse in South Africa: a case of informal settlement communities. *Journal of Critical Reviews*, *7*(19).

McLeod, S. (2007). Maslow's hierarchy of needs. *Simply psychology*, *1*(1-18).

Medicines Control Council (MCC). (2017). *Cultivation of Cannabis and Manufacture of Cannabis-related Pharmaceutical Products for Medicinal and Research Purposes Pretoria.* MCC.

Mizzi, D. (2022). *Cannabis: Legalise it or Criticise it?* THINK Magazine.

Mokwena, K. (2019). Social and public health implications of the legalisation of recreational cannabis: A literature review. *African Journal of Primary Health Care & Family Medicine*, *11*(1), 1–6. doi:10.4102/phcfm.v11i1.2136 PMID:31793317

Munyewende, P. O., & Nunu, W. N. (2017). Patient satisfaction with nurse-delivery primary health care services in Free State and Gauteng provinces, South Africa: A comparative study. African Journal of Primary Health.

Nguyen, N., Wong, M., Delucchi, K., & Halpern-Felsher, B. (2022). Adolescents' and young adults' perceptions of risks and benefits differ by type of Cannabis products. *Addictive Behaviors*, *131*, 107336. doi:10.1016/j.addbeh.2022.107336 PMID:35436697

Organisation for Economic Cooperation and Development. (2021). *OECD Health Statistics*. OECD Publishing.

Paterson, C. (2009). Prohibition & resistance: a socio-political exploration of the changing dynamics of the Southern African cannabis trade, c. 1850 - the present [Doctoral dissertation, Rhodes University, South Africa].

Potter, G. R., Barratt, M. J., Malm, A., Bouchard, M., Blok, T., Christensen, A. S., Decorte, T., Frank, V. A., Hakkarainen, P., Klein, A., Lenton, S., Perala, J., Werse, B., & Wouters, M. (2016). Global patterns of domestic cannabis cultivation: Sample characteristics and patterns of growing across eleven countries. In *Friendly business* (pp. 163–196). Springer VS. doi:10.1007/978-3-658-10329-3_9

Republic of South Africa. (2020). *Government notice R.486-Medicines and Related Substances Act (101/1965)*. Schedules, Government Gazette.

Riley, S., Vellios, N., & Walbeek, C. (2020). An economic analysis of the demand for cannabis: Some results from South Africa. *Drugs Education Prevention & Policy*, *27*(2), 123–130. doi:10.1080/09687637.2019.1581139

Rueda, S., Limanto, E., & Chaiton, M. (2022). Cannabis clinical research in purgatory: Canadian researchers caught between an inflexible regulatory environment and a conflicted industry. *The Lancet Regional Health–Americas, 7.*

Settas, A. (2021). *An Analysis of the Potential Fiscal and Health Benefits of the Legalisation of the Sale of Marijuana in South Africa* [Master's thesis, Faculty of Commerce, South Africa].

Sinha, J. (2001). *The history and development of the leading international drug control conventions*. Library of Parliament.

South African Health Products Regulatory Authority (SAHPRA). (2020). *South African Health Products Regulatory Authority*. Cannabis and Related Substances Frequently Asked Qusetions.

Stahl, S. M. (2013). *Stahl's Essential Psychopharmacology: Neuroscientific Basis and Practical Applications* (4th ed.). Cambridge University Press.

Statistics South Africa. (2021). *Md-year Population Estimates*. Statistical Release, P0302

Theron, F. (1974). *The dagga problem: a sociological perspective with special reference to the question of social policy* [Master's thesis, University of Cape Town, South Africa].

Thomas, F. D., Berning, A., Darrah, J., Graham, L. A., Blomberg, R. D., Griggs, C., & Rayner, M. (2020). Drug and alcohol prevalence in seriously and fatally injured road users before and during the COVID-19 public health emergency (No. DOT HS 813 013). United States. National Highway Traffic Safety Administration. Office of Behavioral Safety Research.

Todd, T. (2018). The benefits of marijuana legalisation and regulation. *Berkeley J. Crim. L.*, *23*, 99.

United Nations Office for Drug Control and Crime Prevention. (1999). *South Africa Country Profile on Drugs and Crime*. United Nations Office for Drugs and Crime.

Vayej, S. & de Lange, A. (2021). *South Africa's Green Gold*. CDCH.

Viviers, H. J., Petzer, A., & Gordon, R. (2021). An assessment of the potency related to Cannabis-based products in the South African market. *Forensic Science International*, *322*, 110754. doi:10.1016/j.forsciint.2021.110754 PMID:33862324

Weihrauch, R. (2021). *Criminalising cannabis in South Africa: a history and post-Prince discussion* [Master's thesis, Faculty of Law, South Africa].

World Health Organization. (2007). *WHO guidelines for assessing quality of herbal medicines with reference to contaminants and residues*. World Health Organization.

Chapter 13
The Process Towards Cannabis Commercialization by Indigenous Communities for Medicinal Purposes in South Africa

Monicca Thulisile Bhuda
University of Mpumalanga, South Africa

ABSTRACT

The possibilities of legalizing cannabis for commercial use in South Africa is investigated in this study using desktop research from documents, newsletters, and existing literature. Indigenous communities would gain immensely from the legalization of producing cannabis-infused products, as it would help to enhance the rural economy by producing jobs and create wealth. Cannabis is a significant component of African religion, culture, and beliefs, having been used by indigenous communities for generations and believed to have curative properties. Moreover, legalizing cannabis for industrial use makes sense not only for economic development but also for further medical research. According to the 2022 February speech of the Republic of South Africa's president, Mr. Cyril Ramaphosa, cannabis has the potential to be industrialized and commercialized in South Africa in the near future. The speech came after the Constitutional Court (ConCourt) in 2018 had already decriminalized and permitted cannabis use for both personal and medical purposes, which was previously illegal.

INTRODUCTION AND BACKGROUND

Cannabis is the source of marijuana and hashish, was introduced to eastern Africa from southern Asia around 1500 and quickly spread throughout the continent as highlighted by (Duvall, 2017). Cannabis was introduced into ethnobotanies in Sub-Saharan Africa, which featured pipe smoking, a habit invented in Africa; in Asia, it was eaten orally. Smoking cannabis has a substantial pharmacological effect, and

DOI: 10.4018/978-1-6684-6346-8.ch013

it was an African innovation that started the now-global practice. Africans created a variety of cannabis cultures, including Central African customs that spread throughout the Atlantic world thanks to slave trade (Duvall, 2017).

People in southern Tanzania prized Cannabis because it is known as a hunger supressing medicine. In 2008, a bioprospector in Malawi reported that cannabis give energy to a point of not needed food than usual (Kalula, 2011; Duvall, 2019). South African labourers have been using Cannabis to quell hunger for at least over a century (Peltzer et al, 2010). Cannabis in the Global North value have effect in the Southern African strains that have entered commercial production, particularly Durban Poison and Malawi Gold (Williams, 2020).

When cannabis was introduced in Africa, it was already used by the indigenous Khoisan and Bantu peoples in South Africa before European settlement in 1652 and was customarily used by Basotho to make delivery easier (de Vos, 2017; Kings, 2014). Cannabis is considered as indigenous traditional medicinal plants in South Africa and largely produced there in the entire continent. Perkel (2005) mentioned that South Africa is the world's third largest cannabis producer and supplies the southern African region.

Riley et al. (2020) argued that cannabis is consumed and grown in South Africa, as well as imported from neighbouring countries such as Swaziland, Lesotho, Mozambique, and Zimbabwe, exported to neighbouring countries such as Namibia and Europe (primarily Holland and the United Kingdom). However, since it is not legal to commercialize cannabis, there is illicit cannabis cultivation and selling which appears to be mostly in the eastern part of South Africa and some northern areas, where cannabis is widely grown.

There are large rural areas where indigenous people live with good conditions for growing cannabis. Indigenous people believe that cannabis is a traditional medicinal plant used for managing nausea, weight loss, treat glaucoma, treat pain and supress hunger. Duvall (2016) stated that in recent years, the estimated area under drug production has been a contentious issue, with the government presenting some unreasonably high statistics. According to current estimations, the amount of land under cultivation is between 1000 and 1200 hectares. According to Interpol, South Africa is still one of the top four herbal cannabis sources in the world. The crop is eradicated, and seizures are made with a lot of effort, with authorities discovering big amounts of it every year. Increased trafficking of illicit cannabis has been blamed on growing cannabis production, insufficient security, little effort on legalising the industrialization of cannabis and a lack of information within the police service.

Over the years, there has been a strong push in South Africa to legalize cannabis production and trade for economic purposes (Lubaale & Mavundla, 2019; Parry et al.,2019). Proponents of the proposal believe that criminalizing commercial cannabis growing and trading has failed to deter illicit cannabis cultivation and trade. The Constitutional Court (ConCourt) authorized cannabis usage for both personal and private medical purposes in 2018. The ConCourt determined that adult cannabis cultivation and personal use before was illegal. It was unconstitutional, as stated in the Drugs Act of 1992 and the Medicines Act of 1965. This verdict means that growing, using, or possessing cannabis in one's own home is no longer illegal but with quantitative restrictions.

Resources have been invested for over a decade exploring cannabis' medical benefits. Before 2016, SAHPRA (formerly the Medicine Control Council (MCC)) classified cannabis as a schedule substance, making it unlawful to consume, grow, possess, or distribute the drug. Lubaale and Mavundla (2019) discussed that decriminalizing private cannabis use and cultivation will certainly bolster calls for full legalization. Decriminalization, on the other hand, may result in increased access to cannabis products in all communities, aggressive marketing, a drop in cannabis prices, the development of high-potency cannabis, and possibly an increase in the ingestion of even higher-potency cannabis extracts, with escalating individual and public health consequences. However, Cannabis legalization, with the right strategies in place, can lead to scientific breakthroughs in disease treatments, allowing people to understand that cannabis can be ingested safely and in suitable amounts (Rothberg, 2017).

Riley et al. (2020) highlighted that there are two possible pricing implications if cannabis is completely legalized in South Africa. First, if the government introduces cannabis excise taxes, prices will rise (and government will generate revenue). Second, since legalization would eliminate the risk associated with buying and selling cannabis, the price of cannabis is likely to drop. Data is insufficient to establish the form of the demand curve for cannabis, or the shift of the demand curve should legalization occur, according to a 2013 article that analyses the limitations of conducting a cost-benefit analysis of cannabis laws (Shanahan & Ritter, 2013). Based on the above reviewed literature, the study investigates the future potential for indigenous communities to commercialize cannabis for medicinal purposes for job and wealth creation.

Cannabis as an African Indigenous Knowledge

The origin and indigeneity of cannabis in South Africa have a highly dubious past. Perkel (2005) argued that the Khoikhoi adopted cannabis as a valuable intoxicant & herbal remedy that was chewed or boiled and was traded from the Xhosa communities living in the eastern parts of South Africa. Scholars like de Vos (2017); Kings (2014) claimed that Khoisan and Bantu peoples in South Africa used cannabis before European settlement in 1652. For the purpose of the study, cannabis is regarded as indigenous knowledge because is perceived as traditional medicine used by indigenous communities to treat different illnesses.

Cannabis has undergone testing through trial and error, just like other conventional medicines, and has been approved as an effective means of treating and curing specific ailments (Masango, 2020). Indigenous knowledge (IK) includes traditional medicine (TM), which is used by people for spirituality, health, and long life. Oral transmission of IK occurs from generation to generation (Anyaoku, Nwafor-Orizu & Eneh, 2015). It is recognized as the traditional education of Indigenous peoples (Nakata et al., 2012).

IK generally refers to established, long-standing customs and practices of specific territorial, indigenous, or cultural groups as well as the wisdom, knowledge, and lessons of these communities, according to a definition given by (Morris, 2010). Indigenous knowledge comes in a variety of formats. It comprises traditional tales, music, dances, and rites that represent ideals about social justice, spirituality, family, and the natural world (Bhuda & Koitsiwe, 2022). It comprises information that could be subject to patent protection related to folk music, handicrafts, traditional foods, farming techniques, and traditional remedies. It entails information about the people, locations, plants, animals, and historical occurrences connected to a specific community (Hunter, 2005).

Traditional medicine (TM) is defined by the World Health Organization (WHO) as the collection of knowledge, skills, and practices based on theories, beliefs, and experiences that are indigenous to different societies, regardless of whether they are reasonable or not, and used to support wellbeing as well as to prevent, diagnose, improve, or treat physical and mental illness (Abdullahi, 2011). Traditional medicine (TM) is a subset of traditional knowledge and an old medical practice that was used in human communities before modern science was applied to health (Bhuda & Khazamula, 2022).

THE MEDICINAL BENEFITS OF CANNABIS

There is evidence suggesting cannabis' potential medical benefits despite the known negative effects of cannabis consumption. Dronabinol and Nabilone, two synthetic cannabinoids, have received FDA approval for the treatment of AIDS-related wasting syndrome and chemotherapy-related nausea and vomiting (dronabinol). According to Ben-Zeev (2020), the FDA authorized the use of cannabidiol (CBD), a cannabinoid produced from the cannabis plant, in 2018 to treat severe childhood-onset epilepsy. Following studies showing that CBD was both safe and effective for treating severe, intractable, childhood-onset, treatment-resistant epilepsy in children and young adults, the FDA approved CBD for this application (Calcaterra et al., 2020; Williams & Stephens, 2020).

Cannabis has been studied by D'Elia et al. (2013) and Mabou Tagne et al. (2020) for the treatment of ailments such pain, spasticity, and nausea and vomiting brought on by chemotherapy. There is conclusive or substantial evidence that cannabis or cannabinoids are effective for the treatment of pain, chemotherapy-induced nausea and vomiting, and for easing patient-reported multiple sclerosis spasticity symptoms, according to a 2017 review of the evidence by the National Academies of Sciences, Engineering, and Medicine.

Cannabis is a psychoactive substance that affects and modifies brain functions related to thought, perception, and behaviour. Other names for psychotropic medications include psychoactive, psychotherapeutic, or psychoactive. Cannabis specifically is a psychotropic substance. Therefore, it is a chemical compound that predominantly affects the central nervous system. By changing how the brain functions, it causes transient changes in perception, mood, consciousness, and behaviour (Cohen et al., 2019).

Cannabis also has psycho-stimulant properties, which means it uplifts mood and induces sensations of exhilaration, enthusiasm, attentiveness, and vigilance. This rise is typically followed by a collision (Dhadwal & Kirchhof, 2018). The three main cannabinoids found in cannabis are delta-9-tetrahydrocannabinol (TCH), cannabidiol (CBD), and cannabinol (CBN) (Andrade, 2016). Cannabinoids are said to provide potential therapeutic advantages, such as the control of stiffness in multiple sclerosis or nausea in chemotherapy for cancer (Zehra et al., 2018).

The primary methods for consuming cannabis are eating, drinking, and smoking (inhalation) (ingestion). Cannabis works fastest when smoked, including when vaped, as THC is transported to the brain in the bloodstream, and a user may begin to feel "high" within seconds or minutes (Hall et al., 2009). To maximize the amount of THC that is absorbed by the lungs, cannabis users hold their breath when they inhale deeply. THC levels reach their peak in around 30 minutes and begin to decline one to four hours later. The effects of cannabis consumption or ingestion occur more gradually than when it is smoked. Typically, there are intervals of between 30 minutes and two hours before the start of the high feeling. The effects linger for up to eight hours.

The Legalization of Cannabis Globally

Cannabis is believed to have come from central Asia and was primarily grown in China for a variety of purposes (Clarke & Merlin 2015). It migrated through East Asia, South Asia, and Europe from Central Asia. The plant was used for a variety of things, including hemp for paper, clothing, rope, animal feed, cooking oil, and religious purposes. The production of fibre and seeds were a priority in European, northern, and eastern Asian cultures. In contrast, it was primarily employed as a hallucinogenic medicine and secondarily as a seed plant and a source of fibre in Middle Eastern, African, South, and Southern Asian cultures.

Over the past ten years, there has been a global movement toward legalizing cannabis. Cannabis commerce and recreational use are legal in Canada and Uruguay. Since 2012, 11 US states including Washington, DC, have made cannabis use for recreational purposes legal. Nine of these jurisdictions also permitted retail sales (Pacula & Smart, 2017). Alaska, California, Colorado, Illinois, Massachusetts, Michigan, Nevada, Oregon, Washington, and other states had granted dispensaries licenses to sell cannabis to adults 21 years of age or older by the beginning of February 2020. Cannabis retail markets that are legal have grown quickly in the US. Cannabis sales in Colorado surged from $683 million in 2014 to $1,545 million in 2018 and from 2014 to 2017 there were roughly 400 percent more permitted shops (Orens et al., 2018).

Orens et al. (2018) further stated that the use of cannabis for medical purposes may be authorized by law. Only cannabis-based medications that have been prepared to pharmaceutical standards and that have been licensed for use due to strong supporting data from controlled clinical trials are permitted to be used by patients under the strongest regulatory framework. Government agencies who choose this route face a number of significant obstacles, including a dearth of medical cannabis products that doctors can prescribe, doctors' hesitation to recommend cannabinoids that have not been approved, and the high cost of using cannabis medicines that have been approved to patients (Pacula & Smart, 2017).

Martin et al. (2020) emphasized that more lenient regulations, such as those that permit medical use with little to no medical supervision and that permit the retail sale of cannabis-based medicines that fall short of pharmaceutical product standards, can make it easier for patients to obtain medical cannabis. By enabling any adult to use cannabis if they have paid a prescriber to certify that they have a medical condition that would benefit from using cannabis, this strategy has been implemented in the US and Canada, legalizing adult cannabis use (Pusiak et al., 2020; Hammond et al., 2022).

Similar research on cannabis in Africa were carried out by Bernstein (1999), who found Ghana to be the second-largest producer of high-quality cannabis in West Africa after Nigeria. Cannabis was found to be mostly sourced from and trafficked through Ghana, Nigeria, and Eswatini (World Drug Report 2018 (Sales No. E.18.XI.9) n.d.). The report also mentioned that most of the marijuana grown in Ghana was intended for export. According to these reports, the nation may be able to supply the legal cannabis industry. The Narcotics Control Commission Act, 2020 (Act 1019) was just approved in Ghana the year 2020. The Narcotic Drugs (Control, Enforcement, and Sanction) Act, 1990, PNDC Law 236 was repealed by this legislation, making it illegal to possess or import drugs (cannabis inclusive). The maximum sentence for breaking the statute was ten years in prison. Act 1019 also makes it legal to utilize cannabis for therapeutic and commercial purposes. Despite numerous studies exploring cannabis use in Ghana, there is little to no information on cannabis as an industrial agricultural crop (Quarshie & Alagidede, 2020).

The legalization of cannabis, also known as weed or marijuana, for personal use in South Africa by the Constitutional Court on September 18, 2018, presents a challenge for the sector of construction where its use has historically been covert or clandestine and in many instances seen to be synonymous with high levels of productivity on sites (Bester & Els, 2021). The decision legalizes an adult's possession, purchase, and production of cannabis, a psychoactive narcotic, for personal use in a home (Riley et al., 2020). South Africa is not the first nation to take this action in the world. Other countries on the list include Belgium, the Netherlands, Portugal, Switzerland, Belize, Jamaica, Spain, Australia, Argentina, Uruguay, and Canada (Orens et al., 2018).

AN OVERVIEW ON THE COMMERCIALIZATION OF CANNABIS

Although the potency of tetrahydrocannabinol (THC), the psychoactive ingredient in cannabis, has increased from about 4% in 1995 to 12% in 2014, according to a study by Calcaterra et al. (2020), the cannabis business continues to promote cannabis as being natural and safe. It is unknown how changes in potency have affected the risks connected to cannabis usage. Most studies looking at the therapeutic potential of cannabis used inhaled cannabis flower with varying THC/CBD ratios or synthetic THC-like cannabinoids, dronabinol and nabilone. THC/CBD concentrations in cannabis sold at dispensaries vary as a result of the cannabinoid extraction procedure. Cannabis is also available in tinctures, lotions, oils, sweets, infused drinks, and inhalation forms.

With the legalization and commercialization of cannabis in places like Colorado, Washington, Spain, and Uruguay, cannabis consumption within the framework of tourism has become more prevalent (Webster, 2017). Cannabis-oriented visitors have become a significant market niche that requires careful analysis for marketing and managerial reasons as a result of the movement toward cannabis consumption in popular tourist locations. Within the In African context, there has been development of commercializing cannabis in different countries.

For instance, according to Duvall (2019), a Canadian pharmaceutical company (EXMceuticals) said in 2019 that it had "obtained a license for producing psychoactive and non-psychotropic cannabis on more than 10,000 acres in the DRC" in January 2017. The contract includes the potential for nearly unlimited farmland expansion. It has cleared 50 acres by the month of August 2018, planted 40,000 plants, and harvested 10,000 of them. Along with photos of its operations, it also published profiles of two of the CEOs of its DRC subsidiaries.

In accordance with current legislation, the government started licensing cannabis cultivation in 2017, however regulations weren't published in Lesotho until May 2018. (Lubaale & Mavundla, 2019). A farming license costs roughly $13,000; manufacturing, testing, and exporting licenses are more expensive. 2017 saw a per capita income of $2,925 for Lesotho. Although the main business is controlled by a British company named Medi Kingdom, at least three other pharmaceutical firms have started exporting their products. These (Australia, Canada, South Africa, the United Kingdom, and the United States) are held by foreigners (Tharoor, 2018; Lamers, 2018).

Agriculture studies of non-psychoactive cannabis produced for fibre and oilseeds were permitted by the Malawian parliament in 2016. The trials were partially funded by a British businessman, whose company intends to begin commercial production. A Canadian-South African investor pushed for a hemp license in October 2018, and soon after that, the legislature started crafting a measure to legalize non-psychoactive cannabis production (Prince et al., 2018; Anywar et al., 2022). Duvall (2019:1) stated that "in February 2019, EXMceuticals announced a deal to grow 2,000 acres of the crop for psychoactive and non-psychoactive medicinal products. In May, it announced the acquisition of a Malawian agricultural processing company".

A parliamentary committee in eSwatini recommended authorizing medicinal plant development in April 2018. In January 2019, a U.S. pharmaceutical company announced a license agreement; in March, the production business structure was disclosed, but the licensing was not yet finalized (Kitchen et al., 2022; Asiimwe et al., 2022). According to regulations released in March 2019, licensees are required to construct high-security grow facilities and pay an estimated US$ 71,000 per license.

Industrial Hemp Uganda (IHU), "a company owned by Ugandans, started marketing hemp fibre goods in 2012. It started cultivating psychoactive cannabis in 2017. After IHU and EXMceuticals announced their agreement in April 2018, IHU bought marijuana seeds from the Netherlands for $42,000" (Duvall, 2019:1). Together Pharmaceuticals stated in July 2018 that it has obtained a license to cultivate medical marijuana. In a facility owned by IHU, together began planting in January 2019 and announced its first harvest in June. More than 90 domestic and international companies have applied to the Ugandan government for permits to engage in commercial marijuana cultivation. It's critical to make an economic argument for the product as consumers and businesspeople, as well as to negotiate the political and ethical landscape (Duvall, 2019).

In June 2017, a Zimbabwean minister of the economy approved a Canadian business' bid to cultivate medical marijuana. Government regulations allowing cannabis producing licenses under current legislation were announced in April 2018 (Anywar, 2022). The application cost $50,000 USD. The initiative was abruptly stopped by the government, but it was restarted in October once the charge was lowered to US$ 10,000. A pharmaceutical business with a Zimbabwean base but an American CEO reported in March 2019 that it had been granted a license for $46,000 USD. Zimbabwe's GDP per person in 2017 was $2,428 (Ibid).

METHODOLOGY

The study relies on secondary data such as news bulletins, government documents and published scholarly works about cannabis's use and commercialization throughout Africa. The study's goal is to look at the future economic benefits that indigenous people would receive as cannabis becomes more industrialized for commercial purposes in South Africa. The research also investigates how indigenous people may protect themselves from having their products and land plundered. The study will examine the IKS policy of 2004, the Biodiversity Act of 2004, DST and CSIR, DSI, NIKMAS, and NRS in the commercialization of indigenous knowledge/ traditional knowledge by custodians.

The State of Decriminalization, Commercialization and Industrialization of Cannabis in South Africa

The South African Constitutional Court upheld a decision in 2018 and went a step further by extending the protection of people who use cannabis for personal purposes. In this regard, the Court decided unequivocally that "an adult individual has the right to consume, cultivate, or possess cannabis in private for his or her own usage." According to the judgement, a home or other private dwelling is not the only place that is protected. With this decision, Mia (2020) stated that South Africa becomes the first and only African nation to allow for the private use of cannabis for personal use.

On the 10 February 2022, President Cyril Ramaphosa pledged that South Africa will soon embrace the economic benefits of the cannabis business during his State of the Nation Address. According to Ramaphosa, cannabis cultivation in South Africa will soon be industrialized, with the government hoping to explore the economic benefits. The Eastern Cape and KwaZulu-Natal provinces have also been chosen as good real estate to kick off efforts to capitalise on products that have proven profitable in neighbouring Lesotho, according to the President (Eyewitness news, 2022). The president stated that:

"Industrial hemp and cannabis will have a pathway to industrialisation for the creation of jobs at farms in the Eastern Cape and KwaZulu-Natal, with production for a number of purposes.

Based on the above statement from the South African president, such will be a good opportunity for indigenous people in Eastern Cape and Kwazulu-Natal provinces to participate in its cultivation and have monetary benefits from the sale of cannabis-infused items. Cannabis commercialization will allow indigenous groups to maintain their livelihoods, generate cash, and create jobs. This will mean opening of rural factories and growing rural economy which is a breakthrough indigenous people need by commercializing their indigenous knowledge (Lubaale & Mavundla, 2019; Viviers et al., 2021)

Policies Supporting the Protection and Commercialization of Indigenous Knowledge

Eastern Cape and Kwazulu-Natal cannabis businesses will guide other areas on how to commercialize their products and grow their businesses (Perkel, 2005). This is supported by the IKS policy of 2004, which emphasizes indigenous knowledge's contribution to the economy, its role in employment and wealth creation, and its interfaces with other knowledge systems, such as how indigenous knowledge is combined with modern biotechnology in the pharmaceutical and other sectors to boost innovation.

It will therefore be vital that indigenous people with interests of commercializing cannabis infused products to seek protection for their items and ask help when appropriate to ensure that they are not exploited in anyway. Malapane et al. (2020) argued that the Council for Scientific and Industrial Research (CSIR) and the Department of Science and Innovation (DSI) are two government entities that help indigenous people with commercialization and protection of their products. Community engagement activities, in which relevant officials visit indigenous people to educate them about commercialization, benefit sharing agreements, and product protection, are essential (Okole, 2021).

Furthermore, the Department of Science and Innovation is pursuing the National Recordal System (NRS) initiative to enable indigenous communities, custodians, and other Indigenous Knowledge holders to document their knowledge holdings for future economic and social gain (Bhuda, 2019). Its goal is to become the top IKS treasure hub in South Africa by documenting, storing, managing, maintaining, disseminating, and protecting IK for communal socioeconomic development.

The National Indigenous Knowledge Management Systems (NIKMAS), which will include a semantic Digital Library with custom-developed metadata schemata and a sophisticated security model to protect and preserve Indigenous Knowledge, an advanced semantic search engine, a sophisticated catalogue system, and an overarching integration architecture that combines the subsystems into a coherent, fit-for-purpose system, will support the NRS (Alberts, Khalala, & Molefe, 2011). Moreover, to ensure that traditional resources are protected in South Africa, the Biodiversity Act of 2004 promotes the sustainable use of natural and indigenous resources, as well as the management and conservation of South Africa's biodiversity through the protection of species, natural environments, and ecosystems, as well as the promotion of indigenous biological resources.

The Biodiversity Act implements ratified international biodiversity accords that are binding on South Africa and establishes the South African National Biodiversity Institute to help achieve the Act's goals (Biggs et al., 2006). The Act as stated by Botha (2004), ensures that the advantages of bioprospecting involving indigenous biological resources are shared fairly and equally. It is critical that indigenous peoples with business interests in cannabis and other indigenous resources understand the function of the Biodiversity Act of 2004, which is why community outreach programs are necessary from government officials.

Potential of Commercializing Cannabis by South African Indigenous Communities

The Eastern Cape government is pressing forward with plans to capitalize on the cannabis market to revive the struggling local economy and generate much-needed jobs. The department committed R4.5 million to grow the cannabis business in the 2021–22 fiscal year. The majority of the estimated 900,000 small-scale dagga growers are thought to be in the Eastern Cape, particularly in Mpondoland, hence the draft master plan's goal of commercializing the sector and making dagga legal will help these farmers (Rothberg, 2017).

KwaZulu-Natal is another province with many of small-scale farmers farming dagga, as was previously highlighted in the report. If accepted as is, a ministerial oversight group made up of farmers, manufacturers, and merchants would oversee its execution. A cannabis council was recommended to be established by the KwaZulu-Natal government to guide the growth of the sector there and assist in carrying out the country's master plan for the plant. The study makes the case that there are indigenous communities in some parts of South Africa that can benefit significantly from the cannabis market, despite the fact that the Eastern Cape and KwaZulu-Natal have been identified as potential provinces to benefit greatly from the decriminalization and commercialization of cannabis (Manu et al., 2021).

For instance, Limpopo and Mpumalanga province can also take a lead in the commercialization of cannabis for medicinal purposes. For decades, indigenous communities with medicinal knowledge have been marginalized from using cannabis and growing the plant. The original indigenous custodians of cannabis in South Africa are now unable to make any type of profit from its trade. Mogoro (2020) mentioned that cannabis has been discussed as a potential stimulus for reviving economically disadvantaged rural communities that are cut off from agricultural value chains and opening chances for canna-tourism.

However, the current law of cannabis restricts indigenous communities from developing markets and sustainable businesses using the product. This means that while the recreational use of cannabis in private is legal, many aspects of producing, processing, storing, possessing, transporting and selling it are still against the law. Luterek (2021) mentioned that the Cannabis for Private Purposes Bill was tabled in Parliament in August 2020. The Bill is still currently under deliberation by the National Assembly following receipt of public submissions (Mogoro, 2020).

The Bill aims to include suitable measures in the pertinent laws to ensure clarity about, among other things, what constitutes "in private" use and the amount that qualifies (Luterek, 2021). According to an interim report on the bill from the Portfolio Committee on Justice and Correctional Services dated March 23, 2022, the National Assembly Rules are asking the National Assembly for permission to expand it to address commercial activities involving recreational marijuana and to allow organizations to cultivate, possess, and supply cannabis plants for religious, commercial, and cultural purposes.

When the extension of the Bill happens, the study argues that government will create ways of supporting indigenous communities in benefiting from the cannabis market. Indigenous communities are likely to commercialise cannabis for medicinal purposes and that will require them to work with the CSIR, DSI and other government bodies to ensure that their products are safe and adhere to all laws associated with the safety of producing medicinal products as suggested by (Patwardhan & Mashelkar, 2009).

Manu and Ntsaba (2016) Indigenous communities who have knowledge of cannabis and want to benefit from its commercialization will need support from organizations that support and recognise rural economic development. Indigenous communities will also have to understand the rights they have towards the commercialization of what they perceive to be their knowledge as according to (Koutouki &

Lofts, 2018). One organization relevant to assist is the Cannabis Development Council of South Africa which is a registered Non- Governmental Organisation founded to represent the interest off the cannabis community in South Africa. Their ultimate objective is to be an all-Inclusive self-regulating Cannabis Industry Association whose duly elected representatives will form part of a National Cannabis Industry Association to help regulate and control the cannabis industry of South Africa.

CONCLUSION

The study's aim was to see whether indigenous communities could eventually commercialize cannabis for medical use in order to generate wealth and create jobs. Sourced and discussed was existing material on the legalization and commercialization of cannabis. The study covered South Africa's current legalization and commercialization of cannabis. It claimed that cannabis was only decriminalized in 2018 for adult private use under specific guidelines. The South African president provided updates and new information about cannabis industrialization in February 2022 through statements and press conferences.

The Eastern Cape and KwaZulu-Natal provinces would take the lead in the commercialization process, the president added. In agreement with the president's assertion, The National Assembly Rules request permission from the National Assembly to extend the Bill to address commercial activities relating to recreational cannabis, provide for the cultivation, possession, and supply of cannabis plants, and address cannabis by organizations for religious and cultural purposes, according to an interim report on the Bill from the Portfolio Committee on Justice and Correctional Services dated 23 March 2022.

The study made the case that indigenous people who view cannabis as an indigenous or traditional medicine must also benefit from its commercialization. The study also covered the existence of policies in South Africa that support the preservation of indigenous knowledge and promote benefit-sharing, wealth building, and job creation based on indigenous knowledge. Such policies must be considered when the process of permitting indigenous people to commercialize cannabis use begins in order to direct the parties who will be deployed in ensuring that the process is equally fair to indigenous people.

This study also revealed that the rights indigenous people have regarding the commercialization of their traditional knowledge are not mentioned in the current The Cannabis for Private Purposes Bill of 2020. As a result, this study hopes that the legislation will be amended/revised and that the process will be governed by current policies that clearly outline indigenous peoples' rights to their traditional knowledge.

REFERENCES

Abdullahi, A. A. (2011). Trends and challenges of traditional medicine in Africa. *African Journal of Traditional, Complementary, and Alternative Medicines*, *8*(5S). doi:10.4314/ajtcam.v8i5S.5 PMID:22754064

Alberts, R., Khalala, G., & Molefe, O. (2011). Collecting structured indigenous knowledge for enhanced exploration: The National Recordal System (NRS), South Africa. *Knowledge Management for Development Journal*, *7*(3), 291–307. doi:10.1080/19474199.2011.649009

Andrade, C. (2016). Cannabis and neuropsychiatry, 1: Benefits and risks. *The Journal of Clinical Psychiatry*, *77*(5), 2250. doi:10.4088/JCP.16f10841 PMID:27249079

Anyaoku, E. N., Nwafor-Orizu, O. E., & Eneh, E. A. (2015). Collection and preservation of traditional medical knowledge: Roles for medical libraries in Nigeria. *Journal of Library and Information Science, 3*(1), 33–43. doi:10.15640/jlis.v3n1a2

Anywar, G., Kakudidi, E., Tugume, P., & Asiimwe, S. (2022). The Cannabis/Marijuana (L.) Landscape in Africa: An Overview of its Cultivation and Legal Aspects. *Cannabis/Hemp for Sustainable Agriculture and Materials*, 297-310.

Asiimwe, S., Tugume, P., Kakudidi, E., & Anywar, G. (2022). Potential Impacts of L. Cultivation on the Environment in Africa: A Review. *Cannabis/Hemp for Sustainable Agriculture and Materials*, 311-325.

Ben-Zeev, B. (2020). Medical cannabis for intractable epilepsy in childhood: A review. *Rambam Maimonides Medical Journal, 11*(1), e0004. doi:10.5041/RMMJ.10387 PMID:32017679

Bernstein, H. (1999). Ghana's drug economy: Some preliminary data. *Review of African Political Economy, 26*(79), 13–32. doi:10.1080/03056249908704358

Bester, P. C., & Els, S. (2021). The legalisation of cannabis: A security-vetting dilemma. *Scientia Militaria: South African Journal of Military Studies, 49*(2), 1–28.

Bhuda, M., & Khazamula, E. (2022). Towards finding a cure for COVID-19: The role of African Traditional Medicine as an indicator of development. *African Journal of Development Studies, 2022*(2, si1), 137–153. doi:10.31920/2634-3649/2022/SIv2a8

Bhuda, M., & Koitsiwe, M. (2022). The Importance of Underpinning Indigenous Research Using African Indigenous Philosophies: Perspectives From Indigenous Scholars. In *Handbook of Research on Protecting and Managing Global Indigenous Knowledge Systems* (pp. 223–248). IGI Global. doi:10.4018/978-1-7998-7492-8.ch013

Bhuda, M. T. (2019). *The role of ethnomathematics in the cultural life of AmaNdebele women at Ekosini village in Mpumalanga Province* [Masters Dissertation, North-West University, South Africa].

Biggs, R., Reyers, B., & Scholes, R. J. (2006). A biodiversity intactness score for South Africa: Science policy. *South African Journal of Science, 102*(7), 277–283.

Botha, M. (2004). The new Biodiversity Act: News from the Conservation Unit. *Veld & Flora, 90*(3), 94.

Calcaterra, S. L., Cunningham, C. O., & Hopfer, C. J. (2020). The void in clinician counseling of cannabis use. *Journal of General Internal Medicine, 35*(6), 1875–1878. doi:10.100711606-019-05612-4 PMID:31898125

Clarke, R. C., & Merlin, M. D. (2015). Small, Ernest. 2015. Evolution and classification of Cannabis sativa (Marijuana, Hemp) in relation to human utilization. Botanical review 81 (3): 189-294. *Botanical Review, 81*(4), 295–305. doi:10.100712229-015-9158-2

Cohen, K., Weizman, A., & Weinstein, A. (2019). Positive and negative effects of cannabis and cannabinoids on health. *Clinical Pharmacology and Therapeutics, 105*(5), 1139–1147. doi:10.1002/cpt.1381 PMID:30703255

D'Elia, R. V., Harrison, K., Oyston, P. C., Lukaszewski, R. A., & Clark, G. C. (2013). Targeting the "cytokine storm" for therapeutic benefit. *Clinical and Vaccine Immunology; CVI, 20*(3), 319–327. doi:10.1128/CVI.00636-12 PMID:23283640

de Vos, P. (2017). *Dagga judgment: there are less drastic ways to deal with its harmful effects*. Constitutionally Speaking.

Dhadwal, G., & Kirchhof, M. G. (2018). The risks and benefits of cannabis in the dermatology clinic. *Journal of Cutaneous Medicine and Surgery, 22*(2), 194–199. doi:10.1177/1203475417738971 PMID:29056081

Duvall, C. S. (2016). Drug laws, bioprospecting and the agricultural heritage of Cannabis in Africa. *Space and Polity, 20*(1), 10–25. doi:10.1080/13562576.2016.1138674

Duvall, C. S. (2017). Cannabis and tobacco in precolonial and colonial Africa. In Oxford Research Encyclopedia of African History. doi:10.1093/acrefore/9780190277734.013.44

Duvall, C. S. (2019). A brief agricultural history of cannabis in Africa, from prehistory to canna-colony. *EchoGéo*, (48). doi:10.4000/echogeo.17599

Eyewitness news. (2022). Taking SA higher: Ramaphosa's plans for the cannabis industry. *EyeWitness news*. https://ewn.co.za/2022/02/10/taking-sa-higher-ramaphosa-s-plans-for-the-cannabis-industry.

Hall, W. (2009). The adverse health effects of cannabis use: What are they, and what are their implications for policy? *The International Journal on Drug Policy, 20*(6), 458–466. doi:10.1016/j.drugpo.2009.02.013 PMID:19362460

Hammond, D., Goodman, S., Wadsworth, E., Freeman, T. P., Kilmer, B., Schauer, G., Pacula, R. L., & Hall, W. (2022). Trends in the use of cannabis products in Canada and the USA, 2018–2020: Findings from the International Cannabis Policy Study. *The International Journal on Drug Policy, 105*, 103716. doi:10.1016/j.drugpo.2022.103716 PMID:35613480

Hunter, J. (2005). The role of information technologies in indigenous knowledge management. *Australian Academic and Research Libraries, 36*(2), 109–124. doi:10.1080/00048623.2005.10721252

Kalula, A. T. (2011). Cannabis use among young people in Dar es Salaam, Tanzania: A qualitative study. *African Journal of Drug and Alcohol Studies, 10*(1).

Kings, S. (2014). *The war on dagga sobers up"*. The M&G Online.

Kitchen, C., Kabba, J. A., & Fang, Y. (2022). Status and Impacts of Recreational and Medicinal Cannabis Policies in Africa: A Systematic Review and Thematic Analysis of Published and "Gray" Literature. *Cannabis and Cannabinoid Research, 7*(3), 239–261. doi:10.1089/can.2021.0110 PMID:34986005

Koutouki, K., & Lofts, K. (2018). Cannabis, reconciliation, and the rights of Indigenous Peoples: Prospects and challenges for cannabis legalization in Canada. *Alberta Law Review, 56*, 709.

Lamers, M. (2019). After decriminalizing cannabis Antigua preps full legislation. *MJ Biz Daily*. https://mjbizdaily.com/after-decriminalizing-cannabis-antigua-preps-full-legalization/.

Lubaale, E. C., & Mavundla, S. D. (2019). Decriminalisation of cannabis for personal use in South Africa. *African Human Rights Law Journal, 19*(2), 819–842. doi:10.17159/1996-2096/2019/v19n2a13

Luterek, J. (2021). Clearing the cannabis haze 3.0: When is cannabis CBD or hemp legal in South Africa? *South African Food Review*, *48*(4), 16–17.

Mabou Tagne, A., Pacchetti, B., Sodergren, M., Cosentino, M., & Marino, F. (2020). Cannabidiol for viral diseases: Hype or hope? *Cannabis and Cannabinoid Research*, *5*(2), 121–131. doi:10.1089/can.2019.0060 PMID:32656344

Malapane, O. L., Musakwa, W., Chanza, N., & Radinger-Peer, V. (2022). Bibliometric Analysis and Systematic Review of Indigenous Knowledge from a Comparative African Perspective: 1990–2020. *Land (Basel)*, *11*(8), 1167. doi:10.3390/land11081167

Manu, E., Douglas, M., Ntsaba, M. J., & Tarkang, E. E. (2021). Perspectives of illicit marijuana growers and traders on commercial legalisation of marijuana in South Africa: Considerations for policy formulation. *Substance Abuse Treatment, Prevention, and Policy*, *16*(1), 1–13. doi:10.118613011-021-00391-w PMID:34174921

Manu, E., & Ntsaba, M. J. (2016). Perceptions of marijuana use: Chronicles of marijuana smokers from two marijuana-Growing communities in South Africa. *Journal of Advances in Health and Medical Sciences*, *2*(3), 82–91.

Martin, J. H., Hall, W., Fitzcharles, M. A., Borgelt, L., & Crippa, J. (2020). Ensuring access to safe, effective, and affordable cannabis-based medicines. *British Journal of Clinical Pharmacology*, *86*(4), 630–634. doi:10.1111/bcp.14242 PMID:32128867

Masango, C. A. (2020). Indigenous knowledge codification of African traditional medicine: Inhibited by status quo based on secrecy? *Information Development*, *36*(3), 327–338. doi:10.1177/0266666919853007

Mia, N. (2020). The problems with Prince: a critical analysis of Minister of Justice and Constitutional Development v Prince. *Constitutional Court Review*, *10*(1), 401-424.

Mogoro, B. M., & Odeku, K. O. (2020). Paradigm Shift from Criminalisation to Constitutional Legal Protection for the use of Cannabis in South Africa: Issues and Perspectives. *African Renaissance (1744-2532)*, *17*(3).

Morris, B. (2010). Indigenous knowledge. *The Society of Malawi Journal*, *63*(1), 1–9.

Nakata, M., Nakata, V., Keech, S., & Bolt, R. (2012). Decolonial goals and pedagogies for Indigenous studies. *Decolonization*, *1*(1).

Okole, B. (2021). CSIR-DSI collaboration yields results for six traditional health practitioners. *CSIR Science Scope*, *17*(1), 6–7.

Orens, A., Light, M., Lewandowski, B., Rowberry, J., & Saloga, C. (2018). *Market Size and Demand for Marijuana in Colorado 2017 Market Update*. Colorado State Web Portal. https://www.colorado.gov/pacific/sites/default/files/MED%20Demand%20and%20Market%20%20Study%20%20082018.pdf.

Pacula, R. L., & Smart, R. (2017). Medical marijuana and marijuana legalization. *Annual Review of Clinical Psychology*, *13*(1), 397–419. doi:10.1146/annurev-clinpsy-032816-045128 PMID:28482686

Parry, C., Myers, B., & Caulkins, J. (2019). Decriminalisation of recreational cannabis in South Africa. *Lancet*, *393*(10183), 1804–1805. doi:10.1016/S0140-6736(19)30011-X PMID:31057166

Patwardhan, B., & Mashelkar, R. A. (2009). Traditional medicine-inspired approaches to drug discovery: Can Ayurveda show the way forward? *Drug Discovery Today*, *14*(15-16), 804–811. doi:10.1016/j.drudis.2009.05.009 PMID:19477288

Peltzer, K., Ramlagan, S., Johnson, B. D., & Phaswana-Mafuya, N. (2010). Illicit drug use and treatment in South Africa: A review. *Substance Use & Misuse*, *45*(13), 2221–2243. doi:10.3109/10826084.2010.481594 PMID:21039113

Perkel, C. (2005). Cannabis-the debate continues: A South African perspective. *The African Journal of Psychiatry*, *8*(1), 25–30. doi:10.4314/ajpsy.v8i1.30181

Prince, M. A., Conner, B. T., & Pearson, M. R. (2018). Quantifying cannabis: A field study of marijuana quantity estimation. *Psychology of Addictive Behaviors*, *32*(4), 426–433. doi:10.1037/adb0000370 PMID:29771542

Pusiak, R. J., Cox, C., & Harris, C. S. (2021). Growing pains: An overview of cannabis quality control and quality assurance in Canada. *The International Journal on Drug Policy*, *93*, 103111. doi:10.1016/j.drugpo.2021.103111 PMID:33478804

Quarshie, E., & Alagidede, I. P. (2020). Cannabis legalization in Ghana: Implications for value-addition in medical and industrial research and applications. *Journal of Indigenous and Shamanic Studies*, *1*(1), 1–14.

Riley, S., Vellios, N., & van Walbeek, C. (2020). An economic analysis of the demand for cannabis: Some results from South Africa. *Drugs Education Prevention & Policy*, *27*(2), 123–130. doi:10.1080/09687637.2019.1581139

Riley, S., Vellios, N., & van Walbeek, C. (2020). An economic analysis of the demand for cannabis: Some results from South Africa. *Drugs Education Prevention & Policy*, *27*(2), 123–130. doi:10.1080/09687637.2019.1581139

Rothberg, A. (2017). Thoughts as we consider the legalisation of cannabis in South Africa. *SAJCH: the South African Journal of Child Health*, *11*(4), 153–153.

Shanahan, M., & Ritter, A. (2013). Confronting the challenges of conducting a CBA of cannabis policies. *Drugs Education Prevention & Policy*, *20*(3), 175–183. doi:10.3109/09687637.2013.763906

Tharoor, A. (2018). South Africa decriminalises personal cannabis use and cultivation. Talking Drugs. *IDPC*. https://idpc.net/alerts/2018/10/south-africa-decriminalises-personal-cannabis-use-and-cultivation

Viviers, H. J., Petzer, A., & Gordon, R. (2021). An assessment of the potency related to Cannabis-based products in the South African market. *Forensic Science International*, *322*, 110754. doi:10.1016/j.forsciint.2021.110754 PMID:33862324

Webster, D. (2017). How to go green for your travel destinations in 2018. *Spokesman Review*. http://www. spokesman.com/stories/2017/dec/29/how-go-green-your-travel-destinations-2018.

Williams, A. R. (2020). Cannabis as a gateway drug for opioid use disorder. *The Journal of Law, Medicine & Ethics*, *48*(2), 268–274. doi:10.1177/1073110520935338 PMID:32631185

Williams, C. M., & Stephens, G. J. (2020). Development of cannabidiol as a treatment for severe childhood epilepsies. *British Journal of Pharmacology*, *177*(24), 5509–5517. doi:10.1111/bph.15274 PMID:32986848

Zehra, A., Burns, J., Liu, C. K., Manza, P., Wiers, C. E., Volkow, N. D., & Wang, G. J. (2018). Cannabis addiction and the brain: A review. *Journal of Neuroimmune Pharmacology*, *13*(4), 438–452. doi:10.100711481-018-9782-9 PMID:29556883

Chapter 14
Possible Employment and Career Development in the South African Cannabis Market

Njabulo Khumalo
University of Kwazulu-Natal, South Africa

ABSTRACT

The aim of the chapter is to provide knowledge on the opportunities that the cannabis market has for South Africa. It further provides new models developed from the current literature on the related subjects. The industry also plans to improve the current products, which requires a lot of training and development from the existing people in the market. Therefore, this chapter will cover a range of topics such as the employment relation act, entrepreneurship competencies, human resource planning, training and development, recommendable diversity and motivational models, national qualifications framework (NQF), as well as to look at the future jobs within the cannabis industry.

INTRODUCTION

Deeper understanding of policy dynamics can assist in developing guidelines for countries like South Africa and other African countries (Kitchen et al., 2022). Unemployment is one of the serious challenges that has been facing South Africa for decades, with no valued resolution at hand for all culture, ages, gender and religions. Areas like rural in South Africa are characterized by high levels of joblessness and very limited in employment specially in agriculture sector. However, those rural areas have potential people with semi and unskilled competencies who are seeking for employment (Makegetla, 2010). Gerwel (2018) indicated that chapter six of the National Development Plan of 2030 reveals that rural areas require a great social, economic and political opportunities to overcome the poverty. The challenge is to achieve the unemployment crises and to close a gap no unavailability of opportunities from the formal market in South Africa. The world of work has already been developing innovative systems to empower graduates with the required competencies such as in-service trainings, internships and graduate programs

DOI: 10.4018/978-1-6684-6346-8.ch014

to prepare youth for work. However, these programs after completion in a year or two, still leave those individuals with no employment, thus adding more to the crises.

Folina, Roussis, Kouneli, Kakabouki, Karidigianni and Bilalis (2019) reveals that the cannabis industry has now many advantages to fill the human resources needs, such as one-hectare unit requires around about 50 scientific staff to operate. This further contributing to healthy area where new medication is produced to manage epilepsy, and other chronic diseases. The literature reveals a need for South Africa to invest in the Cannabis market after it was legalized and it is evident that it has potential to alleviate the employment challenge by providing job opportunities and competencies to the public and also boost the economy through the revenue it will produces. In his State of the Nation address, President Cyril Ramaphosa (2022) estimated that the industry will develop almost 20 000 to 30 000 new jobs in South Africa. However, that will require a proper human resources planning to ensures that the right people are placed in the right positions with the right competences (Khumalo, 2020). The industry also plans to improve the current products which requires a lot of training and development from the existing people in the market such as medicines. Therefore, this chapter covers a range of topics such as Employment Relation Act, entrepreneurship competencies, human resource planning, training and development, recommendable diversity and motivational models, National Qualifications Framework (NQF) as well as to provide recommendations to the market and scholars to research on such as the future jobs within the cannabis industry during the fourth industrial revolution.

Employment Relation Acts

Employment relations refers to the regulations and the Acts, specifically on human or employment relations where there is an agreement between the employer and employee. It is vital for the businesses especially in the cannabis market to understand the implications and regulations of laws changes especially in the area of cannabis and drug policy laws of South Africa. These changes can be very confusing for the business owners within the industry and other spheres (Golegal, 2020). These changes also impact many other businesses since their current policies prohibit the use of drugs in the workplace. Furthermore, the legalization of such products requires the amendments in the policies which are aligned with the Employment Equity Act and Occupational Health and Safety Act. It is vital to promote the constitutional right of equity and exercise of the true democracy by elimination of unfair discrimination in workplace (Kok, 2020). The Act 55 of 1998 stipulates that all citizens should be treated equally and fairly in the workplace, regardless of their gender, race, and social backgrounds. This also regulates the Cannabis market to ensure that they adhere to the terms and conditions of the law especially when recruiting and selecting their employees. All organizations, either public or private sectors need to revise their own policies in favour of accommodating the use of legal cannabis products which were prohibited in the past, going forward. The amended policies need not to be the same, however, it should be aligning to the amendment of laws. It should also be noted that cannabis products have its own side effects which should not affect the productivity of the organisation. Like all other businesses, their main aim is to generate profit and grow the business, therefore, the legalization of cannabis product should not be misused otherwise.

Martinez (2022) reveals a new law of Marijuana Employment Protection Amendment Act of 2022 which will be effective as of July 2023, which prohibit employers from adversely affecting the employment relationship between employees who uses or tested positive for a drug. *"The employer's premises are not a 'private' but a 'public place'. It is submitted that employers may therefore implement rules that regulate the possession and use of cannabis in the workplace. This may, in the opinion of the authors, include a total prohibition on the use and possession of cannabis in the workplace. The draft 2020 Cannabis Bill makes provision for an individual to possess legally (in his or her private capacity) up to a 100 g of cannabis in a public place. Yeates however observes that, if a company has a workplace policy that prohibits any quantity of cannabis, it becomes a workplace rule. If an employee is in possession of any quantity in the workplace, it will then be viewed as a contravention of a workplace policy.108 This may lead to disciplinary action against the employee, not for being in possession of cannabis per se, but because of the breach of a workplace policy. Should the employee be in possession of more than 100 g of cannabis, it will constitute a crime in terms of the proposed legislation, and criminal prosecution will be instituted"* (Bester and Els, 2021:18). Therefore, discrimination based on using cannabis should be prohibited in the workplace. Managers need to know that people uses cannabis for different reasons and they should be allowed.

- ***Basic Conditions of Employment Act (75 of 1997) (BCEA)***

The Basic Conditions of Employment Act stipulates and regulates the conditions of employment and the variation of such conditions such as the written particulars of employment, regulation of working time and leave. The cannabis business owners should adhere to the conditions stipulated by the Act in all they do within the industry. From the contract and agreement, it must be clear in the regulations on how cannabis influence the organization. Further it is crucial for the employer to provide a clear and understandable statement for the employees on what is expected from them prior and during the legalization of cannabis products. This includes relevant conditions of employment and variation of such conditions and also creation of a secure, equitable, non-exploitative and harmonious environment. Lastly, to give fair labour practices (Nel, 2017).

Table 1. Particulars to be provided by the cannabis business

Contract of Employment Example: Mzilikazi Cannabis Business

✓ ***The name of the employer must be clearly provided in the letter head:***
Mzilikazi Cannabis Business, No 202, Stanger Street, Durban, KwaZulu-Natal, 4001, South Africa. www.mzilikazicannabis.co.za

✓ ***The name and the occupation of the job description should be provided:***
Ms Andisiwe Mkhize, Farm Grower, the aim is to dig, plant and water the cannabis every day of the week.

✓ ***The place or places of work:***
Mzinto 101 site in South of Durban 4021.

✓ ***The date of commencement, ordinary working hours and workdays.***
1 February 2021. Work hours are from 6:00am to 14:30pm on weekdays. Part of this the employee should be given an interval time of at least 30 minute a day.

✓ ***Payment in kind and value of such payment:***
An employee will be paid either daily, weekly, monthly e.g. end of 30 each month an amount of R12 000.

✓ ***Wage or salary rate:***
An employee should be made aware that if the payment is calculated hourly, weekly, monthly or commission basis.

✓ ***The overtime rate:***
Overtime should be an agreement between the employer and employee, the rate should also be clear to an employee. Bonuses during your month of employment or birth month.

✓ ***Deduction to be made from the employee's remuneration:***
It must be clear to the employees the deduction to be made on a wage or salary. Such as medical aid, pension fund, pay as You Earn (PAYE).

Component	Employee	Employer	Total
Pension fund	R1000	R1800	R2800
Medical aid	R800 each adult, minor R400	R800 each adult, minor R400	R1600 adult R800 child/ dependent
UIF	R177	R177	R344
PAYE	R2200		R2200
Group life	R250	R250	R500
Total	**R4250**		

✓ ***Leave entitlement:***
Annual leave with 21 consecutive days of paid leave, parental maternal leave of four consecutive months, family responsibility of three days, sick leave of one day every 26 days.

✓ ***Notice period:***
It should be clear to the employee in writing that either part wishes to terminate the employment agreement, at least 14 days or month notice required, depends on the period you have worked.

✓ ***Any other documentation:***
Employee should know where can they access certain information of the business.

- ***Employment Equity Act (55 of 1998) (EEA)***

Kilmer, Caulkins, Kilborn, Priest, and Warren (2021) suggestions is to implement government cannabis stores and use affirmative action policies when they hire and promote especially those groups that were discriminated in the state. The two elements of the Acts prohibit the discrimination from the employers and outlines their duty to implement affirmative action measures by means of employment equity plans. This includes unfair discrimination, the management of sexual harassment, fair discrimination, disputes over unfair discrimination, medical tests, psychological tests and other forms of assessments, testing for HIV and Aids, designated employers and their duties, designated groups and suitably qualified candidates. The cannabis businesses should at all levels ensure that no one is discriminated against based on using cannabis and also the medical tests. Cannabis businesses should ensure that all employees are equally and have similar opportunities for growth in the organisations. Further to that the business should be very vigilant on sexual harassment since it is part of unfair discrimination. Sexually harassment is more of unwelcome conduct of a sexual nature that violates the rights of an employee. If one employee reports such conduct to management and no action taken, the management has failed to adhere in terms of the Acts (Nel, et, al., 2017). It is vital for the cannabis business to understand that if employee feels that he or she has been a victim of unfair discrimination, the matter can be referring to the Commission for Conciliation, Mediation and Arbitration (CCMA) within a period of six months after the act or omission in question.

- ***Labour Relations Act (66 of1995) (LRA)***

*"The authors posit that, as with alcohol abuse, the employer may take disciplinary action against an employee, without any testing, if the effects of cannabis are clearly observable. This can then be included in the employee's personnel file in terms of disciplinary action taken against the employee, which could be considered during the security vetting process. Similarly, in the view of the authors, the employer may introduce a condition of employment that renders it obligatory to undergo regular medical testing if employment conditions justify such testing. This can also be applicable for security vetting to determine whether the applicant is suitable for the job from a security point of view. The authors submit that 'justifiable employment conditions' may be applicable in respect of certain occupations that involve operating heavy machinery, pilots, medical staff, or security services where employees are required to carry weapons or to be alert. Such circumstances may also include incidents where cannabis consumption poses a risk to the property of the employer or the safety of other employees and the public (*Bester & Els, 2021:20).

The LRA seeks to advance economic development, social justice, labour peace and the participation of employees as the stakeholders in the industry. The aim of the Act is to give effect to the rights and obligations of employees and their unions as well as the employers, in according to the fundamental rights of the Constitution and international labour convention. Secondly to promote collective bargaining at sectoral level, employee participation at the workplace and dispute resolution and labour peace. Over and above, the Act has an impact on human resource management such as performance management, training and development, discipline management, retrenchments, collective bargaining and employee participation, and strike handling and dispute resolutions. These Acts above clearly requires a good relationship between the employer and the employee. The amendment Acts indicates that employers must notify employees of their right before the commencement of work and keep on revealing what is expected and not expected from the (Martinez, 2022).

Entrepreneurship Competencies in Cannabis Market

According to Folina et al., (2019) there was no much discussion on medical cannabis few years ago. While these days many are researching and talking about the great opportunity it has such as employment, training and development of people as well as producing health products. Competencies refers to the knowledge, skills, and abilities an individual has. Black (2020) revealed that when Canada legalised cannabis in 2018, there is a strong desire to promote entrepreneurship across the country since the industry tend to be one of those that can contribute significantly in the economy (Deloitte, n.d p.25). Adults can establish businesses by having a number of seeds in their homes, especially if they live alone (Golegal, 2020). Litile and Khumalo (2021) emphasise that for all the projects to be executed, skills transfer expectations need to be defined from the beginning of the project in South Africa. This set the expectations must be clear from the beginning. Schofield (2017) indicate the most fundamental skills the managers should have such as technical, interpersonal, conceptual, diagnostic, communication, decision-making and time management skills. To establish new ventures in the Cannabis market, owners need to demonstrate the following competencies in order to lead effectively:

- ***Communication and interpersonal competencies***: it is vital for new business owners to listen and communicate with all stakeholders who are operating in the new area of specialization. This requires a sound communication, interacting professional and motivating employees, clients, investors and suppliers (Khumalo, 2018). In the cannabis market is essential that everyone treats one another with dignity and in a professional way, regardless of the age, levels and gender. It is essential for everyone in the market to be trained and able to write and speak languages mostly used in the market.
- ***Decision-making and problems solving competencies:*** The industry requires people that can understand that mistakes are part of the development in the learning process to come with unique and innovative ideas. Therefore, new business owners need to be able to take strategic decisions to enhance the business with the aim of maximizing profits and growing the business. Owners need to be trained on how to make wise decisions in the new venture as well to be problem solvers.
- ***Technical competencies***: new owners need to invest more of their time on their employees and ensure that they achieve their goals for the purpose of the business.
- ***Diagnostic competencies:*** new business owners need to visualize the growth of the business and lead in the industry especially in South Africa and globally. This can start by planting a seed of marijuana at home and visualizing the possibility of expanding to be a supplier for big businesses in the country.
- ***Time management competencies***: business owners need to priorities work and family and understand that time is money. The industry must understand that time management is a skill from planning to completion of the projects.

Researchers and academics need to facilitate workshops that can inform people on how to start and run their own cannabis-related businesses, and to provide entrepreneurial innovations to hiring firms as employees and managers (Alicia, Reid Micah, Crump Vikiana, Clement JoAnn and Evers, 2022). Institutions of higher learning need to develop programs that are relevant to cannabis knowledge, which will capacitate individuals to be experts in the field. Black (2020) reveals that "Providing cannabis training to interested and qualified college employees, not just faculty, may positively impact the campus culture regarding an academic cannabis program on campus. For colleges interested in implementing a cannabis program it appears that it may be beneficial to integrate love, passion, relationships, and professionalism throughout their programs".

Human Resource Planning (HRP) in Cannabis Market

According to Arcview Market Research (2020) there is a possibility of hitting 57 billion dollars on cannabis spending through recreation use and medical use. This projected income reflects growth within this industry and the need for a professionally trained workforce. Human Resource Planning refers to planning for the current and future human resources that will be needed in future with the right competencies, in the right positions, and at the right time. Research shows that less than 6 percent of legal cannabis businesses are owned by African Americans (Harris & Martin, 2021). The explosive cannabis industry is thus far dominated by wealthy white men, while black and brown communities that have been disproportionately and adversely impacted by cannabis prohibition are not benefitting substantially (Rahwanji (2019). Therefore, there is a serious need for new business owners and employees at all races and of all genders to own and dominate in this industry. Planning on human resources which can be described as people as resources in the business means to ensure that the right people are placed in the right positions with the related competencies (Khumalo, 2019).

RECRUITMENT

The new law has been introduced prohibit all employers to undermine that recruitment requires planning therefore, in the cannabis businesses they need to ensure that seek for quality personnel (Martinez, 2022). In business, people as employees are required to render their services to the employer in order to obtain a salary or wage for maintaining the standard of living. It should be noted that sometimes the vacant positions get held or frozen for a time in order to save money. The Cannabis market need to be strategic on recruiting in this area by deciding on:

- What type of jobs they need in the Cannabis market?
- Who to perform those job?
- Which skills are required in the Cannabis market?
- Where will those jobs be located?
- Does the Cannabis market need permanent or casual human resources?
- Which retention strategies can be used by Cannabis market?

Business owners in the cannabis market in their planning need to consider the following pre-need hiring strategies which cannot be used at once. From the above cannabis business need to consider strategies such as *Yield model* which estimates how many people the employer may require to reach the target. The business owners need also to consider *Pre-need* hiring people for a particular period. It is also imperative to consider *Rapid-growth* jobs that are estimated to grow rapidly in numbers within a year. Business owners should also consider *Cyclical jobs* of seasonal fluctuations and product cycles not a long time recruitment. In addition, business owners need to consider preparing for promotions jobs. It should be recalled at all times that there are external factors that influence the recruitment such as: *Government or trade union restrictions:* LRA (66 of 1995) regulates the way employer recruits new people and trade unions engage in the development of recruitment policies. *Labour market:* cannabis market should know the trends in the labour market in terms of shortages and surplus of skills. *Image of the company:* cannabis market as it is newly legalized in the country, the owners should protect the image of the industry in order to be the place and employer of choice for people. *Job design and analysis* in the cannabis market industry refer to plan and design of the types of work in a form of functions and relationships. This can be done by writing the descriptions, duties and responsibilities of each job and the specifications needed to do that job. *Advertising and selections:* there are many ways that can be considered for advertising in this industry, either internal or external. The industry should understand the new ways of advertising especially as South Africa is in the 4th Industrial Revolution where people are located in digital networks such as LinkedIn and other ways. Nowadays organizations have changed from traditional ways of doing things which includes selection of potential candidates. The industry can also shortlist people in their own places of work using technology and also interview people via Ms Teams or Zoom till they appoint the suitable candidates. *Orientation:* for high performance in the Cannabis market, owners need to orientate employees to know what is expected from them and where to get help if needed. Familiarising people about the industry can boost them to excel. This also applies in all businesses since their policies need to be amended after legalization of cannabis products. People in the market must be taught about new trends developed from their market. The aim of conducting orientation for the cannabis business is to help people to fit in easily and more quickly, and to make policies and procedure more clear to people.

Training and Development in Cannabis Market

South African economy has many challenges which includes the skills development. Alicia et, al. (2022) highlight that from accounting and logistics to farming and production, some US institutions of higher education are now adding cannabis educational programs to their offerings. These programs are preparing students for cannabis careers in cultivating, processing, researching, analyzing, dispensing, marketing and other ancillary cannabis positions. Alicia et, al. (2022) in Oaksterdam University (OU) in 2007 led this charge to address the cannabis education vacuum and was the first institution to offer cannabis certificate courses. Soon after, other cannabis specific institutions offered practitioner-based instruction on growing and running a cannabis company (Bunting, Garcia, & Edwards, 2013). Next, in the U.S, a small number of four-year colleges and universities stepped in to offer cannabis programs focused on science disciplines to support scientific research, medical practices, and in-depth analysis of cannabis and its various nuances (Alicia et, al., 2022). Many researchers argue that academicians must work very closely with cannabis industry employers to remain current with this rapidly changing industry, and to keep their curriculum up to date (Alicia et, al., 2022) in (Crump, Rolle, Reid, & Brevett, 2020). South Africa is faced with high illiteracy levels and ineffective national education and training system. However, Skills Development Act 97 of 1998 and the Skills Development Levies Act 9 of 1999 are the responses of those challenges. Gerwel (2018) in rural areas like Eastern Cape's and other places there are opportunities for filling a gap of unemployment in South Africa such as planting. The climate of South Africa grows the cannabis well and the GroundUp magazine, once revealed that cannabis is "an important cash crop". The government in South Africa need to design the cannabis cultivating parts to combat the issue of poverty and unemployment.

FOURTH INDUSTRIAL REVOLUTION (4TH I.R)

Technology is making organizations more effective and efficient as industrialization moved from 1.0 end of 18th century, 2.0 begging of 20th century, 3.0 in early 1970s and now 4.0. Cannabis industry should consider investing on artificial intelligence, robotics to perform repetitive and dangerous tasks (Kokt, 2020). After understanding the core of the business owners need to implement a tailored-made plan for the organization (Kokt, 2020). Therefore, career planning and pathing are the ways that ensure that individuals are developed for future (Nel, 2017). Cannabis industry should focus on core values of career management such as empowerment, multiskilling, growth and freedom of occupational choice:

Career management in Cannabis industry can be used for planning and shaping the progression of people according to the needs and preferences. Pathing in the Cannabis industry can be the used as the ongoing process of mapping logical and possible sequences of positions to which an employee can be promoted, transferred or rotated to grow. Below are a few central elements of career pathing: *Education:* refers to educating people about the existing information and recommending new ways that can be added. *Development:* refers to improving the people's skills and knowledge in their careers. *Training:* refers to equipping people from the obtained knowledge into practical. *Promotion:* refer to moving one from one rank to another senior positions. *Transferred:* refers to expanding the experience of one person from one task to another. *Rotation:* refers to continuously doing different tasks.

National Qualification Framework (NQF) levels

There is a need for the institutions of higher learning to develop the curricular cannabis. Moody (2018) indicates that there are colleges who have an opportunity in developing modules and courses in preparation on what can be developed for future in the cannabis industry to grow the revenue of the countries and developing many job opportunities. There is a knowledge gap on legislative and regulatory on the topic of cannabis. Hasses (2019) listed institutions of higher learning that have dedicated resources on providing cannabis education in America such as: Northern 29 Michigan University have a four-year undergrad degree in Medicinal Plant Chemistry, UC Davis have a qualification Physiology of Cannabis class, Daniels College of Business have a qualification in Business of Marijuana at eh University of Venver Class, Vanderbult's Law School have a module on Marijuana Law and Policy, Larner's College of Medicine provide an online course in Cannabis Science and Medicine in the University of Vermont, Ohio State University's had a seminar of Marijuana law in Mortiz College of Law. University of Washington's have a class on Medicinal Cannabis and Chronic Pain, Harvard Law School have a class in Cannabis Law, University of Maryland's School of Pharmacy's have a Master's of Science in Medical Cannabis Science and Therapeutics and, Clark university have a graduate programme in Cannabis Control. Black (2020) said there is huge need of qualified and trained professionals in the booming of cannabis production industry to look at the programs like training in biology and cannabis production including planting nutrition, environment, lighting, climate control.

LEVELS OF EDUCATION IN SOUTH AFRICA

In South Africa in system of higher education is divided into levels. In higher learning institutions, there are traditional universities, universities of technologies and comprehensive university. Table 2 below reveals the categories and levels.

Table 2. Department of Education (2019)

<table>
<tr><th colspan="2">Sub Framework</th><th>NQF Level</th><th>Qualification Types</th></tr>
<tr><td rowspan="5">General and Further Education and Training Qualifications Sub Framework (GFETQSF)</td><td rowspan="7">Occupational Qualifications Sub Framework (OQSF)</td><td>1</td><td>Grade 9</td></tr>
<tr><td>2</td><td>Grade 10/ National (vocational) Certificates level 2/ Occupational Certificates</td></tr>
<tr><td>3</td><td>Grade 11/ National (vocational) Certificates level 3/ Occupational Certificates</td></tr>
<tr><td>4</td><td>Grade 12/ National (vocational) Certificates level 4/ Occupational Certificates</td></tr>
<tr><td>5</td><td>Higher Certificate/ Advanced National (vocational) Certificates/ Occupational Certificates</td></tr>
<tr><td rowspan="5">Higher Education Qualification Sub Framework (HEQSF)</td><td>6</td><td>Diploma/ Advanced Certificate/ Occupational Certificates</td></tr>
<tr><td>7</td><td>Degree/ Advanced Diploma/ Post-Graduate Certificate</td></tr>
<tr><td rowspan="3"></td><td>8</td><td>Honours/ Post-Graduate Diploma</td></tr>
<tr><td>9</td><td>Masters</td></tr>
<tr><td>10</td><td>Doctorate</td></tr>
</table>

According to Manning (2017) there are three principles required to achieve the purpose of facilitating cannabis in the country, foundation from high schools then collaboration with local businesses and lastly, engaging with higher education. For the cannabis industry, people need to be educated and well equipped to be competitive in the market. Therefore, the recommendation is to have a qualification in Cannabis in future related also to agricultural studies and also with management competencies. NQF level 1 referred to someone with grade 9 which was well known as (standard 7, form 2), grade 10 (standard 8, form 3) and grade 11 (standard 9, form 4) can go to the FET and pursuit the NCV on cannabis. NQF level 4 somebody with matric (standard 10) can pursue either a Higher Certificate NQF level 5 (Higher Certificate) or a NQF level 6 (Diploma) or NQF level 7 (Degree/ Advance Diploma) on Cannabis. Senior qualifications can be provided such as NQF level 8 (Honours/ Post Grad Diploma) to professional qualifications such NQF level 9 (Masters) and 10 (PhD/Doctoral studies). Black (2020) reveals that it only one University that has so far produced one PhD graduate on cannabis at the University of Guelph in North America.

Diversity and Motivational Model of using Cannabis

Diversity refers to the engagement of people in the work areas from different backgrounds such as age, gender, ethnicity, cultures etc. Alicia et, al. (2022) in Leafly's 2021 job report: "While cannabis continues its run as America's fastest-growing industry, troubling racial and gender disparities remain. Black Americans represent 13% of the national population, but they represent only 1.2% to 1.7% of all cannabis company owners—a gap that is far too wide." The proposed cannabis education program will address this gap through built in pipelines to mentorships, scholarships, internships, experiential learning opportunities and job placement for students in collaboration with industry collaborators. Kilmer et al.

(2021) government authorities seek to increase workforce diversity in legal cannabis in disproportionately affected communities (DACs) by funding and target recruitment and training effort to people.

A challenges was also posed to licenses to provide an equitable plan on how they make efforts to increase diversity. One of the suggestions is to implement government cannabis stores and use affirmative action policies when they hire and promote especially those groups that were discriminated in the state. So far there are no federal estimates of the number of people working in the state-legal cannabis industry. One industry source put the 2019 figure of workers "who support the marijuana industry" between 165,000-200,000 full-time equivalents ("FTE") and another source estimated that legal cannabis supported 211,000 FTE jobs in 2019 and 243,700 jobs as of early 2020. Owners of the businesses should understand that in this industry many people including employees, customers and other stakeholders are coming from different backgrounds including race, ethnicity, gender and religions with different beliefs and values. However, this is a good initiative to have multi-cultural people in order to learn how cannabis product used in other cultures. For example, some cultures used these products to steam, smoke and drink them. Figure 1 is the proposed cannabis motivational model developed from Bophela's Hierarchy of Stokvels Model which was established using Hayes and Wheels write as well as Maslow's Hierarchy of Needs.

Figure 1. Maslow Hierarchy needs in Bophela's Hierarchy Stokvel Model (Source: Bophela, 2022).

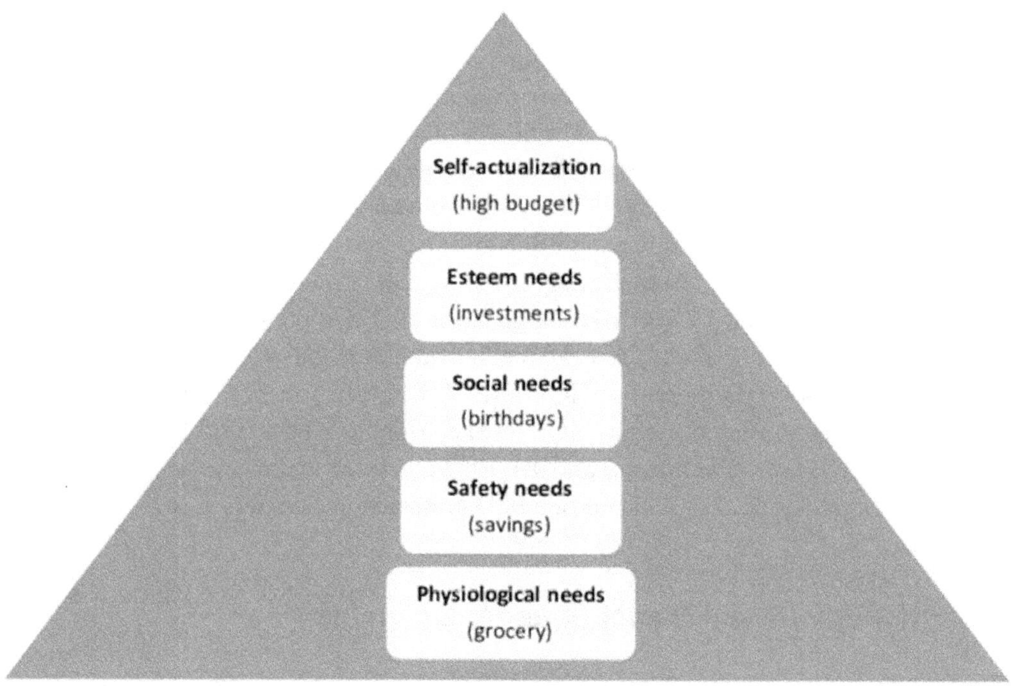

Figure 1 emphasises that people use cannabis products for many different objectives with its own target which is also aligned and concur with Bophela's Hierarchy of stokvels model but not in a hierarchical approach. Bophela (2022) reveals that step one refers to grocery focus, second one refers to savings focus, thirdly, refer to birthdays, fourthly, refers to investments and the last one refers to high budget. While figure 1 reveals cannabis has unique users with different goals, as can be seen in figure 2:

Figure 2. Khumalo's Uses of Cannabis Model

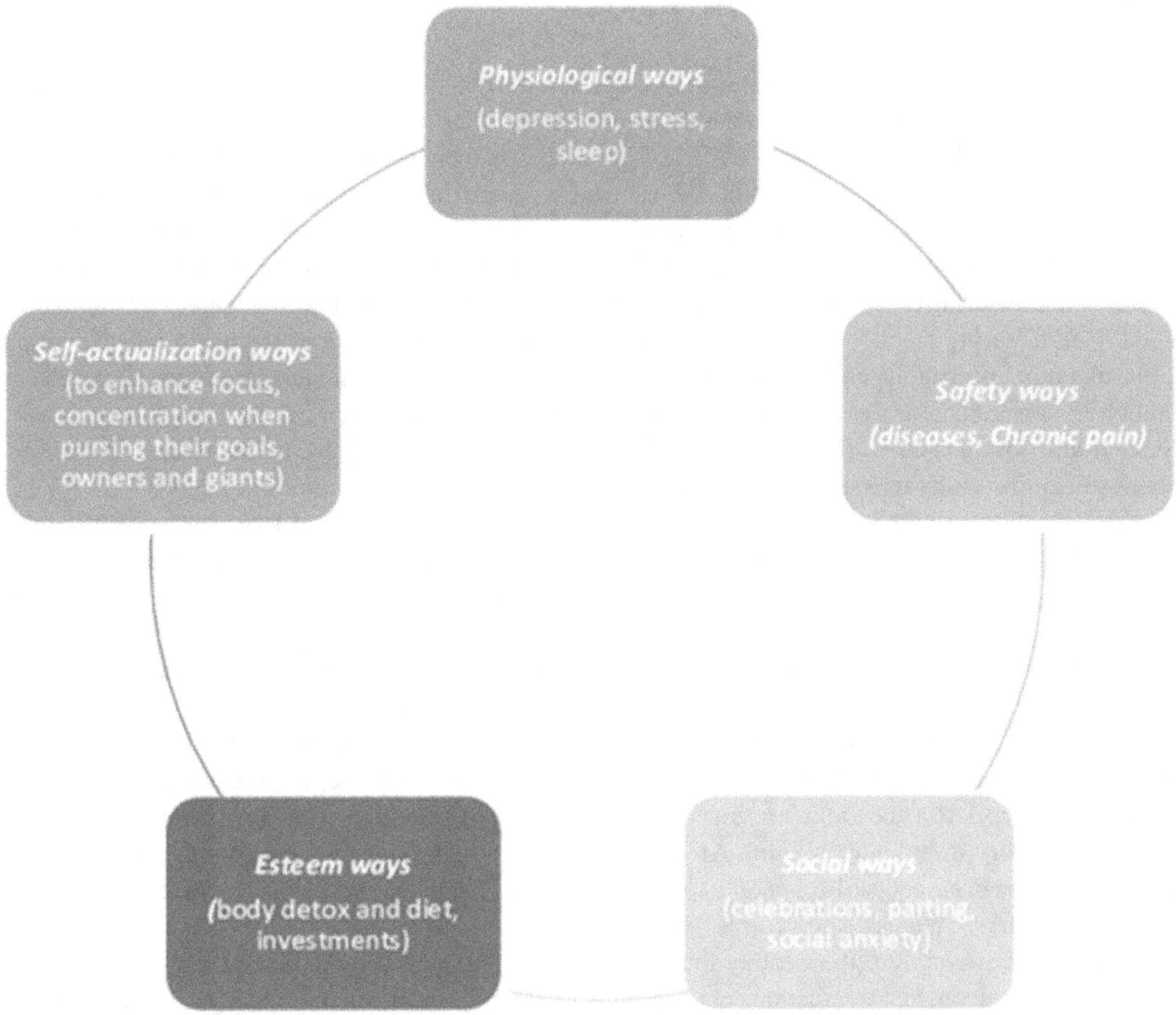

- ***Physiological ways*** of using cannabis product is to help the human body to calm and relax includes depression, post-traumatic stress disorder and sleep problems.
- ***Safety ways*** of using cannabis is to consume medication to heal the diseases that occurred during the span of life such as chronic pain and eliminates some type of cancer.
- ***Social ways*** of using cannabis is to celebrate with peers when people are together and to have fun and ease social anxiety.
- ***Esteem ways*** of using cannabis is for body detox and diet to look more young and fresh. This also contribute on return on investments. Lastly,
- ***Self-actualization ways*** of using cannabis is to enhance focus and concentration, own big and well known business in the market or industry and also to be giants in the industry.

RECOMMENDATION FOR FUTURE JOBS IN THE CANNABIS INDUSTRY IN SOUTH AFRICA

According to Kilmer, et al., (2021) statistics Canada reports that federally licensed medical cannabis producers had $647 million in sales and 9,200 employees, or one employee for every $70,000 Canadian in sales, which is close to one job per $50,000 U.S. at 2020 exchange rates. Black (2020) reveals that in countries like the State of California, the Department of Industrial Relations have already created skills and jobs like Pharmacy Technician Cannabis, Cannabis Nursery Specialist, Manufacturing Technician, Cannabis Distribution Drive. The skills include horticulture, pest management, trimming, extraction processes, manufacturing of edibles, equipment maintenance, building maintenance, regulatory compliance, good manufacturing practices, good lab practices, laboratory analysis, use of Hazard Analysis Critical Control Point, packaging and horticulture technician, pharmacy technicians/budtenders, extractors, laboratory technicians and extract packagers. Other jobs include custodians, as well as delivery drivers. Since South Africa is on 4I. R it is vital for industries to consider future jobs in the market. People have changed from working from employers' environment to work from their homes or anywhere as long as they deliver. To assist the stakeholders of the cannabis industry the following jobs can be considered.

Chat box personnel: the market needs to consider some service on chat box to receive and reply on stakeholders and customer queries on their apps and websites. This service will be sufficient for effectiveness and efficiency of the operation. *Data personnel:* the market needs to have an updated data system which will require people to operate on a continuous basis. *Wellness personnel:* these days South African and the entire country have lost so much on productivity due to Covid 19 implications to the society. About 100,609 people died in South Africa due to Covid 19 which are the families of employees from different organization. Therefore, it is vital to consider more strategies to proceed with this avenue to help employees to cope from stress and other factors via technology platforms. *Policy personnel*: cannabis industry is still new in South Africa, which need to plan on new policies going forward. It is vital that new trained and skillful people to be appointed to align the policies with the requirements of the legalization of cannabis.

Climate change analyst: the weather in the country changes on a daily basis and cannabis are plants which also grow from that weather that changes. It is vital for the market to have analysts who can advise the farm workers on what to expect seasonally. *Supply personnel*: for the industry to be controlled, the supplies need to be centralized and follow one approved procedures of the industry. *Performance management personnel:* the industry also contributes significantly into the country's economy. Therefore, it is imperative that the performance management system is developed to ensure that people deliver according to the standards. *Cannabis grower/famer:* it is evident that there will be number of job opportunities from the cannabis market, therefore, it essential to train number of famers in that area which will be registered in the cannabis industry. *Feedback rater:* to evaluate how the cannabis works for people, it is imperative to have feedback from the society to the industry at large.

RECOMMENDATIONS TO CANNABIS COMPETENCIES

This chapter has provided many angles that need to be considered in the cannabis market in order to be competitive. Therefore, people who wish or already in the cannabis business need to consider the following and plan in advance on who, where and how to achieve the following recommendations. *Choos-*

ing the right location: the area of planting the cannabis cultivation is controlled by the environment in order to grow. Business owners need to choose the area where they can maintain during winter and on summer, in fact in all session of the year by looking at the soil which is required for growth (Mavrogiannopoulos, 2017). *Flowering plant growth:* after having a good place to plant the cannabis and for the plants to grow well, flowering is important at all times. By cutting the plants it reduces crops and get destroyed. It is for people who know something about plant science and understand the principles and fundamentals scientifically of what goes on in a growing environment so we can start the program at a higher level (Dunne, 2018).

Harvesting: by having a timeframe to flowing the plant in order to grow, harvesting is the next step to cut and wrapped good in the large basin to be transported to the relevant areas (Pakes & Silverstone (2012). *Storage:* it is crucial for the cannabis business to train people on how to store the dried inflorescence of cannabis such as in a dark warehouse, 30% H. People working in the cannabis market need to have skills to in terms of the duration of lights since is it one of the important factor for continues production. It should be noted that natural light is not enough but need to be supported by artificial light to supplement. *Ventilation: e*mployee in the cannabis businesses need to be equipped on the ventilation system to ensure a fresh air in the greenhouses. It is a need for the ventilation to be high especially in spring to late autumn. Therefore, it is vital for employees and farmer to be aware that also high air velocities in the area or place can produces high transpiration with negative effect on cannabis clones. *Health and safety: c*annabis businesses owners should be aware that humidity is one of the factors of the greenhouse environment. Humidity produces diseases and other factors in a growing environment while use of insect killer is not allowed in the growing the cannabis environment (Labidi et al., 2017).

CONCLUSION

There is an evidence that other western countries are doing very well in planning for cannabis market such as Canada and America. This is an opportunity for African countries to begin on investing on developing a culture of cannabis from educational level to training purposes. The chapter covers the planning of the human resources form the beginning stage, it provides the perspectives of the amended laws, entrepreneurship competencies that is required within the cannabis market and also to provide opportunities to those who wish to embark in this industry. Further, alluded on planning the human resources, training and development since that are lot of skills people need to have to ensure a smooth running of the business.

At the end the recommendation of the NQF levels in relation to the cannabis that African countries like South Africa should looked at since other countries have produced a PhD graduate in this field. Diversity and motivational models are also considered and bring the attention to the future jobs within the cannabis industry. It is vital for all business people in the cannabis market to abide with the legislations in planning for human resources. By doing so the cannabis market will have the right system with the right people who have the right competencies to operate in the industry. The main of the business owners is to generate profit and grow the business in the market. Therefore, the return on investments should begin from systems thinking at the early stages of the formulation of the cannabis business. Collaboration is very imperative in order to be competitive in the market.

REFERENCES

Alicia, E., & Reid Micah, E. S., Vikiana, R., JoAnn, D., & Evers, R, M. (2022). Introducing cannabis education on a college Campus in 2021 The case of Medgar Evers College. College, New York, U.S. [IJHEM]. *International Journal of Higher Education Management*, *8*(2).

Bester, P., & Els, S. (2021). The Legalisation of Cannabis: A security-vetting dilemma. Scientia Militaria. *South African Journal of Military Studies*, *49*(2), 1–28.

Black, B. E. (2020). *Creating a qualified cannabis workforce: How higher education can support cannabis career pathways*. Kansas State University Manhattan.

Bophela, M. J. K., & Khumalo, N. (2022). The economic contribution factors of stokvels in the local economy of EThekwini Municipality. *Technium Social Sciences Journal*, *29*(1), 343–352. doi:10.47577/tssj.v29i1.5815

Bunting, W. C., Garcia, L. R., & Edwards, E. (2013). *The War on Marijuana in Black and White. PSN: Politics of Race*. Topic.

Deloitte. (n.d.). Open: A society in transition, an industry ready to bloom 2018 cannabis report. *Deloitte.*

Dunne, D. (2018). Implementing design thinking in organizations: An exploratory study. *Journal of Organization Design*, *7*(1), 1–16. doi:10.118641469-018-0040-7

Folina, A., Roussis, I., Kouneli, V., Kakabouki, I., Karidogianni, S., & Bilalis, D. (2019). Opportunities for cultivation of medical cannabis (Cannabis sativa L.) in Greece. *Scientific Papers*. Series A. *Agronomy (Basel)*, *LXII*(1), 293–300.

Gerwel, H. (2018). *Institutional innovation and pro-poor agricultural growth: cannabis cultivation in the Eastern Cape province of South Africa as fertile opportunity*. The 56 Annual conference of the agriculture Economics Association of South Africa. Stellenbosch University, South Africa.

Golegal, (2020). How the Cannabis laws impact your business*? Industry News and Insight.*

Harris, K. N., & Martin, W. (2021). Persistent Inequities in Cannabis Policy. *The Judges' Journal*, *60*(1), 9–13.

Hasse, G. (2019). Do epistemicídio à apropriação: análise da repartição de benefícios na lei da biodiversidade [Master's Thesis, Porto Alegre, Brazil].

Khumalo, N. (2018). The role of human resource planning in producing well-resourced employees to public. *Problems and Perspectives in Management*, *16*(4), 117–125. doi:10.21511/ppm.16(4).2018.11

Khumalo, N. (2019). Obstacles of human resource planning that affect workers in delivering quality services. *Problems and Perspectives in Management*, *17*(2), 114–123. doi:10.21511/ppm.17(2).2019.08

Khumalo, N. (2020). Human Resources Planning strategies implemented by the service institutions in improving employees' competencies. *Gender & Behaviour*, *18*(3), 15991–15998.

Kilmer, C., Kilborn, P., & Warren (2021). Cannabis legalization and social equity: Some opportunities, puzzles, and trade-offs. *Boston University Law Review*, *101*(1003), 1005-1040.

Kitchen, C., Kabba, J, A., Ssekamatte, T., Nelson, E., Adu-Gyamfi, S., Mamatja, M., Yang, C., Chang J., & Fang, Y. (2022). Perceptions of Cannabis in sub-Saharan Africa: Findings from a general population survey in six African countries with different Cannabis policies. *Research Square.*

Kok, Z. (2020). *Cannabis in the workplace*. North West University.

Kokt, D. (2020). *Human Resource Management in the new world of work: meeting the challenges of Industry 4.0.* Van Schaik Publishers.

Labidi, A., Chouchaine, A., & Mami, A. K. (2017). Control of relative humidity inside an agricultural greenhouse. *18th International Conference on Sciences and Techniques of Automatic Control and Computer Engineering (STA)*, (pp. 109–114) IEEE. 10.1109/STA.2017.8314955

Litile, M., & Khumalo, N. (2021). The impact of service providers in the development of the employees' skills in the Government Institution. *Gender & Behaviour*, *19*(2), 18107–18114.

Makgetla, N. (2010). *Synthesis Paper.* South Africa. DBSA.

Manning, F. J. (2017, May 18). CTE program preps high school students in the professional world beyond K12. *District Administration.*

Martinez, A. (2022). Marijuana users offered broad job protections in DC. *Forbes.*

Mavrogiannopoulos, G. N. (2017). *Greenhouses* (4th ed.). Stamoulis Publications

Moody, J. (2018, June, 5). Time for colleges to give cannabis a try? *Forbes.*

Nel, W. (2017). Human Resource Management (10th ed). Oxford University Press Southern Africa (Pty) Ltd.

Pakes, F., & Silverstone, D. (2012). Cannabis in the global market: A comparison between the UK and the Netherlands. *International Journal of Law, Crime and Justice*, *40*(1), 20–30. doi:10.1016/j.ijlcj.2011.09.003

Rahwanji, M. (2019). Hash"ing Out Inequality in the Legal Recreational Cannabis Industry. *Northwestern Journal of International Law & Business, 39*(3), 334-356. https://scholarlycommons.law.northwestern.edu/njilb/vol39/iss3/4

Schofield, I. (2017). Management Sciences: An Introduction. Juta and Company (Pty) Ltd.

Chapter 15
The Industrialization of Cannabis in South Africa:
A State-Led Case for High-Powered Redistribution

Mlondi B. F. Vilakazi
University of Kwazulu-Natal, South Africa

ABSTRACT

This chapter aims to understand the opportunities that are available for the industrialisation of cannabis in South Africa from the developmental state perspective. The exclusion of Black people in the economy is still the main theme of the South African economy 28 years into democracy. Therefore, the intersection between the state and its importance in terms of guiding the private sector to achieve industrialisation and redistribution is a theme worthy of exploring. Interestingly, cannabis being a nascent sector in the economy, can either create opportunities for inclusion of those previously excluded, or it could sustain the dominance of those who presently control the status quo. Hence to facilitate such inclusion the state needs to play a pivotal facilitative role. Therefore, three themes are the focus of this chapter: i) developmental state; ii) opportunity for the cannabis industry in South Africa; and iii) redistribution - what form of distribution is required to occur in the industry to benefit the entire South African population.

INTRODUCTION

We will open up and regulate the commercial use of hemp products, providing opportunities for small-scale farmers; and formulate policy on the use of cannabis products for medicinal purposes, to build this industry in line with global trends.

(Cyril Ramaphosa, 2020 SONA)

While the focus to deregulate the use of marijuana in some parts of the world has been, to a certain extent, influenced by law and order (like in the United States) and, in others, health (like in Uruguay), the focus on the freeing up the use of cannabis in South Africa has been largely about its potential com-

DOI: 10.4018/978-1-6684-6346-8.ch015

mercial value (Baudean, 2022). This leads to an understanding of two broad themes, which, according to New-Frontier-Data (2021: 08), fuelled the expansion of legal access to cannabis globally: the growing acceptance of the plant's therapeutic value, and recognition of its industry's potential as a catalyst for economic growth. The use of cannabis starting with its seeds to all products from dermatology to beverages has been widely practised, albeit under a strict regulatory regime.

In terms of value, globally, the cannabis industry is estimated to grow up to over USD176 billion by 2030 with the United States and Canada being the big role players (Freeman et al., 2019). In Colorado, United States, cannabis legalization created hundreds of millions in tax revenue annually after legalization. The revenue generated assisted in funding state education and health care. It also contributed greatly to employment creation, with about 40 000 jobs created after 2012 (Piispanen, 2022). The growth of the industry across the globe spells opportunity for many regions where the plant grows naturally and where it has been used for centuries for various activities. As these regulations are now getting relaxed, this offers opportunities for those countries that have an advantage on the plant. South Africa has latched on to the wave of relaxation of prohibitions for cannabis and the state is even willing to spearhead the development of industries in this sector. Even though marijuana has been recently decriminalised in South Africa, a large and productive black market already existed - the country did not suffer from any shortage of the plant. While the plant has been planted in secret (because of the previous regulations) and for subsistence purposes, the opportunity presented by the legalisation and change in government policy means that commercialising the crop and growing it on an industrial scale is now open. Already in the 2000s, cannabis' potential was strong, with Emmett and Nice (2009) stating that South Africa was a major producer of cannabis. This was sufficient to service domestic needs and allow for considerable export trade. Although largely in the Black market, the World Health Organisation (WHO) estimates South Africa to be the third-largest producer in the world and with an estimated 900,000 cannabis farmers, this is also on top of the additional 350,000 traditional healers already growing for herb use (Prohibition-Partners, 2019).

What are the crucial factors that the state is expected to introduce for the support and the clearing of the environment for good investment into the industry? This chapter aims to understand the opportunities that are available for the industrialisation of cannabis in South Africa from the developmental state perspective. This takes from the notion of a developmental state's application of the state as not just being a market fixer but also a market co-creator and shaper (Mazzucato et al., 2021). The state occupies a pivotal and powerful role when it comes to economic development and examples in Asia, Europe and North America attest to this notion that where there has been accelerated human progress, the state has been at the forefront (Amsden, 1989). Indeed, the 21st century's realities have called on the use of the state as an enabler for economic development. For all the countries that have developed economically, industrialisation has been the main instrument (Wade, 2012). Where development has lacked it has been because there is slow to no industrialisation. For all the countries that developed in the 20th century, they put, as their main focus, industrialisation. This has been propagated by authors such as Chang (2015), Szirmai et al. (2013) and Mazzucato et al. (2021), and others.

While South Africa has had considerable progress after the 1994 elections; it is industrialisation that has regressed. This poses a challenge for both the state and the private sector as there has not been an agreement on what needs to happen to kickstart industrialisation. When the Chief Justice Zondo Judgment was handed down regarding the use of cannabis in 2018 it did not only incite debate, but it created numerous opportunities for the country confronted with unprecedented unemployment (34%), stagnant economic growth, and stalled development (Sihlobo, 2020). The state, also, seeks to combine this with a redistributive angle which is critical in the South African policy stance by creating the "enabling policy, legal, and regulatory environment for the inclusive economic participation of the previously disadvantaged community enterprises" (RSA, 2021a). The advent of the cannabis promulgation and what forms of industrialisation or development this might spur thus deserve probing. On this, the main thrust of the cannabis takeover will have to be seen in the eyes of all South African as empowering those that were previously disadvantaged. Also, in South Africa, with its history of land dispossession, apartheid, and black underdevelopment, it is important to understand industrialisation as a form of redistribution. This must not only happen in rhetoric but must be in practice as well. It would have been much easier to insert the cannabis de-regulated industry into an already industrialised agro-processing commercialised sector, but such is not the case with SA. What form of distribution is required to occur for the industry to benefit the entire South African population? To facilitate such inclusivity, the state occupies a pivotal facilitative role and this needs to be clear on the policy in licensure, certain prohibitions, and protections that will govern the industry. This chapter begins by raising the framework of the developmental state and how it relates to industrialisation; then it goes on to describe the connection between the cannabis unbanning and industrialisation to show the link needed for the state to direct the industrial development of the cannabis sector. The chapter then moves on to discuss what form of governmental instruments in terms of the policy will be important for the empowerment of the previously disadvantaged to enter the cannabis sector. After which, the chapter will tie in all the discussions as elaborated and then conclude.

DEVELOPMENTAL STATE AND INDUSTRIALISATION

The developmental state offers a framework for understanding the correlation between the state and economic development. It also gives a sufficient understanding of how countries industrialise, especially those that industrialised in the recent past. Capable state, competent state, catalytic state, entrepreneurial state, and other phrases are all the nomenclature of the framework called the 'developmental state' as seminally stated by Chalmers Johnson (1982). Sometimes they are used interchangeably, sometimes stand-alone, but they are in reference to the state that formulates its policies and gives direction to the private sector for the benefit of all in society and to achieve industrialisation. For ease of understanding here, only 'developmental state' is used. Although, the framework is usually used to analyse the nation-state, in recent times it has been used to analyse the policies and sub-state programmes to understand whether they are developmental in their conception (Mazzucato, 2011, Mazzucato, 2015, Mazzucato et al., 2021, Kuye and Ajam, 2012, Bresser-Pereira, 2016, Bresser Pereira, 2019, Khambule, 2019). It is believed that if the policies are developmental, then they may be able to assist the countries towards grand-scale progress in many aspects, thus, by extension, managing to develop the country as a whole. Chu (2016) summarises Johnson (1987) stating that the developmental state is the state that alters incentives, reduces risks, offers entrepreneurial visions, and manages conflicts with the view of helping the businesses capture larger market share rather than aim for short-term profits. From Asian developmentalism, four main conditions need to be satisfied for a country to be considered developmental. For context here, it is important to highlight that the South African government, led by the African National Congress (ANC), has articulated, in policy documents, the espousal for the country to be developmental in its outlook (ANC-NGC-Report, 2015).

These are the conditions that need to obtain for a developmental state to be realised. First, it is the state having a developmental vision that will enable the state to plan toward configuring a developmental state

(Williams, 2014). This is important since the whole notion of the developmental state implies that it is state-driven (centrally). Thus, the conception, vision, direction, and execution need to be formulated at the state level. These are usually in form of grand state policies and programmes. Second is the presence of an autonomous, effective and efficient bureaucracy which is responsible for policy implementation. Bureaucratic effectiveness is very important for the state to function and carry out developmental policies. In East Asia, this was underpinned by good education and well-trained personnel (Tonami, 2018).

The third is the private sector which is committed to the production and is rooted in the partnership between the government, labour, business and civil society. For any state to function for the economy to be efficient, there needs to be a communication of policies between the state and the private sector; this makes it easier for the state's policies to be adopted by the private sector. Both the state and the private sector are in a relationship that Evans (1992) aptly phrased the 'embedded autonomy.' Fourth, is the long-term development plan with an effective industrial policy that is capable of meshing state ambitions with the market's capital accumulation. All these four are very important and none must atop the other in terms of importance; all these have to pull in one direction.

The Role and Importance of Industrial Policy in a Developmental State

With the state being the custodian of all policies and regulations, there is no ambiguity in the state's role in the cannabis industry. Whilst some states, like the United States or Canada, simply removed barriers for trading in cannabis, South Africa is looking to actively play a part in the scope and direction of the cannabis industry cite. This is in essence a developmentalist approach. In terms of the four conditions, the government has really worked to produce the cannabis 'master-plan' to try and spur and direct the industry into productivity. Developmental states of East Asia are famed for their grand development policies (or five-year plans); these include "sub-plans" that are industry based. In a similar style, the South African government has adopted similar processes of placing programmes in public; the difference is that, in South Africa, this is on a consultative basis whereas, in East Asia, these were mostly decreed. Back to the cannabis development, following the pronouncements by the President of South Africa Cyril Ramaphosa and Chief Justice Zondo's 2018 judgement (in *Minister of Justice and Constitutional Development and Others v Prince (Clarke and Others Intervening); National Director of Public Prosecutions and Others v Rubin; National Director of Public Prosecutions and Others v Acton*) (Zondo, 2018); the government has drafted a 'master-plan' in order to "provide a broad framework for the development and growth of the South African cannabis industry in order to contribute to economic development, job creation, inclusive participation, rural development and poverty alleviation" (RSA, 2021a: 04).

While all the four developmental state conditions are important and have to be present in equal measure for the developmental state to take shape, it is important to lift an aspect that is important for this Chapter - the cannabis industry's developmentalism in South Africa and how industrial policy may affect it and what forms of support is needed for it to succeed. In terms of industrialisation, Kelly (2008) and Hayashi (2010b), mention that the primary essence of the developmental state model is state-led industrialisation. For industrialisation to happen, state capacity is pivotal as bureaucrats are executors of industrial policy (Hayashi, 2010b). At a fundamental level, industrialisation is qualified by a move from agriculture industries, mainly manufactured goods; this leads to exports and increased income for the country. Industrialisation is generally understood as a process whereby the share of industry in general, and manufacturing in particular, in total economic activity, is increased (Weiss, 2014). As alluded to above, the manner in which economic development happens is often a result of the state acting explicitly to make this a possibility. Lin and Monga (2010) introduce the difference between the two types of state interventions through industrial policy from both developed and developing countries.

First is the one aimed at facilitating structural change by overcoming information, coordination and externality issues that are intrinsic to industrial upgrading and diversification. This is important in that they aim to provide information, compensate for externalities, and coordinate improvements in the 'hard' and 'soft' infrastructure, that are needed for the private sector to grow in sync with the dynamic change in the economy's comparative advantage. The second one is aimed to protect some selected firms and industries that defy the comparative advantage determined by the existing endowment structure - either in new sectors that are too advanced or in old sectors that have lost the comparative advantage. The state needs to innovatively promote certain 'emerging' industries that could be managed within a more inclusive and equitable manner. This is a notion of induced innovation which is part of the instruments of industrial policy that states pursue (Gerwel, 2018, Ruttan, 1997). The recently legitimate budding cannabis sector easily falls under such emerging industries. In focusing on a few industries and intervening extensively to build them up for export, the state must protect and nurse these industries until they catch up with others in competition and output. An additional, but the important factor, in the developmental state, is the state's ability to fund industrialisation. The need to fund industrialisation is key for developmental states and economic development in general. Industrialisation and innovation take time and are often riddled with uncertainty and thus 'patient capital,' as Mazzucato (2015: 149) puts it, is "required for the full development of radical innovations."

There are two related sets of tensions in industrial policy: government picking and supporting winners and an open architecture approach where support is informed by market-based mechanisms (Sanjaya, 2004). The occurrence in South Africa has been that, in reference to industrial transformation, the country has focussed more on picking and supporting winners (vertical industrial policy) than it has utilised market-based approaches (horizontal industrial policy) (Cuthbert, 2022). These approaches have been done through the Industrial Policy Action Plans (IPAPS) and have largely failed; however, as in any public policy, cause and effect are not always fixed. Therefore, the uniqueness of the cannabis sector and the fact that even globally, this is a budding industry, it may mean that governmental support is warranted and can actually work – and the targeting of this sector may achieve the desired outcomes. The framework that has already been developed sets the motion to cultivate the support needed in the sector.

POTENTIAL CANNABIS INDUSTRIALISATION IN SOUTH AFRICA

When cannabis was legalised in the United States, three things happened. One, there was substantial decrease in the retail price; two, it allowed adults to obtain a regular supply of cannabis without risk of criminal penalty; and, three, it produced a major diversification of the cannabis products for sale (Hall and Lynskey, 2020). With consumers globally spending USD415 billion annually, South Africa is one of the largest producers of cannabis in the world, according to the New-Frontier-Data (2021), placing South Africa as one of the foremost players in the cannabis market. Producing 2300 tons of cannabis annually, South Africa is the third largest in Africa, creating huge prospects for the industry to grow fast. There are an estimated 3,5 million consumers in the country, most of whom consume cannabis for recreational purposes, although the medicinal use of cannabis is beginning to increase, and physicians also prescribe it as treatment (New Frontier Data, 2021). The provinces of Western Cape (WP), Eastern Cape (EC), and KwaZulu-Natal (KZN) are touted by the government as advantaged because they have fair climates for cultivating cannabis and WP and KZN, in particular, have the industrial infrastructure to support it including the those for exporting the finished products overseas. On this issue, the National Development Plan Vision 2030 (NDP, 2012), is clear in stating that "South Africa must tackle the diversification of the economy from a range of angles. It needs to build on state capacity to identify sectors that will improve export opportunities."

The rationale for the establishment of the cannabis industry in South Africa, according to RSA (2021b), is that this can lead to the diversification of the economy and therefore lead to economic growth, creating between 10000 to 25 000 jobs in the entire value chain, and alleviate poverty (cannabis growing in South Africa is viewed as a poor man's business). The cannabis sector has the potential to create more new jobs. That's according to President Cyril Ramaphosa, who said South Africa's government planned to streamline the regulatory process in the sector for it to thrive. Already, the 2019 report stated that one-third of the cannabis users in the world reside in Africa and South Africa has a potentially big cannabis market. This means that the people who already have experience planting it will be in pole position to do so but also it can spring in new players (Prohibition-Partners, 2019).

The production of cannabis for industrial, medical and adult use has the possibility to offer a new base of taxable income for many countries. The legal requirements around the production and sale of cannabis for medical use are onerous, but recent authorized advances specify an attempt to further permit the farming and sale of hemp as a way to boost the economy. In terms of market value, New-Frontier-Data (2021) estimates that Africa ranks 6th in the continent with Nigeria, Ethiopia, Morocco, Angola, and Cameroon being just ahead. According to Prohibition-Partners (2019) market value of cannabis will potentially be worth over USDUS7.1 billion. The SA cannabis master plan states that hemp is one of the fastest-growing biomasses and is used for making various industrial products including rope, textiles, clothing, shoes, ceiling boards, bricks, food, paper, biodegradable plastics, paint, insulation, and biofuels (RSA, 2021a). In the beverages and food market; the size was valued currently at USD427 million globally in 2018 and is estimated to reach USD2,632 million by 2026 (Prohibition-Partners, 2019). There is a reason for optimism from the potential beneficiaries of the lawful possession of hemp, however, Martin and Rashidian (2014) caution that the cannabis industry promises nothing. The work still needs to be done as the industry is one of the most complicated industries.

Of course, this is a big opportunity but also a big health risk factor for those who may continue trading cannabis for smoking (coupled with questions of morality that might arise). Also, adverse effects may increase harmful patterns of cannabis use especially (especially daily use) which may grow with decriminalisation (Hall and Lynskey, 2020). By its own government's admission, in 2022, the country lost billions on taxes during the Covid-19 pandemic because of the tobacco ban. Such figures are not available for products that were already banned like narcotics and hemp products. The public feels that the government should put more restrictions on this industry in order to protect vulnerable groups of society against substance and alcohol abuse. Manu et al. (2021) add, also, that the perceived implications against cannabis legalisation are those small growers may be driven out of a competitive (fear of a fall in the price) and clandestine markets once everything is public. The resistance to any legalisation of cannabis is associated with the belief that it will exacerbate the public security conditions in the country (Bester and Els, 2021). There are also stiff sensitivities that cannabis will abet in being a gateway substance to harder drugs. Indeed, the habit-forming nature of dagga arouses fears. This might have prolonged detrimental effects on health and public order.

This is a fertile industry, for research organisations and R&D companies may take advantage of utilising some of their resources to invest in cannabis research. This means that there are quite several possible upstream and downstream opportunities that can be created using the plant. Usually, serious research would have been published already by governments to try and argue its case for such commercialisation to be widely accepted by society, but in South Africa, this has largely been sluggish. Research alone is important for any industry or development in a sector in order to counter a phenomenon whereby the use by the public outpaces the understanding of the product in question (Hutchison et al., 2019). Possible return on investment is huge for the private sector, especially for those who are fast and first-movers. The growth of interest in the last two decades in cannabis will yield development through renewed research and innovation and is expected to deepen the understanding of the crop (Monthony et al., 2021).

On the policy front; the state, in South Africa, proposed the Cannabis Master Plan. The master plan (falling under the industrial policy) aims to create an export market for the local cannabis producers and attempts to direct the current legislation by removing constraints on the commercial cannabis market to assist with industrialisation. Also, the master plan aims to accelerate investment in the cannabis industry research. Also, the plan is aimed at increasing the support for farmers and indigenous growers of the plant in the cannabis value chain, as well as support for manufacturing and product development. The government of South Africa has envisioned cannabis commercialisation to help industrialise the country, catapult the previously disadvantaged entrepreneurs and contribute positively to the redistribution of the economy. Since 1994, in South Africa, there have been repeated calls for greater industrialisation in the face of lowering jobs in the manufacturing sector and this has evoked all manner of arguments against and for the state intervening to assist the would-be industrialists. It is clear that there is a need for a wide array of interrelated economic activities to prevent the decline of the country's economy and assist in developing various industries, and "contribute to arresting the current trend of deindustrialisation and shift the trajectory of the industrial base into new, sustainable growth areas and value chains" (Lowitt, 2020a). From this cue, the president of South Africa stated that "the hemp and cannabis sector have the potential to create more than 130 000 new jobs" and that the government would be "streamlining the regulatory processes so that the hemp and cannabis sector can thrive like it is in other countries such as Lesotho" (SONA, 2022: 10). It is clear that the government has set its eyes high in terms of cannabis and will be very interested in the establishment and expansion of a vibrant cannabis industry. It is thus important to explore some of the more prominent cannabis sub-sectors.

Medical Cannabis and Pharmaceutical Cannabis

One of the most important longstanding industries sparked by cannabis growth is that on the health sector. There has been widespread praise for the health benefits and effects of cannabis since time immemorial. According to RSA (2021a), medical cannabis refers to the type of cannabis and cannabinoids that are prescribed by physicians for their patients. The modern industries in this sector are separated into medical and pharmaceutical cannabis respectively. Although these industries have stringent barriers; it is here that cannabis has been effective and arguably made an impact on the eventual deregulation. The deregulated market will mean that there will be growth in terms of research on the use of medicinal cannabis; all to the benefit of society. The critical active ingredients in terms of medical cannabis are Cannabidiol (CBD) and Tetrahydrocannabinol (THC). These are important for their use in drug manufacturing as well as the input into the treatments given to different patients. These have been marketed to treat different ailments and potentially more others. These are chronic pain especially joint pain; chest-related problems like Asthma and Tuberculosis (and the Covid-19 virus), glaucoma, epilepsy, cancer, arthritis, and improving appetite.

With all of the above being the main driver in the use of cannabis for health-related reasons, South African Health Products Regulatory Authority (SAHPRA) started welcoming licence applications from cultivators and distributors for the medicinal use of cannabis. Accordingly, the process is very rigorous to obtain a licence from SAHPRA to cultivate cannabis for medical research purposes. Also, the concerns are around uniformity in terms of the cannabis cultivars and assurance that crops can be grown in conditions of strict security. This is because such cultivation needs to be strict because of the International Narcotics Control Board (INCB) regulations, of which South Africa is a signatory. Although this is the case, the major factor is that the people who do get the opportunity to be licenced growers are set to be the first beneficiaries of the commercialisation and the profit for them will be high. The medical cannabis market is set to be worth USD 248.42 billion by 2030 (Globe-Newswire, 2022). For example, the number of patients and prescriptions for medical cannabis greatly surged in the USA and Europe during the COVID-19 pandemic signalling that there are possibilities in this industry. South African industry participants could play a big role in this since South Africa has one of the best health research facilities in the world. The government will have to play a big role in supporting participants in developing further in getting things like the IPs required for African expansion of this industry and also to support localisation.

Cannabis Tourism and Recreational Cannabis

Another concomitant component of the cannabis boom is that of canna-tourism where tourists globally visit to view the varieties of the plant which also creates entertainment opportunities (Sihlobo, 2020). The legalisation of recreational cannabis brings with it changes in the tourism industry as well as in hospitality because of the leisure-related cannabis development (Kang and McGrady, 2020). Much like the health benefits of cannabis, recreational cannabis is one of the oldest in terms of widespread use. Wellness centres and tourism industries (formal and informal) are set to benefit from tourism related to cannabis. Taylor (2019: 52) defines cannabis tourism as "purchasing with the intent to consume marijuana products while temporarily travelling away from one's normal place of work or residence." In addition, Pachmayer et al. (2021), clarifies that tourism in this sector does not have to involve the consumption or use the cannabis, but may merely mean visiting places and facilities where there are exhibitions, expositions, retreats, educational courses and dispensaries. Tan (2021), adds that these, together with the cannabis festivals can only assist in accelerating the spreading and development of this industry. This directly and positively impacts the hospitality, food, and beverages sector as well. This is one of the fastest-growing uses of cannabis because of the growth of leisure industries including spas and areas for entertainment. With South Africa's tourism contributing 3.7% to the GDP, there is still room for expansion in this regard and cannabis tourism may help contribute to this development (RSA, 2022).

From the plant, the seeds and leaves are all used in food and beverages. The products that may come out of this are hemp meal, baked food, sweets and gummies, energy drinks, cookies and muffins, ice creams, animal feeds, and any flavoured or infused food (even water). From this, convenience food stalls like coffee shops, restaurants, and hotels are set to benefit. Also, households would be better suited as end-user outlets. According to Markets (2022), the global cannabis in food and beverage market size is expected to reach USD 3411.43 million by 2030. Bakery products are set to be the leading segment in the food and beverages sector because of the rising demand for THC and CBD-infused stock.

In terms of recreational use, still, the most vital active ingredient is CBD and THC in the leaves and flower buds of the plant. This type of use is done through consumption by smoking, inhaling, or even ingesting. The purpose of this is relaxation and to improve the mood. It is also believed that it is good for creativity. Also, religious people have used it since time immemorial to connect with the higher power or remove bad spirits (used like sage). Southern African countries like Botswana, Swaziland, Zimbabwe, and Malawi have shown interest since there are stalling growth prospects in their respective tobacco industry. Also, removing the stigma associated with the recreational use of the plant and also showing its powerful use in other sectors (other than recreational) will help the region and may create a good environment for trade. In Canada alone, recreational marijuana is currently sitting between USD 4.9 billion and USD 8.7 billion with a potential to be around USD 23 billion (Deloitte, 2016). This can only bode well for the rest of the world as there will be some learning to do from countries like Canada which have successfully managed to do well in this industry where it is projected to become a multi-billion-dollar industry and thus wield "monumental influence on the national economy, health care, the job market, and much more" (Kittel, 2018: 43). Fighting the black market will be key in the recreational cannabis sector. Reducing the black market and creating mainstream business opportunities in the cannabis sector is a welcomed evolution. Easton (2019) observes that the legalization of marijuana consumption is a process and not simply a single event. Easton (2019) continues to warn that while legalisation may assist in decreasing the presence of organized crime, there is a need to guard against the creation of interest groups which will counter the benefits. Increased revenues have to be the main factor and government has to be weary of too much taxes as these may reduce the number of participants in the legal cannabis sector.

Industrial Cannabis

According to Lowitt (2020b), there are four categories where the plant can be utilised in both primary and secondary sectors: 1) a green substitute for various industrial products; 2) food for human consumption; 3) an input (oil extracted from seeds) to personal care and cosmetic products; and 4) therapeutic products (Salentijn et al., 2015). Industrial cannabis has a myriad of uses and can be from different varieties of seeds. In terms of production, Prohibition-Partners (2019), state that there are different routes for this: seed growers and suppliers; production equipment manufacturers and suppliers; cultivation of medical-grade cannabis; cultivation of recreational grade cannabis; cultivation of industrial-grade hemp; and testing and quality control. The need to use cannabis for the industry stems from the fact that all the parts of the plant are useful for the industrial effect; stalks, seeds, and leaves can all be used. The products that are important in industrial cannabis are textiles, building materials, cosmetics, and many others that have not been yet explored. This industry spans the whole cannabis sector and is widely believed to have the potential for growth in the coming years since the plant has been legalised. The farming of cannabis is the most basic and widely understood enterprise. Farmers around the world informal, formal, greenhouse, and indoor have been on the rise since the relaxation of prohibitive laws across the world. This has also called on people who are into cooperatives, or organised farming associations, to come in and participate. As has been mentioned above, in the continent, many African nations' farmers rely on cannabis as the easy and only way to earn an income and assist in meeting basic needs. With the lack of farming implements to carry out most of the sophisticated modern-day farming, the quality of the cannabis produced may be limited and the market may end up flushing out the smallholder producers. This is where the state has to be careful in its support and make sure that they support all the farmers and allow for deviation from the norm so that support is provided where the previously disadvantaged are concerned (Prohibition-Partners, 2019).

THE VALUE CHAIN FOR THE CANNABIS INDUSTRY

Value chains are important for industrialisation. The value chain can be explained by the full range of activities that are required to bring a product or service from conception, to delivery, to the end user, and final disposal after use. Unlocking these would mean that the people, even far down, can be affected positively in terms of cannabis development. Global value chains can be either 'vertically specialized chains' or 'additive value chains.' With vertically specialised chains, different components of the product can be produced in parallel and thus, the process is not costly. These are used mainly in manufacturing. The additive value chains are where the various stages of production are necessarily sequential (more like a factory's conveyor belt) (Zarenda, 2013). The additive value chains are costly and are used mainly in primary sectors (UNECA, 2016). The need to support the cannabis sector is greater because that sector already mixes the primary and secondary sectors. The tobacco industry, whilst worth billions in dollars, cannot compare to the behemoth that the cannabis sector might be worth. This is because of the wide scope that hemp has in terms of products that it can infiltrate. The value chain for the South African cannabis industry has been laid out by the government in the Master-plan. On unlocking the value chain for the industry, the master plan proposes that there will be a division into four parts: production inputs (breeding companies, seed companies, nurseries, chemical companies); primary production (smallholder growers, commercial growers, and contractors); manufacturing and product development (cosmetics and body care products, foods and animal feeds, nutraceuticals, beverages, textiles, building material, paper, and industrial products); and lastly, markets (local markets and export markets) (RSA, 2021a).

Here there will be many small businesses and enterprises that will need to be supported by the industrial policy targeted at the cannabis sector. These will have to involve pricing, licensing (licencing different products and in different provinces (like in the liquor standards and procedures), taxing, etc. However, the state will have to play an oversized role so that there are no businesses (especially rural and previously disadvantaged) that will be side-lined by factors that may be influenced by the policy. This will help especially in the industrial use of cannabis as already the Department of Trade, Industry and Competition (DTIC) in the IPAP aimed to "raise competitiveness, deepen localisation and support job creation across the value chain" (RSA, 2018: 35).

Developmental state demonstrates that support of nascent industries and industrial targeting is important for the state to build up small industries and that the policies directed at these must be clear and run by efficient administrators (bureaucracy). Also, the policy will have to be supported not only by the national departments but will also have to bring in the players in different sectors like finance and land (property). The coterie of supportive structures in the cannabis sector can bring about quick change in the sector whilst bringing in much-needed expertise to assist the new people in the sector. It can quicken access and fast-track development of the sector to be competitive regionally and even globally. This will have effects on the overall economy and help springboard the rural development that the government has previously tried in vain. The important factor here will be on expanding the industrial base and not displacing the already established, and South African budding, and established industries (suppliers). This factor is critical if South Africa is to realise its full potential in the industrialisation of cannabis. Although much criticised (Cuthbert, 2022), the protection of nascent industries and guarding against cheap imports can, used correctly (in a competent, fair, and competitive way), help achieve developmental goals and make the industry competitive globally. The government will have to guard against what happened in the first wave of BEE where connected businesspeople took advantage of the policies to the detriment of developmental goals.

Redistribution Triad (Racial Equity + Spatial Equity + Financial Equity)

If the country is to change its system of accumulation then it has to change the structure of the economy and if that structure does not change, then any returns from growth will add to the ones already in ownership of the economy (Goga et al., 2020, Mondliwa and Roberts, 2020). South Africa's commercial agriculture is much like that in the developed world, which, according to Dillis et al. (2022), is 'capitalist agriculture' which means that it is commercially oriented and profit motivated; secondly, relations among farms are characterized by competition to increase market share and return on investment by lowering costs and increasing productivity. And, now, in addition, and thirdly, industrial agriculture "displays a drive to achieve greater economies of scale through the development and application of technologies in every dimension of production" Dillis et al. (2022: 222). This leaves the industry prone to the vagaries of capitalism where those with deep pockets are in a pole position to benefit from the relaxation of regulations such as in the cannabis sector.

In a country like South Africa where redress and historical disadvantage has taken a racial slant, it is important to address such in a straightforward manner. Seeing that the relaxation of marijuana regulations is happening almost 30 years into democracy, it means that the government will have a chance to display its long-held proposition of redistribution. The fact that the state is itself at the forefront of policy direction (in consultation with all stakeholders) means that any demographic, or sector that will be left out, of the state can be apportioned blame. Black Economic Empowerment (BEE) and all policies that are aimed at redress are state driven, therefore the government has to be at the forefront even on this in the cannabis industry. The argument from the state as to the lack of inclusiveness in the manufacturing sector especially and in business generally, has been that the economy was inherited (from the apartheid regime) and they had little to do with its structure. Now, with a nascent industry to contribute to, this means that the state has to display loyalty to the policies and show the country how much-talked-about redress happens. This will not be easy as the South African government has previously shown a lack of policy execution (if there is execution at all). Where there have been, these instances have been mired in corruption and general disregard for the rule of law.

South Africa, being a middle-income country with a sophisticated economy, combined with a history of abject racism, has struggled to industrialise the economy since the late 20th century. Regarding redistribution, the country has found it challenging to include black people in the economy to become meaningful players that can contribute positively to industrialisation and job creation. It is, thus, encouraging that the government is both committed and supportive of the cannabis sector that is emerging hence their commitment will ensure support of the cannabis industry, its creation and direction, and secondly the deliberate inclusion of Black entrepreneurs in this sector. The exclusion of Black people in the economy is still the main theme of the South African economy 28 years into democracy. The latest data on Black Economic Empowerment paints a bleak picture of redistribution in South Africa. Although Covid-19 may have had a hand to play, the regression is unfortunate (refer to Figure 1). Interestingly the cannabis industry being a new sector in the economy, can either create opportunities for the inclusion of those previously excluded or it could be dominated by those who presently occupy privileged positions.

Figure 1. Sector code analysis - Average Black Ownership (B-BBEEComm-Report, 2022)

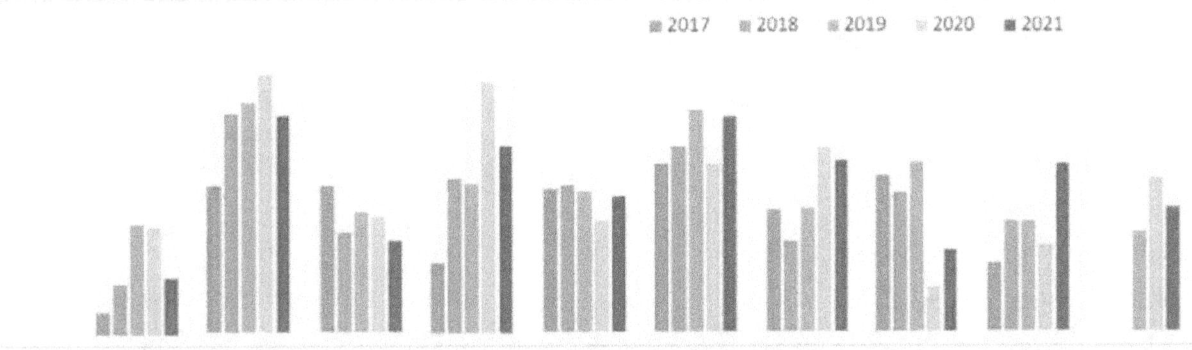

Average Black ownership Data

	Agri-BEE	Construction	Financial	Forestry	ICT	Transport	MAC	Property	Tourism	Generic
2017	**4,90%**	**32,00%**	31,80%	**15,40%**	31,30%	**36,90%**	**26,70%**	34,10%	**14,60%**	**0,00%**
2018	11,20%	48,00%	21,60%	33,70%	32,00%	40,50%	19,60%	30,50%	23,80%	0,00%
2019	24,30%	50,10%	26,00%	32,60%	30,80%	48,60%	27,00%	37,20%	23,80%	21,70%
2020	23,60%	56,40%	25,20%	54,70%	24,30%	36,90%	40,20%	9,90%	18,50%	33,40%
2021	12,27%	47,27%	19,80%	40,95%	29,67%	46,90%	37,45%	17,77%	36,33%	27,20%

Legislation aimed at Redistribution of Cannabis in South Africa

The cannabis industry's operation on the fringes of the mainstream economy meant that the people who operated it were mostly the downtrodden, black and poor. The prohibition on the plant created an underground market that will continue to shape the social dimensions of the industry as it exists today (Kittel, 2018). Some pieces of legislation have been aimed at redistribution in South Africa. These important policies will need to kick in for the cannabis sector to be truly effective in changing the course for participants in South Africa. These policies may help enhance the redistributive factor in terms of the cannabis sector. These will have to be applied to the maximum to make the people who wish to participate in the expansion of the cannabis sector feel that they have made progress.

South Africa is a dual economy and has one of the highest inequality rates in the world. What is most striking is that the poorest 20% of the population consumes less than 3% of total expenditure, while the wealthiest 20% consume 65%, a huge challenge for the government (World Bank, 2017). Although it has done little to halt the situation, the decline in industrialisation is not the post-apartheid government's creation. For example, manufacturing recorded its highest contribution to GDP in 1990 at 24% (TGE, 2022). A steady decline (refer to figure 2) put it at only 13%, thus this impacts many of the country's unskilled workers (NEF, 2014). Although for the developmental state, such policies are crucial, it will be up to the SMMEs and different entrepreneurs' volition to take up the opportunities and achieve success in their cannabis entities. This part looks briefly at some policies that are developmental and aimed at redistribution and what these may achieve in assisting the cannabis sector to be accessed by all demographics.

Figure 2. Manufacturing as a percentage of South Africa's GDP

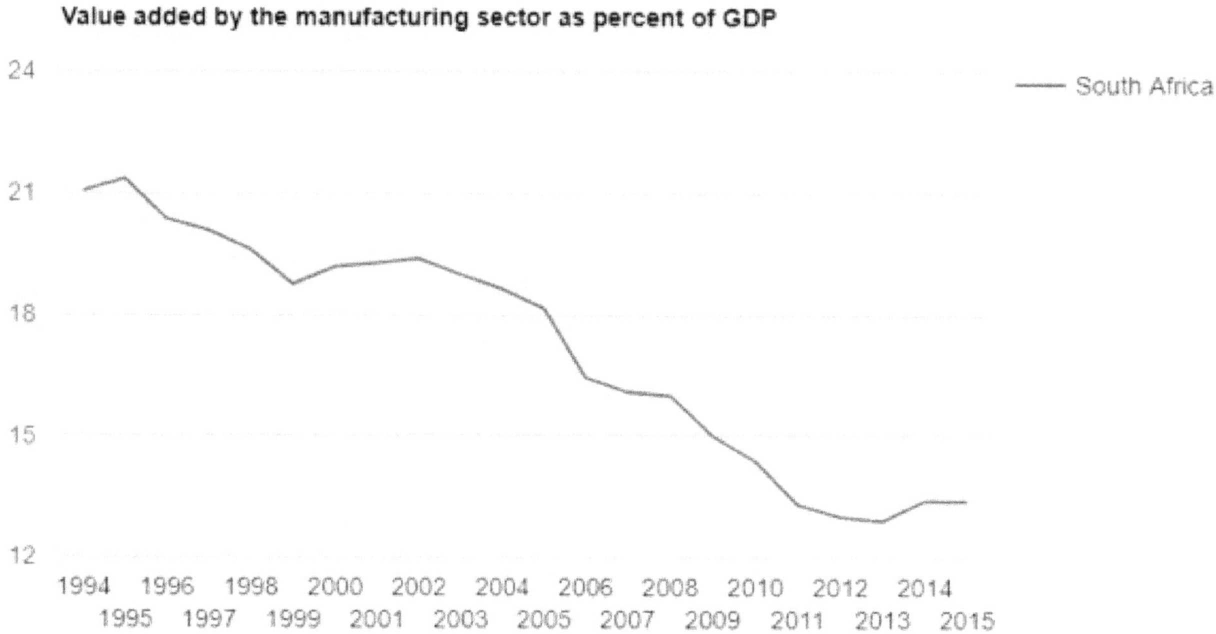

Broad-Based Black Economic Empowerment

Much has been stated about BEE that not much will need to be belaboured again here. However, to appreciate redistribution – the South African way – one needs to understand BEE as it stands as the only policy wholly dedicated to this task. Therefore, it needs to be stated again here. The IDC (2014) defines BEE as the process by which previously disadvantaged South Africans are being empowered through the transfer of ownership, management, and financial control of companies; the multilevel transference of skills and the widespread creation of jobs. Its purpose is to bring the majority of South Africans into the mainstream economy and is the key to the future of the country. However, according to Mondliwa and Roberts (2020), BEE has merely reinforced the status quo instead of challenging the economic structure that keeps the majority of South Africans at bay economically.

Three waves have been observed during BEE policy years. The first wave was a narrow BEE which was empowerment through the acquisition of stakes in already established white companies. This has been termed by Bond (2000) where a coterie of black elites that have strong political connections (mostly ANC) join big established businesses to protect the interest of those businesses and the status quo (Mondliwa and Roberts, 2021). The second was about defining and expanding BEE and giving it a broad-based view. This period was about the development of BEE codes and scorecards, and also industry charters for sectoral compliance. The third and current wave is highlighted by the Black Industrialist Programme and other sub-policies or programmes which seeks to industrialise the economy with blacks at the forefront. With the fact that the cannabis policies are being developed contemporaneously with this third wave, one might assume that this wave will be pivotal to the trajectory of cannabis and its potential to be a redistributing catalyst in the economy. Another policy with an empowering factor that will need to be used in the cannabis industry is that of the PPFA. The Preferential Procurement Framework Act 5 of 2000 is legislation that was passed to secure the participation of preferred groups as a primary driver to stimulate the B- BBEE development (RSA, 2017). This is a policy to advantage black people, youth, women, and the disabled in terms of support from the government. This leans on the supplying of goods and services to the already established businesses and, most importantly, the government.

Rural Development

Few policies in the country are as opaque and lacking in application as that on rural development. The lack of infrastructure and basic service delivery makes any means to support rural areas difficult even for the people charged with delivering those same services. The rural development strategy was promulgated by the government to "attain socially cohesive a stable rural community with viable institutions, sustainable economies and universal access to social amenities, able to attract and retain skilled and knowledgeable people, who equipped to contribute to growth and development" (RSA, 2018: 25). The fact that populations in rural areas are spatially dispersed means that there is an opportunity for agriculture to flourish. The most important factor as far as cannabis industrialisation and rural development is concerned is the issue of land. The land is an important factor for cannabis and South Africa has it in abundance. However, land reform and restitution are politically thorny issues, and traversing them is not easy. For the industrialisation of cannabis to effectively assist rural people and farmers, land will have to be availed for this to happen. This means that government will need to be at the forefront in making sure that people who need access to land are assisted and those who need tenure for it provided. According to IPAP (2018) government identified agro-processing as one of the main nodes for development through upstream and downstream industries. Agro-processing is the most prominent individual sub-sector in manufacturing that is demonstrating a comparatively rapid rise in sales. For upstream, the sector talks about agriculture around a diversity of farming models and products. On the downstream, the products are commercialised across wholesale and retail stores and a wide variety of outlets (RSA, 2018). If the state is to make meaningful progress in the cannabis sector's spatial redistribution, many people need to be assisted where they reside, so that rural development will be the outcome. Through policies directed into it, the government may need to focus the policy on localised farming, cooperatives, rural development and black industrialist policies. The combination of these will allow the smallholder farmers to benefit, community schemes to spring through cooperatives, and agro-processing to happen through potential industrialisation.

Funding

Development finance through direct state funding, Development Finance Institutions (DFI), or commercial entities is the grease that keeps the wheels of industrialisation cranking. Therefore, the most important factor that will be able to cause a shift in terms of redistribution (industrially) is that of funding. Catalytic funding is important to assist businesses that once to upscale to achieve their desired outcomes. The most obvious, especially as far as cannabis farming is concerned, in the primary sector, is the Land Bank. The bank is a Development Finance Institution (DFI) and is mandated to achieve growth in the commercial market, growth in the development market, business efficiency, service delivery, resource management, and sustainability, the bank does this by funding a wide range of people in the agricultural industry including those in farming, commercial farming, cooperatives and all other agriculture-related activities. There is also the Development Bank of Southern Africa (DBSA), established under the DBSA Act, 1997 (Act 13 of 1997). The DBSA's principal role is to promote economic development and growth, human resource development and institutional capacity-building. The other most important funding instrument is that of the Industrial Development Corporation (IDC). Being the financial arm of the DTIC, the IDC has historically played an oversized role in industrial financing in South Africa, and its role in the development of the cannabis sector is expected to be the same. There are other DFIs that are regional and some incentives that are more specific to industries and sectors that will need to be exploited for the cannabis industry players to benefit, especially those participants that are small-scale and not able to fund their enterprises through commercial banks.

CONCLUSION

The developmental state as a catalyst for development is a powerful framework to use in powering new industries. This chapter wanted to raise the intersection between industry and redistribution as a theme worthy of exploring if one is to understand the industrialisation of cannabis and its prospects for the South African political economy. The cannabis industry offers an opportunity for a relatively clean slate from which the government can execute their industrial policy and power the South African economy. The use of the state to spur the private sector to industrialise or redistribute the economy has not been successful because of the structure of the economy inherited from the history of colonialism, dispossession, and apartheid. With an old, sophisticated, and racially unequal economy, South Africa is challenged to include black entrepreneurs in the already established industries that white people continue to dominate and occupy. This opportunity offered by the cannabis industry is that it will afford the South African government to actively consider inclusivity in the present economy.

The developmental state was used as a framework to provide a lens through which to view the budding cannabis industry. The use of the state, its resources and policies to guide the market are at the centre of the developmental state. Thus, with this opportunity that has been offered by the decriminalisation of cannabis, the state is called upon to act to achieve developmental goals. The chapter looked at the role and importance of industrialisation and industrial policy and its usefulness in the cannabis industry and found that there can be no clear success if the state does not play a leading role in the cannabis sector. The sub-industries of medical, recreational, tourism, food and beverages were all discussed and analysed, concluding that the state will have to play a role in all of them. Also, the supportive policies towards redistribution were discussed as a 'triad' – black economic empowerment, rural development, and funding - depicting importance as the special corners that the cannabis industry will have to address for it to be successful.

If this nascent industry is allowed to flourish without the inclusion of black entrepreneurs, it will be representative of the failure of the democratic state to cater for this demographic. If the cannabis industry is allowed to flourish without benefiting the rural people who have planted the 'herb' since time immemorial it will be a failure from the state. If funding is not availed and a special dispensation was given to new participants to access micro-finance, it will be a failure of the government to use available resources for the benefit of society. However, to conclude, the prudent idea is for South African authorities to not intervene too much as to cause constraints but must guide the market to create fair and equitable competition and foster redistribution and participation of the previously disadvantaged population. It will not be through government decree only that one realises the cannabis industry is taking off; the same goes for redistribution. Admittedly, it will be through the mantle of entrepreneurs finding opportunities and synergies of working together and finding a common practice to steer this nascent industry into a fully functioning industry that can drive economic growth and development in all regions of South Africa; hopefully, they will not lose this opportunity.

REFERENCES

Amsden, A. (1989). *Asia's Next Giant: South Korea and Late Industrialization*. Oxford University Press.

ANC-NGC.(2015). Umrhabulo.

B-BBEEcomm. (2022). *National Status and Trends on B-BBEE Transformation Report 2021*. Skotaville Press.

Baudean, M. (Ed.). (2022). *Five Years of Cannabis Regulation What Can We Learn From the Uruguayan Experience?* Routledge.

Bester, P. C., & Els, S. (2021). The legalisation of cannabis: A security-vetting dilemma. *Scientia Militaria: South African Journal of Military Studies*, *49*, 1–28.

Bond, P. 2000. Elite Transition: from Apartheid to Neoliberalism in South Africa. University of Natal Press.

Bresser-Pereira, L. (2016). Reflecting on New Developmentalism and Classical Developmentalism. *Review of Keynesian Economics*, *4*(3), 331–352. doi:10.4337/roke.2016.03.07

Bresser Pereira, L. C. (2019). Models of the developmental state. *CEPAL Review*.

Chang, H.-J. (2015). *Is Industrial Policy Necessary and Feasible in Africa? Industrial policy and economic transformation in Africa*. Columbia University Press.

Chu, Y.-W. (2016). The Asian Developmental State: Ideas and Debates. In Y.-W. Chu (Ed.), *The Asian developmental state: Reexaminations and new departures*. Springer. doi:10.1057/9781137476128_1

Cuthbert, M. (2022). Time has come to ditch vertical industrial policy. *Business Day*.

Deloitte (2016). Recreational Marijuana - Insights and opportunities. Deloitte.

Dillis, C., Polson, M., Bodwitch, H., Carah, J., Power, M. E., & Sayre, N. F. (Eds.). (2022). *Industrializing Cannabis? Socio-Ecological Implications of Legalization and Regulation in California*. Routledge.

Easton, S. T. (Ed.). (2019). *The Legalization of Marijuana and the Remembrance of Things Past*. McGill-Queen's Press-MQUP.

Emmett, D., & Nice, G. (2009). *What You Need to Know About Cannabis*. Jessica Kingsley Publishers.

Evans, P. (1992). The State as Problem and Solution: Embedded Autonomy, and Structural Change. In S. Haggard & R. Kaufman (Eds.), *The Politics of Structural Adjustment: International Constraints, Distributive Conflicts and the State*. Princeton University Press. doi:10.1515/9780691188034-007

Freeman, T. P., Groshkova, T., Cunningham, A., Sedefov, R., Griffiths, P., & Lynskey, M. T. (2019). Increasing potency and price of cannabis in Europe, 2006–16. *Addiction (Abingdon, England)*, *114*(6), 1015–1023. doi:10.1111/add.14525 PMID:30597667

Gerwel, H. (2018). Institutional innovation and pro-poor agricultural growth: cannabis cultivation in the Eastern Cape province of South Africa as fertile opportunity.

Globe-Newswire. (2022). *Medical Marijuana Market Worth USD 248.42 Billion by 2030 at 31.97% CAGR - Report by Market Research Future (MRFR)*. Globe Newswire.

Goga, S., Mondliwa, P., & Roberts, S. (2020). *Economic power and regulation: the political economy of metals, machinery and equipment industries in South Africa. Inequality studies from the Global South*. Routledge. doi:10.4324/9780429282447-7

Hall, W., & Lynskey, M. (2020). Assessing the public health impacts of legalizing recreational cannabis use: The US experience. *World Psychiatry; Official Journal of the World Psychiatric Association (WPA)*, *19*(2), 179–186. doi:10.1002/wps.20735 PMID:32394566

Hutchison, K. E., Bidwell, L. C., Ellingson, J. M., & Bryan, A. D. (2019). Cannabis and health research: Rapid progress requires innovative research designs. *Value in Health*, *22*(11), 1289–1294. doi:10.1016/j.jval.2019.05.005 PMID:31708066

Johnson, C. (1982). *MITI and the Japanes Miracle: The Growth of Industrial Policy, 1925 – 1975*. Stanford University Press. doi:10.1515/9780804765602

Johnson, C. 1987. *Political institutions and economic performance: the government-led business relationship in Japan South Korea and Taiwan*.

Kang, S., & Mcgrady, P. (2020). Support for cannabis tourism: A tale of two states. *Tourism Review International*, *24*(4), 233–250. doi:10.3727/154427220X15990732245691

Khambule, I. B. (2019). *The Role Of Subnational State Institutions In Economic Development: A Case Of Local Economic Development Agencies In Kwazulu-Natal, South Africa*. [Doctoral Studies in Development Studies, University Of Kwazulu-Natal, Africa].

Kittel, J. (2018). Women in weed: Gender, race, and class in the cannabis industry. *The Arbutus Review*, *9*(1), 32–45. doi:10.18357/tar91201818385

Kuye, J. O. & Ajam, T. (2012). *The South African developmental state debate leadership, governance and a dialogue in public sector finance*. African Consortium of Public Administration.

Lowitt, S. (2020a). Industrial Development Projects. *Trade and Industrial Political Strategies*.

Lowitt, S. (2020b). Industrial Development Projects Industrial Hemp. *Trade and Industrial Political Strategies*.

Manu, E., Douglas, M., Ntsaba, M. J., & Tarkang, E. E. (2021). Perspectives of illicit marijuana growers and traders on commercial legalisation of marijuana in South Africa: Considerations for policy formulation. *Substance Abuse Treatment, Prevention, and Policy*, *16*(1), 1–13. doi:10.118613011-021-00391-w PMID:34174921

Markets, R. (2022). *Cannabis in Food and Beverage Market Share, Size, Trends, Industry Analysis Report, By Product Type; By Distribution Channel; By End-Use; By Source Type; By Region; Segment Forecast, 2022 - 2030*. Research and Markets.

Martin, A. & Rashidian, N. (2014). A new leaf: The end of cannabis prohibition. *New Press*.

Mazzucato, M. (2011). The entrepreneurial state. *Soundings*, *49*(49), 131–142. doi:10.3898/136266211798411183

Mazzucato, M. 2015. Building the entrepreneurial state: A new framework for envisioning and evaluating a mission-oriented public sector. *Levy Economics Institute of Bard College Working Paper*.

Mazzucato, M., Qobo, M. & Kattel, R. (2021). *Building state capacities and dynamic capabilities to drive social and economic development: The case of South Africa*. UCL.

Mondliwa, P. & Roberts, S. 2020. Black economic empowerment and barriers to entry. *Opening the South African Economy: Barriers to Entry and Competition*, 215-30.

Mondliwa, P., & Roberts, S. (2021). *From a developmental to a regulatory state? Sasol and the conundrum of continued state support. Ownership and Governance of Companies*. Routledge.

Monthony, A. S., Page, S. R., Hesami, M., & Jones, A. M. P. (2021). The past, present and future of Cannabis sativa tissue culture. *Plants*, *10*(1), 185. doi:10.3390/plants10010185 PMID:33478171

New-Frontier-Data. (2021). *The Global Cannabis Report: Growth & Trends Through 2025*. New Frontier Data.

Pachmayer, A., Switzer, R., & Reilly, S. (2021). Cannabis Tourism and the Community: Resident Attitudes in Humboldt County, California. *IdeaFest: Interdisciplinary Journal of Creative Works and Research from Humboldt State University*, *5*, 6.

Piispanen, R. (2022). *The Effects of Cannabis Legalization on the Economy of State Colorado-a Case Study*. Aalto University.

Prohibition-Partners (2019). The African Cannabis Report.

RSA. (2017). Preferential Procurement Policy Framework Act, 2000. Department Of Agriculture, L. R. A. R. D. (ed.). Pretoria.

RSA. (2018). Industrial Policy Action Plan 2018/19 - 2020/21. Economic Sectors, employment and infrastructre development cluster. Department of Trade and Industry, Republic of South Africa, Pretoria.

RSA. (2021a). Draft national cannabis master plan for South Africa. Department of agriculture, L. R. A. R. D. (ed.). Pretoria.

RSA. (2021b). Update On The Hemp Regulatory Framework For South Africa. Department Of Agriculture, L. R. A. R. D. (ed.). Pretoria: RSA Government.

RSA. (2022). Deputy Minister Lindiwe Sisulu: Tourism Dept Budget Vote 2022/23. In M. O. Tourism (Ed.). South African Government.

Ruttan, V. W. (1997). Induced innovation, evolutionary theory and path dependence: Sources of technical change. *Economic Journal (London), 107*(444), 1520–1529. doi:10.1111/j.1468-0297.1997.tb00063.x

Salentijn, E. M. J., Zhang, Q., Amaducci, S., Yang, M., & Trindade, L. M. (2015). New developments in fiber hemp (Cannabis sativa L.) breeding. *Industrial Crops and Products, 68*, 32–41. doi:10.1016/j.indcrop.2014.08.011

Sanjaya, L. (2004). Reinventing industrial strategy: the role of government policy in building industrial competitiveness. *United Nations Conference on Trade and Development.*

Sihlobo, W. (2020). *Finding common ground: Land, equity and agriculture*. Picador Africa.

Szirmai, A., Naudé, W., & Alcorta, L. (2013). *Pathways to industrialization in the twenty-first century: new challenges and emerging paradigms*. OUP Oxford. doi:10.1093/acprof:oso/9780199667857.001.0001

Tan, C. C. (2021). Learning to Develop a New Industry–Cannabis, with Competitiveness Edge. *Journal of the Association of Researchers, 26*, 1–10.

Taylor, L. L. (2019). Defining marijuana tourism. *Journal of Hospitality & Tourism Research (Washington, D.C.), 43*(3), 438–446. doi:10.1177/1096348018804610

TGE. (2022). *Comparing Economies* [Online]. *The Global Economy.* https://www.theglobaleconomy.com/compare-countries/

Tonami, A. (2018). Exporting the developmental state: Japan's economic diplomacy in the Arctic. *Third World Quarterly, 39*(6), 1211–1225. doi:10.1080/01436597.2017.1415142

UNECA. (2016). *Transformative industrial policy for Africa*, United Nations. Economic Commission for. *Africa*.

Wade, R. H. (2012). Return of industrial policy? *International Review of Applied Economics, 26*(2), 223–239. doi:10.1080/02692171.2011.640312

Weiss, M. L. (2014). *Routledge handbook of contemporary Malaysia*. Routledge. doi:10.4324/9781315756240

Williams, M. (2014). *Rethinking the Developmental State in the Twenty-First Century*. Routledge.

Zarenda, H. (2013). Deriving value from the Global Value Chain (GVC) concept: an approach to regional industrial policies. *Cape to Cairo*, 97.

Zondo, R. (2018). Minister of Justice and Constitutional Development and Others v Prince (Clarke and Others Intervening); National Director of Public Prosecutions and Others v Rubin; National Director of Public Prosecutions and Others v Acton. Constitutional-Court (ed.) [2018] ZACC 30. Johannesburg: The South African Judiciary.

Chapter 16
Envisaged Cannabis Economic Value-Chain for South Africa

John Oupa Hlatshwayo
https://orcid.org/0000-0001-6104-8559
University of South Africa, South Africa

ABSTRACT

The most critical and mainly inherent objective of this chapter is to afford a fresh insight into the economic realm that denotes cannabis potentially through its ploughing, refinery, nurture, multifaceted functions, in relation to job opportunities, employment creation, and subsequently generating revenues. Otherwise, it provides a variety of information depicted from various expert sources regarding the subject matter. Essentially, it presents researched work in the form of surveys which identify not only key debates, challenges, and trends, but also constructs and argue for a future agenda. The selected topic deliberately provides a constellation of perspectives aimed at exploring, yet also debating crucial issues as raised.

INTRODUCTION

The most critical and mainly inherent objective of this Chapter is to afford a fresh insight into the Economic realm that denotes Cannabis potentially through its ploughing, refinery, nurture, multifaceted functions, in relation to job opportunities, employment creation, and subsequently generating revenues. Otherwise, it provides an audience with the variety of information depicted from various sources, thereby becoming a relatively new learning experience, whilst the author is offered an academic opportunity for Businerent writing format as opposed to typical journal articles.

Given that the idea of this Book would be international in its outlook and approach, so the Chapter is set out to provide a state-of-the-art review of the Cannabis' field. Essentially, it presents researched work in the form of surveys which identify key debates, challenges, and trends, but also constructs and argue for a future agenda whilst keeping that target market keen. Such topic deliberately provides the constellation of perspectives, aimed at exploring, yet also debating crucial issues as raised. Thus, a Chapter in its attempt offers more creative academic authoring, focusing on targeted audience members, whilst also developing the 'art and craft' of writing.

DOI: 10.4018/978-1-6684-6346-8.ch016

HISTORICAL BACKGROUND

Cannabis is made from the dried flowering heads and leaves of a plant called Cannabis Sativa (Invest in Cape Town, City of Cape Town & Wesgro, 2019). It is also referred to as Marijuana and Dagga in South Africa (SA, henceforth). A lot has been written about the subject matter, yet views contrast regarding its Businession or decriminilisation in various countries the world-over. Since the 1990s, an international drug-control regime has begun to crumble as societies have decided that drug prohibitions produce more problems than benefits. Cannabis has been the prominent focus of drug-policy reform. Many jurisdictions, especially in Europe, North America, and South America, have Businessio the controls on Cannabis thereby Businessionti and or Businessi some instances of its production, sales, possession, and use. African countries are also participating in this global wave of Cannabis Businessiont (Duvall, 2019).

The nation of South Africa has had a long and complicated history with marijuana. Despite this view Marijuana locally known as "Dagga", was used by an estimated 3.2 million South Africans in 2008. Moreover, South Africa is well known for its role in the global Marijuana trade. Interpol has estimated that South Africa is the fourth largest producer of Cannabis in the world. An agency also suggests that approximately a third of Cannabis seized around the world originates from South Africa (Royal Queen Seeds, 2022). So, a historical account dating back from prehistoric days to date is ushered by Duvall (2019) in that, the Cannabis farming commenced in Africa after this crop arrived from its evolutionary homeland within Southern Asia. Thus, Cannabis came to Africa at least one thousand (1000) years ago to Madagascar and Mediterranean coast. As such the Archaeological evidence is scant, and the continent-wide documentary record principally dates to the nineteenth century.

A contrasting viewpoint is that the recorded history of Marijuana in South Africa goes back to the 1600s when Dutch immigrants first began trading with local nationalities. By 1680, the first ever prohibition laws were already being introduced. Thus, in order to monopolise Cannabis market, the Dutch East India Company prohibited Cape inhabitants from growing Marijuana. However, due to an abundance of this plant in the wild and Cannabis availability thereof through trade with local indigenous nations, such prohibition was then overturned in 1700 (Royal Queen Seeds, 2022). The diverting perspective, yet corroborating above-stated views moves from the premise that, in 1658 Jan van Riebeeck made notes about a certain plant in a personal diary. Such observations were to become famous for the first- written reference to Cannabis in a South African context. However, such documentation does not reveal at first sight that the Herb commonly named Dagga, had been cultivated and used long before that very moment.

At the time of Jan van Riebeeck's arrival in the Cape, clearly the history of Dagga already went back hundreds of years. Bearing such in mind, this idea could suggest that dagga is native to Southern Africa. But this is wrong, as the Plant is originally from Central Asia. The exact diffusion and lines of how it spread are not agreed upon by Scholars, especially when it comes to an exact 'centre of origin' as well as narrowing down the date of its first introduction. There is some consensus though, that by about 4200-4000 BC it had reached China, where records exist about the use of the Plant as Fibre. More so, a further evidence of its ancient use as well as religious Hindu texts describing its creation were found in India which leads to the assumption that the Plant also reached India at an early point in time, if not being native to this area of Asia (Weihraunch, 2021).

Cannabis was initially legal under colonial governments but widely outlawed by 1925, when it became subject to international control under Geneva Opium. There were back-to-back conferences held and separate treaties concluded between 1924 and 1925 (November and February respectively). The first Geneva Convention focused on Opium-producing nations, therefore signatories were permitted to sell the Opium only through government-managed monopolies and required to end trade completely within fifteen (15) years. So, the second Geneva Convention, also referred to as the International Opium Convention (1925 Geneva Convention) was intended to impose global controls over a wider range of Drugs including, for the first time Cannabis described as an "Indian hemp" in Article 11; of that Convention (Sihna, 2001).

Even while Cannabis was legal, colonialists diminished the production capacities of African societies through direct and indirect suppression of the Crop. Colonial governance impelled authorities to seek revenue from controlled territories and for centuries Cannabis has been traded in Africa. Most African colonial governments banned Cannabis before it was listed in 1925 Opium Convention. Thus, additional laws were enacted after such agreement, but drug-law enforcement did not immediately change. Arrests continued where authorities were already watching for Cannabis elsewhere, concern grew gradually. Cannabis became salient in many African locations only after World War Two (2), when returning servicemen and merchant sailors brought it to port cities (Duvall, 2019). State-sponsored marijuana eradication programmes have existed in South Africa since the 1950s. By the 1980s, such programmes took the form of aerial herbicide distribution through helicopters. Since then, numerous public challenges to the use of herbicides especially for this purpose occurred, yet minor change resulted thereof (Royal Queen Seeds, 2022).

In the early twentieth (20th) century, an increasing reprehension did not find its way into law. Even most magistrates' reports from that period did not often engage with Cannabis. More emphasis was on the abuse of alcohol and issues following from that. Although, some magistrates called smoking Cannabis an 'evil habit' generally there was not much attention raised around it. More especially when compared to other issues such as Alcohol, the use of Cannabis was not perceived as that of a major problem according to Weihraunch (2021).

The twenty first (21st) phase of Cannabis agricultural history was a rapidly unfolding move toward its Businessiont. To this effect, news media reported steps towards Cannabis-policy reforms in several countries, wherein agriculture had been the widespread consideration. Hence, proponents promoted a Crop's untapped value, Businessi opportunities blocked by prohibition, and also noted that Global Northern countries were already profiting from its Businessiont. For instance, the notion suggests a politician in the Kingdom of eSwatini asserted that a country was losing potential revenues, unlike the counterparts, 'First world countries' after Businessiont the growing and use of dagga, continues Duvall (2019).

In the beginning of 1950s, African intellectuals developed the concept of 'Neo-colonialism' an attempt to understand how the Political-Economic power is wielded internationally after formal colonialism ended.

The current instances of Cannabis Businessiont in Africa Business Neo-colonialism. As such, mechanism of payment for favourable Cannabis-policies enabled Global Northern organisations to accumulate wealth, by dispossessing citizens of African countries access to the increasingly legal and Global Cannabis Economy (Duvall, 2019). Cannabis ranks as amongst the most frequently used recreational psychoactive substances Globally with an estimated one hundred and ninety two (192) million users recorded in 2018, corresponding to 3,9% of the world population aged fifteen to sixty four (15 – 64) years (Ransing et al., 2022, p. 2).

In a context of Businessio, increasingly Business society, where traditional controls are breaking down, the use of Cannabis has now become a domain of younger user and poly-user. South Africa is a large producer of Cannabis (The world's third largest), most of which is consumed in a Southern African region, but at least some finds its way to Europe. Cannabis is cultivated in South Africa, imported from neighbouring countries (Swaziland, Lesotho, Mozambique and Zimbabwe), exported to some neighbouring African counties such (Namibia, in particular), Europe (Holland as well as UK), and of course consumed in South Africa (Peltzer & Ramlagan, 2007).

LEGAL FRAMEWORK

In September 2018, a landmark decision by the Constitutional Court of SA Business certain acts in relation to Cannabis. In particular, the court ruled that the private cultivation, possession, and use of Cannabis by an adult for personal use should no longer be a criminal offence. This ruling was in recognition of the Constitutional right to privacy. Crucially, any commercial Businessio of Cannabis must be of legal and cultivated under a South African Health Products Regulatory Authority (SAHPRA) cultivation licence. Thus, a Constitutional Court gave the South African parliament about two years in which to develop legislation in line with its ruling. Unfortunately, Covid-19 has caused substantial delays to legislative developments, and so no substantial amendments made to the Medicines and Related Substances Control Act 101 of 1965 in May 2020, which alleviated regulation of certain Schedules. However, the Drugs and Drug Trafficking Act 140 of 1992 is yet to be amended to Businession private cultivation, possession including its use. Furthermore, there are no developments within intellectual property legislation that has been made to date. (Smit & Van Wyk, 2021).

Medicinal Cannabis is a term that refers to legal, high quality, and Businession products that are made from crude or raw Cannabis. Crude Cannabis is a difficult drug for doctors to prescribe because the dose and potency of the drug in each case is not tested or known. Medicinal Cannabis is legally produced under strict pharmaceutical conditions. Doctors and pharmacists know exactly the ingredients of this medicine. By contrast, Illicit Cannabis is usually smoked, contents, potency and quality of Illicit Recreational Cannabis are untested and usually contamination with microbes, pesticides and heavy metals can occur. Medicinal Cannabis products are usually available as oils, sprays, tinctures, and capsules. Differences mean that Cannabis sourced through illicit channels cannot be described as 'Medicinal Cannabis' (Invest in Cape Town et al, 2019).

There are currently no registered Cannabis-containing medicines in South Africa, therefore patients wanting its usage need to follow the procedure for obtaining permission regarding such unregistered medicine. Currently patients are able to obtain Cannabis products for medicinal use in terms of section 21 and 22 of the Medicines Act, which allows medical practitioners to apply towards the South African Health Products Authority (SAHPRA) for permission regarding access and also prescribe unregistered medicines. Under this process Medicinal Cannabis products may be made available, under medical supervision and in exceptional circumstances to specific patients.

To date, patient access to unregistered pharmaceutical products containing Cannabinoids had been enabled by SAHPRA via an importation of such products only. The new licencing framework carves out a possibility for Cannabis-containing medicines to be registered in SA by SAHPRA. Until such time as registered Cannabis-containing medicines are available, access to such products will continue to rely on the section 21 approval process (WESGRO, 2019). It would seem that every single country exercises its own 'strategic' approach in relation to Cannabis, Businession, availability, use and related factors. The process of lifting prohibitions against Cannabis use is known as Businession, while sparing criminal sanctions (E.g. fines, prison, or mandated treatment) against people possessing or using it is known as Decriminalisation. As such Cannabis consumption is legally prohibited in most countries.

Therefore, country-specific details on prohibitions and Businessiontion laws vary. Almost all countries have adopted legal prohibitions as one of core strategies to reduce Cannabis use. Essentially, legal prohibitions seem to have substantially reduced the Cannabis usage in many countries (For instance, before any legal prohibitions, Kathmandu was considered a 'hippie hub' inviting tourists and promoting hashish and tourism eventually). Yet, some countries have harsher policies (Like, Malaysia) whilst others are rather lenient (Spain, in this case). In Spain, Article 368 of the Penal Code distinguishes between drugs that cause, and serious health damage or none at all. So, given that drug-induced harm is related to drug quantity, a person may possess up to hundred (100) grams of Cannabis for personal consumption. Most of the countries thereof have prevalent positive social attitudes towards a future of Cannabis Businession notably among others are South Africa, Morocco, Kenya, Ethiopia, Brazil, Turkey, Iran, France, Italy, Thailand, India. Political and religious factors are however, affecting the implementation of Cannabis Businession in almost all countries (Ransing et al., 2022, p. 5).

The Court Businesng inter alia, that the prohibition on Cannabis use by adults in the confines of private dwellings is inconsistent with the South African Constitution and that provisions of a legislation in question were invalid to that extent. In terms of the ruling such protection is not limited to a home or private dwelling. Thus, with such decision South Africa becomes and is a first currently only African country to make provision for personal consumption of Cannabis in private (Also generally referred to as, Recreational Cannabis). So, Cannabis use for medicinal and recreational purposes is legal, yet remains illegal in most African countries, including Algeria, Angola, Benin, Botswana, Burkina Faso, Kingdom of Eswatini, just to mention but a few (Lubaale & Mavundla, 2019).

A similar perspective moves a premise that Wild Cannabis has been used for centuries by South Africans in particular Indigenous people for recreational, traditional, medicinal and religious purposes. However, the escalation of drug trafficking as well as substance abuse later on resulted in absolute ban towards dealing, cultivation, and possession of Cannabis in South Africa. Thence, prohibitions originated from the International Treaty of Versailles, which required signatory states to establish processes to repress the illicit drug trade of, inter alia, Cannabis. Following the signing of this Treaty in 1919, South Africa promulgated the Customs and Excise Duties Amendment Act in 1922. This Act prohibited the cultivation, sale, possession, use of Cannabis, Cocaine, and a various number of other substances. In 1924, Cannabis was officially added to the International list of habit-forming drugs by the Advisory Committee (Nations League Council) as part of International law. Similarly, the South African Cannabis use was completely Businession in 1928 under the Medical, Dental, and Pharmacy Act. Cannabis prohibition was also included in the Weeds Act in 1937 (Bester & Els, 2021).

Other legislation that prohibits the production, distribution or use of cannabis followed at a steady pace as forthcoming: Medicines and Related Substances Act, 1965; Pharmacies Act, 1974; Criminal Procedure Act, 1974 (Allowing for searches and seizures); and Drugs and Trafficking Act, 1992.

Furthermore, Cannabis was classified as the Schedule 7 substance that is subject to special restrictions and controls, including Drugs and Trafficking Act which allowed people found in possession of more than 115g Cannabis to be presumed guilty of dealing in the Narcotic. In 1995, following an adoption of Interim Constitution, a Constitutional Court declared this presumption unconstitutional, as it unjustifiably infringed on the constitutionally enshrined presumption of innocence, persists Bester & Els (2021).

MEDICAL USE OF CANNABIS

The Clinical evidence of indications for the use of Medical Cannabis is currently supported by a limited evidence base, but this field is evolving. Medical Cannabis has been shown to be effective for certain conditions, but benefits for most investigated indications is limited, in many cases by poor-quality studies, risk of bias, also clinically nonsignificant findings. Notably, three Business controlled trials (RCTs) assessed the effect of a pharmaceutical plant-derived CBD solution (Epidiolex). It was found that when added as adjuvant therapy at the maximum recommended dose, it led to significant reduction in the median frequency of monthly seizures as compared to placebo for Lennox-Gastaut syndrome (van Rensburg et al, 2020).

In essence, an ethical duty on the medical practitioner to ensure responsible prescribing delta-9-tetrahydrocannabino (THC) containing Medical Cannabis products, and a provision of advice to patients. The addition of medicines cannabidiol (CBD) to products containing THC has been shown to reduce the risk of impaired cognition. Some unregulated Cannabis products have been assessed and found to vary in THC and CBD content when compared to information on the label, and some commercially available products sold as pure CBD contain marked amounts of THC. This might affect cognition, for children and adolescents this is particularly important, given the potential for an impact on the brain development, cognitive function and mental illness. Where good evidence of efficacy exists in the context of failed conventional therapy, beneficence would support prescription of a registered safe product, continues van Rensburg et al (2020).

So, high-quality evidence for Medical Cannabis is still in its infancy. Regulatory overview of the use of Medical Cannabis is essential to ensure the availability of safe, effective, and good-quality products. Overall, the current limited benefits of Medical Cannabis for most indications may be outweighed by lack of consistent efficacy and risk of adverse effects, including multiple drug interactions with no data to guide management. Currently, for the majority of the proposed Medical Cannabis indications, safer, and generally more effective pharmacological therapies are regulatorily approved. However, good quality data support the use of Medical Cannabis for some rare forms of childhood epilepsy, resistant to current registered antiseizure medications. So, this may justify facilitated access in SA to Medical Cannabis through Section 21. Medical Cannabis could also be considered for patients with intractable Chemotherapy-induced Nausea and Vomiting and Multiple Sclerosis-associated spasticity. Unfortunately, the cost of Medical Cannabis may be prohibitive for such patient groups (van Rensburg et al, 2020).

Medical Cannabis refers to the use of Cannabis and its constituent Cannabinoids, including Δ (9)-Tetrahydrocannabinol (THC) and Cannabidiol (CBD), as therapy to treat or alleviate symptoms of medical conditions. Although in some countries Synthetic Cannabinoids, such as nabilone (Cesamet) and dronabinol (Marinol) are available for hinted purposes above. Cannabinoids are delivered through various mechanisms, the most obvious being through smoking. Though, smoking Cannabis can be hazardous to health over a long term because toxic compounds are created in the combustion process. In addition, it proves difficult to regulate the amount of Cannabinoids being ingested. However, users report that smoking relieves symptoms quickly. Cannabinoids could be ingested orally, inhaled via vapourisers (Nabidiolex), and used transdermally through suppositories (Parry & Myers, 2014).

The Synthetic Cannabis is most often delivered in the pill format. Obviously, such delivery mechanisms vary in cost and ease of access. In South Africa, smoking is the cheapest and most easily accessible delivery mechanism as Cannabis is widely available to purchase, though not without a risk of arrest. Cannabis oil is also available on the black market, and there are recipes provided by internet for people seeking to be creative too. So, the Medical Cannabis use is now legal in Austria, Canada, Finland, Germany, Israel, Italy, Netherlands, Portugal and Spain, at least according to Parry & Myers (2014).

More recent South African data on Cannabis use were found from the Treatment Centre, that shows Cannabis is the most used drug in South African Treatment Facility cases within a second half of 2016 and a first half of 2017. The Treatment Facility reports though, are limited as only record a number of patients seeking Treatment including Substances with which are treated for. Thus, there is a lack of more recent national population-based data on the prevalence and correlates of daily and non-daily Cannabis use in South Africa. Risk factors for Cannabis use or its disorder are Sociodemographic factors and Health variables. Sociodemographic risk factors for Cannabis use include male gender, divorced, separated, never married, unemployed, lone living (Without a partner), higher education, and lower education. Health variable risk factors include other illicit drug use, alcohol use disorder, psychological distress, having no chronic conditions, and less frequent primary health care Businessio (Ramlagan, Peltzer & Pengpid, 2021).

In concluding this sub-section an interesting perspective below provides some insight. The Businession of Cannabis for medicinal use is a contentious space both politically and in the medical community. The Medical Innovation Bill introduced in a South African Parliament, aimed to shift political and legal positions of Cannabis as an illegal substance, yet available for research and medical use, however to date progress has been slow. Essentially though, Cannabis and Cannabinoid products are currently available for Medicinal use in countries notably, Netherlands and twenty nine (29) Sates in United States (USA). Locally, anecdotal reports suggest that several patients with chronic medical conditions Busines Cannabis and Cannabis-derived or Cannabinoid products for symptom alleviation.

In 2016, the Alcohol, Tobacco and Other Drug Research Unit (ATODRU) of South African Medical Research Council (SAMRC) produced a Policy Brief, evaluated results of a published systematic review for current evidence to inform the discussion. Thus, a review identified moderate quality evidence supported Medicinal Cannabis use. The benefits are for chronic pain, chemotherapy-induced nausea, vomiting, and multiple sclerosis,1,2 however, many formulations, dosages, and administration routes limit recommendations. Subsequently, SAMRC brought key stakeholders representing all nine Faculties (Health Sciences) at South African universities together in 2017, Cape Town, to explore opportunities for conducting research, Medicinal Cannabis clinical trials, and Cannabinoids to inform policy-making. The workshop identified three major research priorities:

- Conduct a national, multisite clinical trial of Cannabinoids following identification of the optimal formulations, dosage and relevant clinical indications from the current evidence base to inform trial protocol development.
- Support exploratory research to quantify prevalence and qualify current use of extracts (E.g. oils) in the community to alleviate pain and other symptoms; methods to include are as follows, firstly, community or clinically-based cross-sectional surveys or online survey of general public, secondly, the cross-sectional surveys of Businessi general practitioners and or specialists mostly at Pain clinics regarding respective knowledge of patient Cannabis extracts through patients' disclosure.
- Conduct qualitative evaluation of the possible barriers and also facilitators to medical practitioners prescribing Cannabis or Cannabinoids (Medically), should it be Business in future.

Further to this meeting, an SAMRC-supported team of researchers evaluated the evidence for a trial of a Cannabinoid for the management of pain related to HIV associated sensory neuropathy (HIV-SN).

The team selected painful HIV-SN as the condition based on:

(1) High burden of HIV and HIV-SN in a South African population, despite availability of improved Antiretroviral drug regimens.
(2) Absence of empirical evidence that supports the efficacy of pharmacological agents typically recommended for the management of neuropathic pain in this population group. Assessment to the high-quality trials of greater than 12 weeks duration was limited, included participants with at least moderate intensity pain at baseline, and that met current recommendations for trial design in the field of chronic pain.
(3) Only three studies all used a fixed dose combination of Tetrahydrocannabinol (THC) and Cannabidiol (CBD) delivered via Oromucosal spray were identified.

The team concluded that Clinical Equipoise exists for a fixed dose THC: CBD oromucosal Cannabinoid spray trial for the management of painful HIV-SN. This was based on the Grade assessment, the absence of demonstrably effective alternative therapies for painful HIV-SN and Clinical need in people living with HIV. In Medical practice, there is a balance between early adoption of the new innovation, and slower considered approach Businession evidence and safety over potential benefit.

Though there are some clear areas where evidence supports the use of Medicinal Cannabis (As reviewed in the SAMRC Policy Brief), this should not imply that Cannabis is the Panacea for all ails, or that it should be freely available without due control of production quality, disease indications and specific dosing recommendations. Research is urgently needed and regulatory changes will promote and allow for high priority, locally relevant research using regionally sourced products. It is imperative that Medical and Scientific community both practitioners and researchers are involved in informing and developing evolving Cannabis policies.

There seem to be much confusion that exists between Medical versus Recreational usage, Medical and Recreational Legal Statutes of possession, the usage and scientific evidence compared to impassioned anecdotal reports of its efficacy in addressing a host of medical conditions. Patients need to be offered a best relief of suffering with all available therapies based on the rational assessment of benefit, cost, and potential harms of Cannabis and Cannabinoid products for Medicinal use (Augustine et al, 2018).

ECONOMIC BENEFITS OF CANNABIS

The South Africa's Cannabis sector is currently worth an estimated twenty eight (28) billion rands. However, as the result of an age-old stigma this industry is not given the attention it needs in order to flourish. Such factor discourages buyers, sellers, potential investors, and that needs to change fast. The biggest stigma associated with Cannabis is the negative perceptions about its uses and effects. The general undesirable picture of Cannabis users being unintelligent, lazy, unhygienic, and even dangerous, it leads to the discrimination in professional and social contexts (Davids, 2021).

Because of the stigma around Cannabis and the history of its illegal status, there has been very little research done on this topic or industry as a whole. Today, South Arica is standing on the cusp of this rapidly growing industry, but not enough is known about it. Thus, this industry deserves focused research since it does not operate the same as other industries. It has different environments and restrictions to overcome, and its consumers think and behave differently.

A fast-burgeoning Cannabis market is needed in South Africa to revive its ailing Economy. Challenges the industry faces have also taken on the arduous task of producing a set of guidelines for how to Businession and navigate the sector to reap the long-term benefits. Despite all hurdles faced, South Africa remains among other largest exporters of Cannabis and this industry in particular is ripe with several possibilities for an Economic growth (Davids, 2021). The above-mentioned raised issues (Hiccups) inspired this Chapter, and its direction in the book. Hence, it will be explored vigorously, detailed, and focus more on the potential, implication, and solution-driven approach.

The legalisation of Cannabis is currently receiving global attention as many countries are considering this policy. In 2018, Canada passed a bill to legalise Cannabis, making it the second country after Uruguay to legalise Cannabis for the Recreational use. In 2018, nine States and District of Columbia in the US allowed Recreational Cannabis use, while thirty (30) others allowed Cannabis for medical use. After Businessi Cannabis in 2014, Colorado started collecting a substantial amount of tax from its sales and One Hundred and Thirteen (113) million Dollars was collected in Retail Cannabis as part of tax revenues. That is twice the amount collected from alcohol taxes.

Seemingly, if Cannabis is fully Business in South Africa there are two possible price effects. Firstly, should the government imposes excise taxes on Cannabis prices will increase (So, government would generate revenue). Secondly, the price of Cannabis is likely to decrease since Businession would result in eliminating the risk associated with buying and selling Cannabis. An investigation conducted (Paper) in 2013 in lieu of challenges associated with conducting a cost-benefit analysis of Cannabis policies, reported that data is insufficient to determine the curve demand shape and or curve demand shift should legislation occur (Riley, Vellios & van Walbeek, 2019).

To this effect a related question becomes whether alcohol and Cannabis are substitutes or complements, and if such varies by age, gender, and use patterns. Evaluation of potential effects that Businession and the imposition of an excise tax might have, an understanding of price elasticity of demand is helpful. For example, the demand for cigarettes in South Africa responds to the changes in a price (With an estimated price elasticity of demand at least between –0.55% and –0.7%). Price Elasticity of Demand, is the ratio of percentage change in quantity demanded of a product to the percentage change in price. Economists usually employ it in order to understand how supply and demand change when a product's price changes (Investopedia Team, James, & Kvilhaug, 2022).

Increased excise taxation curbs the demand for cigarettes for current consumers, reduces initiation among youth, and raises revenue for government. Legalising Cannabis is likely to impact significantly both the demand for and supply of Cannabis. It is unclear at this point how a Business market will be regulated, if at all, yet an understanding of the market dynamics is important. The consumption of Cannabis is significantly affected by price but that the price elasticity falls within an inelastic range (That is -1), neither perfectly elastic not elastic. Thus, the market for Cannabis, even though it operates in a shadow economy, is subject to same economic forces as other consumer products. The price responsiveness of Cannabis is similar to that of cigarettes. Should Cannabis be Business, the government could use some of its experience about the regulation, and especially taxation, of cigarettes as a model for Cannabis, according to Riley, Vellios & Walbeek (2019)._

Clearly views are varied regarding the Businession of Cannabis in South Africa. In another study conducted within a South African context, it was found that the freedom to engage in Cannabis cultivation and trading, capital acquisition to indulge in a commercial Cannabis cultivation and trading, including regulation of Cannabis prices, through Businession were benefits illegal Cannabis growers desired to gain from possible commercial Businession of Cannabis cultivation and trading (Manu et al, 2021).

However, fear of Cannabis takeover business by already established farmers, competition from other small-scale farmers leading to loss of loyal customers, source of livelihood loss, Cannabis perceived fall in price due to lack of bargaining power, and a potential increase in school drop-out rates among children to engage in Cannabis activities were costs that illegal Cannabis growers envisaged from possible commercial Businession of this drug. The point of note therefore is such that, with reference to ease of capital acquisition, historical bottlenecks which hamper small-scale farmers in securing capital for expansion of farms, especially Black farmers, will need to be addressed by both government and union leaders. Some of the challenges include access to land for commercial farming and very few farmers benefit from government funding support programmes. As such, issues of land acquisition and access to capital for would-be Cannabis growers should be improved, a vantage point held by Manu et al (2021).

So, the dual findings as stated above illustrate not only gains yet apprehensions raised by participants in this case study, depicting a less than 'solid' viewpoint pertaining to Cannabis Businession in South Africa in respect of Economics' point of view a 'clarion call' below also bears testimony. The status of Cannabis as a gateway drug to a range of other illicit drugs use among individuals with mental disorders is the major concern for public health in South Africa. Although there have been arguments to emphasise the benefits of Medical Cannabis use, such benefits are outweighed by negative data. For instance, in the USA challenges of Businession include an ineffective overarching federal regulatory structure, including an industry that seeks to exploit loopholes to maximise profit, which are the same issues that apply in South Africa.

More so, in industrialised countries like Canada, with adequate resources for prevention, management, and treatment for Cannabis addiction, its legislation has dismally failed to protect the youth. South African youth is already vulnerable due to widespread prevalence of substance abuse, such as Nyaope, Tik, and Cocaine, that the country has not been able to address satisfactorily. So, lessons learnt from countries which have Business Cannabis indicate that South Africa cannot afford costs of consequences of Cannabis Businession, as it comes with several demands such as infrastructure, human, social, health services, and financial resources brought about by a Highest Court's ruling in the land. Thus, the poor and vulnerable communities, with the least programmes and resources for prevention and treatment will continue to bear the brunt of consequences of this verdict (Mokwena, 2019).

The gateway hypothesis remains a controversial theory which has been debated for years, and states that Cannabis use particularly in adolescence creates a vulnerability to the use and abuse of 'heavier' drugs. Therefore, many have interpreted this association as based on personality and social factors. In essence, that nonconforming adolescents are attracted to Cannabis equally to other drugs, and Cannabis users are pushed by law into the realm of illegal drugs where contact with users and sellers of other drugs becomes inevitable. It seems therefore that, current laws do not work rather snarling up an already overwhelmed resources, criminalise Cannabis smokers and tie it 'heavier' drugs, and have little deterrent effects. People decrease Cannabis use based on health-risk perceptions rather as opposed to fear of being caught. However, many users explore it without problem or progression. Thus, defining the whole Cannabis debate by a small percentage of heavy and problematic users is similar to defining alcohol by alcoholism (Perkel, 2005).

There are four (4) major issues which should be Businessi in relation to the Economic Benefits of Cannabis, namely; net income, net cash flow, return on investment, producer and consumer surplus measures as forthcoming.

Net Income

South Africa's Cannabis Net Worth is estimated twenty eight (28) Billion Rands according to Davids (2021). Another projection was that by 2023, the South African domestic market for Cannabis and related products, excluding consumer Cannabidiol (CBD) products, would be worth around R27 billion (de Wet, 2019). Cannabidiol is a naturally occurring compound found in the resinous flower of Cannabis, a plant with rich history as the medicine dating back thousands of years, a viewpoint maintained by Projectcbd. org (2022). The R27 Billion calculation for the South African Cannabis market is based on growth in markets that have Business it for both medicinal and recreational use, such as Uruguay and Canada, and some American States. It excludes Cannabinol, since there is not yet enough data on sales to predict its market size, continues de Wet (2019).

A varying perspective is that Africa's Cannabis industry could be worth as $7,1 Billion by 2023. This projection focused on the legal ad regulated Cannabis markets in South Africa, Lesotho, eSwatini, Zimbabwe, Malawi, Zamia, Ghana, Nigeria, and Morocco. It is reported that Lesotho became the first nation to legalise Cannabis on the African continent, followed suit by Morocco. The latter's thriving illegal industry sent an estimated $13 Billion worth of pot to Europe annually, and in a process managed to employed approximately, One (1) Million people (Kafeero, 2022).

Net Cash Flow

A report suggests that legal Cannabis sales in the United States of America grew 30% in 2020 to a whopping $22 Billion outpacing the $17,5 billion spent on Wine. It signals a 'healthy' profit-margin in relation to Net Cash Flow. There are few aspects of operating a business in the Cannabis industry dramatically that are variant from managing a typical business. The practicality about cash flow requires steadfast comprehension before even considering launching a Cannabis Enterprise; firstly, Cannabis business is phenomenally expensive to start and maintain, it needs hundreds of thousands to millions of dollars for initial operating licenses, ongoing compliance expenses, property purchases and or leases, equipment, advertising, and security. In essence, considerable liquid funds are a must to possess while taxes are costly too; secondly, a 'going concern' might not be able to open Bank Account, and forced to operate without bank accounts, checks, credit cards, loans, or lines of credit. In a Cannabis industry, cash is critical yet, also a serious liability. The Cannabis 'going concern' has no safety credit bank line net, or that ability to float payments on a credit card; finally, keeping track of cash funds and maintaining meticulous cash earnings, business records, and spending are incredibly hard, especially as Cannabis Enterprises are already under the regulatory microscope. Thus, a solid leak-proof cash flow system is extremely important, according to Pelley (2021).

Return on Investment

A point of note is such that the rapid growth and ever-evolving nature of Cannabis industry has resulted in wild and hyper-inflated business valuations, making it extremely difficult for Enterprises to zero in on a fair valuation as to acquire or be acquired in the 'up-and-coming field', in relation to Return on Investment (ROI), according to Diaz (2019). So, the Cannabis industry is ripe for investors, with more of its organisations joining a Canadian Securities Exchange (CSE), and apparently in the fourth quarter of 2018, about $7,9 Billion Capital was raised by Cannabis companies globally.

As basic investment principle is that, usually the higher is a potential return of investment, the higher the risk as it relates to generating revenues. Several risks are associated with Cannabis business investments that a prospective investor, should take into Businessi when evaluating available investment opportunities. Hence, various Cannabis outlets stake potential successes on future profit and sales. It means that often times, investments are hinged upon the attractiveness of a future business' Profitability.

It is never guaranteed that Enterprises will successfully generate profits or increase stock's value. As a caution and taking risks into consideration, there are still valuable investment opportunities in Cannabis industry. Generally, a solid speculative investment demonstrates the 30% or more ***Return on Investment***, a viewpoint held by Ryan (2018). A Cannabis Tech leader, Dutchie raised another massive financing round. This $350 million Series D values a company at $3,75 Billion and its $200 Million round from March 2021. Dutchie, has raised $603 Million to date, Jane Technologies, raised the $100 Million Series C during August 2021, whilst Kadenwood closed at a $50 Million Series B (Burns, 2021).

The best way to assess viability of an investment is by performing requisite due diligence into understanding such investment, its offerings, and the Businession behind an offering. The forthcoming key elements are extremely critical towards conducting due diligence on:

- Problem-solving, i.e. is there a need for such business, and if it addresses the 'real' customer challenges in a market.
- Organisational Team, i.e. acquired experience if any, is it a multi-disciplinary, and applicable interpersonal-rapport.
- Competitive Advantage, i.e. competitive edge, product differentiation, and value-add.
- Traction, i.e. operations track-record, available customers, and or previous sales.
- Cap Table, i.e. if this institution is private, capital table members, and its split.

As Cannabis business has some risks and positive return on investment (Success) is not a guarantee, prospective investors should be cautious of competition, legal considerations, pricing, taxation, black market, inflated share prices, and dilution a perspective as held by Green Growth (2019).

Producer and Consumer Surplus Measures

Interestingly, United Nations (UN) estimates that an African continent as a whole already produces some 38 000 tonnes of Cannabis per year despite it being illegal to grow including possession, just about everywhere in lieu of producers. Availability of affordable land, low-cost labour, and an experienced agricultural workforce, Africa offers enormous opportunity to local start-ups and foreign organisations expecting to expand, the viewpoint held by de Wet (2019). In the longest outlook there is a definite potential for overall Cannabis market to establish itself as the mainstream business and industry, yet short toward the mid-term prospects some concerns inevitable; firstly, most organisations active in such industry are small caps with little information and research performed on institutions per se, followed suit by low market liquidity especially in United States of America; secondly, a risk remains high both in terms of how the market will consolidate in future and how quickly Businession process would evolve in the United States of America and other countries. In order for the market to Business it needs clear rules; thirdly, Cannabis industry is not uniform, displaying two distinctive businesses namely, medical and recreational the former appears to be more acceptable and successful, although it comes with various hurdles particularly political and regulatory; fourthly, the price evolution for Cannabis is unclear,

Businession process should lead to more demand and higher prices in the short-term. However, the low entry barriers for organisations wanting to enter an industry may lead to an over-supply in the long term. Therefore, such a scenario may have inverse effect on prices, and consequently corporate revenues.

Cannabis and Hotel industry could offer a unique selling proposition for Hoteliers and could take on many different forms. For example, some of United States of America's properties already allow guests to smoke or consume Cannabis on-site, generally providing guidelines regarding acceptable conduct, (Weisskopf, 2022).

CRITICAL ANALYSIS

A recorded history of Cannabis (Marijuana) in South Africa goes back to the 1600s, that is when Dutch immigrants first began trading with local nationalities. By 1680, the first ever prohibition laws were already being introduced (Royal Queen Seeds, 2022). Thus, in order to monopolise Cannabis market, Dutch East India Company prohibited Cape inhabitants from growing Marijuana. To some extent, similar Legislations are still extremely applicable pending some steadfast resolutions and willingness by a current Government. Based on preceding Literature Review, South African Cannabis industry is to date extremely hinged at an 'infancy' phase, yet it operated for centuries ago.

The Constitutional Court afforded a duration of two (2) years to South African parliament towards development of Cannabis Legislation that is congruent to its ruling (Smit & Van Wyk, 2021). To date (September 2022), various other formations (E.g. the Congress of South African Trade Unions; Cosatu) had just only conveyed its submission on May 2022 to parliament according to Businesstech (2022). The 'snail pace' signifies the 'rush' that government is 'speedily' traversing regarding Cannabis Businession. Medical Cannabis has been shown to be effective for certain conditions. So, some Scholars on this subject matter have raised insufficient research conducted. In instances whereby studies were applicable, results proved to be 'laced' with poor-quality, biasness, and also clinically non-significant findings (van Rensburg et al, 2020). It is therefore prudent that Academics at Institutions of Higher Learning to consider such an 'area of focus' mostly, in its pursuit academically. Perhaps, Government should creatively assume a 'speedy' approach in resolving causes of delay.

South Africa's Cannabis sector's net worth is around 28 Billion Rands, a staggering figure by any account, clearly this indication suggests that it could potentially become a 'booming' business, with factors aligned to it considered, and due diligence covered. If United States of America grew 30% in 2020 to $22 Billion, then clearly South Africa is not lagging too far behind regarding prospective revenue generation in the Cannabis market, though a lot of work is still in prospect. It seems that South Africa requires to strategically, legally, and economically devise a Generic Framework (Cannabis) to compete, and trade at the highest level. So, a PESTLE (Political, Economical, Social, Technological, Legal and Environmental) Analysis in lieu of Cannabis market is advised, as the 'blanket' approach towards business-oriented growth and development. Most crucially, in the Cannabis segment is a producer, consumer, sales, demand, surplus, measures, trade, exchange, benefits, including means (Land, Labour, Capital and Entrepreneurship). Essentially, all measures should be carved to benefit all and sundry, yet in the main producers, consumers, entrepreneurs, require to form a 'Triangular Polygon'.

CONCLUSION

It does not seem that there is a consensus regarding the Economic Benefits of Cannabis in South Africa, if any at least by the scholars sampled from literature review hinted above. A common denominator though is that Cannabis has been around for an extremely longest period, currently available, and chances are that it will be prevalent in generations to exist. Perhaps, the premise should be centred around, "how to make it beneficial including but not limited towards financial accruals, to all and sundry within the South African context"?

If Legal Cannabis sales in United States of America grew by 30% in 2020, towards that whopping $22 Billion outpacing $17,5 Billion spent on wine, then South African Cannabis market is not lagging far behind in its 28 Billion Rands worth of world market-share. In Africa, the South African Development Community (SADC) with its all sixteen (16) Member States, more so Kingdom of eSwatini, has in the past traded with South Africa in Cannabis (Illicit and or otherwise). So, eSwatini is reputable to produce the most of 'potent herb' in this Economic Regional Community. South Africa needs to carve and execute an Economic Framework oriented at Cannabis Entrepreneurship.

REFERENCES

Augustine, T.N., Cairns, C.J., Chetty, S., Dannatt, L.G., Gravett, N., Grey, G., Grobler, G., Jafta, Z., Kamerman, P., Lopes, J., Matsabisa, M.G., Mugabo, P., Mulder, M., Parry, C., Rataemane, S., Siegfried, N., Steenkamp, V., Thomas, E., & van Zyl-Smit, R. (2018). Priority areas for cannabis and cannabinoid product research in South Africa. *African Journal of Primary Health Care & Family Medicine.*

Bester, P., & Els, S. (2021). The legalisation of cannabis: A security-vetting dilemma, Stellenbosch University, Scientia Militaria. *South African Journal of Military Studies*, *49*(2). doi:10.5787/49-2-1334

Burns, M. (2021). Cannabis Investment jumps 82% the second half of 2021, 165% over 2020 levels. *TechCrunch.* https://techcrunch.com

Businesstech. (2022). South African Cannabis company details expansion plans following R300 Million cash injection, including Europe and US. *BuisnessTech.* https://businesstech.co.za

Davids, N. 2021. Destigmatise SA's Multibillion-Rand Cannabis Sector to Achieve Economic Growth. University of Capetown News. *www*.news.uct.ac.za

Davids, N. 2021. Destigmatise SA's Multibillion-Rand Cannabis Sector to Achieve Economic Growth. *University of Capetown News.* www.news.uct.ac.za

De Wet, P. (2019). The South African Dagga Industry could be worth R27 Billion within Four years – but export-quality Cannabis may be a problem. *Business Insider.* https://www.businessinsider.co.za

De Wet, P. (2019). The South African Dagga Industry could be worth R27 Billion within Four years – but export-quality Cannabis may be a problem. *BuisnessTech.* https://www.businessinsider.co.za

Diaz, M. (2019). Member Blog: What to Know About Cannabis Business Valuations. *The Cannabis Industry.* https://thecannabisindustry.org/tag/cash-flow/

Diaz, M. 2019. Member Blog: What to Know About Cannabis Business Valuations. *The Cannabis Industry.* https://thecannabisindustry.org/tag/cash-flow/

Duvall, C. S. (2019). *Illegal Cannabis Cultivation in the World: A Brief Agricultural History of Cannabis in Africa from Prehistoric to Canna-Colony*. OpenEdition Journals. doi:10.4000/echogeo.17599

Duvall, C. S. (2019). *Illegal Cannabis Cultivation in the World: A Brief Agricultural History of Cannabis in Africa from Prehistoric to Canna-Colony*. OpenEdition Journals. doi:10.4000/echogeo.17599

Green Growthcpas. (2019). What ROI should you expect when investing in a Cannabis Business? *Green Growth CPAs.* https://greengrowthcpas.com

Green Growthcpas. (2019). What ROI should you expect when investing in a Cannabis Business? *Green Growth CPAs.* https://greengrowthcpas.com

James, M., & Kvilhaug, S. (2022). The Elasticity of Demand. *Investopedia* https://www.investopedia.com

James, M., & Kvilhaug, S. (2022). The Elasticity of Demand. *The Investopedia Team.* https://www.investopedia.com

.Lubaale, E.C., & Mavundla, S.D. (2019). Decriminalisation of Cannabis for Personal Use in South Africa. *African Human Rights Law Journal, Journal,* 819–842, . doi:10.17159/1996-2096/2019/v19n2a13

. Lubaale, E.C., & Mavundla, S.D. 2019. Decriminalisation of Cannabis for Personal Use in South Africa. *African Human Rights Law Journal,* 819–842. . doi:10.17159/1996-2096/2019/v19n2a13

Manu, E., Douglas, M., Ntsaba, M. J., & Tarkang, E. E. (2021). Perspectives of llicit Marijuana Growers and Traders on Commercial Legalisation of Marijuana in South Africa: Considerations for Policy Formulation. *Substance Abuse Treatment, Prevention, and Policy, 16*(1), 54. doi:10.118613011-021-00391-w PMID:34174921

Manu, E., Douglas, M., Ntsaba, M. J., & Tarkang, E. E. (2021). Perspectives of llicit Marijuana Growers and Traders on Commercial Legalisation of Marijuana in South Africa: Considerations for Policy Formulation. *Substance Abuse Treatment, Prevention, and Policy, 16*(1), 54. doi:10.118613011-021-00391-w PMID:34174921

Mokwena, K. (2019). *Social and Public Health Implications of the Legalisation of Recreational Cannabis: A Literature Review*. Afri J Prim Health Care Fam Med., doi:10.4102/phcfm.v11i1.2136

Mokwena, K. (2019). Social and Public Health Implications of the Legalisation of Recreational Cannabis: A Literature Review. *African Journal of Primary Health Care & Family Medicine, 16*(1). doi:10.4102/phcfm.v11i1.2136 PMID:31793317

Parry, C. D. H., & Myers, B. J. (2014). Legalising Medical use of Cannabis in South Africa: Is the empirical evidence sufficient to support policy shifts in this direction? *Article in South African Medical Journal, Vol, 104*(6), 399. doi:10.7196/SAMJ.8135 PMID:25214244

Pelley, A. (2021). 3 Hard Truths About Cash Flow in the Cannabis Industry. *JDSUPRA.* https://www.jdsupra.com

Pelley, A. (2021). 3 Hard Truths About Cash Flow in the Cannabis Industry. *JDSupra.* https://www.jdsupra.com

. Peltzer, K., & Ramlagan, S. (2007). Cannabis use Trends in South Africa. *South African Journal of Psychiatry, 13*(4).

Perkel, C. (2005). Cannabis - The debate continues: A South African Perspective. *South African Psychiatry Review*, *8*, 25–30.

Projectcbd.org. (2022). What is CBD? Learn what CBD is and what isn't, the difference between CBD from Cannabis and Hemp, and more. *Project CBD.* https://www.projectcbd.org/about/what-cbd

Projectcbd.org. (2022). What is CBD? Learn what CBD is and what isn't, the difference between CBD from Cannabis and Hemp, and more. *Project CBD.* https://www.projectcbd.org/about/what-cbd

Ramlagan, S., Peltzer, K., & Pengpid, S. (2021). Prevalence and Correlates of non-daily and daily Cannabis use among persons 15 years and older in South Africa: Results of a National Survey in 2017. *Substance Abuse Treatment, Prevention, and Policy*, *16*(1), 25. doi:10.118613011-021-00364-z PMID:33743758

. Ransing, R., de la Rosa, P.A., Pereira-Sanchez, v., Handuleh, J.I.M., Jerotic, S., Gupta, A.K., Karaliuniene, R., de Filippis, R., Peyron, E., Güngör, E.S., Boujraf, S., Yee, A., Vahdani, B., Shoib, S., Stowe, M., Jaguga, F., Dannatt, L., da Silva, A.K., Grandinetti, P., & Jatchavala, P. (2022). Current state of Cannabis use, Policies, and Research across sixteen Countries: Cross-country Comparisons and International Perspectives. *Trends Psychiatry Psychother, 22*(Suppl 1).

Riley, S., Vellios, N., & van Walbeek, C. (2019). *An Economic Analysis of the Demand for Cannabis: Some Results from South Africa, School of Economics, University of Cape Town: South Africa Drugs: Education.* Prevention and Policy., doi:10.1080/09687637.2019.1581139

Royal Queen Seeds. (2022). The History and Current Status of Cannabis in South Africa. *Royal Queen Seeds.* https://www.royalqueenseeds.com/blog

Royal Queen Seeds. (2022). The History and Current Status of Cannabis in South Africa. *Royal Queen Seeds.* https://www.royalqueenseeds.com/blog

Ryan, M. (2018). Member Blog: What Every Cannabis Needs to Know About Their Finance Function. *The Cannabis Industry.* https://thecannabisindustry.org/tag/cash-flow/

Sihna, J. (2001). The History and Development of the Leading International Drug Control Conventions, Prepared for the Senate Special Committee on Legal Drugs, Law and Government Division, Library of Parliament.

Smit, & Van Wyk, (2021). Legalisation of Private Use of Cannabis in South Africa. www.mondaq.com

Smit, & Van Wyk. (2021). Legalisation of Private Use of Cannabis in South Africa. *MONDAQ.* www.mondaq.com

Statistics South Africa. 2022. South Africa's Youth continues to bear the Burden of Unemployment. *SSA.* https://www.statssa.gov.za/

Statistics South Africa. (2022). South Africa's Youth continues to bear the Burden of Unemployment. *SSA*. https://www.statssa.gov.za/

Stephen, K. 2022. Business is starting to trump morality in Arica's Cannabis Industry. *Quartz*. https://qz.com/africa/

Stephen, K. 2022. Business is starting to trump morality in Arica's Cannabis Industry. *Quartz*. https://qz.com/africa/

van Rensburg, R., Pillay-Fuentes Lorente, V., Blockman, M., Moodley, K., Wilmshurst, J. M., & Decloedt, E. H. (2020). Medical Cannabis: What practitioners need to know. The South African Medical Journal, 110(3).

van Rensburg, R., Pillay-Fuentes Lorente, V., Blockman, M., Moodley, K., Wilmshurst, J. M., & Decloedt, E. H. (2020). Medical Cannabis: What practitioners need to know, The South African Medical Journal, 110(3). Distributed under Creative Commons Licence CC-BY-NC 4.0.

Weihraunch, R. 2021. Criminalising Cannabis in South Africa: A History and Post-Prince Discussion, University of Cape Town, OpenUCT, Theses/Dissertation Masters - http://hdl.handle.net/11427/33974

Weihraunch, R. (2021*). Criminalising Cannabis in South Africa: A History and Post-Prince Discussion.* [Theses/Dissertation, University of Cape Town, South Africa]. http://hdl.handle.net/11427/33974

Weisskopf, J. 2022. Investing in Cannabis: Is the Grass Greener for Investors? https://hospitalityinsights.ehl.edu/investing-in-cannabis

Weisskopf, J. (2022). Investing in Cannabis: Is the Grass Greener for Investors? *Hospitality Insights*. https://hospitalityinsights.ehl.edu/investing-in-cannabis

.WesGro. (2019). *Investing in Cannabis in South Africa: An Inspiring Place to do Business*. WesGro, CCTISSK.

Compilation of References

. Peltzer, K., & Ramlagan, S. (2007). Cannabis use Trends in South Africa. *South African Journal of Psychiatry, 13*(4).

. Ransing, R., de la Rosa, P.A., Pereira-Sanchez, v., Handuleh, J.I.M., Jerotic, S., Gupta, A.K., Karaliuniene, R., de Filippis, R., Peyron, E., Güngör, E.S., Boujraf, S., Yee, A., Vahdani, B., Shoib, S., Stowe, M., Jaguga, F., Dannatt, L., da Silva, A.K., Grandinetti, P., & Jatchavala, P. (2022). Current state of Cannabis use, Policies, and Research across sixteen Countries: Cross-country Comparisons and International Perspectives. *Trends Psychiatry Psychother, 22*(Suppl 1).

.WesGro. (2019). *Investing in Cannabis in South Africa: An Inspiring Place to do Business*. WesGro, CCTISSK.

Abara, E. (2021, February 7). *Africa's cannabis industry could potentially grow beyond $7 billion valuation by 2023 as opportunities abound.* https://africa.businessinsider.com/local/markets/africas-cannabis-industry-could-potentially-grow-beyond-dollar7-billion-valuation-by/evlxmqz

Abbott, B. A., & Zack, J. B. (2018). Current banking issues in the cannabis industry. *CONSUMER FIN. LQ REP, 72*, 390–396.

Abdekalimi, D. (2019). One CPA's Journey from Auditor to Consultant and Fintech Entrepreneur. *The CPA Journal, 89*(10), 11–11.

Abdullahi, A. A. (2011). Trends and challenges of traditional medicine in Africa. *African Journal of Traditional, Complementary, and Alternative Medicines, 8*(5S). doi:10.4314/ajtcam.v8i5S.5 PMID:22754064

Abrams, D. I. (2018). The therapeutic effects of Cannabis and cannabinoids: An update from the National Academies of Sciences, Engineering and Medicine report. *European Journal of Internal Medicine, 49*, 7–11. doi:10.1016/j.ejim.2018.01.003 PMID:29325791

ACCORD. (2021, December 10). The July 2021 Protests and Socio-political Unrest in South Africa. *ACCORD*. https://www.accord.org.za/conflict-trends/the-july-2021-protests-and-socio-political-unrest-in-south-africa/

Acharya, H. J. 2005. Medicine and the recent history of marijuana. *History of medicine days,* 157.

ACO Obstetricians and Gynecologists (2017). Marijuana use during pregnancy and lactation. *ACOG Committee Opinion.*

Adebisi, Y. A., & Olaoye, D. Q. (2022). Medical Use of Cannabis in Africa: The Pharmacists' Perspective. *Innovations in Pharmacy, 13*(1), 8. doi:10.24926/iip.v13i1.4430 PMID:36304681

Adinoff, B., & Reiman, A. (2019). Implementing social justice in the transition from illicit to legal cannabis. *The American Journal of Drug and Alcohol Abuse, 45*(6), 673–688. doi:10.1080/00952990.2019.1674862 PMID:31634005

African News Agency. (2020, February 24). *Tito Mboweni called on to prevent downgrade to junk status, tackle unemployment.* IOL: https://www.iol.co.za/news/politics/tito-mboweni-called-on-to-prevent-downgrade-to-junk-status-tackle-unemployment-43386 368

Agenda.GE. (2016). Norms envisaging imprisonment for marijuana use now null and void in Georgia. *Agenda.Ge*. https://agenda.ge/en/news/2016/3159

AgriColleges International. (2022, August 24). National Certificate in Plant Production – Cannabis & Hemp. *Agricolleges*. https://agricolleges.com/national-certificate-in-plant-production-cannabis-hemp/

Aguilar, S., Gutiérrez, V., Sánchez, L. & Nougier, M. 2018. Medicinal cannabis policies and practices around the world. *Int Drug Policy Consort. Briefing paper*, 1-32.

Aguilar, S., Gutiérrez, V., Sánchez, L. and Nougier, M. (2018*) Medicinal cannabis policies and practices around the world* (Briefing Paper). International Drug Policy Consortium.

Aguirre-Villegas, H. A., & Larson, R. A. (2017). Evaluating greenhouse gas emissions from dairy manure management practices using survey data and lifecycle tools. *Journal of Cleaner Production*, *143*, 169–179.

Ahern, J., Stuber, J., & Galea, S. (2007). Stigma, discrimination and the health of illicit drug users. *Drug and Alcohol Dependence*, *88*(2-3), 188–196. doi:10.1016/j.drugalcdep.2006.10.014 PMID:17118578

Aizpurua-Olaizola, O., Omar, J., Navarro, P., Olivares, M., Etxebarria, N., & Usobiaga, A. (2014). Identification and quantification of cannabinoids in Cannabis sativa L. plants by high-performance liquid chromatography-mass spectrometry. *Analytical and Bioanalytical Chemistry*, *406*(29), 7549–7560. doi:10.100700216-014-8177-x PMID:25338935

Akyeampong, E. (2005). Diaspora and drug trafficking in West Africa: A case study of Ghana. *African Affairs*, *104*(416), 429–447. doi:10.1093/afraf/adi015

Alberts, R., Khalala, G., & Molefe, O. (2011). Collecting structured indigenous knowledge for enhanced exploration: The National Recordal System (NRS), South Africa. *Knowledge Management for Development Journal*, *7*(3), 291–307. doi:10.1080/19474199.2011.649009

Albright, V. A., & Johnson, E. O. (2018). Emerging Topics and Innovative Methodologies in Cannabis Research. *Substance Abuse: Research and Treatment*, *12*, 117822181877426. doi:10.1177/1178221818774264 PMID:29795983

Ali, S., Durrani, H., Naeem, M., Riaz, W., & Shahid, S. (2016). Supporting Pakistani farmers through digital means: An exploratory study. *In Proceedings of the 2016 CHI Conference Extended Abstracts on Human Factors in Computing Systems*. CHI.

Alicia, E., & Reid Micah, E. S., Vikiana, R., JoAnn, D., & Evers, R, M. (2022). Introducing cannabis education on a college Campus in 2021 The case of Medgar Evers College. College, New York, U.S. [IJHEM]. *International Journal of Higher Education Management*, *8*(2).

Ali, M., Tao, L., Shaikh, A. A., & Sajid, M. (2017). The political leadership and corporate governance: An analysis of leadership theories and its influence. *International Journal of Basic and Applied Sciences*, *6*(3), 45–50. doi:10.14419/ijbas.v6i3.7706

Almqvist, I. (2020). *Medicine of the Imagination: Dwelling in Possibility: An Impassioned Plea for Fearless Imagination*. John Hunt Publishing.

Amsden, A. (1989). *Asia's Next Giant: South Korea and Late Industrialization*. Oxford University Press.

ANC-NGC.(2015). Umrhabulo.

Anderson, L. (2022, February 7). *Articles: List of Schedule 1 Drugs.* Drugs.com: https://www.drugs.com/article/csa-schedule-1.html

Anderson, M., & Jiang, J. (2018). ATeens, social media, and technology. *Pew Research Center.* https://www.forbes.com/sites/andrebourque/2019/05/06/under-the-influence-of-instagram-cannabis-in-the-age-of-social-media/?sh=3871ad684746

Andrade, C. (2016). Cannabis and neuropsychiatry, 1: Benefits and risks. *The Journal of Clinical Psychiatry, 77*(5), 2250. doi:10.4088/JCP.16f10841 PMID:27249079

Andrews, N. (2018). Land versus livelihoods: Community perspectives on dispossession and marginalization in Ghana's mining sector. *Resources Policy, 58*, 240–249. doi:10.1016/j.resourpol.2018.05.011

Angulo-Cuentas, G., Ramírez-Vergara, J., & Charris-Polo, M. (2019). Cannabis: Innovation Opportunities for its Medical Use. *Recent Patents on Engineering, 13*(3), 212–223. doi:10.2174/1872212112666181022155150

Anyaoku, E. N., Nwafor-Orizu, O. E., & Eneh, E. A. (2015). Collection and preservation of traditional medical knowledge: Roles for medical libraries in Nigeria. *Journal of Library and Information Science, 3*(1), 33–43. doi:10.15640/jlis.v3n1a2

Anywar, G., Kakudidi, E., Tugume, P., & Asiimwe, S. (2022). The Cannabis/Marijuana (L.) Landscape in Africa: An Overview of its Cultivation and Legal Aspects. *Cannabis/Hemp for Sustainable Agriculture and Materials*, 297-310.

APSA (2019). India Cannabis Industry 2019. *APSA Seed.*

Arowolo, A. L., & Lalude, O. M. (2022). "Their Color is a Diabolic Die," Colonialism and the State of Environmental Justice in Africa. *Society & Sustainability, 4*(2), 1–8. doi:10.38157s.v4i2.418

Arya, S., Ghosh, A., & Kazhungil, F. (2022). Early career psychiatrist's attitude toward medicinal and recreational cannabis legalization in India; findings from an online survey. *Journal of Substance Use*, 1–6. doi:10.1080/14659891.2022.2120424

Asiimwe, S., Tugume, P., Kakudidi, E., & Anywar, G. (2022). Potential Impacts of L. Cultivation on the Environment in Africa: A Review. *Cannabis/Hemp for Sustainable Agriculture and Materials*, 311-325.

Astran, J. (2021, March 17). How Can Blockchain Technology Help The Cannabis Industry? *HealthMed.* https://healthmed.org/how-can-blockchain-technology-help-the-cannabis-industry/

Atakan, Z. (2012). Cannabis, a complex plant: Different compounds and different effects on individuals. *Therapeutic Advances in Psychopharmacology, 2*(6), 241–254. doi:10.1177/2045125312457586 PMID:23983983

Atkins, A., & Catholic Institute for International Relations. (1997). *The illegal drugs trade and development in South Africa: Some observations.* Catholic Institute for International Relations.

Augustine, T.N., Cairns, C.J., Chetty, S., Dannatt, L.G., Gravett, N., Grey, G., Grobler, G., Jafta, Z., Kamerman, P., Lopes, J., Matsabisa, M.G., Mugabo, P., Mulder, M., Parry, C., Rataemane, S., Siegfried, N., Steenkamp, V., Thomas, E., & van Zyl-Smit, R. (2018). Priority areas for cannabis and cannabinoid product research in South Africa. *African Journal of Primary Health Care & Family Medicine.*

Aversa, J., Jacobson, J., Hernandez, T., Cleave, E., Macdonald, M., & Dizonno, S. (2021). The social media response to the rollout of legalized cannabis retail in Ontario, Canada. *Journal of Retailing and Consumer Services*, *61*, 102580. https://doi.org/10.1016/j.jretconser.2021.102580

Ayenigbara, G. (2014). Cannabis sativa: A plant with multiple utilities, misunderstood, and a victim of controversial hypocrisy. *Journal of Emerging Trends in Educational Research and Policy Studies*, *5*, 54–59.

Azarenkova, G., Shkodina, I., Samorodov, B., Babenko, M., & Onishchenko, I. (2018). The influence of financial technologies on the global financial system stability. *Investment Management & Financial Innovations*, *15*(4), 229–238. doi:10.21511/imfi.15(4).2018.19

Azofeifa, A., Mattson, M. E., Schauer, G., McAfee, T., Grant, A., & Lyerla, R. (2016). National estimates of marijuana use and related indicators—National Survey on Drug Use and Health, United States, 2002–2014. *MMWR. Surveillance Summaries*, *65*(11), 1–25. doi:10.15585/mmwr.ss6511a1 PMID:27584586

Bachhuber, M. A., Saloner, B., Cunningham, C. O., & Barry, C. L. (2014). Medical Cannabis laws and opioid analgesic overdose mortality in the United States, 1999-2010. *JAMA Internal Medicine*, *174*(10), 1668–1673. doi:10.1001/jamainternmed.2014.4005 PMID:25154332

Badiola, I., Doshi, A., & Narouze, S. (2022). Cannabis, cannabinoids, and cannabis-based medicines: Future research directions for analgesia. *Regional Anesthesia and Pain Medicine*, *47*(7), 437–444. doi:10.1136/rapm-2021-103109 PMID:35534020

Bakari, S. (2017, August 11). *Why is South Africa Still a Developing Country?* Ideas. https://ideas.repec.org/p/pra/mprapa/80763.html

Bala, A., Rademan, S., Kevin, K. N., Maharaj, V., & Matsabisa, M. G. (2019). UPLC-MS Analysis of Cannabis sativa Using Tetrahydrocannabinol (THC), Cannabidiol (CBD), and Tetrahydrocannabinolic Acid (THCA) as Marker Compounds: Inhibition of Breast Cancer Cell Survival and Progression. *Natural Product Communications, 14*(8), 1934578X1987290. doi:10.1177/1934578X19872907

Balhara, Y. P. S., Mishra, A., Sethi, H., Singh, S., & Khandelwal, S. K. (2016). Time trends of cannabis use among treatment-seeking individuals at government de-addiction centers across India over a period of 7 years. *Indian Journal of Psychological Medicine*, *38*(4), 331–335. doi:10.4103/0253-7176.185961 PMID:27570345

Balhara, Y. P. S., Parmar, A., Modak, T., & Vikram, V. (2020). From "Bhang Shops" to "Cannabis in Coffee Shops": Time to Debate the Option? *Indian Journal of Psychological Medicine*, 0253717620957501. PMID:35656417

Balthazar, C., Joly, D. L., & Filion, M. (2022). Exploiting Beneficial Pseudomonas spp. for Cannabis Production. *Frontiers in Microbiology*, *12*, 833172. doi:10.3389/fmicb.2021.833172 PMID:35095829

Barakabitze, A. A., Kitindi, E. J., Sanga, C., Shabani, A., Philipo, J., & Kibirige, G. (2015). New technologies for disseminating and communicating agriculture knowledge and information: Challenges for agricultural research institutes in Tanzania. *The Electronic Journal on Information Systems in Developing Countries*, *70*, 1–22.

Barney, J. (1991). Firm resources and sustained competitive advantage. *Journal of Management*, *17*, 99–120.

Bartlett, J. (2021,May 11). Smokescreen. *The Boston Business Journal*. https://www.bizjournals.com/boston/ news/2021/05/11/smokescreen-a-lack-of-transparency-in-the-money-c.html

Bartlome, L. R. (2018). *Insurance for the Marijuana Industry.* Dilworth Paxson. https://www.dilworthlaw.com/blog/insurance-for-the-marijuana-industry-pg-38/

Baudean, M. (Ed.). (2022). *Five Years of Cannabis Regulation What Can We Learn From the Uruguayan Experience?* Routledge.

Baxter, B. (2020). Cannabis Companies Tap Top Lawyers as CEOs Amid Legal Challenges. *Bloomberg Law.* https://news.bloomberglaw.com/business-and-practice/cannabis-companies-tap-top-lawyers-as-ceos-amid-legal-challenges

B-BBEEcomm. (2022). *National Status and Trends on B-BBEE Transformation Report 2021.* Skotaville Press.

BBC Visual Journalism Team. (2022, November 14). Ukraine in maps: Tracking the war with Russia. *BBC News.* https://www.bbc.com/news/world-europe-60506682

Beck, R., Müller-Bloch, C., & King, J. L. (2018). Governance in the blockchain economy: A framework and research agenda. *Journal of the Association for Information Systems, 19*(10), 1020–1034. doi:10.17705/1jais.00518

Behera, B. S., Das, T. K., Jishnu, K. J., Behera, R. A., Behera, A. C., & Jena, S. (2015). E-governance mediated agriculture for sustainable life in India. *Procedia Computer Science, 48*, 623–629.

Belackova, V., Maalsté, N., Zabransky, T., & Grund, J. P. (2015). "Should I Buy or Should I Grow?" How drug policy institutions and drug market transaction costs shape the decision to self-supply with cannabis in the Netherlands and the Czech Republic. *The International Journal on Drug Policy, 26*(3), 296–310. doi:10.1016/j.drugpo.2014.12.002 PMID:25655217

Benelli, G., Pavela, R., Petrelli, R., Cappellacci, L., Santini, G., Fiorini, D., Sut, S., Dall'Acqua, S., Canale, A., & Maggi, F. (2018). The essential oil from industrial hemp (Cannabis sativa L.) by-products as an effective tool for insect pest management in organic crops. *Industrial Crops and Products, 122*, 308–315. doi:10.1016/j.indcrop.2018.05.032

Bengtsson, M. (2016). How to plan and perform a qualitative study using content analysis. *Nursing Plus Open, 2*, 8–14. doi:10.1016/j.npls.2016.01.001

Bennett, E. A. (2018). Extending ethical consumerism theory to semi-legal sectors: Insights from recreational cannabis. *Agriculture and Human Values, 35*(2), 295–317. doi:10.100710460-017-9822-8

Bennett, E. A. (2019, April 14). Passing on pot: When environmental organizations disengage from political consumerism in highly stigmatized sectors. *Environmental Politics*, 1–28. doi:10.1080/09644016.2019.1654237

Ben-Zeev, B. (2020). Medical cannabis for intractable epilepsy in childhood: A review. *Rambam Maimonides Medical Journal, 11*(1), e0004. doi:10.5041/RMMJ.10387 PMID:32017679

Berg, C. J. (2018). The Emerging Marijuana Retail Environment: Key Lessons Learned from Tobacco and Alcohol Retail Research. *Addictive Behaviors, 81,* 26-31.

Bernstein, A. (2022, February 7). Ramaphosa's economic reconstruction and recovery plan is a mess – time to throw the baby out with the bathwater. *Daily Maverick.* https://www.dailymaverick.co.za/article/2022-02-07-ramaphosas-economic-reconstruction-and-recovery-plan-is-a-mess-time-to-throw-the-baby-out-with-the-bathwater/

Bernstein, M. (2002). 10 tips on writing the living Web. *A List Apart: For People Who Make Websites, 149.* http://www.alistapart.com/articles/writeliving

Bernstein, H. (1999). Ghana's drug economy: Some preliminary data. *Review of African Political Economy*, *26*(79), 13–32. doi:10.1080/03056249908704358

Bester, P. C., & Els, S. (2021). The legalisation of cannabis: A security-vetting dilemma. *Scientia Militaria: South African Journal of Military Studies*, *49*(2), 1–28.

Bester, P., & Els, S. (2021). The legalisation of cannabis: A security-vetting dilemma, Stellenbosch University, Scientia Militaria. *South African Journal of Military Studies*, *49*(2). doi:10.5787/49-2-1334

Bester, P., & Els, S. (2021). The Legalisation of Cannabis: A security-vetting dilemma. Scientia Militaria. *South African Journal of Military Studies*, *49*(2), 1–28.

Bewley-Taylor, D., & Jelsma, M. (2011). Fifty years of the 1961 Single Convention on Narcotic Drugs: A reinterpretation. *Series on legislative reform of drug policies, 12*, 1-20.

Bhamra, S. K., Desai, A., Imani-Berendjestanki, P., & Horgan, M. (2021). The emerging role of cannabidiol (CBD) products; a survey exploring the public's use and perceptions of CBD. *Phytotherapy Research*, *35*(10), 5734–5740. doi:10.1002/ptr.7232 PMID:34350641

Bhattarai, A. (2021, July 24). Greener pastures: Marijuana jobs are becoming a refuge for retail and restaurant workers. *Washington Post.* https://www.washingtonpost.com/business/2021/07/24/marijuana-dispensaries-jobs/

Bhuda, M. T. (2019). *The role of ethnomathematics in the cultural life of AmaNdebele women at Ekosini village in Mpumalanga Province* [Masters Dissertation, North-West University, South Africa].

Bhuda, M., & Khazamula, E. (2022). Towards finding a cure for COVID-19: The role of African Traditional Medicine as an indicator of development. *African Journal of Development Studies*, *2022*(2, si1), 137–153. doi:10.31920/2634-3649/2022/SIv2a8

Bhuda, M., & Koitsiwe, M. (2022). The Importance of Underpinning Indigenous Research Using African Indigenous Philosophies: Perspectives From Indigenous Scholars. In *Handbook of Research on Protecting and Managing Global Indigenous Knowledge Systems* (pp. 223–248). IGI Global. doi:10.4018/978-1-7998-7492-8.ch013

Bierut, T., Krauss, M., Sowles, S. J., & Cavazos-Rehg, P. A. (2017). Advertising on Weedmaps, a Popular Online Directory. *Prevention Science*, *18*(2), 183–192. doi:10.100711121-016-0702-z PMID:27534665

Biggs, R., Reyers, B., & Scholes, R. J. (2006). A biodiversity intactness score for South Africa: Science policy. *South African Journal of Science*, *102*(7), 277–283.

Bjorgan, Y., & Jimenez, S. (2022, January 1). *Effects of Recreational Marijuana Use in Adolescents.* [Thesis, Bethel University, USA]. Electronic Thesis and Dissertations, 1-64.

Black, B. E. (2020). *Creating a qualified cannabis workforce: How higher education can support cannabis career pathways.* Kansas State University Manhattan.

Boak, A. (2017). Drug Use among Ontario students: Ontario drug use and health survey 1977–2017: Detailed findings from the Ontario Student Drug Use and Health Survey (OSDUHS) *CAMH Research Document Series No.46.*

Bodwitch, H., Polson, M., Biber, E., Hickey, G. M., & Butsic, V. (2021). Why comply? Farmer motivations and barriers in cannabis agriculture. *Journal of Rural Studies*, *86*, 155–170. https://doi.org/10.1016/j.jrurstud.2021.05.006

Boehnke, K. F., Gangopadhyay, S., Clauw, D. J., & Haffajee, R. L. (2019). Qualifying conditions of medical cannabis license holders in the United States. *Health Affairs*, *38*(2), 295–302. doi:10.1377/hlthaff.2018.05266 PMID:30715980

Bogdanovic, V., Mrdjanović, J., & Borišev, I. (2017). A review of the Therapeutic antitumor potential of cannabinoids. *Journal of Alternative and Complementary Medicine (New York, N.Y.), 23*(11), 831–836. doi:10.1089/acm.2017.0016 PMID:28799775

Bond, P. 2000. Elite Transition: from Apartheid to Neoliberalism in South Africa. University of Natal Press.

Bophela, M. J. K., & Khumalo, N. (2022). The economic contribution factors of stokvels in the local economy of EThekwini Municipality. *Technium Social Sciences Journal, 29*(1), 343–352. doi:10.47577/tssj.v29i1.5815

Botha, M. (2004). The new Biodiversity Act: News from the Conservation Unit. *Veld & Flora, 90*(3), 94.

Boudreaux, D. J. (2022, November 11). *Alcohol, Prohibition, and the Revenuers.* Foundation for Economic Education. https://fee.org/articles/alcohol-prohibition-and-the-revenuers/

Bourque, A. (2019). Under The Influence Of Instagram: Cannabis In The Age Of Social Media. *Forbes.* https://www.forbes.com/sites/andrebourque/2019/05/06/under-the-influence-of-instagram-cannabis-in-the-age-of-social-media/

Boyera, S., & Grewal, A. A. (2020). Generic Template for Farmer Profiling. SBC4D.

Bresser Pereira, L. C. (2019). Models of the developmental state. *CEPAL Review.*

Bresser-Pereira, L. (2016). Reflecting on New Developmentalism and Classical Developmentalism. *Review of Keynesian Economics, 4*(3), 331–352. doi:10.4337/roke.2016.03.07

Bridgeman, M. B., & Abazia, D. T. (2017). Medicinal cannabis: History, pharmacology, and implications for the acute care setting. *P&T, 42*(3), 180. PMID:28250701

Brooks, E. (2018). Using the Advocacy Coalition Framework to understand EU pharmaceutical policy. *European Journal of Public Health, 28*(suppl_3), 11–14. doi:10.1093/eurpub/cky153 PMID:30383259

Browne, A. (2018). Power Hungry: The Energy Demands of the Growing Cannabis Industry. *Renewable Energy Law and Policy Review, 8*(4), 7–11. doi:10.4337/relp.2018.03.01

Bryman, A. (2021). *Social research methods* (6th ed.). Oxford University Press.

Budney, A. J., & Borodovsky, J. T. (2017). The potential impact of cannabis legalization on the development of cannabis use disorders. *Preventive Medicine, 104*, 31–36. doi:10.1016/j.ypmed.2017.06.034 PMID:28668544

Bunting, W. C., Garcia, L. R., & Edwards, E. (2013). *The War on Marijuana in Black and White. PSN: Politics of Race.* Topic.

Burchell, J. (2016). *Principles of Criminal Law* (5th ed.). Juta & Co Ltd.

Burdette, A. M., Webb, N. S., Hill, T. D., Haynes, S. H., & Ford, J. A. (2018). Religious involvement and marijuana use for medical and recreational purposes. *Journal of drug issues, 48*(3), 421-434. https://doi/pdf/ doi:10.1177/0022042618770393

Burkhardt, P. (2021, August 26). Govt unveils master plan for R28bn dagga industry. *News 24.* https://www.news24.com/fin24/economy/govt-unveils-master-plan-for-r28bn-dagga-industry-20210826

Burns, M. (2021). Cannabis Investment jumps 82% the second half of 2021, 165% over 2020 levels. *TechCrunch.* https://techcrunch.com

Business insurance. (2022). Liability Insurance. *Business Insurance.* https://businessinsurance.co.za/employer-insurance/liability-insurance/

Business Tech. (2022, April 19). South Africa is looking at legalising medical marijuana – here's how it will work. *Business Tech.* https://businesstech.co.za/news/lifestyle/578102/south-africa-is-looking-at-legalising-medical-marijuana-heres-how-it-will-work/

BusinessTech. (2020, July 3). South Africans are setting up 'cannabis clubs' across the country – are they legal? *Business Tech.* https://businesstech. co.za/news/lifestyle/434401/south-africans-aresetting-up-cannabis-clubs-across-the-countryare-they-legal/

BusinessTech. (2021). New cannabis rules proposed for South Africa – to be introduced within next 2 years. *Business Tech.* https://businesstech.co.za/news/lifestyle/482625/new-cannabis-rules-proposed-for-south-africa-to-be-introduced-within-next-2-years/

Businesstech. (2021, August 26). *South Africa's master plan for cannabis: rules, regulations, and adding it to the school curriculum.* Businesstech. https://businesstech.co.za/news/business/516152/south-africas-master-plan-for-cannabis-rules-regulations-and-adding-it-to-the-school-curriculum/

Businesstech. (2022). South African Cannabis company details expansion plans following R300 Million cash injection, including Europe and US. *BuisnessTech.* https://businesstech.co.za

Butsic, V. (2016, March 18). Cannabis (Cannabis sativa or C. indica) agriculture and the environment: a systematic, spatially-explicit survey and potential impacts. *IOPscience.* https://iopscience.iop.org/article/10.1088/1748-9326/11/4/044023/meta

Butsic, V., Schwab, B., Baumann, M., & Brenner, J. C. (2017). Inside the Emerald Triangle: Modelling the placement and size of cannabis production in Humboldt County, CA USA. *Ecological Economics, 142*, 70–80. doi:10.1016/j.ecolecon.2017.06.013

Calcaterra, S. L., Cunningham, C. O., & Hopfer, C. J. (2020). The void in clinician counseling of cannabis use. *Journal of General Internal Medicine, 35*(6), 1875–1878. doi:10.100711606-019-05612-4 PMID:31898125

Callaway, J. (2004). Hempseed as a Nutritional Resource: An overview. *Euphytica, 140*(1-2), 65–72. https://link.springer.com/content/pdf/10.1007/s10681-004-4811-6.pdf. doi:10.100710681-004-4811-6

Cannabis Big Data. (2021). Integration to BioTrackTHE. Cannabis Big Data. Accesses online at BioTrackTHC - Cannabis. *Big Data.*

Cannabis for Private Purposes Bill B19-2020. (2020). South African Government. https://www.gov.za/documents/cannabis-private-purposes-bill-b19-2020-1-sep-2020-0000

Cannabis Times India, (2020, May 22). Cannabis cultivation legalized in Uttarakhand. *Cannabis times india.*

Carliner, H., Brown, Q. L., Sarvet, A. L., & Hasin, D. S. (2017). Cannabis use, attitudes, and legal status in the US: A review. *Preventive Medicine, 104*, 13–23. doi:10.1016/j.ypmed.2017.07.008 PMID:28705601

Carliner, H., Mauro, P. M., Brown, Q. L., Shmulewitz, D., Rahim-Juwel, R., Sarvet, A. L., & Hasin, D. S. (2017). The widening gender gap in marijuana use prevalence in the US during a period of economic change, 2002–2014. *Drug and Alcohol Dependence*, *170*, 51–58. doi:10.1016/j.drugalcdep.2016.10.042 PMID:27875801

Carnevale, J. T., Kagan, R., Murphy, P. J., & Esrick, J. (2017). A practical framework for regulating for-profit recreational marijuana in US states: Lessons from Colorado and Washington. *The International Journal on Drug Policy*, *42*, 71–85. doi:10.1016/j.drugpo.2017.03.001 PMID:28366598

Cash, M. C., Cunnane, K., Fan, C., & Romero-Sandoval, E. A. (2020). Mapping cannabis potency in medical and recreational programs in the United States. *PLoS One*, *15*(3), e0230167. doi:10.1371/journal.pone.0230167 PMID:32214334

Castro-Granell, V., Garin, N., & Jaen, A. (2021). Prevalence, beliefs and impact of drug-drug Interactions illicit drugs-antiretroviral therapy in people living with HIV in Spain. *PLoS One*, *16*(11), 1–19. doi:10.1371/journal.pone.0260334 PMID:34797882

Caulkins, J. P., & Kilborn, M. L. (2019). Cannabis legalization, regulation, & control: A review of key challenges for local, state, and provincial officials. *The American Journal of Drug and Alcohol Abuse*, *45*(6), 689–697. https://doi.org/10.1080/00952990.2019.1611840

Cavazos-Rehg, P. A., Krauss, M. J., Sowles, S. J., & Bierut, L. J. (2016). Marijuana-related posts on Instagram. *Prevention Science*, *17*(6), 710–720. doi:10.100711121-016-0669-9 PMID:27262456

Chagas, M. H. N., Eckeli, A. L., Zuardi, A. W., Pena-Pereira, M. A., Sobreira-Neto, M. A., Sobreira, E. T., Camilo, M. R., Bergamaschi, M. M., Schenck, C. H., Hallak, J. E. C., Tumas, V., & Crippa, J. A. S. (2014). Cannabidiol Can Improve Complex Sleep-Related Behaviours Associated with Rapid Eye Movement Sleep Behaviour Disorder in Parkinson's Disease Patients: A Case Series. *Journal of Clinical Pharmacy and Therapeutics*, *39*(5), 564–566. doi:10.1111/jcpt.12179 PMID:24845114

Chakravarti, B., Ravi, J., & Ganju, R. (2014). Cannabinoids as therapeutic agents in cancer: Current status and future implications. *Oncotarget*, *5*(15), 5852–5872. doi:10.18632/oncotarget.2233 PMID:25115386

Chang, H.-J. (2015). *Is Industrial Policy Necessary and Feasible in Africa? Industrial policy and economic transformation in Africa*. Columbia University Press.

Chang, J. C., Tarr, J. A., Holland, C. L., De Genna, N. M., Richardson, G. A., Rodriguez, K. L., Sheeder, J., Kraemer, K. L., Day, N. L., Rubio, D., Jarlenski, M., & Arnold, R. M. (2019). Beliefs and attitudes regarding prenatal marijuana use: Perspectives of pregnant women who report use. *Drug and Alcohol Dependence*, *196*, 14–20. doi:10.1016/j.drugalcdep.2018.11.028 PMID:30658220

Chanock, M. (2001). *The making of South African legal culture 1902-1936: Fear, favour and prejudice*. Cambridge University Press. doi:10.1017/CBO9780511495403

Charitos, I. A., Gagliano-Candela, R., Santacroce, L. & Bottalico, L. 2021. The Cannabis spread throughout the continents and its therapeutic use in history. *Endocrine, Metabolic & Immune Disorders-Drug Targets (Formerly Current Drug Targets-Immune, Endocrine & Metabolic Disorders), 21,* 407-417.

Chemerinsky, E., Forman, J., Hopper, A., & Kamin, S. (2015). Cooperative federalism and marijuana regulation. *Ucla L. Rev.*, *62*, 74.

Chen, J. (2020, January 19). Investopedia: Sovereign Credit Rating. *Investopedia*. https://www.investopedia.com/terms/s/sovereign-credit-rating.asp

Childs, J., & Stevens, J. (2021). A cannabis pricing mistake from California to Canada: Government can't tax cannabis optimally. *Applied Economics Letters, 28*(9), 779–783. doi:10.1080/13504851.2020.1781764

Chouvy, P.-A. (2019). Cannabis cultivation in the world: Heritages, trends and challenges. *EchoGéo*, (48). doi:10.4000/echogeo.17591

Chouvy, P.-A., & Macfarlane, J. (2018). Agricultural innovations in Morocco's cannabis industry. *The International Journal on Drug Policy, 58*, 85–91. doi:10.1016/j.drugpo.2018.04.013 PMID:29885594

CHRIS. (2019). A brief agricultural history of cannabis in Africa, from prehistory to canna-colony. *EchoGéo.*

Chummun, B. Z. (2012). *Evaluating business success in the Microinsurance industry of South Africa* [Doctoral dissertation, North-West University, Africa].

Chummun, B., & Ojah, K. (2016). Aggregate savings and financial inclusion: Lessons for developing African economies. *AfricaGrowth Agenda Journal, 13*(3), 4–9.

Chu, Y.-W. (2016). The Asian Developmental State: Ideas and Debates. In Y.-W. Chu (Ed.), *The Asian developmental state: Reexaminations and new departures*. Springer. doi:10.1057/9781137476128_1

Ciolino, L. A., Ranieri, T. L., & Taylor, A. M. (2018a). Commercial cannabis consumer products part 1: GC–MS qualitative analysis of cannabis cannabinoids. *Forensic Science International, 289*, 429–437. doi:10.1016/j.forsciint.2018.05.032 PMID:29954632

Clark, C. (2019, October 14). "People feel betrayed": small-scale dagga growers fear exclusion from legal trade. *GroundUp*. https://www.groundup.org.za/article/people-feel-betrayed-small-scale-dagga-growers-fear-exclusion-legal-trade/

Clarke, R. C., & Merlin, M. D. (2015). Small, Ernest. 2015. Evolution and classification of Cannabis sativa (Marijuana, Hemp) in relation to human utilization. Botanical review 81 (3): 189-294. *Botanical Review, 81*(4), 295–305. doi:10.100712229-015-9158-2

Clark, G., & Clark, G. W. (1999). *Betting on lives: the culture of life insurance in England, 1695-1775*. Manchester University Press.

Clawson, P., & Lee, R. (2016). *The Andean cocaine industry*. Springer.

CNBS. (2019, February 7). Cannabis Technology: The Evolution of an Industry. *CNBS*. https://www.cnbs.org/cannabis-101/cannabis-technology/

Cohen, K., Weizman, A., & Weinstein, A. (2019). Positive and negative effects of cannabis and cannabinoids on health. *Clinical Pharmacology and Therapeutics, 105*(5), 1139–1147. doi:10.1002/cpt.1381 PMID:30703255

Collins, C. J. (2021). Expanding the resource based view model of strategic human resource management. *International Journal of Human Resource Management, 32*, 331–358.

Collins, J. (2020). A brief history of cannabis and the drug conventions. *The American Journal of International Law, 114*, 279–284.

Connor, J. P., Stjepanović, D., Le Foll, B., Hoch, E., Budney, A. J., & Hall, W. D. (2021). Cannabis use and cannabis use disorder. *Nature Reviews. Disease Primers, 7*(1), 16. doi:10.103841572-021-00247-4 PMID:33627670

Consolata, A. (2017). Urban agriculture and the use of ICTS in accessing and disseminating livestock husbandry information in Urban areas of Tanzania. A review of related literature. *Libr. Philos. Pract., 1*, 1–38.

Constitution of the Republic of South Africa. (2018). *Draft White Paper on Science, Technology and Innovation*. Green Gazzette. https://www.greengazette.co.za/notices/constitution-of-the-republic-of-south-africa-1996-department-of-science-and-technology-draft-white-paper-on-science-technology-and-innovation_20180914-GGN-41909-00954

Content, S. (2022, April 12). Catching the Growth of the Cannabis Industry. *Visual Capitalist*. https://www.visualcapitalist.com/sp/catching-the-growth-of-the-cannabis-industry/

Coogan, C. J. (2016). *The South African hemp story: saviour crop or business as usual*. Stellenbosch University.

Coombes, R. (2014). Cannabis Regulation: High Time for Change? *British Medical Journal*, *348*, 1–4. PMID:24850823

Couch, D. (2020). *Left behind: The scale of illegal cannabis use for medicinal intent in the UK*. Centre for Medical Cannabis.

Cova. (2019). *Colorado Medical and Recreational Marijuana Laws and Licensing Procedures*. Cova. https://www.covasoftware.com/us-dispensary-laws/colorado.

Crampton, H. (2015). Dagga: A short history. Johannesburg: Jacana Media (Pty) Ltd.

Crescioli, G., Lombardi, N., Bettiol, A., Menniti-Ippolito, F., Da Cas, R., Parrilli, M., Del Lungo, M., Gallo, E., Mugelli, A., Maggini, V., Firenzuoli, F., & Vannacci, A. (2020). Adverse events following cannabis for medical use in Tuscany: An analysis of the Italian Phytovigilance database. *British Journal of Clinical Pharmacology*, *86*(1), 106–120. doi:10.1111/bcp.14140 PMID:31656045

Creswell, J. W. (2014). *Research Design: Qualitative, Quantitative and Mixed Methods Approaches* (4th ed.). Sage.

Crick, E., Haase, H. J., & Bewley-Taylor, D. (2013). Legally Regulated Cannabis Markets in the US: Implications and Possibilities. Global drug Policy Observatory.

Crini, G., Lichtfouse, E., Chanet, G., & Morin-Crini, N. (2020). Applications of hemp in textiles, paper industry, insulation and building materials, horticulture, animal nutrition, food and beverages, nutraceuticals, cosmetics and hygiene, medicine, agrochemistry, energy production and environment: A review. *Environmental Chemistry Letters*, *18*(5), 1451–1476. doi:10.100710311-020-01029-2

Crosby, A. W. (1965). *America, Russia, hemp, and Napoleon: American trade with Russia and the Baltic,* 1783-1812. Citeseer.

Crowder, M. (2020, June 22). New appellations would celebrate individual terroir of cannabis strains. *San Francisco Chronicle*. https://www.sfchronicle.com/bayarea/article/New-appellations-would-celebrate-individual-15587030.php

Cuthbert, M. (2022). Time has come to ditch vertical industrial policy. *Business Day*.

Cyrenne, P., & Shanahan, M. (2018). Toward a Regulatory Framework for the Legalization of Cannabis. *Canadian Public Policy*, *44*(1), 54–76. doi:10.3138/cpp.2017-026

D'Elia, R. V., Harrison, K., Oyston, P. C., Lukaszewski, R. A., & Clark, G. C. (2013). Targeting the "cytokine storm" for therapeutic benefit. *Clinical and Vaccine Immunology; CVI*, *20*(3), 319–327. doi:10.1128/CVI.00636-12 PMID:23283640

Dada, S., Harker, N., Erasmus, J., Lucas, W., Parry, C. (2022). *South African Community Epidemiology Network on Drug Use (SACENDU): Research Update (Phase 50)*. SACDU.

Dai, Y., Byun, G., & Ding, F. (2019). The Direct and Indirect Impact of Gender Diversity in New Venture Teams on Innovation Performance. *Entrepreneurship Theory and Practice*, *43*, 505–528.

Damsere Derry, J. (2017). *The prevalence of alcohol use among road users and its impact on traffic crash severity in Ghana* (Doctoral dissertation, Queensland University of Technology).

Daniel, L. (2021). Degrees for dagga growers and govt-supplied seeds– inside SA's Cannabis Master Plan. *Business Insider.*

Daniel, L. (2021, August 25). Degrees for dagga growers and govt-supplied seeds – inside SA's Cannabis Master Plan. *Business Insider*. https://www.businessinsider.co.za/south-africa-cannabis-master-plan-for-growers-2021-8

Datta, S., Ramamurthy, P., Anand, U., Singh, S., Singh, A., Dhanjal, D., Dhaka, V., Kumar, S., Kapoor, D., Nandy, S., Kumar, M., Koshy, E. P., Dey, A., Proćków, J., & Singh, J. (2021). Wonder or evil?: Multifaceted health hazards and health benefits of Cannabis sativa and its phytochemicals. *Saudi Journal of Biological Sciences*, *28*(1), 7290–7313. doi:10.1016/j.sjbs.2021.08.036 PMID:34867033

Davids, N. (2021, December 21). Destigmatise SA's multibillion-rand cannabis sector to achieve economic growth. *University of Cape Town News*. https://www.news.uct.ac.za/article/-2021-12-02-destigmatise-sas-multibillion-rand-cannabis-sector-to-achieve-economic-growth

Davids, N. 2021. Destigmatise SA's Multibillion-Rand Cannabis Sector to Achieve Economic Growth. University of Capetown News. *www.*news.uct.ac.za

Davis, S. J., Tzanidis, A., & Saltzman, D. (2018). Medicinal marijuana: Commercialisation and innovation in a complex regulatory environment. *Australasian Biotechnology*, *28*(1), 60–62. https://search.informit.org/doi/10.3316/informit.553969626513007

de Filippi, P., Mannan, M., & Reijers, W. (2020, June 17). Blockchain as a confidence machine: The problem of trust & challenges of governance. *Technology in Society*, *62*, 101284. doi:10.1016/j.techsoc.2020.101284

De Gobbi, M. S. (2022). Exploring decent work in the pharmaceutical industry: job creation in the production of medical cannabis in Lesotho and Zimbabwe. *International Labour Office.* doi:10.54394/isri3535

de Vos, P. (2017). *Dagga judgment: there are less drastic ways to deal with its harmful effects.* Constitutionally Speaking.

De Wee, G., & Asmah-Andoh, K. (2022). Model for Overcoming Policy Analysis Limitation and Implementation Challenges: Integrative Propositional Analysis of South African National Mental Health Policy Framework and Strategic Plan 2013-2020. *International Journal of Public Administration*, *45*(8), 658–674. doi:10.1080/01900692.2021.1878219

De Wet, P. (2019). The South African Dagga Industry could be worth R27 Billion within Four years – but export-quality Cannabis may be a problem. *BuisnessTech.* https://www.businessinsider.co.za

De Wet, P. (2019). The South African Dagga Industry could be worth R27 Billion within Four years – but export-quality Cannabis may be a problem. *Business Insider.* https://www.businessinsider.co.za

Decorte, T. (2015). Cannabis social clubs in Belgium: Organizational strengths and weaknesses, and threats to the model. *The International Journal on Drug Policy*, *26*(2), 122–130. doi:10.1016/j.drugpo.2014.07.016 PMID:25179934

Decorte, T. (2019). *Characteristics of the cannabis market in Belgium. Drugs in Society*. CRC Press.

Decorte, T., Lenton, S., & Wilkins, C. (Eds.). (2020). *Legalizing cannabis: Experiences, lessons and scenarios*. Routledge. doi:10.4324/9780429427794

Decorte, T., & Pardal, M. (2017). *Cannabis social clubs in Europe: prospects and limits. European Drug Policies*. Routledge. doi:10.4324/9781315690384-20

Degenhardt, L., Coffey, C., Carlin, J. B., Swift, W., Moore, E., & Patton, G. C. J. T. B. J. O. P. (2010). Outcomes of occasional cannabis use in adolescence: 10-year follow-up study in Victoria, Australia. The British Journal of Psychiatry, 196, 290-295.

Deloitte (2016). Recreational Marijuana - Insights and opportunities. Deloitte.

Deloitte (2022). *An Industry Makes its Mark: The Economic and Social Impact of Cannabis of Canada's Cannabis Sector*. DeLoitte..

Deloitte. (2020). Nurturing new growth, Canada gets ready for Cannabis 2.0. *Deloitte.* http://www.deloitte.com

Deloitte. (n.d.). Open: A society in transition, an industry ready to bloom 2018 cannabis report. *Deloitte.*

Department For International Development. (1999). *Sustainable livelihoods guidance sheets 1-2*. DFID.

Department of Health. (2022, November 30). SAHPRA - South African Health Products Regulatory Authority. *SAHPRA*. https://www.sahpra.org.za/

Destrebecq, D. (2007). *CANNABIS IN AFRICA; An Overview.* UNODC.

Destrebecq, D. (2007). *Cannibis in Africa; An Overview*. UNODC.

Dhadwal, G., & Kirchhof, M. G. (2018). The risks and benefits of cannabis in the dermatology clinic. *Journal of Cutaneous Medicine and Surgery*, *22*(2), 194–199. doi:10.1177/1203475417738971 PMID:29056081

Diaz, M. (2019). Member Blog: What to Know About Cannabis Business Valuations. *The Cannabis Industry.* https://thecannabisindustry.org/tag/cash-flow/

Diaz, M. 2019. Member Blog: What to Know About Cannabis Business Valuations. *The Cannabis Industry.* https://thecannabisindustry.org/tag/cash-flow/

Dillis, C., Polson, M., Bodwitch, H., Carah, J., Power, M. E., & Sayre, N. F. (Eds.). (2022). *Industrializing Cannabis? Socio-Ecological Implications of Legalization and Regulation in California*. Routledge.

Dippenaar, S. (2017). A joint account – just how legal is marijuana following the High Court ruling? Duperrouzel, J. C., Granja, K., Pacheco-Colón, I., & Gonzalez, R. (2020). Adverse effects of Cannabis use on neurocognitive functioning: A systematic review of meta-analytic studies. *Journal of Dual Diagnosis*, *16*(1), 43–57. PMID:28129086

Disa. (2020). *Map of Marijuana Legality by State.* https://bit.ly/3aM3CPu

Djordjevic, N. (2021). 36 worrisome Global obesity Statistics & Facts for 2022. *MedAlertHelp.*

Donnan, J., Shogan, O., Bishop, L., Swab, M., & Najafizada, M. (2022). Characteristics that influence purchase choice for cannabis products: a systematic review. *Journal of cannabis research, 4*(1), 1-27. https:// doi:10.1186/s42238-022-00117-0

Dorfleitner, G., & Braun, D. (2019). Fintech, digitalization and blockchain: possible applications for green finance. In *The rise of green finance in Europe* (pp. 207–237). Palgrave Macmillan. doi:10.1007/978-3-030-22510-0_9

Dostal, H. (2021). *An Examination of Barriers that Retailers Face to Enter the Legal Cannabis Markets in California*. Northeastern University. doi:10.17760/D20412871

Drozd, M., Marzęda, P., Czarnota, J., Dobrzyński, M., Skubel, T., Dudek, I., & Rybak, N. (2022). The potential of cannabinoids in the treatment of lung cancer. *Journal of Education, Health and Sport, 12*(8), 1100–1110. doi:10.12775/JEHS.2022.12.08.094

Dubey, V. (2019). Fin-Tech innovations in digital banking. [IJERT]. *International Journal of Engineering Research & Technology (Ahmedabad), 8*(10), 597–601

Dufton, E. (2017). *Grassroots*. Basic Books.

Dunne, D. (2018). Implementing design thinking in organizations: An exploratory study. *Journal of Organization Design, 7*(1), 1–16. doi:10.118641469-018-0040-7

Duvall, C. S. (2017). Cannabis and tobacco in precolonial and colonial Africa. In Oxford Research Encyclopedia of African History. doi:10.1093/acrefore/9780190277734.013.44

Duvall, C. S. (2019). A brief agricultural history of cannabis in Africa, from prehistory to cannacolony. *EchoGéo*. http://journals.openedition.org/ echogeo/17599

Duvall, C. S. (2019, July 13). A brief agricultural history of cannabis in Africa, from prehistory to canna-colony. EchoGéo. doi:10.4000/echogeo.17599

Duvall, C. S. (2016). Drug laws, bioprospecting and the agricultural heritage of Cannabis in Africa. *Space and Polity, 20*(1), 10–25. doi:10.1080/13562576.2016.1138674

Duvall, C. S. (2019a). *The African roots of marijuana*. Duke University Press.

Duvenage, A. (2021, November 26). The outlook for 2022. *Finweek*: https://ukzn.idm.oclc.org/login?url=https://search.ebscohost.com/login.aspx?direct=true&db=bth&AN=153857239&site=ehost-live&scope=site

Easton, S. T. (Ed.). (2019). *The Legalization of Marijuana and the Remembrance of Things Past*. McGill-Queen's Press-MQUP.

Ede, C. I., & Jili, N. (2021). Microscopic Examination of the New South African Economic Reconstruction and Post-Pandemic Recovery Plan. *Journal of Political Science and International Relations, 4*(2), 56–65. doi:10.11648/j.jpsir.20210402.15

Ellis, S. (2009). West Africa's international drug trade. *African Affairs, 108*(431), 171–196. doi:10.1093/afraf/adp017

Emmanuel, M., Mbuyiselo, D., Mohlomi, J. N., & Enowbeyang Tarkang, E. (2021). *The perspective of illicit marijuana growers and traders on commercial legislation in South Africa: considerations for policy formulation*. Substance Abuse Treatment, Prevention, and Policy. BMC.

Emmett, D., & Nice, G. (2009). *What You Need to Know About Cannabis*. Jessica Kingsley Publishers.

Erickson, D. (2021). How Will CBD Manufacturers Drive Sector Growth in 2022? *Aptean*. https://www.aptean.com/en-EU/insights/blog/cannabis-manufacturers-drive-growth-2022

Ethiopia, G. (2019). Illegal cannabis cultivation in the world. EchoGéo.

European Monitoring Centre for Drugs and Drug Addiction. (2018). *Cannabis Legislation in Europe: An Overview*. Publications Office of the European Union.

Evans, P. (1992). The State as Problem and Solution: Embedded Autonomy, and Structural Change. In S. Haggard & R. Kaufman (Eds.), *The Politics of Structural Adjustment: International Constraints, Distributive Conflicts and the State*. Princeton University Press. doi:10.1515/9780691188034-007

Eyewitness news. (2022). Taking SA higher: Ramaphosa's plans for the cannabis industry. *EyeWitness news*. https://ewn.co.za/2022/02/10/taking-sa-higher-ramaphosa-s-plans-for-the-cannabis-industry.

Faku, D. (2021, August 22). *Regulatory certainty needed for dope exports to gain momentum*. IOL. https://www.iol.co.za/business-report/companies/regulatory-certainty-needed-for-dope-exports-to-gain-momentum-dcca7629-4273-47a5-a565-3c4d0d1b252f

Fang, K., Heijungs, R., Duan, Z., & De Snoo, G. R. (2015). The environmental sustainability of nations: Benchmarking the carbon, water and land footprints against allocated planetary boundaries. *Sustainability*, *7*(8), 11285–11305. doi:10.3390u70811285

FAO. (2010). *Linking People, Places and Products, A guide for promoting quality linked to geographical origin and sustainable geographical indications*. Food and Agriculture Organization (FAO). https://www.fao.org/3/i1760e/i1760e.pdf

FAO. (2021, November 7). *KARLO Launches 14 Mobile Apps to Transform Agriculture|E-Agriculture*. FAO. https://www.fao.org/eagriculture/news/karlo-launches-14-mobile-apps-transform-agriculture

Farag, R. (n.d.). Provincial Cannabis Legislation, Regulation, and Licensing: Its Effectiveness and Impacts on Municipalities in Ontario. *Scholarship at UWindsor*. https://scholar.uwindsor.ca/major-papers/211/

Farinon, B., Molinari, R., Costantini, L., & Merendino, N. (2020). The Seed of Industrial Hemp (Cannabis sativa L.): Nutritional Quality and Potential Functionality for Human Health and Nutrition. *Nutrients*, *12*(7), 1935. doi:10.3390/nu12071935 PMID:32610691

Farisani, T. R. (2022). The impact of social and institutional networks in sustaining South African rural small, medium and micro enterprises during the crisis. *Acta Commercii*, *22*(1), a1007. doi:10.4102/ac.v22i1.1007

Farmer, C., Monfort, S., & Woods, A. (2022). Changes in Traffic Crash Rates After Legalization of Marijuana: Results by Crash Severity. *Journal of Studies on Alcohol and Drugs*, *83*(4), 494–501. doi:10.15288/jsad.2022.83.494 PMID:35838426

Fazi, A. M. (2021). *A Contextual Study of Regulatory Framework for Blockchain. Regulatory Aspects of Artificial Intelligence on Blockchain*. IGI Global. doi:10.4018/978-1-7998-7927-5.ch003

Fedderke, J. W. (2021, July 29). *Identifying Steady-State Growth and Inflation in the South African Economy, 1960-2020*. South African Reserve Bank. https://www.resbank.co.za/en/home/publications/publication-detail-pages/working-papers/2021/IdentifyingSteadyStateGrowthandInflationintheSouthAfricanEconomy1960-2020

Federal Drug Administration. (2021). *FDA Role in Regulation of Cannabis Products*. FDA. https://www.fda.gov/media/128156/download

Federal Trade Commission. (2018). *Federal Trade Commission Smokeless Tobacco Report for 2016*. Federal Trade Commission. https://www.ftc.gov/system/files/documents/reports/federal-trade-commission-cigarette-report-2016-federal-trade-commission-smokeless-tobacco-report/ftc_smokeless_tobacco_report_for_2016_0.pdf

Felix, J. (2022, April 17). In just five years, SA has borrowed R1.8 trillion from investors - Enoch Godongwana. *News 24.* https://www.news24.com/news24/southafrica/news/in-just-five-years-sa-has-borrowed-r18-trillion-from-investors-enoch-godongwana-20220417

Felnhofer, A., Kothgassner, O. D., Stoll, A., & Klier, C. (2021). Knowledge about and attitudes towards medical cannabis among Austrian university students. *Complementary Therapies in Medicine*, *58*, 102700. https://doi.org/10.1016/j.ctim.2021.102700

Ferrara, M. S. (2021). Peak-experience and the entheogenic use of cannabis in world religions. *Journal of Psychedelic Studies*, *4*(3), 179–191. https://doi.org/10.1556/2054.2020.00122

Fersko, J. (2018, May). The business of marijuana. *ACREL News & Notes*. https://cdn.ymaws.com/acrel.site-ym. com/resource/resmgr/news_and_notes/May/2018-05_Fersko_-_Cannabis_Ar.pdf

Finncann™ (2022). Fintech Solutions and Cannabis Banking: what works and what doesn't?. *Fintech Solutions and Cannabis Banking Opportunities.*

Firth, C. L., Warren, K. M., Perez, L., Kilmer, B., Shih, R. A., Tucker, J. S., D'Amico, E. J., & Pedersen, E. R. (2022). Licensed and unlicensed cannabis outlets in Los Angeles County: The potential implications of location for social equity. *Journal of Cannabis Research*, *4*(1), 1–7. doi:10.118642238-022-00120-5 PMID:35410443

Fischer, B., Daldegan-Bueno, D., & Boden, J. M. (2020). Facing the option for the legalisation of cannabis use and supply in New Zealand: An overview of relevant evidence, concepts and considerations. *Drug and Alcohol Review*, *39*(5), 555–567. doi:10.1111/dar.13087 PMID:32436274

Fishera, E., Moorec, R. A., & Fogartyd, A. E. (2020). Cannabinoids, cannabis, and cannabis-based medicine for pain management: A systematicreview of randomised controlled trials. *International Association for the Study of Pain*, *00*(00), 1–22. doi:10.1097/j.pain.0000000000001929

Fokazi, S. (2015). *Marijuana risks adding to social woes.* The Eastern Star.

Foley, K. E. (2022, July 21). Drug wholesalers shipped 9 million pain pills over two years to a single West Virginia pharmacy. *Quartz.* https://qz.com/866771/drug-wholesalers-shipped-9-million-opioid-painkillers-over-two-years-to-a-single-west-virginia-pha
rmacy

Folina, A., Roussis, I., Kouneli, V., Kakabouki, I., Karidogianni, S., & Bilalis, D. (2019). Opportunities for cultivation of medical cannabis (Cannabis sativa L.) in Greece. *Scientific Papers.* Series A. *Agronomy (Basel)*, *LXII*(1), 293–300.

Francis, S. K. 1996. Hemp (Cannabis sativa L.) as an Alternative Fibre Source. Taylor and Francis Online.

Freeman, T. P., Groshkova, T., Cunningham, A., Sedefov, R., Griffiths, P., & Lynskey, M. T. (2019). Increasing potency and price of cannabis in Europe, 2006–16. *Addiction (Abingdon, England)*, *114*(6), 1015–1023. doi:10.1111/add.14525 PMID:30597667

Freeman, T. P., Hindocha, C., Green, S. F., & Bloomfield, M. A. P. (2019). Medicinal use of cannabis based products and cannabinoids. *BMJ (Clinical Research Ed.)*, *1141*, 11141. doi:10.1136/bmj.l1141 PMID:30948383

Freeman, T. P., & Lorenzetti, V. (2019). 'Standard THC units': A proposal to standardize dose across all cannabis products and methods of administration. *Addiction (Abingdon, England)*, *115*(7), 1207–1216. doi:10.1111/add.14842 PMID:31606008

Friedman, D., & Sirven, J. I. (2017). Historical perspective on the medical use of cannabis for epilepsy: Ancient times to the 1980s. *Epilepsy & Behavior*, *70*, 298–301. doi:10.1016/j.yebeh.2016.11.033 PMID:28089286

Ganjier. (2021). Become a master of cannabis service: Cannabis sommelier certification. *Ganjier.* https://www.ganjier.com/ certified-ganjier-cannabis/

German, L. A., Bonanno, A. M., Foster, L. C., & Cotula, L. (2020, May 8). Inclusive business" in agriculture: Evidence from the evolution of agricultural value chains. *World Development*, *134*, 2. doi:10.1016/j.worlddev.2020.105018

Gerra, G., Zaimovic, A., Gerra, M. L., Ciccocioppo, R., Cippitelli, A., Serpelloni, G. & Somaini, L. J. R. P. O. C. D. D. (2010). Pharmacology and toxicology of Cannabis derivatives and endocannabinoid agonists, *5*, 46-52.

Gerwel, H. (2018). Institutional innovation and pro-poor agricultural growth: cannabis cultivation in the Eastern Cape province of South Africa as fertile opportunity.

Gerwel, H. (2018). Institutional innovation and pro-poor agricultural growth: cannabis cultivation in the Eastern Cape province of South Africa as fertile opportunity. In *Crop Production/Industries.* https://ageconsearch.umn.edu/record/284784?ln=en

Gerwel, H. (2018). *Institutional innovation and pro-poor agricultural growth: cannabis cultivation in the Eastern Cape province of South Africa as fertile opportunity.* The 56 Annual conference of the agriculture Economics Association of South Africa. Stellenbosch University, South Africa.

Gieringer, D. (1999). The forgotten origins of cannabis prohibition in California. *Contemporary Drug Problems, 26*(2), 237–288. doi:10.1177/009145099902600204

Gilpin, E., White, M., Messer, K., & Pierce, J. (2007). Receptivity to Tobacco Advertising and Promotions Among Young Adolescents as a Predictor of Established Smoking in Young Adulthood. *American Journal of Public Health*, *97*(8), 1489–1495. doi:10.2105/AJPH.2005.070359 PMID:17600271

Giombi, K. C., Kosa, K. M., Rains, C., & Cates, S. C. (2018). Consumers' Perceptions of Edible Marijuana Products for Recreational Use: Likes, Dislikes, and Reasons for Use. *Substance Use & Misuse*, *53*(4), 541–547. doi:10.1080/10826084.2017.1343353 PMID:28910182

Global Commission on Drug Policy (2019). *Classification of Psychoactive Substances: When Science Was Left Behind.* GCDP.

Globe-Newswire. (2022). *Medical Marijuana Market Worth USD 248.42 Billion by 2030 at 31.97% CAGR - Report by Market Research Future (MRFR).* Globe Newswire.

Gloyer, G. (2018). *Bradt Travel Guides*. Bradt.

GMP. (2010, November 5) Guide to Good Manufacturing Practice (GMP) for Medicines in South Africa. *SAHPRA.* https://www.mccza.com/Publications/Index/1

Goffman, E. (1963). *Stigma: Notes on the Management of a Spoiled Identity*. Penguin Group.

Goga, S., Mondliwa, P., & Roberts, S. (2020). *Economic power and regulation: the political economy of metals, machinery and equipment industries in South Africa. Inequality studies from the Global South*. Routledge. doi:10.4324/9780429282447-7

Golegal, (2020). How the Cannabis laws impact your business*? Industry News and Insight.*

Goodman, S., Wadsworth, E., Leos-Toro, C., & Hammond, D. (2020). Prevalence and forms of cannabis use in legal vs. illegal recreational cannabis markets. *The International Journal on Drug Policy*, *76*, 102658. doi:10.1016/j.drugpo.2019.102658 PMID:31927413

Gosch, I. (2019, March 1). *5 Key Innovations Driving the Future of Cannabis*. Visual Capitalist. Available at: https://protect-za.mimecast.com/s/cI_0CNx1WPS9Dv97tmIORy?domain=visualcapitalist.com/

Government Communication and Information System (2015). *Media Briefing on Operation Fiela by Inter-Ministerial Committee on Migration.* GCIS.

Government of South Africa. (2020). *South African Economic Reconstruction and Recovery Plan.* Government of South Africa: https://www.gov.za/sites/default/files/gcis_document/202010/south-african-economic-reconstruction-and-recovery-plan.pdf

Gray, B., Babcock, L., Tobias, L., McCord, M., Herrera, A., & Cadavid, R. (2018). *Digital Farmer Profiles: Reimagining Smallholder Agriculture.* USAID.

Green Growthcpas. (2019). What ROI should you expect when investing in a Cannabis Business? *Green Growth CPAs.* https://greengrowthcpas.com

Greydanus, D. E., Hawver, E. K., Greydanus, M. M., & Merrick, J. (2013). Marijuana: Current Concepts. *Frontiers in Public Health, 1.* doi:10.3389/fpubh.2013.00042

Griffith, I. L. (2010). *Drugs and security in the Caribbean: Sovereignty under siege.* Penn State Press.

Groce, E. (2018). The health effects of cannabis and cannabinoids: The current state of evidence and recommendations for research. *Journal of Medical Regulation, 104*(4), 32. doi:10.30770/2572-1852-104.4.32

Grotenhermen, F. (2003). Pharmacokinetics and pharmacodynamics of cannabinoids. *Clinical Pharmacokinetics, 42*(4), 327–360. doi:10.2165/00003088-200342040-00003 PMID:12648025

Guba, E. G., & Lincoln, Y. S. (1981). *Effective evaluation: Improving the usefulness of evaluation results through responsive and naturalistic approaches.* Jossey-Bass.

Guba, E. G., & Lincoln, Y. S. (2005). Paradigmatic controversies, contradictions, and emerging confluences. In N. K. Denzin & Y. S. Lincoln (Eds.), *The Sage handbook of qualitative research* (pp. 191–215). Sage.

Gurewitz, H., Petrillo, M. A., Scott, T., McDonald, B., Weir, A., & Pickman, H. (2019). *Mendocino county 2018–2019 economic assessment.* EDFC.

Hacienda, T. (2021). *The 2021 guide to cannabis laws around the world.* Tribute Content Agency.

Hajizadeh, M. (2016). Legalising and Regulating Marijuana in Canada: Review of Potential Economic, Social, and Health Impacts. [Online]. *International Journal of Health Policy and Management, 5*(8), 453–456. doi:10.15171/ijhpm.2016.63 PMID:27694657

Hall, W. (2020). The costs and benefits of cannabis control policies. *National Center for Biotechnology Information.* https://www.ncbi.nlm.nih.gov/pmc/articles/PMC7605025/

Hall, W. (2009). The adverse health effects of cannabis use: What are they, and what are their implications for policy? *The International Journal on Drug Policy, 20*(6), 458–466. doi:10.1016/j.drugpo.2009.02.013 PMID:19362460

Hall, W. (2020). The Costs and Benefits of the Cannabis Control Policies. *Dialogues in Clinical Neuroscience, 22*(3), 281–287. doi:10.31887/DCNS.2020.22.3/whall PMID:33162771

Hall, W., Leung, J., & Lynskey, M. (2020). The effects of Cannabis use on the development of adolescents and young adults. *Annual Review of Developmental Psychology, 2*(1), 461–483. doi:10.1146/annurev-devpsych-040320-084904

Hall, W., & Lynskey, M. (2016). Evaluating the public health impacts of legalizing recreational cannabis use in the United States. *Addiction (Abingdon, England), 111*(10), 1764–1773. doi:10.1111/add.13428 PMID:27082374

Hall, W., & Lynskey, M. (2020). Assessing the public health impacts of legalizing recreational cannabis use: The US experience. *World Psychiatry; Official Journal of the World Psychiatric Association (WPA), 19*(2), 179–186. doi:10.1002/wps.20735 PMID:32394566

Hall, W., & Weier, M. (2015). Assessing the public health impacts of legalizing recreational cannabis use in the USA. *Clinical Pharmacology and Therapeutics, 97*(6), 607–615. doi:10.1002/cpt.110 PMID:25777798

Hamill, S. (2017). Strengthening Agricultural Market Access with ICT. In *ICT in Agriculture (Updated Edition): Connecting Smallholders to Knowledge, Networks, and Institutions* (pp. 225–265). The World Bank.

Hammond, D. (2019). Communicating THC levels and 'dose' to consumers: Implications for product labelling and packaging of cannabis products in regulated markets. *The International Journal on Drug Policy, 102509*. doi:10.1016/j.drugpo.2019.07.004 PMID:31351756

Hammond, D., Goodman, S., Wadsworth, E., Freeman, T. P., Kilmer, B., Schauer, G., Pacula, R. L., & Hall, W. (2022). Trends in the use of cannabis products in Canada and the USA, 2018–2020: Findings from the International Cannabis Policy Study. *The International Journal on Drug Policy, 105*, 103716. doi:10.1016/j.drugpo.2022.103716 PMID:35613480

Han, L., Alton, K., Colwill, A. C., Jensen, J. T., McCrimmon, S., & Darney, B. G. (2021). Willingness to use cannabis for gynecological conditions: A national survey. *Journal of Women's Health, 30*(3), 438–444. doi:10.1089/jwh.2020.8491 PMID:33667129

Hannah, A. L., & Mallinson, D. J. (2017). Defiant Innovation: The Adoption of Medical Marijuana Laws in the American States. *Policy Studies Journal: the Journal of the Policy Studies Organization, 46*(2), 402–423. doi:10.1111/psj.12211

Hansen, E. M. Ø. (2020). The role of experience exchange groups in farmers' practice transitions: The case of reduced tillage in Danish conventional farming. *Roskilde Universitets Forskningsportal.* https://forskning.ruc.dk/da/publications/the-role-of-experience-exchange-groups-in-farmers-practice-transi

Harper, P. (2020). Cannabis Bill carries harsh penalties. *Mail & Guardian.* https://mg.co.za/news/2020-08-14-cannabis-bill-carriesharsh-penalties/

Harper, C. (2019). All Is for the Best in the Best of all Possible Worlds, *Vermont. Journal of Environmental Law, 21*(1), 55–89.

Harris, K. N., & Martin, W. (2021). Persistent Inequities in Cannabis Policy. *The Judges' Journal, 60*(1), 9–13.

Hartman, M. (2021). Cannabis overview. *National Conference of State Legislators.* https://www.ncsl.org/research/civil-and-criminal-justice/marijuana-overview.aspx

Hart, S. L. (1995). A natural-resource-based view of the firm. *Academy of Management Review, 20*, 986–1014.

Hasse, G. (2019). Do epistemicídio à apropriação: análise da repartição de benefícios na lei da biodiversidade [Master's Thesis, Porto Alegre, Brazil].

Heide, F. J., Chang, T., Porter, N., Edelson, E., & Walloch, J. C. (2021). Spiritual Benefit from Cannabis. *Journal of Psychoactive Drugs, 54*(2), 149–157. https://doi.org/10.1080/02791072.2021.1941443

HempStreet (2022). Cannabis meets Ayurveda: India's First Research to Retail Venture in the Ayurveda Cannabis Sector. *HempStreet Medicare Private Limited.*

Hendricks, B. O., II. (2020). *Cash Management Strategies in the Marijuana Industries* [Doctoral dissertation, Northcentral University, USA].

Herd, T. (2021). How KeefX Is Fueling The Growth Of The B2B Cannabis Industry. *Forbes*

Hill, J. A. (2022). Bank Access to Federal Reserve Accounts and Payment Systems. *U of Alabama Legal Studies Research Paper Forthcoming.*

Hill, K. P. (2019). Medical use of cannabis in 2019. *Jama Insights*, *322*(10), 974–975. doi:10.1001/jama.2019.11868 PMID:31397842

Hodgson, M. (2021, April 16). Santa Barbara County supervisors spend cannabis tax funds on expansion requests. *Lompoc Record.* https://lompocrecord.com/news/local/govt-and-politics/santa-barbara-county-supervisors-spend-cannabis-tax-funds-on-expansion-requests/article_42d8c7a1-110f-5479-86f7-391e0 a5cbd39.html

Hrustek, L. (2020). Sustainability driven by agriculture through digital transformation. *Sustainability*, *12*, 8596.

Hudak, J. (2020). *Marijuana: A short history.* Brookings Institution Press.

Hunter, M. (2022). *The High Cost of Federal Cannabis Prohibition.* Seton Hall University.

Hunter, J. (2005). The role of information technologies in indigenous knowledge management. *Australian Academic and Research Libraries*, *36*(2), 109–124. doi:10.1080/00048623.2005.10721252

Hurd, Y. L., Michaelides, M., Miller, M. L., & Jutras-Aswad, D. (2014). Trajectory of adolescent cannabis use on addiction vulnerability. *Neuropharmacology*, *76*, 416–424. doi:10.1016/j.neuropharm.2013.07.028 PMID:23954491

Hurley, R. (2018). Cannabis, Cannabis Everywhere: UK to Review Medical Cannabis Policy as Cannada plans Imminent Legalisation for all uses. *British Medical Journal*, *361*, 1–4.

Hutchison, K. E., Bidwell, L. C., Ellingson, J. M., & Bryan, A. D. (2019). Cannabis and health research: Rapid progress requires innovative research designs. *Value in Health*, *22*(11), 1289–1294. doi:10.1016/j.jval.2019.05.005 PMID:31708066

Ince, H., Imamoglu, S. Z., & Karakose, M. A. (2021). Entrepreneurial orientation, social capital, and firm performance: The mediating role of innovation performance. *International Journal of Entrepreneurship and Innovation*, 683199960.

Iszatt-White, M., & Saunders, C. (2017). *Leadership* (2nd ed.). Oxforfd University Press.

James, M., & Kvilhaug, S. (2022). The Elasticity of Demand. *Investopedia* https://www.investopedia.com

James, M., & Kvilhaug, S. (2022). The Elasticity of Demand. *The Investopedia Team.* https://www.investopedia.com

James, S. (2020, February 27). Industrial Hemp Market Size Worth $15.26 Billion by 2027. *Cision PR Newswire.*

Jelsma, M., Blickman, T., Kay, S., Metaal, P., Martínez, N., & Putri, D. (2021). *A Sustainable Future for Cannabis Farmers: 'Alternative Development' Opportunities in the Legal Cannabis Market.* Transnational Institute.

Jin, D., Jin, S. X., & Chen, J. (2019). Cannabis Indoor Growing Conditions, Management Practices, and Post-Harvest Treatment: A Review. *American Journal of Plant Sciences*, *10*(06), 925–946. doi:10.4236/ajps.2019.106067

John, K., & Ross, D. G. (2021). How a firm's value capture affects value creation in its ecosystem. *Academy of Management Review.*

Johnson, C. 1987. *Political institutions and economic performance: the government-led business relationship in Japan South Korea and Taiwan.*

Johnson, C. (1982). *MITI and the Japanes Miracle: The Growth of Industrial Policy, 1925 – 1975*. Stanford University Press. doi:10.1515/9780804765602

Johnson, N. (2019). American weed: A history of cannabis cultivation in the United States. *EchoGéo*, (48). doi:10.4000/echogeo.17650

Johnson, R. (2014). *Hemp as an agricultural commodity*. Library of Congress Washington DC Congressional Research Service.

Johns, T. (2015). Managing a policy experiment: Adopting and implementing recreational marijuana policies in Colorado. *State & Local Government Review*, *47*(3), 193–204. doi:10.1177/0160323X15612149

Johnston, L. D. (2016, January 31). Monitoring the Future National Survey Results on Drug Use, 1975-2015: Overview, Key Findings on Adolescent Drug Use. *Institute for Social Research*. https://eric.ed.gov/?id=ED578539

Jonckie (2019). CNN's Marketplace Africa explores South Africa's cannabis industry. *Insurance Chat*. https://www.insurancechat.co.za/2019-07/cnns-marketplace-africa-explores-south-africas-cannabis-industry/

Jorge-Vázquez, J., Chivite-Cebolla, M. P., & Salinas-Ramos, F. (2021). The digitalization of the European agri-food cooperative sector. Determining factors to embrace information and communication technologies. *Agriculture*, *11*, 514.

Kafeero, S. (2021, July 2). Business is starting to trump morality in Africa's cannabis industry. *Quartz Africa Weekly*. https://qz.com/africa/2028012/africas-cannabis-industry-is-set-to-boom-due-to-legalization/

Kafeero, S. (2022, July 20). Business is starting to trump morality in Africa's cannabis industry. *Quartz*. https://qz.com/africa/2028012/africas-cannabis-industry-is-set-to-boom-due-to-legalization

Kalra, S., Pathak, V., & Jena, B. (2013). Qualitative research. *Perspectives in Clinical Research*, *4*(3), 192. https://doi.org/10.4103/2229-3485.115389

Kalula, A. T. (2011). Cannabis use among young people in Dar es Salaam, Tanzania: A qualitative study. *African Journal of Drug and Alcohol Studies*, *10*(1).

Kane, K. (2020, May 26). Cannabis Legalization Is Key To Economic Recovery, Much Like Ending Alcohol Prohibition Helped Us Out Of The Great Depression. *Forbes*. https://www.forbes.com/sites/kriskrane/2020/05/26/cannabis-legalization-is-key-to-economic-recovery-much-like-ending-alcohol-prohibition-helped-us-out-of-the-great-depression/?sh=20d927353241

Kangethe, J. (2022, January 15). Africa's Cannabis Market to Hit U.S.$7.1 Billion By 2023. *All Africa*. https://allafrica.com/stories/202201150144.html#:~:text=According%20to%20Phobition%20Partners%2C%20a,the%20world's%20most%20cultivated%20drug

Kang, S., & Mcgrady, P. (2020). Support for cannabis tourism: A tale of two states. *Tourism Review International*, *24*(4), 233–250. doi:10.3727/154427220X15990732245691

Karch, A. (2021). Filling a vacuum: Subnational governance amid national government inaction. *State & Local Government Review*, *52*(4), 232–240. doi:10.1177/0160323X21999585

Katherine, W. (2021). *4 Top Marketing Trends Affecting The Cannabis Industry in 2021.* Cannabis Marketing Association. https://thecannabismarketingassociation.com/4-top-marketing-trends-affecting-the-cannabis-industry-in-2021/

Katsidoni, V., Kastellakis, A., & Panagis, G. (2013). Biphasic effects of Δ9-tetrahydrocannabinol on brain stimulation reward and motor activity. *The International Journal of Neuropsychopharmacology*, *16*(10), 2273–2284. doi:10.1017/S1461145713000709 PMID:23830148

Kavousi, P., Giamo, T., Arnold, G., Alliende, M., Huynh, E., Lea, J., Lucine, R., Tillett Miller, A., Webre, A., Yee, A., Champagne-Zamora, A., & Taylor, K. (2022). What do we know about opportunities and challenges for localities from Cannabis legalization? *The Review of Policy Research*, *39*(2), 143–169. doi:10.1111/ropr.12460

Kayange, G. M. (2019). *Cannabis Use and Addiction in African Communities; a Value or a Vice? Addiction in South and East Africa.* Springer.

Kay, S., Jelsma, M., & Bewley-Taylor, D. (2020). Fair Trade cannabis: A road map for meeting the socio-economic needs and interests of small and traditional growers. *Journal of Fair Trade*, *2*(1), 27–34. doi:10.13169/jfairtrade.2.1.0027

Kay, S., Jelsma, M., & Bewley-Taylor, D. (2020, November 12). Fair Trade cannabis: A road map for meeting the socio-economic needs and interests of small and traditional growers. *Journal of Fair Trade*, *2*(1), 27–34. https://cronfa.swansea.ac.uk/Record/ cronfa55853/Download/55853__19169__7b6666c 67e5b47758f48e0f6e9656a0e.pdf

Kedem, S. (2019, July 10). *Africa's budding cannabis market.* African Business. https://african.business/2019/07/trade-investment/africas-budding-cannabis-market/

Kellermanns, F., Walter, J., Crook, T. R., Kemmerer, B., & Narayanan, V. (2016). The resource-based view in entrepreneurship: A content analytical comparison of researchers' and entrepreneurs' views. *Journal of Small Business Management*, *54*, 26–48.

Kemp, G. (Ed.). (2015). *Criminal Law in South Africa.* Oxford University Press, Southern Africa.

Kepe, T. (2003). Cannabis sativa and rural livelihoods in South Africa: Politics of cultivation, trade and value in Pondoland. *Development Southern Africa*, *20*(5), 605–615. doi:10.1080/0376835032000149252

Keul, A., & Eisenhauer, B. (2019). Making the high country: Cannabistourism in Colorado, USA. *Annals of Leisure Research*, *22*(2), 140–160. doi:10.1080/11745398.2018.1435291

Khalid, S., Zaidi, W., & Ahmad, F. (2014). Evaluation of the awareness and perception of professional students in medicine, business and law schools of Karachi, regarding the use of (recreational) cannabis. *JPMA. The Journal of the Pakistan Medical Association*, *64*(9), 1025–1030. PMID:25823182

Khalsa, J. H., Maggirwar, S. B., & Bunt, G. (2021). Cannabis/Cannabinoids for Treating COVID-19 Associated Neuropsychiatric Complications. *Journal of Neuroimmune Pharmacology*, *16*(4), 718–721. https://doi.org/10.1007/s11481-021-10013-8

Khambule, I. B. (2019). *The Role Of Subnational State Institutions In Economic Development: A Case Of Local Economic Development Agencies In Kwazulu-Natal, South Africa.* [Doctoral Studies in Development Studies, University Of Kwazulu-Natal, Africa].

Khumalo, N. (2018). The role of human resource planning in producing well-resourced employees to public. *Problems and Perspectives in Management*, *16*(4), 117–125. doi:10.21511/ppm.16(4).2018.11

Khumalo, N. (2019). Obstacles of human resource planning that affect workers in delivering quality services. *Problems and Perspectives in Management*, *17*(2), 114–123. doi:10.21511/ppm.17(2).2019.08

Khumalo, N. (2020). Human Resources Planning strategies implemented by the service institutions in improving employees' competencies. *Gender & Behaviour*, *18*(3), 15991–15998.

Kilin, V., Pini, V., Kasparian, J., Gros, S., & Wolf, J.-P. (2019). Real-time and spatially resolved assessment of pathogens in crops for site specific pesticide reduction strategies. *BIO Web Conf.* EcoSciences. 10.1051/bioconf/20191501019

Kilmer, C., Kilborn, P., & Warren (2021). Cannabis legalization and social equity: Some opportunities, puzzles, and trade-offs. *Boston University Law Review*, *101*(1003), 1005-1040.

Kilmer, B. (2014). Policy designs for cannabis legalization: Starting with the eight Ps. *The American Journal of Drug and Alcohol Abuse*, *40*(4), 259–261. doi:10.3109/00952990.2014.894047 PMID:24853283

Kim, W. C., & Mauborgne, R. (2015). Red ocean traps. *Harvard Business Review*, *93*, 68–73.

Kings, S. (2014). *The war on dagga sobers up"*. The M&G Online.

Kinyungu, N. M., Gikungi, J., & Davson, A. (2022). Medical Marijuana Efficacy: A Survey. *Open Journal of Anesthesiology*, *12*(03), 91–98. doi:10.4236/ojanes.2022.123008

Kitchen, C., Kabba, J, A., Ssekamatte, T., Nelson, E., Adu-Gyamfi, S., Mamatja, M., Yang, C., Chang J., & Fang, Y. (2022). Perceptions of Cannabis in sub-Saharan Africa: Findings from a general population survey in six African countries with different Cannabis policies. *Research Square*.

Kitchen, C., Kabba, J. A., & Fang, Y. (2022). Status and Impacts of Recreational and Medicinal Cannabis Policies in Africa: A Systematic Review and Thematic Analysis of Published and "Gray" Literature. *Cannabis and Cannabinoid Research*.

Kitchen, C., Kabba, J. A., & Sekamatte, T. (2022). Perceptions of Cannabis in sub-Saharan Africa: Findings from a general population survey in six African countries with different Cannabis policies. Research Square, *1*, 1-14. doi:10.21203/rs.3.rs-1241985/v1

Kitchen, C., Kabba, J. A., & Fang, Y. (2022). Status and Impacts of Recreational and Medicinal Cannabis Policies in Africa: A Systematic Review and Thematic Analysis of Published and "Gray" Literature. *Cannabis and Cannabinoid Research*, *7*(3), 239–261. doi:10.1089/can.2021.0110 PMID:34986005

Kittel, J. (2018). Women in weed: Gender, race, and class in the cannabis industry. *The Arbutus Review*, *9*(1), 32–45. doi:10.18357/tar91201818385

Klein, K. (2017). Entrepreneurship, Identity, and the Transformation of Marketing Systems: Medical Cannabis in California. *Journal of Macromarketing*, *37*(1), 85–86. doi:10.1177/0276146716655848

Kobayashi, L. (2012). *Tracy v. USAA Cas. Ins. Co.* Casetext. https://casetext.com/case/tracy-v-usaa-cas-ins-co

Köksal, Ö., & Tekinerdogan, B. (2019). Architecture design approach for IoT-based farm management information systems. *Precision Agriculture*, *20*, 926–958.

Kokt, D. (2020). *Human Resource Management in the new world of work: meeting the challenges of Industry 4.0*. Van Schaik Publishers.

Kok, Z. (2020). *Cannabis in the workplace*. North West University.

Koltai, H., Poulin, P., & Namdar, D. (2019). Promoting cannabis products to pharmaceutical drugs. *European Journal of Pharmaceutical Sciences*, *132*, 118–120. doi:10.1016/j.ejps.2019.02.027 PMID:30851400

Koutouki, K., & Lofts, K. (2018). Cannabis, reconciliation, and the rights of Indigenous Peoples: Prospects and challenges for cannabis legalization in Canada. *Alberta Law Review*, *56*, 709.

Kovalchuk, O., & Kovalchuk, I. (2020). Cannabinoids as anticancer therapeutic agents. *Cell Cycle (Georgetown, Tex.)*, *19*(9), 961–989. doi:10.1080/15384101.2020.1742952 PMID:32249682

Krause, D., & Pullman, M. (2021). Fighting to survive: How supply chain managers navigate the emerging legal cannabis industry. *The Journal of Supply Chain Management*, *57*(3), 50–71. doi:10.1111/jscm.12238

Kuddus, M., Ginawi, I., & AlHazimi, A. (2013). Cannabis sativa: An ancient wild edible plant of India. *Emirates Journal of Food and Agriculture*, *25*(10), 736. doi:10.9755/ejfa.v25i10.16400

Kuppuram, G. (2021). Decriminalizing Marijuana: The Science and Social Sustainability Behind the use of Marijuana (Cannabis) in India. *Journal of the Association of Researchers*, *26*(2), 11–32.

Kurtulmu¸s, B. E., Katrinli, A., & Warner, B. (2020). International Entrepreneurial Orientation and Performance of SMEs: The Mediating Role of Informal Institutional Framework. *SAGE Open*, *10*, 1–9.

Kuye, J. O. & Ajam, T. (2012). *The South African developmental state debate leadership, governance and a dialogue in public sector finance*. African Consortium of Public Administration.

Kyriazis, N. A. (2021). Investigating the diversifying or hedging nexus of cannabis cryptocurrencies with major digital currencies. *Decisions in Economics and Finance*, *44*(2), 845–861. doi:10.100710203-021-00356-5

Labidi, A., Chouchaine, A., & Mami, A. K. (2017). Control of relative humidity inside an agricultural greenhouse. *18th International Conference on Sciences and Techniques of Automatic Control and Computer Engineering (STA)*, (pp. 109–114) IEEE. 10.1109/STA.2017.8314955

LaChance, J. (2019). We can't just be a county that supports inebriants: Voices of the non-cannabis agricultural community. *California Agriculture*, *73*(3), 169–176. doi:10.3733/ca.2019a0016

Lamers, M. (2019). After decriminalizing cannabis Antigua preps full legislation. *MJ Biz Daily*. https://mjbizdaily.com/after-decriminalizing-cannabis-antigua-preps-full-legalization/.

Laohavanich, M. (2022). *Political economy of cannabis in Thailand*. Chula Medical Journal.

Larkin, P. J. Jr. (2021). Cannabis Capitalism. *Buff. L. Rev.*, *69*, 215.

Law for All. (2021). What You Need to Know About the Legalisation of Dagga in South Africa. *Law for All*.

Lawn, W., Fernandez-Vinson, N., Mokrysz, C., Hogg, G., Lees, R., Trinci, K., Petrilli, K., Borissova, A., Ofori, S., Waters, S., Michór, P., Wall, M. B., Freeman, T. P., & Curran, H. V. (2022). The CannTeen study: Verbal episodic memory, spatial working memory, and response inhibition in adolescent and adult cannabis users and age-matched controls. *Psychopharmacology*, *239*(5), 1629–1641. doi:10.100700213-022-06143-3 PMID:35486121

Layton, R. A. (2015). Formation, Growth, and Adaptive Change in Marketing. *Journal of Macromarketing,* 316. Jenkins, M.C., Kelly, L., Binger, K. & Moreno, M.A. (2021). Cyber-ethnography of cannabis marketing on social media. *Substance Abuse Treatment, Prevention, and Policy*.

Leadbeater, B. J., Ames, M. E., & Linden-Carmichael, A. N. (2019). Age-varying effects of Cannabis use frequency and disorder on symptoms of psychosis, depression and anxiety in adolescents and adults. *Addiction (Abingdon, England)*, *114*(2), 278–293. doi:10.1111/add.14459 PMID:30276906

Lee, J. (2020). Do patents lead to an increase in firm value? Evidence from Korea. *KDI J. Econ. Policy*, *42*, 33–52.

Lee, K., & Yoo, J. (2019). How does open innovation lead competitive advantage? A dynamic capability view perspective. *PLoS One*, *14*, e0223405. PMID:31747414

Leinow, L., & Birnbaum, J. (2017). *CBD: A Patient's Guide to Medicinal Cannabis*. North Atlantic Books.

Leins, C., & Alas, H. (2021, June 30). States where recreational marijuana is legal. *U. S. News and World Report*. https://www.usnews.com/news/best-states/slideshows/where-is-pot-legal

Leos-Toro, C., Rynard, V., & Hammond, D. (2017). Prevalence of problematic cannabis use in Canada [Revue Canadienne de Santé Publique]. *Canadian Journal of Public Health*, *108*(5-6), e516–e522. doi:10.17269/CJPH.108.5955 PMID:29356658

Lesch, E., & Adams, A. R. (2016). Couples living with and around alcohol abuse: A study of a farmworker community in the Cape Winelands, South Africa. *Social Science & Medicine*, *156*, 167–174. doi:10.1016/j.socscimed.2016.03.030 PMID:27043369

Levenson, D. (2016). *Asbestos Cases Illustrate Claims-Made vs. Occurrence Insurance Policies*. Insure Your Company. https://www.insureyourcompany.com/blog/asbestos- cases-illustrate-claims-made-vs-occurrence-insurance-policies/

Lewis, M. (2020, June). *Cannabis in the East Cape*. ECSECC - Eastern Cape Socio Economic Consultative Council. https://www.ecsecc.org/documentrepository/informationcentre/cannabis-in-the-eastern-cape-paper-web_76550.pdf

Lewis, P., Thornhill, A., & Saunders, M. N. K. (2019). *Research Methods for Business Students*. Pearson Education, Limited.

Liebenberg, J., du Toit-Prinsloo, L., Saayman, G., & Steenkamp, V. (2019). Drugged driving in South Africa: An urgent need for review and reform. *SA Crime Quarterly*, (67), 7–18. doi:10.17159/2413-3108/2019/i67a4951

Light, M., Orens, A., Rowberry, J., & Saloga, W. C. (2016). *The Economic Impact of Marijuana Legalization in Colorado*. Market Intelligence.

Lindblom, E. N. (2019). How FDA Could Use Its Existing Authorities to Make State Legalization of Cannabis. *Food and Drug Law Journal*, *74*(2), 191–211.

Liput, D., Hammell, D., Stinchcomb, A., & Nixon, K. (2013). Transdermal delivery of cannabidiol attenuates binge alcohol-induced neurodegeneration in a rodent model of an alcohol use disorder. [Online]. *Pharmacology, Biochemistry, and Behavior*, *111*, 120–127. doi:10.1016/j.pbb.2013.08.013 PMID:24012796

Litile, M., & Khumalo, N. (2021). The impact of service providers in the development of the employees' skills in the Government Institution. *Gender & Behaviour*, *19*(2), 18107–18114.

Liu, J., Li, X., & Wang, S. (2020). What have we learnt from 10 years of Fin-Tech research? a scientometric analysis. *Technological Forecasting and Social Change*, *155*, 120022. doi:10.1016/j.techfore.2020.120022

Lloyd, D. H., & Horn, P. G. (2001). Local economic development in rural Eastern cape towns. *Africa Insight*, *31*(1). doi:10.4314/ai.v31i1.22354

Long, A. (2020, November 17). Colorado's summer cannabis sales thrive despite the collapse of the state's tourism industry. *MJBizDaily*. https://Mjbizdaily.Com/Colorado-Summer-Cannabis-Sales-Thrive-Despite-Tourism-Slowd own/

Lopez, G. (2016, August 11). The federal drug scheduling system, explained. *Vox*. https://www.vox.com/2014/9/25/6842187/drug-schedule-list-marijuana

Lowitt, S. (2020a). Industrial Development Projects. *Trade and Industrial Political Strategies.*

Lowitt, S. (2020b). Industrial Development Projects Industrial Hemp. *Trade and Industrial Political Strategies.*

Lubaale, E., & Mavundla, S. (2019). Decriminalisation of Cannabis for Personal use in South Africa. *African Himan Rights Law Journal*, 819-842.

Lubaale, E. C., & Mavundla, S. D. (2019). Decriminalisation of cannabis for personal use in South Africa. *African Human Rights Law Journal*, *19*(2), 819–842. doi:10.17159/1996-2096/2019/v19n2a13

Luterek, J. (2021). Clearing the cannabis haze 3.0: When is cannabis CBD or hemp legal in South Africa? *South African Food Review*, *48*(4), 16–17.

Mabou Tagne, A., Pacchetti, B., Sodergren, M., Cosentino, M., & Marino, F. (2020). Cannabidiol for viral diseases: Hype or hope? *Cannabis and Cannabinoid Research*, *5*(2), 121–131. doi:10.1089/can.2019.0060 PMID:32656344

Mafolo, K. (2019). *Cannabis can create jobs and grow the economy new report argues* [Online]. Daily Maverick.

Maharaj, Y. . (2021). Is SA's cannabis industry predicted to become 'green gold' or 'fool's gold'? *Biz Community*.https://www.bizcommunity.com/Article/196/744/212607.html

Ma, J., Lyoo, I. K., Renshaw, P. F., & Yurgelun-Todd, D. A. (2022). Effect of cannabinoids on brain metabolites: A review of animal and human studies. *Experimental and Clinical Psychopharmacology*. doi:10.1037/pha0000553 PMID:35201831

Makgetla, N. (2010). *Synthesis Paper*. South Africa. DBSA.

Malapane, O. L., Musakwa, W., Chanza, N., & Radinger-Peer, V. (2022). Bibliometric Analysis and Systematic Review of Indigenous Knowledge from a Comparative African Perspective: 1990–2020. *Land (Basel)*, *11*(8), 1167. doi:10.3390/land11081167

Mallinson, D., & Hannah, A. L. (2020). Policy and political learning: The development of medical cannabis policies in the states. *Publius: The Journal of Federalism*, *50*(3), 344–369. doi: us/pjaa006 doi:10.1093/publi

Mallinson, D. J. (2020). Policy Diffusion Results: A New Database for Systematic Review and Meta-Analysis. *State & Local Government Review*, *52*(1), 18–27. https://doi.org/10.1177/0160323x20965682

Mallinson, D. J., Hannah, A. L., & Cunningham, G. (2020). The consequences of fickle federal policy: Administrative hurdles for state cannabis policies. *State & Local Government Review*, *52*(4), 241–254. doi:10.1177/0160323X20984540

Manning, F. J. (2017, May 18). CTE program preps high school students in the professional world beyond K12. *District Administration.*

Månsson, J., Ekendahl, M., & Karlsson, P. (2021). Clashing Perspectives: Cannabis Users and Swedish Drug Policy. In H. Tham (Ed.), *Retreat or Entrenchment? Drug Policies in the Nordic Countries at a Crossroads* (pp. 267–290). Stockholm University Press. doi:10.16993/bbo.k

Manthey, J. (2019). Cannabis use in Europe: Current trends and public health concerns. *The International Journal on Drug Policy*, *68*, 93–96. doi:10.1016/j.drugpo.2019.03.006 PMID:31030057

Manu, E., Douglas, M., Ntsaba, M. J., & Tarkang, E. E. (2021). Perspectives of illicit marijuana growers and traders on commercial legalisation of marijuana in South Africa: Considerations for policy formulation. *Substance Abuse Treatment, Prevention, and Policy*, *16*(1), 1–13. doi:10.118613011-021-00391-w PMID:34174921

Manu, E., & Ntsaba, M. J. (2016). Perceptions of marijuana use: Chronicles of marijuana smokers from two marijuana-Growing communities in South Africa. *Journal of Advances in Health and Medical Sciences*, *2*(3), 82–91.

Maposa, S. (2021, December 22). The complexities of SA's cannabis policy - more integration needed. News 24. https://www.news24.com/news24/columnists/guestcolumn/opinion-siseko-maposa-the-complexities-of-sas-cannabis-policy-more-integration-needed-20211222

Markets, R. (2022). *Cannabis in Food and Beverage Market Share, Size, Trends, Industry Analysis Report, By Product Type; By Distribution Channel; By End-Use; By Source Type; By Region; Segment Forecast, 2022 - 2030*. Research and Markets.

Martin, A. & Rashidian, N. (2014). A new leaf: The end of cannabis prohibition. *New Press.*

Martinez, A. (2022). Marijuana users offered broad job protections in DC. *Forbes.*

Martinez, D. E., Pflueger, D., & Palermo, T. (2022). Accounting and the territorialization of markets: A field study of the Colorado cannabis market. *Accounting, Organizations and Society*, *102*, 101351. doi:10.1016/j.aos.2022.101351

Martin, J. H., Hall, W., Fitzcharles, M. A., Borgelt, L., & Crippa, J. (2020). Ensuring access to safe, effective, and affordable cannabis-based medicines. *British Journal of Clinical Pharmacology*, *86*(4), 630–634. doi:10.1111/bcp.14242 PMID:32128867

Martiroysan, S. (2017). The Decriminalization of Recreational Cannabis in California: Commercial Cultivation Could Cost Growers an Arm, a Leg, and Their Freedom. *San Joaquin Agricultural Law Review*, *27*(2), 187–208.

Marutlulle, N. K. (2021). A critical analysis of housing inadequacy in South Africa and its ramifications. *Africa's Public Service Delivery and Performance Review*, *9*(1). doi:10.4102/apsdpr.v9i1.372

Masango, C. A. (2020). Indigenous knowledge codification of African traditional medicine: Inhibited by status quo based on secrecy? *Information Development*, *36*(3), 327–338. doi:10.1177/0266666919853007

Matavire, M. (2020, February 2020). *Eastern Cape government approves setting up of a cannabis college.* City Press. https://www.news24.com/citypress/business/eastern-cape-government-approves-setting-up-of-a-cannabis-college-20200207#:~:text=a%20cannabis%20college-,In%20a%20move%20to%20develop%2C%20commercialise%20and%20remove%20stigma%20associated,up%20of%20a%20cannabi

Mavrogiannopoulos, G. N. (2017). *Greenhouses* (4th ed.). Stamoulis Publications

Mazzucato, M. 2015. Building the entrepreneurial state: A new framework for envisioning and evaluating a mission-oriented public sector. *Levy Economics Institute of Bard College Working Paper.*

Mazzucato, M., Qobo, M. & Kattel, R. (2021). *Building state capacities and dynamic capabilities to drive social and economic development: The case of South Africa.* UCL.

Mazzucato, M. (2011). The entrepreneurial state. *Soundings*, *49*(49), 131–142. doi:10.3898/136266211798411183

Mbandlwa, Z., & Dorasamy, N. (2020). The impact of substance abuse in South Africa: a case of informal settlement communities. *Journal of Critical Reviews, 7*(19).

Mcata-Mhlauli, N., Ndukwana, T., Mosehla, S. & Christians, G. (2021 July 12). *Briefing to Portfolio Committee on Justice and Correctional Services on Cannabis for Private Purpose Bill.* Pretoria: Department of Trade, Industry and Competition (DTIC).

McCarthy, J. (2017). Record-High Support for Legalizing Marijuana Use in U.S. *GALLUP.* https://news.gallup.com/poll/221018/record-high-support-legalizing-marijuana.aspx

McKenzie, M., Bossuyt, P., Boutron, I., Hoffmann, T., & Mulrow, C. (2021). The PRISMA 2020 statement: An updated guideline for reporting systematic reviews. *BMJ (Clinical Research Ed.), 372*(7), 1. PMID:33782057

McLeod, S. (2007). Maslow's hierarchy of needs. *Simply psychology, 1*(1-18).

McMahon, P. (2018, July 2). Market Dominance. *McMahon Legal.* https://mcmahonsolicitors.ie/market-dominance

Meadows, W. J. (2019). Cannabis Legalization: Dealing with the Black Market. *Electronic Journal.* doi:10.2139/ssrn.3454635

Medical Innovation Bill. (2014, February 19). Republic of South Africa: Medical Innovation Bill. *Pretoria: Government Gazette No 37349.*

Medicines Control Council (MCC). (2017). *Cultivation of Cannabis and Manufacture of Cannabis-related Pharmaceutical Products for Medicinal and Research Purposes Pretoria.* MCC.

Meehan, B., Rusko, C., & Frank Stephenson, E. (2020). (Pot)heads in beds: The effect of marijuana legalization on hotel occupancy in Colorado and Washington. *The Journal of Regional Analysis & Policy, 50*(1), 46–53.

Melchior, M., Nakamura, A., Bolze, C., Hausfater, F., El Khoury, F., Mary-Krause, M., & Da Silva, M. A. (2019). Does liberalisation of cannabis policy influence levels of use in adolescents and young adults? A systematic review and meta-analysis. *BMJ Open, 9*(7), e025880. doi:10.1136/bmjopen-2018-025880 PMID:31296507

Merelli, A. (8 February 2020). India has the world's biggest cannabis industry that doesn't exist yet. *Quartz.*

Merleaux, A. (2020). Drugs, empire, and US foreign policy. *A Companion to US Foreign Relations: Colonial Era to the Present*, 572-595.

Mia, N. (2020). The problems with Prince: a critical analysis of Minister of Justice and Constitutional Development v Prince. *Constitutional Court Review, 10*(1), 401-424.

Miller, A. (2022). Top-rated Reputable Cannabis Seed Companies that Ship to USA *The Sacramento Bee.* https://www.sacbee.com/news/california/california

Miller, R. J. (2013). The cannabis conundrum. *Proceedings of the National Academy of Sciences of the United States of America, 110*(43), 17165. doi:10.1073/pnas.1317663110 PMID:24151330

Minister of Justice and Correctional Services. (2020) Cannabis for Private Purposes Bill, Republic of South Africa. *Government Gazette No. 43595.*

Minister of Justice and Correctional Services. (2020). Cannabis for Private Purposes Bill, Republic of South Africa. *Government Gazette No. 43595.* https://static.pmg.org.za/B19-2020_ Cannabis_for_Private_Purposes6591.pdf

Misaki, E., Apiola, M., & Gaiani, S. (2016). Technology for small scale farmers in Tanzania: A design science research approach. *The Electronic Journal on Information Systems in Developing Countries*, *74*, 1–15.

Miscione, G., Ziolkowski, R., Zavolokina, L., & Schwabe, G. (2018, March 23). *Tribal governance: The business of blockchain authentication*. Scholar Space. http://hdl.handle.net/10125/50455

Misselhorn, A., & Hendriks, S. (2017). A systematic review of sub-national food insecurity research in South Africa: Missed opportunities for policy insights. *PLoS One*, *12*(8), 1–32. https://journals.plos.org/plosone/article?id=10.1371/journal.pone.0182399. doi:10.1371/journal.pone.0182399 PMID:28829787

Mizzi, D. (2022). *Cannabis: Legalise it or Criticise it?* THINK Magazine.

Mogoro, B. M., & Odeku, K. O. (2020). Paradigm Shift from Criminalisation to Constitutional Legal Protection for the use of Cannabis in South Africa: Issues and Perspectives. *African Renaissance (1744-2532)*, *17*(3).

Mohapatra, B., Tripathy, S., Singhal, D., & Saha, R. (2021). Significance of digital technology in manufacturing sectors: Examination of key factors during COVID-19. *Research in Transportation Economics*, 101134.

Mokwena, K. (2019). Social and public health implications of the legalisation of recreational cannabis: A literature review. *African Journal of Primary Health Care & Family Medicine*, *11*(1), 1–6. doi:10.4102/phcfm.v11i1.2136 PMID:31793317

Mondliwa, P. & Roberts, S. 2020. Black economic empowerment and barriers to entry. *Opening the South African Economy: Barriers to Entry and Competition*, 215-30.

Mondliwa, P., & Roberts, S. (2021). *From a developmental to a regulatory state? Sasol and the conundrum of continued state support. Ownership and Governance of Companies*. Routledge.

Monthony, A. S., Page, S. R., Hesami, M., & Jones, A. M. P. (2021). The past, present and future of Cannabis sativa tissue culture. *Plants*, *10*(1), 185. doi:10.3390/plants10010185 PMID:33478171

Moody, J. (2018, June, 5). Time for colleges to give cannabis a try? *Forbes*.

Moorcraft, B. (2018). Outdoor Cannabis Growers Lack Insurance Options-What Can Be Done? Insurance Business Magazine. https://www.insurancebusinessmag.com/ca/market-analysis/outdoor-cannabis growers-lack-insurance-options—what-can-be-done-113996.aspx.

Mootz, F. J. (2018). Ethical Cannabis Lawyering in California. *Mary's J. on Legal Malpractice & Ethics*, *9*, 2.

Moreno, M. A., Gower, A. D., Jenkins, M. C., Scheck, J., Sohal, J., Kerr, B., Young, H. N., & Cox, E. (2018). Social media posts by recreational marijuana companies and administrative code regulations in Washington state. *JAMA Network Open*, *1*(7), e182242. doi:10.1001/jamanetworkopen.2018.2242 PMID:30646364

Morris, B. (2010). Indigenous knowledge. *The Society of Malawi Journal*, *63*(1), 1–9.

Mputing, A. (2020, October 19). *President Ramaphosa Delivers Economic Recovery Plan to Joint Sitting of Parliament.* Parliament of the Republic of South Africa. https://www.parliament.gov.za/news/president-ramaphosa-delivers-economic-recovery-plan-joint-sitting-parliament

Mthuli, S. A., Singh, N., & Reddy, P. S. (2022). Political leadership for improved performance in South Africa: Towards Inspirational and Transformational Leaders. In C. Jones, P. Pillay, P. S. Reddy, & S. I. Zondi (Eds.), *Lessons from Political Leadership in Africa* (pp. 16–31). Cambridge Scholars Publishing.

Mujuru, M., & Sekhejane, P. (2014). Legalising Cannabis for Cancer: Benefits of Indigenous Cannabis Therapeutics (Briefing NO 110 ed.). Africa Institute Of South Africa.

Mujuru, M., & Sekhejane, P. (2014). Legalising Cannabis for Cancer: Benefits of Indigenous Cannabis Therapeutics (Briefing NO 110 ed.). Pretoria: Africa Institute Of South Africa.

Mukeredzi, T. (2021, May 13). *Africa Needs Cannabis to Spark Economic Growth.* Foreign Policy. https://foreignpolicy.com/2021/05/13/africa-cannabis-marijuana-legalization-economy-growth/

Munyewende, P. O., & Nunu, W. N. (2017). Patient satisfaction with nurse-delivery primary health care services in Free State and Gauteng provinces, South Africa: A comparative study. African Journal of Primary Health.

Murphy, K. (2019, May 20). Cannabis is becoming a huge job creator. *Forbes.* https://www.forbes.com/sites/kevinmurphy/2019/05/20/cannabis-is-becoming-a-huge-job-creator/

Mushi, G. E., Di Marzo Serugendo, G., & Burgi, P. Y. (2022, November 16). Digital Technology and Services for Sustainable Agriculture in Tanzania: A Literature Review. *Sustainability, 14*, 2415.

Myers, J., Well, A., & Lorch, R. (2016). *Research design and statistical analysis.* Routledge.

NACB. (2021). The Cannabis Industry's massive under Insurance Gap and Need for more coverage. *NACB.* https://nacb.com/blog/the-cannabis-industrys-massive-under-insurance-gap-and-need-for-core-coverages/

Nair, T. (2012). Understanding livelihoods: A review of major debates. In S. Vipin (Ed.), *State of India's livelihoods report* (pp. 1–12). ACCESS Development Services.

Nakata, M., Nakata, V., Keech, S., & Bolt, R. (2012). Decolonial goals and pedagogies for Indigenous studies. *Decolonization, 1*(1).

Nassiry, D. (2018). *The role of fintech in unlocking green finance: Policy insights for developing countries* (ADBI Working Paper 883).

Nath, M. K., Po-Dergaon, D. & Golaghat, A. (2022). Benefits of Cultivating Industrial Hemp (Cannabis sativa ssp. sativa)-A versatile plant for a sustainable future. MDPI.

National Association of Insurance Commissioners. (2022). *Cannabis and Insurance.* NAIC. https://content.naic.org/cipr-topics/cannabis-and-insurance

National Institute of Health. (2022). Cannabis (Marijuana) and Cannabinoids: What You Need To Know. *National Centre for complementary and integrative health.*

National Institute on Drug Abuse. (2019). What Is Medical Marijuana? *National Institute on Drug Abuse.* https://www.drugabuse.gov/publications/drugfacts/marijuana-medicine

National Prosecuting Authority. (2015, January 29). *The National Prosecution Authority of South Africa Annual Report 2014/2015*National Prosecution Authority of South Africa. https://www.npa.gov.za/sites/default/files/annual-reports/Annual%20Report%202014%20-%202015.pdf

National Treasury. (2019). *Economic transformation, inclusive growth, and competitiveness: Towards an Economic Strategy for South Africa.* National Treasury. https://www.treasury.gov.za/comm_media/press/2019/towards%20an%20economic%20strategy%20for%20sa.pdf

Nel, W. (2017). Human Resource Management (10th ed). Oxford University Press Southern Africa (Pty) Ltd.

New-Frontier-Data. (2021). *The Global Cannabis Report: Growth & Trends Through 2025.* New Frontier Data.

Nguyen, H. V. (2020, May 14). Too young for Cannabis? Choice of minimum legal age for legalized non-medical Cannabis in Canada - BMC Public Health. *BioMed Central.* https://bmcpublichealth.biomedcentral.com/articles/10.1186/s12889-020-08639-z

Nguyen, N., Wong, M., Delucchi, K., & Halpern-Felsher, B. (2022). Adolescents' and young adults' perceptions of risks and benefits differ by type of Cannabis products. *Addictive Behaviors, 131*, 107336. doi:10.1016/j.addbeh.2022.107336 PMID:35436697

Nicholls, A. (2012). Everyday, Everywhere: Alcohol Marketing and Social Media—Current Trends. *Alcohol and Alcoholism (Oxford, Oxfordshire), 47*(4), 486–493. doi:10.1093/alcalc/ags043 PMID:22532575

Nkosi, P. I. (2021). Dagga and Data: Cannabis, Race, and Policing in Midcentury South Africa, 1932–1960. *The Social History of Alcohol and Drugs, 35*(2), 232–259. https://doi.org/10.1086/716209

Nobile, J. (2020, February 11). Report: Cannabis job growth projected to outpace all other fast-growing industries. *Crain's Cleveland Business.* https://www.crainscleveland.com/jeremy-nobile-blog/report-cannabis-job-growth-projected-outpace-all-other-fast-growing-industries

Noël, C., Armiento, C., Péfoyo, A. K., Klein, R., Bédard, M., & Scharf, D. (2021). Adolescent exposure to cannabis marketing following recreational cannabis legalization in Canada: A pilot study using ecological momentary assessment. *Addictive Behaviors Reports, 14*, 100383. doi:10.1016/j.abrep.2021.100383 PMID:34938841

Ntsaba, J. M. M. E. (2016, February 2). Perceptions of marijuana use: Chronicles of marijuana smokers from two marijuana-Growing communities in South Africa. *IDEAS.* https://ideas.repec.org/a/apb/jahmss/2016p82-91.html

Number, R. N. (1975). *1111 of 1975.* Dangerous Drugs Regulations.

Nyembezi, N. (2020, October 10). amaMpondo traditional leaders reject Private Use Cannabis Bill. *SABC News.* https://www.sabcnews.com/sabcnews/ amampondo-traditional-leaders-reject-privateuse-cannabis-bill/

Oduor, M. (2021, May 27). Morocco joins growing list of African countries to legalize cannabis. *Africa News.* https://www.africanews.com/2021/05/27/morocco-joins-growing-list-of-african-countries-to-legalize-cannabis//

Okole, B. (2021). CSIR-DSI collaboration yields results for six traditional health practitioners. *CSIR Science Scope, 17*(1), 6–7.

Omare, M. O., Kibet, J. K., Cherutoi, J. K., & Kengara, F. O. (2021). Current Trends in the Use of Cannabis Sativa: Beyond Recreational and Medicinal Applications. *Open Access Library Journal, 8*(06), 1–17. doi:10.4236/oalib.1107132

Oniwe, L. (2021). *Cannabis.* Revolutionising the Global Consumer Sector.

Orens, A., Light, M., Lewandowski, B., Rowberry, J., & Saloga, C. (2018). *Market Size and Demand for Marijuana in Colorado 2017 Market Update.* Colorado State Web Portal. https://www.colorado.gov/pacific/sites/default/files/MED%20Demand%20and%20Market%20%20Study%20%20082018.pdf.

Organisation for Economic Cooperation and Development. (2021). *OECD Health Statistics.* OECD Publishing.

Otobo, E. E. 1997. The civil service and the private sector in Africa: From relationship of "conflict" to complimentarity. *DPMN Bulletin.* http://www.dpmf.org/civil-service-conflict-ejeviome. html

Oultram, J., Pegler, J., Bowser, T., Ney, L., Eamens, A., & Grof, C. (2021). Cannabis sativa: Interdisciplinary Strategies and Avenues for Medical and Commercial Progression Outside of CBD and THC. *Biomedicines*, *9*(3), 234. doi:10.3390/biomedicines9030234 PMID:33652704

Owens, B. (2019). The professionalization of cannabis growing. *Nature*, *572*(7771), S10–S11. doi:10.1038/d41586-019-02527-2 PMID:31462785

Pacek, L. R., Towe, S. L., Hobkirk, A. L., Nash, D., & Goodwin, R. D. (2018). Frequency of cannabis use and medical cannabis use among persons living with HIV in the United States: Findings from a nationally representative sample. *AIDS Education and Prevention*, *30*(2), 169–181. doi:10.1521/aeap.2018.30.2.169 PMID:29688777

Pachmayer, A., Switzer, R., & Reilly, S. (2021). Cannabis Tourism and the Community: Resident Attitudes in Humboldt County, California. *IdeaFest: Interdisciplinary Journal of Creative Works and Research from Humboldt State University*, *5*, 6.

Packer, C., Crockett, R. A., & Dawson, D. (2022). Not a SAFE Bet: Equitable Access to Cannabis Banking, An Analysis of the SAFE Banking Act. *Ohio State Legal Studies Research Paper*, (721).

Pacula, R. L., & Smart, R. (2017). Medical marijuana and marijuana legalization. *Annual Review of Clinical Psychology*, *13*(1), 397–419. doi:10.1146/annurev-clinpsy-032816-045128 PMID:28482686

Page, R. L. II, Allen, L. A., Kloner, R. A., Carriker, C. R., Martel, C., Morris, A. A., Piano, M. R., Rana, J. S., & Saucedo, J. F. (2020). Medical marijuana, recreational cannabis, and cardiovascular health: A scientific statement from the American Heart Association. *Circulation*, *142*(10), e131–e152. doi:10.1161/CIR.0000000000000883 PMID:32752884

Pakes, F., & Silverstone, D. (2012). Cannabis in the global market: A comparison between the UK and the Netherlands. *International Journal of Law, Crime and Justice*, *40*(1), 20–30. doi:10.1016/j.ijlcj.2011.09.003

Palthe, J. (2014). Regulative, normative, and cognitive elements of organizations: Implications for managing change. *Management and Organizational Studies*, *1*(2), 59–66. doi:10.5430/mos.v1n2p59

Parker, K., Di Mattia, A., Shaik, F., Cerón Ortega, J., & Whittle, R. (2019). Risk management within the cannabis industry: Building a framework for the cannabis industry. *Financial Markets, Institutions and Instruments*, *28*(1), 3–55. doi:10.1111/fmii.12104

Park, S., Choi, H., & Kang, R. (2021). A study on the value relevance and accounting policy of R&D expenditures in accordance with firms' life cycle stages. *Korea Inter. Account. Rev.*, *96*, 73–92.

Parry, C. D. H., & Myers, B. J. (2014). Legalising Medical use of Cannabis in South Africa: Is the empirical evidence sufficient to support policy shifts in this direction? *Article in South African Medical Journal, Vol*, *104*(6), 399. doi:10.7196/SAMJ.8135 PMID:25214244

Parry, C., Myers, B., & Caulkins, J. (2019). Decriminalisation of recreational cannabis in South Africa. *Lancet*, *393*(10183), 1804–1805. doi:10.1016/S0140-6736(19)30011-X PMID:31057166

Paterson, C. (2009). Prohibition & resistance: a socio-political exploration of the changing dynamics of the Southern African cannabis trade, c. 1850 - the present [Doctoral dissertation, Rhodes University, South Africa].

Patwardhan, B., & Mashelkar, R. A. (2009). Traditional medicine-inspired approaches to drug discovery: Can Ayurveda show the way forward? *Drug Discovery Today*, *14*(15-16), 804–811. doi:10.1016/j.drudis.2009.05.009 PMID:19477288

Payan, D., Brown, P., & Song, A. (2021). County-level recreational marijuana policies and local policy changes in Colorado and Washington State (2012–2019). *The Milbank Quarterly*, *99*(4), 1132–1161. Advance online publication. doi:10.1111/1468-0009.12535 PMID:34407252

Pedrazzi, S., Santunione, G., Mustone, M., Cannazza, G., Citti, C., Francia, E., & Allesina, G. (2021). Techno-economic study of a small scale gasifier applied to an indoor hemp farm: From energy savings to biochar effects on productivity. *Energy Conversion and Management*, *228*, 113645. doi:10.1016/j.enconman.2020.113645

Pelley, A. (2021). 3 Hard Truths About Cash Flow in the Cannabis Industry. *JDSupra.* https://www.jdsupra.com

Pelley, A. (2021). 3 Hard Truths About Cash Flow in the Cannabis Industry. *JDSUPRA.* https://www.jdsupra.com

Peltzer, K., Ramlagan, S., Johnson, B. D., & Phaswana-Mafuya, N. (2010). Illicit drug use and treatment in South Africa: A review. *Substance Use & Misuse*, *45*(13), 2221–2243. doi:10.3109/10826084.2010.481594 PMID:21039113

Perkel, C. (2005). Cannabis - The debate continues: A South African Perspective. *South African Psychiatry Review*, *8*, 25–30.

Perkel, C. (2005). Cannabis - the debate continues: a South African perspective: original article. *The African Journal of Psychiatry*, *8*(1). https://doi.org/10.4314/ajpsy.v8i1.30181

Perkel, C. (2005). Cannabis- the debate continues: A South African perspective. *South African Psychiatry Review*, *8*, 25–30.

Perkel, C. (2005). Cannabis-the debate continues: A South African perspective. *The African Journal of Psychiatry*, *8*(1), 25–30. doi:10.4314/ajpsy.v8i1.30181

Perkowski, M. (2018). Marijuana Pesticide Contamination Worries Oregon Farmers. *Capitol Press.* https://www.capitalpress.com/state/oregon/marijuana-pesticide-contamination-worries-oregon-farmers/article_303327ce-fa5d-11e8-b01f-d3b7bdf5bfde.html

Pichler, D. M. (2018). *Political Leadership in Urban Governance: a determinant factor for transformative innovation?* [Masters Thesis, Erasmus University, Rotterdam, the Netherlands].

Pierre, J., & Peters, B. G. (2000). Governance, politics and the state. Macmillan Education UK.

Piet, Bester. & Sonja, Els. (2021). The legalization of cannabis: A security-vetting dilemma. *South African Journal of Military Studies.*

Piispanen, R. (2022). *The Effects of Cannabis Legalization on the Economy of State Colorado-a Case Study.* Aalto University.

Plakias, Z., Jodlowski, M., Giamo, T., Kavousi, P., & Taylor, K. (2021). Pot of money: Characterizing agricultural lending and banking in the California cannabis industry. *Agricultural Finance Review*, *82*(2), 214–246. doi:10.1108/AFR-06-2021-0075

Plant, M. A. (1977). Decriminalising Cannabis. *British Journal of Law and Society*, *4*(2), 252–256. doi:10.2307/1409678

Polson, M., & Petersen-Rockney, M. (2019). Cannabis farmers or criminals? Enforcement-first approaches fuel disparity and hinder regulation. *California Agriculture, 73*(3), 185–193. 0017 doi:10.3733/ca.2019a

Potter, G. R., Barratt, M. J., Malm, A., Bouchard, M., Blok, T., Christensen, A. S., Decorte, T., Frank, V. A., Hakkarainen, P., Klein, A., Lenton, S., Perala, J., Werse, B., & Wouters, M. (2016). Global patterns of domestic cannabis cultivation: Sample characteristics and patterns of growing across eleven countries. In *Friendly business* (pp. 163–196). Springer VS. doi:10.1007/978-3-658-10329-3_9

Potter, G., Bouchard, M. M., & Decorte, M. T. (2013). *World wide weed: Global trends in cannabis cultivation and its control.* Ashgate Publishing, Ltd.

Pourseyed Lazarjani, M., Torres, S., Hooker, T., Fowlie, C., Young, O., & Seyfoddin, A. (2020). Methods for quantification of cannabinoids: A narrative review. *Journal of Cannabis Research*, *2*(1), 1–10. doi:10.118642238-020-00040-2 PMID:33526084

PR Newswire. (2020).. Medical Cannabis Market is Estimated to Rise at a CAGR of 26.6% during the Forecast Period, observes TMR Study. *Zoeken*. https://www.bing.com/search?q=%EF%82%A7+PR+Newswire.+&qout;Medical+Cannabis+Market+is+Estimated+to+Rise+at+a+CAGR+of+26.6%+during+the+Forecast+Period,+observes+TMR+Study.&qout

Pratt, M. A. S., & Thuku, M. (2019). Benefits and harms of medical cannabis: A scoping review of systematic reviews. *Systematic Reviews*, *8*(320), 1–35. doi:10.118613643-019-1243-x PMID:31823819

Prince, M. A., Conner, B. T., & Pearson, M. R. (2018). Quantifying cannabis: A field study of marijuana quantity estimation. *Psychology of Addictive Behaviors*, *32*(4), 426–433. doi:10.1037/adb0000370 PMID:29771542

Prohibition-Partners (2019). The African Cannabis Report.

Projectcbd.org. (2022). What is CBD? Learn what CBD is and what isn't, the difference between CBD from Cannabis and Hemp, and more. *Project CBD*. https://www.projectcbd.org/about/what-cbd

Przybycień, P., Gąsior-Perczak, D., & Placha, W. (2022). Cannabinoids and PPAR Ligands: The Future in Treatment of Polycystic Ovary Syndrome Women with Obesity and Reduced Fertility. *Cells*, *11*(16), 2569. doi:10.3390/cells11162569 PMID:36010645

Pusiak, R. J., Cox, C., & Harris, C. S. (2021). Growing pains: An overview of cannabis quality control and quality assurance in Canada. *The International Journal on Drug Policy*, *93*, 103111. https://doi.org/10.1016/j.drugpo.2021.103111

Qian, Y., Gurley, B. J., & Markowitz, J. S. (2019). The Potential for Pharmacokinetic Interactions Between Cannabis Products and Conventional Medications. *Journal of Clinical Psychopharmacology*, *39*(5), 462–471. doi:10.1097/JCP.0000000000001089 PMID:31433338

Quarshie, E., & Alagidede, I. P. (2020). Cannabis legalization in Ghana: Implications for value-addition in medical and industrial research and applications. *Journal of Indigenous and Shamanic Studies*, *1*(1), 1–14.

Radwan, M. M., Chandra, S., Gul, S., & Elsohly, M. A. (2021). Cannabinoids, phenolics, terpenes and alkaloids of cannabis. *Molecules (Basel, Switzerland)*, *26*(9), 2774. doi:10.3390/molecules26092774 PMID:34066753

Rahman, A. M., Nemoto, K., Matsushima, K. I., & Uddin, S. B., & AKM, G. (2022). A History of Cannabis (Ganja) as an Economic Crop in Bangladesh from the Late 18th Century to 1989. *Tropical Agriculture and Development*, *66*(1), 21–32.

Rahwanji, M. (2019). Hash"ing Out Inequality in the Legal Recreational Cannabis Industry. *Northwestern Journal of International Law & Business, 39*(3), 334-356. https://scholarlycommons.law.northwestern.edu/njilb/vol39/iss3/4

Ramírez, M. (2018). New Mexico tribal cannabis: Policy, politics, & guidance for government-to-Government cooperation in state-tribal cannabis compacting. *Natural Resources Journal*, *58*(1), 75–124.

Ramlagan, S., Peltzer, K., & Pengpid, S. (2021). Prevalence and Correlates of non-daily and daily Cannabis use among persons 15 years and older in South Africa: Results of a National Survey in 2017. *Substance Abuse Treatment, Prevention, and Policy*, *16*(1), 25. doi:10.118613011-021-00364-z PMID:33743758

Rashid, S., & Ratten, V. (2021). Entrepreneurial ecosystems during COVID-19: The survival of small businesses using dynamic capabilities. *World Journal of Entrepreneurship, Management and Sustainable Development*, *17*, 457–476.

Reckner, P. E., & Brighton, S. A. (1999). "Free from all vicious habits": Archaeological perspectives on class conflict and the rhetoric of temperance. *Historical Archaeology*, *33*(1), 63–86. doi:10.1007/BF03374280

ReliefWeb. (2022). South Africa. Floods and Landslides - Apr 2022. *ReliefWeb.* https://reliefweb.int/disaster/fl-2022-000201-zaf

Republic of South Africa. (1992, July 15). Drugs and Drugs Trafficking Act No. 140 of 1992. *Cape Town: Government Gazette .*

Republic of South Africa. (2017, May 26). Medicines and Related Substance Act, 1965. *Pretoria: Government Gazette.*

Republic of South Africa. (2020). *Government notice R.486-Medicines and Related Substances Act (101/1965).* Schedules, Government Gazette.

Republic of South Africa. (2020, August 07). Cannabis for Private Purpose Bill. *Cape Town: Government Gazette No. 43595.*

Reuters. (2022, March 22). South Africa's unemployment rate hits new record high in Q4 2021. *Reuters.* https://www.reuters.com/world/africa/south-africas-unemployment-rate-hits-new-record-high-q4-2021-2022-03-29/

Riley, S., Vellios, N., & van Walbeek, C. (2019). An economic analysis of the demand for cannabis: Some results from South Africa. *Drugs Education Prevention & Policy*, *27*(2), 123–130. doi:10.1080/09687637.2019.1581139

Ritter, S., Zadik-Weiss, L., Almogi-Hazan, O., & Or, R. (2020). Cannabis, One Health, and Veterinary Medicine: Cannabinoids' Role in Public Health, Food Safety, and Translational Medicine. *Rambam Maimonides Medical Journal*, *11*(1), e0006. doi:10.5041/RMMJ.10388 PMID:32017686

Roberts, C. (2018, July 31). Georgia's High Court Removes Marijuana Possession Penalties. *Marijuana Moment.* https://www.marijuanamoment.net/georgias-high-court-removes-marijuana-possession-penalties/

Robinson, R. (1996). *The great book of hemp: the complete guide to the environmental, commercial, and medicinal uses of the world's most extraordinary plant.* Inner Traditions/Bear & Co.

Romano, L. L., & Hazekamp, A. (2013). Cannabis oil: Chemical evaluation of an upcoming cannabis-based medicine. *Cannabinoids*, *1*(1), 1–11.

Romero, P., Peris, A., Vergara, K., & Matus, J. T. (2020). Comprehending and improving cannabis specialized metabolism in the systems biology era. *Plant Science*, *298*, 110571. doi:10.1016/j.plantsci.2020.110571 PMID:32771172

Rosario, J. (2021, July 13). City council members agree on even split of Jersey City cannabis tax revenue between schools, social programs. *The Jersey Journal.* https://www.nj.com/hudson/2021/07/city-council-member-agree-on-even-split-of-jersey-city-cannabis-tax-revenue-between-sc
hool

Rotermann, M. (2020). What has changed since cannabis was legalized. *Health Reports*, *31*(2), 11–20. PMID:32073644

Rothberg, A. (2017). Thoughts as we consider the legalisation of cannabis in South Africa. *SAJCH: the South African Journal of Child Health*, *11*(4), 153–153.

Roussell, A. (2012). Forensic Identification of Marijuana: Suspicion, Mortal Danger, and the Creation of Non-Psychoactive THC. *Albany Law Journal of Science & Technology.*

Royal Queen Seeds. (2022). The History and Current Status of Cannabis in South Africa. *Royal Queen Seeds.* https://www.royalqueenseeds.com/blog

RSA. (2017). Preferential Procurement Policy Framework Act, 2000. Department Of Agriculture, L. R. A. R. D. (ed.). Pretoria.

RSA. (2018). Industrial Policy Action Plan 2018/19 - 2020/21. Economic Sectors, employment and infrastructre development cluster. Department of Trade and Industry, Republic of South Africa, Pretoria.

RSA. (2021a). Draft national cannabis master plan for South Africa. Department of agriculture, L. R. A. R. D. (ed.). Pretoria.

RSA. (2021b). Update On The Hemp Regulatory Framework For South Africa. Department Of Agriculture, L. R. A. R. D. (ed.). Pretoria: RSA Government.

RSA. (2022). Deputy Minister Lindiwe Sisulu: Tourism Dept Budget Vote 2022/23. In M. O. Tourism (Ed.). South African Government.

Rubera, G., & Kirca, A. (2017). You gotta serve somebody: The effects of firm innovation on customer satisfaction and firm value. *Journal Academic Markerting. Science*, *45*, 741–761.

Rueda, S., Limanto, E., & Chaiton, M. (2022). Cannabis clinical research in purgatory: Canadian researchers caught between an inflexible regulatory environment and a conflicted industry. *The Lancet Regional Health–Americas, 7.*

Rupasinghe, H. V., Davis, A., Kumar, S. K., Murray, B., & Zheljazkov, V. D. (2020). Industrial hemp (Cannabis sativa subsp. sativa) as an emerging source for value-added functional food ingredients and nutraceuticals. *Molecules (Basel, Switzerland)*, *25*(18), 4078. doi:10.3390/molecules25184078 PMID:32906622

Rupert Klein & Michel Bédard. (2021). *Adolescent exposure to cannabis marketing following recreational cannabis legalization in Canada: A pilot study using ecological momentary assessment. Kavya, S, (2020). The ultimate guide to CBD marketing*. Cannabis Creative Groups.

Rusenga, C., Klantschnig, G., Carrier, N., & Howell, S. (2022, May 30). Cannabis policy changes in Africa are welcome. But small producers are the losers. *The Conversation.* https://theconversation.com/cannabis-policy-changes-in-africa-are-welcome-but-small-producers-are-the-losers-179681

Russo, E. (2005). Cannabis in India: ancient lore and modern medicine. In R. Mechoulam (Ed.), *Cannabinoids as Therapeutics. Milestones in Drug Therapy MDT.* Birkhäuser Basel. doi:10.1007/3-7643-7358-X_1

Russo, E. B. (2017). Cannabis and epilepsy: An ancient treatment returns to the fore. *Epilepsy & Behavior*, *70*, 292–297. doi:10.1016/j.yebeh.2016.09.040 PMID:27989385

Rutsaert, P., Chamberlin, J., Oluoch, K. O., Kitoto, V. O., & Donovan, J. (2021). The geography of agricultural input markets in rural Tanzania. *Food Security*, *13*, 1379–1391. PMID:34976233

Ruttan, V. W. (1997). Induced innovation, evolutionary theory and path dependence: Sources of technical change. *Economic Journal (London)*, *107*(444), 1520–1529. doi:10.1111/j.1468-0297.1997.tb00063.x

Ryan, M. (2018). Member Blog: What Every Cannabis Needs to Know About Their Finance Function. *The Cannabis Industry.* https://thecannabisindustry.org/tag/cash-flow/

Rychert, M., Emanuel, M. A., & Wilkins, C. (2020). Issues in the establishment of a therapeutic cannabis market under Jamaica's dangerous drugs amendment act 2015. *The International Journal on Drug Policy*, *86*, 102945. doi:10.1016/j.drugpo.2020.102945 PMID:32947242

Rychert, M., Emanuel, M. A., & Wilkins, C. (2021). Foreign investment in emerging legal medicinal cannabis markets: The Jamaica case study. *Globalization and Health, 17*(1), 1–11. doi:10.118612992-021-00687-3 PMID:33794932

Ryu, S. L., & Won, J. (2022, April 22). The Value Relevance of Operational Innovation: Insights from the Perspective of Firm Life Cycle. *Sustainability, 14*, 2058.

SAHPRA. (2019, September 04). Medicinal and Research for Medicinal and Research Purposes. *Sahpra.* https://www.sahpra.org.za/wp-content/uploads/2019/09/SAHPRA-Medicinal-Cannabis-Update_Presentation-to-PC_04Sept2019_Fina
l.pdf

SAHPRA. (2020, January 01). Cannabis and Related Substances. *Sahpra.* https://www.sahpra.org.za/wp-content/uploads/2020/01/Cannabis_and_related_substances_A5_final-1.pdf

SAHPRA. (2020, January 01). *Cannabis_and_related_substances_A5_final.* SAHPRA. https://www.sahpra.org.za/wp content/uploads/2020/01/Cannabis_and_related_substances_A5_final-1.pdf

SAIIA. (2022, August 16). The Dark Side of Foreign Direct Investment: A South African Perspective. *SAIIA.* https://saiia.org.za/research/the-dark-side-of-foreign-direct-investment-a-south-african-perspective/

Saiz-Rubio, V., & Rovira-Más, F. (2020). From smart farming towards agriculture 5.0: A review on crop data management. [CrossRef]. *Agronomy (Basel), 10*, 207.

Salami, S., Martinelli, F., Giovino, A., Bachari, A., Arad, N., & Mantri, N. (2020). It Is Our Turn to Get Cannabis High: Put Cannabinoids in Food and Health Baskets. *Molecules (Basel, Switzerland), 25*(18), 4036. doi:10.3390/molecules25184036 PMID:32899626

Salentijn, E. M. J., Zhang, Q., Amaducci, S., Yang, M., & Trindade, L. M. (2015). New developments in fiber hemp (Cannabis sativa L.) breeding. *Industrial Crops and Products, 68*, 32–41. doi:10.1016/j.indcrop.2014.08.011

Samuel, A.-G. & Edward, B. 2015. The marijuana factor in a university in Ghana: A survey. *Журнал Сибирского федерального университета. Гуманитарные науки, 8*, 2162-2182.

Sanga, C. A., Tumbo, S. D., & Mlozi, M. R. S. (2014). System Design and ICT Adoption in Agricultural Extension Services Delivery in Tanzania. In *Technology Development and Platform Enhancements for Successful Global E-Government Design* (p. 25). IGI Global.

Sanjaya, L. (2004). Reinventing industrial strategy: the role of government policy in building industrial competitiveness. *United Nations Conference on Trade and Development.*

Santomauro, D. F. (2021, November 6). Global prevalence and burden of depressive and anxiety disorders in 204 countries and territories in 2020 due to the COVID-19 pandemic. *The Lancet.* https://www.thelancet.com/journals/lancet/article/PIIS0140-6736(21)02143-7/fulltext

Sarker, N. I., Islam, S., Ali, A., Islam, S., Salam, A., & Hasan Mahmud, S. M. (2019). Promoting digital agriculture through big data for sustainable farm management. *International Journal of Innovation and Applied Studies, 25*, 1235–1240.

Saunders, M., Lewis, P., & Thornhill, A. (2019). *Research methods for business students* (8th ed.). Pearson.

Savundranayagam, M. Y., & Sager, Z. S. (2021). The Experiences, Benefits, and Harms of Cannabis Use in Later Life. *Clinical Gerontologist, 44*(1), 1–2. doi:10.1080/07317115.2020.1855131 PMID:33357131

Scarboro, M., & Bishop-Henchman, J. (2016). Marijuana legalization and taxes: Lessons for other states from Colorado and Washington. *Tax foundation.* https://taxfoundation.org/marijuana-taxes-lessons-colorado-washington/#_ftnref1

Schindler, P. S. (2018). *Business Research Methods*. McGraw-Hill Education.

Schofield, I. (2017). Management Sciences: An Introduction. Juta and Company (Pty) Ltd.

Schultes, R. E. (1974, February 28). Details - Cannabis: an Example of Taxonomic Neglect. *Biodiversity Heritage Library*. https://www.biodiversitylibrary.org/part/168565

Schulz, L. (2019, April 25). The economic impact of developing the adult-use cannabis industry in New York. *Rockefeller Institute of Government*. https://rockinst.org/issue-area/the-economic-impact-of-developing -the-adult-use-cannabis-industry-in-new-york/

Schumpeter, J. A. (1942). *Capitalism, Socialism and Democracy*. Harper Collins.

Scott, W. R. (2013). *Institutions and organizations: Ideas, interests, and identities*. Sage publications.

Seddon, T., & Floodgate, W. (2020). *Regulating Cannabis: A Global Review and Future Directions*. Palgrave Macmillan.

Seltenrich, N. (2019). Into the Weeds: Regulating Pesticides in Cannabis. *Environmental Health Perspectives*, *127*(4), 042001. https://doi.org/10.1289/ehp5265

Semete-Makokotlela, B. (2017, September 17). Cultivation of Cannabis for medicinal use, Cannabis, Pretoria, South African Health Products Regulatory Authority. *Pharmacy and Therapeutics.*

Senovaityte, S., Nguyen, A., Han, S., La, B., Anane-Asane, F., Mohran, R., Lee, S., Monzon, A., Sama-ra, O., Murcia, D., & Purohit, S. (2021). The Safety of Cannabis Use in Pregnancy. *Open Journal of Obstetrics and Gynecology*, *11*(11), 1437–1445. doi:10.4236/ojog.2021.1111133

Settas, A. (2021). *An Analysis of the Potential Fiscal and Health Benefits of the Legalisation of the Sale of Marijuana in South Africa* [Master's thesis, Faculty of Commerce, South Africa].

Shanahan, M., & Ritter, A. (2013). Confronting the challenges of conducting a CBA of cannabis policies. *Drugs Education Prevention & Policy*, *20*(3), 175–183. doi:10.3109/09687637.2013.763906

Sharma, A. (2020). Working with Cannabis, These Indian Hemp Startups are making high profits. *Bingedaily*.

Sharma, S., & Ravikumar, K. V. (2017). Narco-terrorism–A reat to national security. *International Research Journal on Police Science*, *3*(1), 40–45.

Sheefeni, J. P. (2022, June 2). South Africa's economy has taken some heavy body blows: can it recover? *The Conversation*. https://theconversation.com/south-africas-economy-has-taken-some-heavy-body-blows-can-it-recover-183165

Sheel, A. (2021). The Wonder Resources: All Hemp, CBD, and Ayurvedic Cannabis Companies in India. *Itshemp*.

Sihlobo, W. (2020). *Finding common ground: Land, equity and agriculture*. Picador Africa.

Sihna, J. (2001). The History and Development of the Leading International Drug Control Conventions, Prepared for the Senate Special Committee on Legal Drugs, Law and Government Division, Library of Parliament.

Sileyew, K. (2019, January 06). *Research Design and Methodology*. InTechOpen. https://www.intechopen.com/online-first/research-design-and-methodology

Silvaggio, T. (2018). Environmental Consequences of Prohibition: Lessons from California. *International Cannabis Policy Conference organized*. FAAT.

Sinha, S. and Fogla, R. (2020). India's Cannabis Market: Examining Regulatory Frameworks then and now. *Cannabis Industry Journal*.

Sinha, J. (2001). *The history and development of the leading international drug control conventions*. Library of Parliament.

Skliamis, K., Korf, A., & Benschop, D. (2020). Cannabis users and stigma: A comparison of uses from European countries with different cannibis policies. *European Journal of Criminology*, 1–18.

Skypala, I. J., Jeimy, S., Brucker, H., Nayak, A. P., Decuyper, I. I., Bernstein, J. A., Connors, L., Kanani, A., Klimek, L., Lo, S. C. R., Murphy, K. R., Nanda, A., Poole, J. A., Walusiak-Skorupa, J., Sussman, G., Zeiger, J. S., Goodman, R. E., Ellis, A. K., Silvers, W. S., & Ebo, D. G. (2022). Cannabis-related allergies: An international overview and consensus recommendations. *Allergy*, *77*(7), 2038–2052. doi:10.1111/all.15237 PMID:35102560

Small, E. (2015). Evolution and Classification of Cannabis sativa (Marijuana, Hemp) in Relation to Human Utilization. *Botanical Review*, *81*(3), 189–294. doi:10.100712229-015-9157-3

Small, E. (2017). *Classification of Cannabis sativa L. in relation to agricultural, biotechnological, medical and recreational utilization. Cannabis sativa L.-Botany and biotechnology*. Springer.

Smit & Van Wyk. (2021). *South Africa: Legalisation Of Private Use Of Cannabis In South Africa*. MONDAQ. https://www.mondaq.com/southafrica/cannabis-hemp/1107436/legalisation-of-private-use-of-cannabis-in-south-africa

Smit, & Van Wyk, (2021). Legalisation of Private Use of Cannabis in South Africa. www.mondaq.com

Smit, & Van Wyk. (2021). Legalisation of Private Use of Cannabis in South Africa. *MONDAQ*. www.mondaq.com

Smit, S. (2021, February 2). Haze Club case: Cannabis grow clubs allow people to access their rights. *Mail & Guardian*, https://mg.co.za/ business/2021-02-02-haze-club-case-cannabis grow-clubs-allow-people-to-access-th

Smyth, E., & Vanclay, F. (2017). The Social Framework for Projects: a conceptual but practical model to assist in assessing, planning and managing the social impacts of projects. *Impact Assessment and Project Appraisal, 35*(1), 65-80. doi:10.1080/14615517.2016.1271539

Solimini, R., Rotolo, M.C., Pichini, S. and Pacifici, R., (2017). Neurological disorders in medical use of cannabis: an update. CNS & Neurological Disorders-Drug Targets (Formerly Current Drug Targets-CNS & Neurological Disorders), 16(5), pp.527-533.

Sorrentino, G. (2021). Introduction to emerging industrial applications of cannabis (cannabis sativa l.). *Rendiconti Lincei. Scienze Fisiche e Naturali*, *32*(2), 233–243. https://link.springer.com/article/10.1007/s12210-021-00979-1. doi:10.100712210-021-00979-1 PMID:33777341

South African Food Review. (2019, November 4). *Afriplex aligned with prized cannabis cultivation license*. South African Food Review. https://ukzn.idm.oclc.org/login?url=https://search.ebscohost.com/login.aspx?direct=true&db=bth&AN=135842391&site=ehost-live&scope=site

South African Government News Agency. (2020, November 18). Economic Recovery Plan: The key to unlocking SA's growth. *South African Government News Agency*. https://www.sanews.gov.za/south-africa/economic-recovery-plan-key-unlocking-sas-growth

South African Government News Agency. (2021, June 11). Progress made in implementing economic recovery plan. *South African Government News Agency*. https://www.sanews.gov.za/south-africa/progress-made-implementing-economic-recovery-plan

South African Government. (2022). *State of the Nation Address*. South African Government. https://www.gov.za/SONA2022

South African Health Products Regulatory Authority (SAHPRA). (2020). *South African Health Products Regulatory Authority*. Cannabis and Related Substances Frequently Asked Qusetions.

Sprankling, J. G. (2019). Owning Marijuana. *Duke Journal of Constitutional Law and Public Policy*. https://scholarship.law.duke.edu/cgi/viewcontent.cgi?article=1153&context=djclpp

Stahl, N. A., & King, J. R. (2020, September 16). Expanding Approaches for Research: Understanding and Using Trustworthiness in Qualitative Research. *Journal of Developmental Education*, *44*, 1–5.

Stahl, S. M. (2013). *Stahl's Essential Psychopharmacology: Neuroscientific Basis and Practical Applications* (4th ed.). Cambridge University Press.

Statistics South Africa. (2021). *Md-year Population Estimates*. Statistical Release, P0302

Statistics South Africa. (2021, November 30). The South African economy sheds more than half a million jobs in the 3rd quarter of 2021. *Statistics South Africa*. https://www.statssa.gov.za/?p=14922

Statistics South Africa. (2022). South Africa's Youth continues to bear the Burden of Unemployment. *SSA*. https://www.statssa.gov.za/

Statistics South Africa. (2022, March 31). Measuring Food Security in South Africa: Applying the Food Insecurity Experience Scale. *Pretoria: Statistics South Africa*. https://www.statssa.gov.za/?p=15273

Statistics South Africa. 2022. South Africa's Youth continues to bear the Burden of Unemployment. *SSA*. https://www.statssa.gov.za/

Statutory, Z. (2018). *62, Dangerous Drugs (Production of Cannabis for Medicinal and Scientific Use)*. Regulations.

Steinberg, J. N. (2022). *Cannabis legalization: an ethnography of the global movement and market forces*. University of Oxford.

Stein, D. J. (2016). Position statement on cannabis. *SAMJ: South African Medical Journal*, *106*, 569–570. doi:10.7196/SAMJ.2016.v106i9.11222

Stephen, K. 2022. Business is starting to trump morality in Arica's Cannabis Industry. *Quartz*. https://qz.com/africa/

Stiglitz, J. (1997). Reflections on the Natural Rate Hypothesis. *Journal of Economic Perspectives*, *11*(1), 3–10. .3 doi:10.1257/jep.11.1

Stoddard, E. (2020, March 15). Moody's dispenses with SA's investment-grade fiction, the descent into junk is complete. *Daily Maverick*. https://www.dailymaverick.co.za/article/2020-03-28-moodys-dispenses-with-sas-investment-grade-fiction-the-descent-into-junk-is-complete/

Szirmai, A., Naudé, W., & Alcorta, L. (2013). *Pathways to industrialization in the twenty-first century: new challenges and emerging paradigms*. OUP Oxford. doi:10.1093/acprof:oso/9780199667857.001.0001

Tan, C. C. (2021). Learning to Develop a New Industry–Cannabis, with Competitiveness Edge. *Journal of the Association of Researchers*, *26*, 1–10.

Tandwa, L. (2022, September 18). Eskom warns of higher stages of load-shedding as it scrambles to procure power. *The Mail & Guardian*. https://mg.co.za/news/2022-09-18-eskom-warns-of-higher-stages-of-load-shedding-as-it-scrambles-to-procure-power/

Taylor, L. L. (2019). Defining marijuana tourism. *Journal of Hospitality & Tourism Research (Washington, D.C.)*, *43*(3), 438–446. doi:10.1177/1096348018804610

TGE. (2022). *Comparing Economies* [Online]. *The Global Economy*. https://www.theglobaleconomy.com/compare-countries/

Tharoor, A. (2018). South Africa decriminalises personal cannabis use and cultivation. Talking Drugs. *IDPC*. https://idpc.net/alerts/2018/10/south-africa-decriminalises-personal-cannabis-use-and-cultivation

The Business Fortune. (2022 February 16). *Cannabis Market Size, Research | Marijuana Industry Growth 2028*. https://www.fortunebusinessinsights.com/industry-reports/cannabis-marijuana-market-100219

The Department of Agriculture, Land Reform, and Rural Development. (2022, February 8). *Trends in the Agricultural Sector*. https://www.dalrrd.gov.za/Portals/0/Statistics%20and%20Economic%20Analysis/Statistical%20Information/Trends%20in%20the%20Agricultural%20Sector%202020.pdf

The Financial Express. (2020). India's cannabis problem is not just about its use. *Financial Express*

The Lancet. (2021). Global prevalence and burden of depressive and anxiety disorders in 204 countries and territories in 2020 due to COVID-19 pandemic. *The Lancet*. https://www.thelancet.com/journals/lancet/article/PIIS0140-6736(21)02143-7/fulltext

The Medicines and Related Substances Act, 1965 (Act 101 of 1965) as amended. http://www.SAHPRAza.com/Publications/Index/9

The Presidency. (2022, February 8). *State of the Nation Address 2022*. South African Government. https://www.gov.za/SONA2022

The Week, (2021, Dec 14). Where is Cannabis legal?. Malta legalises the drug in in European first. Future PLC. *The Week*.

Theron, F. (1974). *The dagga problem: a sociological perspective with special reference to the question of social policy* [Master's thesis, University of Cape Town, South Africa].

Thingstel. (2021, April 29). IoT in Cannabis Farming *Thingstel*. https://www.thingstel.com/blog/iot-in-cannabis-farming/

Thomas, F. D., Berning, A., Darrah, J., Graham, L. A., Blomberg, R. D., Griggs, C., & Rayner, M. (2020). Drug and alcohol prevalence in seriously and fatally injured road users before and during the COVID-19 public health emergency (No. DOT HS 813 013). United States. National Highway Traffic Safety Administration. Office of Behavioral Safety Research.

Todd, T. (2018). The benefits of marijuana legalisation and regulation. *Berkeley J. Crim. L.*, *23*, 99.

Tonami, A. (2018). Exporting the developmental state: Japan's economic diplomacy in the Arctic. *Third World Quarterly*, *39*(6), 1211–1225. doi:10.1080/01436597.2017.1415142

Trading Economics. (2022). South Africa's unemployment rate. *Trading Economics*. https://tradingeconomics.com/south-africa/unemployment-rate

Trading Economics. (2022, November 04). *Unemployment Rate*. Trading Economics. https://tradingeconomics.com/country-list/unemployment-rate?continent=africa

Tulsyan, A. (2022). Cannabis and the constitution:'High time for amending the NDPS act?. *ILE Human Rights Law Review*, *1*(1).

Uecker-Mercado, H., & Walker, M. (2012). The value of environmental social responsibility to facility managers: Revealing the perceptions and motives for adopting ESR. *Journal of Business Ethics*, *110*(3), 269–284. doi:10.100710551-011-1153-x

UN office on Drugs and Crime. (2021). *INDIA*. https://www.unodc.org/pdf/india/publications/south_Asia_Regional_Profile_Sept_2005/10_india.pdf

UNECA. (2016). *Transformative industrial policy for Africa*, United Nations. Economic Commission for. *Africa*.

United Nations Office for Drug Control and Crime Prevention. (1999). *South Africa Country Profile on Drugs and Crime*. United Nations Office for Drugs and Crime.

United Nations Office on Drugs and Crime (2018, October 31). World Drug Report 2018. Booklet 5. *UNODC*. unodc.org/ wdr2018/prelaunch/WDR18_Booklet_5_WOMEN.pdf

United Nations Office on Drugs and Crime (2018, October12). World Drug Report 2018. Booklet 2. *UNODC*. unodc.org/ wdr2018/prelaunch/WDR18_Booklet_2_GLOBAL.pdf

United Nations Office on Drugs and Crime. (n.d.). *United Nations: Office on Drugs and Crime*. UN. https://www.unodc.org

United Nations. (2021, October 4). *Growing at a Slower Pace, World Population Is Expected to Reach 9.7 Billion in 2050 and Could Peak at Nearly 11 Billion around 2100*: UN Report. https://www.un.org/sustainabledevelopment/blog/2019/06/growing-ata-slower-pace-world-population-is-expected-to-reach-9-7-billion-in-2050-and-could-peak-at-nearly-11-billion-around-2100

UNODC. (2012). *World Drug Report* . United Nations publication.

UNODC. (2016). *World Drug Report.* United Nations publication.

UNODC. (2022, June 01). United Nations Office on Drugs and Crime: World Drug Report part 3. *Drug Market Trends: Cannabis + Opiods*. https://www.unodc.org/res/wdr2022/MS/WDR22_Booklet_3.pdf

USAID. (2021, October 28). *Using ICT to Enhance Marketing for Small Agricultural Producers*. USAID. https://agrilinks.org/sites/default/ files/resource/files/Using_ICT_to_Enhance_Marketing_for_Small_Agricultural_Producers.pdf

Uwakonye, D. (2020). *Strengthening Capacity Of Youth In Support Of Emerging Agricultural Industries In Africa: Lesotho's Cannabis Industry And The Role Of Higher Education In Its Human Resource Development* [Masters Thesis, Cornell University, USA]. https://ecommons.cornell.edu/bitstream/handle/1813/72648/DeAndre_Uwakonye_MPS_Capstone.pdf?sequence=1

Uwiringiyimana, C. (2020, October 14). Rwanda is in talks with EU, and U.S. firms to produce cannabis for export. *Reuters*. https://www.reuters.com/ article/us-Rwanda-drugs/Rwanda-in-talks-with-u-s-firms-to-produce-cannabis-for-exportidUKKBN26Z239

Valachovic, Y., Quinn-Davidson, L., Stackhouse, J., & Butsic, V. (2019). Perceptions of cannabis among Humboldt County timberland and ranchland owners. *California Agriculture*, *73*(3), 161–168. doi:10.3733/ca.2019a0010

Van De Rheede, J. (2020). The Broad-Based Black Economic Empowerment Act 53 of 2003 and the ways in which the commission of fronting practices affects the achievement of its objective. *African Journal of Democracy and Governance*, *7*, 101–118.

Van het Loo, M., Hoorens, S., van 't Hof, C., & Kahan, J. P. (2003). *Cannabis Policy, Implementation and Outcomes*. RAND Corporation.

van Rensburg, R., Pillay-Fuentes Lorente, V., Blockman, M., Moodley, K., Wilmshurst, J. M., & Decloedt, E. H. (2020). Medical Cannabis: What practitioners need to know, The South African Medical Journal, 110(3). Distributed under Creative Commons Licence CC-BY-NC 4.0.

van Rensburg, R., Pillay-Fuentes Lorente, V., Blockman, M., Moodley, K., Wilmshurst, J. M., & Decloedt, E. H. (2020). Medical Cannabis: What practitioners need to know. The South African Medical Journal, 110(3).

Vanek, M. (2022, February 10). *South Africa Looks to Cannabis, Hemp Industry to Create Jobs*. Bloomberg. https://ukzn.idm.oclc.org/login?url=https://search.ebscohost.com/login.aspx?direct=true&db=bth&AN=155177988&site=ehost-live&scope=site

Vasic, A. (2020, March 10). Illegal Cannabis Grows Trigger a Chain of Environmental Disasters on Public Lands. *Greencamp*. https://greencamp.com/illegal-cannabis-grows/

Vayej, S. & de Lange, A. (2021). *South Africa's Green Gold*. CDCH.

Ventura, C., Carrara, B., & Fernandes, R. (2022). General Beliefs About Illicit Drug Use and Stigma: Perspective of People Who Use Illicit Drugs. *Community Mental Health Journal (2022) 58*, 1346–1353. doi:10.1007/s10597-022-00944-8

Vivek, V. (2021). Top 10 Hemp Startups in India. *Hemp Foundation*.

Viviers, H. J., Petzer, A., & Gordon, R. (2022). An assessment of solvent residue contaminants related to cannabis-based products in the South African market. *Journal of cannabis research, 4*(1), 1-10. doi:10.1186/s42238-022-00130-3

Viviers, H. J., Petzer, A., & Gordon, R. (2021). An assessment of the potency related to Cannabis-based products in the South African market. *Forensic Science International*, *322*, 110754. doi:10.1016/j.forsciint.2021.110754 PMID:33862324

Volkow, N. D., Baler, R. D., Compton, W. M., & Weiss, S. R. (2014). Adverse Health Effects of Marijuana Use. *The New England Journal of Medicine*, *370*(23), 2219–2227. https://doi.org/10.1056/nejmra1402309

Volkow, N. D., Swanson, J. M., Evins, A. E., DeLisi, L. E., Meier, M. H., Gonzalez, R., Bloomfield, M. A., Curran, H. V., & Baler, R. (2016). Effects of Cannabis Use on Human Behavior, Including Cognition, Motivation, and Psychosis: A Review. *JAMA Psychiatry*, *73*(3), 292–297. doi:10.1001/jamapsychiatry.2015.3278 PMID:26842658

Vonapartis, E., Aubin, M., Seguin, P., Mustafa, A., & Charron, J.-B. (2015). Seed composition of ten industrial hemp cultivars approved for. *Journal of Food Composition and Analysis*, *39*, 8–12. doi:10.1016/j.jfca.2014.11.004

Wade, R. H. (2012). Return of industrial policy? *International Review of Applied Economics*, *26*(2), 223–239. doi:10.1080/02692171.2011.640312

Waetjen, T. (2022). South Africa's Century of Cannabis Politics, 1922–2022. *South African Historical Journal*, 1–5. doi:10.1080/02582473.2022.2128274

Wallach, O. 2017. Mapped: The Most Common Illicit Drugs in the World. Available: https://www.visualcapitalist.com/mapped-the-most-common-illicit-drugs-in-the-world/.

Walters, D., & Wiseman, H. J. (2022). Self-Regulation in the Cradle: The Role of Standards in Emerging Industries. SSRN 4226081.

Wamba, S., Kamdjoug, J. R., Bawack, R., & Keogh, J. G. (2020). Bitcoin, blockchain and Fin-Tech: A systematic review and case studies in the supply chain. *Production Planning and Control*, *31*(2-3), 115–142. doi:10.1080/09537287.2019.1631460

Wambua, F. N. (2022). *Effect of Fintech Companies on Credit Access among Youths in Nairobi County*, [Doctoral dissertation, United States International University-Africa, Africa].

Wartenberg, A. C., Holden, P. A., Bodwitch, H., Parker-Shames, P., Novotny, T., Harmon, T. C., Hart, S. C., Beutel, M., Gilmore, M., Hoh, E., & Butsic, V. (2021). Cannabis and the Environment: What Science Tells Us and What We Still Need to Know. *Environmental Science &Amp; Technology Letters*, *8*(2), 98–107. doi:10.1021/acs.estlett.0c00844

Webb, J. W., Tihanyi, L. R., Ireland, D., & Sirmon, D. G. (2009). *You Say Illegal, I Say Legitimate: Entrepreneurship in the Informal Economy.* Academy of Management. https://www.jstor.org/stable/27760016

Webster, D. (2017). How to go green for your travel destinations in 2018. *Spokesman Review*. http://www. spokesman.com/stories/2017/dec/29/how-go-green-your-travel-destinations-2018.

Weihrauch, R. (2021). *Criminalising cannabis in South Africa: a history and post-Prince discussion* [Master's thesis, Faculty of Law, South Africa].

Weihraunch, R. (2021). *Criminalising Cannabis in South Africa: A History and Post-Prince Discussion.* [Theses/Dissertation, University of Cape Town, South Africa]. http://hdl.handle.net/11427/33974

Weihraunch, R. 2021. Criminalising Cannabis in South Africa: A History and Post-Prince Discussion, University of Cape Town, OpenUCT, Theses/Dissertation Masters - http://hdl.handle.net/11427/33974

Weisskopf, J. (2022). Investing in Cannabis: Is the Grass Greener for Investors? *Hospitality Insights.* https://hospitalityinsights.ehl.edu/investing-in-cannabis

Weisskopf, J. 2022. Investing in Cannabis: Is the Grass Greener for Investors? https://hospitalityinsights.ehl.edu/investing-in-cannabis

Weiss, M. L. (2014). *Routledge handbook of contemporary Malaysia*. Routledge. doi:10.4324/9781315756240

Wen, J., Kozak, M., & Ying, T. (2022). Cannabis tourists' perceived constraints to engaging in commercial cannabis tourism overseas: A comparison of first-time and repeat tourists. *Asia Pacific Journal of Marketing and Logistics*. doi:10.1108/APJML-06-2021-0411

West, D. P. (1998). *Hemp & Marijuana: Myths and Realities*. The Council.

Whiting, P. F., Wolff, R. F., Deshpande, S., Di, N. M., Duffy, S., Hernández, A. V., Keurentjes, J. C., Lang, S., Misso, K., Ryder, S., Schmidlkofer, S., Westwood, M., & Kleijnen, J. (2015). *Cannabinoids for Medical Use A Systematic Review and Meta-analysis*. American Medical Association. http://hdl.handle.net/10757/558499

Whiting, P., Wolff, R. D., Keurentjes, J., Lang, S., Misso, K., Ryder, S., & Kleijnen, J. (2015). Cannabinoids for Medical Use: A Systematic Review and Meta-analysis. *Journal of the American Medical Association, 1*(24), 2456–2473. doi:10.1001/jama.2015.6358 PMID:26103030

Wilcox, A. (19 July, 2020). Why is Cannabis Illegal? The story of Cannabis prohibition will shock you. *Green Flower.*

Williams, A. R. (2020). Cannabis as a gateway drug for opioid use disorder. *The Journal of Law, Medicine & Ethics, 48*(2), 268–274. doi:10.1177/1073110520935338 PMID:32631185

Williams, C. M., & Stephens, G. J. (2020). Development of cannabidiol as a treatment for severe childhood epilepsies. *British Journal of Pharmacology, 177*(24), 5509–5517. doi:10.1111/bph.15274 PMID:32986848

Williams, M. (2014). *Rethinking the Developmental State in the Twenty-First Century*. Routledge.

Wilson, S., Bodwitch, H., Carah, J., Daane, K., Getz, C., Grantham, T., & Butsic, V. (2019). First known survey of cannabis production practices in California. *California Agriculture, 73*(3), 119–127. doi:10.3733/ca.2019a0015

World Health Organization. (2007). *WHO guidelines for assessing quality of herbal medicines with reference to contaminants and residues.* World Health Organization.

World Wildlife Fund. (2017). *Food Loss and Waste: Facts and Futures.* World Wildlife Fund.

Wright, A. (2020, November 6). What if I build a cannabis business and no one will insure it? *Risk and Insurance.* https://riskandinsurance.com/what-if-i-build-a-cannabis-business-and-no-one-will-insure-it/

Wynn, J. (1998). South Africa Hemp Feasibility Report. Terraforms.

Yang, J., & Yu, M. (2022). The Influence of Institutional Support on the Innovation Performance of New Ventures: The Mediating Mechanism of Entrepreneurial Orientation. *Sustainability, 14*(4), 2212. doi:10.3390u14042212

Yoo, J., Lee, S., & Park, S. (2019). The effect of firm life cycle on the relationship between R&D expenditures and future performance, earnings uncertainty, and sustainable growth. *Sustainability, 11*, 2371.

Zahra, E., Darke, S., Degenhardt, L., & Campbell, G. (2020). Rates, characteristics and manner of cannabis-related deaths in Australia 2000–2018. *Drug and Alcohol Dependence, 212*, 108028. doi:10.1016/j.drugalcdep.2020.108028 PMID:32370933

Zarenda, H. (2013). Deriving value from the Global Value Chain (GVC) concept: an approach to regional industrial policies. *Cape to Cairo*, 97.

Zehra, A., Burns, J., Liu, C. K., Manza, P., Wiers, C. E., Volkow, N. D., & Wang, G. J. (2018). Cannabis addiction and the brain: A review. *Journal of Neuroimmune Pharmacology, 13*(4), 438–452. doi:10.100711481-018-9782-9 PMID:29556883

Zikalala, S., Mutambara, E., & Mthuli, S. A. (2020). The Influence of Credit Rating Agencies on State Governance: The case of South Africa. *Gender & Behaviour, 18*(4), 16732–16752.

Zimmer, M., & Proferes, N. J. (2014). A topology of Twitter research: disciplines, methods, and ethics. *Aslib Journal of Information Management, 66*(3), 250–261. doi:10.1108/ajim-09-2013-0083

Ziolkowski, R., Miscione, G., & Schwabe, G. (2020). Decision problems in Blockchain governance: Old wine in new bottles or walking in someone Else's shoes? *Journal of Management Information Systems, 37*(2), 316–348. doi:10.1080/07421222.2020.1759974

Zondo, A.C.J. (2018, September 18). *Minister of Justice and Constitutional Development and Others v Prince* [and Others] ZACC 30 [court decision]. Constitutional Court of South Africa, Case CCT 108/17, http://www.saflii.org/za/cases/ ZACC/2018/30.html.

Zondo, R. (2018). Minister of Justice and Constitutional Development and Others v Prince (Clarke and Others Intervening); National Director of Public Prosecutions and Others v Rubin; National Director of Public Prosecutions and Others v Acton. Constitutional-Court (ed.) [2018] ZACC 30. Johannesburg: The South African Judiciary.

Zvonarev, V., Fatuki, T.A., Tregubenko, P. (2019). The public health concerns of marijuana legalization: an overview of current trends. *DISA*.

About the Contributors

Pfano Mashau is an academic at the University of KwaZulu-Natal, School of Entrepreneurship and Management. He holds a PhD in Management. He also has various non-degree career development certificates acquired from short programmes (Locally and Internationally). As an academic, he is involved in lecturing at the undergraduate and postgraduate levels. His research focus is on Small Business Development, Innovation, Business Management, Entrepreneurship and Agglomeration Economies. Prior to working as an academic, he worked for JET Education Services, BioRegional and a few small businesses. Prof Mashau has published over 40 research articles, supervised eight doctoral theses to completion, and over 20 Masters dissertations. Some of the research work has been presented in international conferences. He has been an editor for a journal and a book. He is a member of the Pan African Research Council and the Institute of Business Advisors.

Jabulani Nyawo is a Senior Lecturer and the Academic Leader: Teaching and Learning within the School of Management, Information Technology and Governance. Before joining the UKZN, He worked as a Business Coach for Bio-Regional South Africa – an NPO involved in community development by supporting and developing small businesses in South Africa. In June 2014, Dr. Nyawo joined the Department of Cooperative Governance and Traditional Affairs (KZN) as a Development Facilitator. He assisted in facilitating the implementation of social development interventions and ensured the linkages between the traditional institutions and municipalities concerning IDPs. Dr. Nyawo is involved in teaching at the undergraduate level, supervising the Honours, Masters & Doctoral students.

* * *

Monicca Thulisile Bhuda is a culture activist, an indigenous scholar and a lecturer at the University of Mpumalanga. She holds a Bachelor degree (hons) in Indigenous knowledge Systems, a Masters degree in Indigenous Knowledge Systems, both from the North-West University. Currently, she is busy with her PhD also in indigenous Knowledge Systems, registered with the North-West University. Ms Bhuda Specialises in IsiNdebele Ethnomathematics and African cultural expressions. Her work on IsiNdebele ethnomathematics focuses on mathematical ideas and concepts used/found in AmaNdebele beaded attires and mural art. Ms Bhuda believes that AmaNdebele women are ethnomathematicians who never (most) attended formal school yet understand symmetrical geometry. She has been featured on numerous media platforms such as TV, Radio, Magazines and Newspapers that were based on her interests as an indigenous scholar and on Indigenous Knowledge Systems. Her interests include decolonization of education, indigenous knowledge preservation, protection, management and dissemination.

Bibi Zaheenah Chummun is a Senior Lecturer at the University of KwaZulu-Natal (UKZN) Graduate School of Business and Leadership (GSB&L) based on Westville Campus in Durban - South Africa. Dr. Chummun has published several papers in the field of management, microenterprises, microfinance, microinsurance and financial inclusion. She is supervising Masters and PhD students in the field of management She is a Chartered Insurer from the Chartered Insurance Institute in UK. She obtained her MBA from Nelson Mandela Metropolitan University (NMMU- South Africa) in 2010 and her PhD is from North West University (NWU-South Africa). Dr. Chummun is originally from the island of Mauritius.

Thulile Purity Dali is passionate about building resources for the future through knowledge management. She was born in Port Shepstone in KwaZulu Natal and works in a middle management role within the fast-moving consumer goods (FMCG) industry. She has 12 years wealth of experience in various roles within the manufacturing sector. She matriculated at Port Shepstone secondary school and has continued to invest in preparing herself for the workplace environment through education. She holds a National diploma in Chemical Engineering and a Bachelor of Technology in Chemical Engineering from the Durban University of Technology (DUT), from the University of South Africa (UNISA) she has attained a Bachelor of Commerce degree in Supply Chain and Operations Management, an Advance Risk Management (NQF 8) certificate and a Bachelor of Commerce Honors degree in Business management. She is completing her Master's of Commerce in Leadership studies through the University of KwaZulu Natal (UKZN).

Tshililo Ruddy Farisani is a Post Doctoral Research Fellow at the School of Management IT and Governance at the University of KwaZulu – Natal (South Africa). He is a 2019/20 Bergen Summer Research School fellow and a 2018-2021 Researcher in the National Research Foundation's South African Research Chair Initiative (SARCHI) in Sustainable Local (Rural) Livelihoods. His research focuses on the sustainability of local livelihoods through Small Medium and Micro Enterprises (SMMEs).

Jacqueline Grant, currently studying towards a Master of Commerce of Leadership Studies, holds a Postgraduate Diploma in Management (Cum Laude) and a Bachelor of Commerce in Management (Cum Laude). She is dual skilled in property management and financial accounting with 30 years of working experience in various industries, including two R1bn start up organizations in Kwa-Zulu Natal. She aspires to be a lifelong learner and is pursuing a career in lecturing and academia.

Ranson Sifiso Gwala is a PhD Candidate at the university of KwaZulu Natal studying towards a Doctor of Business Administration. He is working for the Department of Agriculture and Rural Development. He is a Provincial Executive Committee member of the South African Communist Party in KwaZulu Natal, heading issues dealing with International Developments affecting the people of the world. He has co-published one peer reviewed article titled, "Corporate governance and firm performance in the fourth industrial revolution: A systematic Literature review. He is an avid reader and an enthusiastic academic want to be. He was born in Ndwedwe KwaZulu Natal but now resides between Durban and Pietermaritzburg.

Sammar Javed has joined University of Derby as Lecturer in Business and Management. Recently she completed an evaluation report for a £6M ERDF funded Greater Manchester Cyber Foundry project (Cyber Security related innovation support for 150 GM Enterprises) and an evaluation plan for a £4M

PrintCity Network (3D printing innovation for 150 GM Enterprises). Prior to that she had successful Research and Knowledge Exchange project worth £32,657 to develop a management KTP (which is in its second year now) and a technical innovation KTP in collaboration of the school of engineering and technology. During the project duration of 6 months, she was successful in bringing direct savings of £219,952 including a winning management KTP bid worth £171,657. Sammar her self-completed a highly successful KTP project for Beds and mattress manufacture based in Huddersfield. The project focused on process innovation utilising SCRUM brought funding's and savings of over £1.8M exceeding the defined 5 year targets. Along this KTP project of worth £132,000, Sammar has achieved successful bids of £216,504.64 including Future Fashion Factory £56,000, Digital Enterprise top 100 for Deluxe Beds, Digital Voucher, LEP, RTC north, Winning Pitch, Department of International Trade (DIT), Collaborative Venture Fund (CVF), Manufacturing Growth Program, Supply Chain Funding etc. Sammar have vast experience of professional and academic research. She started her career from a Pakistani think tank before joining academia in UK. She has participated in over 32 research studies, articles, book chapters and reports as well as presented widely on her topics internationally to diverse audience. Her research interests are: operations, change, innovation, knowledge, culture, leadership and diversity management mainly in manufacturing enterprises.

Njabulo Khumalo is a Fellow in the Institute of People Management (IPM) and an Editor of the International Journal of Human Resource Management. By profession he is an academic and a researcher who have served in all four public institutions of higher learning in KwaZulu-Natal, South Africa. He holds a PhD in Leadership Studies from the University of KwaZulu-Natal, M. Com merit in Industrial Psychology from the University of Zululand, B. Tech Degree and National Diploma cum laude in Human Resources Management from Mangosuthu university of Technology. He graduated more than 22 Masters and 2 PhD graduates from different institutions of higher learning. His research interest is on recruitment, organizational behavior, human resource planning, career development and leadership.

Manono Luthuli is a Social & Behavioural Sciences Researcher at the Africa Health Research Institute, KwaZulu-Natal, South Africa. He holds a Master of Commerce degree in Leadership Studies and a Bachelor of Social Science (Honours) Degree in Psychology - all from the University of KwaZulu-Natal, South Africa. His research interests include men's sexual reproductive health, mental health and adolescent health. He has led and contributed to numerous research outputs in the form of academic journal articles, book chapters, and presentations at local and international conferences, while working in a variety of roles for different research organisations in South Africa.

Nkhensani Maluleke is a Mechanical engineering technologist experienced in HVAC projects. Currently enrolled with the University of KwaZulu Natal for MCom in Leadership studies. Nkhensani was born in Malamulele, Limpopo province of South Africa and she believes in embracing change and diversity. Interested in asset and facility management. The mission is to explore the strategic integration of people, places and processes within the work environment.

Ali Mir was born and brought up in Indian occupational Kashmir. He grew up with lots of ups and downs but finally found his passion with consistency and discipline against failures. He completed his Masters from the University of Huddersfield with majors in Fintech and is exploring to set up a new venture, alongside contributing to his family business of Kashmiri traditional carpet designing and manufacturing industry along the export unit. He has used cannabis and is on medication with cannabis, so better understands the need of cannabis in the right way. He is looking to establish a cannabis industry in Kashmir to help it to reach the right hands.

Thobeka Nomcebo Mnyandu holds a BCom Honours in Marketing Management. Further to this, she holds a Bachelor of Administration degree majoring in Public Administration and Marketing (UKZN). She is an MCom student majoring in marketing. She is currently a Marketing and Communication Intern at the Durban FilmMart Institute. She is keen on finding new opportunities in advertising and communication, social marketing, and green marketing.

Taurai Muparadzi is a PhD researcher at the University of KwaZulu Natal and a lecturer at the University of Zimbabwe with research interests in Public Administration and Banking and Finance. He has extensive teaching and research supervision experience at both undergraduate and master's levels as a lecturer of public sector accounting, fundamentals of public sector finance, theories of organization and management, quantitative social science research methods, local government administration and governance, program management and evaluation, management of public sector finance, public sector reforms and management and e-governance and management information systems. He also has extensive experience in the financial services sector spanning over 10 years with Barclays bank of Zimbabwe and CFX Bank Limited. He is a holder of a Diploma in Business Administration, Bachelor of Commerce Honours Degree in Banking and Finance (GZU), Bachelor of Science Honours degree in Administration (UZ), Master of Science Honours in Public Administration (UZ) and Executive Certificates in Credit Management and Treasury Management (UZ).

Mxolisi Samukele Immanuel Ngcobo was born in KwaNyuswa, Bothas Hill which is located in the outer west of Durban. Completed matric at Mnyameni high school in 2012. In high school is where the passion for reading and research emerged. Currently enrolled for a Master of Commerce degree in marketing from the University of KwaZulu-Natal. The proposed title for the masters dissertation is Consumer purchasing trends during the Covid-19 pandemic and beyond in eThekwini municipality.

Andrisha Beharry Ramraj, lecturer at the University of KwaZulu-Natal, Durban, South Africa, holds a PhD in Management studies majoring in management, leadership and governance. Further to this she holds a Diploma in Higher Education. In 2004 and 2005 she received NRF scholarships to complete her Honours and Masters degrees respectively. She has presented at local and international conference in the areas of Management, Leadership, Marketing, Global Business and Entrepreneurship. She has published in the fields of Leadership, Entrepreneurship, Human Resources and Business Management. She recently published book chapters on entrepreneurial suitability and employee wellness across the globe. In 2016 and 2017 she received best presentation awards for best paper delivered at conferences, she serves on the Teaching and Learning committee within the University of KwaZulu Natal (UKZN) and served as the Bachelor of Business Administrator Programme Manager (Self-Funding Teaching Programme) for a one term. She teaches across levels within the Discipline of Management and Entrepreneurship, from entry level to masters level. She is keen on developing undergraduate curriculum transformation within the discipline. Redesigning curricular to suite the dynamics of the modern world enabling sustainability is fast becoming her passion.

Mlondi Vilakazi, PhD, is a Development scholar with broad interest in developmental states, industrialisation, empowerment policies in post-colonial settings, political economy, economic development, and state programmes.

Index

A

B

C

D

E

F

G

H

I

J

L

M

N

P

R

S

T

U

V

W

Z

www.ingramcontent.com/pod-product-compliance
Lightning Source LLC
LaVergne TN
LVHW060413300926
849162LV00006B/1414
* 9 7 8 1 6 6 8 4 6 3 4 6 8 *